MARKETING MANAGEMENT

PETER R. DICKSON
The Ohio State University

MARKETING MANAGEMENT

PETER R. DICKSON
The Ohio State University
Crane Professor of Marketing

The Dryden Press
Harcourt Brace College Publishers

Fort Worth   Philadelphia   San Diego   New York   Orlando   Austin   San Antonio
Toronto   Montreal   London   Sydney   Tokyo

Publisher	Liz Widdicombe
Director of Editing, Design, and Production	Diane Southworth
Acquisitions Editor	Lyn Keeney Hastert
Developmental Editor	R. Paul Stewart
Project Editor	Karen Carriere
Production Manager	Diane Southworth
Art Director	Jeanette Barber
Photo Editor	Elizabeth Banks
Permissions Editor	Sheila Shutter
Copy Editor	Karen Carriere
Compositor	GTS Graphics, Inc.
Text Type	10/12 Clearface Regular
Cover	© Buck Holzemer Photography, 1993

Requests for permission to make copies of any part of the work should be mailed to: Permissions Department, Harcourt Brace College Publishers, 8th Floor, Orlando, Florida 32887.

Address for Editorial Correspondence
The Dryden Press, 301 Commerce Street, Suite 3700, Forth Worth, TX 76102

Address for Orders
The Dryden Press, 6277 Sea Harbor Drive, Orlando, FL 32887
1-800-782-4479, or 1-800-433-0001 (in Florida)

ISBN: 0-03-096847-X

Library of Congress Catalog Card Number: 93-79572
Printed in the United States of America

4 5 6 7 8 9 0 1 2   069   9 8 7 6 5 4 3 2

The Dryden Press
Harcourt Brace College Publishers

About the cover:
Fancy Footwork The glowing triumph of sleek, fast-moving, smooth-flowing implementation over the winds of change and a turbulent future.

THE DRYDEN PRESS SERIES IN MARKETING

Schnaars
MICROSIM
Marketing simulation available for IBM PC and Apple

Sellars
Role Playing: The Principles of Selling
Second Edition

Shimp
Promotion Management and Marketing Communications
Third Edition

Sisodia and Mentzer
Marketing Decision Systems: Transformation Through Information Technology

Talarzyk
Cases and Exercises in Marketing

Terpstra and Sarathy
International Marketing
Fifth Edition

Tootelian and Gaedeke
Cases and Classics in Marketing Management

Weitz and Wensley
Readings in Strategic Marketing Analysis, Planning, and Implementation

Zikmund
Exploring Marketing Research
Fifth Edition

PREFACE

We are living in a time of extraordinary change. The economic and ecological threat is stark, simple, and very real. American firms must design and make better products and services and find better ways to market them. This demands that we challenge the ways that we have come to think about marketing management. What was once good enough is no longer competitive. What were once limitless resources now have to be used ever more efficiently. Today, either a company is on the leading edge, or it is on the bleeding edge. Have marketing education and marketing management textbooks kept up with change, particularly in developing a much sharper competitive edge? Do the marketing management textbooks focus enough on building customer relationships through delivering benefits and satisfying particular customers better than the competition through total quality management (TQM)? Do they emphasize the constant drive to become more efficient? Are they proposing new ways, such as cross-functional team management, for companies to continuously improve the quality and speed of their market decision-making and implementation processes? Do they discuss the real global marketing and ethical issues?

My 1990 research with the Conference Board on the real-world marketing planning practices of Fortune 500 companies and my 1992 study with The Corporate Design Foundation of the new product management of high-growth firms has tended to confirm the above concerns. Many marketing textbooks are no longer in touch with marketing practice in both small and large firms or with the brutal competitive realities of the new global marketplace. A study of what determines the success of executives has come to an even more alarming conclusion about the added value of marketing training.[1] It found no relationship between having undergraduate training in marketing and career success, as measured by income and title! It also found having an MBA made no difference.

This textbook evolved as a result of 20 years of teaching undergraduate and MBA courses in marketing management at the University of Waikato, a small teaching-oriented business school in New Zealand and The Ohio State University, a large research-oriented business school. The book is designed and written to add value to a senior undergraduate marketing management/strategy course and first- and second-year MBA marketing management/strategy courses taught at both small and large universities. It is also written for market management/strategy courses taught for engineers and industrial design students.

Learning from My Mistakes

In 1973, with another five faculty members who became good friends, I participated in launching a new business school that now has over a thousand students. The dean, Geoffrey Schmitt, one of the first of my many excellent mentors, had been the CEO of one of the most efficient pulp and paper mills in the world, and he taught me a great deal about general management and the real world of business, including international business and business ethics. We worked together, as a cross-functional team,

---

1. See Shelby D. Hunt, Lawrence B. Chonko, and Van R. Wood, "Marketing Education and Marketing Success: Are They Related?" *Journal of Marketing Education* (Summer 1986), 2–13.

developing courses, setting high performance quality standards, recruiting and marketing our graduates, and building crucial relationships with other colleges in the university, as well as businesses, high schools, and government agencies. In many ways, we were launching a new competitive service by applying many of the principles discussed in this book.

My second extraordinary learning opportunity occurred in 1976 when I was fortunate enough to win a special Fulbright-Hays Bicentennial Fellowship to study at the University of Florida. The university's marketing faculty, led by Professor Joel Cohen, was building a reputation for consumer behavior research that is now world renowned. Upon my return to New Zealand, I helped launch a new consumer product, a remarkably comfortable luxury woolen mattress pad that generated thousands of unsolicited letters of thanks from satisfied consumers. One of my responsibilities included a sales mission to the United States where I was "dismissed" from the buying offices of all of the leading department store chains I called on. Our company persevered, began the product testing that established the product benefits, created a Woolrest success story through mail-order catalogs, and within two years the vice-president of a major department store chain had flown across the country to convince us that we should sell to him. During this period I learned a great deal from my friends in the company (particularly Matt Patterson) about managing quality channel relationships and implementing merchandising programs quickly. I also learned that a success story is needed to open doors to the global market.

In 1981, I left the University of Waikato to teach marketing management at The Ohio State University. During the 1980s, OSU graduated more marketing majors than any other university in the United States, and we did so with a marketing faculty far smaller than our respected rivals. I started writing this book in 1986, and my thinking about how to learn and teach the theory and practice of market management has changed a great deal. Early in my career I learned from several great teachers (particularly Bill Wilkie) that if we are to master a topic we must develop simple but powerful frameworks (mental models) around which we think about the topic. Much of my research that has been published in various journal articles has been devoted to developing such frameworks and studying the implications of these frameworks for information providers and decision makers. To this end I have spent a great deal of my career learning about how managers and researchers think about decision making, consumer behavior, competition, ethics, implementation, and many other topics. This is reflected in the organization of this book.

Book Objectives: Addressing Education Priorities

If the latest American Assembly of Collegiate Schools of Business (AACSB) guidelines are to be taken seriously, then textbooks must address a new set of educational priorities. Today's marketing textbooks must prepare students to adopt a global competitive perspective, integrate the total quality and continuous improvement movements with marketing management, present a serious and self-reflective discussion of ethics and the global environment, focus on cross-functional team decision making, and place a heavy emphasis on relationship management. The table on the opposite page outlines how *Marketing Management* addresses these key educational priorities.

Global Competition and Global Marketing

A major issue was how to discuss international or global marketing in the book. Given the extraordinary development of the global economy and global competition, it is imperative that any modern marketing book talk a great deal about global marketing.

Education Priority	How This Text Addresses the Priority
1.* Global Marketing	Almost every chapter in *Marketing Management* concludes with a discussion of ways to apply the material in the chapter to a global marketing environment. Many of the mini-cases and discussion questions deal with global marketing issues.
2.* Cross-Functional Team Management	The textbook assumes that marketing management is primarily handled by a cross-functional team. Cross-functional team management is discussed in detail in Chapters 1, 2, 9, and 14.
3.* Ethics, Environment, Diversity Issues	Chapter 6 on public policy and ethics presents a framework for making ethical decisions. The questions at the end of Chapter 6 cover ethics, the environment, and minority rights.
4. Total Quality Management and Customer Satisfaction	TQM and customer satisfaction are discussed in the sections on the customer satisfaction/quality drive in Chapter 1, measuring quality and customer satisfaction in Chapter 15, and total quality management in Chapters 7, 8, and 9.
5. Relationship Marketing	Relationship marketing is explored in the sections on organization buying in Chapter 3, the relationship market share matrix in Chapter 4, all of Chapter 5 on channel analysis, all of Chapter 10 on managing distribution relationships, and the section on developing external organization networks in Chapter 14.
6. Integration with Computer Decision Support Systems and Software	The textbook offers discussions of DDSs in Chapters 2, 3, 5, 10, 14, and 15. Some 20 Lotus/Excel spreadsheets are integrated into the text and end-of-chapter minicases and discussion questions. STRATMESH, a computer software aid for use in marketing planning, including case studies that teach students how to use the STRATMESH thinking process, can be found in Appendix 2.
7. Integration with Cost and Financial Accounting	Cost and financial accounting are examined in the sections on the competitive rationality cost drive in Chapter 1, understanding of cost structure and costs in Chapter 2, assessing the sales and profitability of a positioning strategy using the Target spreadsheet in Chapter 8, price/cost-based new product development in Chapter 9, cost-based pricing in Chapter 13, and the marginal analysis, variance analysis, leverage analysis, and profitability analysis spreadsheets in Chapter 15.
8. Encouraging Creative Problem Solving	Individual and team creative problem solving is discussed in Appendix 1, which includes a number of creative problem-solving exercises.

*Mandated by the new 1992 AACSB Requirements for Accreditation.

In response to the preference of students and reviewers, *Marketing Management* integrates such discussion throughout the book rather than confining the material to a separate chapter. I personally greatly prefer this approach, for the U.S. economy is part of a global market that is becoming borderless as a result of advances in information technology and the fierceness of competitive forces. A marketing management textbook for the 1990s has to be a whole book about global market management, rather than a book with a chapter about international or global marketing.

The differences between product and service marketing are also discussed throughout the book, and many of the 300 plus discussion questions and minicases deal with services. *Marketing Management* also has a strong efficiency orientation that emphasizes understanding cost structures, profit margins, budgeting, and financial control.

Empowered Thinking and Implementation

Above all else, *Marketing Management* emphasizes getting the most out of people (now called empowering people) by developing an organization "clan" culture, using cross-functional decision-making teams, developing effective relationships with other firms and customers, and teaching executives to think creatively and manage their time, information systems, actions, and processes better. In short, the book emphasizes that competitive rationality, which is thinking and acting smarter, faster, and more ethically, is the essence of success. An emphasis on three driving forces pervades the book: the drive to strengthen customer relations by satisfying customers better than the competition does, the drive to find more efficient and less costly ways of delivering the same customer benefits and service, and the drive to continuously improve decision-making and implementation skills.

This book also emphasizes marketing strategy and competitive strategy. As discussed in several chapters in the book, many market management decisions are made by the most senior executives in the firm. Consequently, a book about marketing management must discuss long-term company goals and senior management leadership. It is also increasingly difficult to separate marketing management decisions from decisions made by design, engineering, production, procurement, and logistics departments and the total quality management and continuous improvement movements. Decisions in these areas almost always influence a firm's market behavior. The mental models developed in this book are also based on a combination of Austrian economics and conventional microeconomics. This should not be surprising, as marketing management is applied microeconomics.

Organization of the Book

The figure on the opposite page illustrates how the fifteen chapters logically flow from one to the next. Our basic objective is to fit a firm's positioning, tactics, and programs to the realities of the market. Chapter 1 presents a STRATMESH decision-making procedure that helps design such a fit (and continue to improve the fit) between strategy, programs, and an ever-changing competitive environment. A firm uses its market research and decision-making processes to develop and continuously update the positioning and tactical programs of a product or service. A firm uses its organization, budgeting, and control to implement its positioning and programs. This explains why *Marketing Management* starts with a discussion of decision making and information gathering, moves on to an analysis of the market, positioning, and tactical programs, and ends with an examination of organization, implementation, and control. The book is strongly anchored in the real world and draws heavily on Conference Board research into actual marketing planning practices, the decision-making practices of great entrepreneurs, and my current research into cross-functional team management.

At the heart of the book is Chapter 8, which explains how to position and develop a product or service that is better than the rival's product or service. The five management chapters (Chapters 9 through 13) that build on the positioning foundation use a whole range of different marketing tactics and programs. Firms that are best at positioning and developing innovative new programs understand their markets better than do their rivals. Their competitive rationality (learning, decision making, and implementation) is better than their rivals. Superior thinking starts with analyzing all of the elements that make up a market, which is why five chapters (Chapters 3 through 7) explore how to analyze buyers, competition, trading channels, public policy, the law and ethics, and the goals, strengths, and weaknesses of the firm. The opening two chapters present the theory and practice of competitive rationality. They discuss, in practical terms, how to make marketing decisions (Chapter 1) and how to gather and use market research and intelligence (Chapter 2). They form the wrench that is applied to the organization and implementation nut (Chapter 14) to fit the behavior of the firm to its market environment.

In the brave new world of continuous improvement, organization and implementation skills are crucial. One study revealed that recruiters believe that marketing

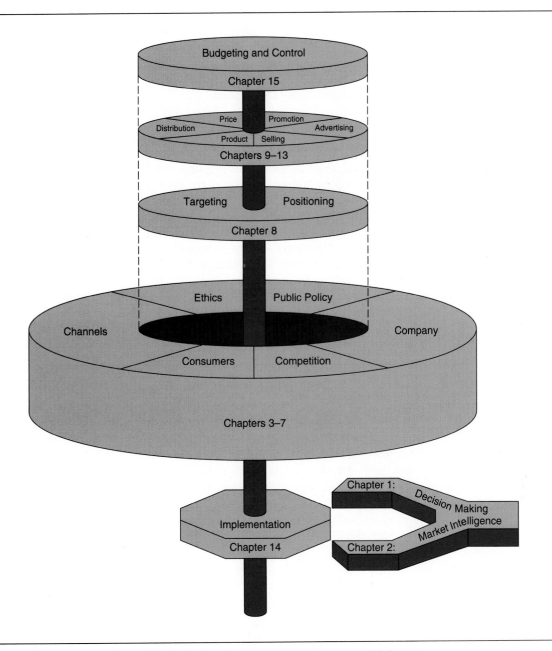

The book has a simple internal structure: five analysis chapters frame the positioning decision chapter, which, in turn, forms the foundation for the five management chapters. The mental models, techniques, rules, and procedures described are decision-making frameworks and routines that, when used, increase a firm's competitive advantage by improving the firm's competitive thinking. The decision maker or cross-functional team has to fit the basic targeting positioning strategy to the five basic elements of the market environment. On top of the targeting-positioning level are the marketing management programs. The whole system is clamped together by implementing, budgeting, and controlling processes.

programs should emphasize teaching students organization and implementation strategies (Chapter 14), ahead of interpersonal, planning, and decision-making techniques.[2] The last chapter (Chapter 15) discusses how to forecast, budget, and control, using spreadsheets and databases.

Using the Book in the Classroom

Instructors will find *Marketing Management* easy and fun to teach for several reasons. First, students like its decision-making orientation and the fact that the book's content complements, but does not overlap too much with the content of prior courses and texts. Second, most of the instructor's time can be spent discussing how to apply the concepts, models, and techniques in the book rather than presenting lectures that merely describe the techniques. Students react positively to such hands-on discussion and assignments. They learn more, and they perceive that they learn more. Third, the discussion questions have been pretested and designed to ensure active discussions that will help students understand the important concepts and models and apply them in the real world. The techniques used in *Marketing Management* lead to a course in which the teacher will worry less about how to structure a detailed lecture and can instead use the discussion questions and cases to help the students best understand and apply what they have learned from the book.

To enable students to gain the most from the many ideas and concepts presented in the text, a number of learning aids are incorporated into each chapter:

- Each chapter opens with a photo montage depicting the themes or perspectives discussed throughout the chapter and several memorable quotes to pique the student's interest.

- Key ideas are color bulleted in the introduction, laying the foundation for a mental map of the material covered in each chapter. These ideas can be returned to again and used as a summary for a lecture discussion.

- The text is interspersed with captioned figures and tables illustrating concepts within the chapter. Pictures and figures are worth more than a thousand words because they greatly enrich the narrative explanation and, in particular, help the reader build a mental model around key figures. The figure captions also help build such models.

- Footnotes are used rather than notes placed at the end of the chapter or book. This makes it much easier for students to locate references and also allows the inclusion of interesting side comments and observations.

- The latter chapters contain computer applications that can be executed using the Lotus/Excel templates that accompany the text. These applications are easily identified in the text by the icon to the left. They are actual marketing management decision aids that enable the user to, for example, practice target return pricing, estimate territorial sales force size based on market potential and workload, allocate an advertising budget to regions, design the best delivery and inventory holding system for a customer, complete a variance analysis, and prepare a budget.

- Color-coded exhibits highlighting competitive rationality in practice are interspersed throughout the text. They illustrate concepts but also are integrative in that they remind the student of the key propositions of the theory of competitive rationality.

---

2. Michael Ursic and Craig Hegstrom, "The Views of Marketing Recruiters, Alumni and Students about Curriculum and Course Structure," *Journal of Marketing Education* (Summer 1985), 21–27.

♦ More than 300 classroom-tested discussion questions and minicases are presented at the end of each chapter that create interesting, lively instruction and debate in the classroom about real-world issues.

Teaching Supplements

To make it even easier to use this book in the classroom, an extensive array of supplements for the professor and students was developed specifically for this textbook.

Instructor's Manual: The extended instructor's manual, written by the author, provides answers to all of the discussion questions and minicases at the end of each chapter and contains additional questions and answers that can be used for testing. It also includes suggested lecture outlines and teaching notes, sample syllabi, and suggestions for integrating computer games, longer cases, and other supplementary items into the course.

Customized Cases: Supplemental cases have been selected to accompany this text. These cases are derived from a wide range of sources and are available from Harcourt Brace Custom Publishing. Many appear in the leading casebooks and this case database will be updated annually. This service enables a school to use the text and cases in a single course or to teach a first course using the text and the STRATMESH cases and then a second course using the 16 to 20 cases selected from the case base. Six comprehensive marketing planning cases are included with the STRATMESH software to teach students the STRATMESH planning process. One of them, the AUTOTEST case study, which also serves as a sample marketing plan, is presented in Appendix 2.

Test Item File: A test item file with over 50 multiple-choice questions per chapter is available on IBM and Macintosh disks.

Transparencies: 80 full-color acetates highlight key figures, mental models, and illustrations from the text and end-of-chapter discussion questions.

Video Series: A video series keyed to concepts and companies discussed in the text is available in VHS format. Alternative formats and specific information on these videos can be provided by your local Dryden sales representative.

Acknowledgments

Without the encouragement and help of my student, friend, and true believer Rosemary Avery, this book would never have been started. Mike Pollard, Hugh Sloan, Joe Urbany, Rao Unnava, and Rosemary Kalapurakal helped through some difficult years and if it wasn't for Joe Giglierano this book would never have been finished. Thank you Joe for your enthusiasm and hard work, particularly your contributions to Chapters 8 through 10. Literally hundreds of undergraduate and MBA students made good suggestions in their course evaluation forms and classroom discussions. There were too many to mention, but several helped me especially. Suzanne Turgeon wrote several of the spreadsheets and did a great job grooming the rest; Tracy Maloney coauthored several of the STRATMESH case studies; and Renee Hytry helped develop the product and service design teaching materials.

My colleagues at The Ohio State University and fellow teachers at sister institutions listed here provided considerable advice and direction as reviewers and contributors. I particularly wish to thank Alan Sawyer for his extensive, pithy suggestions throughout the text, Leslie Fine for her work on sales management, Rao Unnava for his work on advertising management, Joe Urbany for his work on pricing and budgeting, and Wendy Schneier for her work on organization and implementation.

Mark Alpert, The University of Texas at Austin
Danny R. Arnold, Mississippi State University
Neeraj Arora, The Ohio State University
Rosemary Avery, Cornell University
Steve Bell, New York University
Al Belskus, Eastern Michigan University
Gordon Berkstresser, North Carolina State University
Greg Boller, Memphis State University
William Browne, Oregon State University
Dianne S. P. Cermak, Northeastern University
Michael Dotson, Appalachian State University
Jehoshua Eliashberg, University of Pennsylvania
Dale Falcinelli, DF Falcinelli Inc.
Leslie Fine, The Ohio State University
Neil Ford, University of Wisconsin
Marian Friestad, University of Oregon
Joe Giglierano, San Jose State University
Peter Gordon, Southeast Missouri State University
John Grabner, The Ohio State University
Alicia Gresham, Stephen F. Austin University
David Griffith, University of Oklahoma
Jim Grimm, Illinois State University
Janice Gygi, University of North Texas
Linda Hayes, University of Houston
Michael Hutt, Arizona State University
Bernie Jaworski, Harvard University
Rosemary Kalapurakal, The London Business School
Meir Karlinsky, The Open University of Israel
Buddy Laforge, University of Louisville
Bud LaLonde, The Ohio State University
JoAnn Linrud, Mankato State University
Max Lupul, California State University–Northridge
James McAlexander, Oregon State University
Dan McQuiston, Butler University
Paul Miniard, University of South Carolina
Mark Mitchell, Mississippi State University
Bradley O'Hara, Southeastern Louisiana University
Michael Peters, Boston College
Chris Puto, University of Arizona
John Quelch, Harvard University
Brian Ratchford, SUNY–Buffalo
Robert Roe, University of Wyoming
John Ronchetto, University of San Diego
Alan Sawyer, University of Florida
Wendy Schneier, The Ohio State University
Terry Shimp, University of South Carolina
Kimberly Scott, The Ohio State University
Shannon Shipp, Texas Christian University
Allan Shocker, University of Minnesota
Hugh Sloan, University of Mississippi
Ravi Sohi, University of Nebraska

Roger Strang, Quinnipiac College
Donnie Sullivan, The Ohio State University
Eugene Teeple, University of Central Florida
William Thornton, Colorado State University
Dillard Tinsley, Stephen F. Austin University
Rao Unnava, The Ohio State University
Joe Urbany, The University of South Carolina
Russell Wahlers, Ball State University
Bill Wilkie, University of Notre Dame
Dale Wilson, Michigan State University
Gordon Wise, Wright State University

Thank you all very much, and a special additional thank you to the several dozen unacknowledged reviewers and editors that other publishers used to provide feedback.

What can I say to my children Chris and Sarah, to Ann, and to my many friends such as Paul and Debbie, who provided the wonderful caselet on cable TV disservice, and Suzy, who gave me a great deal of good advice and frequently saved me from turning completely and permanently into a Tasmanian devil? Thanking you all for being so very understanding is hardly enough. However I feel about this book, I very much regret how it detracted from our happy times.

I wish to thank Jenny Martin, Karen Carriere, and the good folks at GTS Graphics, Inc., for their patience and skills, particularly Nancy Spear, Daniel Casquilho, and Richard Duncan. R. Paul Stewart, my developmental editor at Dryden, helped a great deal with his suggestions, hard work, and droll sense of humor; Elizabeth Banks did a great job on the photos; Jeanette Barber's design work speaks for itself; Diane Southworth, director of editing, design, and production, lived up to her reputation and was as good as her word; and Lise Johnson has creatively and aggressively managed the marketing of *Marketing Management*. Last, and most, I wish to thank Lyn Keeney Hastert, my acquisitions editor, who talked so many people into believing in this project, and who moved heaven, earth, and even me to make it happen. Her good sense, patience, professionalism, humor, charm, and leadership made it a delight to work with Dryden. I cannot imagine that any other publisher could have done as good a job. Thank you, Lyn, for your fancy footwork.

CONTENTS

Chapter 11   Managing Personal Selling   374

Decision Making and Planning

"There is one thing stronger than all of the armies in the world, and that is an idea whose time has come."

Victor Hugo

"Restlessness and discontent are the first necessities of progress."

Thomas Edison

*T*he greatest **competition** that individuals, organizations, and cultures will face during the next 1,000 years will be the economic competition that comes from the drive to make and sell services and products. The firms and countries that win will deliver a higher standard of living to their employees, owners, and citizens. Their rivals that lose will not. The future economic prosperity and survival of countries and cultures will depend on, and only on, their ability to make and market the right products and services. This most fundamental evolutionary law of modern market economics will determine the destiny of families, firms, and cultures.

This book studies how organizations successfully compete in a market economy. It is about microeconomic decision making, implementation, and control. **Marketing management** is the many and varied organizational activities involved in understanding what consumers want and how they behave. It involves the study and anticipation of competitor behavior, the development of new competitive products and services, and the management of a network of trading relationships with suppliers and distributors. It includes all of the organizational activities involved in interacting with customers and servicing their needs better than the competition does. These activities vary depending on whether the firm's customers are other businesses or households and whether the firms is manufacturing a product or providing a service (such as those provided by banks and insurance companies).

Entrepreneurs, firms, and countries that are effective at marketing management will dominate economically. Enlightened competitive marketing management also makes the market economy work better than any other system of political economics. Superior marketing management not only contributes to the success of an enterprise, but it influences the wealth and health of the society within which the enterprise is undertaken. Marketing management is a crucial organizational and cultural competence.

This introductory chapter discusses marketing management decision making. All organizations can improve marketing decision making, some a great deal. The business, engineering, and design graduate who is excellently trained in marketing management has a great opportunity to suggest and implement change and to be recognized, rewarded, and promoted to a senior leadership role within a firm. But such opportunities are not hanging like cherries on a tree waiting to be leisurely picked by *any and every* graduate who takes a course in marketing management. Being able to identify how an organization can improve its marketing management, and implementing such change, takes a very special skill and drive, some of which cannot be taught—but much of it can.

The Evolution of the Marketing Concept

The general perception of how to compete in the marketplace has changed over the last few decades. The conventional wisdom is that competition has evolved from a *production orientation* (mass producing at a lower cost and hard selling what is produced) to a *customer orientation* (production and selling efforts *must* be based on understanding and serving consumer needs and tastes). Increased competition has forced such an evolution but the evolution has, in turn, increased the fierceness of competition.

The Marketing Concept

The customer orientation demands that a business or corporation serve a clear customer need. Who wants a better mousetrap if you don't have mice? The *marketing concept*—that the corporation's mission is to generate profit for the firm, its employees, and its stockholders by producing goods and/or services that satisfy customer needs—is the natural outgrowth of a customer orientation. The marketing concept puts companies and managers on notice that neither production, nor sales, nor customers exist in a vacuum. As we shall see, production, sales, and customers exist in a competitive marketplace that is becoming more competitive, and it is this competitiveness that really drives the marketing concept.

The Strategic Marketing Concept

The marketing concept, however, is no longer the principle that guides corporate or marketing management. During the business boom of the 1960s and 1970s, the marketplace became increasingly crowded with companies serving the same target markets. This problem is evident in countries like the United States, which protect and promote strong competition in markets. The marketing concept has evolved to meet this threat to a company's well-being. The *strategic marketing concept* can be defined as the corporation's mission to seek a sustainable competitive advantage over competitors by meeting consumer needs. Most sustainable competitive advantages can be traced to superior decision-making and organization, which may not be sustainable.

According to an old business adage, "The sales department isn't the whole company, but the whole company better be the sales department." For today's business environment this needs to be altered to read, "Not everyone in this company is a marketing manager, but everyone here is in marketing management." Everyone also has to understand the fundamentals of competitive decision making.

The free market economy's central principle and driving force is competition between the minds of company leaders to more efficiently and effectively serve and satisfy consumers in the global marketplace. *Competitive rationality* is the marketing decision making of a firm in a competitive market.[1] It is competitive, since the firm operates in a market with many firms making similar decisions. It is rational in that the firm attempts to be logical in developing and servicing exchanges with customers in a continuously evolving market.

Stories about great marketing entrepreneurs such as Cyrus McCormick (farm equipment), DeWitt Wallace (*Reader's Digest*), Ray Kroc (McDonald's), Tom Watson (IBM), Mary Kay (cosmetics), Bill Gates (Microsoft), and Sam Walton (Wal-Mart) are both fascinating and inspirational (see the Rationality in Practice box on page 6). The similarity in their methods of competitive rationality is striking. Accomplished marketing entrepreneurs develop extraordinary insight, often based on years of studying a particular market. They also develop and execute marketing strategies that fit the business environment. Almost all made decisions based on intuition. Few of them left written marketing plans behind to show business historians how these successful decisions were made. They had it all in their heads, or at least a good deal of it.

Great marketing entrepreneurs know how to come up with an idea, run it by the known market facts, and make it work. One of the singular advantages of the driven, autocratic entrepreneur is that his or her visions, personal objectives, or plans clearly define the self-interests of the enterprise and direct its behavior. The entrepreneur's personal drive is infectious and energizes the whole enterprise to strive to become more competitive. Sometimes companies that are not led by the founder or an entrepreneurial chief executive cannot even manage to define their self-interests. When this happens, decision making and management can become hopelessly mired in political

---

1. Peter R. Dickson, "Toward a General Theory of Competitive Rationality," *Journal of Marketing* 56 (January 1992), 69–83.

Rationality in Practice:

DeWitt Wallace and Reader's Digest

Like many great entrepreneurial ventures, the story of DeWitt Wallace is one of triumph over adversity. Many publishing houses had turned down Wallace's idea for a new type of magazine. They told him that publishing condensed, secondhand articles from other magazines would never fly. So in 1922, Wallace launched the venture himself using a direct marketing campaign aimed at potential subscribers. The following are some of the brilliant insights and strategies that have made *Reader's Digest* such a success.

◆ Wallace observed that even people who were bored still skimmed magazine articles. He recognized what later academic research demonstrated: even good writing can be condensed with very little loss of information and *increased* reader satisfaction.

◆ Many magazines adopt a theme and a style that fit the times (for example, *Playboy* in the 1950s and 1960s), but they become dated as societal values change. The articles in *Reader's Digest* are often about freedom, optimism, faith in the goodness of other people, compassion, love, and personal development. These themes are universal and enduring. Maintaining this focus allowed *Reader's Digest* subscriptions to grow throughout the Roaring Twenties, the depression years of the thirties, and the war years of the forties.

THE READER'S DIGEST

THIRTY-ONE ARTICLES EACH MONTH FROM LEADING MAGAZINES ⁓ EACH ARTICLE OF ENDURING VALUE AND INTEREST, IN CONDENSED AND COMPACT FORM

The front page of the first issue of *Reader's Digest* reveals its positioning.

squabbles between the various factions within an enterprise. Many large U.S. companies have such leadership problems.

But successful marketing entrepreneurs do more than invent and market new products and services. They build enterprises that enable them to mass produce and market their products and services. The entrepreneur's creative genius combines with energy, courage, and the ability to lead and manage others culminating in one of the most important entrepreneurial skills—the ability to implement strategy. Entrepreneurs are able to coordinate and schedule the many activities involved in executing their innovative ideas. Other common planning characteristics are listed in Figure 1-1. Marketing entrepreneurs also energize the market economy. They change the behavior of consumers and force rivals to either change their behavior or lose customers, income, and profits.

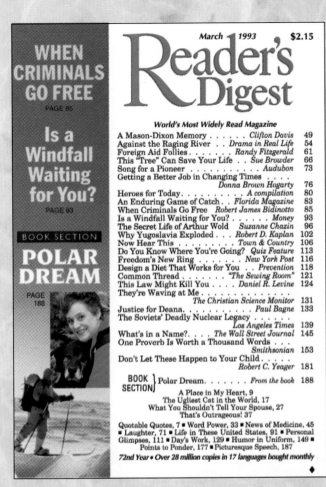

A recent issue of *Reader's Digest.*

◆ Many magazines are directed at either men or women. *Reader's Digest* positioned itself as a family magazine. Wallace's wife was the copublisher, and they balanced the content to be of interest to both husbands and wives. This positioning became extremely valuable in later years when it came to selling advertising to companies marketing products to *both* spouses.

◆ Wallace recognized that he was vitally dependent on his suppliers—competing magazines. Initially, other magazines were happy to receive the free publicity that came from the publication of their articles in condensed form. They let Wallace publish their articles for free, keeping his production costs very low. Wallace could choose the best articles from 100 or more magazines. Perhaps his most brilliant strategy was to refuse to accept outside advertising for the first 30 years of the magazine's existence. It was a great selling point to his consumers and to his suppliers, who were in competition for the advertising revenue. It also meant that *Reader's Digest* could keep a low competitive profile because it did not have to publish its circulation figures.

DeWitt Wallace possessed a unique understanding of magazine readers and their reading behavior. He also understood how to handle his competitors so well that they became the low-cost suppliers of his stories. Few marketers have been able to achieve such a feat.

Sources: Charles W. Ferguson, "Unforgettable DeWitt Wallace," *Reader's Digest,* February 1987, 1–20; and Samuel A. Schreiner, Jr., *The Condensed World of the Reader's Digest* (New York: Stein and Day, 1977).

The basic premise of the theory of competitive rationality is that there are different types of sellers and buyers; some buyers and sellers are innovators, most are followers, and yet others are laggards. Variations in the response rate of buyers *and* sellers to changes in supply and demand create opportunities that can be exploited by the motivated, alert, and hustling decision maker. If every seller were able to imitate an innovator's actions immediately, there would be no advantage to being an innovator. If every buyer responded in the same way, at the same time, economic competition would be very different from what we observe. Figure 1-1 presents a model of the dynamic competitive process in a typical oligopolistic market (a market with only a few major sellers). The model applies to any physical market, from one as small as a country town in Georgia to one as large as the entire global society.

A General Theory of Competitive Rationality

Figure 1-1

**Common Elements in the
Marketing Skills of Great
Entrepreneurs**

1. They possess unique environmental insight, which they use to spot opportunities that others overlook or view to be problems.
2. They develop new marketing strategies that draw on their unique insights. They view the status quo and conventional wisdom as something to be challenged.
3. They take risks that others, lacking their vision, consider foolish.
4. They live in fear of being preempted in the market.
5. They are fiercely competitive.
6. They think through the implications of any proposed strategy, screening it against their knowledge of how the marketplace functions. They identify and solve problems that others do not even recognize.
7. They are meticulous about details and are always in search of new competitive advantages in quality and cost reduction, however small.
8. They lead from the front, executing their management strategies enthusiastically and autocratically. They maintain close information control when they delegate.
9. They drive themselves and their subordinates.
10. They are prepared to adapt their strategies quickly and to keep adapting them until they work. They persevere long after others have given up.
11. They have clear visions of what they want to achieve next. They can see further down the road than the average manager can see.

The Dynamic Process

Each of the statements in the circular flow in Figure 1-2 is linked in a complex cause-and-effect set of relationships. While the cyclical process has no clear beginning or end, we will start with the proposition that the nature and quantity of a seller's offerings are always changing. At any time, some sellers are changing their products/services and production processes faster than others. In some very mature markets, the rate at which suppliers change can be very slow. In other high-growth markets, where there is a great deal of technological innovation (such as the personal computer market) the rate at which suppliers change is very high. Figure 1-3 presents a graphic case study of the competitive rationality of IBM in the personal computer market. In the early 1980s, IBM made the market with superb launches of its PC, XT, and AT. However, by the middle to late 1980s, the quality of IBM's competitive rationality had clearly slipped. Several factors contributed to this decline: bureaucratic complacency, internal pressures from the powerful midsize and mainframe divisions to slow down further innovations that would inevitably cannibalize *their* sales,[2] an inadequate awareness of the evolving market segments, and the innovations of competitors such as Compaq, Apple, Dell, and Toshiba.

The proposition that free markets are constantly evolving through an innovation-imitation process that accelerates, slows down to a trickle, and surges again assumes

2. It is reasonable to assume that IBM was well aware of the parallels between the evolution of the calculator market and that of the PC market; given the geometric increases in the power of the chips, the new generations of PCs that followed the AT would ultimately destroy the market for mid-range and mainframe computers. IBM's fundamental competitive irrationality was that it was not prepared to allow new generations of its PCs to aggressively attack its big-machine markets. The long-term consequence was that even though IBM would not wage such an attack, competitors would. The result for IBM was even more catastrophic than the painful cannibalizing of its highly profitable mature products.

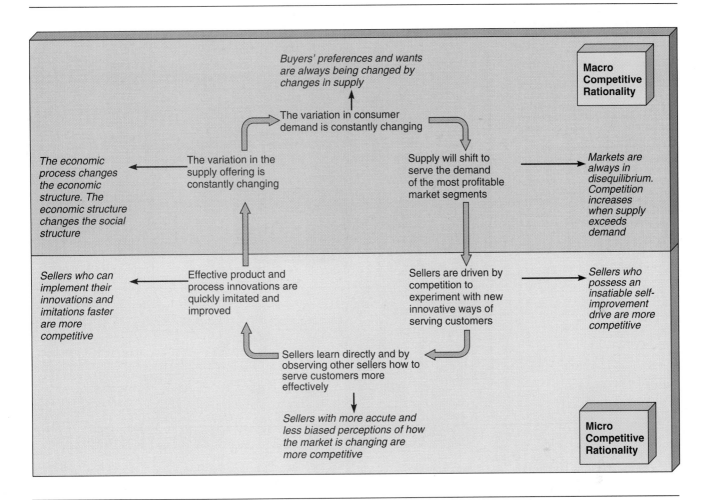

Buyers' preferences and wants are always being changed by changes in supply

The variation in consumer demand is constantly changing

The economic process changes the economic structure. The economic structure changes the social structure

The variation in the supply offering is constantly changing

Supply will shift to serve the demand of the most profitable market segments

Markets are always in disequilibrium. Competition increases when supply exceeds demand

Macro Competitive Rationality

Sellers who can implement their innovations and imitations faster are more competitive

Effective product and process innovations are quickly imitated and improved

Sellers are driven by competition to experiment with new innovative ways of serving customers

Sellers who possess an insatiable self-improvement drive are more competitive

Sellers learn directly and by observing other sellers how to serve customers more effectively

Sellers with more accute and less biased perceptions of how the market is changing are more competitive

Micro Competitive Rationality

The top half of the figure describes macro market behavior; the bottom half describes an individual firm's micro be-havior. The logical consequences and implications of the theoretical propositions *are italicized.* Each proposition serves as a basis for the next proposition. For example, the constantly changing variation in supply leads to a con-stantly changing variation in demand, which leads to supply shifting to serve the demand of the more profitable market segments, which creates a drive to try new ways of better serving the segment. This leads to new learning, which leads to more effective and faster imitation, which creates the constantly changing variation in supply. Unlike most theories, competitive rationality does not have a set of initial premises upon which all other propositions are based. Instead, each proposition serves as a premise for a following proposition. This explains why there is not an obvious starting point in the figure. It also explains why competitive rationality is a dynamic theory of endless innovation-imitation cycles of product forms, distribution channels, and market behaviors, ever advancing in efficiency and effectiveness.

Figure 1-2

The Macro and Micro Theory of Competitive Rationality

that product-markets go through many cycles, rather than a single cycle. Marketers have studied the *product life-cycle,* which is the introductory, growth, maturity, and decline stages of a physical product form.[3] Competitive rationality is a theory of endless innovation-imitation life cycles. The theory emphasizes that sellers are constantly impacting their marketplace environment as well as being impacted. The Rationality in Practice box beginning on page 12 presents a case history of how one company, Bausch & Lomb, has shaped its competitive environment. This example demonstrates

3. See Chapter 9 for an extended discussion of the product life cycle.

Figure 1-3

The Application of Competitive Rationality to IBM and the PC Market

The figure traces the hugely successful competitive rationality of IBM in its early years and its later competitive irrationality. Why IBM faltered is still unclear, but it had a lot to do with internal organizational resistance to the continued development of new super-powerful, networkable PCs, which threatened IBM's highly profitable midsize and mainframe product lines. In 1992, after several earlier attempts to reorganize itself, IBM announced plans to break up into several companies. An independent IBM PC company, with strategic alliances with companies such as Apple, may again become a dominant innovator-imitator, very likely at the expense of the IBM computer companies selling more traditional computers. The story continues.

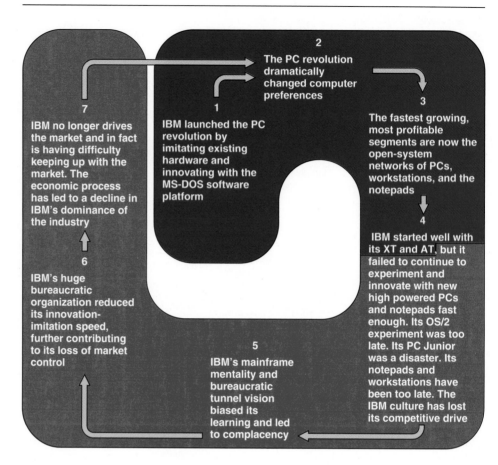

how a market can be impacted by substantial improvements in product design, reductions in production costs, and changes in distribution channels and competition. Consumer attitudes can be changed, public opinion shifted, competitors driven away or acquired, new channels established, and laws changed.

Creating Uncertainty and Change

A firm faces a changing, uncertain business environment. The firm also *creates* uncertainty for itself, and its competition, by its marketplace actions. An innovation in production, product, or marketing will create uncertainty and confusion. Entrepreneurial firms not only love change and doubt, they love creating change and doubt. It plays to their strength, which is dealing with uncertainty.[4] Whether creating change, or responding to change, a company must carefully anticipate the short and long-term effects of its marketing strategies.

The ability to change a market, rather than have to adapt to a market, would seem to be the most successful position for a company to be in, but even this can have its risks. The great business cartels or trusts that were formed in the United States in the

4. Tom Peters, *Thriving on Chaos* (New York: Harper & Row, 1987).

late nineteenth century were considered by many economists of the time to be shining examples of social and economic Darwinism. Most of these cartels became so successful that, like bulldozers, they spent more time shaping their markets than adapting to them. In the end, their competitive rationality failed them in that they did not recognize 1) the extent to which they had alienated the distribution channels, farmers, and other consumers they served, 2) the accommodations they should have made with President Theodore Roosevelt's administration, and 3) the power they had given the Supreme Court to break them up in the general clauses of the Sherman Act, whose passage they had slyly promoted as a sop to public opinion.

How Supply Changes Demand

The changing nature of the market offerings of sellers changes demand. Sony's introduction of the transistor radio and Walkman dramatically changed demand for entertainment appliances. Other innovations, such as color TV, changed demand, but not uniformly across the whole market of interested consumers. Different potential buyers respond in different ways and at different rates to a new innovation or to a change in the supply of a product or service. Such variability in the response of buyers to changes in the offering leads to changes in the different submarkets, called market segments. **Market segments** are groups of consumers who seek the same benefits from a product or service (demand segments) or who have similar buying habits (contact segments). (Market segments will be discussed more extensively in Chapter 3.)

Because sellers want to increase profits, they will target their marketing efforts toward what they believe to be the more attractive market segments. This shifting of sellers' resources and marketing efforts to, for example, a new country, working women, or the elderly creates an imbalance of supply and demand (a *market disequilibrium*). Initially, a move to a new segment by a firm that has a superior fit to that segment results in an increase in demand disequilibrium for the firm's product or service. This in turn leads to greater profits for that firm within the segment. Later on, as more firms recognize this segment and the superior fit of their rival, they imitate, thus creating an increase in supply and an excess supply disequilibrium. An intensification of the rivalry to serve and gain the patronage of consumers in the market segments then occurs, leading us to the micro theory of competitive rationality.

The Micro Theory of Competitive Rationality

This intensification of seller rivalry increases the following three drives.

The Customer Satisfaction Drive

In a changing and competitive environment, in which the behavior of competitors is uncertain, can a decision maker be sure that what is being done today will, indeed, be sufficient tommorow? Buyer preferences, choice, and satisfaction are dependent on the behavior of all sellers. An intelligent seller recognizes that it is in a contest with its rivals. The rivals compete to fulfill the expectations of the target market segment and create higher levels of satisfaction by designing, manufacturing, and delivering the quality performance that the target customer wants. The constant improvement of product and service quality are the first two points in the W. Edwards Deming management method.[5]

---

5. Mary Walton, *The Deming Management Method* (New York: Putnam, 1986). Almost all of the total quality movement gurus emphasize the relentless drive to improve customer satisfaction.

Rationality in Practice:

How Bausch & Lomb Shaped the Soft Contact Lens Market

In 1971, Bausch & Lomb developed and improved upon a Czechoslovakian technique and began making and marketing a soft contact lens through ophthalmologists, optometrists, and opticians. For three years the company had the market to itself (a 100 percent market share) and behaved somewhat like the traditional monopolist. It charged high prices and upset some eye professionals. B&L charged them $25 to attend classes that taught how to fit soft lenses and required them to pay up front for large inventories. When competitors, who offered some design improvements and price cuts, entered the market, many of B&L's clients were eager to do business with the new rivals. By 1978, Bausch & Lomb's market share had plunged to 50 percent.

In 1979, B&L's new chief executive introduced "new, improved" models, soothed upset customers, and cut prices by 28 percent. B&L had claimed that its secret production process was able to injection spin and cast a lens for $2, compared to the $5–$7 it cost the competition to manufacture a lathed lens. In addition, lathed lenses could not be reproduced with the same precision, which was important as the new soft lenses lasted only 18 months on average and individual refitting was expensive and time consuming for the customer.

A price-cutting war ensued, a Federal Trade Commission decision allowed the advertising of contact lens prices, and manufacturers granted big cooperative advertising allowances to retailers. These factors galvanized the big optical chains, such as Pearle and Sterling Optical. The retail price of a pair of soft contact lenses fell from $300 to under $100. The number of wearers doubled in just two years to 5 million. Two-thirds of the new sales went to Bausch & Lomb. However, its competitive onslaught crippled a number of competitors and drove them into the arms of bigger, more market-oriented companies such as Revlon and Johnson & Johnson. B&L's developing relationships with the emerging optical chains also infuriated the traditional channels, the independent optometrists, and opticians.

In 1981, Revlon and Cooper Vision introduced extended wear lenses that could be worn continuously for a whole month. It took until 1983 for B&L to launch its extended wear lens, but when it did, it did so with a vengeance. Within four months, it had its product in 90 percent of the 12,000 eye-care outlets across the United States

and claimed 37 percent of the extended wear market. Its entry wholesale price of $20 was 50 percent or more below the industry norm for such lenses. Clearly, B&L was intent on having price pull demand through the distribution channel (rather than pushing its lens down the channel), as lower prices meant lower overall dollar margins. Bausch & Lomb's production cost was estimated to have dropped to $1.10 per lens. Cooper Vision responded with a $15 price for its top-quality lens, and B&L reacted by dropping its premium product to $10–$15, depending on the distributor volume (thus giving the chains an advantage over the independents). Its sales immediately tripled.

By 1984, the replacement market had become very large, and market saturation was nowhere near in sight. While only a quarter of the 47 million Americans who needed vision correction were wearing soft lenses, many more millions were expected to enter the market when soft lens bifocals were introduced and age caught up with the baby boomers. Tinted lenses have also opened up a fashion market, with many users owning a pair of clear lenses *and* a pair of tinted lenses.

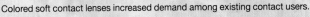
Colored soft contact lenses increased demand among existing contact users.

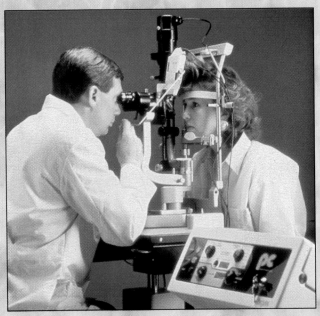
The 30-second laser refractive surgery in process.

In 1987, Viskaton, a small division of Johnson & Johnson, beat Bausch & Lomb to the market with disposable contact lenses that cost $250 per year but do not require the cleaning solutions that cost about $100 per year. Profits were still high, and in 1990 the U.S. Department of Justice started an investigation of competitive practices. A lens cost 50 cents to manufacture, was sold to a doctor at $2.50, then doubled to $5 at retail.

However, the eye-care industry was about to undergo another turbulent period for two reasons. First, Wal-Mart and Kmart (working with Lenscrafters) entered the retail market by opening hundreds of full service outlets within their stores by 1992. Second, corneal sculpting was developed in 1988 to permanently correct nearsightedness, farsightedness, and astigmatism. The laser refractive surgical procedure takes 20 to 30 seconds and the entire operation takes about 30 minutes per eye, all at a cost of $1,000 to $2,000. Some 3,000 patients have had the surgery and

improved procedures are constantly being developed that reduce any slight risks, the cost, and the price. Bausch & Lomb has lost much of its early control of the contact-lens market, and it appears likely that the new surgical service (which is certain to come down in price) will make glasses and contact lenses obsolete.

This history demonstrates how changes in technology, competition, distribution channels, and public policy influenced B&L's strategy. It also describes how B&L's strategy changed the competitive marketplace for both manufacturers and retailers.

Sources: This case was mainly based on the following articles: "Bausch & Lomb: Hardball Pricing Helps It to Regain Its Grip in Contact Lenses," *Business Week,* July 16, 1984, 78–80; Hugh D. Menzies, "The Hard Fight in Soft Lenses," *Fortune,* July 27, 1981, 56–60; "New Disposable Contact Lenses, *New York Times,* July 15, 1987, D4; Rebecca Perl, "Lasers May Mean Sight for Poor Eyes," *Atlanta Constitution,* October 3, 1991, C3; and Iving Arons, *Laser Focus World,* March 1992, 53–62.

The Cost Reduction Drive

Lowering average and marginal costs enables the firm to reduce price, or to increase profits at the present price, and allows more options and slack in decision making. The effects of cost-cutting innovations are particularly attractive, because their resulting effects are more predictable than other innovations. Moreover, a firm has greater control over costs than it does over other aspects of its marketing. Cost innovations are also less likely to be detected and immediately imitated than are product or marketing program innovations. The simple and rational desire for greater profits leads decision makers to seek new ways of reducing costs *without* affecting the potency of the output.[6] Modern information systems, which provide accurate and prompt feedback on price-reduction ideas, have made cost reduction more feasible.[7]

The Improved Decision-making Drive

The competitively rational firm also relentlessly strives to improve its implementation and decision-making routines by using new information technologies and analytical tools and by moving from bureaucratic decision making to the new, cross-functional, clan decision making.[8] In a sense, the firm is searching for ways to increase the quality of its competitive rationality, such as is suggested by the total quality movement (the effort to increase product quality) and the theory of competitive rationality. The advantage of this drive is that it leads to new decision-making and implementation processes that create a unique, very competitive organizational culture that is difficult to imitate. It also eliminates production and decision-making processes that add little or no value.

The firms with organizational cultures that are energized by these three drives strive the hardest in their search for new ways of effectively and efficiently serving consumers. These firms are constantly experimenting with new approaches that increase customer satisfaction, reduce costs, or increase the quality and speed of the firm's decision making and implementation. This ceaseless motivation to improve encourages sellers to learn from their own trial-and-error experiments, rivals' experiments, and the experiments of sellers in very different markets. The sellers that are most alert and able to learn in all three of these ways are the most competitive. Alertness requires an acute, unbiased perception of change and the insightful consideration of the impact of such change on all aspects of market decision making. However, it is normally not enough to be alert. A seller also needs to come up with creative ways to use its organizational resources and competencies to adapt to change and create additional change and further problems for its rival sellers.

The mere formulation of creative new ideas is also insufficient. As mentioned earlier, the enterprise has to implement product and marketing strategies and tactics that are imitations and improvements on what has been learned from studying the market. Companies that are very good at implementing (getting things done) have an inherent competitive advantage. They are able to change and adapt faster. That is why so much emphasis is being given these days to increasing the speed of new product develop-

---

6. As we will see later in the text, the application of the total quality management approach is often able to achieve an increase in quality *and* a reduction in costs at the same time. It is true, however, that a firm has to be careful not to reduce costs that will lead to a reduction in product or service quality that is noticed by consumers.
7. B. Charles Ames and James D. Hlavacek, "Vital Truths about Managing Your Costs," *Harvard Business Review*, (January/February 1990), 140–47.
8. William G. Ouchi, "A Conceptual Framework for the Design of Organizational Control Mechanisms," *Management Science* 25 (September 1979), 833–47; and "Markets, Bureaucracies, and Clans," *Administrative Science Quarterly* 25 (March 1980), 129–41.

ment.[9] If several sellers are equally driven and equally smart, the firm that is fastest at implementation will win. Economic competition does have some parallels with natural evolution and the deployment of resources in military strategy.

The Macro Theory of Competitive Rationality

Finally, the theory of competitive rationality also answers a fundamental question: What are the minimum requirements needed to create and sustain a competitive, progressive market economy? There must be freedom of buyer and seller choice, variability in the rate of change of supply among suppliers, variability in the rate of change of demand among buyers, and the desire for more profits. Under such conditions, a market will continue to increase customer satisfaction and the efficient use of resources. In a sense, it becomes a perpetual motion machine, with each new state of disequilibrium changing seller behavior, which, in turn, creates a new state of disequilibrium. Markets do not mature, they simply ebb and flow in their rate of seller-driven change.[10]

The *marketing concept* is to make sales and profits by focusing on, serving, and satisfying the customer. In many textbooks, the marketing concept frequently takes on the characteristics of a moral maxim that serves to dignify and legitimize the marketing profession and discipline. The theory of competitive rationality explains why the marketing concept is theoretically much more than a moral maxim and morally, much less. The theory of competitive rationality is that oligopolistic *rivalry* forces a seller to serve the interests of customers noticeably better than its competition. Such customer service improvement is a deliberate, relentless process with a clearly intended end; it is not incidental, coincidental, accidental, or unintended (as is suggested by Adam Smith's "invisible hand" explanation of why market economics is the most efficient political economy). The theory of competitive rationality links the marketing concept to the invisible hand by recognizing that it is *competition* that forces a customer or market orientation. The greater the rivalry between sellers, the greater will be the customer's focus and service. The presence or threat of competition results in more customer focus, innovative customer products and services, lower prices, and, consequently, a more efficient utilization of resources.

This proposition addresses the debate as to whether companies should adopt a competitive or a customer focus. A competitive focus is not an alternative to a customer focus: the greater the competition, the greater the firm's need to focus on and serve the customer better than the competition through higher quality, more services, and lower prices. The explicit connection between competition, serving the customer, and self-interest has not been recognized by many scholars, including Smith. A major tenet of his *Theory of Moral Sentiments* is the obligation of the individual to consider and serve the interests of others. But in a fascinating omission, he did not apply this ethic to a sellers' obligation to its customers. Nor did he ever state that, whether or not a seller is morally disposed to do so, competition forces a seller to serve the interests of

9. Brian Dumaine, "How Managers Can Succeed Through Speed," *Fortune,* February 13, 1989, 54–59; Joseph L. Bower and Thomas M. Hout, "Fast-Cycle Capability for Competitive Power," *Harvard Business Review,* November/December 1988, 110–118; George Stalk, "Time—The Best Source of Competitive Advantage," *Harvard Business Review,* July/August 1988, 41–51; and Murray R. Millson, S. P. Raj, and David Wilemon, "A Survey of Major Approaches for Accelerating New Product Development," *Journal of Product Innovation Management* 9 (1992), 53–69.
10. It has also been argued that it is not the "maturity" of an industry that determines the long-term profitability of a firm but rather the vitality and innovation of firms in an industry (that is, their competitive rationality) that determines the vitality and profitability of a market or industry. See Charles Baden-Fuller and John Stopford, *Rejuvenating the Mature Business* (Lordon, Routledge, 1992); and Peter Reid Dickson "Toward a General Theory of Competitive Rationality."

consumers. From the above theory of competitive rationality, the firm also earns profits (entrepreneurial rents) from the insights (private information) that result from a consumer focus.

The marketing concept is theoretically much more than a moral maxim because it is a normative proposition that can be derived from the theory of competitive rationality and (along with its driver, which is competition) explains how the "invisible hand" works. It is much less than a moral maxim because a firm has no choice but to adopt it, if it wishes to succeed in a market economy. The marketing concept is not based on an ethic or a moral value system that is freely chosen, and therefore it cannot be viewed as a moral tenet or maxim.

Marketing Decision Making

Competitive decision making can be characterized as a routine that produces competitive strategy and tactics used against or to counter competitors. Consequently, the study of the competitive rationality of an individual firm boils down to the study of its decision-making routines. It is a crucial first step to improving the quality of management. Such routines are the genes of the firm upon which its long-term success and survival depend.[11] These routines are little understood, having been largely neglected by economists and psychologists, despite their tremendous importance to the competitiveness of firms. But even firms themselves often do not have clear, written, standard operating procedures for decision making or planning. This is so, even though it has been shown that the credibility and use of marketing plans are increased by having rules and procedures that are clearly specified and by the wide participation of relevant personnel in the planning process (that is, the use of cross-functional teams).[12]

So what exactly is the nature of such decision-making routines, and what components most increase the competitive rationality of the firm? The theory of competitive rationality proposes that a clear competitive advantage is to make informed decisions quickly. Thus, one of the first and most interesting concerns is determining how firms update their planned strategies and tactics. In a recent study of major companies, only *half* of the respondents reported that their marketing plans were continuously reviewed and adapted throughout the year.[13] At best, this result suggests that many markets are stable and have very little innovation-imitation; hence, firms do not have to adapt their planned market behavior. At worst, it suggests a mental standstill—a wooden-headed refusal to keep up with changes in the marketplace and a lack of the drive to improve.

An organization's survival depends on its ability to learn and adapt quickly; in practice, this means that plans often must be altered at the very time they are being implemented. But such changes must be carefully considered and reasoned. Tinkering with plans destroys an organization's ability to execute any coherent strategy. The dilemma then is how to effectively implement strategy and yet remain responsive to new market realities? The decision-making and planning routine described in Figure 1-4 addresses

11. Richard R. Nelson and Sidney G. Winter, *An Evolutionary Theory of Economic Change* (Cambridge, MA: Harvard University Press, 1982).
12. George John and John Martin, "Effects of Organizational Structure of Marketing Planning on Credibility and Utilization of Plan Output," *Journal of Marketing Research* 21 (May 1984), 170–83.
13. Peter R. Dickson and Rosemary Kalapurakal, "The 'What to Market' and 'How to Market' Decision-Making Process" (Working Paper, # 92–49, Columbus: Ohio State University, 1992).

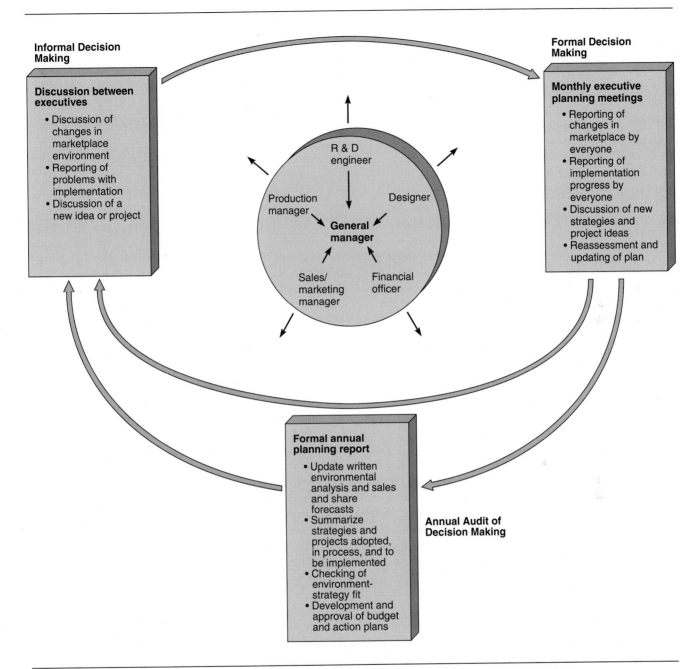

Informal Decision Making

Discussion between executives

- Discussion of changes in marketplace environment
- Reporting of problems with implementation
- Discussion of a new idea or project

R & D engineer

Production manager

Designer

General manager

Sales/ marketing manager

Financial officer

Formal Decision Making

Monthly executive planning meetings

- Reporting of changes in marketplace by everyone
- Reporting of implementation progress by everyone
- Discussion of new strategies and project ideas
- Reassessment and updating of plan

Formal annual planning report

- Update written environmental analysis and sales and share forecasts
- Summarize strategies and projects adopted, in process, and to be implemented
- Checking of environment-strategy fit
- Development and approval of budget and action plans

Annual Audit of Decision Making

Throughout the year, informal decisions impact and are impacted by the more formal decisions made in cross-functional team meetings. The decisions made in these meetings throughout the year are summarized and reviewed in the annual marketing plan. Once established, this plan forms the foundation for decision making in the new year. At the center of this decision-making plan in an entrepreneurial organization is a cross-functional team made up of senior management. In a larger organization, the continuous decision-making process flows around a cross-functional product team.

Figure 1-4

Continuous Marketing Decision Making

this fundamental dilemma.[14] It has two important features. The first is the involvement of key executives of the company (or the division of a large company) in making marketing decisions—not just approving them. The second is the continual updating of decisions, plans, and programs. The continual revision of decision making is consistent with the dynamics of competitive rationality described earlier. It also reflects a constant strive to do better, a key element of competitive rationality.

Cross-functional Decision-making Teams

In the routine described in Figure 1-4, the division manager or chief operating officer chairs an executive committee made up of the managers of the major departments or functions (from here on called a *team*).[15] This team prepares, approves, and oversees the implementation of all functional plans, including the marketing plan. All of the functional plans are integrated into the divisional business plan. This approach is not as radical as it first appears. Senior executive committees have always explicitly addressed major marketing decisions, such as long-term target markets, product positioning, and pricing. Their planning has always involved decisions about new products, the vertical integration of distribution, alliances with suppliers, and other strategic mergers and acquisitions. These are all major marketing strategy decisions. New marketing strategies are also often implicit in major plant expansion decisions. Each of these long-term marketing decisions somewhat constrains succeeding shorter-term marketing strategies and tactics. It is, thus, not a huge step to involve the senior executive team in all market decisions. This involvement has been facilitated by the removal of layers of gate-keeping middle management, thereby increasing the informal contact between senior executives and front-line managers. Another advantage of this approach is that it helps to better integrate marketing strategy with company production and financial strategies. It thus directly addresses the concern that functional silos frustrate communication and timely decision making.[16]

It is not suggested that the marketing function in the firm is eliminated. It is still responsible for market analysis, preparing environment reports, suggesting new strategies and tactics, developing the marketing *action* plans and programs, and implementing them. Moreover, the marketing philosophy of making sales and profits by satisfying targeted customers better than competitors do has become accepted by all firms facing vigorous competition. The reason is simple. Competition has forced the adoption of such a philosophy in the same way that competition has forced an emphasis on quality and efficiency in every element of a firm's behavior, including its decision making.

Senior executives who have become steeped in a product-market often have an intuitive ability to scan the total business environment and identify significant changes in the marketplace. They are also skilled at drawing higher-order strategic implications

14. This model is based on the following research: H. Mintzberg, D. Raisinhani, and A. Theoret, "The Structure of Unstructured Decision Processes," *Administrative Science Quarterly* (June 1976), 246–75; Henry Mintzberg and James A. Waters, "Of Strategies, Deliberate and Emergent," *Strategic Management Journal,* 6 (1985), 257–72; J. B. Quinn, *Strategies for Change: Logical Incrementalism* (Homewood, IL: Irwin, 1980); Frederick Webster, "Top Management's Concerns about Marketing: Issues for the 1980s," *Journal of Marketing,* 45 (Summer 1981), 9–16, 45; Michael D. Hutt, Peter H. Reingen, and John R. Ronchetto, Jr., "Tracing Emergent Processes in Marketing Strategy Formation," *Journal of Marketing,* 52 (January 1988), 4–19; Peter R. Dickson and Rosemary Kalapurakal, "The 'What to Market' and 'How to Market' Decision-Making Process" (Working Paper, Columbus: Ohio State University).
15. For a detailed discussion of team decision making and management, see Appendix 1 and Jon R. Katzenbach and Douglas K. Smith, *The Wisdom of Teams: Creating the High Performance Organization* (Cambridge, MA: Harvard Business School, 1993).
16. Frederick E. Webster, *It's 1990—Do You Know Where Your Marketing Is?* (MSI White Paper, Cambridge, MA: Marketing Science Institute, 1989).

from such new information. In particular, they are adept at interpreting information from many different perspectives and are therefore less subject to framing biases.[17] They are more alert because they are more skilled problem finders and more skilled at recognizing opportunities. Of course, they are not perfect decision makers, but they do not have to be perfect, just better than the competition. Decision making is still uncertain and chancy, but chance favors the prepared mind and the minds of senior executives are better prepared. Senior managers are also able to get things done quickly and implemented right the first time. Their active involvement in marketing management increases the competitive rationality of the firm because it increases the drive to improve, elevates the alertness and learning of the firm, and improves the quality and speed of implementation.

New Product Development Decision Making

New product development decision making requires a greater amount of engineering and design expertise. As a result, many U.S. companies now create special cross-functional teams to plan and develop new products. This team is made up of talented, younger marketers, designers, engineers, operations experts, and logistics executives, all eager to make a name for themselves in new product development. This may be because success in new product development is often the fast track to senior management. These teams operate in a manner very similar to that illustrated in Figure 1-4. The process is called *concurrent engineering*. The group meets constantly to report on progress and the new decisions that have to be made. The meetings are also held as needed, rather than by the calendar. This new product development process is described in detail in Chapter 9. In most cases, the senior management executive committee in a division will be kept informed by a senior manager who is championing, if not heading up, the new product development team. Senior management will also ultimately make the "go" decision, thereby approving the proposed competitive positioning strategy and implementation programs.

While it is important to note the unique composition and behavior of cross-functional teams assembled to develop a new product, it is equally important to note that there is not a lot of difference between new product management and the marketing management of a mature product. New product management is the management of innovation-imitation, with an emphasis on innovation. But marketing management is also managing innovation-imitation. An aggressive, driven firm is likely to create the same sort of cross-functional teams to manage all of its products, whether new or used. This is because a cross-functional product development team is likely to come up with innovations that make an even established product "new." In fact, three out of five marketing plans of industrial and consumer-goods companies contain new product action programs. Almost 80 percent of service firm marketing plans contain new service development action programs.[18]

Continuous decision making takes two forms that vary in formality. The first is the casual discussion between executives, during which new information and ideas are shared and evaluated (this discussion is usually followed up by a memo that proposes

Continuous Decision Making and Improvement

17. Michael J. Prietula and Herbert A. Simon, "The Experts in Your Midst," *Harvard Business Review,* January/February 1989, 120–24; Walter Keichel, "How Executives Think," *Fortune,* February 4, 1985, 127–28; and Daniel J. Isenberg, "How Senior Managers Think," *Harvard Business Review,* November/December 1984, 81–90.
18. Howard Sutton, *Marketing Planning* (New York: The Conference Board, 1990).

a change in plans). The proposal is then discussed at formal meetings that are held regularly throughout the year to monitor progress in implementing the plan and to discuss emerging issues and new strategies or tactics. Continuous decision making does not occur spontaneously. It is driven by a company culture that is itself driven by the three competitive drives. Continuous decision making is demanding and can be time consuming, but the process results in a better plan and the perception of a better plan. This raises morale, esprit de corps, and the enthusiasm needed for successful implementation.

Informal Processes

In many firms, a great deal of information is sought and disseminated on a seemingly casual basis. This crucial determinant of the firm's competitive rationality serves many purposes. It is used to overcome political obstacles and gain cooperation, resources, and control. It often results in the suggestion and enhancement of new tactics and competitive strategy. This emergent process is dynamic, evolving as it goes, depending on what is learned and the behavior of different interest groups and organizational functions. The strategy emerges as a stream of decisions and en route adaptations to changes in the market environment or performance feedback.[19] This informal process seems to describe particularly the behavior of the new product development teams that employ concurrent engineering. Concurrent engineering, also called parallel or simultaneous engineering, involves the design, manufacturing, and marketing departments and suppliers working together on each of their functions concurrently, rather than in sequence. Simultaneous engineering requires considerable informal cooperation and decision making.

A high-tech firm's decision to launch a new avionics product is typical of such an unstructured decision process.[20] Key information from a salesperson triggered the innovation initiative, followed by a great deal of informal information gathering and decision making between R&D and marketing and close, back-and-forth consultations with customers. All of this interaction was driven and lead by the executive who championed the product.

A similar stream of research has described market decision making more generally as one of "logical incrementalism," in which decisions, events, and new information flow together over time to create a consensus for action among the members of an executive committee or cross-functional team.[21] The competitive positioning strategy emerges incrementally, in a way very different from the step-by-step formal planning process described in many marketing textbooks. There is more to the process than simply muddling through, because it involves a very systematic information search and the use of several total quality managment (TQM) procedures. This informal planning process is constantly alert to changes in the product-market, and it adjusts action plans to the new competitive, consumer, or channel circumstances. It is likely to be less subject to serious decision-making biases and, hence, will be more competitive and more profitable.[22] A potential problem with emergent strategy, however, is that it can become

19. Henry Mintzberg and James A. Waters, "Of Strategies, Deliberate and Emergent," *Strategic Management Journal* 6 (1985), 257–72; H. Mintzberg, D. Raisinghani, and A. Theoret, "The Structure of Unstructured Decision Processes," *Administrative Science Quarterly* (June 1976), 246–75; and Henry Mintzberg, "Patterns in Strategy Formulation," *Management Science* 24 (May 1978), 934–48.
20. Michael D. Hutt, Peter H. Reingen, and John R. Ronchetto, Jr. "Tracing Emergent Processes in Marketing Strategy Formation," *Journal of Marketing* 52 (January 1988), 4–19.
21. James Brian Quinn, *Strategies for Change: Logical Incrementalism* (Homewood, IL: R. D. Irwin, 1980), and "Formulating Strategy One Step at a Time," *Journal of Business Strategy* 1 (Winter 1981), 42–63.
22. Robin M. Hogarth, "Beyond Discrete Biases: Functional and Dysfunctional Aspects of Judgmental Heuristics," *Psychological Bulletin* 90.2 (1981), 197–217.

too responsive to the environment. A computer simulation found that reacting to every perceived change in the market is less profitable than only reacting to apparent fundamental trends.[23] In such circumstances, the steadying hand of a senior executive is particularly valuable.

As illustrated in Figure 1-4, the annual marketing plan still plays a vital role in such continuous decision making. First, its environmental analysis updates everyone about the current important issues, the emerging issues, and what has been learned during the year. Annual marketing planning allows for a review of the new strategies and tactics. It also checks the fit between current and proposed strategy and the changing market environment. Finally, it serves to remind the executive committee and others throughout the year of the goals, environmental assumptions, and the priority projects. Much of a firm's competitive rationality depends on the quality of its annual marketing planning.

Annual Marketing Planning

The STRATMESH decision-making process described in Figure 1-5 results in the preparation of the formal annual planning document. It is based on planning approaches used by many leading companies.[24] The routine is called STRATMESH because the distinctive feature of the planning routine is the careful *meshing* of the proposed *strategy* (product positioning and programs) with key facts about the environment.

The process starts with an understanding of the firm's current strategy and tactical programs. It then determines whether or not the firm stuck with its plan, and why it deviated from the plan. This procedure has two benefits. First, it briefs the team about the firm's current strategy, which must now be adapted to new environmental realities. Second, the deviations from what was planned identify 1) the planned programs that were based on incorrect assumptions about the environment, 2) changes that have occurred in the environment during the last planning period that necessitated changes in strategy, or 3) the implementation of unauthorized strategy and programs. Only about one in four of the marketing plans written by divisions of Fortune 500 companies report on implementation of the previous plan.[25] The next step, which can be started at the same time, is the analysis of the different marketplace environments.

The Competitive Importance of Market Analysis

The competitive importance of market analysis and learning was observed in Shell Oil's study of 30 companies that had survived in business for over 75 years.[26] What impressed the Shell planners was the ability of these companies to learn about their changing marketplaces. The cross-functional management teams in these companies were able to change their "shared mental models" of the marketplace faster than their competition did, including their views and models of consumer behavior, competitor behavior, and, perhaps most importantly, themselves. Such fast insight also gave them more time to innovate, imitate, and avoid crisis management. A company with such superior decision-making skills has a clear competitive advantage over its rivals.

23. Donald Gerwin and Francis D. Tuggle, "Modeling Organizational Decisions Using the Human Problem Solving Paradigm," *Academy of Management Review* (October 1978), 762–73.
24. Howard Sutton, *The Marketing Plan* (New York: The Conference Board, 1990).
25. Howard Sutton, *The Marketing Plan* (New York: The Conference Board, 1990).
26. Arie P. De Geus, "Planning as Learning," *Harvard Business Review,* March/April 1988, 70–74.

Figure 1-5

The Annual Planning Process

The bold arrows indicate the process involved in preparing and writing an annual marketing plan. For the sake of clarity, the feedback loops and decision recycling that occurs as a result of senior management review or action-planning problems are not included.

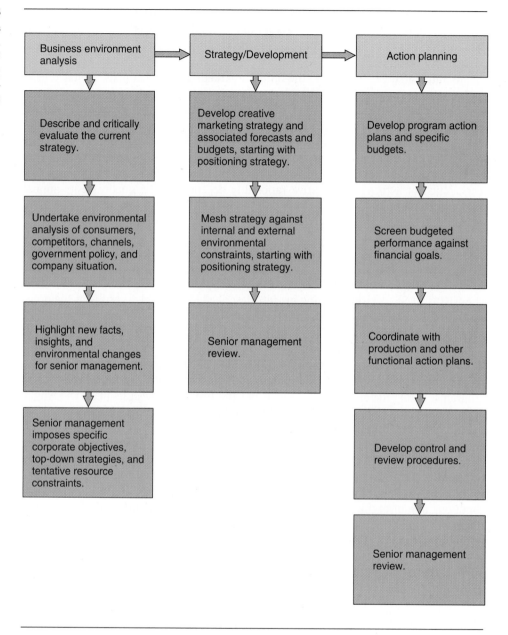

In recent years, some very creative research in economic psychology and marketing has revealed important biases in the use of information and decision making.[27] For example, decision makers tend to frame problems as either threats *or* opportunities,

27. Appendix 1, also J. H. Barnes, "Cognitive Biases and Their Impact on Strategic Planning," *Strategic Management Journal* 5 (April/June 1984), 129–38; Amos Tversky and Daniel Kahneman, "Rational Choice and the Framing of Decisions," *Journal of Business* 59(4) 1986, s251–s278; Robin M. Hogarth, *Judgement and Choice* (New York: John Wiley, 1987); William Samuelson and Richard Zeckhauser, "Status Quo Bias in Decision Making," *Journal of Risk and Uncertainty* 1 (1988), 7–59; J. E. Russo and P. J. H. Schoemaker, *Decision Traps: Ten Barriers to Brilliant Decision Making and How to Overcome Them* (New York: Doubleday, 1989).

and they overweigh certain information and depreciate other information. It seems that decision makers find it hard to view information as both a threat *and* an opportunity.

Framing the Business Environment

A marketplace is a mix of many, diverse players. Some share common interests, but each also has its own distinct interests. Successful decision-making teams do not think about how *the marketplace* will react to a new product or tactic. They think about how *different players in the marketplace* will react to the firm's behavior. It is like a game— you have to anticipate how the different players will react to your move. Some will welcome your moves, others will be indifferent to them, yet others will contest your moves.[28]

A market contains four types of players: consumers, competitors, distribution channel members and exchange facilitators, and regulators. Each of these groups can be further subdivided into segments, types, and individual entities. Consequently, it is generally recommended that the study of the external business environment be divided into four environments: the consumer, competitive, channel, and public-policy environments. If there are any other major players, special interest groups, or environments in the market not falling within these categories, then a separate section of the market analysis should describe the behavior and interests of these groups. The analysis of each of these groups of players is described in detail in Chapters 2 through 6.

The "game" is further complicated by the fact that a company is itself made up of different functional coalitions that represent different internal and external interests (stakeholders).[29] Often, the internal coalitions are linked to different external stakeholders. Each of these internal coalitions have to be considered, consulted, and accommodated during marketing decision making. The cross-functional team enables this consultation to occur immediately, thus saving time and reducing political problems.

Developing the Initial Strategy

A team is likely to develop the initial marketing strategy under general headings such as positioning, product, distribution, logistics, sales management, advertising and publicity, promotions, and price (see Chapters 8 through 13). If the consumer segmentation analysis suggests clearly differentiated strategies for different segments, then a separate marketing plan and planning process may be undertaken for each segment. These can be integrated by recognizing such concerns in the company section of the environmental analysis.

The initial strategy should be based on the current strategy described in the first step of the STRATMESH planning process, assuming the product has already been launched. In the case of a new product, the reality is that during the environment analyses, various product, distribution, promotion, and price tactics will suggest themselves to the team.[30] These ideas should be noted in a planning workbook. Consequently, it is fairly easy to produce a starting strategy, particularly when the team knows that the plan will be fleshed out and even changed in a major way during the meshing stage.

---

28. The problem with most game theories is that they only discuss games between two players (say, two competitors or a supplier and a distributor). Market games involve many players in different win-lose relationships with each other.
29. Paul F. Anderson, "Marketing, Strategic Planning, and the Theory of the Firm," *Journal of Marketing* 46 (Spring 1982), 15–26.
30. Most of these will be imitations of competitor tactics or tactics that have worked in other product-markets or foreign markets.

Meshing Strategy and Programs with the Environment

The first objective of market decision making is to avoid any serious allocation or implementation mistakes. If the decision making cannot at least do this, then the process is flawed, and the decision-making routine is a defective gene. Some argue that the most any decision-making approach can do is reduce the chances of making a serious mistake, because no decision-making approach can produce the one best strategy or most creative strategy.[31] Marketplace information is too limited and imperfect, the future is too unpredictable, company goals too changing, and human judgment too fallible. The research of human decision making undertaken over the last 20 years suggests that even the avoidance of mistakes is a very challenging task. This is because of a common information processing failure: key new facts about the market are identified, but the team fails to consider them when proposing and evaluating strategy and programs.[32] The strategy and the facts are not "fitted" when evaluating whether the strategy will work or not.

Minimizing Marketing Misfits

Some of the competitive difficulties faced by American firms in recent years have resulted from their inability to adapt to changing competitive markets. Many products were made that were no better or worse than new foreign products. Then, there are the really major blunders:

◆ Du Pont failed to consider that retail stores and shoe salespeople might not recommend its Corfam plastic over leather. If the distribution channel needed to sell the product does not believe in the product, then the product will fail.

◆ Time, Inc., launched a television guide that it planned to sell to cable television companies that competed with Time's own cable television network. It was an impossible sell.

◆ The Concorde supersonic passenger jet struggled to survive, not just because of public policy problems with noise pollution, but also because its airport-to-airport time-saving advantage was nullified by travel delays at either end of a trip (stacking, boarding, customs, taxis, and so on). It was a beautiful design and used pioneering technology. The concept failed, however, because too few fliers gained any real utility.

◆ General Electric thought it had the production and selling resources to compete in the computer mainframe market against IBM. It did not.

Twelve of the fourteen companies described as excellent American companies of 1982 in the classic book *In Search of Excellence* soon after stumbled because they failed to adapt to changes in their environments.[33] Between 1973 and 1988, the great marketing company Procter & Gamble lost an estimated quarter of a billion dollars doing business in Japan. It has been claimed that the company's marketing strategy did not fit consumer values, perceptions, and behavior, did not fit the distribution realities, did not respond to public policy environmental concerns, and underestimated

31. Herbert A. Simon, "Rational Decision Making in Business Organizations," *American Economic Review,* September 1979, 493–512; "Rationality As Process and As Product of Thought," *American Economic Review* 68.2 (May 1978), 1–16; "From Substantive to Procedural Rationality," in *Method and Appraisal in Economics,* ed. Spiro J. Latsis (Cambridge: Cambridge University Press, 1976), 129–48; and "On the Concept of Organizational Goal," *Administrative Science Quarterly* 9, June 1964, 1–22.
32. James K. Brown, *This Business of Issues: Coping with the Company's Environments* (New York: The Conference Board, 1979).
33. Thomas J. Peters and Robert H. Waterman, *In Search of Excellence* (New York: Harper Row, 1982) and the follow-up study in *Business Week,* November 5, 1984.

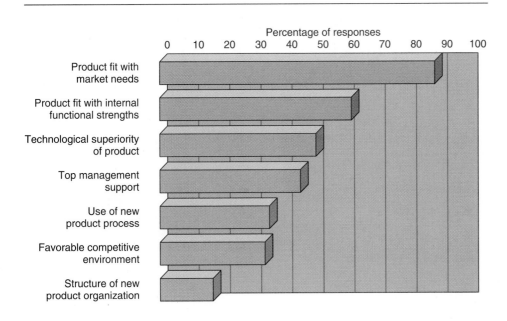

Percentage of responses

Product fit with market needs

Product fit with internal functional strengths

Technological superiority of product

Top management support

Use of new product process

Favorable competitive environment

Structure of new product organization

Figure 1-6

Reasons for New Product Success

The two most important determinants of new product success are whether the product fits market needs (external fit) and whether the product fits organization strengths (internal fit).

Source: Reproduced with permission from Booz, Allen and Hamilton, *New Products Management for the 1980s* (New York: Booz, Allen and Hamilton, 1982).

competition.[34] It is easy to second-guess these decisions. It is impossible to know exactly what went wrong and whether the mistakes could have been avoided. However, it does appear that the above strategies failed because of a critical weakness in team decision making. The product or marketing strategy failed to fit the environment. There were facts about the external marketplace or the company that should have been known and heeded by the team. Figure 1-6 presents the results of a study on what determines new product development success. It dramatically underlines the importance of making sure that a new product fits market needs and organizational strengths.

Figure 1-7 explains how marketing decision making can increase the fit between a proposed behavior and market realities. The proposed marketing strategy and tactics must be run through a series of loops representing what is known about each of the marketplace environments. For instance, if the proposed price does not meet the company's financial objectives, then the price may have to be adjusted and then re-checked to make sure the new price fits the other environmental facts. It now may not. If it is discovered that the proposed distribution strategy does not fit the channel environment, then it must be adjusted and the new distribution strategy checked for its fit with the other marketplace environments. It is best to start with the facts in the environmental analysis that describe the consumer environment. These facts act as prompts to help the planner evaluate the strategy from the consumer perspective. The strategy is then evaluated from the competitive, channel, and government perspectives. Finally, it is evaluated from the perspective of all interest groups in the company.

This meshing exercise is no small task. If the environment report contains five sections and the proposed strategy contains five sections (or programs), then there are 25 different environment-strategy combinations that have to be reviewed. This is

34. *Forbes,* December 15, 1986.

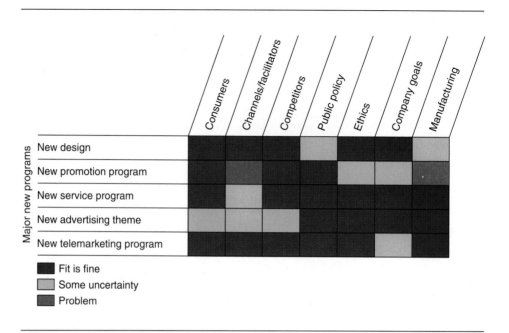

because each of the major tactical elements of strategy or programs (product, distribution, selling, advertising, and price) have to be reviewed from the perspective of each
of the major market players or environments. The task is made easier by constructing
a strategy *a* environment matrix where each proposed element of strategy can be
checked off against important new and old environmental facts (see Figure 1-7).
Another meshing tool can be established by creating a "meshing machine," which has
two rotating disks made of transparent film, one on top of the other. The new strategy
and program ideas are partitioned on the inner disk, and the new market realities are
partitioned on the outer disk. Each new idea can then be systematically rotated by each
of the key facts as described in Figure 1-8. The STRATMESH software can also be used
to mesh strategy against environmental facts (see Appendix 2).

STRATMESH emphasizes the meshing step. The word meshing is used because this
is not just a screening stage. The objective is to fit strategy to the environment. But
sometimes a firm will plan to execute a bold strategy that will change an aspect of the
environment to fit the firm's strategy. Meshing is also a stage for coming up with a
marketing strategy that is even better than the proposed approach. Screening implies
simply evaluating the proposed strategy to make sure it fits the facts. Meshing suggests
a more creative and positive fitting process. If a good strategy-environment fit cannot
be found, then the venture may have to be abandoned. But the planning process will
still have fulfilled its function by stopping the firm from wasting its resources. A tactic
or component of marketing strategy becomes a *problem* or a weakness and an environmental fact becomes an *issue* or a threat when the two do not seem to fit. There
are five ways to respond when this occurs: 1) a different or additional strategy can be
proposed which resolves the problem; 2) the environmental fact can be flagged for
study to ensure that it is correct; 3) the internally imposed constraints can be relaxed
if they are the problem; 4) the misfit can be tolerated and the problem watched very
carefully; or 5) the project can be abandoned. It is ultimately up to senior management
to determine which environmental-strategy problems, if any, should be tolerated. On

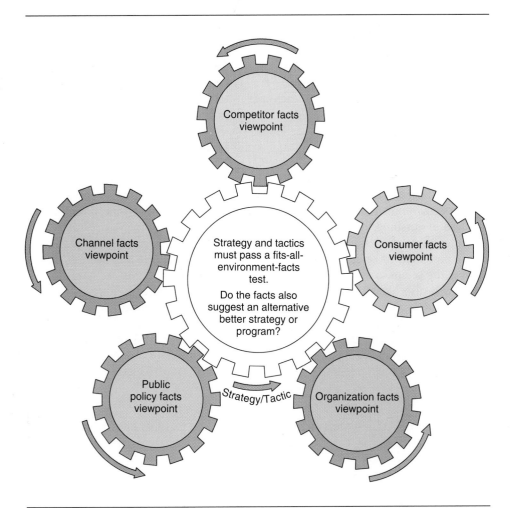

Figure 1-8

Meshing Strategy and Tactical Programs with Business Environmental Facts

A strategy or tactical program that does not mesh with the environmental facts is adapted until it meshes with the facts by considering the strategy from each environmental viewpoint. An environmental fact becomes a *threat* if any one of the viewpoints reveals a problem with the fit. An environmental fact becomes an *opportunity* if, in considering the fact, it suggests a better strategy or program. If several alternative strategies or programs pass the meshing test, then the alternative that is most potent (that will achieve the organization's major objectives most cost-efficiently) should be chosen. In the theory of competitive rationality this is called *bounded optimization*. Bounded optimization is defined as choosing the best option within the bounds of the limited information available, the viewpoints considered, and the current preeminent objectives of the organization.

the positive side, new tactics are almost certain to spring to mind when reviewing the current strategy against the facts.

This meshing approach can also be used in informal, continuous decision making. It contributes to the competitive rationality of both informal decision making and formal planning. For example, when faced with a crisis such as an unexpected external or internal event, the event that precipitated the crisis must be understood by assessing the effects of the event on all of the players. The decision-making team must quickly, but thoroughly, evaluate the effect of the event on existing strategy and propose new solutions. This is done by screening the existing strategy against the new realities detailed in a special report that describes the nature and extent of the crisis. This screening will identify the new problems, focus discussion on understanding why they are problems, and lead to solutions that are themselves screened against the new realities.

Avoiding Repercussion Mistakes

When strategy is changed, the new strategy should be checked for its fit against all environmental facts. This further screening avoids a repercussion mistake, which is similar to what occurs when a doctor prescribes a drug to treat an illness, only to discover that the drug's side effects kill the patient. Similarly, a firm may alter its pricing to cater to the demands of an important customer or customer segment, only to discover that this precipitates a price war, or that it alienates distributors. This is a repercussion mistake that can be reduced by considering any change in strategy or in a program from the perspective of each interested player.

If the marketing plan is important enough to the future of the enterprise, a final precautionary screening can be undertaken. The components of the suggested strategy are reviewed against each environmental sector and the following questions are asked: What change in this business environmental sector would greatly reduce the effectiveness of the strategy (perhaps even make it a foolhardy one), and how likely is it that this could happen? This approach tests the sensitivity of the strategy to changes in the business environment and gives the team a sense of the uncontrollable, downside risk involved in pursuing the strategy.

After completing the business environment-strategy meshing, the adapted strategy is presented to senior management for formal approval. If the decision-making team is the senior executive committee, then obviously this step is not needed. Such a review is also likely to result in a further alteration of strategy. However, the suggested changes proposed by senior executives should be treated the same way as any suggested changes: they should be scrutinized using the STRATMESH evaluation and then tactfully reviewed again with senior management. In the STRATMESH planning process, everyone in the planning team reviews the suggested strategy. If adopted, it then becomes everyone's strategy and everyone learns from its success or failure.

Implementation Planning

Just as the variance in ignorance of sellers and buyers presents opportunities for the marketing entrepreneur, the variance in ability to act or react quickly also presents opportunities. Even if we assume a market with perfect information, where all rivals learn at the same rate, there will still be entrepreneurial opportunities created by the differential implementation abilities of sellers. Conversely, the faster the competition, the fewer the opportunities for exploiting knowledge and response imperfections. Competition is more than just learning; it also involves developing the ability to implement quickly (see Figure 1-2). This hustle view of competitive advantage requires a top-gun mentality:

> Toyota and other fast-cycle companies resemble the World War II fighter pilots who consistently won dogfights, even when flying in technologically inferior planes. The U.S. Air Force found that the winning pilots completed the so-called OODA loop— Observation, Orientation, Decision, Action—faster than their opponents. Winning pilots sized up the dynamics in each new encounter, read its opportunities, decided what to do, and acted before their opponents could.[35]

Consistent with this view, the CEO of Hewlett-Packard, John Young, has introduced a new term, BET (break even time: the time from concept development to the break-even point in the marketplace), in his attempts to improve his company's speed. Many companies are reaching out to firms in other industries to learn how they are able to implement faster. This is a form of technology transfer across industries, but it is the transfer of the technology of how to get things done.

35. Joseph L. Bower and Thomas M. Hout, "Fast-Cycle Capability for Competitive Power," *Harvard Business Review,* November/December 1988, 112; also see George Stalk, "Time—The Best Source of Competitive Advantage," *Harvard Business Review,* (July/August 1988), 41–51; Murray R. Millson, S. P. Raj, and David Wilemon, "A Survey of Major Approaches for Accelerating New Product Development," *Journal of Product Innovation Management* 9 (1992), 53–69.

Routine Rigidity

Organizations can be trapped by prevailing operational routines that limit their ability to innovate, imitate, and implement. Many of these routines add very little value to the competitiveness of a firm's products or services. Such functional rigidity can be psychological, intraorganizational, and/or interorganizational. One of the most powerful psychological human behaviors is the inability to mentally shift from a successful, but inefficient, habitual activity to a more efficient way of solving a problem or achieving a goal.

Such mental inertia is due to more than just habit. It comes from a lack of motivation and the absence of an economic incentive to change behavior. The drive to continue to innovate will be reduced to the extent that innovation is perceived to threaten the sales and profits from past innovations. Thus, a highly profitable firm may be most vulnerable to attack because cautious insiders (often called "tree huggers") are not willing to change their behavior or the firm's behavior. Changing routines within an organization may also be resisted for fear that it would provoke conflict between functions and factions. Here again, the cross-functional decision-making team reduces such conflict.

The need for speed and the habitual tendencies of individuals and organizations requires that formal market planning include completion date deadlines, activity schedules, and the assignment of responsibility for tasks. The final senior management operational review approves these action programs. Sometimes it is discovered at this late stage that the company simply has not got the resources, or the time, to implement the proposed strategy in the plan. This may require a major revision of the planned strategy and tactics.

Table 1-1 presents The Conference Board findings about what types of action programs are most frequently included in marketing plans. First, it is clear that many

Table 1-1
Action Programs Usually Included in the Marketing Plan

	Industrial Products	Consumer Products	Service Firms
Field sales effort	66%	67%	73%
New product/service development	63%	64%	79%
Sales to major accounts	63%	44%	50%
Sales promotions	61%	73%	75%
Pricing policy	52%	42%	46%
Sales training	49%	42%	69%
Export sales	46%	21%	10%
Customer/product service	44%	39%	75%
Product quality	41%	39%	50%
Distributor/dealer relations	39%	39%	31%
Inventories/physical distribution	39%	35%	17%
Advertising themes	35%	52%	56%
Regional selling and promotion	32%	53%	52%
Packaging	23%	44%	23%
Telemarketing	21%	26%	58%
Other overseas marketing programs	22%	12%	17%

Source: Howard Sutton, *Marketing Planning* (New York: The Conference Board, 1990), Table 8.

marketing plans are dominated by sales management and promotion action programs such as field sales programs, major account selling programs, sales training programs, customer service programs, distributor/dealer relations programs, regional selling programs, promotion programs, and telemarketing programs. Marketing plans are more concerned with personal selling action programs than with advertising campaigns. Second, as mentioned earlier, most marketing plans include new product development action programs. Third, there are some logical differences between the marketing plans of industrial product companies, consumer product companies, and service firms. The plans of business-to-business firms include more action programs directed at major accounts and export sales. Service firms give more emphasis to new service programs, sales training (presumably because the provider of the service is often also the most influential salesperson), customer service, and telemarketing. Overall, however, the results of the study do not suggest that the marketing decision making of these different types of firms (as reflected in their written marketing plans) are radically different.

It is also evident that many tactical marketing decisions and execution details (such as advertising themes, physical distribution, and packaging) are not included in the marketing plan. Presumably, if they exist, they are specified as the year progresses, often emerging in response to new environment information about competitor behavior and the success of other company initiatives. Moreover, this process suggests that strategy sometimes opportunistically evolves from tactics, in addition to the conventional evolution of tactics from strategy.

The fact that some firms do not provide action plans for all of their programs in the marketing plan may frustrate efforts to speed up the implementation of decisions. If a major goal of the marketing planning effort is to reduce break-even time (BET), then habitual implementation practices have to be replaced by new, fast-track action plans, which require time-tagged activity sequences that must be documented, circulated, and used as control charts to achieve the deadlines.[36] The natural place for such new fast-cycle action programs would be in the annual marketing plan. Such detailed action planning is described in Chapter 14.

In conclusion, Table 1-2 presents the outline of a typical annual marketing plan. An example of an environment report and strategy report in a format that enables them to be meshed using the STRATMESH software is presented in Appendix 2.

Global Marketing Decision Making

Competitive rationality stresses understanding the business environment and responding to changes quickly. The only reason for not decentralizing decision making to the local executive team managing a regional or country market is because headquarter's decision-making skills are so much better that they more than compensate for the advantages of decentralized decision making. There are four major advantages to decentralized decision making by local teams: they are closer to the foreign market, they are able to understand changes in the foreign market faster, they can develop a better fit between marketing strategy and programs and the foreign market realities, and they are able to implement faster. Seldom do the superior skills of senior management outweigh these advantages. Marketing management must fit the competitive realities of a market, which often vary across foreign markets. Centralized global decision making

36. Murray R. Millson, S. P. Raj, and David Wilemon, " A Survey of Major Approaches for Accelerating New Product Development," *Journal of Product Innovation Management* 9 (1992), 53–69.

Table 1-2
The Typical Contents of an Annual Marketing Plan

Contents	Pages
Executive Summary	1
Environment Report	2–7
Consumer Analysis	
Competitor Analysis	
Channel Analysis	
Public Policy Analysis	
Company Analysis	
Strategy Report	8–12
Positioning Strategy	
Product Programs	
Pricing/Promotion Programs	
Distribution/Sales Programs	
Advertising/Publicity Programs	
Control Programs	
Forecasts and Budgets	13–15

can create suffocating and burdensome bureaucracies and the siren lure of international jet-setting can encourage quick-visit decision making (that is, decision making made during a very brief visit to the market). Continuous decision making cannot be made at arm's length. Decentralized decision making is essential in countries or regions where the pace of innovation-imitation is very high and/or the growth rate of the market is high.

Accepting that the norm should be to allow marketing strategy and programs to vary across global markets, what is the role of the head office in decision making? It can manage at least three programs: 1) the transfer of information and good ideas between markets, 2) the institution, promotion, and standardization of higher-quality decision-making routines in all of its foreign markets, and 3) the global coordination and rationalization of production activities, such as financing, procurement, manufacturing, and advertising creatives, when appropriate. Each of these three activities are now discussed in detail.

Consistent with the innovation-imitation principle of the theory of competitive rationality, it is very important that the head office facilitates the global transfer of good ideas. A communications system needs to be developed by which good ideas about competitive positioning, strategy, cost reduction, and implementation are quickly shared across the different international markets. In practice, this means the use of teleconferences, confidential newsletters, global electronic bulletin boards, and periodic meetings at corporate headquarters where problems, opportunities, and good ideas are shared. If Wal-Mart can use a satellite network to hold teleconferences with all store managers every Saturday, the same technology can be used to manage a global organization. Experts have stressed that the profits from global marketing come from sharing what is learned from experiments and initiatives in one market with sister markets. The result is an exchange of not just technology, but good marketing ideas among all of the global markets that the firm competes in.[37] This process of voluntarily accepting

37. John A. Quelch and Edward J. Hoff, "Customizing Global Marketing," *Harvard Business Review,* May/June 1986, 59–68.

good ideas from other markets may lead to the development of global standards. The important point is that this standardization comes about not because it was imposed by the head office, but because the voluntary acceptance of the idea was universal among the foreign decision-making teams.

Corporate management can standardize the informal decision-making processes and the formal planning process, including the reports, so that the decision-making routines are the same among foreign markets, even if the output is not the same. This is because the key elements of the competitive rationality process are the same in all markets. The standardized decision-making routine should encourage experimentation and creativity and make sure everyone learns from the experiments. It also needs to include the careful and deliberate meshing of the new programs with changing market realities. Most importantly, the disciplines of total quality management and fast implementation need to be introduced in all foreign markets—an easier task in some cultures than others.

Finally, global marketing is often concerned with achieving a competitive advantage by obtaining supply from the least expensive and highest quality global source. This applies to more than raw materials and manufacturing subassembly. It applies to finding the cheapest global source of funds for expansion and to finding the best marketing and advertising consulting advice. When such advantages exist, then such operations can be regionalized or even globalized. The acid test is whether the foreign managers themselves clearly see and initiate such a sourcing strategy, because the competitive advantages are very apparent in terms of higher customer satisfaction, lower costs, faster implementation, and bottom-line profits.

Discussion Questions and Minicases

1. What feature of the STRATMESH planning process is likely to increase the quality of intelligence gathering and environment analysis in a firm? Develop a step-by-step diagram that describes the evolution of higher-quality environment analysis. Theoretically, what does increasing the quality of environment analysis do?

2. Why does senior management need to institutionalize a marketing decision-making process in the firm that inherently demands alertness and adaptability? Isn't it good enough just to have sharp, alert people?

3. The advertisement on page 33 is for Susan B. Anthony coins. How might the STRATMESH process have spared the U.S. Mint, which has been in the sole business of making coins and paper money for 200 years, from the Susan B. Anthony blunder? What *further* mistake did the U.S. Mint make on this project?

4. Why do you think that experts such as Mintzberg and Quinn argue that strategy often opportunistically evolves or emerges from tactics rather than tactics evolving from strategy? Relate your answer to the planning processes described in the chapter.

5. Describe the marketplace constituencies that might be studied in an environmental analysis conducted by a university that is developing a marketing plan to attract more students?

6. Twelve of the fourteen companies described as excellent in the 1982 Peters and Waterman classic *In Search of Excellence* stumbled because they failed to adapt

to changes in their environments. A major conclusion of an earlier Conference Board report on marketing planning practices in large companies emphasized the "failure of senior and operating executives to give issues adequate heed in arriving at investment or marketing decisions." What seems to be wrong with such companies' planning?

Rationality in Practice:

Organization Decision Making in a Crisis

Stage	Planning Behavior	Stage	Planning Behavior
Shock	There is general confusion, panic, and inability to understand the situation. The organization is incapable of reasoned planning. It sometimes reacts impulsively, without exploring alternatives or fully understanding the event.	Defensive Retreat	The threat is minimized, sometimes even dismissed. There is a retreat to old, "tried and true," top-down decision making. Open planning processes are abandoned. Accusations and blaming politicize decision making. The planning team splinters and the decision-making structure disintegrates. The organization then becomes very defensive: programs are cut, budgets are tightly controlled, and all decisions become short term.

7. The Rationality in Practice box above describes what often happens when a firm faces a major external economic or political crisis. The decisions made under crisis can have worse effects than the initial crisis. How does institutionalization of the STRATMESH planning process help in a crisis?

8. The marketing planning process often involves a lot of organizational politics. The risk is that the marketing plan itself becomes a political document, rather than a decision-making document. List all the possible effects on the content and use of the marketing plan when it becomes a political document. What influence do you think politics play in the decision making of U.S. firms?

9. Few organizations undertake marketing planning and produce marketing plans the way most textbooks say planning should be done. Many written marketing plans are nothing more than forecasts of future sales and a budget statement. The presentation of the information in dramatic computer-generated graphics is often very impressive and the written statement may make the reader feel good, but too often it is a triumph of form over function. Although a slick presentation can go a long way in communicating information, it can also mask the superficiality of a marketing plan. Such plans often do not describe the environment or the proposed strategy, nor do they provide implementation directions. This is not to say the company does not have plans. It does, but the plans are in the minds of the decision-making executives. The problem is that the plans are not readily available for scrutiny, improvement, and execution by other executives in the organization. A written plan helps us to remember, make decisions, give directions, and implement. Why then do firms not prepare better marketing plans? Please state and explain all the possible reasons.

10. In 1991, Toshiba held 21 percent of the $3.2 billion laptop computer market, twice the market share of the other big players (Zenith had 10 percent; Compaq, 10 percent; NEC, 9 percent; Tandy, 8 percent; and Sharp 8 percent). But the company

Stage	Planning Behavior	Stage	Planning Behavior
Acknowledgment	The crisis is placed in its proper context and its ramifications are understood. A consensus develops about how the marketplace has changed. There is a constructive call for new solutions from the bottom-up.	Adaptation and Change	New strategies are formulated, evaluated in the light of the new marketplace environment, and implemented. The company returns to its more adventurous and open team decision-making approach.

Source: Stephen L. Fink, Joep Beak, and Kenneth Taddeo, "Organization Crisis and Change," *The Journal of Applied Behavioral Science* 7.1 (1971), 15–37.

was not without its problems. In 1989, American managers asked the parent company in Tokyo to design a small notebook with a hard drive and a 286 chip. They were told it could not be done, but in October 1989 Compaq launched such a computer. Toshiba did not respond effectively until mid-1991 and also missed launching the first 386 notebook. In June 1991, Toshiba fired its exclusive American distributor and returned to Tech Data Corp., which it had fired as its distributor the year before. What appears to have been the problem?[38]

11. An important component of the infrastructure that supports a healthy economy is an efficient and effective legal system to deal with business litigation such as disputes over exchange contracts and private and civil wrongs between competitors and between buyers and sellers (see Chapter 6). Modern governments are expected to provide such a legal system, just as they are expected to provide other types of trading infrastructures such as efficient and effective highways and airports.

Unfortunately, the effectiveness (fairness) of the courts that deal with commercial law in the United States can be questioned.[39] For example, judges of the Texas Supreme court are elected in campaigns primarily funded by the lawyers who appear in their courts. In 1985, the lawyer who won Pennzoil damages of over $10 billion dollars against Texaco for buying a company that Pennzoil wanted to buy made a $10,000 campaign contribution to the judge who presided over the case a few days *after* the judge was assigned the case. The inefficiency of the courts is also scandalous. Everyone agrees that it takes absurdly long for cases to be settled and that the lawyer's fees are often absurdly large.

How might the free market and competitive rationality be used to address this problem/opportunity? Explain the businesses that entrepreneurs and innovators might start, what the keys to success would be, and what effect such businesses

38. Larry Armstrong, "It's a Shakier Perch for Toshiba's Laptops," *Business Week,* August 5, 1991, 62–64.
39. David Frum, "Here Come the Lawsuits," *Forbes,* December 7, 1992, 72.

might have on the traditional legal system that deals with accidents and product liability suits?

12. FX (foreign exchange) speculation exists because governments pursue macro-economic tactics (such as changing central bank interest rates) that are attempts to create a global trading advantage by manipulating exchange rates between currencies (such as between the dollar and the yen).[40] These heavy-handed tactics are immediately arbitraged by FX traders and greatly nullified. The certain result is that the traders will make huge profits, which is like adding a costly friction to the smoothness and efficiency of world trade in products and services that create employment. What macro-economic policy should governments pursue that might be a much more effective way of creating global trading advantages for its firms and a growth in employment?

13. The following example of marketing decision making is a composite of decisions and actions commonly seen in small and large firms launching a new product to be sold to other businesses.

An Example of Marketing Decision Making—How *Not* to Do It

Suppose that a relatively large company that sells products to other businesses is preparing to launch a new product. The product is one whose genesis was in the research and development department of the firm. Developers have talked with potential customers early in the design process, but shortly after the new idea gained some momentum, it was decided by upper-level management to cease talking with all but one customer for fear of divulging information to competitors. The one principal customer has signed a nondisclosure-noncompetition agreement in exchange for receiving proprietary first versions of the product. This principal customer is providing some of the financing for the research and development effort. An initial analysis of secondary data suggests that there is a large potential market for a generic version of the new product. The project gets the go-ahead.

After a year of successive development advances, the company begins work on the generic version of the product. The product manager is still hesitant to talk to potential customers and so does an updated analysis of secondary data and concludes that market potential is still quite large. Planning proceeds on the generic version of the product. Trials with the principal customer are well under way. The product passes through several "go/no-go" reviews and passes, largely because technical progress is being made. The project builds a momentum of its own.

A launch date is set for the generic version of the new product. The product manager provides preliminary specifications of the product to manufacturing. He provides these specifications and the desired positioning of the product to the marketing department and the sales force. The product manager finds he is spending most of his time refining the product's features with R&D and working on pricing.

Upper-level management is getting excited about the new product. Between the principal customer and the broader market, they feel the new product will fill a large role in the company's future over the next three to five years. They tell the director of product marketing, who in turn tells the product manager.

The launch date is approaching. The principal customer is very pleased with the product but is using it less than first anticipated. The product manager is getting anxious about the prospects for the new product, so a market research consultant is called in to verify the size of the market and the chosen target segments, help refine the product's positioning, and forecast the sales of the product. The manufacturing department says that it can probably produce the product for a reasonable cost, somewhere near the cost target. However, the manufacturing department needs updated product specifications and solid sales estimates so that it can plan better. The marketing department says that it needs final specifications and that it has called in its advertising

40. See Kenichi Ohmae, *The Borderless World* (New York: Harper Business, 1990); and "World Economy Survey," *The Economist,* September 19, 1992.

agency to help produce the launch campaign. This will add to the startup cost. The sales force says that it is ready when the product is but will need training on how to sell the product.

The launch date is getting closer. The product manager is still working with engineering to get the product features refined. The preliminary market research results are somewhat ambivalent. Discussions with manufacturing have become heated. The manufacturing cost estimates are going up, and the manufacturing department does not feel comfortable with the lack of details in the product specifications. The sales force is waiting patiently, or as patiently as a sales force can wait. The ad agency has come up with a new idea for positioning the product and the marketing department believes it has merit. Meanwhile, marketing has gone ahead with press conference scheduling and booth design for the industry's major trade show, which will coincide with the product launch.

The launch date is imminent. New market research is now fairly negative and the researchers' suggestions for "re"-positioning the product are judged to be too far afield to be of use. To ensure that the product will reach sales targets, top-level management and the product manager decide to target the product to a broader market than originally intended. Because manufacturing costs appear to be higher than anticipated, the price of the product is raised to maintain the desired profit margin. As positioning has become very vague at this point, the product manager instructs marketing to focus communications on product features. It is rationalized that customers will easily be able to translate for themselves how the product will be useful for them. There is not enough time or money now to produce a full-blown sales training program. Accordingly, the sales force is told that sales techniques used for existing products will work well enough for the new product. Product briefings will be held for the sales force shortly before the trade show.

Shortly afterward, R&D informs the product manager that the first product shipped will have to be a "watered down" version of the original conception of the generic product. R&D is still working on finding ways to provide some features at a cost that "won't break the bank." It is too late to change the advertising or the trade show booth. The sales force is instructed though that the first version of the product will not live up to its billing and that it can offer a discount if the customer is unwilling to wait for the upgraded version.

The launch actually goes smoothly, all in all. Early sales figures are somewhat disappointing. The product manager is actually temporarily relieved at this, since manufacturing ran into problems handling the last-minute product changes, so deliveries are slower than anticipated. The product manager decides to get some post-launch evaluative information to try to pinpoint why the product is not moving as well as desired. Other than sales figures, there is no real data on how the company is doing, except for salesperson call reports. Upon examining the early call reports, the product manager realizes that no one told the salespeople what information to include in their call reports.

At this point, this process can go in any direction. Indeed, the company may have a winner on its hands. More likely, the results will probably be somewhat disappointing and perhaps even disastrous. The point is that there are better ways to handle a product launch that will minimize the chances of making mistakes. The process described in this chapter and discussed in detail throughout this book, if followed, will help keep an organization's marketing efforts focused on the important issues and will help ensure that these efforts are coordinated and move along on a reasonable schedule. Please critique the process described in the example.

14. The citizen army of Napoleon marched and fought at a quick step of 120 paces a minute rather than the orthodox 70 paces of Napoleon's adversaries. Perhaps more importantly, it was the first modern army to be organized into self-contained divisions. It lived on the country instead of traveling with a large supply train of food wagons, and it had a very effective habit of striking at the opponent's supply

wagons and lines of supply.[41] Relate these innovations to the theory of competitive rationality in the global market.

15. Karl Marx argued that the economic process is constantly changing and undermining the economic and political establishments. His mistake was to assume that the major driver of the economic process would be a worker revolution—the revolt of the proletariat. Use the theory of competitive rationality to analyze and explain this mistake.

16. What impact do you think the current innovations and cost reductions in hardware for personal computers are having on software for personal computers?

17. In the mid-1980s, the running fad died and was replaced by aerobics. Soft-leather athletic shoes replaced the clunky jogging shoe both as an exercise and casual fashion shoe. Reebok led the market with its line of aerobic shoes for women. Nike did not recognize the new trend soon enough and was slow to respond. What was the basic problem with Nike's competitive rationality at that time?

18. In 1992, two hundred CEOs of high-growth companies were asked this question: Which of the following would *most* increase your ability to compete against your domestic and global competition?
    a. Buying new manufacturing equipment and a new plant.
    b. Using your current equipment and plant more efficiently by adopting the new approaches to manufacturing.
    c. Adopting the new fast-track quality approaches to designing new products and modifying old products.
    What percentage do you think answered a, b and c? Why?

19. The strategic marketing concept is to seek a *sustainable* competitive advantage over competitors by satisfying consumer needs. An implication of the theory of competitive rationality is that the marketing concept (making sales and profits by focusing on, serving, and satisfying the customer) is driven by competition. The greater the competition among sellers, the greater the customer focus and service will be. In light of this implication, do you see any problem with the strategic marketing concept, as described above?

20. A variation of the following metaphor is often used in the social sciences to explain what can happen when a scholar spends most of his or her career searching for truth by developing and testing a specific theory. A man approaches a somewhat agitated fellow who is down on his hands and knees searching the ground under a streetlight in front of the local pub:

    "Can I help you?"
    "Yes, I nipped round the back of the fence to relieve myself, and lost me wallet."
    "Then why're ya lookin around out here"?
    "Cost there ain't any light back there, ya retard!"

    How is this metaphor relevant to market intelligence generation and use?

21. According the *The Economist* (April 17, 1993, p. 57), in 1992 Japanese companies and individuals filed over 200,000 new patent applications for new products and

---

41. See B. H. Liddell Hart, *Strategy* (New York: Meridian, 1991).

production processes. Sixty thousand new patent aplications were filed by Americans; 30,000 by Germans. Are these differences important? What does this tell us about the competitiveness and competitive rationality of firms in Japan, the United States and Germany? What should the U.S. government do about it, if anything? How should U.S. universities and business schools react to this information?

The Generation and Use of Market Intelligence

"Facts that are not frankly faced have a habit of stabbing us in the back."

Sir Harold Bowden

"What we see depends mainly on what we look for."

John Lubbock

*T*he generation and use of market research enables a management team to *learn* about *changes* in the market *faster* than the competition, making it a major component of competitive rationality and competitive advantage. The question is, how can a decision-making team manage market research and internal self-analysis better than its rivals? This chapter addresses this question.

Market orientation has been defined as "the organization-wide generation of market intelligence, dissemination of that intelligence among departments, and organization-wide responsiveness to it."[1] This definition requires some reinterpretation when decision making and management is undertaken by a cross-functional team. In a cross-functional team, departmental dissemination of information is of minimal concern because decision making is made *within* the group rather than *among* the departments. For such a cross-functional team, market orientation is largely determined by two skills: the generation of market intelligence and the team's use of the intelligence.

The generation of market intelligence primarily involves the gathering of data: searching for secondary sources, choosing a research contractor, developing research technique, framing samples, framing questions, and establishing the right type of analysis and presentation format. Most market research texts and courses focus on the data-gathering technology of market intelligence. How the research is presented to and *used* by the decision-making team has been largely neglected, although it is becoming recognized as crucial:

> There are two elements to information process quality. One has to do with the psychological, sociological, and other organizational dynamics affecting information use. The second has to do with the collection and treatment of data in technically sound and appropriate ways. While each element is important, it is far more likely that a problem will exist with the behavioral element. The technologies for data collection— storage, retrieval, and statistical analyses—are well developed. The technology for putting data into use, however, is in its infancy."[2]

In the traditional bureaucratic organization structure, getting all those involved with a product-market decision closer to the market by getting the latest market intelligence in their hands is a nightmarish responsibility for a product manager and much depends on his or her personal, boundary-spanning abilities.[3] The sharing of relevant, internally generated information between the different functions often can be an even worse problem when individual functions attempt to use information to heighten their own political power. The situation is very different when the new information and inquiry technologies help cross-functional team decision making.[4] Internal and external information sources are interrogated by team members *for* the group, in parallel and back and forth. This collective and consultative intelligence generation is the essence of the information-processing strength of cross-functional team decision making.

Another feature of competitively rational team decision making is that *all* team members spend time talking to customers, distributors, and suppliers, even if these

1. Ajay K. Kohli and Bernard J. Jaworski, "Market Orientation: The Construct, Research Propositions, and Managerial Implications," *Journal of Marketing*, 54 (April 1990), 1–18.
2. Vincent P. Barabba and Gerald Zaltman, *Hearing the Voice of the Market* (Cambridge, MA: Harvard Business School Press, 1991).
3. Some interesting research suggests that the quality of environmental analysis and effort does not depend on market turbulence and uncertainty, but on the boundary-spanning efforts of product managers. See Steven Lysonski, Alan Singer, and David Wilemon, "Coping with Environmental Uncertainty and Boundary Spanning in the Product Manager's Role," *Journal of Consumer Marketing* 6.2 (Spring 1989), 33–44.
4. Rashi Glazer, "Marketing in an Information-Intensive Environment: Strategic Implications of Knowledge As an Asset," *Journal of Marketing* 55 (October 1991), 1–19.

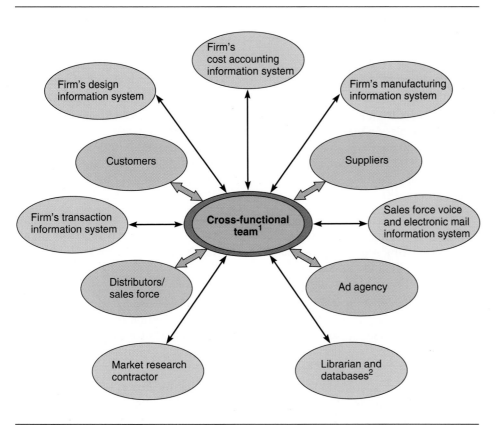

Figure 2-1

Sources of Market Intelligence

1. Information, expert judgments, and mental models of the market environments are transmitted, stored, and assimilated within and across the membership of the cross-functional team. Group members have individual responsibilities and expertise in using and sharing different information systems, such as the transaction IS (order-processing and logistic's information system) and design IS (computer-aided design and costing information system). This occurs both concurrently and sequentially. The closer sources are sources that *all* of the cross-functional team members should interact with continuously. This is often achieved by having the suppliers, sales force, and ad agency representatives attend cross-functional team meetings.

2. A librarian/market research analyst becomes a crucial part of a team's institutional memory, storing reports and relevant documents by cataloging them in a way that reflects the team's agreed upon mental model. The librarian will also be an expert at accessing external databases such as DIALOG, which provides access to some 350 other business databases. The duties of this analyst might also include taking the minutes of the formal cross-functional team meetings. A discussion of running such meetings is presented in Appendix 1. The role of librarian/market research analyst would be a very attractive entry position for a capable new graduate. It combines the duties of an assistant brand manager and market research analyst in more traditional bureaucratic organizational structures.

stakeholders are part of the team. The team has to develop a consensus mental model of how consumers use the product/service: Where do they use the product? How do they use it? What problems do they have with the product? All of this information must be absorbed by *all* members of the cross-functional team. The new electronic decision support systems that link the firm with major customers, scanning services, or global databases can dramatically change the nature and quality of decision making, but they will never be a substitute for the direct learning that occurs when decision makers interact with suppliers and customers.

The cross-functional team also greatly simplifies the concern over how information is used because not only is all important information reported to the team, but team members are delegated to seek out further information, share it with the team, and, most importantly, interpret it (see Figure 2-1). This interpretation teaches other cross-functional team members new decision-making skills. The cross-functional team becomes the organizational inquiry center, where the firm "effectively and efficiently reconciles the voice of the market with the voice of the firm."[5] The following team information processing behavior is typical:

> We gather about ten people in a room, twice a month, in long (think-tank) sessions— anything from three hours to a couple of days. The sessions have no formal structure. We examine and massage the latest competitor and industry information to determine where things are going and what we should be doing.[6]

5. Barabba and Zaltman, *Hearing the Voice of the Market.*
6. Howard Sutton, *Competitive Intelligence* (New York: The Conference Board, 1988), 31.

There are a lot of people in the business unit who know something about a competitor. But it's almost like the three blind men and the elephant: each one examines a small part of the whole. When you put them all together in a room, they are amazed about how much they know. That coalesces into one or two sheets of paper presenting all we know about a competitor's strengths and weaknesses, and our judgments with respect to a competitor's strategies and measures of success. That is the beginning of a competitor file.[7]

A new product team is likely to meet weekly, a more mature product team might meet monthly. Discussion may also be more structured, as was suggested in Figure 1.4. The essential point, however, is that the firm must invest heavily in teams, encouraging them to use market research in their decision making. Such investment is necessary because many factors, such as those that follow, discourage the better use of information.

1. Myopic, short-term perspectives discourage market research that identifies long-term competitor and consumer life-style trends. Most research addresses immediate, fire-fighting problems; longer-term trends that should be researched are ignored. The firm risks being like the frog that is boiled alive in the pot because it doesn't notice the gradually rising temperature of the water.

2. Information that challenges conventional wisdom, beliefs, and mental models is ignored because it threatens the credibility of the intuition of senior managers.[8] The information may be seen as a political challenge, but it may also undermine the confidence of a decision maker who, in making risky, uncertain decisions, needs to believe in his or her existing beliefs and mental models.

3. The fear that listening to the market will mean that the firm is being led by fickle, so-called uninformed consumer tastes rather than by its own radical innovations. In this variation of paralysis-by-analysis fear, the firm becomes hooked on market research rather than managing and mastering research. The perceived dulling effect of market research on creativity is well stated in the following quote:

    Enduringly successful firms focus on being creative, not reactive ... This will be tough for firms nurtured on reactive strategies like market research, the usual method Western firms use to find out what customers want. Car makers are among market research's biggest fans, as the dull similarity of modern cars testifies.[9]

4. Research is often enacted at the eleventh hour to validate (that is, justify) the decision making. It almost invariably does so, but when proven wrong, it undermines respect for research. Only about 1 percent of new products are reasonably successful,[10] and the performance of other advertising and promotion programs are about equally successful. As a result, respect for market research that predicted otherwise has decreased. Results more often fail to meet the expectations created by market research conclusions rather than exceed them. Smoking-gun research undertaken at the eleventh hour that challenges the whole project is even less appreciated. It is hard evidence of the foolhardiness of the project.

7. Sutton, *Competitive Intelligence*, 37.
8. This counter intuitive conclusion has been well documented; see R. Nisbitt and L. Ross, *Human Inference: Strategies and Shortcomings of Social Judgment* (Englewood Cliffs, N.J.: Prentice-Hall, 1980); Blake E. Ashforth and Fried Yitzhak, "The Mindlessness of Organizational Behaviors," *Human Relations* 41 (4) (1988), 305–329; and James P. Walsh, "Knowledge Structures and the Management of Organizations: A Research Review and Agenda" (Working Paper, Hanover, NH: Dartmouth College, June 1990).
9. *The Economist,* December 1, 1990, 7, as quoted in George S. Day, *Learning About Markets* (Cambridge, MA: Marketing Science Institute, 1991), 91–117. To be fair to the auto industry, fuel economy and safety requirements have had much to do with the similar aerodynamic shape of many cars.
10. Alvin Achenbaum, "How to Succeed in New Products," *Advertising Age,* June 26, 1989, 62. More liberal standards of success put the failure rate at about 80 percent.

5. Information in traditional, bureaucratic decision-making situations is devalued because it is generated for its own sake (to justify unnecessary levels of middle management) or to frustrate or delay decision making rather than improve it.

6. The use of mind-numbing complexity and jargon by researchers intimidates users. Also, the third-decimal-point pretension of information creates completely false beliefs about the precision and credibility of costs, market share, or consumer preferences. Researchers often have a different value system. They seek certain types of validity and reliability that are costly in time and money. Users tend to prefer several sequential, quick-and-dirty studies.[11]

In the next section, we describe how market intelligence can be generated by using a number of techniques that vary greatly in their sophistication. Afterwards we will illustrate how such intelligence can be best used by the creation of mental models of the market, which enable pieces of market intelligence to be fitted together by the decision-making team into sensible models of the overall market environment. Figure 2-2 illustrates how these two gathering and use-of-market intelligence sections fit together.

Market Intelligence Gathering

Many methods of gathering market intelligence are available to the decision-making team. Although the degree of complexity among these options varies, they all offer the cross-functional team one of its most indispensable resources—information.

The Customer Visit

Having cross-functional team members visit customers has emerged as one of the most important market research activities a firm can adopt. Talking directly to customers seems so obvious, and yet some firms have lost themselves in sophisticated arm's-length consumer research. The problem with survey research is that too many steps and interpretative judgments separate the consumer and the decision maker. The vivid impact of listening to the customers' own words, of seeing how they use the product, is lost if the customers are not visited in their homes or offices. Consequently, the importance of customers' concerns have less impact in decision making: "Visits allow the voice of the customer to be heard, and they make this voice audible throughout the organization."[12] Furthermore, all the richness of observing the product or service in the usage situation is lost if customers are not communicated with directly. Japanese firms such as Panasonic and Sony prefer hands-on consumer research that focuses on the way current customers use specific products and brands.[13] For example, one appliance manufacturer took 200 photos of actual Japanese kitchens and concluded from the photos that the major problem that appliance manufacturers have to address when designing new appliances is the tremendous shortage of space in many kitchens, an observation he might not have made had he not visited the homes in person and taken the photographs.

11. Mark Landler, "The 'Bloodbath' in Market Research," *Business Week,* February 11, 1991, 72–74; see also Gerald Zaltman, *The Use of Developmental and Evaluative Market Research* (Cambridge, MA: Marketing Science Institute, 1989), 89–107, for an excellent discussion of the lack of trust between researchers and managers.
12. Edward F. McQuarrie and Shelby H. McIntyre, "The Customer Visit: An Emerging Practice in Business-to-Business Marketing" (Working Paper, Cambridge, MA: Marketing Science Institute, 1992), 92–114.
13. Johny K. Johansson and Ikujiro Nonaka, "Market Research the Japanese Way," *Harvard Business Review,* May/June 1987, 16–22; Lance Ealey and Leif Soderberg, "How Honda Cures Design Amnesia," *The McKinsey Quarterly,* Spring 1990, 3–14; and Kenichi Ohmae, *The Borderless World* (New York: Harper Business, 1990).

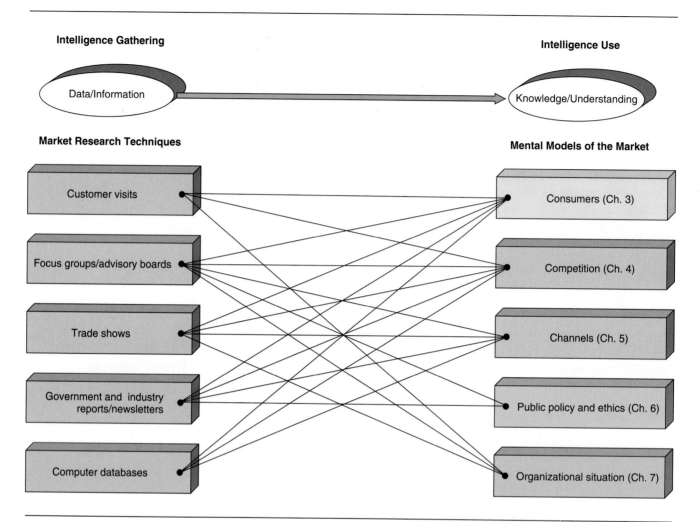

Figure 2-2
How Gathered Market
Information Is Used

An organizational and cross-functional team gathers market intelligence by the use of many direct and indirect research techniques. It is converted into knowledge and understanding when it is interpreted by, stored in, and changes the decision makers' mental models of the market environment. The first section of this chapter discusses market intelligence-gathering techniques. The second section introduces a 5E mental model that interprets and assimilates market information; that is, it uses market intelligence. The mental submodels that can be applied to understanding consumers, competition, channels, public policy/ethics, and the firm itself are detailed in Chapters 3–7. Generally, the most common problem in organizations is the breakdown in the process of converting data and information into knowledge and understanding.

The customer visit is crucial for business-to-business marketing. Marketing's responsibility is to make sure that everyone interacts with customers instead of simply passing on secondhand information about consumers. This explains why the chief executive officer of United Airlines spends time handing out tickets and why senior executives at 3M spend several days a month visiting customers. Some guidelines for such visits are listed here:

♦ Have customer visits arranged by the sales force: cooperation between the factory and the field is crucial.

♦ Talk to from 12 to 20 customers. This reduces the effect of an extreme, atypical opinion.

♦ Only use jargon if the customer is an expert.

- ◆ Learn to listen; do not treat the visit as a sales call.
- ◆ Define your research objectives in advance.
- ◆ Use a discussion guide based on your objectives.
- ◆ Write a report that addresses your research objectives.
- ◆ Report separately on other things that were learned.
- ◆ Observe the product in use.
- ◆ If possible, have two or three members of the team make the visits together.

Trade Shows

Trade shows enable sellers to promote their newest products and services to customers and distributors. They are a great source of information, not only about new products, but also about how interested distributors and customers are in the new products. They also provide an opportunity to network with rival salespeople and to learn about what is happening to other rivals. (For more on trade shows, see Chapter 11.)

Reverse Engineering

To understand a competitor's design and how the product is produced, most companies buy their competitor's products and put them through rigorous performance testing. The products are torn apart (reverse engineering) to see what they are made of and how they are made (see Figure 2-3). Ford dismantled some 50 midsize cars made by

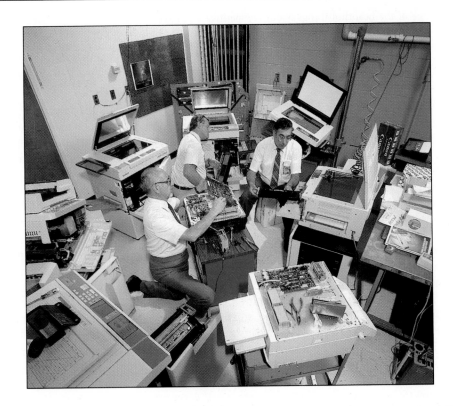

Figure 2-3

Xerox engineers taking apart competitors' products to better understand their design, quality, and how they were made.

its competitors in its effort to imitate and improve on the best features of its rivals.[14] Basic questions were asked while studying the components, the design, and the assembly: 1) How can we do it so the target customer will like ours more? and 2) How can we do it cheaper? These two questions address the first and second competitive rationality drives.

Competitor Annual Reports, 10-Ks, and 10-Qs

While traditional annual reports appear to be glossy self-promotions to shareholders, they often contain valuable information about trends in company goals, missions, and finances that can be tracked by comparing a firm's annual reports over four or five years. Analysts often look for changes in company direction by comparing the comments of the chairperson and chief executive from year to year. The competition's newsletters to distributors and employees also often contain nuggets of information as described by the following executive:

> Two years ago, we found an interesting article in one of our competitor's employee publications. A vice president was saying, "This is what our company is all about, and this is where we want to take the company in the next five years. We want to be this, and this, and this." There was the company's strategy, all spelled out.[15]

The following comments from the same study of competitive intelligence also indicate the value of carefully reviewing a competitor's literature:

> An electronic database is very useful when you have an identifiable question, target, or subject. But to get a sense of the trends in the industry, there's no substitute for what any junior grade intelligence officer does in the CIA: you read the literature, you follow it closely. That's what a sports writer does.

> One of the beautiful things about competitive intelligence is that the competitor has to tell his customers what he wants them to believe . . . If a company does a decent advertising job, the ad campaign will give you a warning signal. The ads will tell you what market segments they're emphasizing and what they're trying to do with their product line . . . If you read their ads and their annual reports—and put them in historic perspective—it's obvious where the company is headed.

The Securities and Exchange Commission (SEC) requires public companies to file annual 10-K reports. The 10-K provides a great deal of financial and competitive information, including analysis by product line, market, and distribution channel (see Figure 2-4). It also includes valuable information on backlogs, patents, licenses granted, and franchises.

The 10-Q reports present quarterly earnings. The pressure from stock analysts has forced a further voluntary disclosure of the marketing plans of companies as chief executives attempt to sell the prospects of their firm to the marketplace each quarter. In doing this, they often reveal their hand to the alert competitor. Firms often subscribe to industry-specific newsletters issued by Wall Street research and brokerage firms to learn the latest facts or speculation about their competition, distributors, or major customers. A service such as the *Value Line Investment Survey* provides brief reports on the state of an industry and the recent moves and prospects of some 2,000 companies in 100 industries. Information about small companies is much harder to obtain; the best sources are the reference librarian in the town where the firm operates or even the local town newspapers, which will have a clippings file on the firm. An illustration

14. Russell Mitchell, "How Ford Hit the Bull's Eye with Taurus," *Business Week*, June 30, 1986, 69–70.
15. Howard Sutton, *Competitive Intelligence* (New York: The Conference Board, 1988), 33.

Figure 2-4

The Form 10-K

An example of the first page of a 10-K form. Very important competitive information is often buried within the form.

UNITED STATES
SECURITIES AND EXCHANGE COMMISSION
WASHINGTON, D.C. 20549

FORM 10-K

(Mark One)

(x)   ANNUAL REPORT PURSUANT TO SECTION 13 OR 15(d)
OF THE SECURITIES EXCHANGE ACT OF 1934 (FEE REQUIRED)
For the fiscal year ended August 31, 1991

OR

( )   TRANSITION REPORT PURSUANT TO SECTION 13 OR 15(d)
OF THE SECURITIES EXCHANGE ACT OF 1934 (NO FEE REQUIRED)
For the transition period from _____ to _____

Commission File number 1-5975

HUMANA INC.
(Exact name of Registrant as specified in its Charter)

Delaware	61-0647538
(State of incorporation)	(I.R.S. Employer Identification No.)
500 West Main Street	
Louisville, Kentucky	40202
(Address of principal executive offices)	(Zip Code)

Registrant's telephone number, including area code: 502-580-1000

Securities registered pursuant to Section 12(b) of the Act:

Title of each class	Name of each exchange on which registered
Common Stock, $.16⅔ par value	New York Stock Exchange
5% Convertible Subordinated Debentures due July 1, 1997	New York Stock Exchange
9½% Subordinated Debentures due October 1, 1998	New York Stock Exchange
10⅛% Senior Notes due September 15, 1991	New York Stock Exchange

Indicate by check mark if disclosure of delinquent filers pursuant to Item 405 of Regulation S-K is not contained herein, and will not be contained, to the best of Registrant's knowledge, in definitive proxy or information statements incorporated by reference in Part III of this Form 10-K or any amendment to this Form 10-K. (X)

Securities registered pursuant to Section 12(g) of the Act:

None

Indicate by check mark whether the Registrant (1) has filed all reports required to be filed by Sections 13 or 15(d) of the Securities Exchange Act of 1934 during the preceding 12 months (or for such shorter period that the Registrant was required to file such reports) and (2) has been subject to such filing requirements for the past 90 days.

YES   X   NO

The aggregate market value of voting stock held by non-affiliates of the Registrant as of November 1, 1991 was $4,313,912,219 calculated using the average price on such date of $28.50. The number of shares outstanding of the Registrant's Common Stock as of November 1, 1991 was 158,412,360.

DOCUMENTS INCORPORATED BY REFERENCE

Portions of Parts II and IV incorporate herein by reference the Registrant's 1991 Annual Report to Stockholders; a portion of Part III incorporates herein by reference the Registrant's Proxy Statement pursuant to Regulation 14A, covering the Annual Meeting of Stockholders to be held January 9, 1992.

---

of the intelligence-gathering process of a firm that is expert in competitive analysis is presented in Figure 2-5.

Government Reports, Industry Reports, and Newsletters

The U.S. Census Bureau, the biggest market research organization in the world, compiles masses of information about household trends. Almost every public library has its reports, and the bureau has offices in large cities with specialists whose job is to help business people find out what they need to know. *American Demographics* magazine also presents analyses of census data, in addition to other analyses on population trends and changes in values, habits, hobbies, and entertainment. The Government Printing Office (Washington, D.C. 20402) has a *Subject Bibliography Index*, which lists free government publications on some 300 subjects. The Library of Congress ((202) 707-5532) also specializes in helping people find information. The U.S. government also produces 3- to 30-page annual industry reports on over 300 industries that cover both national

Stephen J. Bass & Partners Inc.
1335 Dublin Rd. – 200 A Columbus, OH 43215
614–481–3590   FAX 614–481–3501
1–800–323–1427

THE BUSINESS INTELLIGENCE-GATHERING PROCESS

Stephen J. Bass & Partners, Inc. (SJB&P) is a business intelligence consulting firm which gathers and analyzes information enabling executives to make timely, profitable strategic decisions. The methodology SJB&P typically utilizes in developing such intelligence for its clients is outlined below.

SJB&P has determined, based on decades of intelligence-gathering experience, that a synergistic, multi-phased process is often the most efficient approach for satisfying client intelligence needs.

Phase One

In phase one, all readily available published sources pertinent to a client's specific information needs are identified. This substantial secondary research effort encompasses, but is not limited to:

○ Analysis of information and sources already contained in SJB&P and client files.

○ Computer and manual literature searches of appropriate databases and hard copy indexes.

○ Trade association publications and libraries.

○ Federal government publications and libraries.

○ Trade periodicals, and studies and special issues published by such periodicals.

○ Industry/company reports published by research/consulting firms that often specialize in specific industries.

○ Special libraries which focus on particular industries.

○ Industry/company financial and credit performance reports.

○ Industry and company directories and catalogs.

○ Company financial reports, speeches, press releases, testimonies, etc.

○ Wall Street analyst reports on relevant industry segments and/or companies.

○ Records published or made available by relevant state/local government offices, such as state commerce departments and corporation and securities divisions, local building departments, tax assessors, and planning and development offices.

○ Articles and other information available from local sources, such as regional/local business press, daily newspapers, libraries, chambers of commerce, universities, etc.

○ Transcripts of studies of relevant industry segments undertaken by government agencies such as the Federal Trade Commission, U.S. Justice Department or the U.S. International Trade Administration.

○ Case studies, doctoral dissertations, and other academic research published on the industry/company.

Typically, some of a client's intelligence needs will not be fully satisfied by such a comprehensive search for published information. Thus, in order to fill critical information gaps, identified in analyzing phase one's results, a second phase of the research effort is often undertaken.

Phase Two

In phase two, telephone and in-person interviews of experts on the relevant industry segments and companies are implemented to fill these key information gaps. Experts contacted in this phase often include, but are not limited to, individuals employed by government agencies, universities, brokerage houses, trade associations, advertising agencies, consulting firms, periodical/report publishers, newspapers, and industry participants, such as competitors, suppliers, sales representatives, distributors, etc. The results achieved in these interviews are enhanced by SJB&P's substantial network of industry experts covering a wide variety of diverse fields.

Other types of research often incorporated in phase two include: visits to competitors, suppliers, customers, etc; attendance at trade shows; consumer/customer interviews, etc.

To optimize the effectiveness of this phase, part of the research is sometimes carried out in the actual cities and states in which relevant firms/division/plants are located. SJB&P's network of affiliated information researchers, located in key cities in the U.S. and overseas, facilitates this effort.

Phase Three

After the phase two research, SJB&P typically completes phase three. This encompasses analysis and integration of intelligence obtained in previous phases and preparation of a report that concisely profiles the results in a format designed to effectively meet the client's specific needs.

To learn more about the techniques and uses of business intelligence, SJB&P can be contacted the following address: Stephen J. Bass & Partners, Inc., 1335 Dublin Road, Suite 200A, Columbus, Ohio 43215.

Figure 2-5
A Business Intelligence Service

and global trends in supply and competition. These *U.S. Industrial Outlook* reports provide references, which can be followed up, and the names and phone numbers of the government researchers who prepared the report. Other important government publications are *Statistical Abstract of the U.S.* and the transcripts of industry studies undertaken by the Federal Trade Commission, Justice Department, and U.S. International Trade Commission. Calling and asking for information from an expert in government or industry is a very important market intelligence skill. Some general rules are listed here:

♦ The hard part is the introduction. You should politely and cheerfully introduce yourself, give your name and the name of the person who recommended that you call, and state the purpose of your call. Credible compliments go a long way.

♦ Initially, ask specific, easy questions. Be open, enthusiastic, optimistic, humble, courteous, and grateful.

♦ Use a list, but do not sound as if you are following a list. An apparent lack of structure encourages spontaneous insights and allows for bond-forming casual discussions of other ice-breaking topics such as sports, world events, children, or hobbies.

Figure 2-6

Examples of Commercially Available Market Reports

In addition to the hundreds of industry reports prepared by the U.S. Commerce Department each year, market research firms such as FIND/SVP prepare catalogs of research reports that can be purchased. Prices range from the hundreds up to several thousand dollars.

♦ Send a thank you note (you may wish to call again) and offer to return the favor.

♦ Be persistent. Keep generating leads. Calling a cooperative expert is by far and away the best $10 value for money in market research and analysis.[16]

The trade associations, trade journals, and trade newsletters associated with a particular industry can be located through a local reference library or by consulting *The Directory of Directories, The Encyclopedia of Associations, The Encyclopedia of Business Information Sources,* and the *Nelson Directory*. Although trade associations spend much of their time and effort lobbying and running educational programs for their members, they are often a rich source of the history and current trends in a market. There are also firms that specialize in finding relevant articles and news reports (clipping services) and other research firms that sell industry or market reports such as FIND/SVP. A page of its 1991 catalog is presented in Figure 2-6.

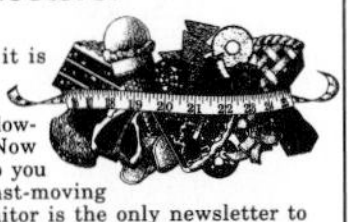

16. This list is based in part on advice from "The Art of Obtaining Information," *Washington Researchers,* Washington, D.C.

Computer Databases

An on-line database allows the user to search for articles, newsletters, or other reports on *key word* topics. Key words, such as *drink mixes* and *Europe* can be combined to obtain information about the drink-mix market in Europe. Four examples of the many databases now available are listed here:

♦ DIALOG Information Services, Inc., which can access some 350 business databases including industry directories and company financial statements.

♦ NEXIS, which can access 400 major newspapers, magazines, and newsletters.

♦ FINDEX, a directory of industry market research reports.

♦ COMPUTER-READABLE Databases, the best directory of databases.

Public libraries and state university reference librarians can help locate and even access several database directories.

Legal Information

Patent applications and awards not only provide information about a competitor's new product developments, but they often describe the technology that enables legal (and illegal) imitations to be made. Several patent databases exist, including *INPADOC*, which have information about some 15 million patents from over 200 countries. Other legal databases describe federal, state, and county regulations that apply to the manufacturing and marketing of products and services. They again can be identified and even searched through law school libraries at local state universities.

Scanning Services

In the last ten years, information on the sales of some 30,000 grocery products have been gathered by syndicated market research companies, such as A.C. Nielsen, SAMI/Burke, and IRI, which process data provided by supermarkets or by households participating in national panels. This data is mainly used by major packaged-goods companies to monitor the behavior of their competitors and test new products, promotions, and advertising appeals. Figure 2-7 presents the effects of store price specials as tracked by scanner data. In the next 20 years, almost all products shipped through distribution channels will have UPCs (universal product codes) that will be scanned to control inventory and order delivery. When this happens, there will be extensive databases on most markets about sales trends, which probably will be available in real-time so that even weekly or daily shifts in market share can be observed.

Decision Support Systems

A decision support system (DSS) is a set of computer software programs that is built into a user friendly interface package such as Windows. It enables a user to answer state-of-the-market questions, market forecasting questions, and to create simulations showing what might happen if tactics were changed. Behind the interactive, user-friendly icons, frameworks, prompts, and pull-down guide screens are major on-line market and accounting databases, communication networks, and powerful spreadsheets, statistical programs, and mathematical models. Figure 2-8 describes the elements and flow of information within a decision support system. The keys to a well designed and frequently used DSS are listed here:

♦ It helps a team make better intuitive decisions by replacing assumptions with facts that can be accessed by pressing a few keys or dexterously moving a mouse.

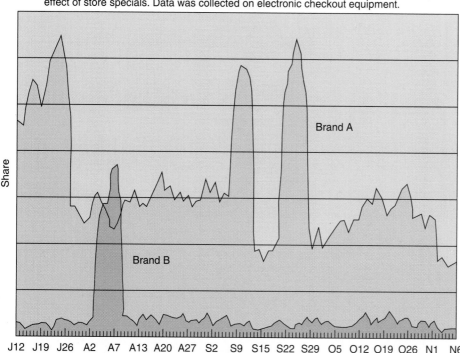

Daily market shares of two national brands in a supermarket chain clearly show the effect of store specials. Data was collected on electronic checkout equipment.

Brand A

Brand B

Share

J12 J19 J26 A2 A7 A13 A20 A27 S2 S9 S15 S22 S29 O5 O12 O19 O26 N1 N6

Day

Figure 2-7

The Use of Scanner Data to Study the Effects of Promotions

In the 1980s, supermarket scanner data was mostly used to study the effects of price and display promotions on sales. Scanner data has also been used by retailers to make their shelf-space displays more productive, increase their stock-turn, and improve inventory control. Scanner data is likely to become available for other markets during the 1990s.

Source: Reproduced with permission from John D. C. Little, "Decision Support Systems for Marketing Managers," *Journal of Marketing* 43 (Summer 1979), 9–26.

♦ It offers simple, decision support aids that reward novices and encourage them to move on to more complex support aids (like computer games that have novice, intermediate, and expert levels of difficulty).

♦ It is designed so that it can be expanded to include new data bases, networks, and aids.

♦ It self-records its use so that its designers know what is popular and what is not. Great care has to be taken to ensure that the evolution of a DSS is driven by usage and not by a compulsion to acquire the latest whiz-bang technology.

♦ It contains the ability to receive, send, and file market intelligence from salespeople, distributors, suppliers, and senior management.

♦ It can be accessed by everyone who wishes to use it (such as regional sales managers).

The initial optimism about the usefulness of decision support systems in the early 1980s has faded a little.[17] It has become clear that the tremendous investment in personal computers during the 1980s (and the associated decision support software) produced, at best, a marginal improvement in the quality of market decision making.[18] In

17. For the early definitive review of DSS, see John D.C. Little, "Decision Support Systems for Marketing Managers," *Journal of Marketing* 43 (Summer 1979), 9–26.
18. At least as reported in the responses to an open-ended question about how and why their marketing planning has improved over the last five or so years by participants in the 1990 Conference Board study; see Peter R. Dickson and Rosemary Kalapurakal, "The Theory and Reality of Environment Analysis in the Marketing Plan" (Working Paper, Columbus: Ohio State University, 1991).

Figure 2-8

A Basic Decision Support System

A decision support system is used for many purposes. Sales managers can look up a customer's purchase history; accountants can use it to do cost analyses, budgeting, and forecasting; managers can use it to evaluate the success of a marketing program (such as an advertising campaign) and to determine the success of positioning (who is taking share from whom). A good DSS is improved by carefully studying who uses the old DSS most and then determining how heavy users would like to see it improved and why decision makers who were expected to use it have not.

Source: Reprinted with permission of the publisher from "What the Hot Marketing Tool of the 80's Offers You," by Michael Dressler, Joquin Ives Brant, and Ronald Beall, *Industrial Marketing*, © 1983, p. 54. Copyright 1983 by Elsevier Science Publishing Co., Inc.

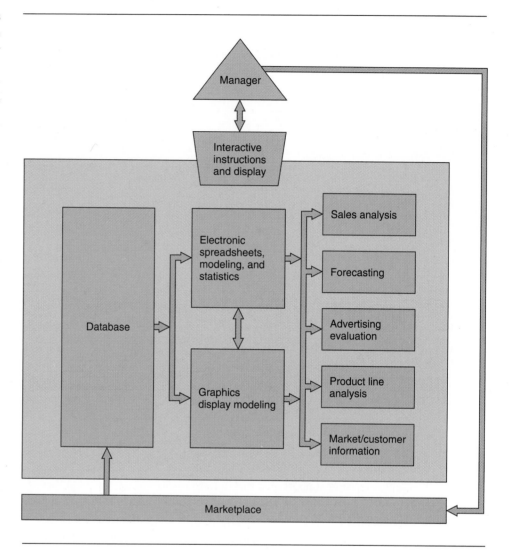

some cases, the use of a DSS has increased paralysis by analysis; in other cases the DSS has not given the firm a decisive competitive advantage over rivals because rivals are using the same or a similar systems.[19] Yet other decision support systems were grafted onto creaky, outdated, and overloaded existing information systems. Finally, some of the mathematical models used to answer "what-if" questions have proved unreliable.[20] It is clear from some of the success stories (such as Frito-Lay's fabulous DSS) that learning to design and use a computer-based decision support system has taken a lot longer than everyone expected. It should also take a great deal of initial conceptualization, because it will influence how generations of users think about the market (their mental models).

19. Louis A. Wallis, *Decision-Support Systems for Marketing* (New York: The Conference Board, 1989).
20. Annetta Miller and Dody Tsiantar, "A Test for Market Research," *Newsweek,* December 28, 1987 32–33.

Transaction-based Information Systems (TBISs)

TBISs link, communicate, and process all of the transactions between a firm's distributors/customers and its suppliers. The TBIS has evolved out of the electronic data interchange (EDI) between businesses (mainly business-to-business, just-in-time delivery relationships). As well as being used to speed quotations, bidding, order processing, and track delivery and billing, these new systems are likely to become an important part of a new generation of procurement and selling decision support systems. As discussed later in this book, some of these DSSs will also include decision support systems for a firm's customers, such as McKesson's ECONOMOST system for its drugstore customers or American Airlines' SABRE reservation system for its travel agents.

Focus Groups

Focus groups result from the careful recruitment of six to twelve people to participate in a free-wheeling one- to two-hour discussion that concentrates on a particular subject. A skilled conversationalist moderates the session, and members of the cross-functional decision team often watch the discussion through a one-way mirror or on closed circuit television. Focus groups are most useful in getting feedback on new product concepts and in understanding consumer product usage and shopping behavior. Focus groups can be used successfully by following these suggestions:

♦ Continue to use focus groups until no new, important insights are learned from the last one. This often means only three or four focus groups need to be run.

♦ Use focus groups during the new product/service development process to check on whether or not you are still on track and to answer questions about usage that arise from design changes.

♦ To gather the opinions of customers who are very different in terms of age, income, education, interests, and values, don't mix them all up in one group. Assemble several groups made up of similar consumers. They will get along a lot better and will be much more open and involved.

♦ Develop a guide that covers the topics that are to be discussed.

♦ Don't let one or two strong personalities dominate; going around the table and getting everyone's thoughts several times early in the focus group will bring everyone out.

♦ Focus group results can only be projected to the wider target segment if there is strong agreement within and among the focus groups on a topic. Otherwise, the focus group should be followed up with survey research, if the issue is important enough.

♦ Focus groups are a research tool—*not* a selling tool.

♦ Customer, distributor, or franchisee advisory councils are permanent focus groups that regularly come together to provide feedback on what is happening in the market and reactions to different ideas and programs. They are often used in business-to-business marketing.

Customer Values, Benefits, Beliefs, and Satisfaction Surveys

Survey research involves the systematic sampling of a population of consumers using a carefully prepared set of questions. Satisfaction surveys monitor customers who have recently purchased a product or service and are contacted by way of telephone call or return postcard.

As described in greater detail in Chapter 15, satisfaction tracking surveys are important for monitoring and controlling the quality of a product or service. If a customer is not *completely* satisfied with the performance of a product or service or with the way a distributor or retailer made the sale, then a good satisfaction survey finds out why by probing to get to the root of the problem. By doing this, the satisfaction survey becomes far more than a crucial quality control device—it can suggest new product/service modifications and new marketing programs.

Major, one-time surveys of individuals or households are normally taken to segment a market by differences in buyer values, life-styles, product usage, benefits sought, and beliefs about product performance. Table 2-1 presents a comparison of the major

Table 2-1
Comparison of Major Survey Research Techniques

Criteria	Direct/cold mailing	Mail panels	Telephone	Personal in-home	Mall intercept
Complexity and versatility	Not much	Not much	Substantial, but complex or lengthy scales difficult to use	Highly flexible	Most flexible
Quantity of data	Substantial	Substantial	Short, lasting typically between 15 and 30 minutes	Greatest quantity	Limited 25 minutes or less
Sample control	Little	Substantial, but representativeness may be a question	Good, but non-listed households can be a problem	In theory, provides greatest control	Can be problematic; sample representativeness may be questionable
Quality of data	Better for sensitive or embarrassing questions; however, no interviewer present to clarify what is being asked		Positive side, interview can clear up any ambiguities, negative side may lead to socially accepted answers	In addition, there is the chance of cheating	In addition, unnatural testing environment can lead to bias
Response rates	In general, low; as low as 10%	70–80%	60–80%	Greater than 80%	As high as 80%
Speed	Several weeks; completion time will increase with follow-up mailings	Several weeks with no follow-up mailings, longer with follow-up mailings	Large studies can be completed in 3 to 4 weeks	Faster than mail but typically slower than telephone surveys	Large studies can be completed in a few days
Cost	Inexpensive; as low as $2.50 per completed interview	Lowest	Not as low as mail; depends on incidence rate and length of questionnaire	Can be relatively expensive, but considerable variability	Less expensive than in-home, but higher than telephone; again, length and incidence rate will determine cost
Uses	Executive, industrial, medical, and readership studies	All areas of marketing research, particularly useful in low-incidence categories	Particularly effective in studies that require national samples	Still prevalent in product testing and other studies that require visual cues or product prototypes	Pervasive-concept tests, name tests, package tests, copy tests

Source: Reproduced with permission from William Dillon, Thomas J. Madden, and Neil H. Firtle, *Marketing Research in a Marketing Environment* (Homewood, IL: Irwin, 1990), 201.

1. Problem Recognition:
   What happened? What is happening? Should we do it?

2. Meet and Define Problem and Determine How to Solve It:
   When is the answer needed? Limits method.
   How valuable is the answer? Limits method.
   How valuable is high accuracy? Limits method.

3. Search Secondary and Syndicated Data Sources:
   Has it happened in the past? Check archives.
   Call outside experts for answers.
   How can the syndicated companies help?
   Is their any published research on the problem?
   Meet and review answers. Stop if satisfactory.

4. Undertake Quick and Dirty Primary Research:
   Conduct an electronic/voice mail survey of the sales force.
   Call on customers/distributors.
   Run focus groups. Meet and review answers. Stop if satisfactory.

5. Undertake Thorough Primary Research:
   Select sampling frame (random sample national panel provided by market research firm). Choose survey technique (personal visit, mall intercept, telephone, mail). Design questionnaire.

6. Analyze Information:
   Review descriptive statistics (such as percentages, means, standard deviations). Conduct relationship analyses (such as cross-tabs, Chi-square, correlational analyses, structural equations modeling, logit, ANOVA, MANOVA, Conjoint).

7. Present Findings:
   Offer progress briefings on important findings.
   Report the presentation.
   Archive findings and data.

Figure 2-9

The Basic Market Research Process

This figure presents the conventional approach to research. Firms often undertake steps 1 through 4. If they require more formal primary research, they will likely hire a market research firm that will take a month or more to do the study at a cost of $5,000–$10,000, sometimes a lot more. This explains why formal primary research is not very common.

survey research approaches. Unfortunately, low response rates are becoming a growing problem. The cooperation of households has been worn thin by telemarketing (sometimes unethically disguised as survey research), political polling, and market research. Figure 2-9 presents the conventional market research process. It indicates that intelligence gathering is often undertaken in an incremental way. The least costly sources of answers to the perceived problem are first searched. Major studies are only taken if satisfactory answers cannot be found from secondary or syndicated sources, if the issue is of great importance, or if a precise answer is required.

Cost Intelligence Gathering

In years gone by, marketers used to grumble that accountants knew the cost of everything and the value of nothing. Accountants might well have responded that marketers know the value of everything and the cost of nothing. In an era of tough competition, when innovation-imitation must reduce costs *and* increase quality, the team must understand costs and cost structure involved in designing a product or service and setting its price. Effective decision making is about allocating scarce resources across product lines and marketing programs.[21] The quality of decision making crucially

21. Budgeting techniques for optimally allocating resources among products and programs (for example, sales management and advertising) are discussed in Chapter 15.

depends on the decision-making team knowing, from the very outset, the cost of the resources it is allocating—that is, the cost of the products and programs it is creating. Understanding the rationality of costs can result in an important competitive advantage. It is a major component of competitive rationality because, as mentioned in Chapter 1, one of the three drivers of competitive rationality is the control and reduction of costs. Moreover, in any market, but particularly mature markets, being the low-cost producer is a huge competitive advantage.

Perhaps one of the reasons why senior executives take the pricing decision out of the hands of lower-level executives more frequently than any other element of the marketing mix, *including* positioning and distribution, is that the executives have a better understanding of costs and margins.[22] Developing such a skill requires a knowledge of the different types of costs, how they are related, and how they affect profit (see Figure 2-10).

Fixed Costs

Costs that are planned and incurred during the planning period no matter what the level of production and sales are called fixed costs. Absolute fixed costs are depreciations on plant and patent amortization. Other fixed costs are somewhat manageable over the long term, such as R&D, rent, insurance, advertising, health benefits, and administrative overheads. Most costs are manageable, but some take more effort to measure and more time to manage.[23] Profits can only be earned after all fixed costs are covered (paid for). The level of sales for a given price that covers all fixed costs is the break-even sales volume. One of the reasons why American companies facing new high fixed costs to be spent on R&D and manufacturing are going global is that the expanded sales base makes the required break-even sales volume more attainable.

Direct Variable Costs

Direct variable costs, such as direct material costs and direct labor costs, are directly associated with the volume of production and sales. These costs increase as production and sales increase. They should also decrease as production and sales decrease, but often they are more sticky on the downside than the upside. They typically include raw material costs, royalties, distribution costs, and sales commissions. Total direct variable cost (TVC) is a function of Q (the quantity sold and produced)—TVC=f(Q). This is an increasing function, but the rate of increase slows down as a firm takes advantage of volume economies in buying, producing, and selling.[24] In marketing we are most interested in the average variable cost of producing and making a product to a specific segment. This cost serves as an absolute floor for a product's price.

Shared Costs

Shared costs include both fixed and variable costs shared among products. Calculating the true cost of a specific product is often difficult because it requires a decision as to

---

22. Peter R. Dickson and Rosemary Kalapurakal, "The Marketing Decision Making Process" (Working Paper, Columbus: Ohio State University, 1991).
23. B. Charles Ames and James D. Hlavacek, "Vital Truths about Managing Your Costs," *Harvard Business Review,* January/February 1990, 140–47. This excellent article emphasizes that, over the long-term, a firm must be a lower-cost supplier and must continuously reduce its costs by correctly measuring them, allocating them sensibly to product/market segments, and making someone responsible to reduce them.
24. As firms produce and sell more, they learn how to make and market products better and cheaper. This effect is called the *experience curve.* The cost of making calculators, computers, hand tools, processing color film, and many other products and services has dropped dramatically in recent years. Such superior learning is a major element of competitive rationality.

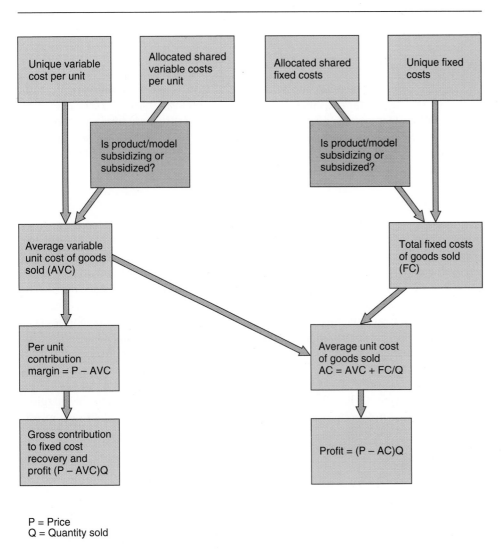

Gross Contribution = (P − AVC)Q
= (P − (AVC + FC/Q)) Q + FC
= (P − AC)Q + FC
= Profit + FC

P = Price
Q = Quantity sold

how to allocate costs among products. It is a particular problem for service costing, as a great deal of the costs of providing services are shared. This may lead to underestimating or overestimating the real costs of products sold to specific segments. If costs are not allocated appropriately, then one product will end up carrying (subsidizing) the cost of another. This can create serious mistakes in promoting particular products or markets at the expense of other products or segments. As many costs as possible should be allocated to a specific product or market rather than sharing the costs among them. That way, each product or market has an incentive to find ways to reduce the cost and to make sure it has been allocated fairly. The traditional way of allocating shared costs by a percentage of direct labor cost involved in making a product can create serious cost and pricing distortions, particularly when shared costs, such as factory support operations, engineering, design, distribution, marketing, and other overheads, make up a significant portion of a firm's cost structure. Activity-based costing (see the following section and Chapter 15) is a much better way of sourcing and allocating costs to a particular product/service.[25]

Average Costs

The average cost of producing and selling is the sum of all fixed and variable costs divided by Q. The greater the ratio of fixed costs to total variable costs, the faster average cost falls as Q increases.[26] This explains why in markets where fixed costs are high, firms try very hard to increase sales and gain market share from each other. Costs fall faster and hence profits increase faster with an increase in sales. Long-distance telecommunications is such a market.

Marginal Costs

Marginal cost is the direct variable cost of producing and selling one more unit over and above the volume that is currently produced and sold. It includes only unavoidable, additional costs. Typical marginal costs include the cost of additional material, direct processing costs, transportation costs, and sales commissions. Fixed and other variable costs already spent on producing and marketing the product are not considered. The direct costs involved in making and selling additional units are usually less than the costs of producing and making what has already been sold. This is due to volume economies in the variable costs of production and selling. The decreasing slope of the TVC curve indicates such economies. The marginal costs of a product are often used to price special orders or export sales. If a firm has no better use of its resources, then any additional sale at a price above marginal cost is worthwhile, provided it does not affect existing sales demand. However, if a firm is producing at capacity, then the marginal cost of increasing production can be prohibitive because it involves major new investments to expand capacity.

Sunk Costs

Costs incurred in the past are called sunk costs. Examples are R&D and the production cost of finished goods in inventory. Sunk costs are relevant in the initial pricing decision and when estimating future profits, but they are not relevant when considering a change in price. This is because such costs will be deducted equally from the sales of each alternative pricing option. They do not vary across pricing options. A pricing decision must focus solely on costs that vary between pricing options, so sunk costs are irrelevant.

Future Costs

When input costs are increasing or decreasing, estimates of future costs rather than past costs should be used to set future prices of products. However, estimating future costs is difficult and can involve subjective judgments that lead to heated arguments among marketing, purchasing, production, and finance managers, particularly during periods of high inflation.

25. Robin Cooper and Robert S. Kaplan, "Measuring Costs Right: Make the Right Decisions," *Harvard Business Review,* September/October 1988, 96–103.
26. Average variable unit costs decrease as volume increase for two reasons that are often confused. The first is *economies of scale* that come from purchasing, manufacturing, distribution, and marketing efficiences that occur with greater sales (the average unit variable cost curve slopes downward when plotted against volume). Second, as an organization *learns* from its accumulated production and sales experience, the whole average unit cost curve changes by shifting down (to be lower than the previous average unit cost curve).

Activity-based Costing (ABC)

Activity-based costing is the latest innovation in management accounting. It is more competitively rational because its focus is the cost of activities. Activity-based costing breaks an organization into activities, and activities into tasks, which then convert materials, labor, and technology into outputs. All of the inputs including direct materials, direct labor, direct machine time, use of facilities, design costs, R&D, and other direct overhead costs associated with the activity are carefully measured. Joint and indirect costs are not assigned to a product but are associated with production and marketing activities. The factors or tasks that drive the costs of the entire activity must be understood. The key measures are cost per output, the time to perform the activity, and the defect rate. Such understanding results in more accurate product/service costing, better make or buy (out-sourcing) decisions, and greater opportunity to control and reduce product costs. The activities of best-practice companies are studied and used as a benchmark to change activity schedules and increase input-output effectiveness and efficiency. Such an analysis is discussed in further detail in the chapters on analyzing the organization (Chapter 7), organizing and implementing (Chapter 14), and forecasting, budgeting, and control (Chapter 15).

Contribution Margin (CM)

The contribution margin is the difference between price and average variable cost, expressed in dollars. When multiplied by sales volume, it is referred to as gross or total contribution (see Figure 2-8). The term *contribution* is used because CM measures the contribution each sale makes toward covering (paying for) fixed costs. After fixed costs are paid, CM measures the contribution each sale makes to profits. The contribution margin percentage (%CM) is equal to the dollar contribution margin divided by the price and expressed as a percentage. To achieve the target contribution margin percentage, either variable costs must be decreased or price must be increased.[27] The above discussion provides a logical framework for gathering, analyzing, and interpreting costs. We now develop a more general framework for using marketing intelligence.

Mental Models of the Market

Very little is known about the mental models that decision makers use when thinking about the market. One way of understanding mental models is to study how decision makers organize information about the market in their decision making and written marketing plans. A case study of ten corporations taken in the 1980s found that *only* two of the ten corporations systematically structured their thinking about their markets.[28] What is even more disturbing is that all of the companies had set up special environmental analysis units in response to the growing importance of tracking changing markets!

Table 2-2 presents two Conference Board studies of the contents of the typical market analyses in the marketing plans of major U.S. companies.[29] About three-quarters of the plans describe a market segment analysis in detail and about half analyze the

27. Different industries use different terms to describe gross contribution (for example, *net earnings* or *revenues*) and contribution margin percentage (sometimes confusingly called margin or profit margin).
28. R.T. Lentz and Jack L. Engledow, "Environmental Analysis Units and Strategic Decision-Making: A Field Study of Selected 'Leading Edge' Corporations," *Strategic Management Journal* 7 (1986), 69–89.
29. Peter R. Dickson and Rosemary Kalapurakal, "The Theory and Reality of Environment Analysis," 119.

Table 2-2
Changes in the Marketing Plan Environmental Analysis of Major U.S. Firms

Variable	1980			1990		
	In detail	Brief mention	No mention	In detail	Brief mention	No mention
Segmentation	60.3	29.6	4.5	75.3	13.5	2.2
Demand forecast	76.0	19.5	2.6	64.6	23.3	4.0
Consumer needs	57.7	36.3	3.0	58.7	30.0	3.1
Competitor M.S.	65.5	24.0	7.9	63.2	22.0	8.1
Competitor information	65.2	28.1	4.5	48.0	39.0	5.8
Technology	41.2	43.4	9.4	43.9	35.9	9.9
Regulation	35.6	43.4	13.9	26.5	39.5	19.3
Environment	30.0	40.4	15.0	25.6	35.4	21.5
BCG analysis*	22.8	23.6	37.8	20.6	25.6	27.8
PLC analysis	14.6	33.7	34.8	17.9	32.3	32.3
Previous plan	19.9	43.4	29.2	14.8	38.1	36.3

*BCG includes mentions of various types of portfolio analyses.

competition in detail. What is even more noteworthy is that despite all of the advances in information technology during the 1980s, the market analyses in the 1990 plans were not more thorough than they were in 1980. If anything, they were less thorough—particularly those analyzing the competition. Figure 2-11 presents a Venn diagram revealing what percentage of the firms in the 1990 study presented market analyses in their plans that detailed changes in the consumer environment, competitive environment, channel environment, and regulatory environment. Only 11.5 percent contained such enlightened insights. It is hoped that the decision makers in the other 88.5 percent of the firms are briefed about such changes during their informal decision-

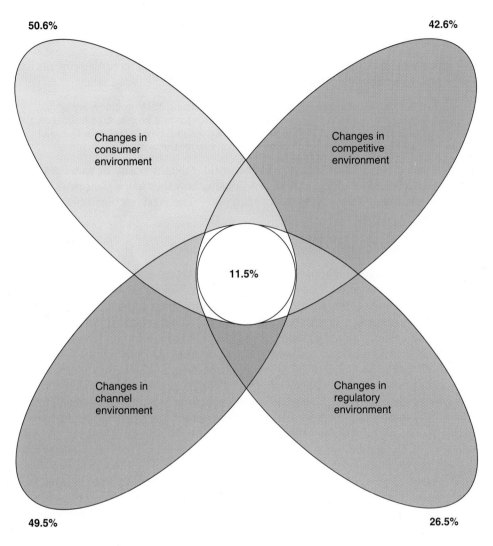

50.6%

42.6%

Changes in
consumer
environment

Changes in
competitive
environment

11.5%

Changes in
channel
environment

Changes in
regulatory
environment

49.5%

26.5%

Figure 2-11

**Environmental Issues Detailed in
the Marketing Plan**

The percentages indicate the proportion
of firms in the 1990 Conference Board
study that include such information in
their typical marketing plan. Changes in
consumer environment include both a
consumer needs analysis and a segmentation analysis. Changes in competitive
environment include both a market share
analysis and an analysis of individual
competitor behavior. Changes in channel
environment were only considered for
those companies that used distributors/
dealers/retailers.

Source: Reprinted from *The Marketing
Plan* by Howard Sutton, The Conference
Board, NYC 1990.

making sessions; otherwise a great deal of market decision making is less informed
than it could be.

A reasonable conclusion is that many firms may be able to gain a considerable
competitive advantage by requiring that their marketing plans include detailed reports
on changes occurring in consumer behavior, competitor behavior, channel behavior,
and public policy. In the words of a marketing manager at a major consumer packaged
goods company:[30]

The most important part of our marketing plan is probably the key learning section,
which is the section that outlines everything that we have learned over the past year

30. These two quotations were derived during research with the Conference Board.

or two about the business and the future of the business. If you don't have a sound basis there, then the rest of the plan is going to falter . . . It's a process of going through and determining what are the key learning points . . . Once we have reached agreement on them, we talk about how they are going to impact the business.

The importance of changing managers' mental models of the market environments was also expressed by another participant in the 1990 Conference Board study:

A lot of people we have coming out of schools with strong MBA programs are people who are brilliant analysts, very, very skilled at understanding how to take businesses apart, but not very skilled at how to achieve market insight, how to trigger action, and most of all, how to change people's paradigm or view of the world.

Whether called a mental model, view of the world, thought world, or paradigm, it is clear that many firms could benefit from rethinking how they frame their market analyses and what they learn from such analyses.[31] The next section offers such a framework.

The Five Environments (5E) Mental Model

There is a great deal of uncertainty involved in marketing planning, even when it is done well. There is uncertainty about whether the descriptions of the marketplace environments are accurate. There is uncertainty about how the marketplace will change in the future. There is often uncertainty as to what are the real objectives of the plan and whether the objectives of the senior executives will change in the future. There is uncertainty as to whether the company has the resources, the will, and the cooperative political climate to implement the proposed action programs. Finally, there is uncertainty about how the marketplace will respond to the strategy. Consequently, a decision-making team can only know a portion of the facts or truths about the marketplace. The planner has a limited knowledge of how consumers behave, how the channels of distribution operate, how competitors behave, what public policy applies to the marketplace, and the capabilities and performance of the company. These sets of knowledge provide insight and reduce decision-making uncertainty.

Figure 2-12 presents a decision maker's mental model of the market. This five-environment market-orientation model extends the three-behavioral-component market-orientation model (customer orientation, competitor orientation, and company orientation) to include channel orientation and public policy orientation.[32]

Each colored ellipse represents what the decision maker knows about each of the five environments that make up the market. If a manager knows a lot about competitors and less about the other market environments, then the manager's perspective or orientation will be colored by this bias. It is as if the manager sees the marketplace through a single colored light—say, green for competition. As a consequence, the manager is less sensitive or alert to changes in other market environments that do not show up in green light. Only by adopting a balanced mental model of the market (that is, a balanced perspective) will the manager see the market through a combination of colored lights that produces a clear white light (the overlapping center of Figure 2-12) with which to view the market. The goal of the decision maker is to increase the size of this enlightened circle in his or her mental model of the market. The goal of the

31. See also George S. Day, *Learning about Markets*, 91–117 (Cambridge, MA: Marketing Science Institute, 1991); and Jeffrey Pfeffer and Gerald R. Salancik, *The External Control of Organizations: A Resource Dependence Perspective* (New York: Harper, 1978).
32. Ajay K. Kohli and Bernard J. Jaworski, "Market Orientation: The Construct, Research Propositions, and Management Implications," *Journal of Marketing* 54 (April 1990), 1–18; and John C. Narver and S. Slater, "The Effect of Market Orientation of Business Profitability," *Journal of Marketing* 54 (October 1990), 20–35.

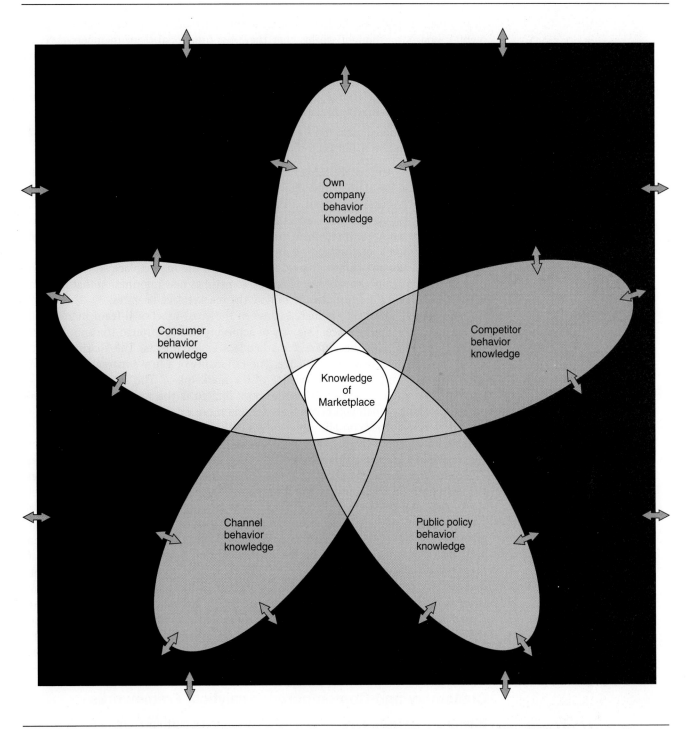

The way a decision maker thinks about a market can be described in terms of what that marketer knows about the consumer, competitor, channel, public policy, and his or her own company's behavior. The proportion of light to darkness indicates how much the decision maker knows about the market. The arrows indicate that the market is always changing, so what a decision maker needs to know is always changing. What *is* known can expand or shrink depending on the decision maker's alertness and interpretative insight. A balanced, enlightened view of the market requires studying a strategic proposal or tactical program in the light off *all five* environments (the white circle in the middle).

Figure 2-12
The Five Environments (5E)
Mental Model of the Market

decision-making team is to increase the size of the enlightened circle in its *collective, shared* mental model of the market. Learning faster than a rival means changing the mental models or thought worlds that the cross-functional team members carry in their heads about the market faster than a rival does.[33] Figure 2-12 makes the following suggestions:

1. A cross-functional team must start with a balanced mental model of the market, which includes knowledge of each of the five business environments.

2. A cross-functional team must continuously update its mental model of the market with information about each of the five business environments.

The actual size of the square, which represents all that could be known about the marketplace, expands as new technology or other events change the marketplace. Their unknown effect increases overall uncertainty. Sometimes, the size of the square is reduced, such as when several competitors withdraw from the market and their behavior no longer has to be predicted. New, correct information about the marketplace increases planners' understanding by providing new insights or confirming and strengthening existing beliefs. It sheds new light on the marketplace and extends the boundaries of a team's knowledge. However, sometimes new information that is wrong will shrink a team's true knowledge of how the marketplace operates.

Competitive rationality is increased when the cross-functional team increases its knowledge of the marketplace. One way of achieving this is through the annual plan's analysis and report of the different marketplace environments. The sharing of such knowledge increases overall knowledge. The rationality of a firm's marketing planning is bounded or limited by its knowledge of the marketplace. The smaller the ratio of light to dark areas in Figure 2-12, the more limited is the rationality of the firm's decision making, which will become riskier and more uncertain.

There is a further complication. Figure 2-12 represents how much an individual or team knows about marketplace truth. Decision makers may have very different perceptions about how much they *think* they know about how the marketplace operates. The more confidence they have that they understand how the marketplace operates, the less uncertain they will feel, the more they will feel in control, and the more likely they will be prepared to make risky decisions. A planning process must try to minimize a team's misperceptions about the market and its misperceptions about how much its members think they know about the marketplace. This is best achieved by having them write down what they know about the marketplace in a report so that it can be challenged or enriched by the knowledge of other members of the cross-functional team or by consultants. Incorrect knowledge or beliefs in the mind of a planner that are never spelled out in writing cannot be changed easily and may never be challenged and changed. It can lead to both overconfident and ineffective decision making. All other things being equal, a firm that possesses the most knowledge about a marketplace and has a correct perception of the knowledge it possesses will make the most rational decisions and hence possesses the highest long-term survival potential.[34]

Customary and Contemporary Analytical Frameworks

Historically, the marketing function has focused on the customer, but in the 1980s the increase in foreign competition and the influence of several best-selling books led to

---

33. Arie P. De Geus, "Planning As Learning," *Harvard Business Review,* 1988; and Deborah Dougherty *Interpretive Barriers to Successful Product Innovation* (Cambridge, MA: Marketing Science Institute, 1989), 89–114.
34. Of course, knowing a lot about the marketplace may not be sufficient if it is not the most important information. Hence, knowledge should be weighed by its strategic importance.

an increased interest in studying the competition.[35] Without exception, today's planning experts all agree that a market analysis should have sections and frameworks describing the consumer environment (see Chapter 3) and the competitive environment (see Chapter 4).

Two other major players in the marketplace are likely to take a keen interest in a company's strategy: the distribution channels (see Chapter 5) and the regulators (see Chapter 6). Changes in these two environments can affect marketing strategy and programs as much as changes in consumer or competitive behavior. Consequently, it is generally recommended that the study of the external environment be divided into four categories: the consumer, the competition, the channel, and the public policy environment. If there are any other major players, special interest groups, or environments in the market not falling within these categories, then a separate section of the environment report should describe the environments, behaviors, and interests of these groups.

The fifth major component of a typical product-market environment report describes the company internal environment (see Chapter 7). This is because a marketing plan for a product or service must be constrained by company goals, strengths, weaknesses, cost structure, and the ability or willingness of other functional areas within the firm (such as production) to supply the inputs and activities required to execute the proposed marketing strategy.

As recommended in Chapter 1, it makes sense to first complete the external market analysis and write up the sections of the environment report describing consumers, channels, competition, and public policy. This report, or at least a summary of the report, is then passed on to senior managers to help them in their corporate planning. Senior management uses the external environmental analysis and operating performance history to develop and impose specific corporate objectives and strategies and tentative production, finance, and personnel constraints on the marketing strategy (see Chapter 7). Production, R&D, and other functional areas are also consulted at this point. The company's internal environment is then analyzed and described to include these top-down objectives and constraints. In this way, the short-term and long-term company objectives for the product or service are stated within the company section of the environment report. In essence, this section describes the voice of the firm.[36]

Writing the Environment Report

It is appropriate at this point to explain that all new environmental information should be presented in what is called an *environment report* within the marketing plan. The proposed strategy is presented in a *strategy report*. These two reports are major components of the written marketing plan (for an example, see Appendix 2). When the environment report is organized by the different interest groups that are likely to be impacted by the strategy, it is much easier to understand the effect of a strategy on the market. It also helps to gather information about each group and to organize the facts into a sensible and meaningful framework, such as the one illustrated in the exhibit on page 68.

Some environment reports will have much larger sections on the consumer and competition because there are limited channels in the product market. There may also be minimal public policy concerns and simple company goals and constraints. Other

---

35. Michael Porter, *Competitive Strategy* (New York: The Free Press, 1980); and Al Ries and Jack Trout, *Marketing Warfare* (New York: McGraw-Hill, 1986). See also the results reported in Table 2.1 of the 1990 Conference Board study.
36. Barabba and Zaltman, *Hearing the Voice of the Market.*

Exhibit:

A List of the Possible Contents of an Environment Report

Consumer Environment

♦ Deep (benefit) segmentation (unfolding causes and effects)

♦ Contact segmentation (media usage and retail shopping behavior)

♦ Analysis of key customer relationships

♦ Trends in values, needs, purchase, and usage behavior

♦ Overall demand forecast

Channel Environment

♦ Technology changes in logistics

♦ New channel trends/channel industry analysis

♦ Short-term economic effects on channels

♦ Key distributor relationship audit

♦ Facilitator audit

Competitive Environment

♦ Market share change analysis/industry analysis

♦ Competitive trends analysis

♦ New technology threats

environment reports will contain extended discussions on these later environments because preliminary analysis reveals their complexity and potential importance.

The environment report should be designed and structured to be most helpful to planners in understanding the environment. This may mean deviating from the above format by creating a separate main section that deals solely with the major competitor or a major customer. The topics and emphasis in the environment report will depend very much on the nature of the product that is being planned and the market that is being served. This point cannot be overemphasized. No two environment reports for different products will ever look the same, and few will approach the detail contained in the exhibit. The initial mental model and detailed categories in the environment report that a cross-functional team adopts may not be the most appropriate. However, a team and a firm with a strong drive to improve the results of its decision making will arrive at an appropriate mental structuring of the market *faster* than its competition by the way it *adapts* its structural view of the market over time. For example, as new issues surface, the structure will change. Issues are discoveries about the environment—normally about consumer, dealer, or competitor behavior—that are news and that have clear implications for future market strategy. As is revealed in the following comments of market decision makers talked to during the 1990 Conference Board study, issues have a big influence on framing the decision making:

> The first half of the process is spent in surfacing issues and the second half is spent prioritizing issues ... One of the issues that is common to all our businesses is the declining efficiency and effectiveness of broadcast advertising.

> The process that we have developed and used at 3M pushes for asking what's different, what's changed, what new issues do we have to address. We also push for what do we anticipate changing, to be proactive when we can.

For example, as environment/habitat concerns become paramount, the green movement will become an important market constituency that changes consumer behavior and public policy. It has already become a major constituency in many forest products and agriculture markets.

- ◆ Backward and forward integration threats
- ◆ Selected competitor audits
- ◆ Anticipated competitor behavior

Public Policy Environment

- ◆ Assistance and support programs audit
- ◆ Regulation/deregulation issues
- ◆ Environmental and other political issues
- ◆ New federal, state, and county regulations
- ◆ Relevant changes in public opinion, values, and ethics
- ◆ Emerging ethical issues

Company Environment

- ◆ Product's long-term role in corporate mission/plan
- ◆ Contribution, ROI, and cash flow objectives
- ◆ Culture and resources, strengths and weaknesses audit
- ◆ Specific manufacturing/logistics constraints
- ◆ Specific budget constraints
- ◆ Internal political and bureaucratic constraints

Writing Style

The writing style of the environment report should be terse, to the point, and punchy. It should read more like an extended memo than an academic research report or a Harvard Business School case study. The report is written for the team and others who already know a lot about the market. Therefore it does not need to present background information that an outsider might need in order to understand the plan. The purpose of the report is to help the cross-functional team adapt strategy to the environmental facts, and it should be written with this in mind. The detailed research, tables, and charts should be available in supporting appendices. Their conclusions should be summarized in the report. This avoids information overload and paralysis by analysis.

Changing the Way We See and Think

The objective of the environmental analysis is to provide insights that enable the team and others to view the proposed strategy from the perspective of each of the major players in the marketplace. To be able to anticipate the acceptance and likely success of an element of marketing strategy, the team has to place itself in the shoes of the consumer, competitor, distributor, regulator, company production manager, and company senior executive. If it understands their situations and objectives, then it will be able to anticipate how they will react. Repeated use of this framework will lead to the categorization and storage of information about the marketplace under these "headings" in memory. This will naturally increase the team's ability to think intuitively, like a consumer, a competitor, a channel member, a regulator, or a production manager, during its informal decision-making sessions. Another highly valued outcome will be an increase in creative ideas.[37]

---

37. Robin M. Hogarth *Judgement and Choice* (New York: John Wiley, 1987); and Henry Mintzberg, "Planning on the Left Side and Managing on the Right," *Harvard Business Review,* July/August 1976, 49–60 and Appendix 1 for a discussion of creativity and perspective in problem solving.

Answers to Five Common Questions

Marketing decision makers who normally organize market analyses in a different way may have a number of questions, which we will now address.

Where Are the Economy and Changes in Technology Described?

Changes in technology and the economy along with changes in population demographics and cultural beliefs, are all vital concerns, but their effects are best tracked by observing *their separate* effects on consumer behavior, channels, current and potential competition, government policy, and the company. Changes in technology, demographics, cultural norms, and the state of the economy can touch all five of these environments. Simply describing the likely state of the economy or new technology in a marketing plan is an incomplete analysis. It leaves it up to the planner to interpret their effects on all the different players in the market.

If such interpretations are unwritten, then an important recorded step in the process of developing strategy is missing. There is also a risk that the impact of the economy and new technology on *all* of the marketplace environments will not be considered. Given Murphy's Law ("If something can go wrong, it will"), overlooking the effect of the economy or new technology on one of the five environments will turn out to be fatal to the venture. When seeking advice from experts about the economy and new technology, it makes sense to have them also forecast the impact of these forces on consumer, competitor, channel, regulator, and your own company behavior. This should be integrated into each of the relevant sections of the environment report.

Where Is the State of the Industry Described?

An overall analysis of the state of the industry should be presented in the competitive analysis section of the environment report. This is because an industry analysis normally involves a description of major competitive trends. Michael Porter, in his best-selling book on competitive strategy, demonstrated the value of applying industrial organization theory to describe general competitive trends in an industry (as well as analyzing specific competitors).[38] Trends in the markets of business customers should be described in the consumer section of the environment report. If there are major industry trends occurring in channels of distribution, then these should be described in the channel section of the report.

This raises another frequent point of confusion. Why does the proposed marketing plan have a section on channels of distribution in the environment report and a section on distribution strategy in the strategy report? The answer is that the environment report describes what is happening in all the channels of distribution that are available. It is not limited to the existing channels that are being used. The strategy report describes proposed distribution programs. Comparing it against the section describing channels in the environment report enables the team to assess what the effect of its proposed distribution programs will be on current channels and other alternative channels. This explains why this text has a chapter on channel analysis (Chapter 5) *and* a separate chapter on distribution strategy (Chapter 10).

Where Are the Opportunities and Problems Described?

The market analysis prepared for the STRATMESH planning process is also different from some other recommended procedures in that a summary of opportunities and problems is not prepared before developing marketing strategy. The reason is that an

38. Porter, *Competitive Strategy.*

opportunity or a problem often can only be defined or evaluated in the context of a particular current or potential strategy. Opportunities and problems are often identified at the meshing stage of the proposed planning process, when specific strategy is being considered. Indeed, a major purpose of the meshing process is to identify problems with the fit of the film's strategy to the market environment *and* identify a new strategy that exploits an opportunity, creates a new opportunity, or even converts a problem into an opportunity.

This is not to suggest that the environment report will not identify possible opportunities and problems. As the environmental analysis proceeds, it is inevitable that problems, opportunities, and exciting new marketing strategies will be discovered. These should be listed in a notebook or workbook, but they must be put aside until the environment report is completed. Otherwise, they may dominate the thinking of the planner and bias the rest of the analysis.

The time to really get excited about new ideas is after the environment report has been completed and the idea has been tested against all of the realities of the marketplace. A related mistake of students and executives alike is to include current strategy in the environment report. A marketing plan's environment report should discuss and explain the environment, and only the environment. When strategy creeps into the description of the environment, it becomes viewed as a given. It discourages thinking about any alternative strategy, and its fit with the marketplace environment is not challenged.

What Should Be the Time Horizon of the Plan?

Many companies undertake an annual marketing planning exercise for each of their products or lines of products. The STRATMESH planning process is designed for annual marketing planning but can be used no matter what planning horizon is adopted. Once the initial investment is made in understanding the marketplace environment, the cost and effort needed to update the environment report annually is a lot less. However, marketing strategy often takes several months, sometimes several years, to implement and take effect. Consequently, the time horizon of the marketing plan is often longer than 12 months. For a new product launch, it may be three to five years. A marketing planner has no choice but to remain open and flexible about time horizons. If the marketing plan is updated annually, then it will build on, extend, and adapt strategy that has been implemented and continues to be implemented.

The environmental analysis and report must, therefore, not only discuss the current environment but look ahead and project how the marketplace will change over the next 12 months and beyond. This is not easy to do, but it must be attempted. Fitting proposed strategy to the current environment, when the environment will certainly change, is like planning to live in the past.

Where Is the Sales Forecast Presented?

The projected industry-wide sales forecast should be presented in the consumer analysis as it is most influenced by the effects of social and economic trends on consumer behavior. Where to present the forecast of the company's sales is a much more controversial issue. The whole purpose of planning is to develop a strategy that, once implemented, will have an effect on sales and profitability. If this is so, then the forecast of company sales should be made *after* the strategy and action programs have been developed.[39] It should appear in the budget and profit projections prepared at the end

---

39. David S. Hopkins, *The Marketing Plan* (New York: The Conference Board, 1981), 20; and David L. Hurwood, Elliott S. Grossman, and Earl L. Bailey, *Sales Forecasting* (New York: The Conference Board, 1978).

of the planning process (see Chapter 15). Consequently, the company's past sales and market share should appear in the company analysis; but forecasts of future sales and share, which depend on strategy, should not appear in the environment report. To do so would be like putting the cart before the horse.

Approving the Environment Report

Obtaining a consensus that the environment report represents a true and fair statement of the expected operating environment is a very important step. When executives disagree on a strategic approach, the basis for the disagreement can often be traced to different views or interpretations of environmental facts. It, therefore, makes sense to settle the "What is the likely state of the operating environment?" question before the "What is the best strategy *given* the likely operating environment?" question so as to avoid unnecessary conflict and frustration. This may require further market research or expert opinions.

Often, strategy will need to be tested against several likely environmental scenarios rather than just the most likely scenario. This happens when an aspect of the environment is so uncertain (perhaps, for example, because of the expected entry of new competition or the passage of new legislation) that a strategy must be able to accommodate each possible environmental circumstance. It is desirable that the alternative environmental scenarios be described and understood at an early stage in the process, rather than lurk as a hidden agenda that may or may not be disclosed by participants late in the process (particularly senior executives privy to information about company constraints). Initial acceptance by everyone of the soundness of the market analysis (even one containing multiple scenarios) reduces the opportunity to challenge a strategy later in the planning process. In the next five chapters, we develop further frameworks and models for thinking about each of the five environments that make up the 5E mental model of the market and for using the market intelligence that is gathered. But before doing this, we briefly review some global marketing intelligence issues.

Global Market Research

Our discussion on the gathering of intelligence about foreign markets is built on the following assumptions. It is assumed that a great deal of the decision making about the marketing programs in foreign markets is decentralized, that is, in the hands of an executive team in charge of regional or national markets. For firms new to exporting, such decision-making activity will be in the hands of local agents or distributors. Thus, much of the previously stated advice on how to gather market intelligence is directed at these executives or agents.

This is not to suggest that market intelligence on foreign markets is hard to find in the United States. The U.S. Department of Commerce publishes two invaluable, brief reports on marketing in over 100 countries: *Foreign Economic Trends and Their Implications for the United States* (semiannual) and *Overseas Business Reports* (annual). Not only are these reports a great buy, they also provide a foundation for seeking further expert advice from the U.S. Department of Commerce and U.S. embassies. If such trade specialists cannot help, they are likely to know and be able to recommend experts in the foreign market who can be called. Thus, the first step in global market intelligence gathering is to use the market intelligence gathered by the U.S. government or by banks (see Figure 2-13).

Whatever the geographical market, be it global, regional, national, or a specific city, it is assumed that the 5E mental model of thinking about a market will hold.

Figure 2-13
Many banks market economic analysis products and services to customers. If they had read their own reports, they might have avoided huge losses on third-world loans in the 1980s.

Having all markets in a multinational enterprise analyzed using the same (5E) mental model makes supervision and oversight a great deal easier. The commonalities and differences between markets, and the trends over time in such commonalities and differences, will be very easy to detect. Thus, the standardization also contributes to the development of major strategic decisions on grouping markets, on transcultural market segmentation, and the standardization of various product lines and marketing programs in the global market. A further advantage of the standardization of the framework for analyzing a foreign market is that when a foreign market is analyzed using such a framework, the market will be perceived to be much less exotic, perplexing, and mysterious. The systematic gathering and use of market intelligence using a familiar mental model takes much of the "foreignness" out of a foreign market.

However, the standardization can be taken too far. In some developing markets that are still under the control of political and economic autocracies (rather than free market forces), a special section of the environmental analysis must be devoted to considering the changing objectives and behavior of those in authority and the changing relationship that the firm or its agents have with such a powerful market constituency. Such concerns are discussed in greater detail in Chapter 6 on the public policy and ethical environment.

Rationality in Practice:

Parkinson's Law, Continued

Or why computers and faxes demand more, not fewer, bureaucrats to feed and comfort them

"It is a commonplace observation that work expands to fill the time available for its completion." With those words this newspaper coined Parkinson's Law in 1955, naming it after the (anonymous) author of the article, Professor C. Northcote Parkinson. Since then, wonderful to report, technology has entirely rescued us from the bureaucratic suffocation envisaged by Mr. Parkinson. The world of administrators has been so transformed by computers, faxes and cheap telephones that their productivity grows ever more prodigious, their numbers ever leaner. Governments have shrunk to mere skeleton staffs of irreplaceable paragons. Obstructive bureaucracy has gone the way of wick-trimmers.

Would it were so. This year, for the first time, more Americans work in government than in manufacturing. Mr. Parkinson's observation that bureaucracies grow inexorably, independent of their workload, is as true today as on the day it was first made. Between 1980 and 1991 the number of officers in the American army grew by 7%, while the total number of soldiers shrank by 3½%. In 1965–85 the number of non-teaching staff in school administration in the United States grew by 102% while the number of students shrank by 8%.

No doubt there are more laws and rules to enforce. But there are also more computers to share the work. Robots have reduced the number of people it takes to make a car. Why have computers—white-collar robots—not reduced the number of people it takes to run a government?

The hard disk effect

Parkinson's Law consisted of two maxims: an official wants to multiply subordinates, not rivals; and officials make work for each other. Or, as explained in *The Economist,* "In any public administrative department not actually at war the staff increase may be expected to follow this formula: $x=(2k^m+p)/n$," with the resulting x then shown to be 5¾% a year. In the 1950s the trouble started with the real, or imagined, overwork of an official whom Mr. Parkinson called A, who came to be the master (and slave) of

The final issue in global market intelligence gathering and use is the value of site visits by senior American executives. Such visits allow the executive to make initial contacts with distributors and agents (often during trade delegation tours led by politicians). They are also symbols of concern and respect for the foreign market and the efforts of local employees. However, they are no substitute for informed briefings on the culture, the purchasing power of target consumers, the existing distribution system, import regulations, and taxes provided by expert nationals or expatriots. If senior executives do not have the time to be so briefed by expert distributors, economists, historians, and cultural anthropologists *before* making the next site visit or *during* the visit, then local management is likely to conclude that the American managers really have neither the time nor the respect to be making the visit.

In short, overseas trips should not be spent on emergency negotiations or used as scouting breaks from the turbulent domestic market. It is not a coincidence that much of the success of Japanese firms in the U.S. market can be traced to their practice of being excellently briefed before and during visits to the United States. Unlike some U.S. firms, who do not listen and take to heart the advice received from Japanese distributors, Japanese companies squeeze all of the market intelligence they can out of the distributors they visit in a foreign market, and they use the information. Consequently, their mental models of the U.S. market are often much closer to the truth than some U.S. firms' mental models of the Japanese market.

his proliferating subordinates, C–H. A's successor achieves the same alphabetical explosion by new means.

The trouble began a few years ago when A first installed a computer in his office. The new computer required A to hire C and D to help him, partly because he was so busy with the computer that he had less time for his other duties, and partly because it was immediately evident that the computer would enable somebody to analyse the information passing through his department in an entirely fresh way.

Nor was A the only one to get a computer. B's group was also technified at the same time, and its overall boss thought it wise that A should see B's memos and vice versa, because there might be—he was rather proud of the word—synergy between them. There was, indeed, synergy. That is to say, C and D found that criticising B's absurd proposals took up more and more of their time. Synergy was soon increasing at an alarming rate, because C had hired two technical wizards, E and F, who plugged the department into adMinNET, the new public administrator's electronic mail service. A was then in no position to refuse D's demand for a new computer since the hard disk of the first one was entirely full of junk mail from Omaha about forthcoming conferences on improving productivity in administration.

This is not to imply that computers reduce productivity. On the contrary, the output of A's department is vastly greater than it was before he got the computer. He could never, in the old days, have generated 80 megabytes of data in a year, even if most of it was repetitious. Nor is it fair to describe this workaholism as make-work. Much of the output is worthy stuff. But running a country, or a school district, is more like digging a hole than cutting down a tree—there is no end to it. The work that could be done is infinite and the capacity for expansion of productive, diligent staff is Malthusian. As Mr. Parkinson put it, 38 years ago, "the number of the officials and the quantity of the work to be done are not related to each other at all."

Let us therefore add a coda to Parkinson's law. Because data expands to fill the hard disks available, and officials proliferate to process the data available, technology is the ally of bureaucratic expansion, not its foe.

Source: *The Economist*, August 8, 1992, 16.

Discussion Questions and Minicases

1. What two negative effects does a recession have on a firm's use of market research?

2. If decision makers prefer market research that confirms their current beliefs, then how do they learn to adapt to changes in the market?

3. All told, do you think it is better for firms employing a lot of brilliant, creative inventors to do market research? Justify your answer. If they should do market research, when should they do it, and what sort of research should they do?

4. Imagine that you were part of the cross-functional team developing the Depend's adult disposable diaper. Several members of the team seem to be having a problem understanding consumer complaints about the existing product in the market. What market intelligence-gathering activity might you suggest to raise their understanding?

5. When researching customer needs, would it be better for a product designer to visit customers personally or to read a survey research report on customer needs, beliefs, and behaviors? What biases are inherent in each approach that will reduce the designer's rationality?

6. The Rationality in Practice box printed above discusses the effect of information technology on an organization. What lessons does it contain about DSSs? (Hint: For information technology to increase productivity, what has to change?)

7. The table below presents an interesting analysis of changes in the cost of living prepared by *Consumer Reports* magazine. The data is based on U.S. Bureau of Labor statistics hourly wage rates and the prices of goods and services in 91 urban areas. The data collectors visited 25,000 stores and service firms to obtain the prices. What does it tell us about the standard of living in America? What does it tell us about changes in price sensitivity over time? Marketers of which products should be most interested in the results?

This table shows how long the average American had to work, before taxes, to earn enough to purchase the goods and services listed. For our calculations, we used the actual prices of items in 1962, 1972, 1982, and 1992 and the average hourly wages in each of those years. For simplicity's sake, we show the inexpensive items in the top third of the list in minutes of work, the more costly goods and services in hours, and the big-ticket items at the bottom in days.

	1962	1972	1982	1992
Small items	**Minutes of work**			
Postage (first class, 1 oz.)	1.1	1.6	1.7	1.6
Newspaper (New York Times, daily)	1.4	2.4	2.3	2.8
Long-distance phone call (3 min., N.Y. to L.A.)	60.8	23.5	13.4	4.3
Apples (Red Delicious, 1 lb.)	3.1	2.9	3.3	4.7
Gasoline (1 gal.)	7.5	5.2	9.1	6.4
Chicken (whole, cut, 1 lb.)	13.5	8.7	7.4	7.4
Milk (½ gal.)	12.5	9.6	8.8	7.8
Ground beef (chuck, 1 lb.)	15.3	13.9	13.0	11.1
Film (Kodak, 35 mm, color prints)	60.0	37.9	27.7	27.2
Barbie doll	81.1	60.8	33.2	31.3
Medium items	**Hours of work**			
Record album	1.8	2.2	1.2	[1]1.6
Consumer Reports (1-yr. subscription)	2.7	2.2	1.8	2.1
Timex watch (men's Mercury model)	3.1	2.1	2.2	2.4
Electricity (500 kwh)	4.6	3.3	4.2	3.9
Theater ticket (Broadway, best seat)	3.4	4.1	5.2	5.7
Television (RCA, 19-in.)	85.1	121.6	42.6	21.7
Dishwasher (GE, midpriced model)	112.2	64.9	55.3	35.5
Washing machine (Sears, midpriced model)	92.3	52.7	58.3	37.8
Refrigerator (Frigidaire, top-freezer)	168.0	99.2	83.7	59.8
Mattress (Simmons, with box spring)	71.6	59.5	44.0	60.7
Large Items	**Days of work**			
Auto insurance [2]	7.1	7.8	7.3	11.3
Income taxes (Federal) [3]	50.0	48.3	63.8	49.0
Child delivery [4]	15.5	37.2	33.3	62.2
College (public) [5]	61.7	64.1	68.9	99.2
Car (average, new)	203.1	131.0	161.0	197.8
College (private) [6]	129.5	140.4	144.0	251.4
House (3-bedroom ranch, Matawan, N.J.)	1125.5	1330.7	1530.0	1777.3

[1] Compact disc.
[2] National average.
[3] Includes Social Security.
[4] Normal delivery (hospital and doctor fees).
[5] University of Michigan (room, boad, tuition; 1 yr.).
[6] Colgate (room, board, tuition; 1 yr.).

Source: *Consumer Reports,* June 1992, 393.

8. Your major competitor is going through a management restructuring, which suggests a change in business direction and corporate culture. Suggest some ways that you might come to a quick understanding about what has happened.

9. A number of car-shopping services (listed in the Exhibit on page 78) have developed in recent years to provide market information to consumers. How might a seller use this information in its short-term market intelligence? In a more interesting long-term, futurist sense, what effect would these services have on car prices if they became very popular and were used by 30 to 40 percent of car buyers?

10. It seems that the more information a firm gives to shareholders and customers, the more it reveals its strategy and programs to its rivals, making it easier for them to learn and imitate. What is the solution? (Hint: What makes a firm more competitive?)

11. If you were a member of a newly formed cross-functional team set up to develop an entirely new product, what is the first market intelligence-gathering activity you would undertake and why?

12. A company has a choice between manufacturing its product in Mexico using a highly labor-intensive process or investing in a new robotic plant and making the product in the United States. The average unit cost of production in Mexico can be expected to stay about constant because although labor rates are expected to rise, productivity and changing exchange rates will compensate for the increase. At current sales levels the proposed capital-intensive U.S. manufacturing unit would operate at about 50 percent capacity, and at that capacity the average unit cost would be about the same as the Mexican product's cost. From a pricing perspective, which manufacturing process would you choose? What market information would help you to make the choice?

13. A highly ambitious product manager is told that senior management is about to introduce a new competitive line that will be managed by another executive. To help launch the new line, she is informed that most of the shared costs will be borne by her product. She considers writing a memo to her superiors suggesting a different approach. Please write the memo for her.

14. An airline uses old planes on one route and new planes on another. The old planes have zero book value. How should this fact affect the airline's pricing on these routes?

15. When the president of Sony, Akio Morita, came to the United States in 1955 to sell his tiny transistor radio, a major distributor expressed interest in selling it under its own name (which Sony wisely refused to do) and asked for quotes on the cost of orders of 5,000, 10,000, 30,000, 50,000 and 100,000 units. The distributor was shocked when Sony quoted a higher per unit price for the 100,000 order. However, when the reason for the price was explained, the distributor was impressed by the unknown Japanese company's business savvy, and it placed the order. What justification did Sony provide?

16. A producer of a well-known brand of canned goods earns a 40 percent contribution margin on its sales to supermarkets. It is approached by a supermarket chain to supply a line of lower-priced canned goods marketed under the store's own brand name. The producer has excess capacity because a current recession has resulted in a slump in sales of its branded line. What factors would you consider when deciding whether to supply such a line? What price would you charge?

17. A publisher of specialized books normally sells its books for $30, which produces a $10 contribution margin. On average, 75 percent of the production runs are sold in the first 12 months. The remaining inventory is eventually sold but on average it takes an additional three years to sell a book that has not sold in the first 12 months. The yearly cost of holding each book is 25 percent of cost (10 percent in

warehousing and utilities, 2 percent in insurance and record keeping, and 13 percent in the cost of capital tied up in the book). The owner is thinking of instituting a continuous clearance sale of all books that he has held for 12 months. What should the sale price be? What would be some of the long-term effects of such a sales tactic? What is the long-term solution?

Widjets	Gadjets
Labor @ $10/hour	
$40	$200
Materials and parts	
300	300
Processing @ $20/hour	
200	40
$540	$540

Source: Cooper & Lybrand

18. A firm makes two types of jets for skis, Widjets and Gadjets. The production costs for these two items are presented in the table on the left.

The firm makes 1,000 Widjets and 1,000 Gadjets a year and its total overhead costs for R&D, design, sales, and administration are $770,000. The selling price for both types of jets is $1,100.

The traditional cost accounting method of allocating overhead and processing costs involves the amount of direct labor cost. Subtract total direct labor and material costs from total costs and divide by total labor costs. This gives the allocation per dollar of labor cost to be assigned to each Widjet and Gadjet. Using this method of costing, what is the cost of producing a Widjet and a Gadjet? Another way of allocating costs is to charge the direct costs of processing to each jet and then allocate the overhead as a function of processing time. Using this costing approach, what is the cost of a Widjet and a Gadjet? What is the more correct way? Does it make a difference to the Widjet and Gadjet product managers? Which is closer to activity-based costing? How could additional activity-based costing techniques be used to correctly cost the Widjets and Gadjets?

19. You have just joined a firm where decision makers have developed a convention of writing up planning market analyses under the following headings: 1) industry trends, 2) market share, 3) economic outlook, 4) technological trends, and 5) threats and opportunities. You propose to introduce the 5E framework. Why can you expect a great deal of resistance, even if the firm accepts that the 5E model is a more logical framework? How will you overcome the resistance?

20. Consider the following situation.

Back in 1980, Mr. Walton and I went into a Wal-Mart in Crowley, La. The first thing we saw was this older gentleman standing there. The man didn't know me, and he didn't see Sam, but he said, 'Hi! How are ya? Glad you're here. If there's anything I can tell you about our store just let me know.' Neither Sam nor I had ever seen such a thing. The store, it turned out, had had trouble with shoplifting. Its manager didn't want to intimidate the honest customers by posting a guard, but he wanted to leave a

Car/Puter. Retail and invoice price hotline, $2 per minute; 900-0370-AUTO. Also retail and invoice price reports and buyer's guide: $20. Car locating service also sells cars from a network of member dealers. Write 1500 Cordova Road, Suite 309, Fort Lauderdale, FL 33316; 800-221-4001 or 305-462-8905.

Consumer Reports Auto Price Service. Lists invoice prices and rebates. Cost: $11 for one car, $20 for two, $27 for three and $5 for each additional car. Box 8005, Novi, MI 48376, or fax 313-347-2985.

Easyquote. Broker, fees included in customer price; 800-635-6466.

Nationwide Auto Brokers. Invoice and retail prices on cars and options. Also sells, finances and arranges delivery of new cars. Cost: $11.95 per quote; 800-521-7257.

USAA Federal Savings Bank Automobile Acquisition Services. Invoice and retail pricing and other information, delivered in one week. Cost: $12 per report; 800-531-8905.

Source: From Brigid McMenamin, "Death of a Salesman," *Forbes*, August 31, 1992, 78.

---

clear message, that if you stole, someone was there who would see it. Well, Sam thought that was the greatest idea he'd ever heard of. We put greeters in the front of every single store. I guess his vindication was that in 1989 he walked into a Kmart in Illinois and found they had installed people greeters at their front doors.—Tom Coughlin, Senior Vice-President, Sam's Club.[40]

In terms of intelligence gathering and use, what does this story teach us? What does it teach us in terms of competitive rationality?

21. The customer survey below is included with every purchase of Rockport shoes. How could Rockport use this information? What other questions might have been included? What questions would you eliminate to make room for the questions you would add?

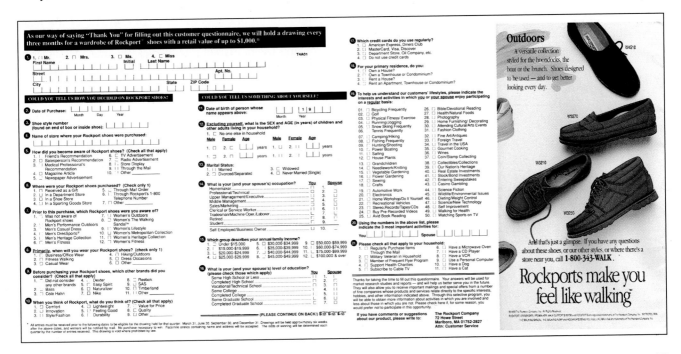

40. Quoted from Sam Walton and John Huey, *Sam Walton: Made in America* (New York: Doubleday, 1992).

22. A survey of 149 major U.S. firms taken in 1989 by the Conference Board asked which research techniques firms used to identify the benefits and outcome performance requirements customers sought from using a product or service. The answer is given below. What does it tell us about the perceived net value (benefit − cost) of different research techniques? Using the theory of competitive rationality, what techniques do you think should be used more often?

Technique	No. of Times Mentioned
Focus groups	40
Surveys of customers' needs, expectations, attitudes, and perceptions by mail and/or telephone. Includes surveys by consultants and in-flight surveys by airlines.	22
Direct contacts with individual customers, including visits by senior executives and technical personnel.	14
Customer and user group councils, forums, panels, advisory groups, and awareness meetings.	12
Use of teams and teamwork between customers and companies.	7
Shopping mall studies, intercepts (exit pools), and interviews.	5
Benchmarking (comparison of a company's performance with that of competitors whose performance is known to be excellent).	4
Analysis of complaints.	4

Source: Francis J. Walsh, *Current Practices in Measuring Quality* (New York: The Conference Board, 1989).

23. A leading supermarket chain surveyed its senior managers to obtain their estimates of consumer price search behavior. The first column presents the results of a major consumer survey, the second column presents the average estimate of the managers, and the third column presents the variation in the managers' answers. What does this tell us about the chain's use of market intelligence, the managers' mental models of consumer behavior, and the firms shared mental model of consumer behavior?

Measure	Consumers (% of sample)	Managers' estimate	Standard deviation	Range
Shop stores' specials regularly	18.6%	33.9%	20.3	5–90
Compare prices weekly	29.6%	36.0%	22.3	1–90
Never compare prices	36.0%	22.7%	20.5	0–98
Scan shelves for specials	78.0%	49.9%	22.6	10–90
Buy larger quantity on special	67.3%	42.8%	22.1	0–100

24. The following tables present information about the usefulness of competitive intelligence and the most useful sources of competitive intelligence. Why is price information more important than strategy information? List several reasons. What do the the results of the most useful sources tell us about how we should set up an intelligence gathering operation?

Best Information and Sources Provided by Competitive Intelligence

Most Useful Source of Information
(by type of market)

Percent Distribution

	Total	Industrial products	Consumer products	Both consumer and industrial
Sales force	27%	35%	18%	23%
Publications, databases	16	13	15	22
Customers	14	13	11	17
Marketing research, tracking services	9	3	24	9
Financial reports	5	7	3	1
Distributors	3	4	1	1
Employees (unspecified)	2	2	6	—
Analysis of products	2	1	3	3
Other	8	6	8	13
No answer	14	16	11	11
	100%	100%	100%	100%
Number of responding companies	308	158	72	78

Most Useful Type of Information
(by type of market)

Percent Distribution

	Total	Industrial products	Consumer products	Both consumer and industrial
Pricing	23%	26%	20%	19%
Strategy	19	20	15	22
Sales Data	13	11	18	12
New products, product mix	11	13	8	10
Advertising/marketing activities	7	3	19	4
Costs	6	8	3	5
Key customers/markets	3	3	6	1
Research and development	2	2	1	3
Management style	2	1	3	1
Other	4	4	—	8
No answer	10	9	7	15
	100%	100%	100%	100%
Number of responding companies	308	158	72	78

Source: Howard Sutton, *Competitive Intelligence* (New York: The Conference Board, 1988).

25. The Secret Service and CIA are likely to become increasingly involved in preserving U.S. company trade secrets and in gathering economic intelligence. Do you think it is a good thing for government secret services to be employed in economic intelligence gathering? Should they be involved in industrial espionage? What if their involvement is needed for the United States to maintain its economic leadership of the world economy? What tactics should the CIA be allowed to employ to obtain crucial intelligence. Should they be allowed to pay for it? To pay bribes? To blackmail? To silence people involved in major scandals that would bring disrespect on the United States and threaten its economic future and, hence, national security? Does your answer change if other nations are already employing their security services in such activities?

Analyzing Customers

"Why and how are words so important that they cannot be too often used?"

Napoleon Bonaparte

"He who would search for pearls must dive below."

John Dryden

*F*or thousands of years most products were custom designed and manufactured for a particular consumer. The first automobiles were made this way, beautiful, expensive works of art. Pioneers of manufacturing processes recognized that standardization and production lines greatly reduced the cost and price of an automobile, opening up the market to middle-income and lower-income consumers. The product would no longer fit the unique needs of each buyer, but that was the price of lowering the cost. The Ford Model T only came in five models and one color but in 1916 its economy model cost only $360. Specialist automobile companies who found they could not compete with the cost advantages of Ford either became very exclusive, were taken over, or went out of business. Ford's compromise between the crafted product and mass production of a single model was the marketing of a line of several models, each designed to meet the needs of different groups of consumers, called market segments (see Table 3-1). General Motors did not invent automobile market segmentation, but in the late 1920s and 1930s General Motors did develop a *better* segmentation framework than Ford and gained a consequential strategic advantage over Ford that it held for several decades. For 50 years, American auto companies segmented the market primarily by making cars for low, medium, and high income households. What a household could afford dominated their mental models of consumer demand. Today, the industry mental models of consumer demand also consider life-style and the benefits that consumers seek from product features (see Figure 3-1).[1]

The mental model that a cross-functional team uses to identify groups of consumers with distinct needs (demand) or behaviors (both usage and shopping behaviors) is called a *market segmentation* framework or model. The firm that chooses a consensus mental segmentation model that best explains how and why consumers differ in their attitudes and behavior toward a product-market has a clear competitive advantage over its rivals. *Market segment analysis* is the search for and understanding of variability in demand (that, in turn, determines customer satisfaction). It is therefore as important a part of a firm's competitive rationality as understanding cost structure. The way a firm thinks about and segments buyers will determine how the firm designs and positions the items in its product line. This positioning will, in turn, determine sales and profits. The firm with a superior mental segmentation model can be competitive, even if it is not the pioneer or low-cost producer. Ultimately, a better segmentation model may enable a firm to dominate the market. Casio segmented the LCD watch market much better than did Texas Instruments, who pioneered the watches but lost the market to Casio. The consensus market segmentation model that is used in market decision making crucially determines the competiveness of a firm's thinking (the firm's competitive rationality).

As you read this chapter, keep the following key ideas in mind:

- Demand varies among buyers and some of this variability can be systematically explained by *segmenting* buyers and their uses of the product.

- All members of a cross-functional team need to develop a consensus mental model that shows how to segment the market and describes the different behavior of buyers in each segment.

- Demand varies among buyers because they seek different benefits and features from products. Four basic needs (physical, emotional, intellectual, and spiritual)

1. Peter Drucker, "The Big Three Miss Japan's Crucial Lesson," *Wall Street Journal*, June 18, 1991, A18. Japanese auto manufacturers were able to break into the U.S. market by segmenting the market more by life-style than socioeconomics.

	Touring	**Runabout**	**Coupe**	**Town**	**Sedan**	**2-Door**	**4-Door**
1909	$850	$825	$ 950	$1,000			
1910	$950	$900	$1,050	$1,200			
1911	$750	$680	$1,050	$1,200			
1912	$690	$590		$ 900			
1913	$690	$590		$ 900			
1914	$490	$440	$ 750	$ 690	$975		
1915	$440	$390	$ 590	$ 640	$750		
1916	$360	$365	$ 505	$ 595	$640		
1917	$360	$345	$ 505	$ 595	$646		
1918	$425		$ 500		$775		
1919	$525	$500	$ 650		$775		
1920	$575	$550	$ 850		$975		
1921	$415	$370	$ 695		$760		
1922	$348	$319	$ 580		$645		
1923	$393	$364	$ 530			$595	$725
1924	$295	$265	$ 525			$590	$685
1925	$290	$260	$ 520			$580	$660
1926	$380	$360	$ 485			$495	$545
1927	$380	$360	$ 485			$495	$545

Table 3-1
Models and Prices of the Model T

A 1914 Ford ad for the Coupe and Sedan.

The basic 1915 touring Model T.

The 1917 Town Car or Landaulet for buyers who had a chauffeur do the driving.

The above table and illustrations reveal that, contrary to legend, Ford made and sold more than one type of Model T that was based on a segmentation of the market by usage situation and income. As indicated from their prices and design, Ford made an economy model, a sports model, a middle-of-the-road model, and a luxury model. Ford also made Tourster, Topedo, and Fore (sic) Door models between 1909 and 1913. Extracted from Gordon Schindler, *Ford Model T Catalog of Accessories* (Osceola, WI: Motorbooks International, 1991).

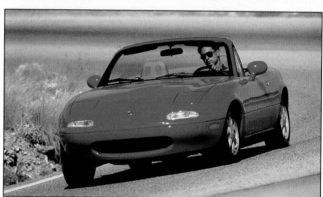

Figure 3-1

Different Life-Style Vehicles

These vehicles are all priced in the $15,000–$20,000 range (depending on options). While similarly priced, they are clearly designed to provide very different benefits.

determine the benefits each buyer seeks. The first step in developing a mental model of market segments is to identify the different benefits and features buyers want.

■ Benefits sought and buyer behavior are functions of personal differences (P) and usage situation differences (S): Benefits sought = $f(P \times S)$, Buyer behavior = $F(P \times S)$.

■ Benefits sought and features desired determine beliefs about the choices, how the choice is made, and preferences. Preferences determine usage, brand loyalty, price sensitivity, and shopping behavior.

■ Buyers spend money and time buying and using products. Time-poor consumers value higher quality. The time-saving benefits of products and services are very important.

■ Buyers can be segmented by the way they make choices. Some undertake a thorough search and make comparative evaluations, others use feelings and choose by impulsively trying alternatives and experiential learning, yet others choose by simply following habits.

■ There are many types of brand loyalty behavior. Each type of brand loyalty has a different implication for a seller trying to change such loyalty and can be used to segment the market.

■ The different reasons for price sensitivity can be used to segment the market.

- Buyers can also be *contact* segmented by the media they use, where they buy, and their attitude toward shopping.

- The unique needs of major business buyers and the benefits they seek from product usage are often custom serviced. This goes beyond market segmentation.

- The business market can often be segmented by whether the business buyers want to develop a close partnership relationship or low-bid buy from many sources.

- The global marketer must understand the cultural and economic reasons why demand varies from one country to another and how the segmentation model must change.

Mental Models of Market Segmentation

Numerous articles have been written about how markets can be segmented by demographic classifications such as income, class, age, or geographical region, and almost all marketing texts list a large number of segmentation variables. However, increasingly enterprising marketers are *combining* the variables they use to segment consumer demand. For example, some large packaged-goods companies segment demand by using a combination of demographics, values, and interests called psychographics.[2] This makes sense because segmentation variables such as personal differences, usage situation differences, benefits sought, beliefs about products, and behavior are *theoretically* related, as described in Figure 3-2. The unique behavior, beliefs, benefits sought, and life-style of a market segment are described because they are related to each other. This deep segmentation creates a richer mental model of the consumer compared to a simplistic mental model, which uses only a single segmentation variable.

Figure 3-2 also suggests an ordered procedure that a decision-making team can use to create a mental model of consumers and their behavior. The first step is to start with benefit segmentation by deciding whether groups of buyers seek different product benefits and hence value different product features.[3] The second step is to determine whether there are differences in life-style or usage that cause the distinct benefit segments. Such information may suggest new features and innovations that might be appealing to a buyer segment. The third step is to explore whether the benefit segments hold different beliefs about the product and competitive brands. Most importantly, the analysis needs to determine whether the benefit segments differ in their buying loyalties, shopping behaviors, media usage, and sensitivity to various marketing tactics. If they do not, then it will be very difficult to reach a broad range of benefit segments with a targeted and specially designed marketing campaign.

Some marketers prefer to begin the segmenting process by categorizing consumers by their usage behavior (for example, heavy, moderate, light, or nonuser) or brand loyalty and work backward to see if beliefs, benefits sought, and general life-style measures explain the difference in behavior. In such an analysis the behavior is treated as a symptom, and the analysis searches for causal explanations. The above analysis processes are

2. According to Russell Haley in 1965, an advertising executive studying the demographics, life-style, benefits sought, and behavior of a market segment provided by a survey research study said, "Boy, this stuff goes way beyond standard demographics. Why, you're showing us people's psychologies! These are psychographics." Psychographic questions measure buyer and nonbuyer interests, life-styles, hobbies, self-images, and values. Unlike standard personality measures or measures of social class, sets of psychographic questions are usually designed and assembled to study buyers in a particular product market. The study of psychographics was one of the first major advances in measuring differences in consumer demand and behavior in a product-market.
3. As we shall see later, establishing the benefits that different consumer segments seek is a crucial first step to designing quality into a product or service.

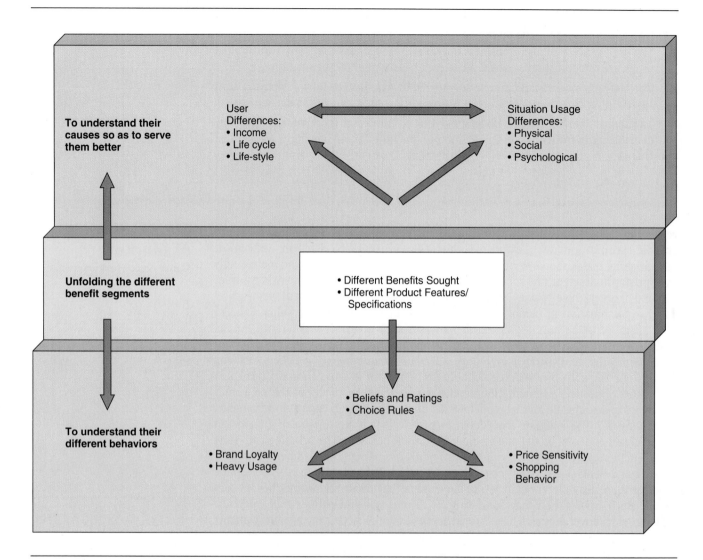

Figure 3-2

A Model of Consumer Behavior for Deep Benefit Segmentation

This model explains that user and usage situation differences combine to determine behavior (Behavior = F(P×S)). In between are benefits sought from using the product. The benefits sought determine how the alternatives are perceived and rated. These perceptions determine product choice and use. Deep segmentation starts with benefits and works forward and back, or starts with behavior and works back. Each segment is then described in terms of its behavior, preferences, benefits sought, usage situations, user demographics, geographics, and user life-style. This can be an intuitive process that uses managerial experience and judgment or it can be a process that uses sophisticated statistical analysis.

very similar to what some advertising people do when they construct means-end chains as a way of organizing and understanding.

Linking different segmentation variables does not need to be as complex as that described in Figure 3-2. Many firms simply focus on the connections between heavy usage or brand loyalty (see the bottom of Figure 3-2) *and* the buyers' responses to different products, distribution channels, media, advertising message strategies, or price promotions (such as coupons). We now describe each of the above steps and elements of deep segmentation in detail.

Benefit segmentation was originally used to identify groups of consumers who were particularly responsive to specific advertising strategies and creatives.[4] However, benefit segmentation can be also used to design a product. For example, a group of former Hewlett-Packard executives formed Tandem computers in 1974 to satisfy the needs of computer buyers who desired an ultrareliable computer. Hospitals, banks, and airline reservation systems cannot afford to have their computers crash. To service this need, Tandem linked two central processing units together. If one went down, the other automatically took over the processing until the first unit was repaired. In 1986, sales of Tandem's "crash-free" computers reached $800 million. The company profited greatly from identifying a need and then creating a product that serviced the need.

Most product-markets can be segmented by the benefits sought. Table 3-2 reports the different beverage preferences of students. It reveals that each beverage satisfies a very specific physical need. The reason why the colas dominate the young adult beverage market, rather than, say, milk, is because the students surveyed needed to pep themselves up, stimulate their taste buds, or quench their thirst much more often than they needed a sleep aid or to obtain nutrients and vitamins.

The Four Basic Human Needs

Consumers require that a product or service satisfy one or more of four basic human needs: physical, emotional, mental, and spiritual needs. Within each of these categories are many subcategories (see Table 3-3). Products and services are purchased or rented to satisfy these needs. However, consumers tend to be extremely goal-directed, and once they have fully or partially satisfied one need, they promptly turn their attention to another need or goal. In our day-to-day and year-to-year lives we normally use a multitude of products and services to satisfy a wide range of short- and long-term needs.

Consumer Benefit Segmentation

Table 3-2
Student Preferences for Beverages by Benefit Sought

Which of the following would you choose to meet each benefit/need?

	Coffee	Tea	Milk	Beer	Cola	Noncola	Other
Need a drink to relieve throat irritation	5%	30%	11%	2%	16%	6%	30%
Need a drink to help your digestion	6%	13%	46%	0%	12%	8%	18%
Need a drink to provide energy and pep you up	32%	5%	5%	1%	42%	3%	11%
Need a drink to help you unwind and mentally relax	3%	5%	2%	38%	11%	3%	39%
Need a drink to settle an upset stomach	0%	14%	33%	0%	20%	23%	10%
Need a drink to provide nutrition and vitamins	0%	0%	63%	2%	0%	5%	31%
Need a drink to stimulate your taste buds	3%	5%	7%	13%	32%	12%	27%
Need a drink to relieve a headache	4%	24%	9%	5%	10%	10%	38%
Need a drink to quench your thirst	0%	5%	3%	8%	35%	11%	38%

4. Russell I. Haley, "Benefit Segmentation: A Decision-Oriented Research Tool," *Journal of Marketing* 32 (July 1968), 30–35. To measure how different buyers value the different benefits and features of a product offering, see Paul E. Green and Yoram Wind, "New Way to Measure Consumers' Judgments," *Harvard Business Review*, July-August 1975, 107–17.

	Table 3-3 Basic Benefits, Specific Benefits, and Products	
Fundamental benefits	**Specific benefits sought**	**Means or paths used to achieve the benefit**
Physical/bodily benefits	Health	HMOs, vitamins, new drugs
	Physical fitness	Jogging shoes, spas
	Beauty	Cosmetics, Nautilus machines
	Procreation	Artificial insemination
	Sex	Spouses, X-rated movies
	Safety	Seat belts, security systems
	Thirst	Nonalcoholic beverages
	Hunger	Food
	Mobility	Automobiles, airplanes
	Sleep	Bedding, drugs
Emotional benefits	Love	Family, flowers
	Friendship	Friends, social clubs
	Pleasure	Music, drugs, food
	Humor	Jokes, situation comedies
	Aggression	Professional boxing, football
	Power	Wealth, career promotions
Mental/ intellectual benefits	Curiosity	Tourism
	Problem solving	Games, detective stories
	Education	College, TV documentaries
	Control	Yoga, religion, TV news
	Creativity	Artwork, gardening tools
	Truth	Nonfiction books
Spiritual benefits	Peace	Meditation, nature trails
	Communality	Churches, charitable clubs
	Philosophy	Books, religion, discussion
	Patriotism	Flags, political parties
	Ritual	Christmas, engagement rings
	Guilt	Grace, good works, hair-shirts

The perceived quality of a product or a service depends on its effectiveness and efficiency in achieving the benefits desired.[5] One new market research technique, *conjoint analysis*, has been effectively used to identify segments that seek different benefits. In the box titled "Benefit Segmenting the Food Processor Market," conjoint analysis was employed to identify benefit segments and position new product models; each model was specially designed to offer the qualities desired by a specific benefit segment.

Often products are purchased to achieve several benefits. For example, going to a restaurant with friends may satisfy hunger, a need for friendship, a need to be seen in

---

5. The words *quality, utility,* and *instrumentality* (as in an instrument used as a means to an end) all have pretty much the same meaning, although some scholars argue about the differences.

the right places with the right faces (the status benefit), and a need to do something different (the novelty benefit). An automobile provides physical mobility that earlier civilizations would have envied. However, it also can be seen as a thing of beauty in itself or used to confer status, power, and sex appeal. Some people use cars as an outlet for aggression (speeding and racing) or as an outlet for curiosity and problem solving (a restoration or tinkering hobby). Different cars are designed to provide different benefits and these benefits are, as already mentioned, often related to an individual's life cycle and life-style. This leads us to a discussion of life cycles and life-styles.

If consumer needs are to be served, they must be anticipated. The major, long-term driver of many predictable trends in our economy is the changing distribution of ages in the population of the United States. These trends in the size of age categories and associated life-cycle stages are important to the marketer for several reasons:

1. Age categories can be predicted with reasonable reliability. If we know how many five-year-olds there were in 1990, we can use current mortality rates to accurately forecast the number of 15-year-olds in the year 2000.

2. Both the needs and wealth of individuals and households change as they progress through the family life cycle (see Table 3-4).

Consumer Life-Cycle and Life-Style Segmentation

Table 3-4
Changing Priorities and Purchases in the Family Life Cycle

Stage	Priorities	Major Purchases
Fledgling: teens and early 20s	Self; socializing; education	Appearance products, clothing, automobiles, recreation, hobbies, travel
Courting: 20s	Self and other; pair-bonding; career	Furniture and furnishings, entertainment and entertaining, saving
Nest building: 20s and early 30s	Babies and career	Home, garden, do-it-yourself items, baby-care products, insurance
Full nest: 30–50s	Children and others; career mid-life crisis	Children's food, clothing, education, transportation, orthodontics, career and life counseling
Empty nest: 50–75	Self and others; relaxation	Furniture and furnishings, entertainment, travel, hobbies, luxury automobiles, boats, investments
Sole survivor: 70–90	Self; health; loneliness	Health-care services, diet security, and comfort products, TV and books, long-distance telephone services

Rationality in Practice:

Benefit Segmenting the Food-Processor Market

In June 1983 the Sunbeam Corporation undertook a benefit segmentation study using conjoint analysis to identify the benefit segments in the food-processor market. More than 500 women were interviewed in four different sites around the country. The interviews took place in high-traffic shopping malls and produced a complete preference ranking for 27 different model designs. The conjoint analysis of the preference rankings of 500 women were then clustered into the benefit segments. This produced four clusters of consumers. Within each cluster the consumers shared similar preferences for different design features in a food processor; that is, they sought similar feature benefits. The differences in benefits sought between clusters can be illustrated by comparing which features the "Cheap" segment wanted in a food processor with which features the "Multispeed" segment wanted.

It is clear that a new $49.99 product designed with a 4-quart bowl and very little else would appeal to one segment, and a new $99.99 blender/mixer model with seven speeds and a 2-quart cylindrical bowl would appeal to the other. Sunbeam launched two such models in 1984 that appear to have been successes. Note that Sunbeam also used life-style and brand loyalty information to develop a deep understanding of each segment, as suggested by the procedure in Figure 3-2. For further details on the conjoint analysis technique, see Chapter 9: Managing the Product.

Source: For the full case study, see Albert L. Page and Harold F. Rosenbaum, "Redesigning Product Lines with Conjoint Analysis: How Sunbeam Does It," *Journal of Product Innovation Management* 4 (1987), 120–37.

	The cheap and large segment	The multi-speeds and uses segment
Very important features	$49.99 price 4-quart bowl	Seven speeds Can be used as a blender and a mixer
Moderately important features	Two speeds Seven processing blades Heavy-duty or professional power motor Cylindrical bowl Pouring spout	$99.99 price 2-quart bowl Cylindrical bowl Regular discharge bowl
Other demographic and psychographic and brand-loyalty features of the segment	Least likely segment to already own a food processor Higher than average ownership of Oster and Sears brands Most likely segment to give a food processor as a gift Older in age Midrange incomes Comprise 22% of the food-processor market	Most likely to own a GE brand food processor Younger in age Lower incomes Comprise 28% of the food-processor market

Life-style segmentation is a type of psychographic segmentation. The best known of the commercial life-style classification techniques is called VALS. Introduced in 1978, it was later discovered that shifting values and life-styles had created problems with the original classification.[6] The VALS2 segmentation framework was offered in 1989. Its segment sizes are roughly equal and its creators claim that VALS2 will be more stable over time. The new framework is also more directly linked to age and income. The basic problem with general life-style profiles such as VALS or VALS2 is that they suffer from the same limitation that affects general personality inventories—they do not apply to all life situations. A grizzly bear at work may turn into a teddy

6. See Martha Farnsworth Riche, "Psychographics for the 1990s," *American Demographics,* July 1989, 24–31.

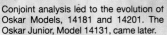

Conjoint analysis led to the evolution of
Oskar Models, 14181 and 14201. The
Oskar Junior, Model 14131, came later.

bear at home. One of the latest commercial segmentation research services, PRIZM,
can locate life-style segments by zip code, even down to the city block. Although very
expensive, it is possible to obtain a map of the U.S. market that identifies concentrations of households by their life-style, values, and demand for various products and
services. This is obviously useful for targeting mailings and locating attractive retail
outlets.

Life-style segmentation has also been affected by the changing role of women in
American life. World War II, the birth control pill, the high divorce rate, new laws
against sex discrimination, and the writings of the feminist movement have created
nothing less than a cultural revolution. Contemporary women often choose to work or
have to work and maintain their homes at the same time. The increasing opportunities
for women have created many stresses on professional and social relationships, in large

An early competitor in the gourmet pre-pared-meal market aimed at the time-poor consumer. A primitive ancestor was the TV dinner. Today, the products must also be low in both calories and fat.

For people who have more taste than time.

Chicken Teriyaki from scratch: 1 hour, 39 minutes.

Chicken Teriyaki from McCormick®/Schilling.® 20 minutes.

Now you can fit great cooking into a busy schedule with Chicken Sauce Blends from McCormick®/Schilling® There's no faster, easier way to turn ordinary chicken into a variety of extraordinary entrees. Whether it's the taste of Teriyaki, delicious Dijon, zesty Cacciatore, a Mesquite marinade, the cajun accent of Creole or a mild and creamy Curry, you can't go wrong. And it won't take long.
For more taste in less time, try Chicken Sauce Blends from McCormick®/Schilling.®

McCormick®/Schilling® The heart of great cooking.

part because some men have been very slow to adapt to the new roles women play in pursuing a career or helping earn enough money to put bread on the table.

This trend has greatly affected product innovation and marketing strategies. In 1990, more than 36 million women (more than half of all women between the ages of 18 and 64) spent approximately nine hours a day at work or commuting. This is time they no longer had for teaching their children to read, cleaning, waxing, polishing, mending, weeding, writing, delivering, cooking, shopping, and socializing. As a result, convenience-food sales have soared, the telephone call has replaced the letter, refrig-erator-freezers have grown in size, dishwashers have become more efficient, and micro-wave ovens have become standard appliances in households throughout the country. Supermarkets stay open late at night and have become one-stop shopping centers for the busy woman. Catalog shopping has increased in popularity because of the conve-nience it offers. Other important life-style trends, such as Hispanic immigration, the flight to the suburbs, and the decline of public education, have created new, distinct life-style segments based on subculture, literacy, employment, and income.[7]

7. The magazine *American Demographics* provides excellent articles and statistics on how changing life cycles and life-styles influence demand.

One of the most ignored aspects of segmentation has been the importance of a product's usage situation. Usage situation is an important determinant of benefits sought and features desired (see Figure 3-2). In this form of segmentation, analysts identify and study how a product or service is used in different situations and then market it accordingly. For example, drinks are *packaged* for their usage situation (lunches, picnics, and so on) and many products are *designed* for a specific usage situation (for instance, Sony Walkmans, bicycles, and lawn mowers are designed for usage situations). Richardson-Vicks Inc. entered the very competitive cold-remedy market by focusing on nighttime cold relief with its brand Nyquil. Congestion and discomfort from a cold usually increases at night because nasal passages do not drain as well when sleeping. Cold symptoms also become more of an irritant when relaxing than when one is very active. Nyquil was specially designed for nighttime use and was effectively advertised to appeal to such problems. Once it was strongly established in this usage segment, the company then rolled out Dayquil for daytime use. While the drowsiness side effect was an advantage for a nighttime cold remedy, Dayquil was designed to minimize such side effects—for obvious reasons. The usage-situation factor has many obvious dimensions, such as the way temperature and weather might affect how a product is marketed. However, in the following section we discuss the not-so-obvious effects of situation-induced time pressure on the benefits sought from products and services and on buying behavior.

Consumer Product Usage-Situation Segmentation

The Effect of Time Pressure on Consumption

In leisurely paced societies, there is a lot of free time for play, a midday siesta, and recreational pursuits such as fishing, hunting, and sports. Time is not of great importance, no one is punctual, and what can be postponed may as well be. In North America, the situation is very different for most adults and households. Punctuality is important, scheduling is a must, and whatever leisure time there is available is often spent recovering from the rat race.[8] Time is a highly valued commodity for two groups in particular: high-income couples who are pursuing dual careers and low-income couples and single parents who are struggling to pay the rent and raise children so that they too can survive in the rat race. Many marketers have yet to fully appreciate this fact. Some manufacturers do not place an extremely high priority on designing products that are easy to use and to *learn* to use. Some retailers have reduced rather than increased in-store customer services that save time. Income and time pressure have the following important interaction effects on consumption.

Income and Household Behavior

As a household's income and the hourly wage of its members rise, families buy homes, then larger homes, a second home, a swimming pool, more cars, recreational vehicles, boats, vacations, skis, and so on. However, most of these goods take up more personal time to buy, enjoy, and maintain. As income rises, more activities can be or have to be squeezed into leisure time. The result is that the perceived value of free time increases and produces what has been called the harried leisure class. Leisure-time management has some significant effects on decision making, particularly on each of the following:

8. See Staffan B. Linder, *The Harried Leisure Class* (New York: Columbia University Press, 1970).

Risk Taking. If the wealthy are more harried in their work and family life, then they may not be novelty seekers and innovators when they make purchases. They already have enough stimulation and excitement in their lives. What the wealthy often want are not the latest products but the high-quality, low-maintenance, high-reliability products. They do not want to waste time returning goods or waiting for a new innovation to be repaired. Further, many of the working wealthy do not have time to invest in a hobby or to become an expert, enthusiastic do-it-yourselfer. The real innovators are likely to be the consumers who have more leisure time to devote to their interests. The wealthy are, hence, more likely to be imitators who buy only after the early adopters have identified the reliable, high-quality, high-status brands.

Search and Shopping. Consumers have developed a series of informal buying rules to save time but still ensure satisfactory purchases. For example, consumers tend to buy quality brand name products, follow the advice of friends, buy from quality catalogs, and remain loyal to high-service stores. The latter not only reduces shopping time and effort, but increases personal service at restaurants, dry cleaning services, florists, and so on. Two of the biggest pet peeves of American shoppers are waiting in line while other windows or registers are closed and waiting at home for a no-show delivery or a service call.[9] Seventy-five percent of consumers who earn $50,000 or more a year boycott stores because of such poor service.

Product Expertise. One of the ironies of the wealth-time trap is that some higher income consumers may not get the most out of their purchases because they do not have the time to learn to use the products properly. They do not learn how to adjust an expensive camera or use all the features on their sound system or VCR. As a consequence, some of the advantage they gain from buying quality products is lost by not learning to use the product for maximum effect. In an interesting role reversal, teenagers often teach their parents how to use some luxury products, particularly electronic equipment.

The implications for usage instructions, service, and safety are important. The equipment owned by the wealthy may need higher than expected servicing because the new owners do not learn to use or care for the product the way the supplier recommends. Such servicing must be prompt and preferably door-to-door, as wealthy consumers perceive time spent on equipment repair as particularly wasteful. Also, when equipment needs servicing, the wealthy are likely to regard that equipment as unreliable and of low quality, rather than view themselves as impatient or unskilled consumers. Such user-caused service problems will be particularly frustrating because the consumer paid for quality in order to avoid such equipment malfunction. The lack of time spent learning how to use a product safely may also increase the risk of accidents or injury (such as those caused by the improper use of chain saws or off-road vehicles). Furthermore, the dollar amounts of product liability claims made by the wealthy are likely to be a lot higher and their lawyers more skilled. What this suggests is that usage instructions and foolproof features may be as important for quality products as they are for economy products designed for the less educated, lower income consumer.

Demand for Quality. Although members of the harried leisure class pay top dollar for time-saving, high-quality devices and services, they do so not just because they can afford to, wish to conspicuously display their wealth, or want very reliable performance. When time is very scarce, consumers try to squeeze the very most out of their free time. They therefore demand goods that increase the enjoyment and quality of their leisure. A large-screen television with a super sound system increases the quality of

9. David Wessel, "Sure Ways to Annoy Consumers," *Wall Street Journal*, November 6, 1989; and Francine Schwadel, "Shoppers' Blues: The Thrill Is Gone," *Wall Street Journal*, October 13, 1989.

television viewing time. A high-quality tennis racquet enriches exercise time. A sports or luxury car enhances the time spent in recreational driving. Higher incomes enable consumers to buy higher quality items, but it is the perceived value of *leisure time* that often motivates the demand for high-quality products.[10] This is one of the reasons why higher quality products and services have increased in value and will continue to appreciate as leisure time becomes more of a precious commodity.

Returning to the mental model illustrated in Figure 3-2, we see that the benefits consumers seek from a product or service determine their beliefs and choices. Belief segmentation uses consumers' beliefs about a product to segment demand. Beliefs are usually measured to explain heavy usage or brand loyalty. However, if all sellers target the heavy user, it may be worthwhile to look for opportunities among current nonusers. Such a strategy is particularly appropriate for the market leader interested in expanding the market or for a smaller company interested in finding a new market segment that is separate from the rest of the competition.

Figure 3-3 presents a potential segment categorization framework of nonusers of a product category and/or brand. It compares nonusers who are simply unaware of a product or service with potential consumers who either do not know where to buy the product, are in a state of inertia about the product, or have negative opinions about the product. These different market segments will suggest very different marketing tactics. It may be possible to develop a new product and image that overcomes the

Consumer Belief Segmentation

Figure 3-3
A Nonusage Belief Segmentation Framework

Nonuser of Product Category

- Unaware of product/service
- Aware but has never seriously considered purchase
- Aware but product/service is unavailable in channels
- Aware but habit and inertia prevent trial
- Aware but a perceived risk prevents trial
- Aware but rejected because of believed poor performance
- Aware but rejected because of high price
- Tried and rejected because of poor performance
- Tried and rejected because of low value for money
- Previously used but no longer needed

Product User But Non-Brand User

- Unaware of brand
- Aware but has never seriously considered purchase
- Aware but brand is unavailable in channels
- Aware but habit and inertia prevent trial
- Aware but a perceived risk prevents trial
- Aware but rejected because of believed poor performance
- Aware but rejected because of high price
- Tried and rejected because of poor performance
- Tried and rejected because of low value for money

10. We are, in effect, talking about the pleasure productivity of leisure time. A leisure good is more productive when it produces more pleasure per minute in use.

objections of the consumers with even the most negative beliefs, particularly if the beliefs are wrong. A campaign that raises the awareness of the segment that is unaware of a particular brand would be very different from a campaign targeted at the segment that has specific negative beliefs about a particular brand.

The tactics used to change specific beliefs also depend on the ways consumers choose between alternatives. We now discuss three different ways consumers make purchase decisions. The first is based on logic, the second on emotions, and the third on habit. Different segments may predominantly use each of these methods for making purchases; for example, subcompact cars are most likely to be bought on logic, sports cars on emotion, while older consumers buy on habit.

Consumer Choice Rule Segmentation

Logical Choice Behavior

An information-processing choice model assumes that human decision making and problem solving is more or less rational.[11] It suggests that we use reason and logic to carefully evaluate alternatives. Many choice models and rules have been developed to describe such decision making. Generally, the information-processing choice model is based on the type of decision logic that appears in computer programs. It suggests that consumers:

1. Identify and evaluate the choice options (brands and models within brands) on several abstract dimensions. For example, the consumer may rate several automobile models on such characteristics as fuel efficiency, acceleration, top speed, braking and cornering performance, interior noise, mechanical reliability, comfort and convenience features, price, and financial terms.

2. Add up the ratings to create an overall quality score or use some other algebraic rule to decide which alternative is most preferred. For example, the consumer may assess an automobile's overall quality by adding up its scores on each of the choice dimensions, weighted by the importance of each dimension.

Choice rules may be applied in sequence. We often know what we definitely do *not* want in a product. This "no way" elimination process quickly whittles down the set of choices. A more complex preference rule may then be used to identify the best of the acceptable alternatives.[12]

Experiential Choice Behavior

Experiential choice behavior occurs when the benefits we seek from a product are driven by our fantasies and emotions. Fantasies are our wishful thoughts about who and where we would like to be and what we would like to own. Emotions are our feelings of pleasure, pain, excitement, relaxation, fear, and stress, among many others. People, pets, and our physical environment (such as a warm bakery or a steamy sauna) create such reactions. Many products and services are designed to arouse pleasure, excitement, and relaxation. For example, rock music might make us feel energized, while woodsy fragrances might make us feel romantic, or the latest fashions might make us feel confident. The function of these products is to create feelings, imagery,

11. James R. Bettman, *An Information Processing Theory of Consumer Choice* (Reading MA: Addison-Wesley, 1979); Brian Sternthal and C. Samuel Craig, *Consumer Behavior: An Information Processing Perspective* (Englewood Cliffs, NJ: Prentice-Hall, 1982).
12. Dennis A. Lussier and Richard W. Olshavsky, "Task Complexity and Contingent Processing in Brand Choice," *Journal of Consumer Research* 6 (September 1979), 154–65.

or fantasies that give pleasure and lift the user to a higher experiential plane. Brands are also often given personality associations and images whose congruence with the ideal or actual self can motivate users to purchase one brand over another.[13]

Fantasizing creates and enhances emotional experience. Sometimes fantasies recreate the past. Nostalgia products are often popular at times of heightened emotion, such as during the Christmas holidays. For example, favorite holiday movies and television dramas are shown each Christmas. They become part of the symbolism of the season. Special products in our home can become almost sacred, because they express and celebrate treasured memories, connections with ancestors, or associations with a loved one, a special group, or a very special time in one's life. The value of the symbolism and meaning of these products far exceeds their replacement cost or the value of their more functional uses.[14] Other products allow users to fantasize about a world where they are much more powerful, beautiful, or wise than they are in reality. Young children spend a good deal of their play acting out such fantasies with their toys. Many adults also act out such fantasies using cosmetics, fashion, and exotic vacations. When we cannot afford to play with the toys or they do not have the desired effect, we may escape through projection, that is, by reading romantic novels or watching the adventures of others at the movies or on television.

Habitual Choice

Reptiles are slaves to routine. They do pretty much the same thing at the same time every day and they cannot help it. They behave this way instinctively. To a certain extent, so do we. There is a little bit of the crocodile in all of us. As a result, a good deal of consumer behavior is habitual and routine. Many of us do the same thing at the same time every day. We have many routines and rituals and we give many of these activities about as much thought as a reptile does mindlessly mooching around its swamp. This is not all bad. Consumption habits have survival value for several reasons:

1. What has worked in the past is likely to work again in the future.

2. Habits allow us to save time making decisions.

3. Habitual routines can be executed more efficiently than new behaviors.

4. Habitual behavior frees the mind to think about other things while executing the behavior.

5. Habits bring a sense of discipline, order, and control to a person's life and self-perception.

Evolution also helps us understand when many of our habits are formed. Most of the behavior patterns of primitive man and woman were learned before the individual reached maturity. In ancient times, a person seldom lived beyond the age of 30, so there was very little evolutionary value in continuing to develop thinking skills that kept people learning through old age (30 plus!). Unfortunately, our memories are still designed to learn that way today. Of course, we can keep learning, but curiosity and

---

13. Elizabeth Hirschman and Morris B. Holbrook, "Hedonic Consumption: Emerging Concepts, Methods and Propositions," *Journal of Marketing* 46 (Summer 1982), 92–101. Russell Haley, the father of benefit segmentation has pointed out, however, that it is much more difficult to segment the market for products that involve sensory or emotional benefits because so much depends on the execution of the advertising appeals. See Russell I. Haley, "Benefit Segmentation—20 Years Later," *The Journal of Consumer Marketing* 11 (1986).

14. Sidney J. Levy, "Symbols for Sale," *Harvard Business Review* 37 (July/August 1959), 117–24; "Interpreting Consumer Mythology: A Structural Approach to Consumer Behavior," *Journal of Marketing* 45 (Summer 1981), 49–61; Dennis W. Rook, "The Ritual Dimensions of Consumer Behavior," *Journal of Consumer Research* 12 (December 1985), 251–64; Russell W. Belk, "Possessions and the Extended Self," *Journal of Consumer Research* 15.2 (September 1988), 139–68.

learning are greatest when we are young. The best time to influence human consumption behavior, such as diet, sports, and artistic interests, is before the age of about 15, which partly explains why the debate over the influence of recreational reading versus MTV has raged for more than a decade.

How We Learn Habits

Habitual behavior is common in the buying and usage of products and services ranging from groceries to dry cleaning. It normally starts with a trial, experiential purchase. If the product is not liked, it is never tried again; new products and services seldom get a second chance, which is why a new consumer product must get it right the first time. A successful new product is likely to produce a very enthusiastic reception, such as the "Yumm, this is really good" reaction to a new food product. Consumers may actually say this to themselves, and this positive verbal reaction is clearly remembered the next time the consumer is in the market for a product in that category. When consumers volunteer such a remark out loud in a product test, the marketing team really knows it has a winner. By about the fifth trial, the habit of buying will be firmly in place, and much of the initial reinforcing buzz will have faded.[15] But not all habitual buying routines and loyalties are "mindlessly" created. Sometimes we very deliberately plan a course of action through information gathering and alternative comparison. We then execute this consumption or production process over and over again, for instance, when choosing where we eat lunch during the work week. In such cases, consumers may be able to explain very rationally what appears to be "mindless" routines and loyalties.

Consumer Brand Loyalty Segmentation

The creation of consumer loyalty to a brand or service is akin to domesticating the consumer. The buyer's behavior becomes routinized and, in that sense, tamed or controlled by the seller.[16] This is achieved through a stream of marketing activities and exchanges that results in an enduring *relationship* between the seller and the consumer. Some buyers can be so domesticated that they will allow themselves to be "branded." For example, they will pay extra to have the firm's brand advertising on a T-shirt, hat, or other article of clothing (notice how often you see the logo for Nike or Panama Jack T-shirts).

However, brand loyalty and repeat purchasing does not always involve such high involvement with the brand. Table 3-5 describes different brand loyalty segments and the marketing implications of each. It is important for a firm to understand the different loyalty segments in the market because the *type* of loyalty as well as the size of the segments determines not only a firm's marketing tactics, but also the potential value of its brand name (called brand equity; see Chapter 9). Some habits and loyalties are relatively easy to change because the habit is only superficial, sustained by buying convenience or the fact that the brand is the first to come to mind (top-of-mind brand familiarity). While apparently loyal, buyers may be very open to trying a new product. This raises a related issue of the buyer's price sensitivity and how this can vary across market segments.

15. For a review of learning theories, see Michael L. Rothschild and William C. Gaidis, "Behavioral Learning Theory: Its Relevance to Marketing and Promotions," *Journal of Marketing* 45 (Spring 1981), 70–81; and Walter R. Nord and J. Paul Peter, "A Behavior Modification Perspective on Marketing," *Journal of Marketing* 44 (Spring 1980) 36–47.
16. The concept of market domestication has been discussed by Johan Arndt, "Toward a Concept of Domesticated Markets," *Journal of Marketing* 43 (Fall 1979), 69–75. His focus was on imperfectly competitive seller-reseller markets and did not connect brand loyalty to domestication of demand as we suggest.

Table 3-5
Types of Brand Loyalty/Relationship Segments

Nature of Loyalty/Relationship	Marketing Implications
Emotional loyalty: Unique, memorable, reinforcing experiences create a strong emotional bond with brand. Examples: hospital that saves child's life, fragrance given by future husband.	Goodwill is immune from attack by competitors or company mismanagement. Positive word-of-mouth is likely to be very high.
Identity loyalty: The brand is used as an expression of self, to bolster self-esteem and manage impressions. It becomes part of the extended self. Examples: Porsche cars, L.L. Bean clothes, Chicago Bears caps.	This loyalty resists attack, but a firm can hurt itself by brand mismanagement over a long time. Brand extension prospects into related product categories are good.
Differentiated loyalty: Brand loyalty is based on perceived superior features and attributes. This perception may be outdated because of a lack of recent search. Examples: appliances.	Goodwill can be undermined if competitor proves superior performance. Demonstrations and trials are very important tactics.
Contract loyalty: Consumer believes that continued loyalty earns him or her special treatment or that the seller is trying very hard to keep customer loyalty. Such a "I'll stay loyal if you keep trying hard" social contract applies in retailing and service markets.	Competitor can question whether the consumer's trust is being exploited. However, loyalty is most likely to be lost by a single or series of experiences that expose the seller's efforts or claims as insincere.
Switching cost loyalty: Consumer is loyal because effort involved in considering alternatives and adapting to a new alternative is not worth the expected return. Example: loyalty to the Apple Macintosh operating system. Sometimes the consumer may even be dissatisfied but will remain loyal because competition is perceived to be same. Example: slow bank service.	Competitors can undermine loyalty by making it easy to switch through product design, training, and terms. If loyalty is based on both attitudes and behavior, it can be used in product extensions (for example, the Macintosh power notebook).
Familiarity loyalty: Loyalty is the result of top-of-mind brand awareness. Brands are perceived to be similar. Example: colas.	Loyalty is defended and attacked by constant, attention-getting advertising that builds top-of-mind brand awareness. This loyalty is very vulnerable to promotions.
Convenience loyalty: Loyalty is based on buying convenience. Example: cola sold by favored food outlet. Frito-Lay snacks are available at most convenience stores.	Loyalty is attacked by expansion of competitor into convenience channels.

When segmenting market demand by price sensitivity, a seller has to recognize that price sensitiviy has many determinants, a number of which are described below:

Consumer Price Sensitivity Segmentation

Expenditure Importance

The higher an item's price relative to the buyer's income, the greater the buyer's price sensitivity. Housing starts are very sensitive to interest rates for this reason. With each percentage point decrease in the prime rate, thousands of home buyers enter the market. In contrast, the typical consumer is not very price sensitive to the cost of a can of oil. However, the lube service business segment is very sensitive to the price of oil because it greatly affects its cost of doing business.

Sensitivity of the Buyer's Market

This sensitivity only applies when the buyer uses the items purchased as inputs to the items it makes or resells. If their marketplace is price sensitive, then buyers will also be price sensitive when purchasing their input products. For this reason, the discount store chain segment is likely to be more price sensitive in its buying habits than the prestigious department store chain segment.

Economic Circumstances

Consumer expectations of future wealth can influence price sensitivity. The stock market crash of October 1987 severely affected Christmas sales of luxury goods and other non-necessity items. The anticipation of hard times makes market segments more conscious of spending habits and hence more price sensitive. On the other hand, when a market segment experiences windfall profits (for instance, a greater than expected tax refund because of a change in the law that favors a profession or property owners), the segment is likely to be less price sensitive in the expenditure of the windfall profits.[17] The anticipation of inflation may also reduce sensitivity to current prices, because differences between current competitive prices are not as important as differences between current prices and future (higher) prices.

Product Differentiation

The more distinct the image positioning and performance of a product or service on dimensions desired by the segment, the lower the price sensitivity of the segment will be. As such product differentiation (unique positioning) is more common in growth markets than in mature markets, growth markets are likely to be less price sensitive.

Awareness of Substitutes

Shoppers may believe a product has unique features or is of high quality simply because they are unaware of alternatives. In general, less informed segments are less price sensitive. When it is easy and inexpensive to try alternatives, price sensitivity is likely to be low for truly differentiated products and high for similar ("me-too") products.

Ease of Access to Substitutes

Price sensitivity, therefore, can change dramatically depending on whether potential buyers can easily find substitutes in different retail outlets. The reason why generic cans of fruit are not usually sold alongside name brand fruit cans is because sales of all branded cans of fruit (including the store's private labels) would become much more price sensitive. The harder it is for a segment to find substitutes the less price sensitive the segment will be.

17. Richard R. Thaler "Toward a Positive Theory of Consumer Choice," *Journal of Economic Behavior and Organization* 1 (March 1980), 39–60.

Ease of Substitution

Substitutability depends on more than just quality differentiation. If the switching costs of using the substitute are high (that is, the user has to change his or her behavior too drastically in order to switch or the switch involves financial costs), then price sensitivity is less in the short term. For example, if a consumer has to modify existing equipment in order to use the alternate product (such as switching from a gas furnace to an electric one) or if he or she has to learn new operating procedures (such as special microwave cooking directions for a new brand of rice), then the switching costs may be too high and the consumer will be less likely to switch to the alternate product. Market segments that do not have the skills or time to invest in the switching costs will be less price sensitive.

Ease of Storage and Postponability

The demand for products that can be stored easily will be more price sensitive. This is because an item's current price is compared with and competing against its expected future price as well as any current price substitutes. The same product purchased in the future can be a perfect substitute for a product that is purchased today and is stored for the future. For similar reasons, the market segment that can postpone the purchase is more price sensitive than the segment that cannot.

Price/Quality Signaling

When a product is purchased to signal power, prestige, or quality, a higher price helps position the product. The higher priced product is a signal to the target market that greater value comes at a higher price. In order to buy a product with high quality, the buyer has to spend more. The more a segment believes that a higher price signals greater value or quality, the less that segment's price sensitivity will be.

Consumer Search Behavior and Contact Segmentation

Most market segmentation practices emphasize isolating the differences in product demand among buyers. However, the market can be usefully segmented even if consumer demand for a product and its price does not vary. Buyers sometimes differ in their *search* behavior: they use different retail outlets, they use different shopping styles, they are exposed to different media, and their sensitivity to advertising creatives varies. This search behavior is called *contact* sensitivity, in contrast to *demand* sensitivity, to product features, services, and price.

It is important to study what types of retail stores buyers patronize and are loyal to.[18] Buyers may evaluate the services, convenience, and pricing of retail stores differently. It is also possible to segment buyers by the way they shop, such as reviewing how much comparison shopping they do, or determining whether they shop for price, value, service, or use catalogs and other sources of written information.[19] Shopping behavior may be a more enduring personality characteristic than other life-style or psychographic measures. If differences in retail store or catalog loyalty are evident, then

---

18. Fitting the product and marketing campaign to the unique consumer franchise of particular specialty stores is discussed in greater detail in Chapter 10: Managing Distribution.

19. Jack A. Lesser and Marie Adele Hughes, "The Generalizability of Psychographic Market Segments across Geographic Locations," *Journal of Marketing* 50, (January 1986).

The shopper for a major investment, such as a house, automobile, or major appliance, will often spend several days actively shopping, and may find the experience stressful because of the expense involved and the shopper's lack of current knowledge about the market.

it is important to pursue several different distribution strategies, even if you, as the marketer, offer the same product to each distribution channel. Otherwise, you will not reach all of the market. When demand and contact sensitivity both vary, then you may offer different product forms or promote different product features in different distribution channels and advertising media. In retail stores where buyers are concerned with quality and reliability, you may emphasize your extended warranty. In retail stores where patrons are more price sensitive, you will emphasize value in point-of-purchase displays and offer economy packages.

In mature markets it may be more effective not to segment by demand sensitivity at all, but instead to segment by contact sensitivity. Much depends on the variability of buyer search and shopping behavior. Contact segmentation may also be less obvious to competitors and hence will be more difficult to imitate. But to segment the market by shopping behavior, a firm needs to develop a better understanding of how consumers shop. A firm with a better understanding than its rivals is more competitive.

Complex Search and Shopping Behavior

Inexperienced consumers may not be able or willing to make time to undertake complex analyses of product information, but that does not mean they make foolish or wasteful purchase choices. For one thing, consumers know that there are many experts in the marketplace who can help them make decisions. Such experts were used to help solve problems long before the computer was invented. Realtors, stockbrokers, accountants, travel agents, interior designers, wardrobe consultants, car salespeople, and appliance sales associates are used by people who are short of time, lack confidence in their choice ability, or lack knowledge of what is available and where it is available. The success of professional advice agents depends on their expert knowledge of the product or market and their ability to

1. Understand what benefits the consumer really wants.

2. Help define the features wanted and *not* wanted.

3. Show and explain the alternatives.

4. Find or make the consumer a deal that makes it unnecessary for the consumer to look any further.

Figure 3-4 demonstrates a model of the search and shopping behavior of buyers that recognizes the important role of professional advice.[20] Some event arouses the buyer to start actively shopping. Shopping activity may be prompted by a product failure, a change in family circumstances, the purchase behavior or recommendation of a friend, a magazine article, a television program, or an advertisement. Naturally, shoppers use their past direct and vicarious experiences to help decide what to do next. This normally involves first deciding what is wanted or where to look for what is wanted. Brand and store loyalty has its greatest influence at this stage. Friends, advocate sources such as *Consumer Reports,* and catalogs may give helpful advice on how to choose and identify the options. The store visit comes next, perhaps triggered by a sales advertisement.

The good salesperson helps the buyer to define the purchase requirements precisely, explains features, and suggests what may be best for the consumer. Folklore often portrays the salesperson as an adversary of dubious integrity. It is true that most of us have been deceived at some time by a dishonest sales pitch, but what we tend to forget is that the great majority of exchanges we have with sales clerks are helpful and rewarding. We are often unaware of the obstacles they have piloted us past in order to help us make good purchase choices! The bottom line is that a decision-making team should not assume a salesperson's role is to hard-sell. Instead, the salesperson should be viewed as playing a partnership role in a joint purchase decision. The successful salesperson soft-sells by discussing the pros and cons of the options, indicating which models are popular and why, explaining how to judge quality, and sharing personal experiences and insights with the prospective buyer.

If the salesperson cannot convince the buyer that he or she has exactly what the buyer is looking for, or that no one else has a better deal, then the salesperson often does not get paid for the effort. This is a very strong incentive for the salesperson to gain the buyer's confidence and make the sale. The more a salesperson expects the chance of repeat business, the greater the incentive for the salesperson to give honest, helpful advice. This economic survival incentive explains why the salesperson often plays a major role in the purchase and why shoppers lean fairly heavily on the salesperson's expert advice. It is important that the shopper know just enough to decide whether the salesperson is expert, sincere, and well meaning. The consumer who cannot confidently spot the salesperson who is a sham or a shark will often shop with a relative or friend who has such skills. Alternatively, such a consumer will go to a quality store where such expertise is known to exist, and then may use the advice obtained there to shop the discount stores!

Recreational Shopping

A major limitation of the model in Figure 3-4 is that it does not pay enough heed to shop-till-you-drop recreational shopping. It is human nature to develop recreational interests and hobbies, including shopping. They provide a sense of competence and

20. William L. Wilkie and Peter R. Dickson, "Shopping for Appliances: Consumers' Strategies and Patterns of Information Search," *Marketing Science Institute Working Paper,* Cambridge, MA, 1985.

Figure 3-4
An Adaptive Model of Shopping and Decision Making

The first store visit leads to interaction with a salesperson, which frequently leads to a respecification of what is wanted (this often occurs with appliances, automobiles, furniture, furnishings, fashion clothing, cosmetics). The salesperson helps identify satisfactory alternatives. If one of them is not exactly what was wanted, the shopper has to decide whether shopping elsewhere will be worth the effort. The process is adaptive because decision making and behavior intentions change as new information is learned.

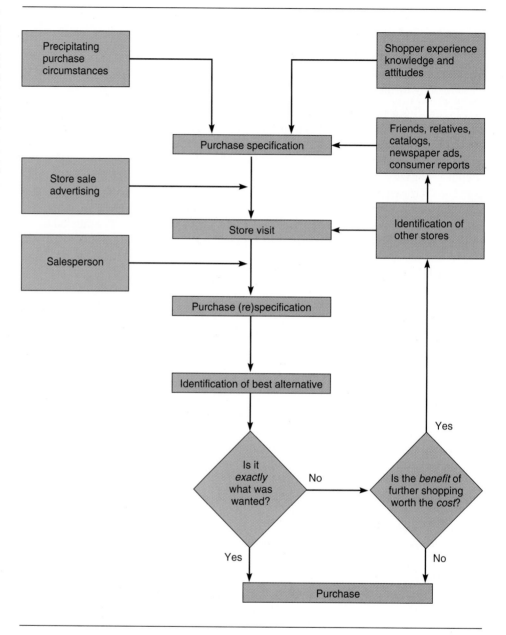

mastery over a small part of an extremely complex and uncertain world. As children, teenagers, and adults, we become experts through reading about, using, and buying products associated with our hobbies. Such hobbies include many types of arts and crafts, antiques, photography, gardening, cooking, fishing, or activities that involve computers, cars, and boats, to name a few. An important recreational aspect of such hobbies is going shopping for supplies and new equipment. Such shopping is frequently done at specialty stores and personal relationships often develop with store owners and their salespeople. A two-way learning process takes place in which customers and salespeople exchange information about what is going on in the marketplace, new trends, what works, and what does not.

After a shopper learns the layout of a supermarket, grocery shopping becomes a habitual activity. It's done with very little thought and is consequently hard to change.

The product-enthusiast market segment is important because hobbyists are heavy users, important influence agents, and can be targeted. They often gather together in clubs where information about new products, new distribution channels, and special deals offered by retailers is exchanged and discussed. But their influence extends well beyond the immediate group of heavy users. Product enthusiasts are consulted by friends, relatives, and work associates.[21] They often give advice and even help others shop, as enthusiasts derive some of their self-esteem from their expertise. The skilled marketer can harness the tremendous pool of knowledge and product involvement that exists among enthusiasts by offering workshops, special credit terms, and even part-time employment to the enthusiast.

Media Use

Buyers may also be segmented by the media they use heavily. To make sure they are reached, different media schedules may have to be developed to advertise to buyers who have been segmented by their media habits. There are heavy users of products, and there are heavy users of particular media. According to the advertising agency Needham, Harper and Steers, the regular (heavy) readers of magazines use more ideas from magazines, spend significantly more time reading magazines, and record higher ad page exposure levels and significantly higher verified recall of ads than do less active readers.[22] Regular television viewers are also more likely to recall advertising than

21. Lawrence F. Feick and Linda L. Price, "The Market Maven: A Diffuser of Marketplace Information," *Journal of Consumer Research* 13 (June 1987), 119–26. For insights into the different decision-making practices of experts, see also Joseph W. Alba and J. Wesley Hutchinson, "Dimensions of Consumer Expertise," *Journal of Consumer Research* 13 (March 1987), 411–54.
22. Needham, Harper, and Steers, *The Core Audience Concept: A Media Position,* White Paper, February 1983, New York.

Shopping is often a recreational activity associated with a particular hobby or interest, such as interior decorating, fashions, or collecting particular objects. Such a shopper will often spend several days a month enjoying such activities. Unlike habitual shoppers, recreational shoppers are interested in shopping in new stores and finding out about new products and services.

casual viewers. If these heavy media users are *also* heavy product users, then a firm can target them very effectively with repeated advertising in the magazine sections, newspaper sections, television programs, and radio shows that are popular with the heavy product user. Some advertisers have a long history of doing this by associating themselves with specific television programs; for example, Mutual of Omaha has been associated with "Wild Kingdom" and Prudential Assurance with the "College Football Scoreboard." In summary, it may be worthwhile to segment the market by its regular and heavy contact with different media.[23]

Another possibility is that buyers may not differ in their evaluation of the product, their buying behavior, or their media use, but they may respond differently to features of specific advertising pitches. For example, when marketing to both men and women and a range of age groups it may make sense to use spokespeople or models that specific segments of buyers can relate to—young men will respond more to young male models in the advertising campaign, young women to young female models, and older buyers to older models. This way you can segment the market by applying buyer sensitivity to features of the advertising creatives. A frequent question in advertising is whether the basic message theme should be logical or emotional. A "This is how we are better than them" message will be more effective if the market segment prefers to use a logical choice rule and process a lot of factual information when making a decision. A market segment that is more "right-brain" dominant and experiential will be more persuaded by a campaign that expresses "Wow! What an experience" message themes.

23. The matching of heavy product users with heavy media usage is discussed in greater detail in Chapter 12: Managing Promotions and Advertising.

Table 3-6
The Relevance of Consumer Segmentation Bases

Segmentation Basis:	Actionable Relevance to
Demographics	◆ Choice of sales regions ◆ Estimating segment size ◆ Choice of local channels or channels that cater to different age, income, and education groups ◆ Choice of media that serve different age, income, and education groups
Usage Situation	◆ Product performance specifications ◆ Delivery service ◆ Advertising themes ◆ Brochure design ◆ Written and video usage instructions
Benefits Sought	◆ Different models with different features ◆ Different advertising messages that emphasize different benefits ◆ Sales training
Beliefs	◆ New offerings that solve a previous problem ◆ Campaigns that raise awareness ◆ Campaigns that change image and positioning
Heavy Product Usage	◆ Special products (sizes and quality) ◆ Special services ◆ Special frequent-user promotional programs ◆ Special financial terms
Channel Loyalty	◆ Choice of distributors ◆ Different product mix for different channels
Heavy Media Usage	◆ Promotion tailored to media ◆ Media buying ◆ Message tailored to media

This completes the review of the segmentation variables described in Figure 3-2. To summarize, market segmentation is undertaken for a purpose: to profit by targeting the product and marketing to particular groups of buyers. Table 3-6 summarizes the actionable relevance of different segmentation variables in consumer markets. It should be recalled, however, that all these variables are related to each other and deep segmentation analysis describes *each* segment in terms of its level of consumption, brand loyalty, shopping behavior, media use, sensitivity to different message themes, price sensitivity, choice rules, beliefs, features preferred, benefits sought, usage situations, life-style, life cycle, income, and geographical concentrations. The use of the mental model of consumer behavior described in Figure 3-2 helps sellers really get to know their different consumers and satisfy them more effectively and efficiently than the competition.

Segmenting Business-to-Business Markets

In markets where buyers are other businesses (often called accounts), the first two natural segmentation variables are the size of the account and the growth potential of the account.[24] When a firm does 80 percent of its business with three or four accounts, it cannot help but adopt a special-relationship marketing approach that actually goes well beyond traditional segmentation. Moreover, buyers are directly and constantly in contact with the seller. The seller can tailor the marketing campaign to the consumer by promoting the items in the line that will be of most interest to the consumer, providing the relevant brochures, and adapting to the unique aspects of the buying firm's purchasing procedures. Each account is likely to be provided with special products and services that fit its unique requirements. Today, the consumer is likely to ask the selling firm if it can be involved in helping design the product. An ordering schedule that minimizes the transportation and inventory holding costs can be especially designed for the customer. This sort of unique relationship marketing makes talking about broader segment strategies somewhat irrelevant. The above realities help explain why business-to-business market segmentation (sometimes called industrial market segmentation) is not as complex as business-to-individual consumer market segmentation.

Standard Industrial Classification Segmentation of Business Markets

Usage situation segmentation is often used to target particular industries or groups of accounts within industries where there are hundreds of businesses. One useful approach is to study the different uses of the product or service by the industry and to rate the potential of such usage situations in terms of long-term growth potential and the competitiveness of substitutes in each usage application. One manufacturer, 3M, has dominated the industrial adhesive market for several decades by adopting such an approach.

The Standard Industrial Classification (SIC) coding system is used by the government to describe the line of business of a specific firm. In a way, having access to SIC data that the Commerce Department provides is equivalent to knowing the demographics, life-style, and product usage situations of consumers or households, all rolled into one. SIC information can also be used to determine how many potential buyers exist in a region. However, a full understanding of the different usage situations and benefits sought by the different industrial markets requires a close working relationship with several companies in each SIC created segment.

Purchasing Style Segmentation

The cross-functional decision-making team should find it relatively easy to view the business buyer's purchase decision from two cross-functional perspectives: the engineering-user view and the purchasing view. This is because both perspectives are likely to be encountered in the different individuals the team has to deal with and satisfy in the buying organization. The segmentation of a business-to-business market by usage and purchase behavior is similar to the distinction between demand and contact segmentation in consumer markets. The end users in a buying firm are more sensitive

24. In Chapter 11: Managing the Sales Force, a spreadsheet is described that categorizes accounts into A,B,C, or D segments depending on their size, growth potential, and the service they receive from competitors. This segmentation is used to determine the annual number of sales calls on the account and other relationship services.

about product performance and hence can be segmented by demand sensitivity. The purchasing agents in a buying firm may vary in their sensitivity to selling approaches and use of trade media and, hence, can be segmented by their readership of different trade magazines and newsletters.

More fundamentally, there may be wide variations in the way that firms make the purchase decision and their standard purchasing procedures. The short- and long-term financial position of each customer within such a submarket may also influence the way that customers respond, as will the unique personalities and socio-political climates that exist within a buying firm at any time. Indeed, it may be very hard to generalize and aggregate industrial buyers based on their purchasing characteristics because each of them uses a different bidding and buying process. This again emphasizes why an adaptive sales force is needed to spearhead the marketing effort.

To handle such complexity, a systematic analysis of a key buying account should proceed through a step-by-step description of the people involved, the organization's use of the product or service, the major players' perceptions of the benefits sought, and perceptions of the competitive offerings. The firm's standard buying behavior can even be mapped out in a flowchart. If lucky, such a buying guide may even be provided by the buying firm.

Low-Bid Buying

Much of the literature on organizational buying suggests that buyers play a rather passive, receptive role in the purchasing process by responding to the seller's marketing efforts. In fact, this is far from the truth. Business buyers generally search for information more actively than do households or individuals. They go out and solicit bids. Competition has forced many companies to search for new, economical sources of supply. Purchasing agents and entrepreneurs from the United States have carried samples of parts and finished products to Pacific Rim countries to be copied by Asian manufacturers. The growth in off-shore sourcing of high-tech components came about by economic necessity for many American manufacturers.

The typical process of seeking bids and then evaluating bids can initially appear *very* complicated (see Figure 3-5). However, after a purchasing agent has learned the ropes, the process becomes very routine depending on the yes or no answers to a series of questions presented in the different sections of the flowchart. The process is an application of a series of activities and rules that make the decision making much more systematic, orderly, and predictable. Such activities and rules include the following:

1. Actively seek new sources when the number of suppliers on the bid list is less than three.
2. Keep using current suppliers when their performance is satisfactory and the number of suppliers on the list is greater than three.
3. Toughen acceptable performance standards when the number of suppliers on the list is greater than three.
4. Relax standards when a new vendor is minority owned or suggested by top management.
5. Drop the existing vendor with the worst performance when new vendors are included on the bid list.

Product performance specifications and rules such as those in the above list are likely to have evolved from past group decision-making sessions that involved technical experts and senior management. For some purchases undertaken by very large

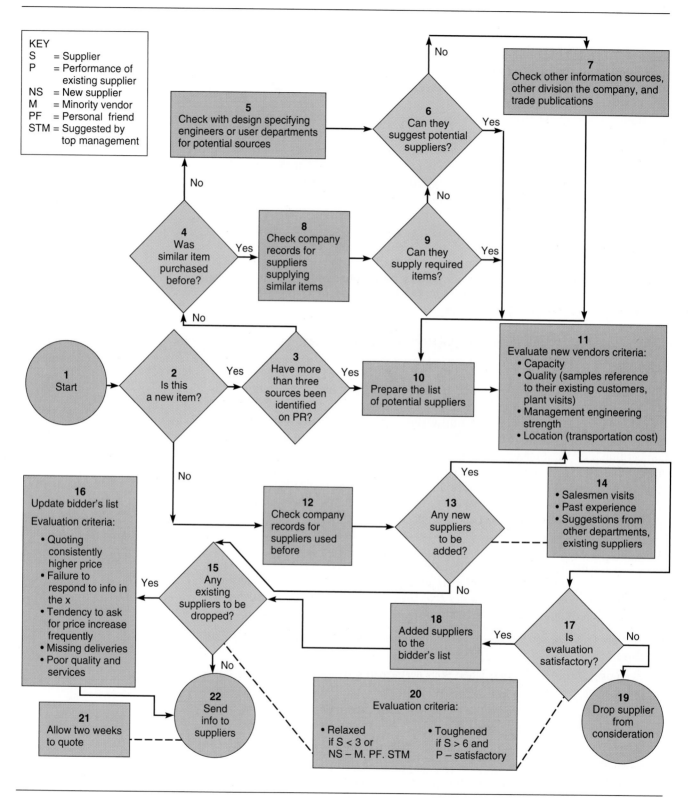

KEY
S = Supplier
P = Performance of existing supplier
NS = New supplier
M = Minority vendor
PF = Personal friend
STM = Suggested by top management

5 Check with design specifying engineers or user departments for potential sources

6 Can they suggest potential suppliers?

7 Check other information sources, other division the company, and trade publications

4 Was similar item purchased before?

8 Check company records for suppliers supplying similar items

9 Can they supply required items?

1 Start

2 Is this a new item?

3 Have more than three sources been identified on PR?

10 Prepare the list of potential suppliers

11 Evaluate new vendors criteria:
• Capacity
• Quality (samples reference to their existing customers, plant visits)
• Management engineering strength
• Location (transportation cost)

16 Update bidder's list

Evaluation criteria:
• Quoting consistently higher price
• Failure to respond to info in the x
• Tendency to ask for price increase frequently
• Missing deliveries
• Poor quality and services

12 Check company records for suppliers used before

13 Any new suppliers to be added?

14
• Salesmen visits
• Past experience
• Suggestions from other departments, existing suppliers

15 Any existing suppliers to be dropped?

18 Added suppliers to the bidder's list

17 Is evaluation satisfactory?

19 Drop supplier from consideration

21 Allow two weeks to quote

22 Send info to suppliers

20 Evaluation criteria:
• Relaxed if S < 3 or NS – M. PF. STM
• Toughened if S > 6 and P – satisfactory

Figure 3-5
Developing Requests for Bids

This flowchart, which describes the decisions and actions that have to be taken to solicit bids for a purchase, reveals just how complex organization buying can get. The shortest path is 1-2-12-13-15-22. What is the longest path? Reproduced with permission from Niren Vyas and Arch G. Woodside, "An Inductive Model of Supplier Choice Processes," *Journal of Marketing* 48 (Winter 1984), 30–45.

companies or government, it is even possible to develop computer-based expert systems that guide a purchasing officer through a purchase decision, according to rules set up by expert buyers and the original design and production engineers.[25] Future expert systems are likely to integrate information from production that rates a supplier in terms of defect rates, on-time delivery, and other performance criteria. This will make buying a much more objective process.

A striking characteristic of most bidding processes is their emphasis on encouraging competition between suppliers by seeking bids from three or more vendors (see Figure 3-4). The explanation is simple: Industrial buyers often find it difficult to locate more than two or three suppliers who will bid, and a bidding competition between suppliers is in the interests of the buyer. It is not a coincidence that there is a bias toward always accepting the lowest bid, rather than the bid that offers the most value for price. This bias is encouraged by company audit procedures that require purchasing agents to file a written justification if they do not accept the lowest bid. There are, however, often powerful arguments for choosing superior quality and service rather than the lowest price. Furthermore, the whole process of bid buying has started to be questioned by many organizations.

Sole Sourcing and Relationship Marketing

In an attempt to become more competitive in their markets, many manufacturers are now reaching back up the supply channel to help their suppliers develop more innovative materials and components, establish more efficient production processes, and produce a product that exceeds the buyers desired quality and performance specifications. As described in later chapters, it makes a great deal of sense to involve suppliers in the development of new products. Rather than taking over their key suppliers, firms set up joint ventures that give them exclusive rights to any product or process innovations developed in cooperation with the supplier. The logic behind the idea of the supplier and buyer working together is that two independent, innovative, and entrepreneurial firms are better than a single, vertically integrated firm. The continued independence between the supplier and buyer enhances enterprise and keeps the entrepreneurial leadership in both the selling and buying firms happy.

Joint venturing can also produce major cost savings for both parties. Ongoing selling and purchasing costs are reduced to a minimum and cooperation on product design can significantly reduce costs. Perhaps the most publicized advantage is that the inventory holding costs of both the supplier and buyer can be dramatically reduced by developing a just-in-time (JIT) delivery system. JIT is a supply system where the seller delivers its product as it is needed to the production line of the buyer. JIT offers the following features:

1. Items purchased are designed and produced according to buyer specifications.

2. All delivered items are inspected by the supplier before delivery, reducing defect rate to zero for the buyer.

3. Delivery is frequent and very reliable. Suppliers often relocate close to an account to provide such service.

4. Initial negotiation of terms and operating procedures between senior executives is extensive.

5. Likelihood of repeated contract renewal is very high.

---

25. Mary Kay Allen, *The Development of an Artificial Intelligence System for Inventory Management Using Multiple Experts* (Oak Brook, IL: Council of Logistics Management, 1986).

The development of such relationships involves a very different sort of selling to organizations that wish to buy this way. The emphasis is on the long-term relationship rather than the immediate transaction. Sellers that have developed this relationship skill, and already have a track-record of being able to smoothly implement such relationships, have a clear advantage over sellers that are novices. This advantage will be particularly important when selling to buyers who are new to joint-venture buying.

A further point is that switching costs from one supplier to another can be very high in joint-venture buying. Seller joint-venturing experience therefore becomes particularly valuable because the sellers who are the first to develop such relationships with buyers often get to keep the business for a very long time. It is safe to predict that the sellers who serve multiple industrial markets and are first to offer buyers joint ventures in product development and JIT delivery will end up with a very important and sustainable long-term competitive advantage.[26]

Social Network Segmentation of Business-to-Business Markets

A firm's line of business describes its market, within which often exists powerful social networks that can become the basis for contact segmentation. While word of mouth is important in the selling of any product or service, the following sociological characteristics of the business-to-business marketplace make it critical:

1. Generally, the most influential members of the buying firms received similar training in engineering or trade schools. They think in similar ways, which enables them to communicate more readily with each other. Their similar training also instills similar values, as well as similar skills and mental models.

2. Industry trade associations encourage the exchange of ideas and learning within an industry (even between competitors) through conferences, trade shows, seminars, and annual meetings.

3. Executives who move on to a position with a competitor, supplier, or major customer often maintain personal friendships with their previous coworkers.

4. Consultants act as word-of-mouth megaphones; they often pass on what they have learned to others. A consultant's advice to one company is also often noted and copied by other companies.

5. Sellers often use testimonials and encourage prospects to contact satisfied customers. Finding and talking to dissatisfied customers is harder, but the competition will often find them and encourage them to talk to other buyers about their dissatisfaction.

6. Keeping up with what the competitors are buying is a necessity because the survival of the firm may depend on the early adoption of new technology. The buyer also knows that even if the purchase is not a success, the rival whose purchase behavior was imitated is likely to be in the same sinking boat.

The reasons listed above explain why a letter of introduction or an open endorsement from an opinion leader in an industry can be a very powerful marketing tool.

---

26. The significance of the long-term rewards that will be achieved from being a pioneer in offering such a service to buyers and transferring this managerial and technological skill across to other markets may not be fully appreciated by marketers and Wall Street investors. On the other hand, situations arise in which a buyer who develops close relationships with several suppliers can play them against each other even more than the buyer could before the close relationships were established. We will discuss this further in the context of the retailer's global sourcing of supply.

Conversely, in a close-knit industry that has strong personal networks, a supplier and its sales force cannot afford to make any major blunders. The word will get around. Well-established social networks may be important enough and stable enough in a market for a supplier to invest the time and effort necessary to map them out. A social network can then be divided into niches based on influential individuals and organizations that then become the targets of a coordinated selling effort. In fact, experienced salespeople already know these social networks and use them constantly. When they exist, they should become a formal basis for contact segmentation because they are powerful in the diffusion of new ideas and products in an industrial market.

Table 3-7 presents other potential business-to-business market segmentation criteria and the elements of marketing management most shaped by each criterion. Segmenting by whether a major account's purchasing is decentralized or centralized will influence whether the account is serviced by a regional sales force or treated as a national account. An industrial sales force is often regionally structured and managed. Region or geographical location is therefore another natural way of segmenting the market and may indeed also reflect different usage situations based on concentrations of particular types of industry in different regions and sales territories. Also, distinct, regionally based management subcultures (styles, etiquette, and protocol) can make doing business in New York very different from doing business in Los Angeles, Atlanta, or Houston. The sales and marketing campaign must be sensitive to such business

Table 3-7
The Actionable Relevance of Industrial Segmentation Bases

Segmentation Basis	Actionable Relevance to
Account size and growth potential (A,B,C, or D)*	◆ Account and relationship management
SIC usage code	◆ Geographical sales territory allocation ◆ Product design ◆ Choice of trade journal to carry advertising ◆ Choice of trade show attendance
Usage situation	◆ Product design ◆ Sales force training ◆ JIT delivery service ◆ Advertising theme/brochure design
Purchasing process is centralized/decentralized	◆ Organization of sales force
Location	◆ Organization of sales force
Low-bid buying versus joint venturing	◆ Involvement of senior management ◆ Emphasis on design versus low price
Automation of buying	◆ Timing of selling ◆ Electronic linkage

*In a mental segmentation model of a business-to-business market, each account may be given a code such as A6P where A stands for an A account, in terms of size and growth potential, 6 is a code for the SIC/usage situation, and P stands for a low-bid price orientation, rather than a joint-venturing on innovation orientation.

subcultural differences. Accounts can be further rated in terms of their sensitivity to personal relations and service or price promotions, and managed accordingly. Ultimately, the credit ratings of buyers must also be integrated into any segmentation strategy as slow or no payers may have to receive special attention (or nonattention).

An important feature of business-to-business segmentation is the instability of the segment structure. Industrial markets are usually more volatile than consumer markets. First, industrial markets are often based on derived demand from other markets. If the economy hesitates or new competitors enter the served markets, then demand in an industrial market can collapse and radically change a firm's segment framework. Second, important new product, service, or process innovations in technology occur more frequently in industrial production than in household production. Such innovations are likely to radically change the usage situation of a product or service, perhaps eliminating its use altogether in one industry sector and opening up a new use for the product or service in another industry sector. This leads us into a more general discussion of some other limitations to using mental segmentation models in decision making.

The Limits of Market Segmentation

If a firm's product or service positioning and marketing tactics are not directly influenced by the way it segments the market, then its segmentation approach is useless. But a mental model of how a market is segmented must do more than influence strategy and tactics. It must increase sales and profits.[27] Offering a single product and undertaking a single marketing strategy enables economies of scale. Design costs, start-up production costs, production variable costs, administration costs, inventory handling costs, and advertising and promotion costs will all be lower per unit sale than when multiple products are offered and multiple marketing strategies are implemented to serve several market segments. Things can also get out of control rapidly if marketers in a company are asked to juggle too many balls in the air at once.

The profitability of identifying and pursuing market segments may also be here today but gone tomorrow because of changes in input costs and new competition. Changes in consumer values, demographics, and life-styles add to the uncertainty and instability. For example, during a recession, consumers may become more price sensitive and want to trade product features or quality for a more standard product with a lower price. After the recession is over, they become less price sensitive and return to their old behavior. What this means is that the market segment mental model has to be updated often, leading to the merging of old segments and the creation of new segments.

At what state in the life of a product-market is market segmentation most important? The best time to segment a market is at the rapid market growth stage when other competitors have yet to segment the market. When growth slows down, most market segments are already being well served by a competitor and are too expensive to attack. The rapid growth stage is also the time when new types of buyers are entering the market in large numbers. Often they are entering the market for the first time precisely because an innovative seller has designed a new model that nullifies their previous objections to purchasing or offers a feature or price that tips the scales. The

---

27. Frederick W. Winter, "A Cost-Benefit Approach to Market Segmentation," *Journal of Marketing* (Fall 1979), 103–11; Shirley Young, Leland Ott, and Barbara Feigin, "Some Practical Considerations in Market Segmentation," *Journal of Marketing Research* 15 (August 1978), 405–12; Peter Resnick, B. Turney, and J. Barry Mason, "Marketers Turn to 'counter-segmentation'," *Harvard Business Review* (October 1979), 100–106.

seller may also have discovered a previously unused distribution or media channel to reach a virgin market segment. Markets often expand precisely because such new market segments are developed. In summary, a growth market often meets all the requirements for profitable segmentation: different segments are responsive to different benefits and product characteristics, vary in their price sensitivity, and use different buying channels.

Consumer Analysis in Foreign Markets

Foreign consumers often differ from American consumers in conspicuous ways. They speak different languages, and when the listener is unfamiliar with the language they seem *very* different. They dress in different ways, eat different foods, and have different customs. However, foreigners do *not* all behave the same way. Some are rich, many are very poor. Some are very highly educated and live in industrialized environments, many are illiterate and lead very simple lives. The segmentation mental model described in Figure 3-2 can be applied just as well to a foreign market as it can to a U.S. market. In fact, a case can be made that it is more applicable to foreign markets because it provides structure and discipline to a decision-making team's thinking that reduces its nationalistic prejudices.

The problem lies in obtaining information that is insightful and results in a segmentation of consumer behavior that leads to superior competitive strategy. The greatest danger is that, like the early missionaries and sociologists, the decision-making team imposes its own values, beliefs, and behavior on the analysis. Executives who find it impossible to empathize with consumers who have "foreign" ways should be kept well away from global marketing decisions. On the other hand, sellers also need to beware nationalists and expatriots whose romantic or idealistic views can be just as dangerously biased.

Perhaps one of the greatest problems facing American firms in dealing with global consumer behavior is the reaction of distinctly different cultures to the encroachment of American culture. For example, the Islamic religion has dominated and enriched civilizations for centuries. But like other religions, some factions of Islam are going through a period of hatred and violence directed at the United States. The very global appeal of American products is a threat to some:

> It should by now be clear that we are facing a mood and a movement far transcending the level of issues and policies and the governments that pursue them. This is no less than a clash of civilizations—the perhaps irrational but surely historic reaction of an ancient rival against our Judeo-Christian heritage, our secular present, and the worldwide expansion of both. . . . From constitutions to Coca-Cola, from tanks and television to T-shirts, the symbols and artifacts, and through them the ideas, of the West have retained—even strengthened—their appeal.[28]

Companies and their global marketing decision-making teams are becoming increasingly aware that while segments of foreign cultures, particularly the young in Asia, South America, and the Middle East, are very enthusiastic consumers of American culture, other segments, particularly the elderly or deeply religious, are quite antagonistic toward the effects of American influences on their culture. This creates special marketing segmentation problems in such countries.

28. Bernard Lewis, "The Roots of Muslim Rage," *The Atlantic Monthly*, September 1990, 47–60.

Discussion Questions and Minicases

1. Imagine that your first assignment on your new job is to create a segmentation model for your firm's major service market. You spend four weeks working through piles of secondary data, old market research, and talking to industry experts, sales managers, and distributors. Halfway through your presentation to the senior executive team and other junior marketing and operation's executives it is evident that you have lost control of the presentation. A vigorous, sometimes heated discussion about market segmentation ensues between the executives in your audience. You have a sinking feeling in your stomach but it is quickly replaced by exaltation. Why did you have the sinking feeling, and why is it replaced by a feeling of exaltation?

2. Figure 3-1 presents pictures of several very different life-style vehicles. Imagine you are working for an auto company and you decide that one way to really make your point about life-style segmentation is to ask your colleagues to imagine what sort of music would be played on the sound systems in each of the cars. What would be your guess? How might such judgments be used to gain a competitive advantage?

3. What evidence is there in Table 3-1 that the Ford Motor company used a socio-economic market segmentation model to developing its Model T product line? Can you see any evidence of life-style segmentation as well?

4. The basic psychological theory used in Figure 3-2 to analyze demand structure is that behavior results from the interactions between individuals and the different situations they face. Buying behavior is a function of the person times the situation (B=f(P×S)). This is called Lewinian Field theory. Individual differences that we are born with (nature) or are the result of our unique life experiences (nurture) determine how we view our physical and social situation and how we behave in the situation. We do things for a purpose and it is our values and beliefs that give direction to our buying behavior. Thus differences in beliefs and values explain why consumers behave differently. What are the implications of this theory for market segmentation?

5. Market researchers undertook a test to determine how different variables affected the explanation and segmentation of demand.[29] Of the 37 cases studied, the benefits consumers wanted from a product was the most important purchasing factor in 19 of the cases, product beliefs were most important in 15 of the cases, and the consumer's life-style was most important in only three of the cases. How do these results support the mental model presented in Figure 3-2? What is fundamentally wrong with the test?

6. In the box on benefit segmenting, why do you think that lower income users preferred the more expensive food processor?

7. The 20th century has seen a radical change in home economics brought about not just by the many labor-saving appliances but also by numerous food-preparation and cleaning innovations. Many older people alive today can still remember their grandmothers hand-washing clothes, making home preserves, and even stoking a wood-burning stove and buying ice. Why is it safe to predict that the changes in household products and consumption over the next few decades will not be nearly as great? What impact will this slowdown have on brand loyalty?

8. At what market segment is the *Reader's Digest* advertisement on the left aimed? Do you think it is effective?

29. Russell I. Haley, "Benefit Segmentation—20 Years Later," *Journal of Consumer Marketing* (1986), 5–13.

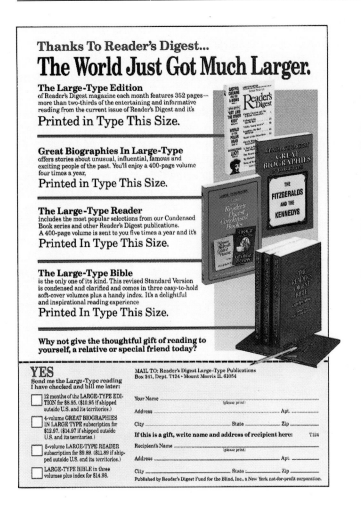

9. Some futurists are paid very large fees to give speeches about how technology will change transportation, housing, leisure, food, and health care over the next 20 years. Make your predictions (in less than 200 words) for each of these markets.

10. An association of peach growers in Georgia has requested your help with a marketing campaign aimed at increasing the consumption of peaches among young, upscale adults, particularly university students. The association figures that fruit consumption habits, once established, tend to continue for life. How might you segment the students' consumption of fruit into three usage situations? How would you guess the following fruits would be ranked in terms of popularity in each of the usage situations: apples, bananas, grapes, kiwifruit, oranges, peaches, plums, and strawberries? Would you agree that fruit preferences, once established in early adulthood, do not change very much? Think of your parents' or grandparents' tastes.

11. The advertisement on the right above is for a line of multivitamins targeted to four different user segments (children, teens, women, and men) and two different usage situations (women under stress and men under stress). Please identify the unique benefits that each formula is meant to satisfy. Why might it be difficult to sell such a line to a family?

12. The household cleaner market has been segmented into distinct usage situations, with different brands and products serving each situation. List all of the uses. Why has such niche marketing worked? Why do households now have four to five bottles under the sink when they once only had one? What trend helps explain this phenomenon?

13. The following is a rather simple example that illustrates a typical information processing choice rule. Let us imagine that two consumers are interested in buying a pair of running shoes. *A* is an overweight yuppie who has been told to exercise. *B* is a lean, serious runner. They consequently rate the importance of the choice attributes of running shoes differently (see table below). Buyer *A* emphasizes comfort and appearance while buyer *B* emphasizes comfort and functional performance characteristics.

There are three alternative shoes, *X, Y,* and *Z* whose ratings on each of the attributes by the magazine *Runner's World* are also presented in the following table:

Features	Importance Weight (Low 1 ⟷ 10 High)		Rated Performance of Shoe (Low = 1, Avg.= 2, High =3)		
	Buyer A	Buyer B	X	Y	Z
Comfort	10	10	Avg.	High	Avg.
Appearance	10	2	Avg.	High	High
Durability	7	5	High	Avg.	Low
Shock absorbency	5	10	High	Avg.	Low
Arch support	5	10	High	Avg.	Low
		Price	$50	$50	$25

Predict which shoes *A* and *B* would choose? What if they chose based on value for their money? What if *B* would not buy a shoe that did not rate high on comfort? What if *A* could only afford a $30 shoe?

14. Some experts believe that benefit segmentation does not work with fantasy feeling goods. What segmentation approach might you use for a woman's fragrance?

15. How might you use the belief measures in Figure 3-3 to segment retail store patronage? Construct potential segments.

16. What are the implications of the shopping model in Figure 3-4 for retailers and manufacturers?

17. Why might it be a good idea for Ford to buy a toy company and make and market toy models of its cars?

18. Coupons and price reductions are often used to encourage consumers to try out a new product or store. How could they be used to encourage not only trial but also repeated purchases and long-term loyalty? Develop a price promotion plan for launching a new toothpaste and for opening a new store. In the latter case, recognize that having too big a crowd on the opening day could badly hurt the service image of the store.

19. How good are you at intuitively matching food preference with demographics? On the left are the demographic descriptors of five segments. On the right are the food preferences of the segments. Match up the food preferences (1–5) with the demographics (A–E) and name each segment.

Demographic Descriptors	Food Preferences
A. Larger households More blue-collar workers From smaller towns More high school graduates Female head less likely to be employed	1. Fresh fruit Rice Natural cold cereal Wheat germ Yogurt Granola bars Bran/fiber bread
B. Lower income More likely to be retired More nonwhite Older Fewer children More two-person households	2. Wine Mixed drinks Beer Butter Rye/pumpernickel bread Bagels Swiss cheese
C. More upper income More younger people More one-person households More college grads More professionals More people from West Coast	3. Whole milk Pork Roast beef Boiled potatoes Gravy Pies
D. Below-average income Above-average age Fewer professionals More nonurban More nonwhite	4. Skim milk Diet margarine Salads Fresh fruit Sugar substitutes
E. Upper income More one-person households Fewer children under 18 Female heads employed full time More college grads More professionals and white-collar workers Larger cities	5. Lunchmeat sandwiches Hot dogs Bologna Soda pop Fruit drinks Spaghetti Pizza

20. From a market segmentation perspective, which is more effective and efficient: to offer advertising coupons to reduce the price of a product or to give a trade discount that results in a "sale" price? Hint: Review the definition of market segmentation and think about who benefits from a sale price and how different buyers react to a sale price.

21. Executives involved in major equipment and material purchases often see things very differently. Why should these different perspectives be expected? What motives and biases are frequently present in design engineers, production engineers, finance and accounting executives, senior management, and purchasing agents?

22. Computers and expert systems are automating routine buying. Orders are automatically placed with approved suppliers when buyer inventory levels drop to a minimum order level. Such automatic ordering systems have been operating successfully for a number of years in the hospital supplies, pharmaceutical, and book

markets. Their ability to collect and analyze information, such as reject rates and on-time delivery, is awesome. Over the long-term, how is such automation likely to affect marketing?

23. Often influential people within an organization have conflicting objectives and amicably disagree over the following questions:
    a. Whose product, if any, is really superior?
    b. Can a supplier's claims and promises can be believed?
    c. What is the added performance really worth to the organization?
    d. What is wrong with accepting the low bid?
    How do you think such uncertainty and disagreement influences how the organization makes its choice? What implications does this have for marketing?

24. The chart below shows the percentage of users of different products who are loyal to one brand. What types of products seem to have the highest brand loyalty?[30]

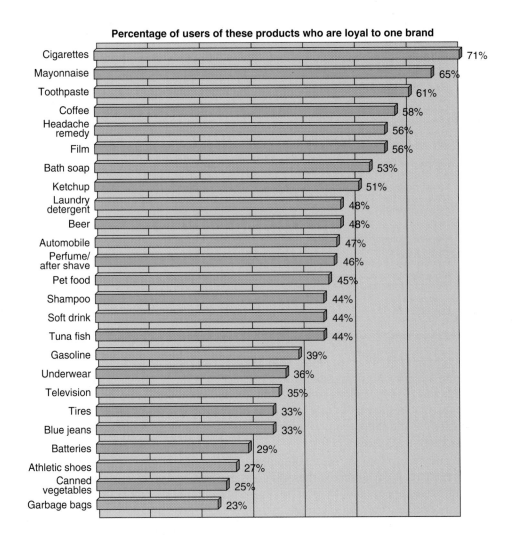

Percentage of users of these products who are loyal to one brand

Product	%
Cigarettes	71%
Mayonnaise	65%
Toothpaste	61%
Coffee	58%
Headache remedy	56%
Film	56%
Bath soap	53%
Ketchup	51%
Laundry detergent	48%
Beer	48%
Automobile	47%
Perfume/after shave	46%
Pet food	45%
Shampoo	44%
Soft drink	44%
Tuna fish	44%
Gasoline	39%
Underwear	36%
Television	35%
Tires	33%
Blue jeans	33%
Batteries	29%
Athletic shoes	27%
Canned vegetables	25%
Garbage bags	23%

25. In the discussion of purchasing style segmentation, two basic approaches were described. The first, bid buying, is a systematic bidding process in which the bulk of the contract normally goes to the lowest bidder. In the second, joint venturing, a supplier is selected and the buyer and supplier work together to develop product specifications, product design, and the production and delivery process. There is no competitive bidding. Advocates of the relationship buying approach argue that to be competitive a buyer does not have to be constantly encouraging price competition between its suppliers. Sole sourcing can reduce costs and create a climate of long-term cooperation that leads to greater innovation in product design and production processes. Working as a supplier-buyer team can make a buyer more competitive—in terms of its product innovativeness, quality, and price—compared to using multiple suppliers. Why might it be predicted that buyers will polarize into either a tough low-bid buying approach or a relationship buying approach? What market life-cycle conditions might determine which buying approach will be most successful?

26. Northern Telecom has developed single sourcing partnerships that have resulted in a reduction of its previous order-delivery cycle by half, a 49 percent reduction in its inspection staff due to a higher quality incoming product, and a 97 percent reduction in shop floor problems caused by defective material.[31] Hearing about this, you decide to approach one of your major customers, Hewlett-Packard, with the notion of developing a sole sourcing relationship. You, however, will have to make the company a deal it cannot refuse. What might it be?

27. Some companies have abandoned the centralized buying approach and have returned the purchasing responsibility to the line production managers who are responsible for quality and cost control. What are the advantages and disadvantages of such a move? What implications does it have for a seller?

28. A seller of computer software has had a lot of trouble making progress with a large company in an industry that is very close, very traditional, and in which everyone knows everyone else. It has sold its software to one of the major companies and is making good progress with several other accounts. How might the seller creatively use the social network in this market to make a breakthrough with this difficult customer?

29. When can market segmentation hurt a firm's competitive advantage? How must you consider competitors' behavior in segmenting a market?

30. International marketers are often concerned that the executives who are making decisions about what to sell and how to sell do not really understand consumer behavior in foreign markets? How might you test to see if this problem exists?

31. Roy Merrills, "How Northern Telecom Competes on Time," *Harvard Business Review* 67 (July/August 1989), 108–14.

Analyzing Competition

"You get out in front, you stay out in front."
A.J. Foyt

"When you've got good, strong competition,
you drive harder."
Roger Maris

*C*ompetitiveness is how effective and efficient a firm is, relative to its rivals, at serving customers and resellers. Effectiveness has to do with the quality of products, market share, and profitability; efficiency has to do with response speed and low costs. Both effectiveness and efficiency ultimately depend on competitive rationality—the strength of the firm's competitive drives and its decision-making skills.

American firms have been exhorted by almost everyone—government agencies, associates oversees, and industry insiders among others—to become more competitive. But becoming more competitive is like losing weight or converting fat to muscle. It is easy to talk about, but not that easy to do. The task is almost impossible if it is not based on a thorough competitive analysis. The analysis should start with a general overview of the competitive structure and dynamics of the product-market. This includes a market share analysis, a review of the history of the market, and a search for new competitors that threaten to drive existing firms and their products into extinction. The analysis should then zoom in on major rivals and their likely behavior.

It is surprising how often companies, even the best run companies, take their eyes off the competition. Throughout the late 1970s and early 1980s, the DEC Vax computer architecture made major inroads to the mid-range computer market previously dominated by IBM. It took until 1986 for IBM to set up a task force (with its own war room) to really respond to DEC. By then it was too late: the new unrecognized threat was from networkable PCs.

One problem with talking about competitiveness is that we have very ambivalent attitudes toward it. We admire competitiveness in sport, but often disparage it in the classroom. American executives often use up all their energy fiercely competing with each other for promotions. Management can sometimes become more fixated on the competition than it is on staying close to its customers. A competitive orientation involves understanding the competition and gaining advantage from exploiting its weaknesses. It does not mean attacking the competition at every opportunity, no matter what the cost.

Remember these key points when reading this chapter:

- Competition is a dynamic concept. It used to be measured by market share, mind share, voice share, and R&D share. It now is measured by *changes* in these shares.

- *Relationship market share* and its changes measure the strength of a seller/reseller *trading partnership*. Tracking this market share is a priority because the net changes in relationship market share determine changes in both the sellers' and the distributors' market share.

- The threat of new competition depends on the many types of barriers that block newcomers from entering the market.

- Many markets that were once separate are now merging as new technologies create head-to-head competition.

- New competitive threats come from new technologies, buyers or sellers becoming competitors or encouraging new entries, and the takeovers or mergers of current competitors.

- The strengths and weaknesses of existing competitors should be identified by studying their specific skills and competencies across the added-value chain (from buying to after-sale service) and throughout the order-delivery cycle.

- Anticipating competitor behavior is very difficult but must be attempted. No one can afford to ignore what the competition may do next.

■ Globalization means there will be a lot more competition to supply the U.S. market and other wealthy economies. This competition will increase as labor and management skills increase in emerging economies such as China and Eastern Europe.

Competitive Structure

Michael Porter's pioneering text on competitive strategy changed the way many companies think about their competition.[1] Porter identified five forces that shape competition: current competitors, the threat of new entrants, the threat of new substitutes, the bargaining power of customers, and the bargaining power of suppliers. This structure can be reduced further to include simply *current* competitors and *potential* competitors and substitutes. This is because, as we will discover, the bargaining power of customers depends very much on the extent to which rivals are competing to supply these customers. The bargaining power of suppliers also depends on how actively rivals are biding for their supplies. Hence, the bargaining power of suppliers and distributors depends on the rivalry between firms in a market. What Porter overlooks is that this is not a one-way process. The bargaining power of a firm over its suppliers and customers also depends on the rivalry between suppliers in the supply market and the rivalry between customers in their markets.

The way customers and suppliers behave determines the threat posed by immediate and potential competition. Customers and suppliers are therefore not separate competitive elements but moderators or amplifiers of competition (see Figure 4-1). Generally, suppliers and distributors are used to gain competitive advantage and should be seen in this light. That is why the customer and channel environments are separately analyzed (see Chapter 5) and given much more attention than Porter's framework suggests. It is true that at times customer and suppliers have to be directly considered in a competitive analysis, but *only* when they threaten to become a new, direct competitor by supplier forward integration or customer backward integration. This is not to belittle Porter's considerable contribution, which encouraged firms to analyze both the current and potential competitive environment.

Market Share Analysis

The first question almost every company asks in its decision-making process is who has what share of the market? Market share is measured as a percentage of total industry sales over a specified time period. About 70 percent of the companies in the *1990 Conference Board* study tracked their competitor's market share. The reasons are fairly obvious. Market share identifies who the major players are, and changes in market share identify who has become more or less competitive in the marketplace, that is, who gained share from whom.

There are clearly problems in defining the market. A company's market share can change dramatically depending on whether the market is defined as global, a particular export market, the U.S. market, a region of the United States, a city, or a segment of users or usage. The scope of the market is normally specified by a realistic assessment of company resources and by company growth objectives. Operationally, the market is often specified by the way market researchers are able to collect sales and market share information.

1. Michael E. Porter, *Competitive Strategy* (New York: The Free Press, 1980). Porter's work is largely based on industrial organization economics. He merged it with marketing literature on competitive analysis and the product life-cycle. His work is a clear presentation of these frameworks with many excellent examples.

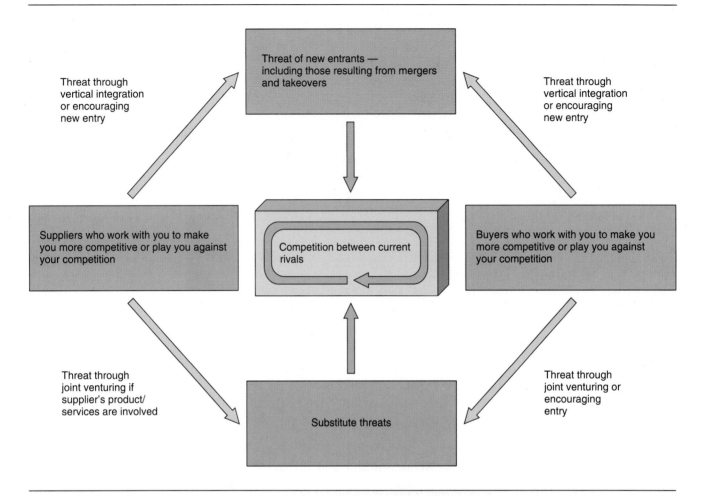

Figure 4-1

Competitive Forces

Competition occurs among current rivals. Buyers and suppliers can help or hinder a firm's efforts to become more competitive (see Chapter 5). Sometimes, they even encourage a new entrant or the development of a new substitute. They seldom, if ever, discourage such entry or the development of a new technological substitute. However, buyers and suppliers are not competitors. In fact, as we shall see in Table 4-1, the trading relationship a firm has with a supplier or a buyer is a cooperative effort that competes with other trading relationships in the market.

The change in market share over time is a vital indicator of competitive dynamics, particularly during the growth stage of a product-market. It indicates whether a firm is ahead, abreast, or behind the market's total growth rate. Part of the reason that Japanese companies are concerned about gaining market share is that they often compete in high-growth markets, and they understand that this is the crucial time to develop brand loyalty. For example, the Japanese production of calculators grew 200 times during the 1970s. A firm had to expand its sales by this multiple just to keep its market share—Casio raced ahead of its rivals and grew its market share from 10 percent to 35 percent.[2]

During a market growth stage, market share competitiveness really pays off. Having a large percentage of an infant market means having a lot of very little. In a mature market, it is often too expensive for firms to go after market share because every move draws fierce retaliation. The activity among firms during a growth stage is akin to the behavior of competing species when a new habitat has been discovered. The firm that multiplies the fastest and establishes a dominant hold through new models that command different niches, wins. In evolutionary theory this is called adaptive radiation.

2. Subrata N. Chakravarty, "Economic Darwinism," *Forbes,* October 6, 1986, 52–56; and J. W. Brittain and D. R. Wholey, "Competition Coexistence in Organizational Communities: Population Dynamics in Electronics Components Manufacturing," in *Ecological Models of Organizations,* Glenn R. Carrol, ed. (Cambridge, MA: Ballinger, 1988).

However, market share is not the only measure of competitiveness. The following measures are often used as leading indicators of a likely change in future sales and profits.

1. *Mind share:* The percentage of customers who name the brand when asked to name the first brand that comes to mind when they think about buying a particular type of product. This indicates the consumer's top-of-mind brand awareness and preferences.

2. *Voice share:* The percentage of media space or time a brand has of the total media share for that industry, often measured simply as dollars spent on advertising. This is likely to lead to a change in mind share (but not always if the creatives are weak).

3. *R&D share:* A company's research and development expenditure as a percentage of the total industry R&D expenditure. This is a long-term predictor of new product developments, improvements in quality, cost reductions, and, hence, market share. It is a very important measure of future competitiveness in many high-technology markets.

Relationship Market Share Analysis

A new type of market share analysis measures the competitive importance and influence of *relationships* in a market. An example of a relationship matrix is presented in Table 4-1a.[3] Let us assume there are three major manufacturers: *X, Y,* and *Z.* Manufacturer *X* has a market share of 50 percent, *Y* has 30 percent, and *Z* has 20 percent of the sales in the product category. There are also five major resellers/distributors/retailers: *A, B, C, D,* and *E.* The resellers, in their sales of the product to the end user, have the following market shares: *A* has 50 percent, *B* has 20 percent, *C* has 10 percent, *D* has 10 percent, and *E* has 10 percent.

One way of appreciating the competitiveness of the relationships between the manufacturers and resellers is to estimate each relationship's market share. For example, the business that *A* and *X* do together (that is, *A*'s sales of *X*'s products) constitutes 20 percent of total market sales. *A* might be the giant retailer Wal-Mart, *X* might be the giant laundry detergent manufacturer Procter & Gamble. *X-A*'s market share would then be the estimated share of total laundry detergent sales that the Wal-Mart/P&G relationship has achieved. According to conventional economic theory, in Table 4-1a, *X* and *A* exercise countervailing power on each other and consequently make the market more competitive. The *X-A* relationship has a 20 percent market share, and this is matched by the equally large *Y-A* and *X-B* relationships. The remainder of the relationships are much smaller and five potential relationships do not even exist.

The competitive situation, however, could be very different, even though the market shares of the manufacturers and retailers stay the same; that is, the market shares at the end of the rows and bottom of the columns are the same. What if 40 percent of the total market share was generated by the *X-A* relationship? In the situation illustrated in Table 4-1b, it is clear that rather than counter-balancing each other, seller *X* and reseller *A* are now in a position to work together to dominate the market with their pricing and marketing practices. This illustrates the importance of estimating the market share of relationships, rather than just measuring market share at the seller or reseller level.

A relationship matrix provides us with a foundation for developing a deeper understanding of competitive market structure. For example, in Table 4-1a, the trading

3. This discussion develops and extends the channel dependence matrix concept presented in Peter R. Dickson, "Distributor Portfolio Analysis and the Channel Dependence Matrix: New Techniques for Understanding and Managing the Channel," *Journal of Marketing* 47 (Summer 1983), 35–44.

Table 4-1						
Measuring Relationship Market Share Using the Relationship Matrix						

Table 4-1a

Major sellers		Major resellers A	B	C	D	E	Seller's share
	X	20%*	20%	5%	0	5%	50%
	Y	20%	0	5%	5%	0	30%
	Z	10%	0	0	5%	5%	20%
Reseller's share		50%	20%	10%	10%	10%	100%

Table 4-1b

Major sellers		Major resellers A	B	C	D	E	Seller's share
	X	40%*	0	5%	0	5%	50%
	Y	10%	10%	5%	5%	0	30%
	Z	0	10%	0	5%	5%	20%
Reseller's share		50%	20%	10%	10%	10%	100%

*The term *seller* is used to describe a manufacturer or importer selling to a reseller who is a distributor, wholesaler, or retailer. The trading relationship *X-A* has a 20 percent share of the market. The business *X* does with *A*, and *A* with *X*, constitutes 20 percent of all of the sales of the product category. In some cases, it may be useful to group sellers and resellers into types rather than treat them as individual entities. The individual relationships are then aggregated into a set of relationships with some common characteristic.

relationship *X-B,* with a 20 percent market share, has presumably flourished because *X* and *B* have worked together to generate such sales. It may be relatively easy for *B* to switch to new sources of supply, but it is more likely *B* has built its reputation by selling manufacturer *X*'s line exclusively. It would be expensive, in both effort and goodwill, to switch suppliers or to add another line. Distributor *B* is clearly very important to *X*, but *X* does have some alternative trading relationship options. Hence, it appears that *B* is relatively more dependent on *X* than *X* is on *B*. Of course, other issues may change this diagnosis, including sales of other product lines. Reseller *B* may also serve a very special segment that cannot be reached any other way. Consequently, the competitive advantage provided by *B* to *X* is not readily substitutable. Further, *X* may highly value the exclusivity of *B*'s buying and hence *X* may be very responsive to any move *B* makes to introduce a competitive line. It may also be important to look beyond market share and examine the profitability of the trading relationship for each party. Despite these limitations, estimating the relationship matrix can be a good starting point for assessing the competitiveness of trading relationships. The relationship market share provides a lot more information than conventional seller and reseller market share data that are used to measure conventional market structures. It is also more important in determining longer-term sales because the market share of a seller is the sum of its relationship market shares with resellers. Similarly, the market share of a reseller is the sum of its relationship market shares with sellers. It is therefore very important to understand how such relationships are changing.

Entries, Exits, and Competitiveness

The dynamic effects of the entry of a new supplier or a new reseller can also be tracked in the above relationship matrix to determine who is going to be hurt and who is going to be helped. This raises a very important fact in the balance of power between suppliers and resellers: the entry of a new seller increases the power of resellers. First, it allows resellers to negotiate better terms as part of the price that the new supplier has to pay to enter an established distribution channel and to cover the increased effort and cost of adding its new line. Alternatively, resellers can discuss the situation with their current suppliers to explore ways to sweeten current trading relations so as to reduce the incentive for the reseller to add the new supplier—a move that would clearly threaten the existing supplier's sales to the reseller.

The flood of manufacturing imports in recent years (particularly in the clothing industry) has not only taken market share away from domestic suppliers but has also enabled resellers to extract better terms. The net effect is that domestic suppliers are selling less and making even less on what they sell. A similar power shift can occur when the number of resellers shrinks because of mergers or failures. On the other hand, when the number of resellers increases or the number of independent suppliers is reduced, power will shift in favor of the supplier. For example, when Hines finally gave up and pretty much turned over the canned soup market to the Campbell's Soup Company, power shifted dramatically in favor of Campbell's Soup.

The relative incidence of entries and exits over time at various trading levels (particularly between manufacturers and retailers) directly determines long-term shifts in power between levels in a channel. It leads to the renegotiation of contracts and terms that reflect the new power. This power-shift theory of competitive dynamics makes the following arguments:

1. When a seller's market becomes more competitive, the resellers, who are free to choose who to do business with, become more powerful. A seller's market becomes more competitive with the entrance of new sellers or an increase in the production and distribution capacity of existing sellers.

2. When a seller's market becomes less competitive, the resellers become less powerful. A seller's market becomes less competitive by the exit of sellers, a reduction in production and distribution capacity, or the merger of current sellers thus reducing the number of buyers.

3. Power is most effectively exercised at the time of a structural shift in the amount of competition in the seller's or reseller's market.

4. The above propositions also apply to changing competition among suppliers and manufacturers.

The History of the Market

A study of the recent history of the product-market identifies the dimensions on which sellers have competed most strongly to serve the interests of the resellers and consumers. In some markets, this competition may have resulted in a price war. In others, sellers have competed with each other to improve product and service quality. Often, a technological improvement made by an innovator forces every competitor to respond. This occurred when Duracell introduced the alkaline battery. All of the competitors were forced to match the new technology. The start of heavy sales promotions in a market also often results in a major shift in industry marketing tactics away from image advertising and, more seriously, away from product innovation.

Rationality in Practice:

Waking Up a Sleeping Giant

When Philip Morris bought the Miller Brewing Company, it intended to shake down what it saw as a sleepy product-market. It did change the rules of competition in the industry, but it did so in ways that it did not and could not have anticipated. In the end, it was Anheuser-Busch who proved to have the better marketing plan.

Behind the beguiling appeal of the television beer advertisements, a knock-down, drag-out fight for market share and profits has been going on for over a decade. Beer prices have fallen and advertising agencies have been changed frequently. The big winner by far has been Anheuser-Busch, whose market share rose from 25 percent in 1978 to 40 percent in 1988. Miller Brewing Company, which started the new marketing era with its intensive advertising of Miller Lite, went from a 19 percent to a 21 percent market share over the decade. Schlitz, Stroh's, G. Heileman, and dozens of regional breweries have been the big losers.

Beer is a mature market and the changing demographics are against it. The postwar baby boomers have grown out of the heavy beer-drinking stage. Wine coolers have cut into beer's summer sales. Fitness and nutritional awareness has resulted in a reduction in beer bellies. Tougher drinking and driving laws and an increase in the legal drinking age to 21 in most staes (in part from a Federal threat to withhold highway construction subsidies)

The study of competition as a process, a series of events over time, tells us a lot more about the dynamics of the marketplace than a single here-and-now snapshot view that is assumed, often incorrectly, to describe the market in equilibrium.[4] The box titled "Waking Up a Sleeping Giant" describes such a process. The history of the product-market is seldom recorded. It is often carried around in the heads of experienced executives and the invaluable insights they can provide are lost when they retire.

An industry often has standard marketing tactics and rules that are universally adopted. Examples are certain formulas for cost-plus pricing and spending a certain percentage of the previous year's sales on advertising in the next year. Sales force commissions and incentives are also often standardized in an industry. These rules of doing business make the market more predictable and stable. If the market "learns" and has over time been moved by competitive innovation toward more efficient ways of making and marketing its products, then these rules should reflect such learning and, hence, make sense.

Knowing how and why standard industry practices and decision rules came about enables a firm to better understand whether the rules are based on competitive logic or whether they have simply become "established" practice to keep from rocking the boat.[5] If they are based on logic, then a competitor can better understand what works and what does not in the marketplace and why. However, if the rules are based on old-fashioned agreements to restrain competition, then violating them represents an opportunity for the aggressive firm.

As we shall see in many of the examples of innovative marketing tactics described later in this text, the innovator often profits from breaking the established rules of doing business. These risk-taking new entrants often have little regard for the old rules of the game.

4. Richard N. Langlois, ed., *Economics as a Process* (Cambridge, England: Cambridge University Press, 1986). This view of competition is more consistent with the theory of competitive rationality than conventional economic static equilibrium theory.
5. Gloria P. Thomas and Gary F. Soldow, "A Rules-Based Approach to Competitive Interaction," *Journal of Marketing* 52 (April 1988), 63–74.

have also taken their toll. In 1972, Miller got a jump on the competition by launching its very successful Lite beer and later its classic TV sports advertising campaign. Until that time, Schlitz had been the most profitable brewery with its emphasis on cost control, but it had become too greedy and had begun reformulating its beer using cheaper ingredients. The consumer noticed the change about the time Miller launched its marketing offensive.

Anheuser, crippled by a 90-day strike, was also temporarily stopped in its tracks. But over the next five years the Budweiser ad budget was tripled and the company sponsored, and dominated, every sporting niche it could. The strategy worked brilliantly. The slogan "This Bud's for You" matched the appeal of the "Miller Time" and the humorous old jocks claiming "Great taste, less filling" in the Miller Lite ads. A network of efficient refrigerated warehouses also gave Bud the best distribution system in the country, and a new generation of management, led by August Busch III, has had a lot to do with Anheuser's current success. The new managers have proven to be excellent hands-on marketing planners and implementers.

Sources: G. Bruce Knecht, "How Bud Won the Battle," *Dun's Review*, February 1982, 83–85; "A Shrinking Market Has Beermakers Brawling," *Business Week*, August 20, 1984, 59, 63; William Dunn, "Where the Beer Industry Is Heading," *American Demographics*, February 1986, 37–39.

The Threat of New Competitors

Once established in an industry, a firm must extend its vigilance beyond its current competitors and identify potential competitive threats. The first question the established firm must ask is, how difficult is it to enter this product-market? Economists have analyzed this difficulty in terms of barriers to entry. Barriers to entry are created by the advantages of established competitors. Figure 4-2 lists twelve barriers to entry and examples of individual firms whose strengths (sustainable competitive advantages) create such barriers.

Sometimes entry barriers appear to be overwhelming, until one newcomer or another recognizes that a barrier has two sides. Huge investments in particular raw material resources, processes, distributors, and consumer goodwill can also become barriers to an existing competitor's mobility, that is, its ability to change and adapt. The great 19th-century railway companies have often been criticized for being myopic, too production-oriented, and not noticing the threats posed by new technologies. They were constrained by the very resources that made them great—the thousands of miles of track and rail and their rolling stock and expertise in running a railway. How could they readily dispose of such assets and invest in trucking or aircraft? A forest products company that owns thousands of acres of forest must similarly grow and market forest products.

Consumer attitudes and habits may also pose a barrier to mobility. Banks have found it more difficult than expected to sell products such as insurance and airline tickets to their customers. Consumers see banks as banks. They want their bank to stick to providing safe investment returns, loans, and check-cashing services—not economy travel packages. There are some other less obvious barriers to mobility. For many years oil companies have possessed powerful franchised dealer networks, but this competitive advantage has constrained their ability to supply independents, who are often neighborhood competitors, with their franchised dealers. AT&T faced a similar problem when it launched into the personal computer market. Not wanting to offend

Figure 4-2

Different Types of Barriers to Product-Market Entry

1. Economies of scale and scope in research—Boeing (aerospace and defense contracts).
2. Economies of scale and scope in production—General Electric (light bulbs).
3. Economies of scale and scope in distribution logistics—Anheuser Busch (beer).
4. Locked in distribution channels—General Motors (car dealerships).
5. Advertising expenditure—Procter & Gamble (laundry).
6. Proprietary patents—Polaroid (instant photography), Proprietary processes—Bausch & Lomb (contact lenses).
7. Ownership of raw materials—Exxon (oil reserves).
8. Location advantages—McDonald's (fast food).
9. Government regulation—Utilities and television cable companies.
10. Management expertise—Merck (pharmaceutical).
11. Customer switching costs—General Dynamics (nuclear submarines).
12. Brand franchises (customer loyalty)—IBM (computers).

its telecommunications sales forces, AT&T was far too tentative in developing exclusive dealer relationships with computer and office equipment retailers. Some companies find their product differentiation and brand franchise both a tremendous advantage and a straitjacket. McDonald's has been forever constrained by its Ronald McDonald image. Billions of dollars of advertising spread over 20 years has firmly established McDonald's positioning in the American psyche. Other companies are constrained by fears that others will cannibalize their established products. IBM was so protective of its PC that it launched a PCjr that threatened neither its PC nor, for that matter, any rival's product.

While history has shown that some markets are very difficult to break into (for instance, the pharmaceutical and automobile markets) without considerable resources, this perceived difficulty can lead to dangerous complacency. These days, an aggressive new entrant can turn to many sources for resource assistance. Global suppliers and venture capitalists can assist overcoming any financial and production barriers. Even powerful distribution channels can sometimes be circumvented. Many small manufacturers are finding that specialist mail-order catalogs provide one way to launch a new product that department and chain stores will not touch until it has a proven sales record. New companies can also supply private label and generic brands to retailers, thereby sidestepping the need to invest in a brand image and opening channels and shelf-space that otherwise would be closed. Even regulations prohibiting entry can be end-run. Stockbrokers were able to offer a mutual fund with checking services by contracting banks to run the customer accounts while they operated the investment portfolio.

There is also increasing evidence of a competitive trend that can be summed up by the phrase, "marketing muscle in search of product-markets." Consumer marketing firms such as R.J. Reynolds, Procter & Gamble, Gillette, and Campbell's Soup are stalking the marketplace looking for small companies with new products. They have superb distribution and marketing organizations, massive R&D resources, and access to funds that can be used to take a small company's product or service and roll it out nationally.

Figure 4-3

Federal Express's ill-fated Zapmail service never really caught on.

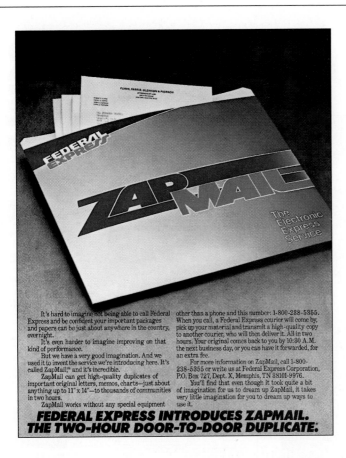

Converging Technologies and Merging Markets

In many markets today, new entries are often established companies with new technology that has expanded the boundaries of their traditional market.[6] The express mail market is experiencing a clash between converging technologies. In 1974, Federal Express launched its overnight letter and package delivery service, which is now a $5 billion-plus market. Beyond its direct competition, such as the U.S. Postal Service, Federal Express faced threats from several other technologies. Western Union, the original telegraph company, launched an Easylink electronic mail service that could also converse with Telex, the long-established conventional business-to-business electronic mail system. Easylink failed, but the really serious threats were posed by the fax machine and the integration of telephone and computer systems that enabled organizations and individuals to create and operate their own electronic mail services. MCI has attempted to foster such networks. Ironically, Federal Express indirectly encouraged fax competition by developing a Zapmail service based on facsimile machines (see Figure 4-3). Although this service failed, it was meant to protect Federal Express from the long-term threat of customers owning their own fax machines.[7] Instead, it helped manufacturers of facsimiles sell their product (see Figure 4-4).

6. This is akin to a species (firm) mutating (innovating) in such a way that it can flourish in a new habitat (market).
7. "The Zapping of Federal Express," *Newsweek*, October 13, 1986, 57; and John P. Tarpey, "Federal Express Tries to Put More Zip in Zapmail," *Business Week*, December 17, 1984, 110–11.

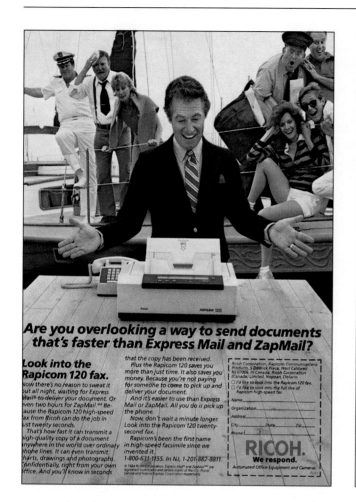

Figure 4-4

A Potential Supplier Becomes a Competitor

Federal Express's Zapmail faced a severe threat from the very fax machines that were used to provide the Zapmail service. Electronic mail now threatens fax machines and Federal Express–type services.

The Competitive Threat of Vertical Integration

Sears Roebuck offers several case studies of how to enter markets by backward vertical integration. Its Craftsman tools, Kenmore appliances, DieHard batteries and Roadhandler tires are leading national brands. It does not own any factories outright, but it has owned large shares of some of its suppliers (for instance, Sears owns about 30 percent of Roper, its range maker, 30 percent of DeSoto, its paint manufacturer, and 20 percent of Swift, its textile provider). Sears product development and testing labs have produced over 1,000 patents since 1930.

Even distributors who do not undertake R&D or product development are often in a position to take advantage of the new ideas of small domestic or foreign manufacturers who are not adequately protected by patents or binding nondisclosure agreements. It is not unusual for even quite respectable retail chains or mail-order companies to take samples (requested for "testing" purposes) to another original equipment manufacturer (such as OEM) and have it manufacture a "me-too" copy under the reseller's own private label.

Sears' startlingly aggressive move into the financial services industry is an example of innovative vertical integration.[8] Although considered a risky move by many (seemingly vindicated by Sears' decision to sell its financial services in 1992), it was a natural extension of a long-established financial service. Sears has for decades been one of the biggest consumer credit granting, and hence personal financing, institutions in the United States. It is also one of the biggest insurance companies through its Allstate company, founded in 1931. The purchase of Dean Witter in 1981 and other financial service acquisitions finally woke up the complacent banking industry. Sears became a major competitor in a new market that is merging banking, insurance, and investing: full-service personal finance management. Other players are the deregulated national and regional banks such as Citicorp and Ohio's Banc One, stockbrokers Merrill Lynch, and the credit card company American Express. This is another example of traditional boundaries collapsing and markets blending as the result of 1) deregulation, 2) breakthroughs in electronic banking and financial services technology, 3) innovative products, and 4) vertical integration. This new financial market will produce a number of new and highly volatile competitive interfaces. One significant result may have already occurred. New competition has hastened the extinction of the traditional savings and loan as an economic species.

Suppliers may also become competitors when they see opportunities for making higher returns by adding value themselves or when they become frustrated with distributor or customer behavior. An obvious example was the cloning of IBM personal computers by off-shore component suppliers. Another example occurred in 1978, when Cuisinart launched its $140 food processor in the United States, a product actually made by French supplier Robot-Coupe. The Cuisinart was so successful that it attracted dozens of competitors who flooded the market with cheaper imitations. Cuisinart extended its product line by turning to a Japanese supplier who provided an even more competitive new product that was less expensive and offered more features. By 1980, the new Japanese model was outselling the original Robot-Coupe model. Unhappy with such sales cannibalization, Robot-Coupe launched its own distribution network and advertising campaign. The result was a nasty war of words in their advertising and a messy court case. Cuisinart's U.S. operation went bankrupt under Chapter 11 in 1992.

The above examples clearly illustrate that a company must be on its guard against the threat of new entrants from merging markets and from others up and down the channel. This concern is best addressed in the marketing plan by asking and answering the questions presented in Figure 4-5. Such questions force a company to look beyond its traditional competitors. They also require the marketing decision maker to test the traditional assumptions about entry barriers, ask how they might be overcome, and determine who might do it.

Auditing Current Competitors

For most companies it is not possible to put all current competitors under the microscope and undertake an in-depth analysis of their competitive strengths and weaknesses. However, particular competitors are always worthy of such attention, either because it is clear they are attacking the established company's market share with a new product or because the company has decided, in a previous plan, to attack them.

8. Steve Weiner, "The Rise of Discover," *Forbes*, May 4, 1987, 46–48; and John Heins, "Name Recognition," *Forbes*, November 30, 1987, 137.

Figure 4-5
New Competitive Threats Audit

New Technology—Converging Markets Threat

- What price changes in other technology markets appear to influence our sales? Is this effect changing?
- Which new technology or service is starting to be considered as a substitute for our product or service by consumers? Is this occurring in any particular usage situation or by any particular group of buyers? Are our existing channels encouraging such substitution?
- What is our closest new technological or service competition?
- Who is the major mover and shaker in this new industry?
- What appears to be its current objective and strategy?
- What is its growth rate?
- What has been its effect on our sales?
- What further threat does it pose?
- What constraints does it face?

Channel Integration Threat

- Which supplier is most likely to become a downstream direct competitor in the near future? Why? How would it do it? Is there any evidence of this occurring?
- Which customers are most likely to become upstream do-it-themselves competitors in the near future? Why? How would they do it? Is there any evidence of such plans?

Competitor Takeover—Merger Threat

- Which mergers, takeovers, or trading coalitions among competitors or from inside pose the greatest threat to our position? What evidence exists that this is likely to occur?

The isolation of aggressors or targets usually requires a preliminary analysis that identifies from which rivals you are gaining business and to which competitors you are losing business. This is the way you identify your immediate current competition, which may or may not be using similar technology.[9]

Many major U.S. cities now only have one daily newspaper and yet such monopolies have not created super profits for the publisher. The reason is simple. Although other newspapers may have died, competition for advertising has increased from the suburban weeklies, direct marketing, and other media. TV, radio, and local magazines have also become more competitive with their news and features. The mistake the newspaper publishers made was not identifying these competitors early on when they could have been countered.[10]

In a new venture it is useful to study the position of a typical, apparently successful, major company and the position of a small, but high-growth, company. The analysis may reveal that an established company is not as successful as initially assumed, and some of the reasons for its less than impressive position and performance will also emerge. The initial investment in time, effort, and expense necessary to audit competitors may be very high (amounting to several weeks or even months of an executive's or consultant's time), but it should be treated as an investment. The results will produce a file and a word-processed report that can be built on from year to year with constantly expanding details and insights. This file then becomes part of the collective memory of your organization to be passed on to successive managers.

9. Thomas W. Dunfee, Louis Stern, and Frederick D. Sturdivant, "Bounding Markets in Merger Cases: Identifying Relevant Competitors," *Northwestern University Law Review* 78 (November 1983), 733–73.
10. Subrata N. Chakravarty and Carolyn Torcellini, "Citizen Kane Meets Adam Smith," *Forbes,* February 20, 1989, 82–85.

A Competitor Analysis Template

Figure 4-6 presents a very comprehensive competitor analysis form that is still not exhaustive. It is better characterized as a template that a company can use as a basis for developing its own unique competitor analysis form. The analysis should start with a general assessment of the competitor's product positioning, current objectives, strategy, major strengths and weaknesses, and likely next moves. The specific vulnerabilities of the competitor during the planning time horizon and what is going to be the competitor's major growth and response constraints should also be highlighted. A very important part of this summary will be an assessment of the rival's goals and basic innovation-imitation competitive strategy. This information will enable predictions to be made about the competitor's future behavior and reactions. It is not sufficient to describe how the competitor is performing in terms of market share and profits. A competitive analysis must diagnose how the competitor has managed to generate such performance outcomes, be they good or bad.[11] The following research suggests that firms do adopt a general competitive strategy that is reflected in their new product development behavior.

New Product Strategy: Cultural Attitude to Innovation and Imitation

The direction and tone established by top-level management shapes the way that the firm will pursue new product opportunities. A company can pursue two general strategies with its product development activity.[12] In the first approach, the firm attempts to achieve a continuous stream of modestly successful new product introductions. Each of these new products builds on the firm's knowledge of its customers and its technology—the firm never strays far from its core competencies. Individually, these new products do not remake the market or the organization itself. However, in sum, they add up to a consistently successful performing company. This approach requires a modest, but continuous investment of resources to sustain such an effort.

The second strategy is to search for a revolutionary product that changes the market and the company. Such an approach often requires a substantial commitment of resources and a relatively long development period. The result, though, is a discontinuity in the performance of the firm. This is probably accompanied by the reshaping of the product-market, or even the creation of a new one. A hybrid approach can also be pursued, in which the firm attempts to produce the occasional discontinuous innovation while generally pursuing a series of incremental ones. Such an approach will take even greater resources than the "big hit" approach.

The amount of innovation and new product development that a firm undertakes will depend very much on the organization's overall strategy, its entrepreneurial aggressiveness, and its focus. Miles and Snow have categorized companies by their willingness to launch into new markets with new technologies and products.[13] The categories are as follows:

11. George S. Day and Robin Wensley, "Assessing Advantage: A Framework for Diagnosing Competitive Superiority," *Journal of Marketing* 52 (April 1988), 1–20.

12. Robert G. Cooper, "The Impact of New Product Strategies," *Industrial Marketing Management* 12 (1983), 243–56; and Robert G. Cooper, "Predevelopment Activities Determine New Product Success," *Industrial Marketing Management* 17 (1988), 237–47.

13. R. E. Miles and C. C. Snow, *Organization Strategy, Structure, and Process* (New York: McGraw-Hill, 1978); also see Daryl O. McKee, P. Rajan Varadarajan, and William M. Pride, "Strategic Adaptability and Firm Performance: A Market-Contingent Perspective," *Journal of Marketing* 53 (July 1989), 21–35; and Carolyne Smart and Ilan Vertinsky, "Strategy and the Environment: A Study of Corporate Responses to Crisis," *Strategic Management Journal* 10 (Summer 1984), 149–71.

Competitor_____ Analyst_____ Date_____

SUMMARY OF COMPETITOR'S POSITION

* Goals _____
* New product development strategy _____
* Decision-making skills _____
* Product and process R&D _____
* Innovation/imitation skills _____
* Implementation skills _____
* Current success story _____
* Current mistakes _____
* Advantage with buyers _____
* Disadvantage with buyers _____
* Cost advantages _____
* Cost disadvantages _____

COMMENTS AND RATING OF COMPETITOR'S ADDED VALUE CHAIN

Financial position
* Importance of this profit center to rival _____
* Short term liquidity _____
* Access to working capital _____
* Access to capital for major expansion _____
* Contribution margin _____
* Fixed cost/breakeven _____
* Marginal cost structure _____

Market position
* Major geographical markets _____
* Major target markets _____
* Way they segment the market _____
* Current expansion efforts _____
* Current holding efforts _____
* Overall strength _____

Product position
* Raw material quality _____
* Workmanship quality _____
* Design quality _____
* Design effeciency _____
* Durability _____
* Ease of servicing _____
* Feature innovations _____
* Appearance _____
* Brand strength _____
* Product range _____
* Fit to segments _____
* Packaging effectiveness _____
* Overall strength _____

Pricing
* How much above/below average _____
* % increase in last year _____
* Increases in last 2 years _____
* Margin to trade _____
* Volume discounts _____
* Payments terms _____
* Promotional discounts _____
* Leasing terms _____
* Buy back allowance _____
* Overall strength _____

Figure 4-6
A Competitor Analysis Template

Inbound logistics
- Sources of supply _____
- Purchasing skills _____
- Raw materials inventory control & effeciency _____
- Overall strength _____

Production
- Production capacity (long-term & seasonal) _____
- Production efficiency _____
- Labor relations _____
- Labor turnover _____
- Ability to retool/adapt _____
- Quality control _____
- Production costs _____
- Overall strength _____

Outbound logistics
- Finished product stock control & effeciency _____
- Warehouse/storage method _____
- Transportation method _____
- Order-delivery lag _____
- Back order lost sales _____
- Logistics service features _____
- Overall strength _____

Trade relations
- Major channels used _____
- Image of channels _____
- Trade loyalty _____
- Trade promotions _____
- Trade advertising _____
- Overall strength _____

Advertising and promotion
- Message theme _____
- Past message themes _____
- Media used _____
- Schedule/seasonality _____
- Effectiveness _____
- Cost effeciency _____
- Consumer promotions _____
- Overall strength _____

Sales force
- Selling strategy _____
- Salesforce management _____
- Salesforce morale _____
- Salesforce turnover _____
- Salesforce selection _____
- Salesforce training _____
- Salesforce discipline _____
- Territory allocation _____
- Salesforce calling cycle & patterns _____
- Use of new technology (telemarketing, etc.) _____
- Service reputation _____
- Overall strength _____

Figure 4-6 continued.

Prospectors

Companies that follow the prospector strategy are aggressive innovators prepared to risk failure. Prospectors respond quickly to new ideas and seek them out from every possible source. They place high value on being first in the marketplace with new products or first into new markets. They emphasize the *innovation* component of innovation-imitation.

Analyzers

Firms that emphasize the analyzer strategy monitor the prospectors and adopt their ideas by coming out with their own products, which may have additional superior features, may be lower priced, or may be offered through a superior marketing program. Analyzers often make a commercial success out of a prospector's idea. They may well end up being perceived as the pioneering entrepreneur because they "made the market" for a product that an innovating prospector invented. They emphasize the *imitation* component of innovation-imitation.

Defenders

Firms that can be described as defenders stick to a market or market segment that they know, and they defend it by raising quality and lowering price. Their distinctive characteristic is their single-minded focus on meeting the needs of their existing customers and potential customers who are like their existing customers. They know these people very well and make the most of that knowledge. They innovate and imitate narrowly.

Reactors

Reactor companies are complacent. They only respond to competitive innovations when they absolutely must, which is often too late.

The first three types of companies are active scanners of the marketplace for information about new product ideas, although they tend to scan different types of information. Prospectors look everywhere, analyzers focus on what the competition is doing, and defenders focus on their specific markets. Reactors do very little environmental scanning. The central lesson from the ideas of Miles and Snow is that top management creates the internal environment for the pursuit of new opportunities.

However, much still depends on the quality of the individuals or teams making the current decisions. If they are fixed in their ways, then their thinking may be rigid and old-fashioned and their vision myopic. On the other hand, if they are young and inexperienced, then they may be too impulsive and trigger happy. Assessing decision-making skills involves identifying the skills of the old hands and any new executives who may have been recently hired. When a company is taken over or merges with a strong marketing-oriented company, this often results in an injection of managerial strength that is likely to lead to at least a lot of sound and fury (this occurred when Philip Morris took over the Miller Brewing Company). Sometimes, however, it can lead to the disillusionment of current quality managers who may then resign, leaving an experience vacuum during the transition and the competitor very vulnerable. It is important to base the evaluation of a company's experience and knowledge on the reputation of the managers *currently* making the decisions rather than any general reputation the firm has earned over the years. The firm's current decision-making *processes* also need to be assessed; for example, have they recently moved to decentralized, cross-functional team decision making?

The quality of a firm's intelligence gathering and R&D is not necessarily related to years of experience in the market. By investing shrewdly, a new entrant in these areas can quickly acquire a lot of knowledge and experience, and through the right combination of imitation and innovation, it can leapfrog ahead of established firms. Consequently, a competitor's major market research and R&D projects are often early warning signals of a major new strategic effort or change of direction.

Added-Value Chain Competitive Analysis

Michael Porter has argued that competitive advantage in product and service quality and costs can come from one or more of the following stages in the added-value chain:[14]

1. Inbound logistics
2. Operations
3. Outbound logistics
4. Marketing and sales
5. Service

The implication is that a rival's competitive standing at all stages of the added-value chain from inbound logistics through to after-sales service must be studied. The analysis form presented in Figure 4-6 addresses each of these stages of the order-delivery cycle.

Before proceeding to discuss the headings in Figure 4-6, the comments and ratings used to evaluate the competitor need to be explained. The comments should be as specific and concrete as possible, stating facts and, when considered necessary, referencing the source. This will help establish the validity and reliability of important conclusions and will enable the interested reader to follow up and obtain more information. Assumptions and rumor should be stated as such to avoid confusion with fact. The rating is proposed as a tool to make comparisons between competitors and your own enterprise. This relative rating (say on a scale of 1 to 10 with 5 being average) highlights both the direction and the extent of the difference on each of the dimensions of added value. Finally, the reality is that few competitive analyses will be as detailed as suggested in Figure 4-6. Often, there is not even enough information available to make a good assumption about a competitor's particular skill. In reality, comments are likely to focus on aspects of a rival's competence or behavior that has recently changed. Hence, the headings in Figure 4-6 are provided as prompts to help thoroughly review a rival's competitive situation.

Financial Position

The financial importance of the product-market to the competitor tells us how aggressively it is likely to respond. In hindsight, Procter & Gamble may have regretted taking on General Foods in the coffee market because Maxwell House was a very important profit earner for General Foods. General Foods fought tooth and nail against the market expansion efforts of P&G's Folgers brand.

Cash flow problems may increase the possibility that the competitor will dump stocks by slashing prices or using trade deals to pump inventory down the channel. But it may also mean the competitor will not be able to maintain its voice share and mind share against an aggressive advertising or promotional assault on its market

14. Michael E. Porter, *Competitive Advantage* (New York: The Free Press, 1985).

share. A competitor's potential access to long-term capital through its parent company—by borrowing (as indicated by its leverage or its debt to assets ratio) or by issuing more shares (indicated by its share earnings ratio and stock price)—enables some predictions to be made about whether it can keep investing in an expanding market or new production and distribution technology. The leveraged buyout frenzy of the 1980s left more than a few major companies up to their necks in debt. It is likely that the resulting inability to raise money to invest in the business will greatly affect their long-term competitiveness. A rival's estimated average contribution margin, marginal costs, fixed costs, and capacity utilization all indicate its ability to sustain a price war and expand its market share.

Market Positioning

What is the competitor's targeting-positioning strategy? How well is this executed in the sense that the competitor's positioning really appeals to the target segment or segments? These truly fundamental questions must be answered at the time a firm decides on its own positioning and are discussed at length in Chapter 8 when we discuss the positioning strategy. Apart from talking to distributors and buyers, much can be deduced about a rival's target audience from the advertising media it chooses. What it says in its advertising claims tells a lot about how it is positioning and differentiating its products and services.

A study of a competitor's entire product line or service offering may enable you to understand which segmentation framework has been used to develop its product positioning and marketing tactics (is it demographic, benefit, usage situation, heavy user?). This knowledge will help anticipate a competitor's reactions and in particular its blind spots.

The operating performance and durability of the competitor's product can be established in the laboratory, in market research user trials, or surveys of distributors and independent service outlets. Consumer testing organizations such as *Consumer Reports* can also provide some free and independent evaluations of a competitor's products.

Pricing

List prices often have little relevance because of promotions and special discounts. Consequently, it is important to establish what is the lowest, typical, and highest billed prices of each item in the competitor's product line. This variation tells you something about its choice of loss leaders, the problem items in its line, and its high demand items (these will be the least discounted). Price trends over time may suggest a deliberate repositioning of the line. It may also simply reflect cost control problems. An understanding of how the competitor sets its prices (for instance cost-plus or competitive parity) may enable you to further interpret changes in price. Information on the recency of price changes, particularly during periods of price inflation created by cost increases, may enable you to anticipate a competitor's price increase in the planning period and develop contingency plans.

Your analysis of pricing must often go beyond purchase price to a consideration of the life-cycle cost to the consumer of the competitor's product. A rival may be very competitive on the purchase price but, because of service charges or running costs, it may be a very expensive buy over the life of the product compared with your product (or vice versa). This is a particularly telling analysis in industrial marketing and is often the basis of the competitive advantage for the seller producing the highest quality, most reliable product.

Production

In recent years, production and operations have become a major strategic concern in many markets. Automation and workflow innovations have dramatically lowered costs, boosted productivity, and reduced reject rates and wastage. Production performance characteristics are leading indicators of changes in the quality image of a competitor's product and pricing.

Knowledge of short-term production capacity enables some estimate to be made of constraints on a competitor's likely behavior. If a competitor is working at or near to its production capacity, it is not in a position to capture new business in an expanding market or to threaten a rival's market share if the competitor raises prices. On the other hand, if a competitor has slack capacity, the competitor may be tempted to lower its prices.

The period during which a company is in the process of retooling or renovating is a good time to make an assault on its market. General Motors was given its golden opportunity by Henry Ford when he closed his factories down for a good part of 1928 to retool his plant to produce the Model A rather than the Model T. Many of Ford's loyal customers who wanted to buy a new car that year turned to GM and never returned to Ford. The effect on Ford's distribution network and channel goodwill was very serious.

A competitor's labor relations and labor turnover may have a number of implications for the short term. High labor turnover may indicate low morale, lower average worker skills, and a consequent decline in product quality and productivity. Poor labor relations may also have a creeping debilitating effect on quality and service. The effects of labor relations can also be sudden and dramatic in a unionized industry when a union picks on a particular competitor and the result is a strike or a lockout. To the extent that such events can be anticipated in the short term, preparations can be made to serve that competitor's customers. A further very serious effect is that labor unrest can so preoccupy management that it neglects the interests of resellers and customers. When management becomes less alert and less responsive to changes in the market, then the company is always more vulnerable to attack.

Distribution and Logistics

Inventory levels and the stock control methods of competitors give clues as to the vulnerability and problems of a competitor. High inventory levels may suggest problems with product acceptance, but they could also mean that the competitor is about to launch a special promotion campaign. The efficiency of the competitor's stock control system indicates the likelihood that the competitor will ultimately hurt itself by either tying up too much working capital in stock or investing too little in finished stock, which results in poor service and stock-outs. Some competitors will operate a system that is chronically overstocked or understocked. Other competitors will fluctuate between the two extremes by constantly overreacting to overstocking or stock-out crises.

Sources of supply should be looked at because the price and quality of raw materials are often the basis for product differentiation and cost competitiveness. Skilled purchasing for competitive advantage has been a neglected area of business policy and marketing management and will become even more important with the globalization of supply sources. When a rival changes its source of supply, it is particularly important to find out why (perhaps from the old sources) as it may suggest a change in product design, a technological breakthrough, a significant raw materials price advantage, or the possibility that the competitor knows more about long-term reserves of raw material than you do.

The competitor's transportation and storage system says a lot about that competitor's service tactics, which will be reflected in its average order-delivery time and its spare parts service. The geographical positioning and size of new warehouse facilities gives clear leading indicators of a firm's long-term logistics strategy. What is often overlooked is that a firm's logistics and distribution system may face undercapacity and overcapacity problems that are just as important to costs and service as a firm's production under- or overcapacity. A firm's distribution-logistics system can also be less adaptive than its production system because it involves agreements and contractual arrangements with third parties who, in their own self-interest, may become very inflexible.

Advertising and Promotion

The reasons for studying a competitor's advertising and promotions are obvious. What is of particular interest is how its product positioning has changed over time. Changes may suggest 1) problems with previous product positioning, 2) new insights resulting from market research, or 3) simply a new advertising agency that has suggested a new campaign theme. The agency may have come up with a campaign that, while creative and attention-grabbing, is not well integrated with the competitor's overall marketing tactics and product positioning. The creativity and attention-grabbing appeal of a competitor's advertising is obvious and often intimidating. What is not so clear is whether its positioning is really getting through to the customer. Consequently, it is just as important and useful to ask target customers to explain and give their reactions to competitor's advertising and promotions as it is to ask the same target customers to react to your own advertising and promotions.

The competitor's media tactics measured in terms of volume and size (extent of campaign), choice of media (indicating its target market), and seasonality need to be studied so that the company can plan its own purchase of media space and the timing of its campaigns in the next planning period. Much of this part of the competitor analysis should be prepared, as a matter of course, by the advertising agency.

Trade Relations and Sales Management

This area, along with promotion, is probably the easiest part of a competitor analysis to undertake because information is so readily obtainable from trade sources. The problem is in getting information that has not been filtered or deliberately distorted by resellers intent on playing one supplier against another. The first aspect in this area that needs to be identified is the overall nature of the competitor's distribution system (for instance, is its emphasis on franchising, particular types of retailers, image, or location) and how it is changing. This often requires an understanding of how the distribution system evolved historically. Monitoring trade loyalty may reveal a sharp difference in goodwill between different types of resellers toward the rival or problems in a particular region or at a particular time, such as after a bungled promotion or product introduction.

It is important to establish whether the competitor's loss of loyalty and channel cooperation is the result of a weak positioning strategy or poor execution before any attempt is made to exploit the competitor's misfortune. The idea may have had merit, and with a little modification and much better execution, your company could benefit from the competitor's learning experience. Trade advertising, trade promotions, trade shows, in-store or warehouse promotions, displays, and new competitor shelf-space management programs need to be watched carefully so as to spot new competitive thrusts and product repositioning before it is too late to react effectively.

Sales force selection criteria and training indicate the importance the competitor places on sales management in its long-term competitive strategy. Changes in the reward system (particularly the basis for bonuses) and the sales control system are indicators of likely changes in the resourcefulness and aggressiveness of the competitor's sales force. The reward system, calling-cycles, and sales territories often give away the competitor's target segments, selling priorities, and its overall marketing objectives.

Anticipating Competitor Behavior

Even after you have gone to great lengths to assess a competitor's strengths and weaknesses and to predict its behavior, you cannot view these results as a given. Competitors will be responsive to your behavior and the more your behavior is effective the more it will disturb market equilibrium and almost guarantee a competitive response. An analysis of the competitive environment can tell you what likely initiatives rivals can and will mount and their ability to respond. What it cannot tell you is what the final outcome will be of the interaction between your initiatives, their initiatives, and the sequence of counter-responses.

The first step in anticipating a competitor's likely behavior is, as explained earlier, to understand its current objectives, its self-perceptions, and how it thinks about the product-market, that is, its competitive rationality. A second step is to study the past decision-making and general personal style of the competitor's key decision makers. Have they sent signals in the past indicating how they would respond to having their market share and brand image attacked? Are such threats credible in that they have always followed through or do they frequently blow smoke? Do they respond rationally or emotionally? If the competitor's marketing planners are fixed in their thinking and ways, as many executives are, then studying their past behavior and reactions (even if they occurred in different product-markets) will very likely be a good predictor of how they are likely to behave in the future. Senior executives are often very good intuitive judges of the mindsets of rivals as they have played against them for years.

A third step is to become fully acquainted with any "game playing" rules that may exist in the industry and that may enable you to predict competitor response. Regrettably, there are few, if any, analytic tools available to predict a competitor's response. Such a predictor would require a computer-based simulation that accurately anticipates all of the moves of players in the marketplace, which is impossible. One of the ironies of economic theory is that so many of the models assume that the marketplace will quickly settle into a steady state equilibrium.[15] It is ironic because the theory of competitive rationality asserts that a marketing planner's mission in life is to constantly find ways of profiting from disturbing such equilibrium. If a new marketing strategy does not disturb competitive equilibrium, then it is not having any impact on the market. The box titled "Swept Along and Swept Away by the VCR Boom" demonstrates the dynamic and complex interplay between competitors that occurs in a market.

While trying to predict competitor behavior by using analytic models does not seem feasible, it is still sensible to attempt to anticipate and play through the most likely consequences of your planned strategy. This can be done by asking and answering the following questions:

15. K. Sridhar Moorthy, "Using Game Theory to Model Competition," *Journal of Marketing Research* 12 (August 1985), 262–82.

Rationality in Practice:

Swept Along and Swept Away by the VCR Boom

In 1984, some seven million VCRs were sold in the United States, raising the proportion of U.S. households that own a video cassette recorder to about 20 percent. Market penetration had hit 40 percent by 1986 and in 1989 over 60 percent of U.S. households had a VCR. Over a period of about five years, the evolution of the VCR product-market had a dramatic effect on complementary and substitute products such as the sales of color television sets and blank video tapes, video movie rentals, library usage, and network television viewing. It also helped revive the sagging audio-TV retail sector.

The video disc product-market was the big loser. RCA took a $580 million loss on its disc player, which it doggedly marketed from 1981 through 1984. RCA chose to develop disc rather than tape technology because it 1) did not believe the consumer really wanted a recorder/player and 2) did not believe that a mass-produced tape pickup head could be manufactured that would record and reproduce a quality picture. Sony and JVC proved them wrong. Despite the fact that for two decades Japanese ingenuity had time and time again demonstrated its ability to halve, and halve again, the production costs of electronic equipment, RCA also did not expect the VCR to drop in price so rapidly (from over $1,000 in 1979 to under $300 in 1984 and $200 in 1988). All is not lost for the video disc, however; the product has found a new market niche, changed its appearance, and developed new organs. It has mutated into a splendid computer data-storage device.

Sony also made its biggest marketing mistake with VCRs (according to founder Akio Morita) by sticking with its Beta format, which it had hoped to make the industry standard. The switch in standard from Beta to VHS caused only a hesitation in the development of the product-market. For too long Sony fought the new standard. Pride dominated pragmatics and profits.

The VCR software business boomed in the 1980s. By 1984 some 120 million video cassettes were being sold annually at a market value of $700 million. But the industry was heading toward a major price war and shake-out between such daunting competitors as Polaroid, Kodak, 3M, Fuji, Sony, Memorex, Maxell, and Basf. As distribution moved from the appliance store to the already crowded shelves of the drugstore, supermarket, and discount store, some manufacturers were beginning to sell solely on price. Others were desperately attempting to establish a brand image before it was too late by marketing heavily promoted high-grade, high-margin tapes. This turned out to be unsuccessful as buyers were not able to perceive any difference between the tapes. Blank VCR tapes have become a commodity product. In 1987, 300 million blank VHS tapes were sold at a market value of just over $1 billion.

In 1984, the Video Software Dealers Association's annual convention attracted 2,000 people, triple the 1983

1. What will be the competitive responses to our new strategy?
2. What impact will this have on the market?
3. How will we respond?
4. What will be the repercussion of our response on (a) the marketplace and (b) our financial performance goals?
5. Return to number 1.

It is often useful for members of a marketing team to role play as competitors in such an exercise. A sufficient number of such iterations often leads one to conclude, "I think I'd better think it through again." For example, Pepperidge Farm certainly wished it had thought its plan through once more after launching its branded, high-quality, premium-priced blended apple juice. Other juice manufacturers slashed retail prices by more than 40 percent, reducing their price to 99 cents a gallon. This particularly hurt Pepperidge Farm as it had invested up-front to make the juice on its own rather than contract it to outside producers and packers. In 1981, Honda and Yamaha each had a 35 percent share of the motorcycle market. That same year, Yamaha announced its intentions to become number 1 and introduced 60 new models. Honda launched 63 new or modified models and announced that Yamaha had stepped on the

Blockbuster Video was the big winner in the shakedown of the video-rental market.

attendance. Some 12,000 specialty video outlets were selling and renting video cassettes, but they were facing increasing competition from thousands of bookstores, grocery stores, movie theaters, and even U-Haul rental agencies moonlighting as video cassette rental outlets! Many of the nonconventional outlets were charging as low as $2 for a one-night rental, half the fee the video stores were charging, but they did not offer the same selection. Start-up costs were low and profits were high. Everything looked rosy.

In 1985, some 50 million videos were sold and 1.2 billion were rented, more than the 1.1 billion books checked out from public libraries. Sales of color television sets were

up 40 percent in 1983 and up another 25 percent in 1984. More than 100 million movie videos were sold in 1987 as prices of box office hits were slashed from $89.95 to $29.95 to encourage buying rather than renting. Sales did not stop the renting, however, which experienced similar growth. Major chains such as Kmart and 7-Eleven were now renting for as low as 99 cents a night.

The writing was on the wall for most of the 25,000 rental outlets. Sales started to level off. Most households had seen *Top Gun, Gone With the Wind,* and every other movie they had wanted to see as many times as they could stand. The pool of software was running out. Worse, by 1989 some discount stores were renting three tapes for a dollar. The video rental business had boomed and busted in five years, leaving Blockbuster Video the big winner.

The growth of the VCR product-market resulted in the extinction of the video disc product and laid the foundation for the dynamic growth of the video movie rental market. The evolution of the VCR product-market created a wave that washed into several other new and mature markets. Even the marketing experts did not anticipate the rapid rise and fall of the video tape rental industry.

Sources: "The Anatomy of RCA's Videodisc Failure," *Business Week,* April 23, 1984, 89–90; "The VCR Boom Puts Blank Tapes in Fast Forward," *Business Week,* August 6, 1984, 92–93; Susan Spillman, "Videocassette Rental Sites in Darndest Spots," *Advertising Age,* August 30, 1984, 1–5; Alex Ben Block, "Hard Dollars in Video Software," *Forbes,* June 17, 1985, 128–32; Stephen Kindel, "Goodbye, TV Hello, Video," *Forbes,* July 1, 1985, 100–101; and Randy Pitman, "A Tale of Two Cultures: The Video Business and Libraries," *Wilson Library Bulletin,* May 1988, 27–28.

tiger's tail. Over the next eighteen months, Honda introduced 81 new models, Yamaha 37. The market was flooded and prices were slashed. In 1983, Honda introduced 110 more models. Yamaha introduced only 23 models in 1983 and in 1984 had to sell assets and cut salaries.[16] If Yamaha had understood how fiercely Honda would react, it probably would have pursued a less aggressive and outspoken strategy.

Predicting What-If Effects Using a Relationship Matrix

If changes in reseller trading relationships are planned, then a relationship matrix can also be used to study likely competitive repercussions. For example, in Table 4-1a, an attempt by manufacturer Y to sell to distributor E may well be seen by Manufacturer Z as threatening its sales to the distributor and its overall market share. The most likely retaliatory action could be the establishment of a trading relationship between Z and C. The net effect could give new trading relationship Y-E a 2 percent market share taken from Z-E but in return the new relationship Z-C could grow to 2 percent (taken from Y-C). A Y-E move might produce reactions as well from X and the other

16. R. B. Kennard, "From Experience: Japanese Product Development Process," *Journal of Product Innovation Management* 8 (1991), 184–88.

distributors, which would disturb all the channel relationships. The new situation might indeed be preferred, but situations may arise in which a supplier or reseller will think twice after following through the likely repercussions of such a move. Of course, the profitability of any change in trading relationships must also be considered. P&G's much publicized close working relationship with Wal-Mart has led to the growth in Wal-Mart's sales of P&G products, somewhat at the expense of P&G's trading relationships with its more traditional distributors. The problem for P&G is that the expanding business relationship with Wal-Mart may ultimately be less profitable than the old business relationships because the profit margins may be lower.

It is encouraging when strategy and tactics stand up to such an analysis. However, it should be recognized that the analysis is still highly speculative. In truth, there does not seem to be a way around this planning problem. That is why so much emphasis was placed on alertness and speed of response in the opening chapters. Every firm should constantly update its competitive analysis and re-evaluate its behavior in the light of the new facts. Foresight is better than hindsight, but fast hindsight (seeing things as soon as they have happened) is a lot better than slow hindsight.

Analyzing Competition in Foreign Markets

Much has been written about global competitiveness but few generalizations or conclusions can be made. Each foreign market differs in its competitive structure, as analyzed using Figure 4-1. What we do know is that fierce domestic rivalry produces firms that are superbly conditioned to compete in foreign markets and the general global market. This is the major argument against government policy that protects long-established domestic firms.

In foreign markets such as Southeast Asia, the labor cost has been low and the labor productivity has been high. In other foreign markets such as Japan, the cost of capital has been low and hence the cost of investing in new plant and equipment has been low. The basic theory of how production functions in economics tells us that output is determined by labor and capital inputs. The powering coefficients associated with labor and capital reflect the efficient and effective use of labor and capital (that is, competitive rationality). As long as the United States is prosperous, its semiskilled and unskilled labor force will never be price competitive with the labor forces available in emerging countries. As long as its saving rate is low (a cultural characteristic) compared to Japan and Germany, the U.S. cost of capital will never be lower. The solution is clear. U.S. firms must employ superior technology and management to overcome their labor cost and capital cost disadvantages. American scientists, engineers, and managers must be more insightful, innovative, and adaptable, particularly when it comes to working together on product design and flexible manufacturing. U.S. manufacturing skills fell far behind those in other countries in many industries from the mid-1960s to the mid-1980s.[17] For example, GM senior management was stunned when Toyota managers (in a joint venture) made a mothballed California assembly plant with old equipment into GM's most efficient factory; in fact, it was twice as productive as a typical GM plant.

American firms must also be prepared to become global enterprises by using cheap labor and cheap capital where they can be obtained. The global market has a larger and more diverse group of players, but competitiveness in the global market is no different in theory or in practice than competitiveness in the domestic market—it still comes down to outthinking, outrunning, and outlasting rivals.

17. "Can America Compete," *Business Week*, April 20, 1987, 44–69.

There has been a lot of brave talk about making American companies more competitive. But in reality, many of the companies whose leaders are talking this way will budget tens, even hundreds of thousands of dollars on consumer research but will balk at the suggestion that a fraction of this money should be spent on gathering competitive intelligence. For many firms, market research means only consumer research. This situation must change. If American companies are going to become competitive, they must know what they are up against. They need to be informed and stay informed about their competition in every market around the globe.

Discussion Questions and Minicases

1. Researchers at the Wharton Business School presented students with a simple problem involving a choice between the following:[18]
   a. Keeping the price of a product low, causing competition to suffer substantial losses; or
   b. Maintaining a higher price that would produce higher long-term profits but would also allow the competition to prosper.

   The results of over 30 experiments were very disturbing. Some 40 percent of the students preferred to hurt the competition rather than maximize profits for their owners. Why do you think the students were so aggressive?

2. Given the following shares, please analyze the competitive position of *A*.

	1989 (%)				1990 (%)				1991 (%)			
	A	B	C	D	A	B	C	D	A	B	C	D
R&D share	30	20	25	25	25	25	25	25	20	30	25	25
Voice share	30	25	25	20	40	25	15	20	40	20	20	20
Mind share	40	30	20	10	50	25	15	10	50	30	10	10
Market share	40	25	20	15	40	25	20	15	30	30	20	20

3. A relationship matrix would not provide any useful information if each seller's market share of each reseller's sales were equal to the seller's overall market share and vice versa. Such a balanced relationship structure is an extremely unlikely event. Please change Table 4-1a so that all of the relationships are so balanced, and contrast it with the original Table 4-1a and Table 4-1b.

4. How might the types of consumer loyalty identified in the last chapter be used to assess the competitive position of rivals? What questions does this raise about market share?

5. Name two different technologies that are competing with the greeting card business? What do you think is going to happen in the long-term as these product-markets converge?

6. The local baby bell telephone companies and the cable TV companies appear to be converging on the broad-band, fiber-optic, communication and entertainment market. In 1992 Congress was trying to decide whether to allow telephone

18. J. Scott Armstrong, Robert H. Colgrove, and Fred Collopy, "Competitor-Oriented Objectives and Their Effects on Long-term Profitability," Working Paper, Wharton Business School, University of Pennsylvania, January 1993.

companies to offer cable TV services. What strengths and weaknesses do the two types of companies bring to the impending clash in the marketplace?

7. In 1984, American Express Merchandise sold over $200 million through its mail-order business. Its best selling items were VCRs, Gucci watches, grandfather clocks, and IBM typewriters. About 6 million cardholders got billing inserts and two million hot prospects got solo mailings, including catalogs. By 1989, Amexco's direct marketing sales were higher than L.L. Bean's mail order sales. What sort of competitive move has Amexco made? What is its big advantage?

8. AT&T and IBM appear to be inevitably converging as competitors. AT&T has taken over NCR to add to its Olivetti investment in computers. IBM is developing new networking hardware that links computers by optical fibre and standard telephone lines. Ultimately, in what product-market do you think they will compete the fiercest?

9. Give two examples of industries or specific corporations that generally present formidable barriers to entry but also tend to be trapped by their resources. Why is this so? When does it matter?

10. A competitor threat audit reveals a possible threat from a new entrant firm into a product-market. What is likely to be its motive? If you were in the competitor's shoes, what would be your major reason for entering the market? What implications does it have for existing competitors and what dilemma does this create for public companies compared to private companies?

11. General Motors purchased Electronic Data Systems for $2.5 billion. GM is EDS's biggest customer as it streamlines and integrates its own morass of computer systems, including its linkages with suppliers and dealers.[19] This variant of backward integration (of a service rather than a raw material or component's supplier) into the $20 billion computer services industry will inevitably bring GM into competition with the hardware-software systems giants. In another transaction, Exxon invested over $1 billion in venture capital in office automation ideas for over a decade. In 1980 the objective of its information systems division was to become a major supplier of advanced office systems and communication systems to large customers within 3 to 5 years. But in late 1984 Exxon sold the business.[20] What is your theory as to why General Motors purchased Electronic Data Systems? What opportunities for GM might emerge from this transaction? On the other hand, what might GM learn from Exxon in this particular market?

12. Managers of mutual funds often talk about investing in companies with superior management. Use the theory of competitive rationality to develop a list of criteria to evaluate the superior management of a rival or investment opportunity. Does it matter whether the superior management is the result of superior systems, superior processes, or superior people?

13. What might changes in a competitor's advertising message themes over time reveal? What might an analysis of its media strategy reveal?

14. Some product-markets maintain rules of behavior called industry or professional practices. List some examples. How and why do you think they have come about?

15. The two boxed cases in this chapter present a brief history of two markets: the mature beer market that experienced the Lite beer innovation and the relatively

19. Stephen Koepp, "Driving into the Computer Age," *Time,* July 9, 1984, 65.
20. Marilyn Harris, "Exxon Wants Out of the Automated Office," *Business Week,* December 17, 1984, 39; and "Exxon's Next Prey: IBM and Xerox," *Business Week,* April 28, 1980, 92–103.

new VCR and video tape markets. These examples demonstrate the importance of being able to anticipate competitor behavior. Using library reference sources, write a one-page report that brings these two case studies up to date. Do you think that what happened in these two markets could have been anticipated? How?

16. Below are two very prescriptive learning propositions. How are they supported by the competitive rationality theory premises and propositions presented in this chapter and Chapter 1? (Hint: Consider Figure 1.1 and the Third Competitive Rationality drive.)

    PD Proposition: A firm should *constantly* study its ongoing product development (PD) process with the objective of improving the quality of the decisions made in the PD process and increasing the effectiveness of the implementation routine scripts within the overall process.

    OD Proposition: A firm should *constantly* study its order-delivery cycle (OD) process with the objective of improving the quality of the decisions made in the OD processes and increasing the effectiveness of the implementation routine scripts within the order-delivery cycle process.

17. What sorts of mental skills do you think are required to undertake the competitive conjecture described on page 147? Do you think that engineering training provides such skills more than training in accounting, law, or parenting? (Hint: See Chapter 14.)

18. Use the section on anticipating competitors' behavior to explain why competition is a lot more intense when a company has two or more competitors rather than just one competitor. Why is the drive to innovate with new products and the drive to reduce costs so much stronger and more constant when a company has more than one competitor? What does this suggest about the number of sellers it takes to make a market competitive and keep it competitive?

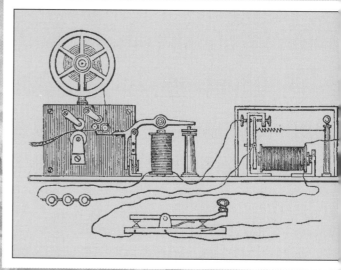

CHAPTER

5

Analyzing
Market Channels

"Open the windows, let in the year we're living in."
Kitty D'Alessio

*"You on the cutting edge of technology have
already made yesterday's impossibilities the
commonplace realities of today."*
Ronald Reagan

*T*he majority of marketplace exchanges made today involve the use of a trading channel—third-party legal entities that are separate from the original seller and the final buyer. The trading channels marketers use play a critical role in determining competitive advantage. The obvious channels are resellers, such as wholesalers, importers, retailers, commission agents, and brokers, but any entity that is employed to facilitate the exchange process can serve as a trading channel. Banks and shipping agents help the payment process, advertising agents and trade show organizers facilitate the flow of information, and common carriers and the public warehouses facilitate the flow of goods.

In a marketplace, where the players are free to choose what to sell and what to buy, channels survive and flourish because both buyers and sellers pay them to perform particular functions. The services of the many and varied organizations that can make up a marketing channel are not just important to the individual seller. Economic history demonstrates that channel intermediaries have, through their entrepreneurial marketing innovations, played a crucial role in creating and shaping the modern U.S. economy. Many of the significant differences between today's international economies can be traced to the evolution of very effective trading channel relationships.

Because the choice of channel partners, be it up or down the channel, has a profound effect on the profitability of a business, a marketing plan for a venture in a market that uses trading channels should include an analysis of current and potential channel members and exchange facilitators. This analysis can prove to be as important as an audit of the consumer or the competition.

In order to address the economic and political problems that may arise from trading channel relationships, marketers must maintain the following:

1. A macroeconomic understanding of how and why the different types of channel services and participants evolved.

2. An understanding of the major changes occurring today in channels of distribution.

The first section of this chapter traces the origins of some of the major marketing intermediaries in the United States. Understanding how channels evolved helps to explain how and why they are likely to change in the future. The development of trading channels is also an excellent demonstration of evolutionary economics. Much of the change in the organization of marketing channels can be traced to the ways that entrepreneurs have used technological inventions to increase the effectiveness and efficiency of the flow of money, information, goods, and services. Social and political events have also created entrepreneurial opportunities.

The second section discusses how some of the technological and institutional changes occurring today are likely to reshape distribution channel relationships. The third section describes the basic function of intermediaries. The final section presents a general audit template that can be adapted to evaluate suppliers and distributors. The chapter concludes with a discussion of some of the issues involved in evaluating channel facilitators such as banks.

Keep the following key issues in mind as you read through this chapter:

■ The modern market economy was created by wholesale merchants and retailers, not by large manufacturers.

■ Technical innovations, such as the development of the telegraph and railroads, changed the village economy into a national economy. New technologies, such as computers, satellites, and jumbo jets, are changing national economies into a global economy.

■ Physical distribution channels are becoming integrated by information and transportation conglomerates.

■ New, low-cost distribution channels, such as Wholesale Clubs, are changing the nature of some product-markets.

■ Franchising enables a new retailing innovation to spread rapidly into new geographical markets.

■ Many different forms of channel intermediaries exist. They vary in their skills and competence, cost efficiencies, and willingness to allow a manufacturer to control what they do.

■ Channel resellers should be evaluated on the history of their trading performance, market positioning, competitive effort, and purchasing behavior.

■ A seller needs to monitor how its trading relationships with its portfolio of distributors or types of channels is changing.

■ Even sellers who do not use distribution channels use facilitator relationships that help them find and serve customers more competitively.

■ The global marketer has to find the key to the unique distribution channels that exist in each national economy.

■ An increase in global sources of supply increases the power and potential profits of well-managed and well-positioned distributors and retailers in the United States.

Marketing Channels That Created the Modern Economy

The folklore of marketing has held that mass marketing came about as a result of mass production. In truth, it was the other way around. In his Pulitzer Prize–winning book, *The Visible Hand,* Alfred Chandler convincingly argues that the evolution of distribution channels in the United States can be traced to changes in the transportation and communication infrastructure, largely caused by the huge investment made in developing the national railway system.[1] The improvements in physical distribution provided by the railway and steamship over the sailing ship, canal barge, and wagon, and the improved communication provided by the telegraph over the primitive mail service, enabled the creation and growth of the large centralized wholesaling companies. These institutions, in turn, created mass production.

Until the mid-19th century, there were no economies of scale in mass production because, simply put, the cost of distributing beyond local markets was prohibitive or physically impossible. No economic entities existed that could undertake the necessary distribution functions. Banks, insurers, and local common carriers had evolved, where previously the general merchant had undertaken all of these functions, but the standard operating procedures of commerce were basically little different from those developed by the Venetian merchant dynasties back in the 15th century. The colonial merchant families funded shipping ventures, built ports and warehouses, financed crops and goods in transit, and loaned money to local artisans. In essence, almost all businesses still served local markets.

1. Alfred D. Chandler, *The Visible Hand* (Cambridge, MA: Harvard University Press, 1977). Chandler presents an excellent history of the development of modern management.

A Change in Scale

A sudden change in scale of operations occurred between 1840 and 1870. The largest importers in the 1840s had annual sales of around $250,000 and employed fewer than 20 employees. By 1870, Alexander T. Stewart, the largest dry-goods wholesaler/importer, had annual sales in excess of $40 million and employed a buying and selling organization of 2,000 persons.[2] Prior to the transportation revolution, merchants sold the products of local manufacturers, local agriculture industries, and imported goods to storekeepers, some of whom had to trek hundreds of miles every six months to buy their supplies. Having purchased the goods, the storekeepers then had to arrange a complicated and risky delivery chain involving numerous regional carriers and storehouses so that goods could be unloaded and prepared to await the next barge or wagon. There was much spoilage, damage, theft, and delay.

By the 1860s, a new form of merchant, the wholesale jobber had evolved. Wholesalers did not sell on a commission of 2 to 5 percent but instead took title to the goods. The sellers were happy because they now received prompt payment. The buyers were happy because the railway brought the wholesaler's traveling salesman to the buyer's door with samples, catalogs, and a more reliable and less expensive delivery service. The wholesaler system also resulted in further cost savings because safety inventories needed to avoid the stock-outs caused by delivery uncertainty could be reduced. Of even greater significance, the wholesaler could now define its markets in national terms and gain huge economies of scale from bulk purchasing and buying expertise.

The wholesalers also flourished because of fortuitous political events. As Europe returned to economic stability after the ravages of the Napoleonic Wars, its production rose and it sought export markets. A flood of imports came in and were auctioned off to the wholesale jobbers (at bargain prices) instead of being presold to the traditional merchants. Between 1821 and 1830, 40 percent of the imports through the port of New York (20 percent of all imports into the United States) were sold by auction, mostly to the new wholesale jobbers. The tragic Civil War further benefited the jobbers supplying the armies. In these ways, domestic and global politics spawned and nourished an economic innovation.

The Wholesale Buyer: Large Orders and Mass Production

The wholesaler's traveling sales forces spearheaded the mass marketing revolution. They introduced new products, spread merchandising innovations, and taught local retailers the rudiments of bookkeeping and retail management. The sales forces also reported back on regional economic conditions, new products and ideas, changes in demand, and retailer credit ratings.

It is interesting to note that at the very time these economic pioneers were helping to build a new industrial state, Karl Marx was characterizing this new class of "bourgeois" traders as economic leeches in *Das Kapital* and quoting no less than Thomas Jefferson in support of his argument that channel intermediaries only make their money from lying and thieving. The characterization of manufacturing as more honorable and productive than distribution has its roots in such ill-informed, if well-intentioned, slanders.

The large sales force was a new phenomenon, but just as important was the emergence of a new breed of buyer who had developed expert knowledge of a particular product group. These buyers were given total autonomy and were often involved in profit-sharing plans. The fortunes of the wholesalers depended on their skills. The

2. Chandler, *The Visible Hand.*

buyer's expertise, built over years of experience, became greater than that of either the manufacturer (who often maintained a limited, parochial, local vision) or the end-user and was, consequently, worth paying for. Many wholesalers set up buying offices in Europe where they searched for better buys or new products. Separate traffic departments handled the shipping and negotiated special bulk rates with the railway and steamship companies. Credit and collection departments were set up that introduced standardized payment terms. The sheer scale of the wholesalers' operations gave them not only great buying power, but also the opportunity to encourage manufacturers to expand so as to be able to fill the wholesaler's large orders. In this sense, it is clear that mass distribution led and fostered the development of mass production.

Making Money From Stock-Turn Rather Than Margins

The wholesalers made even more money when they learned the basic law of retailing: profits come from margin *and* stock-turn. **Margin** is price minus direct manufacturing and marketing costs. **Stock-turn** is the number of times a firm's inventory turns over in a year (annual dollar sales divided by the dollar value of the annual average inventory). These new measures of performance were introduced in the 1860s, and the wholesalers particularly focused on stock-turn.

By 1880 the dominance of the wholesaler had peaked as enterprising local retailers vertically integrated up the channel by buying or merging with wholesalers or setting up their own wholesale operations. By now the consumer was also becoming more urban, sophisticated, and demanding. In such changing market conditions, the retailer benefited by being closest to the consumer.

Consistent with the theory of competitive rationality, when the market environment changes, the players who are first to notice such changes and adapt gain an initial, and perhaps permanent, advantage. The first department stores were set up in New York and quickly spread to the major urban centers. Profits were made on sales volume and stock-turn rather than on margins. In 1887, Macy's recorded an average stock-turn of 6 over six months—double the typical stock-turn of today's department stores, even with computerization. The department stores' lower prices wiped out many small retailers. The merchandising practices of the department store were little different from what they are today: extensive local advertising (that itself spawned the formation of advertising agencies), money-back guarantees, and mark-down sales of slow-turning items.

Mail-Order Houses and the Chain Store

Mail-order companies served rural buyers who found it difficult to shop locally, let alone visit the big-city department stores. Sears Roebuck was able to take advantage of the rapid improvement in postage and railway service in the 1890s. Its revenues increased geometrically from $745,000 in 1895 to $37,789,000 in 1905.[3] The mail-order houses were such a threat that the extension of the parcel post service introduced in 1912 was vigorously opposed by traditional wholesalers and retailers.

As the small towns and suburbs grew in the early decades of this century, other entrepreneurs saw the opportunity and grew their wholesaling or regional retailing operations into national chain stores. The first chain stores were grocers, drug stores, and furniture stores in urban markets where the department stores concentrated on clothing and furnishings. For example, in 1865 the Great American Tea Company (later

---

3. In fact, Sears' sales increased so rapidly that during the Christmas season of 1905 the company almost collapsed from within because it started to lose control of all of the orders and its shipping department became impossibly overloaded and chaotic. Great success can threaten a firm by overwhelming its logistics system.

A&P) sold only tea in 26 stores in downtown New York. The Great Western Tea Company (later Kroger) and the Jewel Tea Company started from a similar base of operation. Woolworth started the first five-and-dime variety store, in which all items were priced at either five or ten cents. By 1913, 680 such stores had sales of $66 million.[4] Other specialty chain stores flourished, such as the United Cigar Stores Company with 900 stores nationwide in 1914.

The chain stores operated in a way similar to the department store except that they required greater control over operations and logistics. The newly invented telephone and truck greatly assisted the management of these two activities. Many of the chains were also innovative in their management style. They gave managers a minority ownership of their store, and they operated the businesses in a manner similar to today's retail franchises. The competitive advantage of the chains came from their buying power, lower margins but higher stock-turn, scientific selection of store locations, standardized advertising, standardized store arrangement, window displays, sales training, inventory control, and cash-and-carry setup.[5] By the 1920s, the growth of the chain store had become so threatening that the two major mail-order houses, Montgomery Ward and Sears Roebuck, responded by opening their own chain stores. Other merchants attempted to have tax and price control legislation passed to combat the enterprise and initiatives of the chain stores.[6]

The Supermarket and Modern Retailing

The spread of the suburbs during the prosperity of the 1920s, coupled with increased automobile ownership, led to the development of the first suburban shopping centers (anchored by a supermarket) and shopping malls (anchored by major department and chain stores). During the Great Depression of the 1930s, which killed a lot of small merchants, the lower-priced supermarket flourished. For the first time, a single store sold meat, produce, and dry foods. Previously, the consumer had to shop at the butcher shop, the green-grocer, the bakery, the dairy, the drugstore, and the grocery store. Now they were all combined in a one-stop location that provided parking. The new refrigeration technology that provided in-home, in-store, and in-transit storage of perishables was also essential to the success of the supermarket.

Another innovation, self service—in which most of the inventory was stored on the display shelves rather than in a back storeroom—reduced labor and inventory holding costs, encouraged consumers to experiment with new products, and paved the way for brand-image marketing by manufacturers such as Pillsbury and Betty Crocker. This, coupled with the introduction of new advertising media (radio, magazines with superior graphics, and finally television), launched the golden era of household brands marketing (1950–1990).

In the 1950s, suburban shopping started to overshadow downtown shopping. Inner-city congestion and decay diminished the entertainment value of what had once been a special family event (dressing up to go shopping downtown on Friday night). By the mid-1960s, the shopping mall had evolved into its current form—anchor stores

---

4. Ralph S. Butler, *Marketing Methods and Salesmanship* (New York: Alexander Hamilton Institute, 1914), 47. This book was one of the first marketing management texts ever published.
5. Butler, *Marketing Methods.*
6. The Robinson-Patman Fair Pricing Law was the result. It required a manufacturer to administer its prices so that it sold its products at much the same price to all retailers. This law, which obviously runs counter to the spirit of the Sherman Act's *price-fixing* clauses, protected the interests of economically inefficient but politically powerful local merchants.

surrounded by specialty boutiques and service stores. Self-service discount stores, furniture warehouses, and catalog showrooms were launched by entrepreneurs who took advantage of improvements in mass distribution and computerization. Other forms of discount shopping have since evolved, such as hardware superstores (Home Depot), off-price clothing outlets, and, of course, the most successful of all, Wal-Mart. Most of these forms of discount stores have succeeded because an increasing number of knowledgeable and skilled shoppers prefer price discounts and a wide selection of choices over a convenient location—especially when they don't have to sacrifice good service. However, for their purchases in other product-markets, these same consumers have displayed a willingness to pay for time and place convenience, and this led to the growth of the gas station convenience store, the supermarket specialty counters, and the specialty recreational and fashion stores (for instance, The Limited).

During the 1970s and 1980s, the major changes in consumer marketing channels largely resulted from the new channels of distribution being created by existing retailers, not from new forms of retailing. Pharmaceutical and health-care products are now sold in convenience stores, discount drug chains, supermarkets, and department stores, as well as family-owned pharmacies. Soft goods and fast food are increasingly being sold in supermarkets. The traditional general mail-order companies (for instance, Sears, Penney's, and Spiegel) took a large share of the expensive camera market away from the specialty stores during the 1970s. Department stores were being squeezed by discount and off-price clothing stores on one side and the premium fashion chains, such as The Limited and Lands-End, on the other side. This explains why many ended up in bankruptcy in the 1990s.[7] Warehouse Clubs are currently making major inroads into the sales of more traditional supermarkets, drugstores, and discount stores (see Figure 5-1). According to the Food Marketing Institute, because of their lower labor and facility costs, the operating expenses for Warehouse Clubs are about 7 to 9 percent of sales, compared to 19 to 21 percent for traditional grocers.[8] This is a considerable advantage.

Changes in Industrial Channels

The above discussion focused on evolutions in consumer product channels. Changes in industrial marketing channels have not been as dramatic. The wholesaler may have faded in importance in the marketing of consumer goods over the last 100 years, but this is certainly not so in many industrial markets. Wholesalers are still personally responsible for much of the customer problem solving, pioneer selling, and introduction of new products.

In many firms that competed in industrial markets prior to the 1970s, distribution was fragmented, and the responsibility was divided among several functional departments such as accounting, manufacturing, and marketing. However, over the last two decades the distribution function has been integrated, leading to major changes in order-processing, transportation, and warehousing. Industrial suppliers have only recently made advances in distribution and channel management for several reasons.[9]

7. The polarization of large retailers into general low-cost merchants and specialized, high-service retailers is predicted by Management Horizons (a prominent retail consulting firm) to continue.
8. Linda L. Hyde, "Catalysts for Change in Retail Strategy," in *1992 Strategic Outlook Conference* (Columbus, OH: Management Horizons, 1992).
9. Bernard J. LaLonde, John Grabner, and James F. Robeson, "Integrated Distribution Systems: Past, Present and Future," in *The Distribution Handbook* (New York: The Free Press, 1985), 15–27.

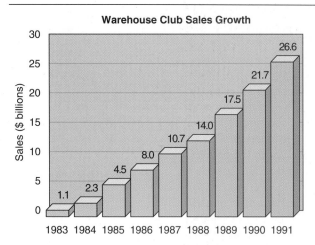

Warehouse Club Sales Growth

Source: Management Horizons Division of Price Waterhouse

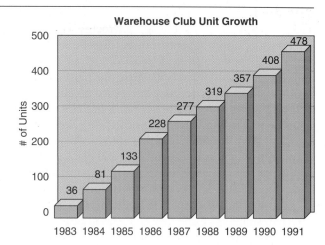

Warehouse Club Unit Growth

Source: Management Horizons Division of Price Waterhouse

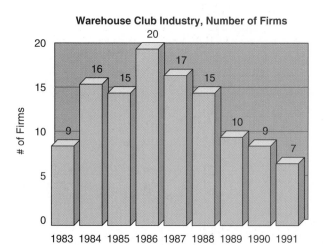

Warehouse Club Industry, Number of Firms

Source: Management Horizons Division of Price Waterhouse

Warehouse Club Industry, 1991

Company (Parent)	Net Sales ($ Million)	Share of Total	# of Stores	Share of Total
Sam's Club (Wal-Mart)	$ 9,430	35.4%	208	43.5%
The Price Company[1]	6,598	24.8	69	14.4
Costco Wholesale Club[2]	5,216	19.6	71	14.9
PACE Membership Warehouse (Kmart)	3,646	13.7	87	18.2
BJ's Wholesale (Waban)	1,432	5.4	29	6.1
Warehouse Club	243	0.9	10	2.1
Wholesale Depot	67	0.3	4	0.8
Total	$26,632	100.0%	478	100.0%

[1] Includes the results of 11 Canadian units.
[2] Includes the results of 9 Canadian units.

Source: <u>Discount Merchandiser</u>, company annual reports and Management Horizons Division of Price Waterhouse

Figure 5-1
The Growth of the
Warehouse Club

The growth of the Warehouse Club took the grocery industry by surprise. The big question is, when will it stop growing? It already may be too late for major supermarket retailers to establish a strong presence in the market unless they buy into Price or Costco.

Source: Management Horizons and the Food Marketing Institute.

First, compared with manufacturing and promotion, distribution has been neglected. Marketers gradually realized that the cost reduction and/or service differentiation that might result from paying more attention to distribution could create a considerable competitive advantage. Second, inflation in the 1970s and high interest rates in the early 1980s also focused attention on distribution management. Third, as increasing competition and the recession made it difficult to increase sales, managers started to really appreciate the profit leverage that came from reducing distribution costs rather than trying to increase sales. Fourth, the computerized integration of order processing, warehousing, and dispatching functions did not become common until the early 1980s. Fifth, global marketing places a premium on logistic efficiencies.

Several major forces are likely to change channel relationships in the future. Technological changes in communications and third-party transportation services will influence who is involved in distribution. The political economy of channels is also likely to change as a result of the continued growth in franchising and the formation of channel buying groups. Each of these is discussed in the following sections.

Future Channel Relationship Trends

Integrated Channel Information Systems

Electronic information technology has greatly reduced inventories and dead stock. For example, P&G is linked to Wal-Mart by computers, and orders for its personal-care and cleaning products are received, processed, and dispatched automatically. This relationship is similar to the just-in-time management of raw materials by a manufacturer whose production process computers are linked to its suppliers' order processing and dispatch computers. The advantages in market forecasting, inventory management, and production scheduling are obvious. The savings in time, documentation, and paperwork are profound.

The availability of electronic information has affected marketing channels in other ways. For example, industrial buyers can consult electronics catalogs, which are constantly updated with information about new lines, availability, delivery, volume price breaks, and innovative payment terms. The use of UPC-type coding allows a firm to track the progress of an order through the channel in real time.

Integrated channel information systems will enable a company to assess the performance of channel members, the profitability of doing business with them, and the success of promotional programs and new, more efficient operating procedures. Not being a part of such an information system may become a real barrier to entering some markets. On the other hand, being part of the system may also limit the managerial options of the participant by limiting the company's ability to switch to alternative distribution options. These and other inter- versus intra-channel competition antitrust issues have yet to be adequately addressed by managers and legislators. The outcome of such judgments will profoundly shape the way business-to-business relationships are conducted. For instance, the electronic revolution in channel relationship marketing has allowed retailers and distributors to greatly reduce their *number* of supplier relationships. For example, Federated, a major department store chain, reduced its number of suppliers from 14,000 to 200 in the late 1980s.[10] The effect on suppliers can be imagined.

Integrated Transportation Conglomerates

Continued innovations in transportation technology and regulation are also likely to have a major impact on channel structures and relationships. Containerization and automated warehousing have already changed the competitive dynamics in the marketing channel. Warehouse automation has made the large merchants much more competitive against the local specialty store and large department stores. The redesigning of international and domestic transportation infrastructure around the container has reduced costs for the original shipper and the final buyer. Not only was intermediate handling reduced, but containers reduced loss due to spoilage and theft.

10. Linda L. Hyde, "Catalysts for Change in Retail Strategy," in *1992 Strategic Outlook Conference* (Columbus, OH: Management Horizons, 1992), 14.

They also serve as useful short-term mini-warehouses for storing inventory. Perhaps most importantly, the integration of competing modes of transportation around the container has introduced much more competition among these modes (rather than just within each mode). Before the container, it was very labor intensive, expensive and time consuming to switch from one transportation mode to another (for example, truck to rail or rail to truck).

Containerization has forced the different transportation modes (ship, rail, air, and truck) to focus on the haulage activities that they undertake most efficiently and to introduce and adapt new technologies. Freight forwarders (transportation specialists) now mix and match the modes to offer a much greater variation in service and price to customers than was previously available. All of this has occurred somewhat at the expense of the intermediate public warehouse and most certainly at the expense of the domestic supplier. Technology has now made it much easier and cheaper for importers and manufacturers to physically move their goods and off-shore assembled components into and around the United States. In short, innovations in physical distribution have made the global marketplace much more accessible.

Deregulation and standardization in technology between transportation modes has opened up the opportunity for the full-service, integrated-transportation freight forwarding company.[11] It will ship, warehouse, and even handle international funds transfer. These companies offer many different distribution options and services to channel participants seeking to increase their asset productivity, including innovative delivery systems such as just-in-time (JIT). There is even the possibility that such transportation service companies will decide to take title to some of the goods and services that they move or will offer lease-back arrangements with customers (whereby inventory is pooled and managed by the intermediary). Ryder Systems offers an aircraft parts inventory management service that most airlines use.

The Growth of Franchising Relationships

The United States Department of Commerce has estimated that by the year 2000, 50 percent of retail sales will be made through franchised outlets. A franchise is a trading relationship in which the franchisor (the seller or supplier) gives a franchisee (a reseller) the rights to sell its product, often including exclusive rights to a particular geographical territory. The franchisor also supplies the services described in Figure 5-2. In return, the franchisee agrees to buy exclusively from the supplier. In addition to paying for the supplies, the franchisee pays the franchisor a commission on all of its sales and an initial franchise fee. Franchising is the major channel that industries such as pest control use to deliver their service. With services, the franchisee is required to follow prescribed service delivery scripts and train its employees to follow such scripts. (See Chapters 8, 9, and 14.)

Franchising effectively places the entrepreneurial decision making and marketing planning for many separately owned enterprises in the hands of a few. The franchisor, as explained in Chapter 1, had better continue to be very good at marketing decision making, for its own sake and the sake of all its franchisees. This necessity has become starkly apparent in the auto, petroleum, and fast-food industries, which accounted for over 80 percent of all franchise sales in 1985. When the franchisor's marketing planning loses its competitive edge, as happened with General Motors in auto sales and Burger King in fast food, the franchisees feel very uncomfortable about their lack of control over their destiny. This often results in attempts to loosen the terms of the

---

11. Bernard J. LaLonde, "Transportation in the 21st Century," *Journal of Physical Distribution,* Presidential Issue, (1985), 76–82.

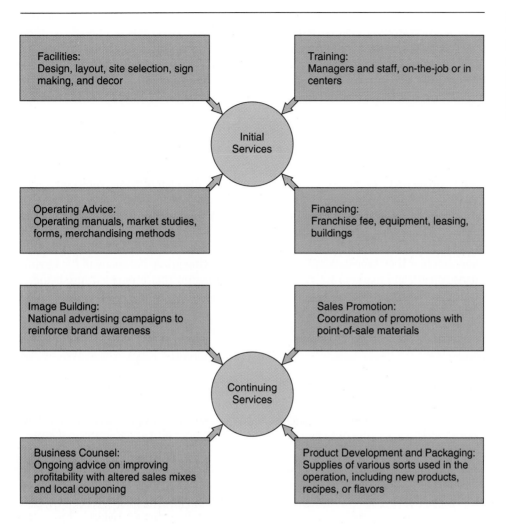

Figure 5-2

Typical Services Franchisors Provide Franchisees

Source: From *Marketing Channel Management: Strategic Planning and Tactics* by Kenneth G. Hardy and Allan J. Magrath. Copyright © 1988 by Scott, Foresman and Company. Reprinted by permission of HarperCollins Publishers.

legal contracts that bind the parties together. Alternatively, the franchisees may pressure the franchisor to copy new innovations or to buy out the new competitive threat.

The rise in the number of franchises means that while the ownership of individual retail businesses will not be in fewer hands, their success or failure will depend on the entrepreneurial decision-making skills of a smaller number of individuals. As the original marketing innovators are replaced by professional managers, the innovativeness and hence competitiveness of the franchisor is likely to be reduced. The marketing and production planning systems introduced must compensate for the loss of the personal creative flair (competitive rationality) that the original entrepreneurs and their management teams provided. Another solution is for the franchisor to reward franchisees richly for suggesting new operational and marketing ideas that can be adopted generally by the franchise network.

Franchising enables entrepreneurs to quickly, economically, and efficiently launch their ideas into many other local markets. The advantage to a franchisee is that franchising provides a way to profit from the innovative creativity and early risk taking of a marketing entrepreneur. The franchisee is, in a sense, paying an up-front fee and continuing royalty for a sure thing. Franchising is a way of quickly spreading a good idea and accelerating change across an economy and society. It is one of the most efficient mechanisms of the free market and capitalism. But what happens when the initial franchisors cease to be the innovators? Both the franchisor and franchisee are at risk from new marketing entrepreneurs who improve on an idea and set up their own new franchises.

The Growth of Channel Buying Groups

The growth of buying groups such as Tru Value Hardware stores is another excellent example of evolutionary competitive economics. Buying groups form when a major chain threatens to dominate a market through economies of scale. Individual businesses that could not survive on their own combine to form an economic "herd" that initially seeks and obtains volume buying discounts from sellers. It then develops cooperative management, merchandising, and marketing programs. Figure 5-3 not only highlights the advantages gained from such middleman buying groups but also describes how they evolve. When fully evolved, a buying group has many of the buying, management, and marketing strengths of the competitor that brought it into being. A buying group requires cooperation and some conformity, but its integrated organization increases the chances of survival.

Mass Market– Mass Distribution

Before discussing the functions of a distribution channel, it is important to recognize that different products require different distribution systems. The distribution strategy for many convenience products, such as batteries and soft drinks, is very simple: Make your product as convenient to buy as possible by getting it into as many channel outlets as possible. Convenience products are called that because shoppers will not go out of their way to buy the preferred alternative. When that product or service is not available, then the next most preferred alternative will do. Consequently, the best distribution for a convenience product is to be everywhere the competitors are, and are not. Mass distribution is best suited for products with the following characteristics:

♦ inexpensive
♦ easy to try
♦ frequently purchased
♦ nondurable
♦ low risk
♦ a mature product-market

The distributor adds very little to the product besides low cost and access convenience. Product knowledge and purchase preferences are cultivated through the manufacturer's advertising and trial. The benefits of shopping at and buying through a select channel are minimal for convenience products because reseller image, services, and marketing add very little value.

Economies of Scale and Scope

Mass distribution often means more levels are required in the channel to reach, service, and control the merchandising and sales of the ultimate resellers. This means giving away added margin (trade discounts) to distributor wholesalers, manufacturer

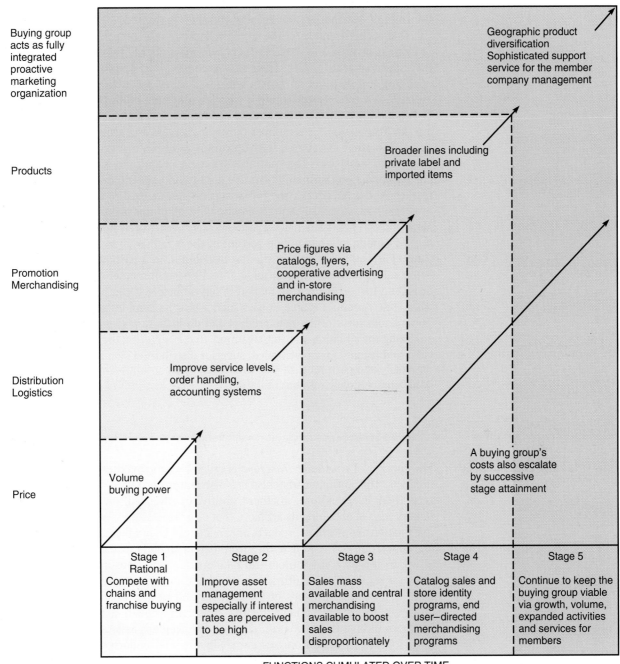

FOCUS OF EFFORT

Buying group acts as fully integrated proactive marketing organization

Products

Promotion Merchandising

Distribution Logistics

Price

Geographic product diversification Sophisticated support service for the member company management

Broader lines including private label and imported items

Price figures via catalogs, flyers, cooperative advertising and in-store merchandising

Improve service levels, order handling, accounting systems

Volume buying power

A buying group's costs also escalate by successive stage attainment

| Stage 1 Rational Compete with chains and franchise buying | Stage 2 Improve asset management especially if interest rates are perceived to be high | Stage 3 Sales mass available and central merchandising available to boost sales disproportionately | Stage 4 Catalog sales and store identity programs, end user–directed merchandising programs | Stage 5 Continue to keep the buying group viable via growth, volume, expanded activities and services for members |

FUNCTIONS CUMULATED OVER TIME

Source: From *Marketing Channel Management: Strategic Planning and Tactics* by Kenneth G. Hardy and Allan J. Magrath. Copyright © 1988 by Scott, Foresman and Company. Reprinted by permission of HarperCollins Publishers.

Figure 5-3
The Evolution of Middleman Buying Groups

representatives, brokers, or rack-jobbers to have the product delivered to the retailer. Consequently, in mass distribution, much of the focus of competition is on reducing the costs of distribution and keeping the shelves stocked.

One of the strengths of the large packaged-goods companies is that the significant economies of scale and scope in their own mass distribution system reaches down to the individual retail outlet. Their new products share the fixed and variable costs of operating this distribution system with established products. Systems and procedures are also well established (through past learning) for rolling out new products. Such distribution systems have been recognized as an undervalued asset in recent years and are the justification for a number of major mergers and acquisitions.

At the other extreme, a start-up company with a new convenience product must either cut a deal with the centralized buying organizations of a major chain store, piggy-back on another manufacturer's distribution system, or saturate a very localized market. In the latter case, the initial success can be used to roll out the product progressively, first regionally and then nationally. All of this is much easier said than done. Many entrepreneurs and naive marketers have prematurely licked their lips at the prospect of gaining one half of one percent of the U.S. market in a particular product category. The reality is that a particular distributor, in a particular market, needs much better sales performance (probably a 5 to 10 percent market share) in its local market or among its customers (the market it serves) before it can push the new entry. Even when a new product is able to pass such a test, its troubles are really only beginning. The manufacturer of the new product can do little to prevent a major company from analyzing the situation and slipstreaming, that is, entering the market behind the innovator and using its own well-oiled, superior distribution channel machinery to roll out nationally and earn most of the "entrepreneurial" profits. This is an example of profitable competitively rational imitation.

Specialty Distribution

The concept of *consumer franchise* is critical when thinking about how to distribute products. The consumer franchise is a distributor's or retailer's customer goodwill and reputation. Every culture, whether primitive or advanced, ancient or modern, has customary ways of obtaining its artifacts, that is, products and services. In most economies, information about where products or services can be purchased or leased is passed from one generation to the next (either from parent to child or from senior to junior executive). In this way, distributors and retailers develop a consumer franchise that is created as a result of both cultural influences and individual enterprise. A consumer franchise is measured in terms of the number and type of existing customers and their loyalty to the reseller. The more the consumer believes a retailer contributes to a product's ultimate performance (through the retailer's assistance in problem recognition, solution specification, recommendations and endorsements, tangible services, warranties, and an intangible image), the more the consumer is likely to seek out and be loyal to this retailer. This is the essence of its consumer franchise.

For mass market products, a reseller's consumer franchise is based on convenience and price image. In specialty markets, expertise, service, and image also shape the nature and loyalties of a reseller's consumer franchise. A specialty reseller, be it a distributor or a retailer, opens a door for a supplier into a unique submarket: the reseller's consumer franchise. Each retail store's assortment of customers has varying degrees of uniqueness measured in terms of individual differences (such as age or income),

The Limited is a specialty clothing store that has spawned several new store concepts (The Limited Express and Limited Too) that cater to the children of its original customers.

product usage, needs, perceptions of the competitive offerings, sensitivity to different promotional strategies, and loyalty to the store.

Specialty distributors are generally used for expensive, specialty products where design, choice of technology, and after-sales service are important. For a supplier of a mass distribution product, the basic problem is how to get into the mass distribution channels. For the marketer of a specialty product aimed at a specialty market, the problem is more complex. The choice of distributor can make or break the ultimate competitiveness of its offering. As discussed in Chapter 10, there must be a match between the supplier's strengths and weaknesses and the resellers strengths and weaknesses.

Sharper Image has expanded from a catalog selling expensive toys to yuppies to a successful modern chain store.

The Basic Functions of Channel Participants

Because of the increasing competition between channels and the ever present possibility of technological or economic change, it is imperative for an enterprise to be prepared to adapt its distribution system. This requires a sound understanding of the basic functions of a channel.[12] The players may change, the technology may change, where and how the functions are undertaken may change, but the fundamental activities of a channel (see Figure 5-4), and the economic principles governing a channel do not change. Sometimes this truth is lost in the adaptation process.

The most common function of a marketing channel member is to resell the product into a market that could not be reached as efficiently or effectively by the original seller. Intermediaries have already established goodwill with their customers, and those customers trust the intermediary's buying judgments. As mentioned earlier, this is called the reseller's *consumer franchise*. Retailers often have multiple selling outlets that are in prime geographical locations and have the right image. This gives the manufacturer both *physical* and *psychological* market positioning.

Intermediaries play a major role in bringing the product or service to the end user at the right place and right time by *transportation* and *storage*. Many intermediaries also work with the manufacturer to provide customer *training, education,* and after-sales *maintenance and repair services*. The *risk-taking* and *financing* activities of channel intermediaries have been greatly reduced over the last 100 years. Nowadays, many new products are sold to retailers on consignment (retailers pay for what they sell and return the rest) or purchased with buy-back deals in the contract. Some retailers are even demanding up-front cash payments (shelf-slotting allowances) to compensate for the cost and the risk of placing a new product on their shelves. With established products, the credit allowances given to the wholesaler or retailer are such that a high-turn product is often sold by the retailer before the manufacturer is paid.

Sometimes merchants do take risks with seasonal products and are caught with stock at the end of a season that has to be sold at a loss or carried over to the next year. Many retailers also offer their shoppers no-questions-asked money-back guarantees. On the other hand, the manufacturer usually provides a product performance warranty even though the retailer or wholesaler is the new legal owner of the product. Under common law, unless explicitly qualified as "where is, as is," the merchant is responsible for the merchandisable quality of anything it sells. However, a consumer usually has to deal with the manufacturer, rather than the retailer when a product needs repair.

Today, very little *breaking down, repacking,* or further *processing* is undertaken down the channel. Fabricator wholesalers do assemble doors, windows, and other fixtures for building contractors, and paint is tinted at the point of purchase. Postponement of processing down the distribution channel greatly saves the cost of carrying inventory and, at the same time, offers the consumer an expanded product offering. Usually, however, the advantage the manufacturer offers in processing specialization and economies of scale mitigates against such postponement of processing.

Channel members are able to provide valuable customer feedback back up the distribution channel, but often the manufacturer also provides information down the channel to retailers that creates interest and support for its product. Hence, *market research* and information flows form a two-way street with findings and data often

---

12. For an excellent discussion of channel functions see Louis Stern and Adel El-Ansary, *Marketing Channels,* 3rd ed. (Englewood Cliffs, NJ: Prentice-Hall, 1988).

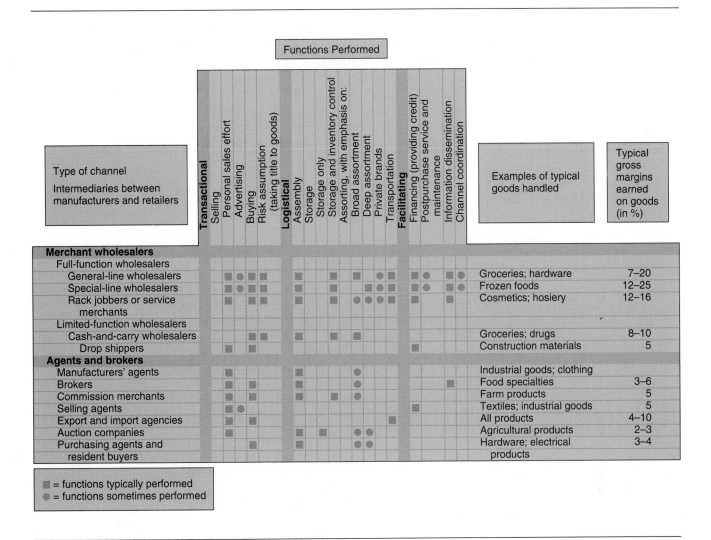

Figure 5-4

The Varying Functions of Channel Intermediaries

These different types of middlemen have come about because different sellers and buyers had a need for their various services. Their long-term survival and competitiveness depend on a continuing need for their bundle of services. This need may be threatened by technological innovations that change the added value of channel intermediaries.

Source: Reprinted with the permission of Macmillan Publishing Company from *Marketing* by James Heskett. Copyright © 1976 by Macmillan Publishing Company.

being interpreted in different ways by the different parties. It is also not necessarily in the interests of retailers to provide all the information a manufacturer wants about its competitors' sales.

Competence, Cost, and Control

Just who should undertake the above distribution and marketing activities depends essentially on three factors: competence, cost, and control. Each of these criteria has to be considered before deciding whether a particular function should be done in-house or undertaken by a channel partner. Marketing expertise and competence can be provided immediately by an intermediary, but this often results in a higher cost and a loss of some control over the marketing of the product. Determining whether it is less expensive to subcontract marketing responsibilities to channel partners is similar to deciding whether to subcontract or manufacture a product in-house. A channel member may, through economies of scale or scope, be able to provide service at a lower cost. But whether these cost savings are passed on to the manufacturer or are retained as profits by the channel participant depends very much on the competition among channel members to serve the supplier.

Competence and control have to be evaluated from two perspectives: the fit between the fundamental competitive strategies of channel partners and the channel members' ability to execute the planned joint marketing strategy. Each alternative channel participant can be evaluated on the competence, cost, and control dimensions for each of the different functions described above. The problem is that often the channel functions cannot be unbundled. They are offered in a take-it-or-leave-it package by a reseller. This makes channel selection very difficult because a reseller may be strong on one function but weak on another function compared with the other channel options. Figure 5-4 illustrates the variety of different channel intermediaries that exist, their functions, and typical gross margins earned.

Predicting the Future Fit of a Relationship

Channel decision making depends on long-term plans. Once the consumer connects a branded product with a particular seller, a dissolution of the trading relationship can be very expensive. But, like a marriage in which one party outgrows the other, many channel relationships eventually fall apart. A manufacturer, having used a particular channel to obtain a foothold in the market, turns to alternative channels to provide greater efficiencies, sales volume, or profits. Similarly, a retailer may choose to reposition its lines of business or offer its own private label and abandon a supplier. Consequently, the prudent marketing manager attempts to anticipate how potential channel partners are likely to change and makes the choice not just on current strengths and weaknesses but on an estimate of a partner's value over the entire expected life of the trading relationship.

Evolutionary Rigidity in Trading Relationships

In distribution channels, traditional trading practices, rituals, and trappings are frequently maintained to resist new competitive challenges, ease anxiety, or save face. This is called channel evolutionary rigidity. Such cautious change can be best seen in the recent, but long-delayed, computerization of stock trading. Almost all product markets mix archaic trading practices with modern innovations. Cultural change generally lags behind technological or economic change. The stronger the trading traditions in a market, the less adaptable the market will be to change. But because others in the market will be slow to adopt and adapt, the innovator can reap tremendous rewards. Hence, there is a strong incentive to innovate in nonadaptive markets. Such incentives will ultimately "break" the evolutionary rigidity of a market.

Over the last decade, advances in physical distribution, communications, and information processing technologies have also radically reduced the need for some of the customary activities undertaken by channel intermediaries such as brokers and wholesalers. As markets mature, the pioneer personal selling-and-order-taking efforts of the channel are no longer needed and are replaced by direct selling and billing. Less inventory is carried in the channel because sales stabilize and orders are often drop-shipped (bypassing the intermediary). The problem is that margins, payment terms, and other traditional trading practices are sticky. The renegotiation of terms often puts considerable strain on relationships. A relationship that does not have enough give and take ultimately results in a channel fracture, and the manufacturer or retailer breaks out of its traditional relationship only to face the internal and external adjustment problems of breaking into different levels of the channel or breaking into a completely new channel. Another serious consequence of evolutionary rigidity is that a channel member's failure to move with the times drags down its suppliers and resellers, whose loyalty may prevent them from keeping up with the competition. The reverse can happen when an innovative retailer is slowed by suppliers who are reluctant to change their products and trading practices. It often takes a new generation of executives to fully adapt to the new trading channel realities and relationships.

The Channel Relationship Audit

The suggested procedure for auditing the channel is to address first a number of questions about general changes in the channel and then to zero in on a detailed audit of key resellers. Figure 5-5 presents several questions that address the impact on the channel of 1) changes in technology, 2) new entrants, 3) changes in established channel relations, and 4) changes in the way existing channel members do business. The first three types of change were described earlier. The recorded music market provides an excellent example of the impact on manufacturers of the way channel members do business.

In the 1950s and early 1960s, record retailers allowed consumers to play new records in the store. This was an important way of exposing a new artist or title to the public, as the enthusiasts and opinion leaders did most of this in-store sampling. But as popular music took off with rock 'n' roll and the spending power of the baby boomers

Figure 5-5
Channel Change Audit

- *Who are the latest new entrants in the reseller market?*
  What is their competitive advantage?
  Which existing resellers are being most affected?
  How has it affected us?

- *What new trading coalitions between resellers are occurring?*
  What will be their competitive advantage?
  How will it affect us?

- *What changes in order-processing technology are now occurring?*
  What impact will they have on the way business is done?
  What competitive advantage do they provide?

- *What changes in transportation technology are now occurring?*
  What impact will they have on the way business is done?
  What competitive advantage do they provide?

- *What changes in warehousing technology are now occurring?*
  What impact will they have on the way business is done?
  What competitive advantage do they provide?

- *What changes in payment technology are now occurring?*
  What impact will they have on the way business is done?
  What competitive advantage do they provide?

increased, chain stores opened record bars that did not provide the sound booths for sampling but undercut the record stores on price. Consumers would often listen to the music in the record store and buy at the chain store. To compete, the record stores dropped the sound booths but offered a generous return policy. Eventually, the return policy was dropped.

As a result of the termination of in-store sampling, popular radio stations now became not just important but critical in marketing records. Radio was also going through a transition. Increased competition was forcing the stations into Top 20 or Top 40 formats where the hit-parade music was played continuously at the expense of new artists and songs. This program format kept the audiences and advertisers happy, but it forced the recording companies to buy airtime in order to advertise their new releases (where previously such exposure was free). This increased the cost of launching a new release, thus giving a major competitive advantage to the larger recording studios and distributors. MTV pulled the recording industry out of the doldrums in the early 1980s, but this new channel has forced the studios into a whole new marketing activity—video production. The music video component has become an important new competitive element in selling compact discs and tapes, and a further entrance barrier for new competition.

Many channels of distribution have changed dramatically in recent years. Figure 5-6 illustrates how cut-flower distribution changed between 1970 and 1984. Importers from all around the world entered the market and now produce more than 40 percent of the cut flowers sold in the United States. At the other end of the channel, mass marketers, such as supermarkets, have expanded their market share from 2 percent to 20 percent (and that percentage is still growing). Caught in between, wholesale florists are facing a radically changing supplier and reseller market and all sorts of new competitive channel mutations.

Once the general audit has been undertaken, the important resellers and suppliers will have been identified for further study. Clearly, not all resellers and suppliers can be studied, and some good managerial judgment is needed to make sure greater attention is paid to the major players and innovators. When a company's sales force uses an account management approach for its major customers, it should be relatively easy to complete audits of such resellers. However, care must be taken that day-to-day operating relations do not drive the valuations of those who are in constant contact with representatives of suppliers and resellers. The reseller audits require the auditor to stand back so as to assess the changes that have occurred over the last trading year and explain some of the basic reasons for predicting longer-term changes.

The reseller audit presented in Figure 5-7 starts with a summary evaluation that can also be used as a short-form audit when the planners and auditors do not have the time or interest to fully evaluate particular resellers. A paragraph can be written to provide responses to each of the concerns listed. The evaluation can be updated on a regular basis (normally annually) so the major investment is in preparing the initial evaluation. The detailed evaluation questions have been categorized into those dealing with the reseller's trading performance, marketing positioning, competitive effort, and purchasing behavior. Understanding what is going right and what is going wrong in a channel relationship almost always involves taking information and putting it together like a jigsaw puzzle. That is why it is important to add depth to the audit by answering as many questions as possible using facts, good judgment, and best guesses. Trying to understand the reasons for a channel member's change in performance or behavior often has to be traced back from its buying behavior, through trading and operating indicators, to its competitive effort and market position. The audit of the reseller must also forecast its future competitive strengths and weaknesses.

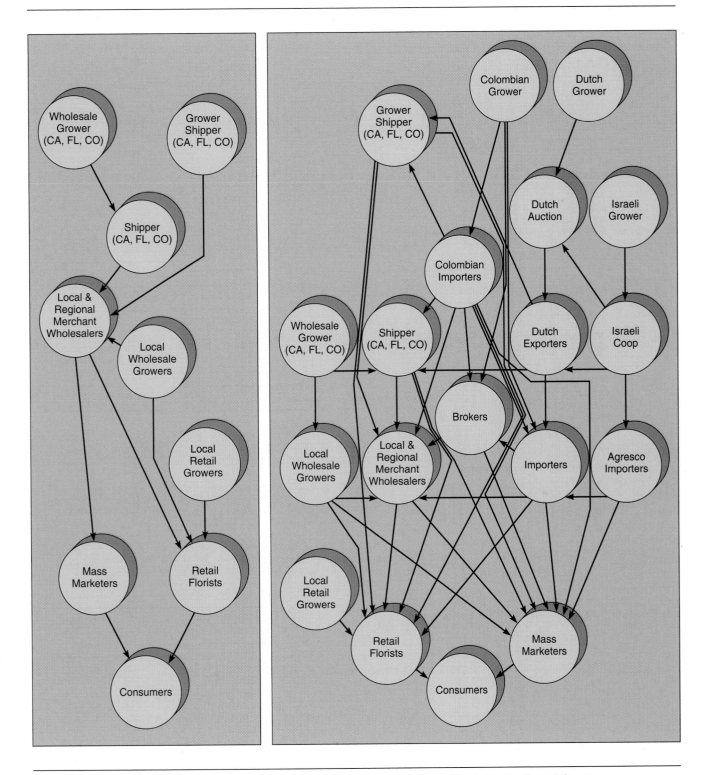

The entry of supermarkets and other retail chains into cut-flower retailing and the growth in size of some of the whole-sale florists opened up the market for bulk contracts with foreign suppliers. Without the Boeing 747, the globalization of this market would not have occurred.

Source: Thomas L. Prince, *An Empirical Investigation of Market Power and Channel Conflict in the Cut-flower Distribution Channel,* Unpublished Master's Thesis, The Ohio State University.

Figure 5-6

Changes in the Cut-Flower Distribution Channel 1970–1984

Reseller Audit

Company name: _____ Date: _____

Summary Evaluation

- Major strength, unique value, and importance of this seller _____
- Major weakness and failure of seller _____
- Change in reseller's dependency on us as a supplier _____
- Change in our dependency on reseller _____
- Reseller's perceptions of its dependency on us _____
- Reseller's pxerceptions of our dependency on it _____
- Special personal relations with supplier _____

Detailed Evaluation

Trading Performance

- Current annual sales _____
- Current annual sales of our products _____
- Current contribution earned from sales to this reseller _____
- Recent growth in sales _____
- Growth in sales of our products _____
- Previous 12-month contribution earned from sales to this reseller _____
- Changes in product mix sold _____
- Current average stock-turn of our products _____
- Past average stock-turn of our products _____
- Most recent profit performance _____
- Credit rating _____

Marketing Positioning

- Years in business _____
- Current image and reputation _____
- Past image and reputation _____
- Geographical markets served _____
- Customer segments served _____

Competitive Effort

- Recent investment in new plant, premises, and technology _____
- Recent marketing strategy _____
- Quality of locations _____
- Quality of advertising _____
- Quality of premises _____
- Quality of buyers _____
- Extent we are treated as a preferred supplier _____
- Quality of sales staff _____
- Sales-staff knowledge of our products _____
- Standard pricing strategy _____
- Price promotion selling of our products _____
- Inventory management _____
- Order-delivery lag to its customers _____
- Special marketing efforts and cooperation _____

Purchasing Behavior

- Recent ordering history _____
- Recent payment history _____
- Volume deals/discounts sought and given _____
- Other allowances and considerations sought and given:
  - Freight _____
  - Cooperative advertising _____
  - Promotions _____
  - Returns _____
  - Push money and sales contests _____
  - Special credit terms _____

Figure 5-7
Reseller Audit

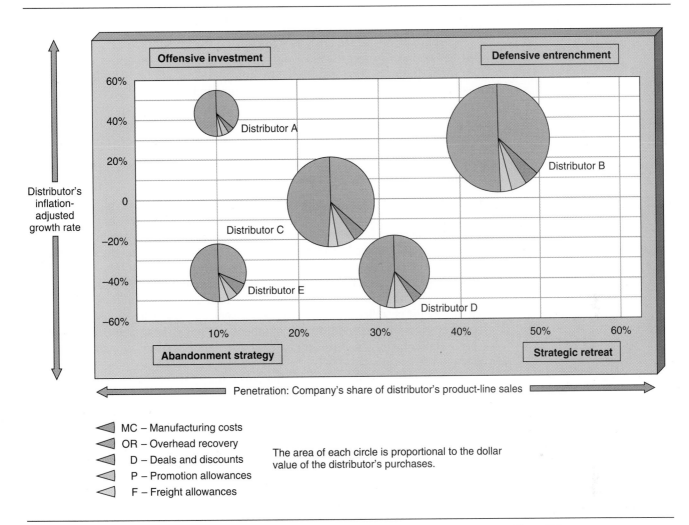

MC – Manufacturing costs
OR – Overhead recovery
D – Deals and discounts
P – Promotion allowances
F – Freight allowances

The area of each circle is proportional to the dollar value of the distributor's purchases.

Figure 5-8
A Distributor Portfolio Analysis

This figure presents a great deal of information about channel trading relationships. It indicates which distributors are thriving, which distributors are giving a lot of their business to you, and which distributors you depend on most for sales and profits. It also indicates how the distributors are being rewarded differentially in terms of the extra discounts/allowances they received as a percentage of sales.

Distributor Relationship Analysis

Some of the audit information should automatically be compared across resellers. An example of such a visual comparison is provided in Figure 5-8.[13] A distributor portfolio analysis can be undertaken by reviewing the information on a reseller's growth rate (the y axis), the company's share of its sales in the particular product-market (the x axis), and the percentage of the company's total sales that are made through the reseller. The latter is represented by the area of the circle, best visualized as a cross-sectional view of trading channel "pipes," down which the company's sales "flow."

The deals and discounts that the company has given the distributor are the sections of the pie chart. The remaining two slices of the pie are the manufacturing cost and the gross margin that the company earns on sales to the distributor. These calculations

13. Peter R. Dickson, "Distributor Portfolio Analysis and Channel Dependence Matrix: New Techniques for Understanding and Managing the Channel," *Journal of Marketing* 47 (Summer 1982), 35–44. See also Patrick M. Dunne and Harry I. Wolk, "Marketing Cost Analysis: A Modularized Contribution Approach," *Journal of Marketing* 41 (July 1977), 83–94.

depend on the mix in sales to the distributor and requires use of internal management accounting information.

The purpose of such an analysis is to visualize the actual trading *relationships* that exist between a firm and its major distribution channels. Often a firm discovers that its current dealings with a distributor are outdated. They are based on its past performance and long-established personal relationships and loyalties rather than on current trading realities. The real advantage of such comparative analyses emerges over time. The dynamic changes that have occurred can be tracked and future performance can be projected based on the trends that emerge.

Facilitators and Alliances

Finally, a thorough channel audit should also give status reports on all other channel facilitators that are vital to sustaining sales. For example, often a service company relies on the assistance of other enterprises or individuals to provide introductions, recommendations, and help deliver and market its line of services. Two services (for example, a law firm and an accounting firm) develop a relationship in which they cross-sell each other's services. The marketplace, standing, and situation of such facilitators are consequently very important and should be investigated and detailed in the environmental report. The list of such facilitators includes brokers, bankers, insurers, lawyers, accountants, senior executives and directors of other companies, the Chamber of Commerce, federal, state, and local government officials, advertising agencies, shipping agents, and common carriers.

It is also worthwhile to explore the possibility of developing a business alliance with another company that sells a complementary product (products that are used with each other). Microsoft used IBM as a facilitator to launch its MS-DOS operating system. Apple Computer worked with ADobe Systems to develop its desktop publishing. Now Apple and IBM are working together to develop new networking software. The key to the success of such alliances is to take full advantage of the skills and resources each party brings to the alliance, overcome cultural differences between organizations, and protect joint investments and trade secrets with legal contracts that anticipate future problems.[14] Alliances that facilitate trade and increase the competitiveness of the joint offering are likely to increase with the globalization of markets. Figure 5-9 presents a list of questions that need to be answered when evaluating the potential of various parties who, although not part of a standard or conventional channel, may be able to play a critical role in planned marketing and selling efforts.

Channel Relationship Analysis in Global Markets

There is increasing suspicion and some evidence that the hidebound tradition and inertia of the distribution channels in Japan, Europe, and emerging third-world economies have been turned into a competitive barrier against foreign competition. Trading loyalties and practices are often used to protect the domestic market from the rapid entry of foreign competition. As a result, exporters often have to enter foreign markets through a backdoor, such as Schick using Seiko's distribution network to sell its razors in Japan, Olivetti distributing directly to retailers, and Melitta selling coffee makers

14. Louis P. Bucklin and Sanjit Sengupta, *Balancing Co-Marketing Alliances for Effectiveness* (Working Paper, Cambridge, MA: Marketing Science Institute, 1992), 92–120.

Figure 5-9
Potential Facilitator/
Alliance Audit

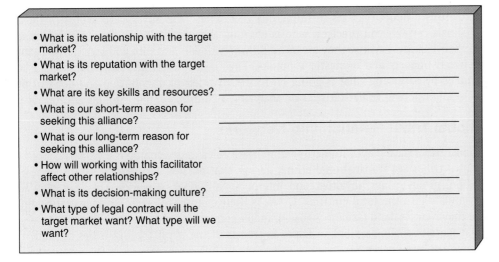

- What is its relationship with the target market? _____
- What is its reputation with the target market? _____
- What are its key skills and resources? _____
- What is our short-term reason for seeking this alliance? _____
- What is our long-term reason for seeking this alliance? _____
- How will working with this facilitator affect other relationships? _____
- What is its decision-making culture? _____
- What type of legal contract will the target market want? What type will we want? _____

through coffee bean channels. In these cases, the traditional appliance channels were controlled by Japanese manufacturers.

For many years, international marketing textbooks have stressed the need to understand foreign distribution channels and how they operate. The failure of export initiatives is frequently attributed to the arrogant, ignorant attitudes and behavior of U.S. exporters toward foreign distributors and markets. While sometimes this is so, in reality it is often quite the reverse. U.S. companies and regulators have often been exploited by foreign distributors and governments. Publicly, the exporter receives endless excuses, condolences, advice, and exhortations to try harder. Privately, the foreign distributors and governments are working to launch or boost domestic, low-cost, me-too competition. Such opportunistic behavior not only reduces the U.S. imports (hence saving foreign exchange), but it also offers the possibility for foreign distributors to enter the U.S. marketing channels and attack the home base of U.S. companies.

Ironically, U.S. distribution channels have been very accommodating to foreign suppliers. Indeed, a number of foreign manufacturers of consumer and industrial electronics may have benefited from *not* having evolved within the hidebound channel subcultures of many U.S. industrial markets. Their radical suggestions and innovations in distribution may be forgiven and even considered more favorably by distributors, mass merchandisers, and retailers looking for new sources of supply. As outsiders, these foreign manufacturers were not breaking any rules that they had previously accepted. A domestic supplier, who should know better, would be perceived to be arrogant, pushy, and breaking the rules if it made the same suggestions.

In the current global trade war, the most effective strategic defensive initiatives are not being built on the geographical borders between countries. They are already in place in the distribution channels of an economy. Channel barriers are much less obvious than border barriers and less likely to provoke political retaliation. Everyone studying macroeconomics follows the daily, weekly, or monthly trade statistics to make predictions about the health of different national economies and their competitiveness. But such statistics reflect the consequences of decisions made in trading channels months, even years, before.

Meanwhile, the current international trade war that will determine the future balance of payments and employment patterns is being fought in the trading channels of numerous product-markets in numerous economies. The buyers and sellers in these channels can tell you precisely who is winning and who is losing the latest skirmish in their channel because they are *deciding* who will win and who will lose in the battle between imports and domestic suppliers. That is why international trade should be studied by observing what is going on in the channels of distribution and not just by belatedly tracking trade statistics or analyzing a country's import quotas and tariffs.

Global Tribal Relationship Networks

Global tribes have played immensely important roles in developing the global economy. Global tribes are transnational ethnic groups that possess very strong group identification, group values, loyalties, and interpersonal global networks. They are slow to assimilate into the local cultures. Home is their country of origin or ancestral origin, be they New Zealand farmers whose grandparents migrated from Scotland or Japanese managers of a Honda plant in Ohio. Examples of the great trading tribes of modern times are listed here:[15]

The Jewish Tribal Network

Their forced dispersion around the globe made the Jews the classic global trade intermediaries and merchants. Their common culture and shared estrangement and alienation led to a shared trust and deal-making rules that were necessary for survival. Such trust and trading conventions settled on a handshake and led to low transaction costs and low risks when trading with merchants within and across borders who shared their culture and trading conventions. The Jewish merchants also emphasized education (human capital) as they were often not allowed to own land or were frequently dispossessed of their property. Ironically, this gave them greater mobility, enabling them, as traders and financiers, to follow and expand the flow of international commerce and to become worldly wise and intensely skilled and competitive in their trading.

The British Tribal Network

The British Empire spawned and spread much of the modern global culture, such as its common trading and scientific language and its law, science, and arts. Britain's advantage over its larger European rivals (France and Germany) was its emphasis on international trade and its ever restless search for new resources, new markets, new lands to colonize, and new technologies. Britain gained a first mover advantage into new markets through an aggressive colonial policy between 1600–1900 that expanded its empire into India, North America, the Caribbean, Africa, Southeast Asia, and Australasia. The more unruly, maverick, and adventurous sons of the aristocracy sought their fortunes abroad, and they exhibted a Calvinist acceptance of the merchant profits in their competitive rationality and concern over idleness expressed best by Benjamin Franklin: "Remember, that time is money."[16] Britain did more than spread new technology, such as steam engines and railways, around the globe. It also led in competitive rationality skills, such as cost accounting, financial accounting, and all types of management and marketing decision-making activities.

---

15. The following summaries are mostly abstracted from Joel Kotkin, *Tribes* (New York: Random House, 1993); and Philip D. Curtin, *Cross-Cultural Trade in World History* (Cambridge: Cambridge University Press, 1984).
16. Max Weber, *The Protestant Ethic and the Spirit of Capitalism,* translated by Talcott Parsons (New York: Scribners, 1958).

The Japanese Tribal Network

The Japanese used the manufacturing and distribution innovations of its Anglo-American conquerors to help forge the greatest modern global tribal network. Japanese trading companies send scouts out on global wanderings and management assignments of two to five years, supported by a network of Japanese-owned hotels, spas, bars, restaurants, schools, and golf-clubs. The modern Japanese tribe has its basis in the corporate family clans that were formed 300 years ago during the period of Japan's great isolationism from the world. These clans are linked by a tribal ethos of mutual self-help that has transcended international borders. Another important value was the emphasis on reinvesting almost all profits back into expanding the family business, into new markets, or into new technologies. This resulted in large networks of extraordinarily adaptive, efficient, and aggressive small firms.

The Chinese Tribal Network

Led by merchants from Taiwan, Hong Kong, Malaysia, and Singapore, the new Chinese traders have expanded the already existing Chinese community networks around the world. Coupled with their extraordinary energy and enterprise is a great willingness to cooperate with local business partners. Like many Asian immigrants, they focus on building family businesses and investing in children's education. An extended family "clan" system that emphasizes discipline, self-control, work ethic, and frugality pervades the network of Chinese communities around the world.

Politicians, social scientists, and business scholars have consistently underestimated the importance of the above trading tribes. The European aristocracy vilified the Jews. France and Germany dismissed the British as a nation of shopkeepers. The British, in turn, did not see the emerging Asian trading networks as a threat and allowed rigid laborer job titles to rule while allowing jobs for the titled (company directorships for the aristocracy) to reduce the competitive rationality of Britain's manufacturing industry just as the competitive rationality of its Asian rivals was advancing in leaps and bounds. Even more recently, East African nations, such as Kenya and Tanzania, learned a bitter lesson about the importance of global tribal networks when they expelled their Indian communities and their export trade promptly collapsed.

The importance of global tribal trading networks is hardly ever discussed in books on international marketing or economics, even though one of the biggest problems faced by emerging nations such as Russia, India, Pakistan, Egypt, and Brazil is that they have to build such networks. The alternatives are to develop a close facilitating relationship with one of the existing global tribal networks or to operate at a severe and sustained competitive disadvantage.

Global Communication Networks

Operationally, success in global distribution comes from communicating electronically and finding ways of shipping goods in containers as quickly as possible. The tremendous improvements in communication and transportation have opened up the world as a source of supply for the American distribution system. What this means is that the number of potential global suppliers for retailers such as Wal-Mart, Kmart, Sears, The Limited, and Toys Я Us has increased much faster than the number of new retailers in the United States. The natural consequence of this, as illustrated in Figure 5-10, is a shift in power and potential long-term profits to the existing successful distribution

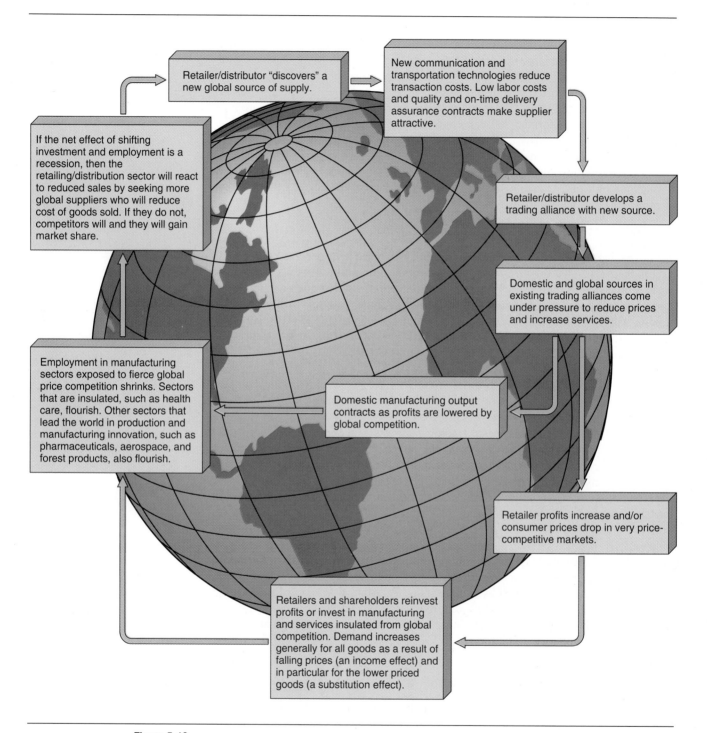

Retailer/distributor "discovers" a new global source of supply.

New communication and transportation technologies reduce transaction costs. Low labor costs and quality and on-time delivery assurance contracts make supplier attractive.

If the net effect of shifting investment and employment is a recession, then the retailing/distribution sector will react to reduced sales by seeking more global suppliers who will reduce cost of goods sold. If they do not, competitors will and they will gain market share.

Retailer/distributor develops a trading alliance with new source.

Domestic and global sources in existing trading alliances come under pressure to reduce prices and increase services.

Employment in manufacturing sectors exposed to fierce global price competition shrinks. Sectors that are insulated, such as health care, flourish. Other sectors that lead the world in production and manufacturing innovation, such as pharmaceuticals, aerospace, and forest products, also flourish.

Domestic manufacturing output contracts as profits are lowered by global competition.

Retailer profits increase and/or consumer prices drop in very price-competitive markets.

Retailers and shareholders reinvest profits or invest in manufacturing and services insulated from global competition. Demand increases generally for all goods as a result of falling prices (an income effect) and in particular for the lower priced goods (a substitution effect).

Figure 5-10
The Dynamics of Globalization

channels that have strong consumer franchises.[17] The same power-shift effect in favor of an economy's existing distribution channels is occurring in every major economy. This power shift is producing an extensive restructuring of the U.S. economy as investment leaves sectors facing fierce global competition. U.S. manufacturers have responded by developing close working relationships with retailers and distributors, moving manufacturing off-shore, and developing their own new distribution channels, such as was the case when Van Heusen, the shirt manufacturer, developed a very successful chain of outlet stores. If the 1960s was the decade of focusing on the consumer, the 1970s the decade of focusing on new public policy, and the 1980s the decade of focusing on the competition, then this power shift is likely to make the 1990s the decade in which businesses focus on their marketing channel relationships.

Discussion Questions and Minicases

1. Why was it so important for the Communists to wipe out the bourgeois middlemen and traders soon after the 1917 revolution?

2. A decade ago, a wheel-of-retailing theory was in vogue. It argued that as forms of retailing mature they become less cost efficient and trade up by increasing services and positioning themselves to service the less price-sensitive consumers. New forms of lower-cost retailing enter the market and, in time, they move upscale in their positioning, and so the wheel rotates. What might be the real explanation for what appears to be a wheel effect? Can you think of any successful retailers who are exceptions to the wheel theory?

3. A large part of the success of Wal-Mart can be explained by the orthodox economic theory of competition. What is it?

4. A retailer is currently selling disposable diapers at a 30 percent margin for $10 a box and has 12 stock-turns a year. What price could it charge for the diapers if it received a delivery of diapers to its stores every week and it increased its stock-turn to 36 a year?

5. In 1976, 6.8 percent of convenience-store sales came from gas. By 1981, that share had grown to 23 percent and it is still climbing. The reasons for this dramatic swing in line of business can be traced to changes in the economy, technology, demographics, and traditional gasoline marketing. In the 1950s and 1960s the major gasoline companies heavily promoted their branded gasoline, often making somewhat dubious product superiority claims. The credibility of such product differentiation was wearing thin by the early 1970s, when the price of gas doubled. Consumers, scrambling to stretch their budgets, economized by first using less gas and then turning to self-service and independent unbranded gas.

   The erosion of their brand franchises and margins and the doubling of the cost of holding gas in their underground tanks hit the major dealerships very hard. Many had to extend their opening hours to increase revenues and match the service of the independents. A desperate survival search began for new ways of paying

17. Peter R. Dickson and Carl Steidtmann, *Globalization 2000* (Columbus, OH: Management Horizons, 1992).

the increased bills. New chains, such as Sears and Midas, had eliminated the opportunity for gas dealerships to profit from auto maintenance. The aftermarket in tires and batteries had also been lost to discount merchants. The most promising new line of business was the sale of convenience products such as tobacco, soft drinks, beer, candy, and snack foods—products that the traveler would buy or the local consumer would purchase late at night when many of the conventional outlets for these products were closed. What effect did the above events have on competing channels?

6. What growth technologies gave the mail-order business a big boost in the 1970s and 1980s?

7. What effect do direct electronic-funds transfers between businesses have on banks? What might the banking industry's response be?

8. Electronic shopping has been forecast as the future wave of retailing for the last 20 years. Why has the wave never come in, and what cautionary lesson is there in this story?

9. Two major economic drivers of distribution logistics costs are very volatile. What are they, and how do they affect costs and innovations?

10. What might be discussed in the channel section of an environmental analysis for a service company that does not use conventional distribution channels?

11. What determines seller dependency on a channel reseller? Is it true that if a seller is very dependent on a middleman then the seller lacks power?

12. Investment will move from low return on investment markets to high return on investment markets. What implications does this have for channel profitability and power given what we know about the relative ability of retailers and manufacturers to switch product-markets?

13. Explain why franchising is so successful using the theory of competitive rationality.

14. What advantage does the UPC information that retailers gather from their check-out scanning systems give them over their suppliers?

15. Please study the growth of the cut-flower market in Figure 5-6. How do you think this market evolved? What impact do you think its evolution has had on the channel power of the different players over time? Why do you think supermarkets like Kroger entered the market?

16. What are two reasons that governments protect the interests of the distribution channels in their economies against foreign threats?

17. Many experts suggest that developing a close trading relationship with a distributor or retailer through automatic ordering, electronic information links, and new product development joint ventures is a way of building a sustainable competitive advantage. But most of the time it is assumed that the supplier will be the sole supplier. What do you think happens when a distributor or retailer develops such close working relationships with several suppliers? How can a supplier prevent this from happening?

18. Blockbuster Video dominates the video rental market with its many locations, large selection, and convenient hours. It has millions of customers, whose purchase history can be tracked. Blockbuster's problem has been maintaining demand by finding a way to effectively promote its latest releases. How might it develop a facilitating relationship with national magazines? What might the magazine, in turn, get out of the relationship/alliance that would make the magazine even more competitive?

Analyzing Regulation and Market Ethics

"To see what is right and not to do it is a lack of courage."
Confucius

"Always do right. This will gratify some and astonish the rest."
Mark Twain

*A*s individual citizens, our behavior is constrained by the law and our considerations of right and wrong. It is no different for firms and marketing decision makers. The marketplace is full of rules. Many are written into law, some are stated in professional codes of ethics, and others are stated in company rules of good conduct. Finally, we all have some sense of what is honest, decent, and fair. The interpretation of morality may vary greatly among individuals, but it still exists. In business, what we decide to make and how we market it are also constrained by our perceptions of the law and our mental model of what is right and wrong—that is, our code of ethics.

Marketing plans seldom feature legal concerns and almost never raise ethical issues. The law and ethics still influence marketing decision making. It is usually assumed that marketing planners are familiar with marketing law and that their decision making is ethical. What others might see as enlightened knowledge is part of a professional marketing planner's general expertise. Any new law or potential litigation that must be paid attention to because of recent events in the marketplace is likely to be singled out and described in the environment sections of plans. This might include the recent actions of a government agency, a consumer lawsuit against a competitor, or impending legislation. Plans should also note current ethical issues that have been raised by public interest groups or consumers.

Foundations for a Policy and Ethical Mental Model

This chapter does not list all of the possible laws and ethics that might apply to a marketing decision. Instead, it asks you to think about the legal issues that affect marketers in certain ways in order to lay a foundation or framework for your understanding of marketing law.[1] Such considerations may seldom be revealed in actual written marketing plans or decisions, but they are important.

Despite the fact that the U.S. marketplace is one of the most open and free in the world, federal and state laws and agencies impose numerous constraints. The great surge in public policy activity that occurred in the 1970s resulted in several new agencies (for example, the Product Safety Commission) and numerous new laws. More regulation means more restrictions, and more crusading regulators means higher legal expenses and the risk of a company losing its reputation if it is tried by the press. The Library of Congress has calculated that the annual cost of completing, filing, and handling an estimated 15,000 different government forms is $40 billion, well over the national expenditure for *all* research and development. Clearly, some of this paperwork is worth the cost, but much is not. We also should recognize that much of this red tape resulted from requests made by businesses themselves. Keep these key ideas in mind as you read this chapter:

■ Public policy can both improve and impair seller behavior.

■ Deregulation can create market chaos that slows the seller's learning process.

■ Patent regulation encourages invention and non-price competition.

■ In many markets, safety regulations are required to protect the consumer because competition has failed to do so (a free market failure).

■ Free markets always have laws against misleading pricing and price fixing, which reduce price competition.

■ Distribution regulations are designed to encourage competition between resellers (called intrabrand competition).

---

1. For details, see Robert J. Posch, Jr., *The Complete Guide to Marketing Law* (Englewood Cliffs: Prentice Hall, 1990).

- Selling and advertising regulations seek to eliminate deception and dishonesty.

- Seller behavior is actually expected to be more ethical than that required by law, which only provides a framework for moral considerations.

- The principle of utility says that when faced with a moral dilemma, a seller should choose the option that does the most good for the most. In practice, this is very hard to determine.

- The categorical imperative suggests that to determine if a behavior is unethical, one should ask, "Would it be wrong if everyone did it?" Most of the time we know the answer to this question, but sometimes we do not.

- We have ethical standards when we have the courage to ask hard questions about our behavior. How we choose to resolve ethical dilemmas tells us a lot about ourselves.

- Trade quotas, import taxes, and the ways in which governments manipulate currency to enhance the competitiveness of domestic products are issues of concern in global marketing. This is bound to continue.

- The establishment of universal marketing ethics is a problem because the global marketplace is made up of different cultures with different ethics.

The Positive Side of Public Policy

While the law and paperwork can frustrate initiative, public policy, in general, is positive for business. The exhibit on page 190 outlines some ways in which government benefits the marketplace. The point is that marketers can be just as shortsighted about the role played by public policy in the marketplace as they can about changing consumer needs or technological innovations in production. A hostile attitude toward regulation that is generalized into a hostile attitude toward public policy is unreasonable, and if it encourages a marketing strategy that willfully frustrates the letter or intent of the law, it can be disastrous.

We start with a discussion of why some markets are heavily regulated. This is followed by an analysis of what happens when these markets are deregulated. The remaining sections describe regulations that apply to all markets. These regulations cover product, price, distribution, advertising, and selling. Each subsection can be matched with later chapters that discuss these elements of marketing strategy.

A completely regulated market is one in which the number of sellers is controlled and any marketing strategy must be approved by a controlling authority. Many of the widely accepted reasons for completely regulating a product-market are primarily economic or associated with public safety. In some markets, it does not make sense to have competition. Imagine if we have several local phone companies, each with its own lines. We would need a telephone line for each phone company.

Industry Regulation and Deregulation

Natural Monopolies

When a monopoly results in lower costs, it is called a natural monopoly. Monopoly is often associated with higher prices, but monopolies do not always result in higher prices. Whenever the fixed costs of a service are very high and there are large economies of scale, a monopoly service can result in lower prices than if competition existed. Most

1. *Protective tariffs, subsidies, and tax breaks.* While we take pride in being a free market system, some 30 percent of U.S. product-markets are protected by tariffs and import quotas. Even more are protected by threats of action, which result in voluntary constraints by overseas competitors (such as the Japanese auto manufacturers). Prices in some markets are subsidized (such as the agricultural product-market). Our tax laws are such that many billion-dollar companies pay little or no taxes. In fact, some of the tax breaks have grossly distorted the investment and marketplace behavior of companies.

2. *Contract laws and fair trade practices.* The law and the courts provided by our government are essential to maintain the integrity of legal contracts. The importance of this legal infrastructure is often taken for granted until a business faces inept or corrupt courts of law, as can exist in some third-world countries. Nothing discourages investment and closes down a marketplace faster.

utility markets fall into this category. They allow a single seller, but they regulate its prices and other marketing and production strategies. Other markets allow competition but are heavily regulated to assure orderly competition and to maintain adequate safety standards. The broadcast media (television and radio) are regulated. Each station is allocated a band of radio wave that it uses to transmit its signal. Without such control, the airwaves would be congested. The airline industry was initially regulated to help it get started. Its later regulation was justified on the grounds of public safety.

Unnatural Monopolies

The problem with protected monopolies is that the enterprise, vitality, and change provided by the forces of competition are no longer present. The absence or limitation of competition discourages innovation, risk taking, and efficiency. For several decades it seemed that several industries could not resist convincing legislators to pass laws that effectively restricted new competition, even competition between existing firms. In recent years, public policymakers have taken a hard look at the industries listed in Figure 6-1 and decided to rejuvenate them by allowing free-market forces to operate again. The effects have been dramatic and in some cases unexpected.

The Chaos of Industry Deregulation

In a typical competitive marketplace, it is possible to determine the impact that might occur if one firm makes a change in strategy while the competition is conducting business as usual. Let us imagine the opposite extreme, however: Suppose *everyone* in the market changes strategy. To make the situation even worse, what if there is no past history that can be used to forecast the impact of any of the players' new strategies? We might also introduce some completely new and unpredictable players into the market. This is the sort of extreme shock a decision-making team faces when a market is deregulated.

A regulated market, by definition, restrains and controls competition; it imposes order. When a market is deregulated, the players are allowed to attack each other's

3. *Government agencies.* The services of government agencies range from setting standards to checking for accurate measure at the gas pumps (in both volume and rated octane) to ensure that advertising claims made about competitors' products can be substantiated. Such accurate information makes the market fairer and more competitive. The law also protects extremely valuable patents, trademarks, and brand names.

4. *Government as a source of market research.* Through its Census Bureau and Department of Commerce, government provides invaluable free information to marketers about consumers, suppliers, distributors, competitors, technology, and economic trends. In addition, the government subsidizes higher education and research establishments that provide technological research and development, market research, and career and occupational training.

market share, change pricing strategies, and undertake competitive product differentiation and advertising. Deregulation introduces a state of chaos into the market:

1. Many of the players take new competitive positions and launch new strategies. These moves intersect and interact with each other, creating an unpredictable and volatile market. Based on the initial performance of their new moves, some participants have second thoughts and change their positioning and strategy. This creates new disturbances in the market.

2. Everyone in the deregulated market is inexperienced. The players, including the consumers and channels, must adjust to new competitive realities. As they learn to cope, their behavior and loyalties change, which further alters the dynamics of the market.

Observing the impact of a risk taker, an initially conservative competitor may then throw caution to the wind and quickly mimic the innovator or pursue a different but equally extreme strategy. In the process, it may bump heads with another company pursuing the same target market with a similar strategy. Both may recoil and back off or both may dig their heels in, expecting the other to withdraw. Meanwhile, another competitor that elected to pursue a different target market with a different strategy may reap the greatest benefits, partly because it may also have had time to gain a dominant presence in this market segment.

The competitive inexperience of the marketing strategists may also lead to major mistakes in strategy known as competitive irrationality. Certain environmental constraints may be overlooked simply because they never had to be considered in the good old days when the market was regulated. For example, when the airlines were initially deregulated, the ability of each airline to compete on price was now constrained by fuel efficiency, the suitability of its fleet for the new markets (routes), and labor costs. Continental was the first major carrier to fail because its pricing strategy was unrealistic, given its cost structure. Its bankruptcy, however, may have been a blessing in disguise because its initial failure to adapt to the new competitive realities gave it the opportunity and courage to 1) restructure its debt and fleet and 2) renegotiate its labor contracts with its pilots and other labor unions. The new company that emerged was better adapted to the new market realities, even if it was taken over by another company (Texas Air).

Banking

- The freeing of interest rates led to the introduction of interest-bearing check accounts, a greater variety of savings accounts, and generally higher rates of interest.
- Direct costs were raised, charges for checkbooks and bounced checks were raised.
- Banks initially lengthened the holding period for checks and used the extra "float" as a no-cost source of funds.
- A shocking failure rate in the savings and loans industry was caused by competition for funds, risky investments, foolish tax and accounting policy, lax regulation of bank solvency, and fraud. Customers were not selective and vigilant because the security of their deposits was still assured by the government. Thus, an important determinant of competitive efficiency was not present.
- Labor costs were trimmed. Fewer full-service branches and more automated teller machines were provided.
- Enterprising banks focused on market niches, for example BancOne in Columbus, Ohio, specialized in processing cash management accounts for brokerage firms that by law could not issue and process checks themselves.

Telephone Services

- Long-distance rates fell by at least 20 percent and are still dropping.
- The local cost of calls increased by over 30 percent but so did the volume; therefore the cost per call increased less.
- The number of telephone suppliers increased from 25 to over 200. Innovations and variety greatly increased.
- Introduction of fibre optics in long-distance networks accelerated, led by Sprint as a point of differentiation.
- Service complaints increased. Many consumers were confused and unhappy with the AT&T breakup—"if it works, why fix it."
- AT&T kept more than 60 percent of the long-distance market. MCI and Sprint struggled to make the necessary billions to invest in new networks and still make a profit.

Railroads

- The industry was restructured into several national railroad systems with regional feeder carriers.
- Concentration increased from 11 major companies in 1978 to six in 1986 who carried 86 percent of the freight.
- Investment in new rolling stock and profitability increased. Railroads invested in other transportation modes to offer integrated services.
- The quality of service increased with automation and superior information systems.

Trucking

- Since 1980, 17,000 new trucking companies (mainly small fleets of one to three vehicles) have been launched; 6,500 have failed.
- Services were broadened, new terminals were built, and rates were lowered.
- Concentration in the less-than-truckload (LTL) market increased with about five companies dominating.
- Highway accidents increased per haulage mile, caused by desperate operators driving dangerous vehicles.

Air carriers

- Between 1978 and 1988, 215 new air carriers entered the market. The number of airlines authorized to fly planes with more than 60 seats rose from 36 in 1978 to 123 in 1984 and then decreased to 74 in 1987.
- Tickets were estimated to be 40 percent cheaper in 1987 than they would have been under regulation. However, fares were much cheaper on major competitive routes, much higher on other routes. Continued price wars and promotions drove three major airlines into bankruptcy in 1991.
- The number of domestic passengers increased from 255 million in 1978 to 393 million in 1986.
- Low airfares forced a merger between the two major bus companies, Greyhound and Trailways, creating a monopoly.
- More than 900 previously monopoly routes were made competitive.
- Airlines restructured around hubs with commuter airlines expanding to serve abandoned routes and feed the hubs.
- Airline labor costs were reduced significantly.
- Service deteriorated as infrastructure airports and air traffic control did not expand to cope with increased demand. Reduction in service personnel also reduced service.
- Travel agents became more powerful as airlines competed on routes. Agents increased their commission percentages.
- Frequent-flier programs were introduced to encourage loyalty among heavy users.
- Air safety per mile flown initially decreased but then increased.

Figure 6-1
The Effects of Deregulation on Selected Product-Markets

Sources: Howard Banks, "The Start of a Revolt," *Forbes,* October 7, 1985, 41–42; Lewis M. Schneider, "New Era in Transportation Strategy," *Harvard Business Review,* March/April 1985, 118–26; Chris Welles, et al., "Is Deregulation Working," *Business Week,* December 22, 1986, 50–55; Stephen Koepp, "Rolling Back Regulation," *Time,* July 6, 1987, 50–52; Edward J. Kane, "The Unending Deposit Insurance Mess," *Science* 246 (October 27, 1989), 451–56; Joel A. Bleeke, "Strategic Choices for Newly Opened Markets," *Harvard Business Review,* September/October 1990, 158–65; Richard J. Herring, and Ashish C. Shah, eds., *Reforming the American Banking System* (Philadelphia, PA: The Wharton Financial Institutions Center, 1991).

The Fruits and Thorns of Deregulation

The initial purpose of regulation was to ensure adequate service for *all* at a reasonable cost in industries where economists believed competition would not lead to such an outcome. However, the price of regulation was often bad management, inefficient operations, inhibited innovation, discouraged segment marketing, and unrealistic franchise values because of restricted entry to the industry's supply sector. Deregulation was meant to produce more competition, lower prices, increase efficiency, and provide more choices for the consumer. As can be seen in Figure 6-1, deregulation achieved some of its goals. However, some effects were unexpected.

In several of the deregulated industries, major competitors have quickly reorganized and created networks that tend to monopolize certain geographical markets. For example, Northwest Airlines, with its hub in Minneapolis, TWA in St. Louis, and USAir in Pittsburgh control more than 80 percent of the business through these airports. The major airline hubs are fed by minor players. In these symbiotic relationships, the small airlines feed the large carrier, and the larger carrier provides reservation and check-in services, ground and baggage handling, and advertising.

A Tendency to Concentrate and Monopolize

Public policymakers worry most that the networks formed in the restructuring of several deregulated markets will create formidable barriers to entry, mobility, and innovativeness—the very things deregulation attempted to remove from the market. However, even if these barriers occur, the major competitors will still compete on the boundaries of their niches, keeping the market more competitive than it was under regulation. New technologies will also disturb any equilibrium. It is not at all clear that an oligopoly market (one with a few large competitors) can maintain a stable equilibrium anyway. Differences in the ambitions and competitiveness of the participants in an oligopoly market are inherently and ultimately destabilizing.

Finally, some policymakers believe that new regulations may be necessary in the trucking and airline markets to protect consumer and public safety. It is possible that competition can become too desperate in markets and lead to lower maintenance on equipment and overworked employees, both of which can endanger public safety. Other policymakers are unhappy that the advantages of deregulation are not distributed equitably. The faster, smarter, and wealthier consumers have reaped most of the benefits, but this is to be expected in any free and competitive market. Survival of the fittest affects both sellers and buyers. The hard facts are that not all sellers benefit the same from their selling practices and not all buyers benefit the same from their buying practices. We now turn to a discussion of specific regulations and policies.

The specific laws applying to products cover packaging requirements, ingredient labeling, instructions labeling, usage warnings, minimum quality or performance standards, mandatory warranties, product ratings, and production and marketing licenses and permits. Industry Associations, often active in shaping such laws, can be of great help in providing information on relevant laws and recommended compliance procedures. This section focuses on two of the most important product policy issues: patent regulation and product safety.

Product Regulations

Patent Regulation

The U.S. patent system is the result of a balance achieved between competing economic forces and the judiciary in order to maximize the total benefit to society. Much of the intent, legal prescription, and interpretation of marketing law involves the evaluation of several different arguments, each with merit. Marketers have to become familiar with these arguments in order to adapt to the law. Patents also provide a nice example of the problems inherent in implementing marketing law. Before expanding on these points, we note an important concept in marketing law: the law itself adapts to changes in the economy and specific markets.

The Rule of Reason

This rule, first applied in the early 1900s by the Supreme Court, says that the law should be interpreted to fit the prevailing competitive, political, and social situations. It should not be interpreted rigidly (called *per se* judgment). Instead, the interpretation should be flexible so that the original intent of the law can be achieved, even if the new precedent conflicts with the letter of the law. Reason and reasonableness are used to judge whether the law has been broken. The rule of reason permits the law to keep up with technological and social innovations and be progressive in its fostering of competition and protecting consumers. The disadvantage is that it may be difficult to predict how a law will be interpreted by the courts. Old precedents may not apply. The rule of reason increases uncertainty and risk for a company thinking about a groundbreaking marketing strategy. The rule of reason has been exercised in the following debate.

Innovation Competition versus Price Competition

A patent allows the holder to extract monopoly profits for an invention or design for up to 17 years. No one else is allowed to design a product or service using the patent without the inventor's permission. A patent rewards creative genius. It is meant to encourage the development of new processes and products that will ultimately benefit society. By protecting a good idea from immediately being copied by competition, patent law encourages an important type of competition. New inventions create obsolescence and force competitors to upgrade their technology, service, and marketing. Without patents, the incentive to invest in risky R&D that leads to new and improved products would be greatly reduced. Without patents, the number of new products would decline, ultimately reducing competition.[2] On the other hand, patents restrict competition in the sense that only the holder of the patent or companies that pay royalties to the patent holder can manufacture and market the invention. This results in higher prices.

The conflict between long-term, new-product competition and short-term price competition has been debated and partially resolved in the pharmaceutical market. Many patented drugs now have a much shorter patent protection of only seven years. This is to enable free-market price competition, particularly with generic substitutes, much sooner than was possible in the past. On the other hand, legislators accepted the argument that the United States would lose its international leadership in pharmaceuticals if some reasonable patent protection was not in place to recover the huge costs and risks involved in developing, effectively testing, and marketing not only successful new drugs but also less successful drugs that never made it to the market.

---

2. Weak patent protection encourages imitative price competition and discourages innovation competition.

Name of Drug	AARP Pharmacy Service (by mail)	America's Pharmacy (by mail)	Walgreens (chain store)	OSCO (chain store)	Independent Pharmacy
Apresoline 25mg/100 tablets	$25.90	$25.14	$29.99	$27.99	$25.92
Generic hydralazine	4.25	4.55	6.99	7.93	3.71
Calon 80mg/100 tablets	37.40	40.66	43.99	43.39	41.92
Generic verapamil	15.95	4.64	15.99	16.39	19.98
Diabinese 100mg/100 tablets	29.60	30.58	34.95	32.99	29.95
Generic chloropropamide	8.90	1.49	8.99	8.39	8.66
Dyazide 100 capsules	28.95	34.14	31.99	28.99	36.20
Generic triamterene & hydrochlorothiazide	16.75	16.82	19.99	19.99	19.98
Elavil 50mg/100 tablets	54.50	59.44	63.99	60.99	46.97
Generic amitriptyline	6.90	4.10	9.99	8.39	13.06
Lasix 40mg/100 tablets	16.95	17.70	16.99	16.99	23.00
Generic furosemide	5.95	4.50	7.99	6.99	9.45
Motrin 400mg/100 tablets	12.95	18.07	15.99	19.99	29.11
Generic ibuprofen	8.45	5.20	9.99	10.99	15.45
Nuprosyn 375mg/100 tablets	79.90	82.76	88.99	84.39	99.80
Generic none available	—	—	—	—	—
Procardia 20mg/100 tablets	82.45	94.01	87.99	88.99	100.00
Generic nifedipine	45.95	43.66	54.99	55.99	70.00
Valium 5mg/15 tablets	8.75	7.78	11.79	11.39	14.52
Generic diazepam	2.50	.74	5.29	5.39	7.71

Figure 6-2

Comparing Drug Prices

The originally patented drug still often sells at a huge premium over the generic competition. Prices vary less among stores than between the brand and generic drug. This suggests that doctor loyalty to the original drug explains the huge price premium and not the fact that consumers have little incentive to search because they do not pay for the medicine directly.

Source: Elliott H. McCleary, "How and Where You Can Save Over 50% on Prescription Drugs," *Consumer's Digest*, November/December, 1992.

The evidence suggests that the initial patent protection from competition continues after the expiration of the patent (see Figure 6-2). The medical profession tends to remain loyal to the pioneering brand of a drug and a pioneering brand's price remains higher than the generic substitute. Although some may argue that the original brand dissolves faster or provides some minor advantage, the Federal Drug Administration believes that many of the superiority claims are false. As a consequence, all fifty states have passed laws that give pharmacists the discretion of substituting a less expensive generic unless the doctor specifically forbids it. In Florida, pharmacists are required to inform consumers about how much they can save if they purchase the generic equivalent.

The problem in the drug market is that the buying expert consulted (the doctor) has no financial incentive to recommend the cheaper generic substitute. In fact, due to the extent that the drug industry provides conference expenses and other promotions to the medical profession, the incentive is quite the opposite. The consumer often does not pay directly for the medication, further reducing the price sensitivity of the competition. Cost is also not a very salient concern when health is at stake. The lesson that can be learned is that patent protection gives a company a chance to establish strong consumer and channel loyalty. If the patent holder markets its product well, this loyalty will carry on past the period of legal monopoly into the free market.

Patent Piracy and Weak Policing

Unfortunately, United States patent law often does not function the way it should. Firms get away with patent infringement by pleading ignorance or by claiming that the damage to the patent holder is minimal. Larger enterprises steal patents and then wear down the patent holder in the courts. A small company or individual who holds a patent hardly stands a chance against a big domestic or foreign company in court.

Some critics argue that the patent law hurts, rather than helps, the protection of inventions. The required disclosure of working drawings is helpful to competitors. Because the courts have been so weak in upholding the rights of the holder, some companies would rather keep certain processes a secret than "protect" them with a patent. Today, many people believe that our economic survival depends on maintaining a lead in technological inventiveness and initiative. This means that public policy is likely to shift in the direction of making patent law much tougher, particularly on low-cost, off-shore patent pirates. The courts are likely to take a much harder line on patent infringements by all competitors, whether foreign or domestic, leading to an increase in returns from innovations that can be patent protected. This will produce an increase in R&D investment.

Consumer and Environmental Protection

Much of our consumer and environmental protection legislation has come about as the result of horrific cases in which companies marketed dangerous foods, medications, cosmetics, or machines that eventually killed or maimed users or polluted the environment. We need to be protected against dangerous products, but how much protection do we need?

A further problem with consumer and environmental safety is that sometimes the long-term consequences of product use cannot be determined beforehand. The discoverer of DDT won a Nobel prize for his invention. The insecticide saved hundreds of thousands of lives by killing the malaria-carrying mosquito. However, the product was so successful that excessive and possibly irresponsible agricultural use led to a buildup of DDT in the food chain of birds, particularly the bald eagle (our national symbol). DDT was banned, and pesticides now require much more testing before being allowed on the market. Companies cannot anticipate all of the consequences of product use (and misuse). They cannot be blamed for doing their best, but marketers have a responsibility to remain vigilant in their effort to sniff out emerging problems. They should be open and responsive to questions about product safety and environmental pollution raised by users and the public. Figure 6-3 presents an example of a positive approach to environmental protection by one of the leading waste-disposal service companies.

A major problem with safety and environment regulations is that companies, regulators, and opinion leaders (such as Ralph Nader and the media) find it difficult to keep the relative risks and benefits of regulation in perspective. Some of the misperceptions are surprising. They can be partially explained by the ways consumers view risks and dangerous products. It seems that consumers are prepared to accept *voluntary* risks, in which the users of the product *knowingly* balance the risks against the benefits (such as skydiving, skiing, hunting, swimming and smoking), but risk perceptions may still be wrong. This explains why ski resorts advertise the risks of skiing and why the cigarette manufacturers did not violently object to the strengthened warning messages on their packaging. The cigarette and asbestos industries have discovered that such risk disclosure reduces (but does not necessarily eliminate) their liability.

It is quite another matter when users and the general public belatedly discover that they have been exposed to involuntary risks through their use of a product (such

Environmental Principles of Waste Management, Inc.

1. **Environmental Protection and Enhancement**
The company is committed to improving the environment through the services that we offer and to providing our services in a manner demonstrably protective of human health and the environment, even if not required by law. We will minimize and strive not to allow any releases to the atmosphere, land, or water in amounts that may harm human health and the environment. We will train employees to enhance understanding of environmental policies and to promote excellence in job performance on all environmental matters.

2. **Waste Reduction, Recycling, Treatment and Disposal**
The company will work to minimize the volume and toxicity of waste generated by us and others. We will operate internal recycling programs. We will vigorously pursue opportunities to recycle waste before other management practices are applied. The company will use and provide environmentally safe treatment and disposal services for waste that is not eliminated at the source or recycled.

3. **Biodiversity**
The company is committed to the conservation of nature. We will implement a policy of "no net loss" of wetlands or other biological diversity on the company's property.

4. **Sustainable Use of Natural Resources**
The company will use renewable natural resources, such as water, soils and forests, in a sustainable manner and will offer services to make degraded resources once again usable. We will conserve nonrenewable natural resources through efficient use and careful planning.

5. **Wise Use of Energy**
The company will make every reasonable effort to use environmentally safe and sustainable energy sources to meet our needs. We will seek opportunities to improve energy efficiency and conservation in our operations.

6. **Compliance**
The company is committed to comply with all legal requirements and to implement programs and procedures to ensure compliance. These efforts will include training and testing of employees, rewarding employees who excel in compliance, and disciplining employees who violate legal requirements.

7. **Risk Reduction**
The company will operate in a manner designed to minimize environmental, health or safety hazards. We will minimize risk and protect our employees and others in the vicinity of our operations by employing safe technologies and operating procedures and by being prepared for emergencies. The company will make available to our employees and to the public information related to any of our operations that we believe cause environmental harm or pose health or safety hazards. The company will encourage employees to report any condition that creates a danger to the environment or poses health or safety hazards, and will provide confidential means for them to do so.

8. **Damage Compensation**
The company will take responsibility for any harm we cause to the environment and will make every reasonable effort to remedy the damage caused to people or ecosystems.

9. **Research and Development**
The company will research, develop and implement technologies for integrated waste management.

10. **Public Policy**
The company will provide information to and will assist the public in understanding the environmental impacts of our activities. We will conduct public tours of facilities, consistent with safety requirements, and will work with communities near our facilities to encourage dialogue and exchange of information on facility activities.

11. **Public Education**
The company will support and participate in development of public policy and in educational initiatives that will protect human health and improve the environment. We will seek cooperation on this work with government, environmental groups, schools, universities, and other public organizations.

12. **Participation in Environmental Organizations**
The company will encourage its employees to participate in and to support the work of environmental organizations, and we will provide support to environmental organizations for the advancement of environmental protection.

13. **Monitor and Report Environmental Matters**
The Board of Directors of the company will evaluate and will address the environmental implications of its decisions. The Executive Environmental Committee of the company will report directly to the CEO of the company and will monitor and report upon implementation of this policy and other environmental matters. The company will commit the resources needed to implement these principles.

14. **Annual Report**
The company will prepare and make public an annual report on its environmental activities. The report will include a self-evaluation of the company's performance in complying with all applicable environmental laws and regulations throughout its worldwide operations.

This progressive approach to protecting the environment might be expected from a leading waste-disposal company.

Figure 6-3
Environmental Principles of Waste Management, Inc.

Source: Reproduced with permission from Joan V. Bernstein, "Environmental Policy and Strategic Planning," in *Corporate Stewardship and the Environment*, ed. Barbara H. Peters and James L. Peters (New York: The Conference Board, 1991), 20.

as the risks created by pesticide use or nuclear power). When it is also revealed that suppliers have attempted to cover up such hazards, a major scandal may be in the making. Corporate dishonesty and disregard for consumer or environmental safety seems inexcusable, and yet desperate firms often appear to prefer this route.

Manufacturers and marketers should argue that cost has to be considered and compared to the incremental increase in safety. But an appeal to common sense and reason in regulation will not wash if regulators believe that an industry or company has not shown genuine concern and good faith for consumer safety in the past. The rather obvious reason that we have product safety laws and the Food and Drug Administration is to protect the public from rogue firms or even whole industries who, far from serving the consumer interest, have endangered the health and well-being of their customers.

Price Regulations

The laws that apply to pricing are primarily aimed at preventing unfair and deceptive practices. Avoiding price competition and charging different buyers different prices for the same products are considered unfair practices. Price deception occurs when an actual selling price turns out to be more than was claimed.

Price Fixing

Price fixing between suppliers is the best-known illegal marketing tactic. It is an obvious conspiracy against the free market, unless of course the government does it in its regulation of a market. Price fixing has occurred in many and varied markets from giant electricity generating turbines to school milk programs to Ivy League colleges. Price fixing can have dire consequences for the firm and individual executive. In ancient Rome, price fixers were put to death. Today, they may go to jail. The real economic threat is that if a company is found liable, it can be forced to pay triple damages to the aggrieved party to cover not only the consequences of its own actions but even the consequences of the actions of all of its co-conspirators. Price fixing has resulted in huge fines (in the hundreds of millions of dollars).

Price Signaling

Some industries fix prices less blatantly by having the market leader report its intended future prices to the other suppliers, who then set their prices only after they know what the leader's price will be. Illegal price signaling can be hard to determine. Everyone agrees that a market is more efficient and competitive when suppliers and consumers have information about market prices. Advertising prices helps achieve this, but some critics argue that suppliers should be required to make public their actual selling prices, not just their list prices. A rule of reason is therefore applied to judging whether any potential price signaling is illegal. The private exchange of price information between suppliers (with or without the assistance of a trade association) is illegal if it results in a period of stable or rising prices. However, when prices are signaled in public and a price war results, such price signaling between competitors is judged not only legal, but desirable.

Discriminatory Pricing

A supplier is allowed to respond to changes in demand by charging different prices for a product or service in different situations and at different times. Charging two customers different prices for exactly the same type and amount of goods in the same situation and time period is not allowed. The Robinson-Patman Act, passed in 1936, is the major law banning price discrimination. It prevents manufacturers from selling their goods at lower prices to major chain stores unless the company can prove proportionate cost advantages for selling to such large customers. The act was passed to protect smaller, inefficient, but possibly more service-oriented family stores.

Resale Price Maintenance

While manufacturers are required to *sell* their products at the *same* wholesale prices to different retailers, they are not allowed to enforce *standard* resale prices. Attempts to enforce a minimum retail price may encourage a retailer (often a discounter) to sue. Any pressure in the form of threats or acts, such as the withdrawal of service or delivery tardiness, can be damning. A manufacturer, however, can print its manufacturer recommended price (MRP) on its packaging. Resale price maintenance is a vexing problem, because other retailers often are upset with a manufacturer for not discouraging competition from undercutting them on price.

Predatory Pricing

In order to drive fledgling competition out of the market, the classic tactic is for a market leader to cut its prices to the bone. When monopoly is achieved, the predator, faced with no competition, raises prices. Such a predator must have deep pockets or a lower cost structure. It must also have a good deal of confidence that other entrepreneurs with superior products or production processes will not enter the market in the future. The standard evidence of predatory pricing (which is very hard to obtain) is that the price is below marginal or average cost, whichever is the lower. Such a price is clearly unprofitable, and the obvious inference is that it has been applied solely to hurt the competition more than it hurts the predator. However, a seller can match (but not undercut) the prices of competitors even if the price is below cost. Size and success also have a lot to do with establishing a predatory pricing case. It is difficult to accuse a company with a small market share of predatory pricing.

Price Misrepresentation

Public policy makers have long been aware of the competitive practice of quoting or stating prices in ways that make price comparisons between options difficult. Competitors do this to reduce the sensitivity of the market to price and hence price competition. A number of laws require the standardized presentation of price. Lenders are required to state the terms of their loan offerings in annual simple interest rates and some states require unit pricing of supermarket packaged goods to make it easier for consumers to compare the prices of different sizes. With the advent of the universal product code (UPC) and checkout scanning equipment, many state laws also require the prominent shelf-labeling of prices, detailed cash-register receipts, and even the continuation of individual item pricing. Special introductory pricing offers must be new offerings and must last a reasonable period of time. They must also offer genuine savings in that the final price actually rises to the level that will substantiate the claim of the introductory offer. Finally, the words *economy, budget* or *bargain* can be used to describe a price only if other package sizes in the same product line are priced at least 5 percent higher per unit volume.

Distribution Relationship Regulations

The law that applies to distribution relationships covers franchising and exclusive dealing. These practices restrict competition among outlets selling the same brand (intrabrand competition). It also addresses the tricky situation of trading with distributors or customers who are also competitors.

Franchising and Exclusive Relationships

Franchising is a long-term trading contract or partnership with another party. The fundamental legal issue is whether a franchising arrangement substantially reduces competition in the relevant market. In part, this is determined by the relative strength of the competitors and the market share involved. As in other areas of marketing law, judgments have been inconsistent.

The Brown Shoe Company arranged with its dealers (who made up about 1 percent of all shoe retailers) to provide group insurance, assistance with shop design, and other marketing help. In return, the dealers agreed to concentrate on the purchases of Brown shoes. Even though the agreement was not binding and could be terminated by the dealers at any time, the Supreme Court supported the Federal Trade Commission's claim that this arrangement potentially injured competition. Thousands of franchise contracts are more binding. The difference is that normally they are made between a supplier and an entrepreneur who is setting up in business. Consequently, the arrangement does not affect existing suppliers.

A Shift in Legal Power

The general view is that franchise contracts greatly favor the franchisor or supplier. This may no longer be true. In early 1984, Porsche AG attempted to break from its Volkswagen of America franchised dealers so that it could sell through factory-owned outlets. It hoped to be able to better control its marketing, service, and pricing. However, a dealer group representing about 80 percent of Porsche cars sold in the United States sued, claiming $1 billion in damages. Porsche quickly backed down.

Franchisee gas stations won a major settlement with the oil companies allowing them to shop for the cheapest gasoline available. For example, a Texaco dealer can now buy Mobil gas, but it must inform its customers that the gas comes from a different company. There is evidence that unhappy franchisees are now joining together and using the threat of an antitrust suit to obtain what they want from the franchisor. This situation is another indication of the growing influence of retailers and distributors over suppliers.

Tying Contractual Relationships

You cannot use demand for one product to sell another. For example, motion picture distributors once required television stations to buy films such as *Gorilla Man* if they wanted to purchase popular features such as *Casablanca*. This tying arrangement was deemed a violation of the Sherman Antitrust Act. However, companies are allowed to offer cheap financing tied to a purchase. Forced reciprocity, in which a consumer is forced to sell its product to the supplier on particular terms as part of the price of obtaining a desired product, is also regarded as illegal tying. Tying arrangements are illegal when monopoly or economic power is used to force the consumer to purchase an otherwise unattractive product or service.

Restricting Intrabrand Competition

While the courts may frown on the exclusive franchising of existing distributors, they have allowed manufacturers to deliberately restrict their number of product resellers in a particular market, be it a regional territory or a group of customers. Refusal to supply other resellers is acceptable if such a tactic increases or is likely to increase competition *between* manufacturers' brands—that is, if it increases interbrand competition.

While the purpose of antitrust regulation is to promote competition, the law is unclear when intrabrand competition (competition between retailers selling the same product and brand) should be traded off against interbrand competition (competition between manufacturers' brands). Applying the rule of reason, the Supreme Court objected to the refusal of Schwinn Bicycles to deal with new distributors wanting its bikes. The court ruled that increasing the number of Schwinn outlets in the market would increase service and reduce the retail prices of this (then) leading brand. Expanding the outlets would increase intrabrand competition without materially hurting the interbrand competitiveness of Schwinn.

On the other hand, in a case involving Sylvania, the television manufacturer was allowed to restrict distribution of its product. At the time, RCA, along with Zenith and Magnavox, dominated the market. Sylvania argued that it could improve its distribution efficiency and competitiveness in the market by restricting its outlets to only two per metropolitan center. The court agreed that in this case interbrand competition would very likely be increased, even if at the expense of intrabrand competition.

Other acceptable grounds for restricting sales to resellers include when the product is highly perishable, is inherently dangerous to handle, or requires considerable investment on the part of a reseller to service the product. Distributors who sell the product and send their customers to a competitor's authorized service outlet are unfairly taking a free ride on the competitor's investment in customer service. When a distributor has to make a similar considerable investment to handle a product's perishability or risk of handling, it expects to recover such investments by being offered a larger, exclusive sales territory.

Selling Regulations

Apart from the laws of contract that apply to business-to-business marketing, the major laws affecting personal selling apply to door-to-door, or in-home, selling. Once very common, this type of marketing has declined because of its high cost and the dramatic increase in the numbers of working women. Over the years, it has fallen into disrepute because of hard-selling tactics involving harassment and misrepresentation. The law now requires door-to-door salespeople to immediately make clear the true purpose of the sales call. Market researchers report that such misrepresentation has become so well known that many people asked to participate in surveys are suspicious that the real intent is to make a sale, not conduct a survey. The unscrupulous behavior of a few has hurt the ability of all marketers to study consumers.

The law also requires a cooling-off period of three days during which the consumer can withdraw from a signed agreement or contract. This regulation also applies to dance studios and health clubs, some of which have been accused of being too successful at talking potential customers into long-term contracts. The greatest problems with personal selling, however, are caused by the thieves who prey on the elderly or feebleminded. A typical ruse is to inspect victims' chimneys and declare them a safety hazard. The victims are then charged thousands of dollars for so-called repairs that can never be inspected and amount to nothing more than cleaning the chimney. The best protection for such vulnerable consumers may not be federal or state law but a friendly, caring, old-time banker who flags major withdrawals from the elderly's savings, discreetly determines the purpose, and reports anything suspicious to the police. This example serves to remind us that the law often has great difficulty preventing the behavior of those with clear criminal intent. It often requires a great deal of public cooperation.

Advertising Regulations

The major concern of the government regulation of advertising is the control of deceptive practices. Initially, such regulation was justified on the grounds that advertising deception was unfair to competitors and, hence, came under the jurisdiction of anti-competition laws (for example the Wheeler-Lea Amendment). Not until the 1930s was deception declared illegal because it was unfair to consumers.

The Federal Trade Commission was set up in 1914, but it did not become an advertising regulatory agency until the 1960s. This commission investigates complaints and is empowered to make rules that advertisers must follow. Most advertising deception cases are settled out of court by withdrawal of the offending advertisement, but occasionally advertisers are required to make restitution to consumers or undertake corrective advertising to change false consumer perceptions.

What Is Deceptive?

The definition of a deceptive advertising claim has been argued in the courts and academic journals for a number of years. Initially, advertising was considered deceptive if the claim was related to an important product characteristic and was not literally true. The question was answered by consulting dictionaries. Today, however, with television and magazine advertising involving few words and much imagery, deception is more often judged by measuring the impact of the advertising on consumer beliefs and attitudes. If the advertising creates beliefs that cannot be supported by the advertiser (using market research or product testing), then the ad may be judged to be making false representations.

False representation can include not telling all, as well as telling lies. For example, a television advertisement for an acne remedy was considered deceptive on two counts. First, the endorsers, Pat Boone and his daughters, had not actually used the formulation (as some viewers inferred). By law, an endorser must have used the product and continue to use the product. Second, the advertisement did not disclose that Pat Boone was president of the company marketing the product. The advertisement must disclose whether the endorser has been paid to endorse the product or is receiving a commission on sales.

Expert endorsers must possess expertise relevant to the product claims and must have legitimately evaluated the product, and its competitive substitutes. Advertising deception applies to product characteristics, price claims, information about product availability, and any promotional contests and sweepstakes. For example, sweepstakes advertising must disclose the number of prizes and the odds of winning.

Substantiation of Claims

The long era of using superlatives in advertising, such as "the best," "the cheapest," and "the easiest to use," may be drawing to a close. Such general positive claims (called puffery in advertising) were long considered acceptable, because advertisers were expected to praise their product. Most of us learned at an early age to be suspicious of advertising claims. Our parents taught us, and we learned from experience. Even so, increasingly, advertisers are asked either to provide substantiation for their claims or to stop making them. For example, comparison advertising must be based on valid laboratory tests, market research, or other objective information.

Deceptive advertising by sellers also needs to be put in perspective. How many of us strenuously object to deceptive advertising, but do not think twice about using enticing words to attract buyers when we are selling cars that have become, for one undisclosed reason or another, too expensive to maintain? Honesty in advertising presumably applies across the board, whether you are the buyer or the seller.

Marketing Ethics

Ethics are our beliefs about what is right and what is wrong. The planning process recognizes responsibilities to consumers, channel members, and the company. This responsibility is accomplished by designing a marketing strategy to satisfy the needs of each of these groups. The law and general public-policy issues also come into play. However, personal beliefs about what is right and what is wrong should also constrain our decision making. It is called exercising ethical standards.

Ultimately, marketing planners must live with their professional behavior and decisions in the same way that they must live with their personal behavior and decisions. An implication of the theory of competitive rationality is that the ethics and values of marketing planners greatly influence society. Because supplier behavior shapes consumer behavior, the values of marketing planners expressed in what they make and how they sell set a moral tone in and beyond the marketplace. The ethical dilemmas can be complex.

The Law Is a *Minimum* Ethical Standard

Why do we need ethics when we have the law, which tells us what we can and cannot do? One answer is that the letter of the law is generally considered to be only a minimum ethical standard. Another answer is that the law often does not work the way it should. As aptly stated in the code of ethics of Caterpillar Tractor, the law is a floor, and must not serve as the *only* basis for individual and corporate ethics.[3]

Company and Personal Ethics

Despite the general public image, many companies are moral enterprises, led by men and women of impeccable character. Such enterprises have written codes of ethics and unwritten company cultures that influence marketing decision making. A company code of ethics is actually a type of company constraint on marketing decision making similar to a production constraint or a financial goal.

Figure 6-4 presents a summary of the business conduct guidelines of IBM and P&G. Figure 6-5 summarizes the content of some 200 company ethics statements.

3. Gene R. Laczniak and Patrick E. Murphy, *Marketing Ethics* (Lexington, MA: Lexington Books, 1985).

Figure 6-4

Business Conduct Guidelines for IBM and P&G

Source: Gene R. Laczniak and Patrick E. Murphy, *Marketing Ethics* (Lexington, MA: Lexington Books, 1985), 117–23, and Jan Willem Bol, Charles T. Crespy, James M. Stearns, and John R. Walton, *The Integration of Ethics into the Marketing Curriculum* (Needham Heights, MA: Ginn Press, 1991), 27.

IBM

- Do not make misrepresentations to anyone you deal with.
- Do not use IBM's size unfairly to intimidate or threaten.
- Treat all buyers and sellers equitably.
- Do not engage in reciprocal dealing.
- Do not disparage competitors.
- Do not prematurely disclose an unannounced offering.
- Do no further selling after competitor has the firm order.
- Keep contact with the competition minimal.
- Do not illegally use confidential information.
- Do not steal or obtain information by willful deceit.
- Do not violate patents or copyrights.
- Do not give or accept bribes, gifts, or entertainment that might be seen as creating an obligation.

P&G

- To provide customers with superior benefits.
- To listen and respond to customer opinions.
- To ensure products are safe for intended use and anticipate accidental misuse.
- To strive for fair and open business relationships with suppliers and retailers.
- To help business partners improve performance.
- To reject illegal or deceptive activities anywhere in the world.
- To safeguard the environment.
- To encourage employees to participate in community activities.
- To be a good neighbor in communities in which business is done.
- To provide employees a safe work place.
- To show concern for the well-being of all employees.
- To create opportunities for employee achievement, creativity, and personal reward.
- To provide a fair annual return to the owners.
- To build for the future to maintain growth.

Such company-imposed constraints on business practices might be reported in the company constraints section of a product-market environment report, but often they generally are assumed to be applied to all decisions made, so they may go unstated. The narrower and more prescriptive the code of ethics of a company, the less the ethical discretion of the marketing strategist and planner. However, many ethical dilemmas are situational, involving trade-offs between different interest groups or between the means and the end, so company codes of ethics are often general. Specific interpretation is left to the individual executive. Ethical dilemmas also arise in the implementation of strategy. Decisions often must be made without an opportunity to consult superiors. Such situations throw heavy responsibility on the cross-functional team, marketing manager, product manager, and salesperson.

Ethical stress on the marketing executive is greatly heightened by the presence of a double standard. Executives must meet performance goals. A company must make clear what action it will take against unethical behavior and establish credibility by following through. If actions are taken *only* when a company's behavior is publicly challenged, then the company sends the wrong signals to its marketing executives. What it says is that we do not really mind what you do to achieve your financial goals, as long as someone from outside does not raise hell. If this happens, we will piously

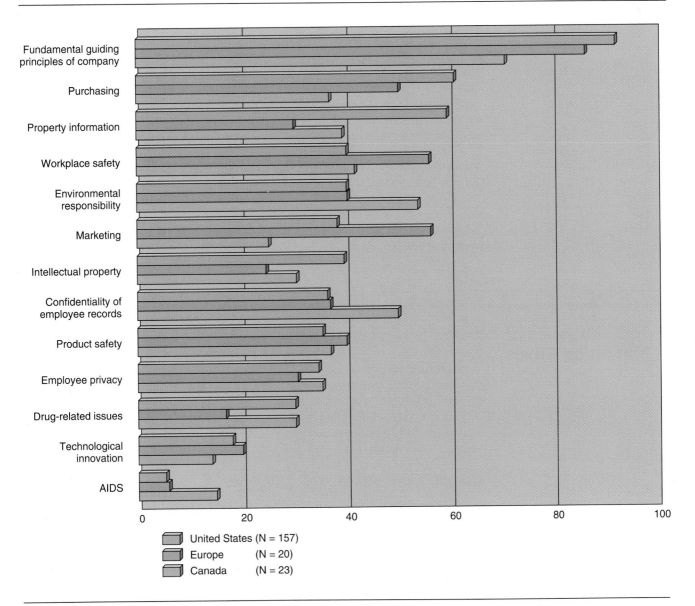

It seems that companies are more concerned that their purchasing is ethical than they are that their marketing is ethical. In the cross-cultural comparison, U.S. firms are more frequently concerned about proprietary information, Canadian firms more frequently concerned about environmental responsibility, and European firms more frequently concerned about workplace safety.

Source: Reproduced with permission from Ronald E. Berenbeim, *Corporate Ethics Practices* (New York: The Conference Board, 1992).

Figure 6-5

Issues Addressed by Company Ethics Statements

stick it to you. Unfortunately, many marketing decision makers face this conflict to varying degrees. It places great demands on their personal codes of ethics.

Junior marketing executives should also have strong personal codes of ethics. Subordinates are responsible for their own behavior even if following orders or under the threat of dismissal. Ignorance is also no excuse. There is no easy way out. To take a stand may put at risk a promotion or even your job. To not take a stand is to sell out your values, your self-respect, and your soul. To pass the responsibility on to senior executives may be construed as weakness or, worse, setting up your boss. When orders and ethics collide, a trusted mentor in an organization can be invaluable.

On a more positive note, many companies' mission statements contain core ethical values that have become part of the enduring corporate culture. The values have become so ingrained that they are automatically applied to the evaluation and implementation of strategy. They do not have to be stated in the marketing plan, as they are accepted by all concerned as a given.[4] Where do such values and rules come from? The next section discusses some of the issues and models that underlie personal and organizational ethics.

Theories of Marketing Ethics

This section discusses models of business ethics. One model argues that we do not really need ethics and another argues that there can be no tried-and-true code of ethics. We then turn for guidance to the underlying religious values of our society. Yet even this approach has problems. It seems that the best we can do is to confront ourselves honestly with a series of questions to challenge our thinking. Such an approach will at least stop us from avoiding or shelving the questions of ethics. We may also come away from the experience with a better understanding of who we are and why and how we made our choices.

Competition, Ethics, and Efficiency

Social Darwinism was used to excuse the sharp trading practices of the so-called robber barons who dominated American business at the turn of the century. These industrialists, financiers, and entrepreneurs helped make the United States a superpower. They left endowments that built some of the finest universities in the world. But they were also quite unscrupulous at times. On a similar theme, some marketers and economists have used Adam Smith's economic philosophy to argue that it is right to pursue self-interest (read selfish interests) in the marketplace, using any means within or around the law. It is true that competition makes the market efficient, but only in an ethical environment. For example, if suppliers conspire to reduce competition, then competition ceases to exist. Competition is also reduced if suppliers are not honest in their product or service claims. If advertising is deceptive or contractual promises are not kept, then the competitive pursuit of self-interest will no longer be efficient and serve the interests of consumers and society. When ethics do not exist, the visible hand of government regulation must ensure that competition works honestly and openly.[5]

4. Donald P. Robin and R. Eric Reidenbach, "Social Responsibility, Ethics, and Marketing Strategy: Closing the Gap between Concept and Application," *Journal of Marketing* 51 (January 1987), 44–58.
5. This argument is based on the philosophies of Thomas Hobbes and Jean-Jacques Rousseau, which state that society needs sets of rules (morality) that are accepted by all (the social contract) for it to funciton effectively.

The Shifting Sands of Situational Ethics

The famous philosophers David Hume, Jeremy Bentham, and John Stuart Mill developed the principle of utility: the right action is that which produces the most good for the most people in a specific situation. This is a very useful guide as ethical problems often arise because there is a trade-off between rights and interests. The guiding principle is relativistic and situational, in that one action is judged against another instead of an absolute standard. This relativism raises a number of problems.

First, how does one calculate the most good for the people? A problem with the principle of utility is that it does not help in measuring good or bad. Obviously, a decision maker cannot assess the total good of an action if the total good and bad cannot be measured. A second concern is whether we can measure good by adding up all the positive outcomes and then subtracting all the negative outcomes. For example, is it allowable to have one out of 10,000,000 consumers die from the side effects of a new drug if the drug is twice as effective at relieving the headache pain of the other 9,999,999? Third, how do you avoid mixing what is good for others with what is good for me? How does a decision maker avoid overweighing the benefit that he or she is likely to receive personally from pursuing one strategic option over another? It is not easy to separate one's desires and goals from the judgment of what is right.

Situational ethics can also result in sinking to the lowest ethical standards among a group of competitors, when each rationalizes that it is at least as ethical as the competition. "If we were to be any more ethical" a company might argue, "we, as a good guy, would go out of business, and what good would be gained from that? We did not start it, so what has occurred is also not our fault." This kind of thinking can become moral quicksand. Another harsh reality is that the more desperate the company or personal situation, the lower the ethical standards applied will be and the more the decision maker will be fixated with how his or her company will benefit. Sometimes it seems that only successful companies and executives can afford a conscience. In practice, it can mean being dragged down to the ethics of the most desperate competitor.

The Categorical Imperative

Emmanuel Kant's famous categorical imperative offers an alternative to situational ethics. His approach is to ask whether the proposed action would be right if everyone did it. What would happen to the social fabric? What would happen if you were constantly on the receiving end of such ethics? This approach takes most of the situation or context out of the ethical evaluation and, in that sense, is more explicit than the utilitarian principle. But the categorical imperative still requires the decision maker to *see* the universal wrong or evil in the act if everyone did it. Immoral or amoral individuals, caring nothing for society, may answer that yes it would be fine for society and that others are welcome to act in the same way toward them. Both situational ethics and the categorical imperative still require a basic set of values. Such values are normally based on religious beliefs.

The Religious Foundations of Marketing Ethics

It is no accident that both primitive and advanced civilizations have ethical and moral codes that constrain group and individual behavior. The enlightenment of a civilization is often measured by its underlying ethics. When ethical codes break down, societies cease to function and ultimately collapse from within (for example, the decline and fall of the Roman Empire) or under external pressures (for example, the defeat of the Third

Reich in World War II). How do such ethical codes come about? The history of civilization reveals that they are based on a society's predominant religious creed. As the obvious source of a marketing decision maker's code of ethics is the society's general code of ethics, this suggests that marketplace ethics will have a religious basis. The predominant religion of the United States is Christianity. The Judeo-Christian creed has greatly influenced the constitution, common law, and the system of justice in the United States. Thus, it can be argued that marketers in the United States should at least evaluate, if not adopt, a code of marketing ethics based on Judeo-Christian religious beliefs.[6]

Conflicts can result when this theory is applied to societies in which freedom of worship and thought is a right. It is to be expected, and appropriate, in a free society that a believer of another religion will apply his or her religious ethics to all situations, including marketing decision making. This exercise of different religious beliefs and values increases the variability in ethics that we are likely to observe in the marketplace. One reason we should use the predominant religion's values as the common core for our society's ethics, even if we are not followers of that religion, is that the universal acceptance of its code enables us to anticipate the likely behavior of other parties in the market. This anticipation leads to an increase in trust and a sense of confidence and control that the market is orderly and fair. If the clearly dominant and underlying religious creed in our society is *not* to be used as the foundation for a generally accepted code of business ethics, then what should be used? It would be extraordinarily difficult to argue that some other religious or moral philosophy should be substituted.

Questions and Issues for Marketing Decision Makers

We now discuss the set of general questions in Figure 6-6, which can be asked by the decision maker or decision-making team seeking to develop its own ethical standards. While most questions are self-explanatory, others need some brief justification or raise issues worth exploring.[7] It seems that the least society should require of marketing executives is that they *ask* such questions. Sometimes not asking a question can be as wrong as asking and giving a poor answer. For example, not considering the safety of a toy being marketed is as irresponsible as considering and deciding to sell the toy anyway. The effects are the same. One of the most common situations in which marketing executives suffer a lapse of ethics is when they have to make a quick decision and are preoccupied with other concerns. The ethical sufficiency of the decision is simply not examined.

Unfortunately, relaxing our ethical vigilance can have as serious a consequence as relaxing our competitive vigilance. We must ask ourselves why we use situational ethics to justify our ethical standards. It is important to confront our excuses and our reasons for violating personal ethics. Avoiding or shelving the answers to such questions is no solution. Asking ourselves why we do or do not behave in certain ways helps us to be more honest with ourselves about our true intentions. This is the essence of executive responsibility, and it can also be the first step down the path of change. It leads us to recognize that most of us have at least two codes of ethics: 1) the set that we espouse

---

6. That the moral norms in a democracy are determined by the community standards of the majority (the social contract) has also been argued by Lawrence Kohlberg, "The Just Community Approach to Moral Education in Theory and Practice," in *Moral Education: Theory and Application,* ed. Marvin W. Berkowitz and Fritz Oser (New York: Lawrence Erlbaum, 1985).

7. Some of the questions are based on the thinking of Gene R. Laczniak, "Framework for Analyzing Marketing Ethics," *Journal of Macromarketing* (Spring 1983), 7–18; and William David Ross, *The Right and the Good* (Oxford: Clarendon Press, 1930).

1. Am I violating the law? If yes, why?
2. Are the values and ethics that I am applying in business lower than those I use to guide my personal life? If yes, why?
3. Am I doing to others as I would have them do to me? If not, why not?
4. Would it be wrong if everyone did what I propose to do? Why?
5. Am I willfully risking the life and limb of consumers and others by my actions? If yes, why?
6. Am I willfully exploiting or putting at risk children, the elderly, the illiterate, the mentally incompetent, the naive, the poor, or the environment? If yes, why?
7. Am I keeping my promises? If not, why not?
8. Am I telling the truth, all the truth? If not, why not?
9. Am I exploiting a confidence or a trust? If yes, why?
10. Am I misrepresenting my true intentions to others? If yes, why?
11. Am I loyal to those who have been loyal to me? If not, why not?
12. Have I set up others to take responsibility for any negative consequences of my actions? If yes, why?
13. Am I prepared to redress wrongs and fairly compensate for damages? If not, why not?
14. Are my values and ethnics as expressed in my strategy offensive to certain groups? If yes, why?
15. Am I being as efficient in my use of scarce resources as I can be? If not, why not?

Figure 6-6
A Personal Ethics Checklist for Marketers

and want others to apply in their behavior toward us and 2) the code of ethics that, for whatever rationalizations, we actually live up to. The more we recognize the differences between them, the closer we come to understanding how easy it is talk about ethics in black and white while practicing them in tones of gray.

The list of questions in Figure 6-6 is organized in approximate order of importance and by the nature of the ethical or moral principle involved. The first question in the figure is the first and last question the ethical minimalist will ask. The second question addresses the application of a double standard and the basis for such a double standard. The third question addresses the extent to which we apply the Golden Rule: "Do unto others as you will have them do unto you." A prominent British chief executive officer has suggested that a better way of posing the question is to look at oneself and ask, "What would I think of someone who has my business ethics or took the action that I propose to take?."[8] The fourth question argues that if it would be wrong for everyone to do it, it is wrong for anyone to do it. Why are you the exception that makes it right? For example, if you are considering paying a bribe to a foreign businessperson, would it be right if, from now on, everyone had to pay bribes to do any sort of business? Would this change your view of the ethics of the single action?

Marketing planners have to decide whether they live in a society where they are expected to care about the welfare of others. It has been called the social contract by philosophers. A free market does not mean suppliers and consumers are free to do what they like. Competition forces sellers to serve the interests of consumers. Also, competition benefits from laws that enforce contracts and at times needs to be constrained by codes of conduct. The interests of society at large and future generations also have to be promoted and protected by informal ethics and formal laws. Today, there are so

8. Sir Adrian Cadbury, "Ethical Managers Make Their Own Rules," *Harvard Business Review,* vol. 87.5 (September/ October 1987), 69–75.

Figure 6-7

The Legal and Ethical Constraints on Marketing

The marketing decision should be constrained by the law and professional, company, and personal codes of ethics. An inverse relationship often exists between the standard and enforcement. The law is a floor on ethics, but it can be enforced. The personal code of the enlightened citizen, in theory, should be the most demanding but is only enforced by personal values and conscience.

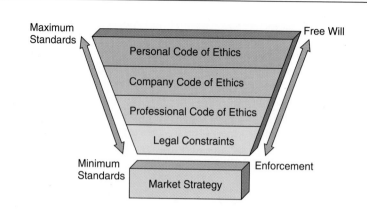

many complex laws that it pays to have an expert lawyer screen any proposed strategy that is questionable. It is in the interest of both the firm and society at large that the firm sensibly constrains its planned competitive behavior rather than have to defend it later in overloaded courts, involving expensive litigation.

The ethical standards of morality that constrain marketing decision making should be a product of the combination of personal conscience and the morality of the company as stated in its code of ethics. Figure 6-7 illustrates the several layers of ethical standards that apply to marketing decision making. Ethical behavior is required to make the market work efficiently and to keep it free and open. Marketing planners must therefore respond to the almost universal ethical codes involved in trading: to be honest and not conspire to cheat and steal. But their decisions as to what to offer the marketplace and how to offer it also have an impact on the prevailing values and ethics of a society. Some products and marketing practices are ethically questionable. This heavy responsibility cannot be simply shrugged off. The enlightened leadership that marketing planners are expected to display is most put to the test when faced with ethical dilemmas created by conflicts of interests between customers, employees, and owners. How we choose to resolve such dilemmas tells us a lot about ourselves.

Public Policy, Ethics, and Global Marketing

Into the foreseeable future, the world will be engaged in a trade war that will lead to new types of public policy. In theory, an open, free-trade global market works to the advantage of all nations if each nation trades goods that they are best at making and marketing. Even if one nation erects trade barriers, it is still best if other nations do not. But in practice, what happens if some nations make some of the product, and other nations market the product to the rest of the world and make most of the profits? What happens if nations erect barriers to protect special interest groups out of spite and frustration? What we have is the world we live in. As large, new free-trading blocs emerge and the global economy develops, politicians will experiment with new types of interventionist policies to save their jobs by saving their citizens' jobs. This is because the innovative-imitative competitiveness of firms increasingly will be judged by global, rather than national standards. Firms that are superior to their global competition will flourish, firms that are inferior will perish. This will lead to large shifts in investment from uncompetitive sectors of a national economy to globally competitive sectors. Financial and human capital will flee from economies that lack sectors that are globally competitive. Such economic restructuring will lead to the rapid growth of some economies and the stagnation and decline of other economies. Responding to public pressure, politicians will resort to four basic strategies:

1. Investment in research, education, and infrastructure with the goal of boosting the innovative-imitative competitiveness of national industry (a competitive rationality strategy).

2. Financial management that results in an economy that is trim and fit (low inflation, low interest rates, near-balanced budget) rather than bloated with election-promised giveaways.

3. The creation of taxes on imports (tariffs) and less obvious and more discreet trade barriers that protect domestic products, services, and jobs.[9]

4. Direct support for export enterprise in the form of tax subsidies and geo-political arm-twisting.

In the worst-case scenario, the overprotection of industries will lead to major barriers between trading blocs. Today the barriers to the international marketplace are no longer only distance, language, or ideology. The major barriers are often economic and political, erected to protect domestic products and services that are not competitive in the global marketplace. In short, this age of great uncertainty places a premium on understanding the current and future trading policies of nations and the thinking (competitive rationality/irrationality) of their leaders.

The need to understand the commercial law of foreign markets, as it is practiced, is also critical. For example, foreign competitors, suppliers and distributors are often able to infringe patents with immunity. Some third-world and emerging economies have very attractive labor costs and are responsive and cooperative. But if anything goes wrong with the relationship, it is often very difficult to get legal redress from their justice systems, which are often either corrupt, very political, or very slow.

More generally, a serious and unresolved situational ethics problem occurs in global marketing. There is no international code of business ethics, because each society's ethics vary, some slightly, others greatly. Some cultures have different religions and, hence, different codes of ethics. Bribery, kickbacks, lying, and other behaviors considered unacceptable in our culture are more acceptable in some cultures. How should we behave in such a market? If we do not tolerate such standard practices, we risk not doing any business and may be criticized for imposing our values where they are not wanted. The quick and easy answer, "When in Rome do as the Romans do," is no answer for at least two reasons. First, international trade is not done in the buyer's country alone. It is done in New York and Rome at the same time. Second, this philosophy suggests abandoning personal ethical standards and replacing them with the ethical standards of the parties with whom one is dealing. What is the social contract in this situation? Is it determined by the accepted norms of your political economy or the accepted norms of your trading partner's political economy? With the increase in global

---

9. Tariffs are better than import quotas because they raise money for governments, whereas quotas raise prices and the excess profits then go to the foreign seller. Quantity quotas on automobiles and clothing also encourage foreign competition to sell high-quality, high-profit items rather than economy, low-profit items. Thus, U.S. quantity quotas on autos and clothing encouraged foreign competition to compete in the most attractive market segments, an unintended outcome that reveals that the policy was not well thought through. This demonstrates that the success of a nation in the global trade war depends on the competitive rationality of its trade policy, as well as the competitive rationality of its firms.

marketing comes a pressing need to adopt an international code of ethics that applies to international marketplace behavior. Unethical behavior will always exist, but it can be greatly reduced if it is defined the same way and condemned by every society.

Discussion Questions and Minicases

1. Canada Dry launched a caffeine-free cola in 1967. The product was ordered off the market by the Food and Drug Administration (FDA) because Coca-Cola and PepsiCo convinced the regulators that a cola without caffeine was technically no longer a cola drink. Coke and Pepsi later launched their own noncaffeine colas, but they had the clout to change the FDA's mind. What problems does this incident reveal and how might it be redressed?

2. What predictions would the theory of competitive rationality make about the consequences of the deregulation of an industry?

3. In a move that they perhaps now regret, the airlines strategically withdrew from the ticket-booking business several years before deregulation. By default, they passed on much of the business to travel agencies, whose offices grew in number from 12,000 to 26,000 between 1975 and 1985. The travel agencies have loved deregulation because, along with competing in the air on most routes, the airlines have had to compete on the ground for the agent's attention and favors. The travel agents have also become more important to the consumer who simply cannot keep up with the changes in airfares and route services. In their attempt to sew up the loyalty of the agents, companies such as United and American have provided free use of their computerized booking systems (Apollo and Sabre) for up to three years, free training, and even initial adoption bonuses. Despite protestations to the contrary, it is clear from their actions that these airlines believed that the use of their system would give them *some* competitive advantage. It appears they were right. Overall, the commissions paid to travel agents have risen from an official commission of 10 percent to an average of 14 percent. What lessons can we learn from this case about deregulation?

4. What do you think should be done with our patent law to encourage more American invention and innovation? Be decisive and creative in your suggestions.

5. The Japanese Patent Office is years ahead of the U.S Patent Office in computerization. Describe the desirable characteristics of a new computer system for the U.S. Patent Office that would greatly reduce the cost of patent searches, make it easier to file a patent application *correctly*, and reduce both the cost and time involved in getting a patent. What would be the major cost of developing such a system? How much would it be worth to develop such a system? Justify your answer theoretically. (Hint: See Chapter 1.)

6. A competitor's disgruntled employee has just mailed you plans for what looks like a promising new product. Should you throw the plans away? Send them to your R&D people for analysis? Notify your competitor about what is going on? Call the FBI?

7. Late in the 19th century, acetylsalicylic acid was a new medicine. Its discoverer, Hermann Dreser, claimed that it relieved headaches, reduced fever, and alleviated the aches and pains of arthritis. Typical of the period, the claimed effects were not scientifically proven. It was then discovered that acetylsalicylic acid produced

severe reactions in some users. Even moderate overdoses were likely to produce dizziness, vision problems, severe gastric irritation, nausea, vomiting, and psychological confusion. Larger overdoses were fatal. How does modern-day regulation protect the consumer from such drugs? Do you agree with the regulation?

8. Cigarette manufacturers add a chemical to cigarettes to make them burn faster and to make them easier to smoke. Fire prevention offices around the country have convincingly demonstrated that the use of this chemical also results in more bedding and upholstery fires, which kill or injure hundreds of Americans each year, because cigarettes treated with the chemical continue to burn longer and hotter when dropped. Some manufacturers have reacted to potential lawsuits by running advertising campaigns that discourage smoking in bed. Such advertisements are meant, in part, to signal the company's good intentions to the courts and to help reduce any settlements against the manufacturer, if it is found liable. Should manufacturers remove the ingredient? What about the advertising?

9. After almost a decade of sales, the Dalkon intrauterine device (IUD) was found to be defective and unreasonably dangerous to use. On the other hand, the medical community considered the Searle IUD a safe, quality product. This distinction was lost on a number of lawyers who hounded Searle with lawsuits. In one case, Searle spent $1 million defending itself—successfully. Many women who cannot use other forms of contraception would like to use the Searle IUD. What should Searle do to stay in business?

10. All-terrain vehicles (ATVs) were involved in 1,500 deaths and 400,000 serious injuries during the 1980s—20 percent affecting children 12 and under. The automobile industry stopped selling the three-wheel version and notified dealers to instruct buyers that the vehicles should not be driven by children under 16. However, many dealers have ignored the direction. The industry view is that because state laws allow children to use the vehicle, it is the parents' responsibility to supervise their children's use. Should the product be banned?

11. Punitive damages were introduced in order to punish firms for deliberately and knowingly breaking the law and causing harm to consumers and employees. However, in recent years, huge punitive damages, over and above assessed compensatory damages (those that compensate the injured party for loss of income, pain and suffering, and so on), have been awarded by juries. As a result, litigation in this area has increased, casting a paralytic effect on many enterprises. How might the law be changed to discourage the unscrupulous behavior of both eager lawyers and of firms that knowingly and calculatingly endanger consumers?

12. The figure on page 214 indicates how consumers perceive the risks of different activities. Based on your own intuition and what you know about the activities that are high on each characteristic, please label the ends of each dimension by identifying characteristics 1 and 2. What does it tell us about how the public views safety risks?

13. In some high-income, highly educated segments of our society, consumers are prepared to pay more for products and services that are "earth friendly." The problem is that it is difficult for consumers to understand terms such as biodegradable, photodegradable, or organically recyclable and to understand the environmental impact of different production processes. Many companies are exploiting this lack of understanding by making exaggerated claims about the earth friendliness of their products. What free-market solution might help (not including government regulation)?

Source: Based on Paul Slovic, "Perception of Risk," *Science* 236 (April 17, 1987), 280–85.

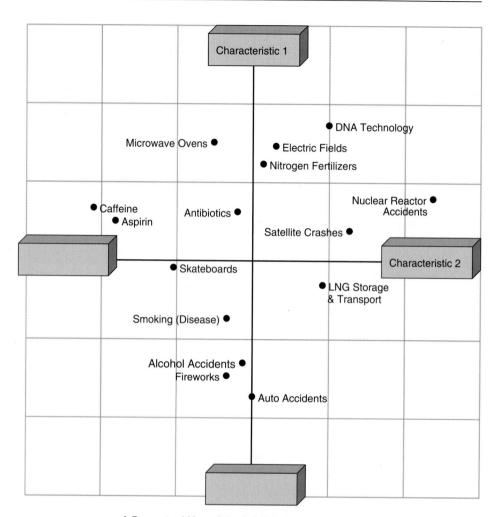

A Perceptual Map of the Public's Perception of Risks

14. American Can Company invented rolled-steel beverage cans in the late 1960s. They take at least 20 percent less energy to produce than aluminum cans, and they are cheaper and biodegradable. But while recycling rolled-steel cans is not cost effective, recycling aluminum cans is. Recycling also produces important income for street people and social organizations such as the Boy Scouts. Many Coke bottlers were using steel cans in the mid-1970s but, reacting to pressure from vocal critics, switched back to aluminum. What would you have done? How would you respond if we were facing a landfill crisis? What if we were facing another energy crisis?

15. The only way for many third-world countries to develop their economies is by exploiting their natural resources (such as cutting down the rain forests) or by using very dirty energy sources (such as the use of high-sulphur coal in China). Do you think it is hypocritical for advanced economies to complain about such environmental crimes when each went through a similar stage in its own history? What is the long-term solution, assuming that unlesss some solution is found we will all run out of air to breathe?

16. What is the intrabrand versus interbrand issue in distribution law really all about? How is it an example of the rule of reason? What sort of experts do judges have to become to make such judgments?

17. In the late 1970s, credit-card interest rates rose to between 18 and 20 percent because of inflation. Through the 1980s, many credit-card interest rates remained at around 18 to 20 percent, long after inflation had cooled and the cost of money had dropped to under 10 percent. Many banks have argued that the cost of servicing credit-card debt is high, but some banks charge only 13 percent on their cards. The merchant is charged a fee (2 to 5 percent) for each purchase made on a card. This covers the cost of the transaction and some of the risk of card theft and bad debt. Is still charging 18 to 20 percent ethical?

18. A manufacturer of tables and chairs always increases its prices when the cost of timber increases. It does not lower its prices when the cost of timber decreases. Is this pricing rule ethical? Is it fair? What other rule might the manufacturer use?

19. A supermarket serving a low-income black market charges higher prices for its staples (such as bread and milk) than do supermarkets in the suburbs. Consumer groups have complained that this practice exploits the poor. The store argues that suburban shoppers buy more profitable luxuries, allowing surburban stores to lower their prices on staples. The store's management also can prove that there is a greater incidence of shoplifting and vandalism in its store, resulting in hardly any profit, even at the higher prices. Should the store lower its prices? Should it simply close down, if it would lose money by lowering its prices? What other creative options does the store have?

20. Why do you think services such as airlines and movie theaters are allowed to price discriminate based on customer age (such as when lower rates are offered to seniors and students), but when hiring are not allowed to discriminate based on age? Do you think it would be acceptable to price discriminate based on race? Why is age different from race?

21. Consumer product testing research undertaken for a major lawn-care company revealed that putting two parallel rows of holes on a lawn sprinkler increased consumer perceptions of the products performance and quality. However, tests show that performance actually is not improved. Should the company produce a sprinkler with one or two rows of holes? If it uses two holes should it feature them in the advertising as a point of product differentiation? Research shows that if the company charges a higher price for a product, the consumer will believe it is of higher quality. Should the company charge a higher price?

22. The cartoon on page 216 presents an ethical dilemma. Please answer the questions listed. In addition, why do you think that using cartoons to present dilemmas is effective in ethics training?

23. To make used cars safer and shopping more efficient, the Federal Trade Commission proposed a rule in 1981 that would require dealers to disclose a used car's known defects on a window sticker. The dealers argued that any prospective buyer could have the vehicle mechanically checked at his or her own expense. They argued that since few buyers actually have the vehicles checked, then the information is not really needed. The dealers gave millions of dollars to the election campaigns of numerous senators and congressmen who overwhelmingly, and with very little explanation, voted down the rule. Was what the dealers did ethical?

24. A marketer of orange juice added the word *fresh* in its brand name and the following phrases on its cartons: "Pure, squeezed, 100% orange juice . . . We pick our

This cartoon strip, which presents an illustrative, hypothetical ethics situation in cartoon form, was used by Armstrong World Industries, Inc. in "ethics awareness" seminars conducted for its employees.

1. How is Armstrong's reputation affected by a retailer's misrepresentation? How could Armstrong be affected by Jenny taking action? not taking action?

2. If you were Jenny, what would you do and why: talk or write again to the retailer? raise your concerns with the Division staff in Lancaster? ignore it?

Source: Reproduced with permission of Armstrong World Industries from Ronald E. Berenbeim, *Corporate Ethics Practices* (New York: The Conference Board, 1992), 40.

oranges at the peak of ripeness. Then we hurry to squeeze them before they lose their freshness." The juice is made by adding water to concentrated orange juice, pulp, and "orange essence." Do you think the behavior was lawful? Do you think it was ethical?

25. A Save the Children Fund (SCF) ad features little Pedro with the sad eyes and Joanne Woodward saying "Imagine, the cost of a cup of coffee, 52 cents a day, can help save a child." But SCF has not been in the business of directly sponsoring children for many years. It is involved in community development work, such as building playgrounds and providing start-up loans for small businesses. The problem is that community development does not pull cash donations the way that little Pedro does. Only about 35 percent of the funds raised are actually spent on charitable projects—the rest is spent on marketing and overhead. Was SCF's behavior ethical? Should SCF be held to a higher or lower standard than would be applied to a profit organization?

26. What double standard seems evident in Figure 6-5, which presents the contents of company ethical guidelines?

27. You are in a foreign country where bribing government officials and businesspeople is essential to do business, and bribery is not outlawed as it is in the United States. Officials from the country approach you, saying that there are many buyers for your products and you could make good profits in their country. Would you do business and pay the bribes? Would you hide the practice, hoping that no one in the United States would find out? Would you pay a distributor in the country a set fee to take care of everything for you, pretending not to know what taking care of everything means?

28. A major U.S. bank in Chicago has been approached by an oil sheik who wishes to make a major investment in its New Ventures Mutual Fund that has been brilliantly managed by a 35-year-old female executive. The bank is keen to make the sale, but the sheik will only do business with men. Normally, the female mutual-funds manager would travel to meet such a client. Should the bank send her anyway? What if a major commission is involved in making the sale? Would it make any difference if the sheik was visiting the United States and refused to meet the female executive?

29. Dagonet, a diversified manufacturer, is introducing its products in Latin American markets. The company has been asked by several potential distributors to underbill and remit the differences to their companies' accounts in Switzerland and the Cayman Islands. The practice is customary in these countries because local taxes are confiscatory and the local exchange rates make it very difficult for local distributors to achieve profitable results. What should Dagonet do? What if Dagonet has received similar requests in the past from U.S. and European firms and has always refused?

30. Now that the cold war is over, and the global trade war is heating up (our jobs versus their jobs), do you think it is appropriate that the Central Intelligence Agency change its mission and recruit economists and market researchers to help gather economic intelligence? What should be the limits to the CIA's involvement in industrial espionage? What agency should be responsible for making sure that international environmental protection laws and free-trade laws are obeyed? Why is any United Nation's agency likely to be very ineffective?

Analyzing the Organization

*"The greatest difficulties lie where we
are not looking for them."*
Johann Wolfgang Von Goethe

"Structure is not organization."
Robert H. Waterman

*I*n addition to looking outward at the marketplace, marketing planners must also turn inward and look at their own companies. This involves studying the company's strengths, weaknesses, objectives, and how it makes decisions. Company issues can often be identified more readily than external environmental issues relating to consumers, competitors, channels, and public policy. Also, they are usually more controllable than aspects of the external environment.

In the first section of this chapter, a procedure for integrating the marketing planning activities into the overall corporate plan is proposed. This discussion deals with how the corporate mission statement and resource allocations guide and constrain marketing strategy. The following sections describe various ways of identifying specific internal company issues that a marketing planner should be aware of before developing strategy. First, an audit of the physical assets, human resources, marketing goodwill, and the company's current position in its specified product target market should be taken. Second, the cultural and political climate within the organization must be assessed. Third, the bottom-line performance objectives must be specified. Keep the following key ideas in mind as you read this chapter:

- The way senior management in a large corporation makes decisions greatly influences the practice and effectiveness of marketing decision making in the product divisions.

- Cutting through the bureacracy, time wasting, and miscommunication is a major problem that is best solved by the formation of special cross-functional teams focusing on ventures, products, or projects.

- Corporate mission statements are meant to provide broad direction to marketing decision makers. In fact, senior management often goes much further, making top-down marketing decisions about marketing strategy and tactics.

- Senior management must choose one of four basic financial objectives for a product-market: short-term, low-risk; short-term, high-risk; long-term, low-risk; and long-term, high-risk.

- A company should identify its strengths and weaknesses the same way it identifies its competitors' strengths and weaknesses.

- Companies cannot afford to look into the mirror and judge themselves because the capacity for self-deception is so great. Obtaining independent evaluations through consultants or using the opinions of customers, suppliers, even competitors produces a more sobering perspective and identifies issues that otherwise would not surface.

- The role of senior management is to create company culture and politics that encourage competitive rationality.

- Important synergies between production and marketing have to be created.

- A company culture *can* enhance quality, increase the speed of implementation, and reduce costs all at the same time.

The Corporate Planning Process

Traditional corporate planning in a large, diversified company involves distinct stages that are illustrated in Figure 7-1. The first stage involves an environmental analysis. In the second stage, the corporate mission is developed and the divisional and product-market objectives are set. The third stage involves the development of divisional and

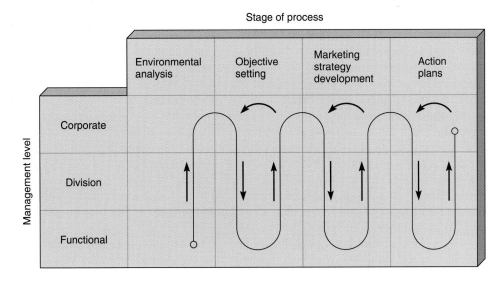

Figure 7-1

An Opportunistic Corporate Planning Process

In the traditional large, bureaucratic company with several operating divisions, planning should start with a bottom-up analysis of the market environments. Corporate management then develops the corporate mission and sets objectives for the divisions. The strategy and action-plan cycles are then started. The corporate planning of most large organizations more or less operates this way. The big differences are in the formality of the process. As discussed in Chapter 1, some organizational divisions operate informally and combine the stages into a dynamic, continually adaptive process.

functional strategies, including marketing and production strategies. Product and marketing managers develop marketing strategy within the guidelines imposed by senior management in the first planning stage. Senior management then reviews and approves the strategy. The final planning stage or cycle involves the development and scheduling of action plans and budgets. This stage is, again, primarily a bottom-up process involving coordination between marketing and other operations.[1]

Top-down, Bottom-up

The interplay between levels of management in this complex consultative process is critical.[2] The top-down initiation, bottom-up response in each of the second, third, and fourth stages is closed by a senior management review. The difference between the top-down expectations and the bottom-up projections is the planning gap. The existence of such a gap indicates that the proposed strategy does not satisfy the company goals. Corporate planners emphasize the need to close this gap before advancing to the third stage of strategy formulation. In actual practice, corporate planning is an iterative top-down, bottom-up accommodation process not only *within* each stage in Figure 7-1 but also *between* stages. It can become such a constant to-and-fro activity that the stages cannot easily be distinguished from each other. When this happens, marketing planning is imbedded into corporate or business planning, and it is very difficult to separate the processes.[3] This explains why the continuous planning process used by an executive committee described in Chapter 1 is, in reality, a combination of marketing and corporate planning.

1. Peter Lorange, *Corporate Planning* (Englewood Cliffs, NJ: Prentice-Hall, 1980). Figure 7-1 adapts Lorange's model in that it starts with an environmental analysis as suggested by H. Igor Ansoff in *Corporate Strategy* (New York: McGraw-Hill, 1965).
2. Howard Sutton, *The Marketing Plan* (New York: The Conference Board, 1990).
3. George Day, *Strategic Market Analysis: Top-Down and Bottom-Up Approaches* (Working Paper, Cambridge, MA: Maketing Science Institute, 1980), 80–105.

Marketing and the Environmental Analysis

An important issue involves determining who should prepare the environmental analysis. It seems sensible that this initial external environmental analysis should be prepared via a bottom-up process involving the company's junior marketing executives, market researchers, and sales force. Information on consumer trends, new market opportunities, new ways of segmenting the market, competitive threats and opportunities, channel changes, and changes in public policy need to be synthesized, integrated, and summarized for corporate management by the people who are close to these issues on a day-to-day basis. The bottom-up information on all the markets served by a division and the division's resource constraints has to be combined with the corporate manager's perceptions of existing overall company strengths and weaknesses. Out of this process should emerge (after several iterations) the company's business definition, mission statements, and performance objectives.[4] Such a corporate planning approach is opportunistic in that it takes advantage of the issues revealed by the annual external environmental analysis.

The marketing function has to play a major, but not exclusive, role in putting together the bottom-up environmental analysis. This will ultimately involve very little extra work for product managers, sales mangers, and marketing managers, because such analysis needs to be undertaken in developing the divisional product-market strategy anyway. The only inconvenience is that the analysis will have to be completed earlier and especially packaged for corporate executives. Production, engineering, R&D, and finance functions should also provide their environmental insights and perspectives, which, when shared with marketing, will enrich and expand the product-market specific environmental analyses undertaken and used in Stage 3 of the corporate planning process.

The Corporate Mission Statement

The second stage starts with a corporate mission statement. Corporate planning texts and articles emphasize the important role of the corporate mission statement.[5] Without its direction, marketing managers, along with functional managers who seek direction from others higher in the management hierarchy, will use their own personal beliefs about the corporate management's company vision, or corporate mythology, to guide their planning. This will result in unnecessary internal uncertainty, conflict, and a waste of resources on tangential projects.

The purpose of the corporate mission statement is to direct the planning and strategy of the enterprise by broadly describing how the organization intends to fulfill its basic responsibilities to its owners. In doing so, it should help resolve the competing, conflicting, and contradictory demands made on the company's resources. No corporate mission, even if written by Solomon, can resolve all of the inherently conflicting interests of shareholders, customers, management, employees, suppliers, and government. However, a corporate mission statement can go a long way toward expressing and achieving a consensus.

The generally accepted opinion of experts is that the corporate mission should describe the target markets, the basic product or service, the principal technologies to be mastered, and the competitive competencies that will be employed. Figure 7-2

4. Peter Doyle and John Saunders, "Market Segmentation and Positioning in Specialized Industrial Markets," *Journal of Marketing* (Spring 1985), 24–32. In their real-world case study, the authors report that unrealistic top-down objectives were replaced by objectives based on a competitive market appraisal (p. 31).
5. Derek Abel, *Defining the Business: The Starting Point of Strategic Planning* (Englewood Cliffs, NJ: Prentice-Hall, 1980); and John A. Pearce, "The Company Mission As a Strategic Tool," *Sloan Management Review* (Spring 1982), 15–24.

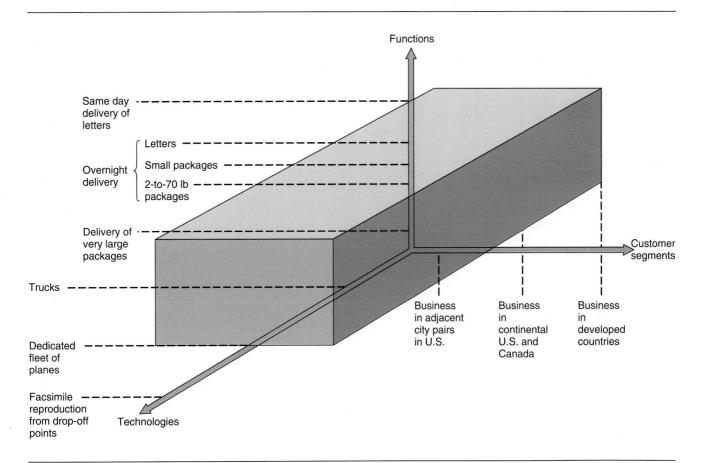

Figure 7-2

The Business Definition of Federal Express

The above three-dimensional framework defines the corporate mission of Federal Express in terms of target market segments, the benefits provided, and the technologies used to deliver such benefits to the segments. Federal Express also pioneered the hub-and-spoke logistics strategy (later imitated by the passenger airlines) and a superb computerized tracking system. Both of these management technologies enable it to deliver, as promised, "Absolutely, positively, overnight."

Source: Reprinted by permission from George Day, *Analysis for Strategic Marketing Decisions* (New York: West Publishing Company, 1984).

presents such a statement in visual form for Federal Express. Statements like "Providing energy for a better America," "Maximizing profits through consumer satisfaction," "Making tomorrow happen," "Preserving and improving human life," or "Making people happy" are too vague and sound more like public relations statements. They are not corporate mission statements for the simple reason that they do not provide explicit direction. A great example of a goal statement was that given to NASA by President Kennedy: "achieving the goal, before this decade is out, of landing a man on the moon and returning him safely to earth." The goal was ambitious, yet achievable, and had a clear objective and deadline. Its vision inspired not only NASA but a nation. A less profound but equally clear goal is that of Home Depot: "To go national with $10 billion in sales and 350 locations by 1995."[6]

While the mission statements of NASA and Home Depot are clear and inspiring, both are somewhat lacking in that they do not describe the competencies or technologies that needed to be employed to achieve the goal. Jack Welch, the CEO of General Electric, outlines the sort of competence he seeks by describing how he plans to change his company's culture: "As we succeed in ridding the company of ritual and bureaucracy, we are now better able to attack the final, and perhaps most difficult challenge

6. C. Hawkins, "Will Home Depot Be the Wal-Mart of the '90s?" *Business Week,* March 19, 1990, 124.

Rationality in Practice:

Corporate Mission Statements

The Prudential Mission Statement

The Prudential is, and will remain, the No. 1 insurance company in America. Leading with this strength, we will become the No. 1 financial services company in this market and a leader in global financial markets. We will achieve this goal by enhancing our core businesses and by entering related businesses that either reinforce our core businesses or provide superior returns. We will actively explore global markets and will enter those where we can leverage our strengths. We serve our clients through four core businesses:

♦ Individual Insurance

♦ Individual Investments

♦ Institutional Asset Management

♦ Institutional Employee Benefits

Our strategies will build on the competitive strengths that distinguish The Prudential:

1. Our name and reputation, based on public recognition of our integrity and rock-solid foundation;

2. Multiple distribution channels, including the largest full-time sales force in financial services;

3. Financial size and the skills to capitalize on it; and

4. A range of products and services that gives our clients the advantages of choice and our company the benefits of diversification.

We will be aggressive and market driven. We will operate through distinct business units, targeting specific market segments with coordinated strategies. We will emphasize accountability and reward accomplishment while stressing ethical behavior. We will continue Prudential's tradition of social responsibility.

As a mutual company, we will act always in the long-term interests of our policyholders. We will measure our performance by balanced growth among earnings, revenue, and market share, and by our competitive ranking on these measures.

Source: The Prudential Vision Statement is reproduced from John C. Shaw, *The Service Focus* (Homewood, IL: Dow Jones Irwin, 1990), 55.

Extracts from Hewlett-Packard's Corporate Mission Statement

1. **Profit.** To achieve sufficient profit to finance our company growth and to provide the resources we need to achieve our other corporate objectives . . . Our objective is to rely on reinvested profits as our main source of capital . . . This can be achieved if our return on net worth is roughly equal to our sales growth.

2. **Customers.** To provide products and service of the greatest possible value to our customers, thereby gaining and holding their respect and loyalty . . . Products must be designed to provide superior performance and long, trouble-free service . . . A prime objective of our marketing department is to see that the finished product is backed by prompt, efficient service . . . Our customers must feel that they are dealing with one company with common policies and services, and that our company is genuinely interested in arriving at proper, effective solutions to their problems. Confusion and competition among sales teams must be avoided.

of all. And that is the empowering of our 300,000 people, and the releasing of their creativity and ambition; the direct coupling of their jobs with some positive effect on the quality of a product or service."[7]

Three complete mission statements are presented in the box above. They all provide a vision, delineate company values and ethics, and describe the nature of the target markets and products. They also outline the strengths that will empower the competitiveness of the enterprise, and they place constraints on management decision making.

7. General Electric Company (Schenectady, NY: *The General Electric Company,* 1989), 128.

3. **Fields of Interest.** To enter new fields only when the ideas we have, together with out technical, manufacturing, and marketing skills, assure that we can make a needed and profitable contribution to the field.

4. **Growth.** To let our growth be limited only by our profits and our ability to develop and produce technical products that satisfy real customer needs.

5. **Our people.** To help HP people share in the company's success, which they make possible; to provide job security based on their performance; to recognize their individual achievements; and to ensure the personal satisfaction that comes from a sense of accomplishment in their work . . . The objective of job security is illustrated by our policy of avoiding large ups and downs in our production schedules, which would require hiring people for short periods of time and laying them off later.

6. **Management.** To foster initiative and creativity by allowing the individual great freedom of action in attaining well-defined objectives.

7. **Citizenship.** To honor our obligations to society by being an economic, intellectual, and social asset to each nation and each community in which we operate.

Source: Extracts from Hewlett-Packard's company mission statement are reproduced from William G. Ouchi, *Theory Z* (New York: Avon Books, 1981), 193–99.

GIRO Sport Design Vision Statement

Values and Beliefs

◆ Customer satisfaction is first and foremost.

◆ It takes great products to be a great company.

◆ Integrity is not to be compromised; be honest, consistent, and fair.

◆ Commitments made are to be fulfilled.

◆ Never cut corners; get the details right.

◆ The golden rule applies to peers, customers, and employees.

◆ Teamwork should prevail; think "we," not "I."

◆ There is no reason to make any product that is not innovative and high quality.

◆ Style is important; all of our products should look great.

Mission Our mission is to become a great company by the year 2000—to become to the bicycling industry what Nike is to athletic shoes and Apple is to computers.

The best riders in the world will be using our products in world-class competition. Winners of the Tour de France, the World Championships, and the Olympic Gold Medal will win while wearing Giro helmets. We will receive unsolicited phone calls and letters from customers who say, "Thank you for being in business; one of your helmets saved my life." When you ask people to name the top company in the cycling business, the vast majority will say "Giro." Our employees will feel that this is the best place they've ever worked.

Source: The Giro Sport Design Corporate Vision Statement, 1991, quoted in James C. Collins and Jerry I. Porras, "Organizational Vision and Visionary Organizations," *California Management Review* (Fall 1991).

Mission Drift

A company's purpose can drift because of weak leadership, purpose, and direction. This often occurs in a transition between the original entrepreneur and second-generation management. The most common problems in this situation are as follows:

1. The enterprise outgrows the management skills of the original founder.

2. The founder loses interest in the humdrum of day-to-day management.

3. The entrepreneur grows old, a little cranky, and out of touch with the competitive market but continues to stay at the helm.

The situation is worsened by a tendency for strong leaders not to prepare years in advance for the succession crisis so as to avoid the possibility of an angry civil war between rival political factions within the company. Another type of mission drift occurs when senior executives focus on the stock market rather than on the product-markets their company competes in. A number of critics of American management have argued that American companies spent far too much time in the 1970s and 1980s first conglomerating, then divesting, and finally pursuing leveraged buyouts. A third type of mission drift occurs when an organization such as NASA achieves its initial mission and is literally at a loss as to what to do next. Ford had a similar problem, after "democratizing" the motor car.[8]

Mergers and takeovers can also cast a company adrift. There is no doubt that company restructuring shakes up complacent management and introduces new efficiencies. But there is also evidence that a number of companies lost their direction during this era and sometimes were whipsawed by the wheeling and dealing of their leadership. The business magazines *Business Week, Forbes,* and *Fortune* were full of such stories over these two decades.[9]

Mission Adjustment

Another problem that can occur with a company mission is that while it must be enduring enough to provide stable direction, even it must change from time to time in response to changes in technology and the competitive marketplace. It is at such times of corporate transition and repositioning that the senior executives really exercise their vision and earn their salaries. Recently, Procter & Gamble made a number of acquisitions that clearly indicated that much of its future growth will come from marketing over-the-counter health-care products to an aging population. Ryder International was quick to recognize that deregulation led many airline companies to search for ways of trimming costs and financial risk. The truck rental company is now a major player in aircraft leasing, aircraft engine overhaul and maintenance, and aircraft spare parts supply.

Top-down predetermination of the markets to be served and how to serve them is not without its critics. If such direction includes specific marketing strategies or focuses on a specific market or technology, it can reduce the peripheral vision of lower-level planners.[10] They only look for opportunities under the light provided by senior management. This reduces the organization's foresight and adaptability. A McKinsey and Company study suggests that competitively successful companies have the ability to pool the environmental insights of their antennae employees such as salespeople, engineers, and shop floor workers. Successful companies seem to make strategic accommodations to numerous environmental changes rather than only executing the grand strategy of senior management, imposed from the top-down. The results of the 1990 Conference Board study of marketing planning suggest that many senior executives do much more than set financial objectives for the marketing plans. Figure 7-3 indicates the top-down direction that is given at the outset of the formal marketing planning exercise. In more than 20 percent of the firms surveyed, the respondents (mostly vice-presidents) reported that senior executives set marketing management strategy and tactics at the *outset* of the planning exercise.

Senior executives predetermine the planning and decision making. Such top-down direction may reflect a continuation of previous strategy or the superior insight and

8. James C. Collins and Jerry I. Porras, "Organizational Vision and Visionary Organizations," *California Management Review* (Fall 1991).
9. "Do Mergers Really Work?" *Business Week,* June 7, 1985, 88–100; and Robert H. Hayes and William J. Abernathy, "Managing Our Way to Economic Decline," *Harvard Business Review,* July/August 1980, 67–77.
10. Richard Pascale, "Our Curious Addiction to Corporate Grand Strategy," *Fortune,* November 2, 1982, 148–56.

	1980	1990
Broad strategic objectives for marketing are determined by senior management before the plan is prepared	71.5%	84.5%

1990 Study: Topics checked as included in this top-down instruction.

Goals and Constraints

Profit goals	74.4%
Budget constraints	62.6%
Sales goals	58.1%
Market share goals	44.8%
Cash flow goals	29.6%
Production constraints	22.2%

Marketing Strategy

Choice of target markets	42.4%
New product/service development	38.9%
Market penetration strategy	27.6%
Pricing strategy	44.8%
Product/service positioning	35.0%
Distribution strategy	27.6%
Advertising strategy	26.1%

Figure 7-3

Goal Setting and Top-Down Directions by Senior Management

The above percentages indicate that most marketing planners have profit goals. Some planners are also given explicit sales, market-share, and cash-flow goals, which further constrain their options. Furthermore, in about one in four companies, senior management prescribes the marketing strategy that should be pursued *before* the marketing plan is put together. It is hoped that this direction does not come as a surprise to the marketing planner and is the result of earlier consultations.

wisdom of senior executives. In other cases it may not. A more basic question is why senior management direction occurs before the preparation of the marketing plan rather than during the preparation of the plan. It suggests a rather bureaucratic and hierarchical decision-making process. What may be preferred is a combination of bottom-up adaptation and top-down integration. Senior executives have a better understanding of the strengths and the weaknesses of the enterprise and can see the forest rather than just the trees. They understand and are concerned about production constraints, working capital, cash flow, costs, and contribution control. Experienced senior managers are also better at crisis management.

The challenge is to find a way to make senior executives aware of changes in product-market environments that may have company-wide strategic implications before they develop corporate objects and strategy. One solution is to decentralize all decision making to divisions and then combine marketing and all functional planning into divisional planning as described in Chapter 1. Another solution is to introduce a company-wide information system, in which new information about the marketplace is cataloged and constantly disseminated in reports that are specially designed for different levels of management.

Portfolio Analysis and Financial Goals

Almost all of the contemporary corporate planning and marketing management texts describe various product portfolio models designed to assist the senior executive in evaluating the company's overall strategic position and to guide the allocation of the enterprise's resources across the competing demands of divisions or product groups. About 20 percent of the companies participating in the 1990 Conference Board study of marketing planning reported that they used a product portfolio in their planning. There has been much discussion about the validity of the different models and how to design the most useful portfolio.[11] Not as much attention has been paid to the claim that a portfolio serves as a link between corporate strategy and marketing planning.

Portfolio models generally evaluate strategic business units (SBUs), divisions, product groups, or product-markets on two dimensions:

1. The attractiveness of the industry or market.
2. The competitive position of the company within the industry or market.

The Boston Consulting Group used specific measures of market growth and market share. General Electric has used composite, categorical measures of industry attractiveness and business strength. Much of the criticism of the portfolio technique has centered on the appropriateness of the evaluative dimensions. Analyses that focus on specific dimensions are criticized for ignoring many other important environmental facts relative to competition, channels, public policy, and regulations. On the other hand, analyses that are composite evaluations of the operating environment are considered by some managers to be too abstract. The undertaking of a bottom-up external environmental analysis before the portfolio analysis stage of planning provides senior executives with a much better option. As recommended earlier in the chapter, the entire environmental analysis for a product-market or division can be summarized and a portfolio made up of these summaries. Senior management can then study these market profiles before deciding the role and financial objectives of each product-market or division and allocating resources.

As well as being used to compare the operating environments of the different product groups, portfolio analysis may be a somewhat useful tool for identifying the overall strengths and weaknesses and the resources needed. For example, the portfolio analysis may suggest that, whatever the competitive strategy pursued, most of the businesses are going to be cash hungry, and to feed them, senior executives must find external rather than internal financial resources. Finally, if portfolio analysis is going to be used for prioritizing resources, it would seem sensible for it to be based on *strategy-driven* performance forecasts and risk-return analysis. The performance forecasts should be made after the environment has been analyzed and the new strategy and marketing management projects proposed, not before such activities.

Project Evaluation Using Shareholder Value

A recent trend has been the growing effort by managers of diversified companies to search for ways of increasing the value of shareholders' stock in the company.[12] This effort has made an impact on marketing planning by creating a new measure of bottom-line performance called shareholder value. It is measured by evaluating an overall marketing strategy, plan, or project in terms of its ability to generate cash flow and the initial additional debt that must be incurred to pursue the plan. The formula is as follows:

PROJECT VALUE = Present value (PV) of Net after-tax **CASH FLOWS** over estimated life + PV of **DEPRECIATION** of the assets employed over life + PV of the **RESIDUAL VALUE** of the venture at the end of its life − PV of Incremental **INVESTMENT** in fixed and working capital that have to be made over its life − Any other initial project **DEBT** incurred

11. Roger A. Kerin, Vijay Mahajan, and P. Rajan Varadarajan, *Strategic Market Planning* (Boston: Allyn and Bacon, 1990). Chapters 2 and 3 provide excellent coverage of different product portfolio models.
12. George Day and Liam Fahey, "Valuing Market Strategies," *Journal of Marketing* 52 (July 1988), 45–57; and Roger A. Kerin, Vijay Mahajan, and P. Rajan Varadarajan, *Strategic Market Planning* (Boston: Allyn and Bacon, 1990), chapter 9.

While complicated, this formula directly connects a marketing project's performance to the shareholders' interests. As with estimating all future performances, there are severe problems inherent in forecasting cash flow, future costs, and the final residual value of the venture. Predicting residual value is particularly difficult to do if the venture plans to create or enhance customer goodwill. Future customer goodwill is an important asset or equity, but estimating it in a highly competitive market is often based on pure speculation. However, simply understanding how this formula is calculated does provide the marketing planner with very useful guidelines on what financials are of greatest concern. Such an approach may also be useful in making decisions as to which product-markets appear to offer the most attractive investment prospects. But again, it can be seen how dependent this technique is on forecasts.

Investing or Directing?

The issue of how to allocate resources across the product portfolio begs a fundamental question: To what extent should an enterprise spread risk and resources across a range of products? The advice "stick to your knitting" runs counter to investment portfolio theory, which suggests that the larger and more diversified the portfolio, the lower the risk. Risk can also be reduced by the insightful combination of product-markets. Take, for example, the south-sea island trader who invests in ice cream and umbrellas. Whether it rains or shines, one of his investments will profit, and he is not so vulnerable to major fluctuations in weather. The island trader's business portfolio, however, may benefit from some further shrewd environmental insight and strategy. Perhaps the rainfall and sunshine vary over time or between islands, suggesting locational advantages. The umbrellas may also be designed so they can be used as sunshades. Strategy is being driven no longer by simple risk reduction but by recognizing environmental issues and technological competencies that can be turned into competitive advantages.

This example demonstrates an important difference between a product and an investment portfolio. An investor has little control over the destiny of his or her portfolio. A corporate and marketing planner has considerable influence on the performance of the products in his or her portfolio. Indeed, they are paid to exercise such influence. Senior executives who allocate resources across a portfolio of ventures as if they were just investments are denying the influence they can have on outcomes. They are either taking little advantage of the unique competencies and economies of scope and experience of the firm or they are, in effect, admitting that the firm, under their stewardship, has no such competitive advantages.

If, in fact, senior executives approach their product-market planning from an investment perspective, then a provocative question is whether they should exercise any strategic influence on marketing strategy at all. It might be better to allow the individual product groups to market their products the best way they can and allow corporate headquarters to pursue their real interest in investment banking, mergers, and acquisitions. The downfall and takeover of AMF (a 1970s prototype of the successful conglomerate) was blamed, in part, on its senior management, which ran its divisions like a financial portfolio rather than understanding and playing to the divisions' individual strengths and needs.[13]

Important Time and Risk Trade-offs

When a company operates several divisions or profit centers that operate in different product-markets, the financial performance objectives for each of the product groups are not likely to be the same. In this sense, every diversified company has a portfolio

13. *Business Week,* August 12, 1985, 25.

of products with different financial objectives. Consequently, marketing planners often have to accept the role their product must play. One of the least desirable roles is as a source of cash flow and funds for another product group pursuing a growth strategy. There is, however, a situation that is even worse than knowing your product-market is being treated as a so-called cash cow. It is when corporate management demands high performance on conflicting objectives. The result is confused divisional or product-market management, planning, and strategy. Clear top-down financial directives are a must. The corporate mission statement is often open to interpretation, resource constraints can be bent, compromises with manufacturing can be made; but at the end of the year, the financial targets always come back to haunt, if not hang, the marketing planner. That is why it is so important to seek clarification and realism at the time the directives are given. The alternative is to search for excuses later or have to explain why concerns were not raised about the impossibility of the objectives at the outset.

Most simply put, two critical trade-offs occur in financial goal setting: a trade-off between long-term growth and short-term profit taking and a trade-off between assured, stable financial performance and the high-risk, adventurous strategy that may either strike oil or fail disastrously. The challenge is to have senior executives accept the responsibility for the financial goals they set for the marketing planner by answering the two basic questions presented in Figure 7-4. The answers to these two questions should be constantly in the back of the minds of marketing planners when developing their marketing strategy. Marketing decision makers may find that senior management will resist providing such explicit direction because it forces them to reveal their priorities and to take responsibility for their leadership and direction.

As Figure 7-4 illustrates, the goals of a division or a product group are defined by the following basic questions which need to be answered by senior management:

1. When faced with a choice, should the marketing plan aim to reinvest for growth and develop marketing strategies and tactics that build goodwill and sales or should its goal be to generate short-term cash and profits that enable the company to siphon off the cash flow and profits?

2. When faced with a choice, should the marketing plan aim for assured but modest financial performance or should it attempt to achieve uncertain but possibly spectacular performance?

Figure 7-4
Alternative Financial
Performance Goals

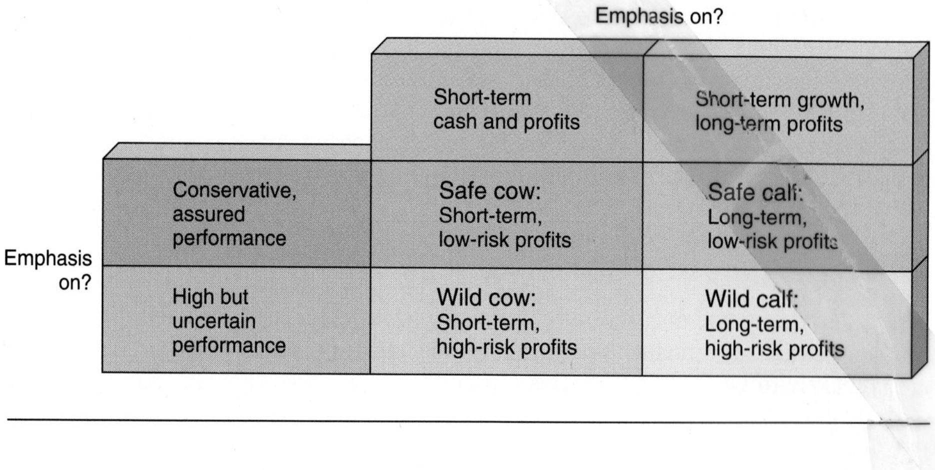

In short, senior management must choose a goal from one of the quadrants that then defines the financial role of the product or product group in the company plan.

Derivative Marketing Goals

The financial goal setting just described can be reduced to derivative goals. For example, a company might seek to increase, by a particular percentage, the numbers of a particular type of account, the size of particular accounts, a particular product item or market segment, or the number of inquiries. It might also aim for an increase in awareness, a decrease in complaints, a decrease in service time, and the achievement of many and varied sales force performance and cost control goals.

The mistake that some marketing planning approaches make is to prescribe these marketing goals at the outset in great detail and to search for a strategy that bridges the gap between current performance and target performance. Planners sometimes forget that strategy and performance expectations drive each other. Rather than being bound and fettered by a hundred lilliputian marketing performance and cost control goals, it seems to make more sense to step back and develop strategy that meshes with all of the environmental issues and the overall performance goals. If it does, then the implementation of the strategy has to be monitored and controlled using marketing performance indicators that are related to the bottom-line target. In summary, although it sounds like quite a radical proposition, detailed marketing goals and performance targets may be best used to control and monitor marketing's effectiveness rather than to derive strategy. These issues are further explored in the discussion of budgeting and control in Chapter 15.

The first step in identifying a company's strengths and weaknesses is to conduct a realistic audit of its resources, which can be applied to the product-market plan. The audit should include the following assessments:

1. Physical assets: land, buildings, plant, patents, inventory, stocks, bonds, and cash.
2. Market goodwill: channel goodwill, consumer goodwill, and investor goodwill.
3. Human resources: senior and middle management, research and development engineers, sales force, skilled production staff, other support staff.

It is important to place a value on all of these resources in terms of a specific purpose, presumably that defined by the company mission statement and objectives for the product-market. If the realizable value of the assets is higher than their value in furthering the corporate mission, then perhaps they should be sold to purchase assets that contribute more to the furthering of long-term objectives.

When a company's mission changes, its assets need to be reaudited and some very harsh appraisals need to be made about the skills of management and the labor force, goodwill, and physical assets. Such zero-based, balance-sheet appraisals often occur after a takeover or merger. If such appraisals had been taken earlier, they might have prevented the takeover or merger.

Also, it is dangerous to take a snapshot approach to assessing company strengths and weaknesses. Trends are often critical, and past, present, and future resources need to be compared and contrasted. For example, plans may be based on a very strong and capable sales force that once existed. However, the company may recently have lost a

Assessing Company Strengths and Weaknesses

very competent leader and may be about to suffer a loss of experienced sales people. Not recognizing that the sales force is not what it once was is courting disaster. Strengths and weaknesses of an organization need to be assessed at the time they are needed. This requires a dynamic, rather than static, view of company resources. We now discuss how to identify such company competencies. They can be classified as general competencies and competencies that are specific to a product-market.

Identifying General Competencies

Corporate missions that describe target markets and technologies may successfully guide plans and strategy. However, they may still provide insufficient direction because they do not explicitly state the unique competitive competencies that are to be developed by the organization. A company should search for a common thread in its activities and acquisitions.[14] This thread should be its general competitive competence. Such competencies, be they involved in purchasing, production, technology, manpower, materials, logistics, or marketing, have to then be added to the corporate mission statement. During the first and great diversification period of modern management in the 1920s, chemical companies such as Du Pont, Union Carbide, Allied Chemical, Hercules, and Monsanto all diversified from a common specific technological base. General Electric and Westinghouse also diversified around production and technological strengths.

The further a company gets from its current products and markets, the less likely it is to make a profit.[15] This is a logical consequence of the firm's inability to utilize its existing competitive skill and cost competencies. In the 1970s and 1980s, a number of companies rediscovered the importance of synergy. Johnson Wax diversified from packaged goods into recreational equipment in the early 1970s by acquiring 15 different companies. In the process, it lost momentum in its mature floor polish (Pledge), insect repellant (Raid), and shaving-cream (Edge) markets by overpricing (up to 25 percent higher than its competitors) and underpromoting.[16] It returned to what it knew and did best and regained lost market share in its core product-markets by launching new products, such as Spinfresh (an air freshener that fit into a toilet roll). Efforts by Gillette, Coca-Cola, Philip Morris, Mobil, Beatrice, and General Foods to diversify into very different markets have failed, despite these companies' undisputed marketing skills.

For many years, IBM's corporate mission was to be the best service organization in the world. This competence, when applied to the information-processing market, provided the company with an outstanding early competitive advantage. Many other companies, such as UNIVAC and RCA, had competitive products but did not appreciate the importance of service. Marriott determined that its special competence was in hospitality management and food-service operations. It sold its cruise ship, travel agency, and theme park businesses and even sold its hotels to investor groups. It found its most profitable niche was managing hotels rather than owning them.[17] Service is not one of the competencies of the highly successful BIC Pen Company ("What BIC proposes, the world disposes"). This is because the company seeks to manufacture and sell products that are cheap, used relatively briefly, and then discarded. Instead, the company's competencies lie in quickly adopting and improving on competitors' innovations and then efficiently mass producing, distributing, and promoting such products.

14. H. Igor Ansoff, *Corporate Strategy* (New York: McGraw-Hill, 1965). This is the classic work on the subject.
15. Thomas J. Peters and Robert H. Waterman, *In Search of Excellence,* (New York: Harper and Row, 1982).
16. *Business Week,* June 8, 1987, 130.
17. Walter Kiechel, "Corporate Strategy for the 1990s," *Fortune,* February 29, 1988, 34–42.

Specific Product-Market Competencies

When a company already has a presence in a specific product-market, then an audit similar to that made of competitors should be taken to identify its product-market specific competencies. The possible dimensions of such a self-audit are presented in the competitor analysis template (see Figure 4-6 in Chapter 4: Competitive Analysis), where they are discussed in detail. Because of the sensitivity of some of the evaluations, this audit should preferably be under the supervision of senior management and perhaps involve outside consultants to provide objectivity and perspective. It should also incorporate suppliers' and distributors' perceptions of the company's strengths and weaknesses. Table 7-1 presents the results of an audit taken for a distributor of veterinary supplies. It can be seen that on some performance characteristics, customers and suppliers had a less positive view of the company than the company had of itself.[18]

18. Murray Young, "The Company Audit," Ph.D. dissertation, Ohio State University, 1988.

**Table 7-1
Seeing Ourselves As Others See Us**

Characteristic	Distributor's evaluation of self	Competitor's evaluation of distributor	Supplier's evaluation of distributor	Customer's evaluation of distributor
Minimal backordering	10.0	8.0	7.4	8.2
Timely payment of invoices	8.8	8.5	8.5	NA*
Purchasing expertise	9.0	7.9	7.3	8.3
Managerial competence	9.6	7.9	7.5	8.1
Flexibility/adaptability	9.6	8.0	7.9	8.5
Overall profitability	9.6	8.3	7.3	7.5
Inventory management	7.3	7.5	7.3	8.2
Off-the-shelf availability	9.7	8.0	7.3	8.3
Quality of products	10.0	8.7	8.1	8.7
Wide range of products available	8.7	7.5	7.9	8.6
Large number of options for each product	7.0	7.0	7.2	7.8
Competitive pricing	7.7	7.8	7.5	7.6
Convenient ordering system	9.3	8.3	8.1	8.6
Timely notification of order status	9.0	8.0	6.9	7.6
Consistent timely delivery of regular orders	10.0	8.1	8.0	8.5
Responsive to special handling requests	9.3	8.1	7.5	8.6
Rapid delivery of rush orders	9.3	8.1	7.5	7.9
Territory coverage	8.0	7.0	6.7	NA*
Technical knowledge of sales force	9.0	7.9	6.7	7.7
Assertive sales personnel	7.7	7.6	7.1	7.0
Appropriate frequency of contact with veterinarians	8.7	7.9	6.9	6.6
Detailing and demonstration skills	8.7	7.9	6.6	7.4
Flexible return policy	8.3	8.0	7.1	7.9
Professional ethics	10.0	8.8	7.6	8.3

*NA = Not Asked

When a company evaluates its own competitiveness it often does not view its own strengths and weaknesses the way that its suppliers, customers, or competitors do. The above 1–10 ratings report on the competitiveness of a distributor of veterinary supplies as seen by a survey of the company senior managers, suppliers, competitors, and end consumers (veterinarians).

A new approach to studying a company's skills in particular functional areas is called benchmarking. It involves going beyond competitors and even the industry to find companies that are excellent at a particular function to use as a benchmark. Companies such as Ford and Xerox have used this approach to improve their production processes, customer service, and logistics functions.

Company Culture and Politics

No internal audit is complete without an assessment of a company's unique organizational culture and its likely impact on marketing strategy. Company culture is defined as the shared values and beliefs that help individuals understand how an organization functions and thus provide norms for behavior within the organization.[19] It is primarily the responsibility of senior management to develop and nurture the right company culture. Figure 7-5 presents some characteristics of excellent corporate cultures. These characteristics have been identified by a number of consultants and researchers.[20] Marketing planners must evaluate how their division or company performs on these characteristics in determining whether the strategy they propose will be acceptable to the rest of the company and can be implemented. The impact of company culture on implementation is further discussed in Chapter 14: Organization and Implementation.

Company politics also often play a major role in determining whether something can be done. Company politics, which are an outgrowth of a company's culture, involve conflict and cooperation among various members and factions of the organization. The most important internal politics involved in marketing planning are the politics between the marketing function and production, which we now discuss.

Marketing and Production Synergy

In recent years, as many companies have evaluated their strengths and weaknesses and strategic posture, the classic confrontation between marketing and manufacturing has re-emerged. What marketing planners need to recognize, however, is that a production-oriented culture can provide important competitive advantages, including a special type of peripheral vision.[21] Engineers not only can answer the question, "Are we doing the job right?" but can and should also address the question, "Are we doing the right job?" There are times when a change in technology or process confers significant competitive advantages to the innovator. The use of the continuous-process cigarette manufacturing machine in the 1880s reduced the cost of manufacturing a cigarette to one sixth of its previous cost. The first two users of this technology, James B. Duke in the United States and the Wills brothers in the United Kingdom, very quickly dominated their product-markets. The Japanese became fierce competitors in the automobile and home electronic markets in large part because of innovations in operations: inventory management, work flow, quality control, and automation.[22]

19. Rohit Deshpande and Frederick E. Webster, Jr., "Organizational Culture and Marketing: Defining the Research Agenda," *Journal of Marketing* 53 (January 1989), 3–15.
20. This list of excellent cultural characteristics is based on the work of William G. Ouchi, *Theory Z* (New York: Avon Books, 1981); Thomas J. Peters and Robert H. Waterman, *In Search of Excellence* (New York: Harper and Row, 1982); Carol J. Loomis, "Secrets of the Superstars," *Fortune,* April 24, 1989, 50–62; Carol J. Loomis, "Stars of the Service 500," *Fortune,* June 5, 1989, 54–62; and Modesto A. Maidique and Robert H. Hayes, "The Art of High Technology Management," *Sloan Management Review* 26 (Winter 1984), 1–31. See also Roger A. Kerin, Vijay Mahajan, and P. Rajan Varadarajan, *Strategic Market Planning* (Boston: Allyn and Bacon, 1990), chapter 11.
21. Robert H. Hayes and Steven C. Wheelwright, *Restoring Our Competitive Edge: Competing Through Manufacturing* (New York: John Wiley & Sons, 1984); and Alan M. Kanthrow, "The Strategy-Technology Connection," *Harvard Business Review,* July/August 1980, 6–21.
22. Steven C. Wheelwright, "Japan—Where Operations Really Are Strategic," *Harvard Business Review,* July/August 1981, 67–74; and Robert H. Hayes, "Why Japanese Factories Work," *Harvard Business Review,* July/August, 1981, 57–66.

1. They are able to introduce change and adapt to change in the marketplace very quickly. This involves the ability to make decisions quickly and implement the decisions faster than their competition. They have a do-it, fix-it, try-it culture.

2. They are market driven. They are close to their customers who they listen to and respond to with relevant product features and service.

3. They are market leaders in specific product-markets and the use of specific technologies. They have become expert at doing something very well, and they find other uses for this skill.

4. They have few layers of management and have a lot of informal contact up, down and across the organization.

5. They decentralize decision making and encourage autonomy and entrepreneurship.

6. Everyone in the organization is very cost conscious.

7. Senior managers take a hands-on approach. They manage by walking around the production plants, visiting customers and talking informally with the managers and other employees. They are active managers and are experts on their product-markets.

8. The organization is more like a clan rather than a bureaucracy.

9. Special venture teams of marketing, engineer, and production specialists are informally and formally formed to find innovative or imitative solutions to quality and cost problems.

Figure 7-5

The Characteristics of Excellent Company Cultures

The Growth-Choke and Adaptation-Efficiency Trade-offs

Inevitably, a strategic accommodation must be made between marketing and production. The two commonly occurring situations that create conflict are the growth-choke and the adaptation-efficiency trade-offs.

In a growth market, marketing activity can often overheat demand. Order backlogs build, supply is worked to capacity and then overcapacity, costs rise, and quality drops. For these reasons, competitors are able to gain a toehold with copycat entries. Marketing effort often has to be turned down or even turned off, and the market momentum is lost while expansions in the manufacturing process and materials management are made. Such changes then produce sharp-break increases in capacity and a tendency to oversupply. Marketing is then asked to raise demand again. Such swings can happen several times in a rapid growth market and can create enduring tensions between marketing and production. Turning market demand off and on is just as frustrating to the sales force, the channel, and advertising agency as asking production to first overstretch itself and then operate at below capacity and optimum efficiency. Both marketing and production are also expected to control costs so as to produce profits and cash flow to fund further market or production expansion. This often leads to finger pointing, as one functional area accuses another of inefficiency. Ironically, such inefficiencies can often be traced to accommodating the demands or constraints of the finger pointer.

In any market, cost efficiencies and high quality conformance (few rejects) come from bedding down a production process, cranking it up in long, uninterrupted production runs, and stretching the life of the plant by creative maintenance. New products involve investment in retooling, changing work flow, adding downstream and upstream inventory during the transition, retraining staff, start-up operating inefficiencies, numerous quality control problems, and extra marketing expenses. But product change may be needed to increase competitive product differentiation or to match a competitor's new product features. Traditionally, this has resulted in an adaptation-efficiency trade-off that often had to be resolved by senior management.

Recently, however, a new manufacturing strategy has emerged that bridges production's demands for low costs with marketing's demands for product innovations. Termed *flexible manufacturing,* this strategy emphasizes manufacturing many different products on the same line and switching from one product to another without set-up time and at a low cost. The objective is to make as much profit on short runs as ordinarily would have been obtained only on long, uninterrupted runs while gaining the ability to adapt quickly to market demands. To make this strategy work, however, a culture must promote close cooperation between manufacturing and marketing. There are two additional areas in which marketing and production can work together to each other's mutual advantage: improving quality and decreasing the sluggishness of all company routines.

Total Quality Management

American manufacturers have only recently recognized that as production quality goes up, costs can come down. It has been claimed that 20 to 25 percent of the operating budgets, 25 percent of the labor costs, and up to 30 percent of the final production costs of U.S. manufacturers are spent on finding, fixing, and compensating for production mistakes.[23] Companies can learn to remove the causes of variation in the production process through statistical process control (SPC), which spots defects where and when they are made rather than after the fact.

A drive for improved quality requires a change in the whole company culture. Quality improvement must become a major focus of the business plan, part of each manager's annual review, and involve all workers in job and production process design. It requires increased quality control from suppliers and requires that everyone on the production line understand that the person operating the next added-value process is the customer that they must satisfy. Computer programs are now being developed that enable engineers to evaluate how they can manufacture a rough design and determine its production costs. Such computer assistance allows engineers to make clear the trade-offs between form, function, cost, and the likelihood of zero-defect production of the component. The input-output matrices used in quality function deployment (QFD) and described in Chapter 8 and 9 also increase inter-function communication and the employee's understanding of how to create quality and reduce costs.[24] Such frameworks enable marketing, engineering, and manufacturing to see all of the facets of design, manufacturing, and marketing in one big picture that they can all review and agree on. This increases communication and suggests ways of resolving disagreements. It is claimed that Toyota has used QFD very successfully to increase quality, lower costs, and bring products to market much faster. American companies have had mixed success using the approach, but the problems appear to stem less from QFD and more from the organization's commitment to change and making QFD work.

While it may take several years for a company to benefit from making quality a major corporate goal, the long-term benefits can be considerable. Ford started a quality drive in 1981. Five years later, the company's costs were down, quality was up, customer satisfaction was up, and profits were even greater than those of General Motors, which had almost twice the market share of Ford. Who can object to investing in quality when it helps sell the product, makes production more efficient, *and* reduces costs.

23. *Business Week,* "The Push for Quality," June 8, 1987, 130–43.
24. Abbie Griffin, *Evaluating Development Processes: QFD As an Example,* #91–121 (Cambridge, MA: Marketing Science Institute, 1991), 91–121; and John R. Hauser and Don Clausing, "The House of Quality," *Harvard Business Review,* May/June 1988, 63–73.

Implementation Speed: A Sustainable Competitive Advantage

If a company can accelerate the pace of change in the marketplace, then it makes it more difficult for competitors to keep up with its moves. If a company can move faster than its competition, then this speed creates a sustainable competitive advantage. Sometimes a company will make mistakes, but its ability to rectify such mistakes quickly and regain momentum will put it out in front again. Implementation speed enables a company to be more aggressive, to stay out front, and to defend itself better in highly turbulent markets. Implementation speed reduces costs by eliminating wasted time and effort. It also increases cooperation within the organization because greater cooperation is needed to get things done quickly. Finally, it lifts the overall image of the company's service and innovativeness. Increasing the overall pace of operations in a company results in faster response to leads, faster fulfillment of orders, faster design and manufacture of special orders, faster delivery, and faster repair services. Speed kills the competition.[25]

As pointed out in Chapter 2, action or reaction time first involves seeing change in the marketplace before others and understanding its implications faster. The second component involves adapting and implementing faster. The CEO of Hewlett-Packard, John Young, introduced a company-wide program called BET (break-even time), which was the time it took to move a product from concept development to its break-even position in the marketplace. He recognized two important trends: 1) the company that gets new technology to the market first can charge a premium until competitors catch up and 2) manufacturing typically takes up only 10 percent of the time between when an order is placed and when the new product reaches the customer. The rest of the time is consumed by administrative duties; this time can be greatly reduced. A McKinsey & Company consulting study found that it is more profitable to get high-tech products out on time but over budget than to get them out on budget but late.[26] Figure 7-6 presents a benchmarking process designed to improve an organization's responsiveness.

1. What are Black & Decker's core markets and what technology has it mastered? (Hint: Name some of its major products and then think of what technology they have in common.)

2. What problems arise when setting performance objectives for a product group? In answering this question, consider what is wrong with the use of portfolio analysis to allocate resources and provide strategic direction?

3. Your boss refuses to give clear direction as to whether or not a project should be given short- or long-term attention, but your boss wants high, assured profits. Your boss promises to make the tough decisions, but you know that if you keep running to your boss, he or she will soon lose confidence in your leadership and management skills. What should you do in this situation?

25. This is one of the key propositions of competitive rationality theory. See also Derek F. Abell, "Strategic Windows," *Journal of Marketing* (July 1987), 21–26; Tom Peters, *Thriving on Chaos* (New York: Harper & Row, 1987); Walter Kiechel, "Corporate Strategy for the 1990s," *Fortune*, February 29, 1988, 34–42; Amar Bhide, "Hustle as Strategy," *Harvard Business Review*, September/October 1986, 59–65; and George Stalk, Jr., "Time—The Next Source of Competitive Advantage," *Harvard Business Review*, July/August 1988, 41–50.
26. Brian Dumaine, "How Managers Can Succeed Through Speed," *Fortune*, February 13 1989, 54–59.

Figure 7-6

**Implementation Speed
Benchmarking**

This flowchart, developed by Kaiser Associates, Inc., describes seven steps involved in improving the action and reaction speed of a firm. The best in class need not be in the firm's industry. For example, companies such as Xerox have turned to the catalog company L. L. Bean to learn how to improve the responsiveness of their customer service operations.

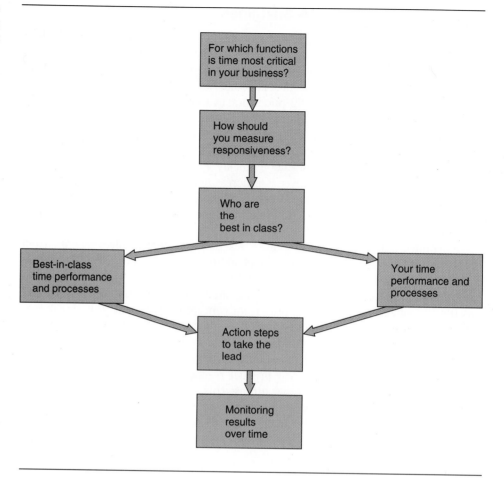

4. Which of the goals in Figure 7-4 is likely to end up being a "bum steer"? When the S&Ls got into more and more desperate trouble, which of the four goal quadrants did they end up in, and why did this decision seal their fate?

5. What disturbs you about the statistics in Figure 7-3? What aspect of the theory of competitive rationality might reduce your concerns?

6. A number of years ago, corporate planners in the General Electric Company appliance division looked at the demographics and assumed that the demand for smaller appliances would increase because family size was shrinking. Because they were not in touch with home builders and retailers, they did not understand that kitchens and bathrooms were the two rooms in the house that were not shrinking and the working woman wanted bigger refrigerators to cut down supermarket trips. Senior management listened to the planners but then discovered that the demand for smaller appliances was not there. What lessons can we learn from GE's experience?

7. In the 1980s, Pan Am proposed to sell its New York headquarters to save the company from a cash-flow crisis. This evoked angry protests from shareholders who,

at the annual meeting, insisted that the board was made up of a "bunch of dum-mies" who should have kept the building and sold the airline. How was selling the building a right decision? How was selling the airline a right decision?

8. Why is an ounce of prevention worth a pound of cure when it comes to quality control? What is the recommended recipe for prevention?

9. Explain in detail what can happen when there is not a strategic accommodation between marketing and production.

10. Why do you think it so difficult for marketers, engineers, and production people to work together in teams? Suggest solutions to the problems you identify.

11. On what performance characteristics in Table 7-1 is the distributor perceiving itself to be doing better than reality? What impact is this likely to have on the firm's competitiveness?

12. A chief executive of an operating division of a small company is paid a lot because of his or her leadership and thinking skills. How should such a CEO explain how she or he thinks about the dynamics of the competitive market to subordinates? Do you think that this is an important function of a CEO over and above providing the mission statement and setting objectives?

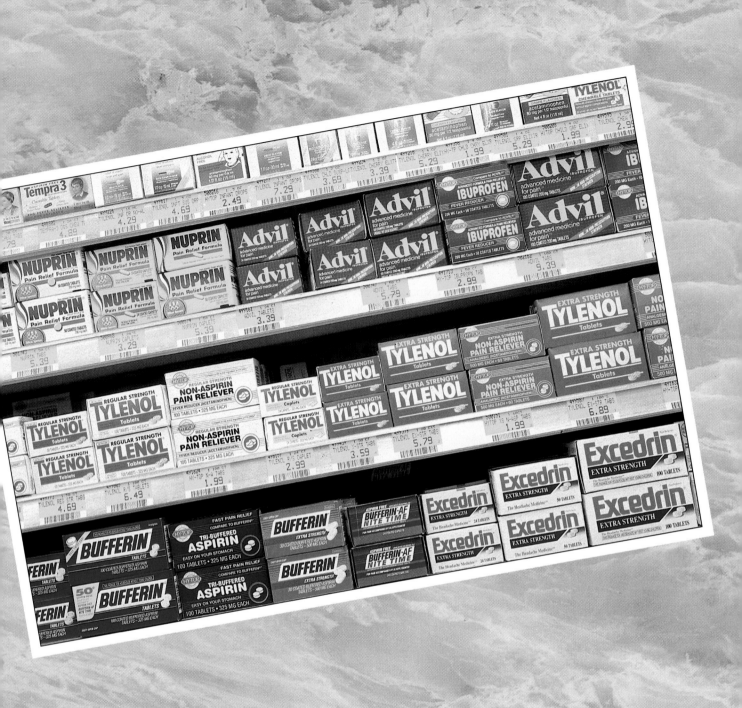

Positioning Strategy

*"The pessimist sees the difficulty in every opportunity,
the optimist sees the opportunity in every difficulty."*
Winston Churchill

"Chance favors the prepared mind."
Louis Pasteur

*A*fter studying and understanding the market environment, the first and most critical strategic decision to be made is the choice of the target benefit segment. Once this segment has been chosen, the market management team must determine its product's competitive positioning. These two strategic decisions are pivotal, in that they influence all of the marketing decisions that follow them.

How is it that a small start-up company such as Apple succeeded in an industry dominated by hugely successful computer manufacturers? The answer is positioning. The first Apples were distinctively positioned as stand-alone personal computers. During the time of Apple's rise, the rest of the manufacturers were in a race to build ever larger, faster computers. While other start-up companies such as Osborne came and went, Apple flourished by targeting the education market, which it later came to dominate. The entry of IBM opened up another segment—the business market for personal computers. Even though its operating system and software was totally incompatible with IBM and MS-DOS, Apple was able to compete. Why? Because it targeted a business segment that demanded graphics applications, report preparation, and desktop publishing. Apple's mouse, pointers, software, and early laser printers ideally positioned its computer to serve these usage segments. Later the company added a further positioning advantage—the Apple was user-friendly and it was marketed as the system that was easy to learn. The success of Apple, first in the education market and then in the business market, had a lot to do with its focus on distinct usage-benefit segments and the positioning of its product to deliver the desired benefits.

The ability to spot a positioning opportunity in a market tests the true genius of an entrepreneurial marketer. Positioning skill can make entrepreneurs into millionaires and chief executives out of middle managers because clever positioning can produce above-average profits (see Figure 8-1). In the first section of this chapter we will discuss the targeting decision because at some point every company must ask itself, "Which consumers do we want to target and what benefits do they expect from the product or service?" The second section discusses positioning and differentiating: What benefits do we want to deliver to the consumer, and how will our product deliver better benefits compared to the competition? The third section discusses the use of positioning to attack and defend a market. The fourth section explains how a positioning concept on a competitive map is converted into an actual differentiated product or service: How will our product or service be designed to deliver the desired quality? The fifth section explains how to estimate a price using quality-added analysis: How much are our target consumers prepared to pay for the superior quality of our product? The process concludes with a method of assessing the financial feasibility of the proposed positioning: Will the proposed positioning, design, and price produce sales forecasts that are attainable and that will meet company financial goals? Finally, a number of positioning issues that arise in global marketing are discussed. The recommended approach to developing a positioning strategy is detailed in Figure 8-2.

Keep these key ideas in mind as you read this chapter:

- Positioning starts by segmenting the market based on the different benefits that each consumer group seeks from the product.

- Positioning is often intuitive. Sophisticated analysis techniques help, but they are not needed. Rough-and-ready techniques are better than *no* systematic thinking about positioning strategy.

- It helps to develop a mental map of where the competitors are positioned in terms of determining factors like benefits and quality features.

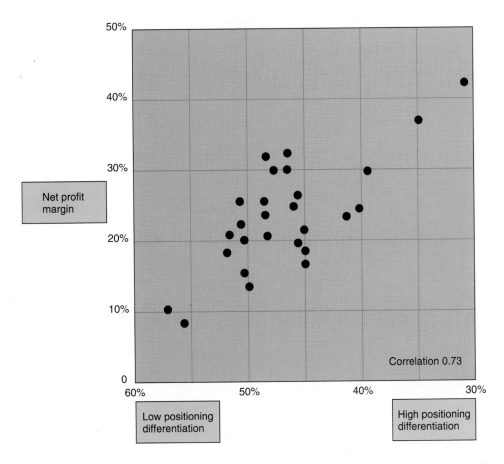

Figure 8-1

The Profitability of Distinctive Positioning

The basic objective of competitive positioning strategy is to design and promote an innovative product so that it is perceived by a market segment to be attractively distinct. In economics, this is called distancing oneself from the price competition of inferior substitutes. Such a reduction in substitutability enables a company to monopolize a market segment, charge a higher price, and earn extra profits (economic rent).

The economic advantages of such a strategy are demonstrated in the above figure. A clear relationship exists between successful differentiation and net profit margin. Brands that are perceived by target consumers to have no or few substitutes (higher differentiation) generally earn higher margins. A lot of money can be made from unique positioning. A lot of money can also be lost by ending up a close substitute to other competitors (the "me-too" situation) and having no sustainable cost advantage over the competitors.

Source: *Product Line Strategy,* The Conference Board, New York, 1982.

- A positioning map can be used to identify opportunities and specify the current and desired positioning of the product or service.

- The goal is to develop a differentiated product that creates a unique mind share, particularly in the target market segment.

- Positioning involves careful thinking about all of the models in a company's line.

- Positions are best attacked by focusing resources and promotion on a particular positioning or quality feature.

- Positions are best defended by an aggressive, mobile counterattack involving repositioning existing products and introducing new models.

- When designing the product, make sure that quality is incorporated into the features that most affect the desired competitive positioning of the product.

- Set the price for the positioned product or service by estimating how much extra quality the product will possess over and above the competition and how much the target consumers are prepared to *pay* for this extra quality, over and above the competition's actual selling price.

Figure 8-2

The Major Steps in Positioning Strategy

The differentiated positioning concept is developed after the benefit market segments are identified. This concept is then converted into a product or service blueprint using quality function deployment (QFD). The QFD blueprint is then quality added (QA) and tested to establish its price differential superiority. Finally, the feasibility of the strategy is tested by estimating the sales and market-share goals and assessing whether the goals are achievable.

Positioning Strategy Steps	Useful Analytical Techniques
Benefit Segmentation: Identify the nature of the benefit segments including forecasts of size and growth of segments, demographics, usage context, beliefs, and behavior.	• Deep segmentation (See Chapter 3)
Mapping Competitive Position: Position the product/service concept against competitive alternatives on a positioning map that also shows the clusters of consumer ideal points (that is, benefit segments).	• Intuitive mapping • Substitution mapping • Preference mapping • Attribute ratings • Conjoint analysis • Cluster analysis
Quality Function Deployment (QFD): Convert positioning concept into an engineered product or service.	• Quality functional deployment (QFD) • The QFD product specification matrix • Input-output process mapping of a service activity schedule
Quality Added (QA) Analysis: Test monetary value of quality added compared to competitors	• QFD benchmarking • Quality added (QA) analysis • Conjoint analysis • Taguchi methods
Feasibility Analysis: Evaluate the financial feasibility of the positioning: Can the sales and share targets be achieved?	• Break-even analysis • Target return analysis • STRATMESH planning

■ Roughly estimate the financial feasibility of the proposed positioning strategy. Will the expected sales and share meet targets?

■ When marketing on a global scale, a product is often first positioned in a similar foreign market the same way it is positioned in the home market. The positioning is then adjusted to the local segment structure and competition. Eventually, products may be positioned for benefit segments that cross borders and cultures.

■ Global marketing requires constant repositioning to counter new entrants from other foreign markets. It also involves counterattacking in the new entrant's home market.

Targeting Benefit Segments

The competitively rational positioning process summarized in Figure 8-2 starts with identifying the nature and potential of benefit segments, as described in Chapter 3. Customers are grouped together (clustered) by the benefits they seek from using the product or service. This includes the features and other specifications that are a must or are highly desired in the product and service. In this way, the benefit segments are created. Deep segmentation then uses individual differences and usage context to explain why different customers belong in a particular benefit segment. It also studies

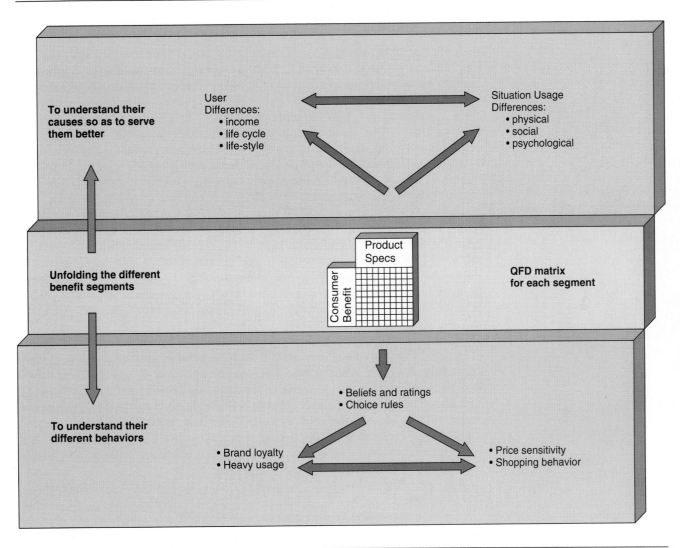

User
Differences:
• income
• life cycle
• life-style

Situation Usage
Differences:
• physical
• social
• psychological

**To understand their
causes so as to serve
them better**

Product
Specs

Consumer
Benefit

**QFD matrix
for each segment**

**Unfolding the different
benefit segments**

• Beliefs and ratings
• Choice rules

**To understand their
different behaviors**

• Brand loyalty
• Heavy usage

• Price sensitivity
• Shopping behavior

Figure 8-3

**Benefit Segmentation and
Quality Functional Deployment**

Chapter 3 discussed how to segment the
market starting with the different benefits
and levels of outcome performance that
consumers seek from using a product or
service. The QFD matrix shows the relationships (correlations) between consumer benefits and product design and
engineering specifications. A product or
service is then designed, engineered,
and manufactured to the specifications
that are most related to a specific segment's desired benefits and levels of performance. This is called positioning a
product to satisfy the needs of a target
segment or market niche.

the beliefs, choice behavior, brand loyalty, and shopping behavior of each benefit segment (see Figure 8-3).

Having identified and developed a deep understanding of each benefit segment, a
cross-functional team must then decide which, if any, segment or segments the company should attempt to serve. This involves more than estimating the size and growth
potential of each segment. It requires an understanding of how well the existing competitive products and services are positioned to serve the benefit segments. How well
are competitors' products and services fitted to the needs of each benefit segment? Are
the existing products and services in the market designed and engineered to specifications that will deliver the desired benefits to the target segment? If they are not well
designed and engineered, then an opportunity exists to introduce a new product model
or service that is positioned to better serve the needs of the target benefit segment
than the existing competition. The question then is whether such a target segment can
be profitably served and the positioning defended over the long term. This question

cannot be answered with certainty, but it is best answered by evaluating the environmental factors, as described in the STRATMESH process in Chapter 1.

A market niche is another name for a segment of the market. The word *niche* means a state of nature that is well suited to the holder ("With her writing skills, she has found her niche as a journalist."). Market niching means finding, understanding, and serving a target segment that *fits* the competitive strengths or objectives of the company. Ideally, the niche should be such that there is only room for one supplier or there are significant barriers to entry, as described in Chapter 4. For example, the National Hole in One insurance company, run by a golf enthusiast, insures sponsors of hole-in-one prizes and earns a profit of a million dollars a year doing so.[1] McKee Food's Little Debbie Cakes dominate a small but highly profitable segment of the food market—children who want a low-priced, extremely sweet product that can be purchased at convenience stores. It sells for 50 percent less than competing products.[2] The company is the best there is when it comes to the low-cost manufacturing and distribution of snack cakes to children. Lee, the number three manufacturer of jeans, targeted the female market niche and became the number one supplier to this market segment. Zenith gave up competing in the general personal computer market and instead focused on the university and government agency market niches. A women's health service clinic in a major city offers many service conveniences to its 10,000 patients, including a free lending library with books on women's physical, psychological, and social concerns.

Clever segment targeting and product positioning can bring success to companies of any size. Even very large companies can be rewarded by creative positioning strategies. Anheuser-Busch offers several different brands of beer in a range of containers that are carefully positioned to appeal to different beer drinkers and different drinking situations. These brands each have a distinctive taste, image, advertising campaign, and promotion strategy. Not only does Anheuser-Busch have major economies-of-scale, but it also has an excellent target-positioning strategy that is difficult to attack. In recent years, its market share has grown, despite the best efforts of domestic and foreign competitors.

Mapping Competitive Positions

The easiest way of visualizing the positioning of competitive products is by using a two-dimensional map to compare the consumer's image of competing products on two critical performance features.[3] These product positions can then be compared to where a consumer's ideal product would be positioned on the map. An *ideal point* indicates the combination of the two features that the consumer would like most, if it were available. If some consumers' ideal points cluster together, then they form a potential target benefit segment. Figure 8-4 illustrates and explains such a map. The three major benefit segments in the analgesic (painkiller) market were discussed in Chapter 3. Figure 8-4 is the same figure, except that the major competitive brands of analgesics are rated on the two most important features: effectiveness and gentleness. The reason why Tylenol has 30 percent of the total analgesic market is obvious. It is the best known brand of acetaminophen, a powerful painkiller with very few bad side effects. Evidence

1. Rita Koselka, "The Best of Both Possible Worlds," *Forbes,* July 23, 1990, 52–74.
2. William Stern, "Mom and Dad Knew Every Name," *Forbes,* December 7, 1992, 172–74.
3. The competitive map can be based on consumer ratings of each brand's performance on each dimension. It can also be derived from consumer judgments of brand similarity, brand preferences, and brand switching behavior.

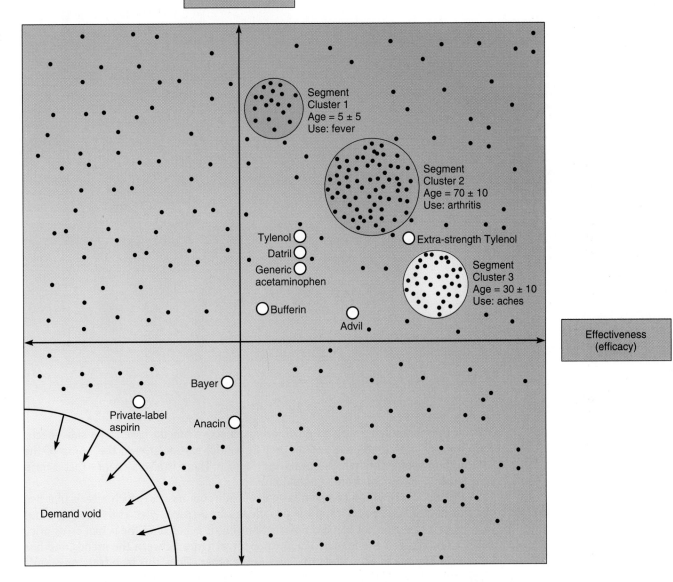

This map shows three major benefit segments: children, for whom gentleness is a priority, the elderly who seek to reduce the aches and pains of old age and need medication that is gentle to the stomach (which aspirin is not), and a younger segment of the population that seeks relief for occasional sharp pain. Tylenol's positioning explains why it gained such a large share of the analgesic (painkiller) market. This intuitive map illustrates the value of using competitive maps to decide which benefit segments to target.

Figure 8-4

An Intuitive Competitive Map of the Analgesic Market

Figure 8-5

A Competitive Map of Bathroom Tissues

In this map, the distance between brands is determined by measuring the effect of changing one brand's price on the sales of the other brands. The greater the effect, the higher the cross-price elasticity and the closer the brands are positioned on the map. Charmin and Soft N Pretty are close together because their cross-price elasticities are high. A change in price of one has a strong effect on the sales of the other. On the other hand, Coronet's and Scott's sales do not change very much at all when the prices of Charmin or Soft N Pretty change. They have distanced themselves from the price competition of their rival brands. The major difference is that Scott is sold by the roll and Coronet in 8-roll packs. All of the rest are sold in 4-roll packs. It seems that Scott and Coronet have differentiated themselves with their packaging. Charmin has emphasized softness in its promotion, but it has not been able to achieve a differentiated position in the market because Soft N Pretty has also emphasized softness.

Source: Greg M. Allenby, "A Unified Approach to Identifying, Estimating and Testing Demand Structures with Aggregate Scanner Data," *Marketing Science* 8.3 (Summer 1989), 265–80.

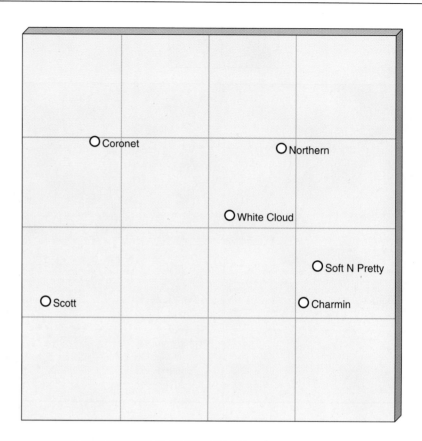

shows that ibuprofens, such as Advil, are as effective but do have some side effects. Aspirins are not as effective and are not as gentle, particularly on the lining of the stomach of young children and heavy user adults. There is also a chance that aspirin can produce Reyes Syndrome in children.

Figure 8-5 presents a competitive map of bathroom tissues, which reveals that two brands have unique positions in the two-dimensional space. What is interesting about this map is that it is not based on perceptions but it is based on the actual cross-price elasticities between the brands. The greater the distance between the brands, the less a change in price of one affects the sales of the other. Thus, this map truly represents how well a brand has distanced itself from the price competition of other brands. It reveals that some brands of bathroom tissue have used the number of rolls in a pack to successfully differentiate themselves from competition. Two brands that have promoted their softness quality are positioned closely together.

Drawing Intuitive Maps

Very complex statistical techniques can be used to identify opportunities and to position products competitively, but most positioning is based on intuition—an important component of the competitive rationality of the decision makers. While analytic methods of drawing competitive maps can be very useful in the real world of marketing decision making, they are only used by a tiny fraction of marketing planners. Most positioning decisions are largely based on intuition. Unfortunately, this intuition is often not spelled out or mapped out on paper. It can be very useful for a cross-functional team to create its own intuitive map of the major benefit segments and the positioning of the competition. For instance, a cross-functional team might gain a great deal of insight by taking the two most critical buyer choice dimensions and positioning the competitive products in the resulting two-dimensional map. The position and size of the market segments could then be estimated and drawn in on the map. The result is a competitive positioning map similar to that in Figure 8-4. The chosen dimensions and resulting maps of the different executives involved in the decision making will make interesting comparisons as they reflect how the different planners think about the market. This consensus map is a very important mental model that can form a basis for product development and other marketing decisions.

Product Differentiation

When a firm positions its offering to serve a target segment or niche, this positioning may either be unique or, at the other extreme, be exactly the same as a competitor's offering. Two products may be positioned to serve the same segment and be very similar in design and the image they attempt to present. They are positioned, but because they are not *uniquely* positioned they lack product differentiation. Product differentiation is the act of distinguishing a product from its competitors on one or more basic performance or image features.

A clever way to expand the demand for aluminum wrap is to position it as a product that goes *in* the dish as well as *over* the dish.

The objective of a differentiation strategy is to convince the target market that your product or service is clearly the best choice to achieve the target buyer's particular end or ends. Differentiation requires that your positioning be unique. This is because if any alternative is positioned close to your image, then your product will no longer be perceived as clearly the best choice. It is important to note that such differentiation provides a very important way for a firm to gain competitive advantage and make extra profits by distancing its products from the price competition of less well positioned substitutes. But it is not the only way of competing and making profits. If a firm has a lower cost structure than its rivals, it might find it very profitable to offer a product or service with exactly the same performance positioning as the competition but at a significantly lower price. If it can sustain its cost structure advantage it can continue to differentiate and compete purely on price.

For example, as mentioned earlier, McKee Foods makes Little Debbie, the number 1 snack cake with a 54 percent market share. It mostly sells its cakes and cookies to kids under 15 for a price that is at least 50 percent less than its competition. Its cost advantage comes, in part, from using natural preservatives that give its products a shelf life of 30 days, three times longer than Hostess Twinkies.[4] This means that McKee does not need to employ its own expensive sales force and logistic's system to make weekly deliveries. Instead, it uses lower cost, independent distributors. McKee Foods also employs nonunion, lower cost labor, has low management overheads, and enjoys other economy-of-scale advantages over its competition (the next largest being Hostess, with 18 percent of the market). The low-price positioning fits with the benefit that most kids and parents seek from such snacks—economy rather than gourmet flavor and quality.

Differentiation has been called the establishment of a *unique mind share*—creating unique images and perceptions of a product in the minds of the market that will, in time, convert into market share.[5] The greater the uniqueness of a product or service's image (measured by the noticeable differences in image between the product and its competitors), the greater the product or service's differentiation will be. Image is very important in positioning, but it is *not* everything. The image often has to be created, supported, and authenticated by superior quality, design, and performance in use—not just by celebrity endorsements or clever advertising.

Coke and Pepsi have had to work very hard to differentiate themselves from one another in the perceptions of many customers. They have matched each other in advertising dollars spent to create an image of superiority in the taste and "fun to drink" dimensions. After several decades of competition, they still remain very similarly positioned on taste and image. As a result, many buyers regularly switch between the two, depending on which one is on sale in the market. Coke and Pepsi are trying to avoid having to compete on price by developing distinct images. Pepsi, in particular, has targeted the younger generation by positioning Pepsi as more invigorating and modern. Most of the true innovation in this market has come from more convenient packaging and the diet and no-caffeine alternatives. The successful innovations of each have been quickly imitated by the other. Coke was the first to offer a diet cola and has kept its lead in this market.

4. William Stern, "Mom and Dad Knew Every Name," *Forbes,* December 7, 1992, 172–74.
5. Al Ries and Jack Trout, *Positioning: The Battle for Your Mind* (New York: Warner Books, 1982). It is important to note that a *unique* mind share occurs when consumers are aware of a brand and perceive it as unique in some way. Mind share is when consumers are simply aware of a brand but do not perceive it as having a unique image.

Product Differentiation in a Competitive Positioning Map

Product differentiation implies that a firm has unique positioning, that it has come up with a design or image innovation that has successfully differentiated it from the competition in the eyes of the target market. A differentiated strategy is therefore a more subtle and complicated type of positioning strategy, which, if it works as planned, is highly desirable.

To be successful, a product must be differentiated on a dimension that is important to at least one segment of the market. Importance without differentiation is not sufficient; neither is differentiation without importance. Manufacturers of telephones found this out in 1977 when it became possible to buy, rather than rent, phones from AT&T. Phones with multiple features and functions did not sell nearly as well as expected. The features that differentiated them were only desirable and important to a small usage segment. In the late 1980s, a quarter of the phones sold to the public were still the basic dial models and a further 20 percent were the basic push-button models. Also, although AT&T's prices were comparatively high, 40 percent of homes still rented from AT&T, and 25 percent of the phones sold were marketed by AT&T.[6]

One of the dangers of competitive positioning maps produced by intuitive judgment or various multivariate statistical techniques is that an unoccupied space or hole in the surface may or may not represent a new positioning opportunity. It can also indicate a combination of features that nobody wants (a "demand sinkhole"). A company that designs and markets a product into such a sinkhole can lose a great deal of money. Product positioning often boils down to determining whether or not there is enough actual or potential demand for a product with such a new positioning. Sometimes it is easy to avoid such risks. For example, in Figure 8-4 there is no analgesic positioned in the bottom left quadrant because there is no demand for a painkiller that does not kill pain and has unpleasant side effects! At other times it is more difficult to recognize a demand void or sinkhole. For example, a number of major news media companies spent hundreds of millions of dollars attempting to market various computer-based information and shopping videotext systems. However, the demand for the product they offered did not exist, even after the companies gave months of free trials to potential customers. Existing alternatives were at least as convenient to use.

New Combinations of Benefits

Sometimes an area of a competitive positioning map shows little demand because buyers believe that it is not possible to obtain such a combination of benefits. The task of the positioning strategy is to convince the dubious consumer that the new brand does indeed successfully combine these features. The Miller Lite beer "less filling, great taste" campaign was an example of such positioning. Attempts by breakfast cereal companies to convince a suspicious market that high-fiber cereals can also taste good (with the addition of fruit) is another example. General Foods appears to have convinced a sufficient number of consumers that its Post Fruit & Fiber is good for you and tastes good, too. If successful, such differentiation will be particularly powerful because what was previously believed to be a trade-off between two desired but contradictory features now becomes a combination of the two desired attributes. Whereas once a plus on one important choice dimension meant a minus on another, now the brand that positively links the two attributes receives a double plus in positioning.

---

6. Nicholas Shrady, "When More Is Not Better," *Forbes*, May 6, 1985, 94–95.

Service Differentiation and Positioning

Differentiation of a service rather than a product depends on understanding customer needs and attempting to meet such needs on a one-to-one level with genuine consideration and caring. A new service can quickly be copied by competitors, but being the first to introduce such new services conveys a genuine concern for customers. Continuous innovation in customer service creates an image that is not easily copied.

The necessity to provide consideration and caring in the delivery of the service poses a tricky problem for a substantial portion of service providers. As the service market has expanded, providers have had to choose between the customization of their service to suit individual consumer needs and the trend toward standardization and lower prices. When service positioning involves offering a standardized service or a reduced level of service for a lower competitive price, success hinges on the service provider's ability to provide a satisfactory level of service for the target market segment. But even at lower levels of service, the provider must pay attention to the personal interaction aspects of service if he or she is to maintain customer satisfaction.

Charles Schwabb is a good example of a company that offers a reduced set of services (securities brokerage, without the investment advice) that are appropriate for its target customers (those people who follow their own investment strategies and pick their own securities to buy). Meanwhile, Schwabb still offers a number of service features, such as 24-hour access, that contribute to its customer's total satisfaction. Figure 8-6 illustrates how some mass-delivered services have catered to the market by becoming more standardized and, hence, more affordable.

Service Quality, Expectations, and Satisfaction

The central goal of service quality is meeting or exceeding the expectations of customers, particularly on the determinant positioning dimensions.[7] However, viewing quality positioning from such an expectations perspective raises a very interesting issue. Customers develop service expectations based on past service experiences, the price they are paying, and other factors. Service satisfaction, then, depends on the difference between the service customers expected to receive and the service they actually received. A service is judged to be very good if it exceeds such expectations. But what this means is that a service with a high-quality reputation (that is, achieved positioning) may not generate high satisfaction, even though it is perceived to be very high quality.

Therein lies the rub. With each positive experience there builds up, bit by bit, expectations of even better performance in the future. The service or product's quality positioning increases. Consequently, the ability to pleasantly surprise and satisfy customers reduces as these expectations build, and the chances of unpleasantly surprising and dissatisfying customers increases. If service then slips badly, it can create such dissatisfaction that the customer is lost forever. That is why restaurants lose business when a favorite waitress or waiter leaves. It also explains why stockbrokers are constantly hustling to improve the timeliness and quality of their advice and why a sudden collapse of the stock market after a sustained and prosperous climb (that is, a long period of "good advice") creates panic among brokers. Along with a long climb in the stock market goes a long climb in customers' expectations and trust that the advice they receive will continue to make them money. This tricky expectation-performance

7. Valerie A. Zeithhaml, A. Parasuraman, and Leonard L. Berry, *Delivering Quality Service: Balancing Customer Perceptions and Expectations* (New York: Free Press, 1990).

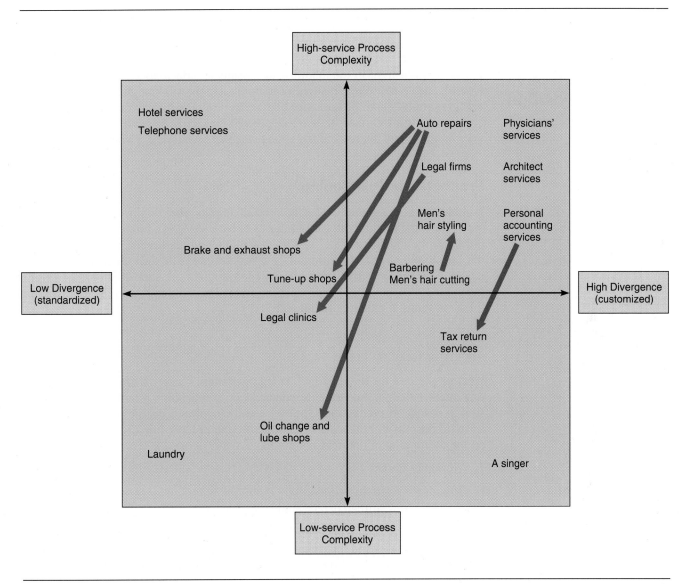

Figure 8-6

The Development of Standardized Services

This competitive positioning map shows how a number of services have evolved from being complex and highly customized to being less complex and more standardized. An exception to the trend is men's hair-cutting services, which moved in the other direction.

Source: This figure is based on a framework developed by G. Lynn Shostack, "Service Positioning Through Structural Changes," *Journal of Marketing* 51 (January 1987), 34–43.

relationship poses a problem. Should a service company set high service expectations with its marketing and just meet such expectations with its performance, or should it be more modest in its marketing claims and then offer a service that greatly exceeds expectations? The first marketing strategy will attract more business immediately, but the second marketing strategy will lead to stronger loyalty and sustained growth through customer referrals. Whichever long-term strategy is pursued, conformance (consistent delivery of quality service) becomes much more important as overall quality expectations rise. This is because a downside deviation (a negative decline in service quality) can be very serious. It may be better for a service provider to *meet* expectations rather than continually exceed ever-increasing expectations, because to do the latter is to raise expectations to a level that is hard to attain and maintain.

Attacking and Defending a Competitive Position

The objective of positioning is to find an attractive niche, occupy it with a distinctive innovation, and then use innovation-imitation to defend it against all competition. As will become apparent in the following discussion, an attack on a position is often very focused, and defense often involves a counterattack. We will first discuss the traditional defensive strategy and then describe how it can be attacked and counterattacked. However, since the attack defense is often initiated by adding new models to the product line, we must first understand the strategy behind positioning a line of products.

Product-Line Positioning

A product line is a group of specific product models marketed by one company that are in the same product category (in terms of basic design and function). They vary in price, quality, and features and are targeted at different market segments. The items in the line also vary in competitiveness and profitability with each other and with rival models. The questions that propel product-line strategy are simple: Should we expand the product line, contract the product line, or reposition items in the line? Answering these questions is much more difficult.

Adding or Deleting Items

Whether you are on the offensive (going after more market share or expanding the total market size) or defensive (responding to a competitor's recent or current offensive), a change in product-line strategy usually involves a decision to add or remove an item. Success in expanding or contracting the product line consequently depends on the positioning of the item relative to

1. consumer needs,
2. specific competing products, and
3. existing items in the current product line.

The profitability of adding or repositioning an item depends on what happens to overall market size, the demand for competitor's products, the demand for existing items in the line, and the overall product-line fixed and variable costs. We will now consider each of these in turn.

Expanding Sales

Consumers who are currently outside the existing product-market may be drawn into the market by the new offering. This will expand the market size, increase the company's overall market share, and generate higher earnings that will contribute to fixed costs and overhead recovery. When diet colas were introduced, the cola market grew because diet colas attracted adults back into the market.

Forecasting how much a market will grow in size or how much market share will be gained from competition is not easy. It depends very much on the success of the marketing campaign and the response of the competition. In some markets, the competitors do not respond at all to the loss of market share. In other markets the reaction of competitors is swift and effective. This uncertainty highlights the importance of analyzing the competitive environment.

Cannibalizing Sales

It is also very likely that a new item or repositioned item will cannibalize the market share of existing items in your line. Every time Gillette introduces a new wet shaving system it takes most of its sales from existing Gillette products. Why? First, Gillette dominates the market. It has over 40 percent of existing sales, so naturally it is likely to be most affected by its own innovation. Second, a new Gillette product will appeal more to Gillette's loyal users than to consumers who are loyal to Schick, BIC, or another manufacturer. The new product is almost certain to increase administration fixed costs and involve expensive advertising and trade promotions (to obtain more shelf space and change buyer perceptions and attitudes). However, the new item is presumably being introduced because it has particularly attractive features. This may enable the company to charge a premium price that compensates for the added expenses and the cannibalization of existing sales. It may also fill a gap in a product line that, if left unfilled, may enable a competitor to gain a foothold in the market.

At first, the introduction of Miller Lite beer in 1973 seemed to be a great marketing success. However, over time it became clear that much of the market share Miller gained was cannibalized from the brewer's premium beer, Miller High Life. It was still a good decision, however, because the introduction of lite beers by the competition was inevitable. In summary, the advantages and disadvantages of product-line expansion are as follows:

Potential Advantages
♦ Expands total market size
♦ Takes market share from competitors
♦ Blocks competitor entry
♦ Preempts competition
♦ Increases gross margin on each dollar sale

Potential Disadvantages
♦ Cannibalizes market share of existing items in the product line
♦ Increases operating overheads
♦ Requires extra management time and skill
♦ Involves major launch expenses

Most new product failures in the market are due to unsuccessful product-line extensions. They generate very little extra revenue and cost a great deal in management effort and costs. Many of these failures could be prevented by the adoption of a more hard-nosed approach when considering the introduction of a new item in the line.

Product-Line Tactical Issues

In highly competitive markets, particularly those that are driven by continual technological innovations, product-line repositioning, expansion, and pruning are constant. It is a fact of life, a consequence of continual innovation-imitation. Repositioning is the sign of healthy competition and a healthy marketplace. The question, therefore, is not whether to change the product line, but how to change it so as to remain competitive and best meet overall company objectives. In doing so, it pays to consider the following issues and tactics.

Differentiation Shrinkage

Technological innovations in product features and production processes coupled with cost reductions can quickly shrink the differences between the models in a line and the justification for price differences. For example, consider the dilemma faced by companies that marketed both dot matrix and laser computer printers. Technological advances improved the quality of $300–$400 dot matrix printers to near letter quality. Meanwhile, competition and reductions in production costs put severe price pressure on $2,000 laser printers. The net effect was that laser printer prices dropped to under $1,000 and are still dropping. This technology-driven price squeeze has led to an appropriate pruning of manufacturer product lines.

Economy Substitutes

While the decision as to whether to add an item to a product line should generally focus on the items in the line that are closest to the new model in the competitive-feature map, such a narrow perspective can be a mistake. If the consumer uses value for the money to decide which item in a line to choose, then the model or service package that is closest to the planned new model may not be the most competitive substitute. Instead, a very competitively priced option much lower down or much higher up the product line may be what the buyer would otherwise buy. This implies that best selling items in the product line may dominate other models because they are underpriced in terms of value for the money. They are economy substitutes, in that they may not be as close to the new item as others, but they are more price competitive. For example, low-priced, low-octane gas poses more of a threat than medium-priced, medium-octane gas to high-priced, high-octange gas. The solution may be to eliminate the dominated items or to adjust the relative prices.

Repositioning a Whole Product Line

Sometimes a manufacturer systematically moves the whole of its product line positioning, up or down, by adding items at one end and pruning at the other. Honda started off with a line of relatively inexpensive automobiles. The rapid development of its reputation for features, finish, and reliability (a change in consumer perceptions) and the setting of import-volume quotas rather than dollar-value quotas (a new public policy constraint) led to a strategy of upgrading the price/quality of the whole line. In addition, Honda successfully launched Acura, an even more upscale brand.

Image Anchors

Very low and very high priced items in the line can be used as general image anchors. The objective is to drag the perceptions of the whole line in a desired direction. Bottom-of-the-line specials are often advertised to attract customers into a store with the intention of having them trade up to a more expensive model. This "bait and switch" is illegal only when the bait item is not available for purchase, either immediately or by a rain check. At the other end of the line, some brands advertise an extreme high-quality, high-priced item in the hope of enhancing the quality image of their biggest-selling models. Fisher electronics had a $2,500 video-audio system, which it advertised in *Time* and *Newsweek*. While sales of such a top-end system might barely pay for the campaign, the incremental enhancement of the entire Fisher brand name and line of audio-video equipment by such an image anchor may well have made it a very worthwhile product-line strategy. Exclusive department stores such as Neiman-Marcus and Saks Fifth Avenue use expensive display porcelain, jewelry, and perfumes to enhance the image of a thousand more modest items of merchandise.

New Items That Merge Market Segments

An attractive feature in a new model may actually lead to a merging of several previously distinct segments. The minivan, which offered maneuverability without sacrificing capacity, had such an effect. It drew together the two respective target segments of the traditional family station wagon and the full-size van. Now they are largely one segment. A new item in a line can have unexpected effects on other long-standing positioning relationships.

Attacking by Concentrating Resources

Now that we understand some of the important aspects of product-line strategy, let us return to the question of how an existing market might be entered. Rather than embarking on an all-out assault, the entrant may prefer to target an attractive segment of the market where the competition is weak. This is often a growth segment, because often the competition does not yet have a strong image in the minds of the new users.

The new users of a product or new uses for a product may also change what is valued in the product or service, opening up an important new positioning or differentiation opportunity. Pepsi started its major assault on Coca Cola's brand loyalty in the 1950s by concentrating its push in specific regions and by targeting the take-home market, a market that, up to then, Coke had largely overlooked. Once such a positioning weakness in the market is found, the attacker must position itself as superior on a consumer choice dimension that the competition will find difficult to counter. The objective of the new entrant should be to become number 1 on quality, economy, style, or some other important choice dimension in the minds of the consumer.[8] This will require new product design and a saturated advertising campaign directed at the heavy users in the target market. The above resource concentration strategy is most evident in the behavior of small companies that focus on a regional market. They develop a local consumer franchise and often use the local media and distribution channels more effectively than large competitors whose marketing tactics are devised at national headquarters and applied nationwide.

Attacking with a New Performance Feature

One leading economist has argued that most markets can only be entered successfully by a massive launch of a whole new product line.[9] The history of marketing campaigns suggests otherwise. An existing market is most vulnerable to the introduction of an important new feature. Such a competitive move can have an effect equivalent to undermining a fortress by crumbling the walls around the rival's competitive positioning. It fractures and transforms the current competitive positioning map. The defender has to scramble, often at great cost, to cope with the upheaval and repair the damage.

Cuisinart, the innovator of the food processor, had a decision to make in 1985 when Sunbeam launched Oskar, a compact food processor/blender, for $60. Cuisinart had taken the high road in the late 1970s with its large, powerful, feature-laden processors that caught the gourmet cooking fad. It successfully gambled that it could expand the company's product line to unheard of price points of $200 plus for a glorified chopper/blender. Cuisinart became chic among gourmet cooks. But in the early

8. Al Ries and Jack Trout, *Marketing Warfare* (New York: McGraw Hill, 1986). Some might argue that if you have more than one differentiation advantage you should promote them all. Ries and Trout point out that you must be superior on at least one important choice dimension and this must be clearly and effectively promoted.
9. Kelvin Lancaster, *Variety, Equity and Efficiency* (New York: Columbia University Press, 1979).

1980s, as the economy recovered, eating out increased by 50 percent, and while gourmet cooking was still in, the Cuisinart was increasingly in the kitchen cupboard. It was too bulky and too difficult to clean. Enter Sunbeam with its compact, convenient, and low-priced Oskar. Cuisinart chose not to respond, fearing the damage to sales of its larger processors would not be offset by increased sales. The company badly underestimated the demand for convenience and compactness. Sunbeam sold 700,000 Oskars, 25 percent of all food processors sold in 1985. Cuisinart's volume share dropped from 20 percent to 10 percent. In the fall of 1986, Cuisinart responded belatedly with the $40 Cuisinart Mini-mate chopper/grinder. But the damage had already been done to both market share and the company's image—consumers no longer saw Cuisinart as a cutting-edge innovator and, just as importantly, neither did retailers.[10]

If a new feature innovation can quickly be adopted by established competitors, the successful assault of the new entrant may be short-lived. The best that the attacker can hope for is that it gets a toehold into the market channels and consumer consideration set (the set of brands a consumer will choose from) that it can build on. In the financial services market, competitors are constantly hustling to develop innovative offerings and services to investors because new product competitive advantages are usually impossible to sustain. For example, the Reserve Fund of New York invented money market mutual funds in 1972, but by 1986 they had over 300 competitors and only 0.8 percent of the market for such funds. Competing in the marketplace, particularly service markets where product imitation is relatively quick and easy, requires relentless innovation-imitation repositioning and cost control.

Defensive Positioning

A defensive "island fortress" strategy is one in which a firm protects its most profitable line items by surrounding them with a wall of flanking models that stave off competitive threats. Such a strategy will work best if the line is positioned on top of a concentration of demand: a benefit cluster in a positioning map (see Figure 8-4 for examples of benefit clusters). A company so positioned on top of such a peak of demand then occupies the high ground. It can develop a coordinated image directed at its captive market segment and may realize production, R&D, and marketing economies of scale and scope.

Kellogg's, the 800-pound gorilla in the breakfast cereal market, pursued an island fortress strategy. In 1983, Kellogg's was being written off as a company past its prime, even though it had 36.7 percent of a $3.7 billion market. By 1988, it had 41.7 percent of a market it had helped grow to $5.4 billion. What did Kellogg's do? First, it focused on the 80 million baby boomers who were looking for a convenient and nutritious breakfast. In five years, consumption of cold cereal by 25- to 49-year-olds increased by 26 percent. In 1987, Kellogg's introduced 47 new cereals worldwide, spending $40 million on R&D and $600 million on advertising. Kellogg's is so dominant in its category that it does not have to pay shelf-slotting allowances (shelf-space rent) to get retailers to stock its new products. This gives the company a considerable advantage over competitors who may have to spend up to one-third of a new product's first-year budget on such allowances. But Kellogg's costs advantages do not stop there. Its gross margin rose from 41 percent to 49 percent thorough automation and relentless cost control. The rest of the industry averaged 35 percent. The other competitors are no slouches

10. A. Pomice, "Losing the Cutting Edge," Forbes, October 6, 1986, 162. Cuisinart declared bankruptcy in 1992.

(for example, General Mills, Ralston Purina, RJR Nabisco, and Quaker Oats). Kellogg's dominates a fiercely competitive market by being the complete competitor. It targets, it positions, and it controls its costs.[11]

Flanking Brands and Price-Point Brands

A flanking brand is often used to protect a premium brand from price competition. It is launched as an economy brand to pick up the price sensitive consumer and to offer distributors an alternative (and hence blocking competitors out of the channel). Offering a flanking brand is considered a better option than extending the product line of the premium brand down to lower price points. It is possible, however, that such a move might undermine the quality image of the premium brand. Even private branders such as Kroger have recognized this in its marketing of a premium Kroger brand of coffee and a separate Cost-Cutter flanking brand of coffee. However, sometimes price-point brands can be mismanaged. The original intent of General Motors was to sell Chevrolet, Pontiac, Oldsmobile, and Cadillac at increasing price points so that the buyer would graduate up the brand/status ladder as his or her income increased. The plan went astray when these divisions became too independent. It led to Chevrolet offering economy cars, sports cars, luxury sports cars, and family sedans. These GM brands, designed to flank each other, ended up tearing each other's markets apart and opening opportunities for new foreign brands that had distinct and focused images.

The above defensive strategies can become very expensive and difficult to manage. The number of boundary items required to protect the interior cash cows increases at least geometrically with the number of features used by consumers to make their choices. For example, a product with a unique advantage on one key benefit may require two flanking items to protect it from a higher-quality competitor at a higher price and a lower-quality product at a lower price. A two-dimensional product may require at least four flanking-fighting items, a three-dimensional product may require nine, and so on. The cash cow profits may be entirely consumed to support its own defenses.

As explained above, the island fortress strategy is also still vulnerable to attack by a completely new feature. For example, Gillette's market share was successfully attacked by BIC's introduction of the disposable razor. An alternative strategy is to identify several market niches and position items or brands on top of each of them. When a niche is attacked, new items are introduced as a defensive counterattack on an as needed basis. The defensive strategy discussed below requires that a firm possess the competitive rationality skill of quickly adapting to the new competitive threat.

The Mobile Counterattack

Perhaps the best method of defending a market niche is with a reactive, adaptive counterattack. This places a premium on the defender's ability to marshall its reserves (resources) and counterattack quickly. Following this strategy, you do not build island fortresses. Instead, you introduce new counterattacking products and brands when and if needed. This strategy depends on superior alertness and imitation-implementation speed.

The way Tylenol defended itself against the entry of Datril into the over-the-counter painkiller market is a classic example of such a defense. The core benefit of analgesics is the relief from pain. Tylenol came along in 1955 and offered superior painkilling performance compared to the traditional aspirin-based products. Rather than relying

11. Patricia Sellers, "How King Kellogg Beat the Blahs," *Forbes*, August 29, 1988, 54–64.

on a big advertising pull campaign, Tylenol used a conservative push campaign by encouraging doctors to recommend Tylenol over aspirin. Tylenol slowly replaced the previous market leader, Bayer, and by 1974 had 10 percent of the market. It was not seriously challenged by another acetaminophen until Bristol-Myers launched Datril at a dollar a bottle less. Datril matched Tylenol on painkilling power and mildness but was sold at a much lower price. McNeil, the marketers of Tylenol, counterattacked quickly and strongly. The price of Tylenol was immediately lowered by 30 percent, thus removing Datril's price positioning advantage. Extra-Strength Tylenol was also launched in 1976. Now Tylenol was offered in a form that also outperformed the new competition on the core competitive benefit—painkilling power. Datril was effectively out-positioned in the marketplace. Tylenol also gained the most from the advertising war that accompanied the attack and counterattack. By 1977, its market share had grown to 20 percent (compared to Datril's 2 percent), and by 1981, Tylenol had 30 percent of the analgesic market.

If superior competitive rationality and an aggressive counterattack are key elements of a defensive positioning strategy, then even market share leaders might profit from adopting a multiple niching strategy. It forces them to become more efficient at targeting and positioning and, hence, at retargeting and repositioning. They effectively do this by selling several brands and making brand managers responsible for a particular target-positioning strategy. Such a strategy can sometimes backfire. The history of military disasters is full of stories of separate armies forgetting their missions or being led by headstrong generals who refused to cooperate with each other. There are parallels in the history of brand management, even in such great companies as General Motors and Procter & Gamble. When a company has several brands that are positioned differently, it is essential that the brands work together in attacking a competitor's position or defending against an attack. Such coordination and cooperation must be made explicit in the marketing plan and exist between cross-functional teams.

Total Quality Management and Quality Function Deployment (QFD)

A product or service is an instrument or means used in a production or consumption process to achieve a buyer's particular end or ends. This was explained in Chapter 3. The product positioning strategy should convince the targeted consumers that the offering has the product features, characteristics, or specifications necessary to satisfy their desires. To create and sustain such a positioning image, the product or service must be designed and manufactured to quality specifications that live up to its intended positioning concept and promotional image.

Developing a differentiated positioning *concept* is one thing, converting the concept into a competitive differentiation in the *design* of the final product or service is quite another. Quality function deployment (QFD) was developed by Yoji Akao, a Japanese professor, in the late 1960s and was being used by over half of the 135 largest Japanese manufacturing companies by the mid 1980s.[12] QFD is the deployment of quality, reliability, technology, and cost so that the design features of a product or service deliver the desired customer benefits and satisfaction. QFD takes a positioning concept and converts it into an engineered product or service that is competitively superior in performance on the desired differentiation dimensions. It also involves seamlessly con-

---

12. John R. Hartley, *Concurrent Engineering* (Cambridge, MA: Productivity Press, 1992).

necting such product specifications to the appropriate manufacturing and production process. (This aspect of QFD is explained in the new product development section in Chapter 9.)

Designing Quality Differentiation

It is said that beauty is in the eye of the beholder. In terms of marketing decision making, quality is in the eye of the target benefit segment. Buyers will choose a product based on quality (or quality and price) when they perceive that a product's quality is higher than a competitor's quality on the product benefits, characteristics, features, and specifications important to them. It is therefore essential that target customers are constantly consulted about what they want and their answers, in their own words, are always in the minds of the marketing decision makers.

The reputation of Japanese products over the last 30 years may help us understand what it means to make a quality product. In the 1950s and early 1960s, most Japanese exports were of a trinket nature sold in discount stores. They were poorly designed and soon broke. However, in the 1960s, Americans started to become aware of a change. Japanese electronic products, such as transistor radios, began to flood the market. Everything about them was quality. They came in higher-quality packaging. They came with batteries that often lasted longer than the replacement American batteries. They had more features, more range, and a superior tone. The Japanese radios also looked more impressive and were better assembled. In summary, the radio was better constructed and offered superior performance. This was achieved by caring about design details and assembly quality control. The same image developed for Japanese motorcycles, cars, and almost everything else.

Input Engineering Quality and Perceived Output Quality

Quality should be defined in terms of inputs and outputs. Superior design, superior materials, superior assembly, and quality control are all inputs that are deployed (used) to contribute to quality output, which is the bundle of benefits that the product or service provides the consumer. However, these inputs may not contribute additively. The development of an image of quality requires all input to be of a high standard. If just *one* of these elements is weak, then the overall quality rating may be weak. For example, the design may be excellent and high-quality materials may be used, but if assembly is poor, then the product will *not* develop a quality reputation. Making a quality product demands a lot of cooperation and coordination through the value chain of activities within an organization to produce value for buyers.[13] QFD is an unforgiving and very demanding process. One weak link and the whole effort can be wasted.

Consumers also use various cues to judge quality that may be different from an engineering or design view of quality. This is because most consumers are not aware of the quality of the inputs, as judged from an engineering or technical perspective. For example, consumers judge the quality of a pencil from its output: its ease of holding, lack of smudging, and time lapse between sharpening. Note that children may evaluate pencil quality differently than adults do. An engineer evaluates input quality in terms of product specifications (see Figure 8-7). The relationships between benefits and the engineering specifications described in the QFD product specification matrix will be the same for all benefit segments, but the importance of the relationships will change because the importance of the benefits changes between the segments. The product specification matrix is key to designing a product to deliver the desired

---

13. John R. Hauser and Don Clausing, "The House of Quality," *Harvard Business Review*, May/June, 1988, 63–73.

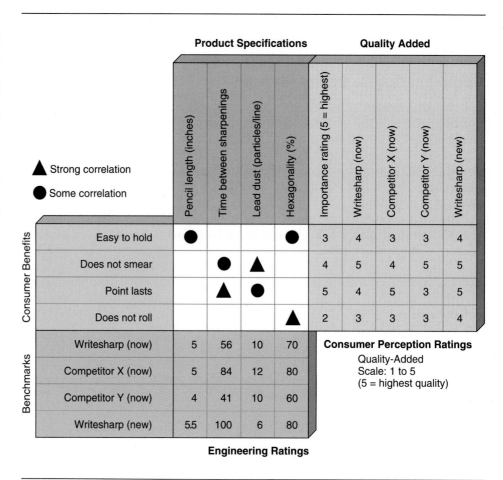

Figure 8-7

Positioning Using Quality Functional Deployment (QFD)

This figure was constructed by a staged process called quality function deployment (QFD) that involves 1) finding out the benefits and outcomes the customer wants 2) identifying what engineering specifications are most related to the benefits and levels of outcome the customer most desires, 3) determining which product features, characteristics, and attributes (product specifications) are most important to the target segment, 4) measuring consumer perceptions of relative competitive performance, and 5) measuring the relative competitive product specifications (benchmarking). The figure presents three matrices: a QFD product specification matrix, a quality-added matrix on the right, and a benchmarking matrix at the bottom. This enables the new product to be positioned against the competition in terms of consumer perceptions and engineering specifications.

Source: Based on an example presented in Robert Neff, "No. 1—And Trying Harder," *Business Week*, October 25, 1991, 23.

positioning benefits, and that is why it is placed at the *core* of the deep segmentation process presented in Figure 8-3. Benefit segmentation is not based on segmenting by benefits sought *and* product features, characteristics, and specifications desired. Benefit segmentation is based on benefits or outcomes desired. A QFD product specification matrix then converts the benefits desired into the engineering specifications desired. In this way, benefit segmentation can be seamlessly linked to the QFD process.

A product will develop a consumer image of quality if it excels on the cues used to judge output quality. The task of market research is to provide R&D and product designers with information on how consumers judge such quality so that it can be engineered into the offering. For example, the quality of jeans may be judged by the number of brass studs used, the weight and thickness of the denim, and whether double or even triple stitching is used at the seams. For fashion knitwear, even the label may be an important cue of quality. This is because the buyer will often read the label to find out what the garment is made of. If such information is presented on a very high-quality label, it will enhance the image of the clothing. Quality foods and beverages are often packaged in glass, rather than plastic or cans, because the glass container conveys a quality image.

The question is not whether to make a quality product, but which inputs produce the most quality outputs for the cost. For example, the best way to enhance the quality

1. Performance:
   Measured on specific dimensions, such as the quietness of an automobile's ride. It depends very much on the primary benefit sought from using the product.
2. Features:
   This refers to the ancillary features that provide secondary benefits—the bells and whistles.
3. Reliability:
   Normally measured as the mean time to the first failure, the mean time between failures, and the failure rate per unit of time.
4. Durability:
   A measure of product life and robustness under stress.
5. Serviceability:
   The speed, courtesy, competence, and ease of repair.
6. Aesthetics:
   The sensory appeal of the product—how it looks, sounds, feels, tastes, and smells.
7. Reputation:
   The reputation inferred from company name or brand image.
8. Conformance:
   Whether the product or service meets specified design and operating standards, and how often and how much the product or service diverges from the target standards.

Figure 8-8
Eight Ways of Defining Quality

These eight dimensions of quality are based on David A. Garvin, "Competing on the Eight Dimensions of Quality," *Harvard Business Review,* November/December 1987, 101–109. It should be noted that a number of these dimensions overlap. For example, durability, serviceability, reliability, and features are often associated with performance. Perceived quality might be viewed as covering perceptions of all of these dimensions. The last dimension, conformance, is the most distinct because it deals with production consistency and product uniformity instead of a perceived or average performance characteristic.

image of a sports car may be to fit it with the highest quality tires, gauges, steering wheel, and shift knob. The best way to enhance the quality image of a family sedan may be to equip it with a quality sound system and interior carpeting. The makers of minivans found that customers used the number of cupholders as an important indicator of the quality of the product. It is not good enough to bury quality in a product. It must be *seen* and *experienced* to be recognized and believed. There is also something intangible about quality. It resides in the feel, the look, the sound of an item. We may not be able to explain it, but we know it when we see it.

Performance, whether functional or symbolic, is an important component of quality. Figure 8-8 lists some of the other dimensions that have been used to measure quality. If the conceptual positioning of a product emphasizes durability and reliability, then quality must be related to long-term performance. If the positioning of a product emphasizes a particular benefit, then QFD should be used to emphasize the feature or attribute that provides the benefit.

The Symbolic, Intangible Dimensions of Quality Management

Some market segments buy quality as a *symbol*—quality merchandise says something about the owner. Just as most humans take pride in a job well done, we also take pride in owning someone else's job well done. It suggests we have standards and are discriminating. That is why we treasure ancient works of art. In fact, part of the national concern over becoming competitive on quality has a lot to do with national pride. There is some residual satisfaction for all of us in knowing that we have the best universities and make the best computers in the world. We are not happy when the quality of our automobiles suffers in comparison with foreign competition. We take pride in the output of our culture, which we believe produces a lot more than great sports teams or

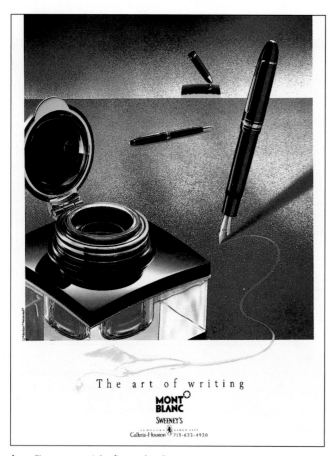

The art of writing

MONT BLANC

SWEENEY'S
Galleria-Houston 713-622-4920

"Official Rolex Jeweler."
It's not just a title; it's a
commitment we take seriously.

There's more to being an Official Rolex Jeweler than simply displaying the crystal prism. We are full partners in the Rolex heritage of quality, integrity, and service.

Our sales staff participate in special training seminars so that they are better able to help you select the Rolex that's right for you. And as part of the Rolex Worldwide Service Network,

we will give you a service warranty and a guarantee that we use only official Rolex parts and accessories. When you're looking for a Rolex timepiece, be sure to look for an Official Rolex Jeweler. For just as the Rolex name tells you what to expect from the watch you're buying, the Rolex prism tells you what to expect from the jeweler who displays it.

ROLEX

A quality pen or watch often makes its owner feel like a higher-quality person. It also raises the quality reputation of the retailer selling the brand.

smart weapons. The quality of many of our culturally significant products and services—such as automobiles, clothing, art, music, films, high-technology items, and education—is an important symbol of national self-esteem.

However, as discussed in Chapter 3, the main reason we prefer quality products is that we get more satisfaction from using them and have to spend less time repairing them. The more valuable our time, the more we will value quality in a product or service. From the marketer's perspective, quality means less customer service, more customer goodwill, and an important basis for building brand equity.

A product is often endowed with *intangible* characteristics, such as performance guarantees, delivery, before- and after-sales service, finance terms, status, style, or some other image associated with its brand name and price. Often such seemingly peripheral features are keys to successful product positioning. This occurs when there is little difference between competitors' products on the core benefits and features.

Almost any product, including commodities, can be differentiated on service dimensions such as delivery, terms, training, and usage advice.[14] De Havilland built the first passenger jet to provide faster travel, but it did not design its capacity and range for routes on which the airlines wanted to use a fast aircraft (a basic targeting-positioning mistake). Further, the company did not offer attractive financing terms and

---

14. Theodore Levitt, "Marketing Success Through Differentiation—Of Anything," *Harvard Business Review,* January/February, 1980, 83–91. This article argues that even in a commodity market, a seller can differentiate its product.

He may give you
diamonds
this holiday season.

You can give him
a star.

ENGINEERED LIKE NO OTHER
CAR IN THE WORLD
© 1993 Mercedes-Benz of N.A., Inc., Montvale, N.J.

Mercedes has always connected satisfaction and quality to engineering, as is
recommended by the QFD process.

ultimately lost to Boeing and Douglas, who entered the market with more competitive
purchase packages.[15] Boeing and Douglas matched De Havilland with their planes and
then differentiated their payment terms.

The Dimensions of Total Service Quality Management

Services vary in quality on *performance* dimensions, such as dependability, speed, competence, courtesy, caring, customization, and accompanying products (for example, the
shampoo and conditioning a hairdresser uses).[16] *Conformance*, which is delivering the
same dependable service consistently over time to the same customer and to different
customers (for a standardized service), is also very important. However, service conformance is particularly hard to manage compared to manufacturing conformance.
This is because services are produced by people who are much harder to control and
regulate than machines.

Service quality can be measured as an input process involving the functional
deployment of resources and activities. The output is the delivered service benefits.
Consequently, a QFD type input-output framework can also be used to study services.
Such a service quality framework has been developed and is presented in Figure 8-9.
It employs a gap analysis, which has very close parallels with positioning and QFD. The

---

15. Peter F. Drucker, "The Discipline of Innovation," *Harvard Business Review,* May/June, 1985, 67–72.
16. For a more complete description of quality service features, see A. Parasuraman, Valarie A. Zeithaml, and Leonard L. Berry, "A Conceptual Model of Service Quality and Its Implications for Future Research," *Journal of Marketing*
49 (Fall 1985), 41–50. More recent work by Joseph J. Cronin and Steven A. Taylor, "Measuring Service Quality: A
Reexamination and Extension," *Journal of Marketing* (1992), suggests that the importance of different quality features varies among different services such as banking, pest control, dry cleaning, and fast food.

Figure 8-9

A Model of Service Quality

The top of the model describes the factors that determine service expectations and demand. The bottom of the model describes how a company generates the service it provides. Gap 1 indicates a benefit segmentation problem—management beliefs about consumer expectations are wrong; Gap 2 indicates a positioning problem; Gap 3 indicates a QFD problem—the delivered service does not meet operational specifications of service quality; Gap 4 indicates a promotion positioning problem—the promises do not match the performance; Gap 5 indicates a satisfaction problem—the supplied service fails to meet expectations.

Source: For details see Valarie A. Zeithaml, A. Parasuraman, and Leonard L. Berry, "A Conceptual Model of Service Quality and Its Implications for Future Research," *Journal of Marketing* 49.4, Fall 1985, 41–50.

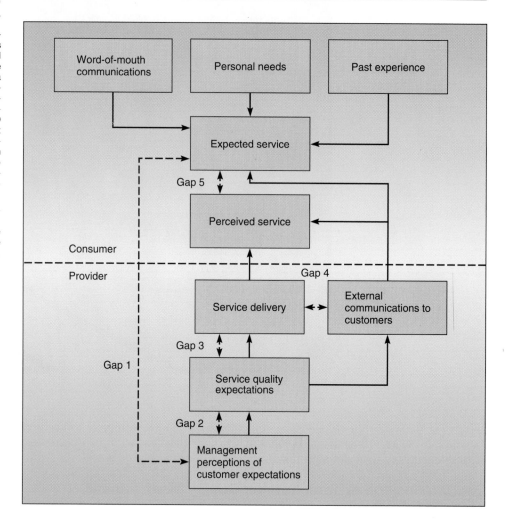

task is for the service provider to identify and reduce the following gaps that have been identified by researchers as significant barriers to delivering a quality service:

Gap 1: *Management beliefs about consumer expectations are wrong.* Management's benefit segmentation analysis is flawed.

Gap 2: *Management operational specifications of the desired service do not match management perceptions of the target consumer's desired benefits and expectations.* Management's QFD service specification matrix is wrong.

Gap 3: *The delivered service does not meet management operational specifications.* The implementation and control of the service production script is basically flawed.

Gap 4: *Promises do not match performance.* The *promoted* positioning does not match the delivered service.

Gap 5: *Consumer perceptions of the delivered service do not meet consumer expectations.* Consumers are dissatisfied.

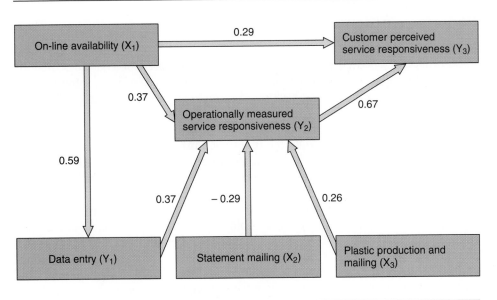

Figure 8-10

An Input-Output Process Map of a Service

Four operationally distinct activities make up the service process: on-line service, data entry, statement mailing, and plastic production. The error-rate and other operational performance measures (X1, Y1, X2, X3) can be used to assess the month-by-month quality of the execution of each of these activities. These ratings can then be connected to an overall operational measure of service responsiveness (Y2) and surveys of customer perceptions (Y3). The size of the weightings indicate the relationship between activity performance and operational quality and the perceived quality of service. The actual relationships are as follows:

$Y_1 = 0.59X_1$
$Y_2 = 0.37X_1 - 0.29X_2 + 0.26X_3$
$\quad\quad + 0.37Y_1$
$Y_3 = 0.29X_1 + 0.67Y_2$

Source: For further details, see David A. Collier, "A Service Quality Process Map for Credit Card Processing," *Decision Sciences* 22 (1991), 406–16.

As a service is often made up of a sequence of distinct activities (a production script), Gaps 2 and 3 can be reduced by studying the correlations between the actual operational performance on each service activity and the quality ratings of the overall service by the customer. Figure 8-10 presents a service quality process map for credit card processing which indicates the relationship between the customer's perceived service performance and operational performance on four activities that make up the credit card service. Service process maps are equivalent to the QFD product specification matrix. They indicate which feature or activity performances are most crucial in delivering perceived quality to the customer, as well as specifying the flow of activities that constitute the service production script.

Maintaining Service Quality

The meeting of customer service expectations depends on the design of the service, employee training, employee rewards, and control. Because service is personally delivered, its implementation depends on the performance of many people in an organization. It is therefore particularly important that a service company create a company-wide culture that encourages all employees to present a quality service image during their personal interaction with customers and to conform to the expected standards. An airline does not help its service image by keeping callers on hold waiting for information on flight arrivals. It conspicuously improves its service image by helping young families and the elderly get their luggage to and from their ground transportation, free of charge.

Interestingly, service companies often direct their advertising at both their customers and their service employees. Such advertising positions the product not only in the mind of the consumer but also in the minds of the service providers out in the field. It spells out what the service provider promises to deliver and reminds the field service staff of what they are expected to deliver to the customer. In this way, service advertising acts as an employee motivator and a control program (encouraging service quality conformance to the service production script), as well as a selling device.

Service Worker Morale and Performance/Conformance Slippage

Maintaining service quality conformance is particularly important when a service organization faces a financial squeeze.[17] When a company cares for and looks after its employees, it sets an example for its employees to follow in servicing customers. The opposite can also occur. Cutting back on staff, raises, benefits, expenses, and general overhead support can lead to a deterioration in morale, which quickly shows up in a deterioration in customer service quality. As morale drops, employees are less likely to go the extra mile or do things right the first time. Customers then become dissatisfied because service is not what they had come to expect, and this results in lost sales. The lost sales then lead to further belt-tightening and a further decrease in morale and service.

It is imperative that service firms think carefully about how decisions made in other aspects of the business may affect employee service performance.[18] For example, efficiencies in the productivity of service employees can be achieved through extensive practice training and productivity incentives. Employees can be taught from a production script where they mechanically execute a routinized service step by step. This training increases quality control and standardization, but may do so at the expense of servicing the unique needs of particular customers. A service company has to decide on its service positioning and be very careful to keep all of its operations and marketing strategies consistent with this positioning.

Quality-Added Analysis

A product's price is justified based on its perceived quality to the target market segment. Products offering more quality than alternative products can be sold at higher prices. Having developed a positioning concept and used benefit segmentation and QFD to design quality into the product or service, a marketing executive must then assess whether the new or modified product is economically feasible. This feasibility analysis involves two steps. The first is to price the product against the competition; the second is to estimate what sales levels will have to be achieved at the proposed price to meet financial targets.

Quality-added (QA) analysis attempts to estimate the extra price the target market segment is prepared to pay to obtain the added quality (benefits and performance outcomes) that a product offers over and above its competitive alternatives. The quality added can be measured in engineering terms, such as output, reliability, and durability, or it can be symbolic and intangible. It is easier to undertake a QA analysis when the quality output can be measured in engineering terms because it can be computed based on objective performance tests. However, the difference in quality between two brands can still be measured using a simple test that asks target buyers to state how much more they would be willing to pay for the quality added compared to other brands. It becomes more difficult to measure QA when the target buyers are not familiar with the alternatives.

If the quality added is symbolic or intangible, then consumer research should be taken to assess the average dollar value the target market places on the differentiation.

17. Christian Gronroos, *Strategic Management and Marketing in the Service Sector* (Cambridge, MA: Marketing Science Institute, 1984).
18. Leonard A. Schlesinger and James L. Heskett, "The Service-Driven Service Company," *Harvard Business Review*, September/October 1991, 71–81.

The difference in price between the QA product and the standard product is then set so that the majority of the target buyers gain a noticeable and significant net value advantage (benefit-cost) from buying the new product. QA analysis is most successful for pricing capital equipment, raw materials, components, or supplies to be sold to original equipment manufacturers (OEMs), farmers, or the government.

Examples of QA Analysis

The QFD analysis of pencils in Figure 8-7 presents a simple but effective quality-added analysis. On the right of the product specification matrix is a QA matrix. It presents the results of target consumer test ratings of the new pencil and the competition on important quality dimensions. It also shows that the new pencil will cost no more to produce than its substitutes, so it is clear that it can be priced the same as its competition and promoted as offering the added quality identified in the QA matrix. Underneath the product specification matrix is a benchmarking comparison of the prototype's performance on objective tests. These engineering benchmarking tests would be taken *before* the consumer tests because there would be little point in testing consumer perceptions of the new pencil's added quality if the pencil did not outperform its rivals on key technical specifications that are known to be correlated with the performance benefits and outcomes that the target segment desires.

Added output quality can come from superior product performance or from cost savings in the use and disposal of the product. Table 8-1 compares the performance of the new product with that of the current standard product (the benchmark product). The choice of the benchmark is important. For now, we will assume it is the best-selling product in the target market. The price of both products is $500, but the new product costs 50 percent less to install and 20 percent less to operate. The new product

Table 8-1
An Example of Quality-Added Analysis

Price, cost, and quality added	Benchmark product	New product		
		Price A Plan	Price B Plan	Price C Plan
Purchase price	$ 500	$500	$600	$ 700
+ Start-up cost	$ 100	$ 50	$ 50	$ 50
+ Post-purchase costs (maintenance & operations)	$ 500	$400	$400	$ 400
− Net disposal value (disposal sale price less disposal cost)	$ 100	$150	$150	$ 150
Life cycle cost	$1,000	$800	$900	$1,000
Added dollar value of superior performance over lifetime compared to reference product		$200	$200	$ 200
Net gain to buyer		$400	$300	$ 200

also uses more advanced technology that results in lower operating costs. Therefore, its disposal value is $50 more. The total cost savings for installation, operation, and disposal amounts to $200 over the life of the product. The new product is also more productive than the standard product, thus increasing productivity by $200. Under price plan A, buyers stand to gain an extra $400 in value added by buying the new product instead of the standard product. They pay the same purchase price, $500, but receive $200 in cost savings and $200 in added productivity. Price plan A pursues a market penetration pricing strategy in that many sales are made quickly. The firm does not profit from the quality-added differentiation by charging a higher price, but its high quality/low price should lead to higher sales and market share.

Factoring in Cost

Until now we have assumed that the new product and the standard product cost the same to make. Suppose the new product costs $50 more to manufacture than the standard product. Price plan B covers such extra costs and also gives an extra $50 in contribution margin. A salesperson can still sell the new product on its life-cycle cost advantages of $100 and extra performance utility of $200. Under price plan C, the salesperson is likely to have more difficulty. At a purchase price of $700, the new product is 40 percent more expensive than the standard product. The new product can also no longer be sold on its total life-cycle cost savings.

The salesperson must try to convince the customer that the added quality (performance utility) of the new product is worth its price. This is a difficult task for several reasons. First, the cost savings and performance superiority are future benefits that may be discounted because of their uncertainty. What is certain is that the new product costs $200 more than the standard product. Second, future dollars earned are worth less than current dollars because current dollars can be invested today to earn profits for tomorrow. Third, there is a natural tendency to stick with the status quo if the status quo is adequate (a psychological switching cost).

For these reasons, plan B is likely to be the best choice of the three alternative price plans. It offers two selling points—life-cycle cost savings and superior performance—and adds a healthy extra margin for the seller. Both buyer and seller share the added benefits and value of the new innovation. At a price above $600 and below $700, the product would only be targeted at and sold to the buying segment who value the product's differentiation most (its superior performance and life-cycle cost savings). Such a price would mean the buyer has to pay for most of the added quality.

How to Measure Quality Added

Quality added should be measured by target consumers and not company engineers, designers, or accountants. This may well be the most common and biggest competitive rationality mistake made by marketing decision makers. They convince themselves that a product or service has a quality advantage over its competitors, which, in the minds of consumers, simply is not true. Alternatively, a product may have a quality advantage that is not needed by the target market (for example, a buyer neither needs the added productivity nor considers the whole life-cycle cost of the product).

Market researchers have developed a method of establishing the buyer's perceived worth of extra features, performance, and life-time cost savings. The method, called conjoint or trade-off analysis (see the "Conjoint Analysis" exhibit on page 274), is based on customer ratings of product alternatives described in terms of their selling features.

From these ratings, incremental utility of improvements in performance, quality, or cost savings can be calculated in terms of current dollars.[19]

Sometimes marketers can provide independent confirmation to back up their claims of superior product performance. For example, marketers of herbicides, insecticides, fertilizer, and hybrid grains often have universities run tests that compare the performance of their products to alternatives under different field conditions. They can use this information to support their claims, thus increasing buyer confidence. In fact, agricultural scientists first used conjoint analysis over 50 years ago to test for differences in actual test performance rather than differences in farmer perceptions of performance.

Choice of the Benchmark Product

In QA everything hinges on the choice of the benchmark product. Common sense suggests it should be the most competitive current offering. What, exactly, does most competitive mean? Does it mean the product with the largest market share? This makes sense, because the added-value price then appeals to the largest number of current buyers. However, if an aggressive competitor launches a new product offering superior value for the money over the current market leader, a QA analysis may also have to be applied to the new entry so as to set a price that heads it off at the pass.

It makes no sense to compare the new product against a clearly weaker product. The comparison will have no meaning to buyers of more competitive products and, in fact, may lead customers to question the firm's integrity. Thorough marketers may undertake QA analyses against all of the major competitors' offerings. This will help to ensure that the quality for price is superior to any major competitor. Alternatively, it may lead to a change in targeting toward the loyal customers of the competitive products or services that are discovered to be the least competitive using QA analysis.

Feasibility Analysis

At this stage of decision making, the manager has done initial positioning, QFD, and QA competitive analyses of the product or service. These analyses suggest a competitive market price that, along with relevant cost information, can be used in a target return analysis to determine the number of units that must be sold to either break even or achieve a specified profit target. This is the point at which bottom-line considerations play an important part in assessing the attractiveness of the proposed positioning. A *feasible position* is a differentiation position that can be made into a product (using QFD) and sold at a price (using QA analysis) such that the required sales to meet the financial goals are feasible.

If the financial feasibility of a new or modified product or service is to be established before it is launched, then some sort of profitability analysis must be taken. Without it, how can a company decide whether or not to proceed? Some sort of financial feasibility analysis, however rough, should be made before developing detailed tactics. The analysis can be repeated again when all the details have been developed and the cost estimates are much better. Fortunately, personal computer spreadsheet programs are ideally suited to do such analyses. They are a variation of old-fashioned break-even analyses (see Figure 8-11).

19. The Japanese use a variation of conjoint analysis called *Taguchi* methods; see A. Bendell, J. Disney, and W. A. Pridmore, eds., *Taguchi Methods: Applications in World Industry* (Kempstone, England: IFS Publications, 1989).

Figure 8-11
Using TARGET to Test the
Feasibility of a Price

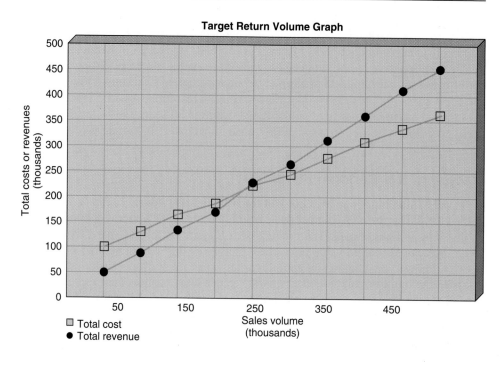

Target Return Volume Graph

□ Total cost
● Total revenue

Target Return for a Given Price
(units in 000's)

Fixed Costs		
Manufacturing		
• R&D	$10,000	
• patent	10,000	
• other	10,000	
Total Fixed Manufacturing		$30.000
Marketing		
• advertising	$10,000	
• sales expense	5,000	
• distribution	5,000	
• other	0	
Total Fixed Marketing		$20,000
Administrative Overhead		10,000
Other Fixed Costs		0
Total Fixed Costs		**$60,000**
Target Return on Assets Employed		20.0%
Value of Total Assets Employed		**$60,000**
Enter target selling price		*$1.00*
Estimated variable cost per unit		*$0.60*
Size of total target market		*1,000*
Target break-even volume		*180*
Market share at break-even volume		*18.0%*

The Formula

Break-even volume (Q_{pBE}) is the sales volume needed at selling price p that generates a contribution equal to estimated fixed costs. At Q_{pBE} all fixed and variable costs are covered.

$$\text{Break-even sales} = QE_{pBE} = FC/CM = FC/(\text{Price} - AVC),$$

where CM = Contribution margin from each unit sold
FC = Fixed costs
AVC = Average variable cost

If a specific target return on assets employed is desired then

$$\text{Target return sales} = Q_{pTR} = (FC + ROA{\times}AE) / (\text{Price} - AVC),$$

where ROA = % target return desired on assets employed,
AE = Value of assets employed

These formulae can be converted into a visual graph called a break-even chart or target sales chart (see Figure 8-11). It can also be used in a spreadsheet. The TARGET spreadsheet presented in Figure 8-11 allows a decision maker to test a price by computing the target sales and market-share required to cover costs and meet return on assets (ROA) goals.

Establishing Feasibility

Having determined the target sales volume for a given price, the pricing decision maker must now answer the following questions:

1. Given the target market, competitive positioning, sales effort, likely distribution coverage of the market, advertising reach, and estimated share of industry advertising spending ("voice" share), what is the likelihood of achieving the required market share and unit sales at the proposed price?

2. Is there a good chance of achieving the required sales, given the results of the QA analyses?

3. How long would it take to reach the target sales and market share? Is this time reasonable?

If the answers to these questions are positive, then the positioning is feasible. The QA analysis helps establish the credibility of the sales and, particularly, the share targets, because the sales must come at the expense of the current popular substitutes. Estimates about where the sales will realistically come from (an expanded market or a competitor's market share) will also help establish the credibility of achieving the sales and share goals. This suggests that when assessing the feasibility of achieving the sales needed, decision makers should identify where the sales will come from—what percentage of the sales will come from which competitors, including the firm's existing products or services? Feasibility assessments that do not detail where the majority of the sales will come from are less realistic and credible. When executives start to predict where the sales are going to come from, they start to think about how the competitor's will react (see Chapter 4) and this will temper their estimates and optimism.

Other elements of marketing strategy must also be considered. For example, the planned distribution strategy may not reach sufficient potential customers to attain the sales goal. The planned advertising budget may not produce the unique mind share

Exhibit:

Conjoint Analysis

Conjoint analysis is a popular marketing research technique that allows one to generate quantitative measures of the relative importance of attribute levels, which are called utilities. Based upon these individual level utilities, it is possible to segment the market into groups of people with similar benefits sought (needs, tastes, or preferences), as discussed in Chapter 3.

This benefit segmentation can be used to make design changes to existing products or to determine optimal designs for new products. The utilities also influence key marketing mix decisions, such as pricing and promotion, by providing insights on the price sensitivity of consumers and by identifying attributes that are valued more by the consumers.

The simplest approach to conjoint analysis is called the full profile approach. An example can best illustrate how this approach works. Consider a product such as an alarm clock/radio with the following attribute or feature options:

Attribute/Feature	Attribute Levels
1. Brand	Sony
	AT&T
	Unbranded
2. Frequency available	a.m. only
	f.m. only
	Both a.m. and f.m.
3. Price	$15
	$20
	$30

Based upon these three attributes, each with three levels, one can come up with 27 different full profiles. One profile, for example, could be a Sony alarm clock with a.m. and f.m. and a price tag of $30.

In order to obtain the utilities for each level of the three attributes, the respondents to the conjoint task are asked to rate each of the 27 profiles on a 1 to 100 scale that measures the likelihood of purchase or the overall positive reaction. This ratings data, along with the specification of each profile that the respondents rank, acts as an input to the estimation procedure used to generate the utilities.

The estimation procedure itself is fairly simple and uses a dummy regression approach. For our example of the alarm clock/radio, this results in the following regression model:

$$y = \beta_0 + \beta_1 \text{ sony} + \beta_2 \text{ att} + \beta_3 \text{ fm} + \beta_4 \text{ amfm} + \beta_5 \text{ twenty} + \beta_6 \text{ thirty} + \epsilon$$

where y is the profile rating on a scale of 1 to 100 and variables Sony, att, fm, amfm, twenty, and thirty capture the attribute levels of each profile presented to the respondent. These variables are defined as follows:

$$\text{sony} = \begin{bmatrix} 1 \text{ when the brand is Sony} \\ 0 \text{ otherwise} \end{bmatrix}$$

$$\text{att} = \begin{bmatrix} 1 \text{ when the brand is AT\&T} \\ 0 \text{ otherwise} \end{bmatrix}$$

$$\text{fm} = \begin{bmatrix} 1 \text{ when the frequency available is f.m. only} \\ 0 \text{ otherwise} \end{bmatrix}$$

$$\text{amfm} = \begin{bmatrix} 1 \text{ when both a.m. and f.m.} \\ \quad \text{frequencies are available} \\ 0 \text{ otherwise} \end{bmatrix}$$

needed to generate the market share required to break even or reach the desired ROA. The plausibility of achieving the target sales and market share required depends on much more than price. An executive must test the feasibility of the sales goal, given the proposed marketing strategy and everything that is known about the size of the market, consumer behavior, competition, and channels of distribution. In effect, the fit of the required sales goal is tested against every marketing fact the marketing planner possesses. The problem is that at the positioning stage, the rest of the logistics and marketing tactics have yet to be developed. This means that the estimates of their effectiveness and costs have to be roughly estimated and fined-tuned at a later date.

If the required sales and market share goals are clearly not attainable, then marketers must reevaluate the offering. If a feasible positioning-price-sales target combi-

$$\text{twenty} = \begin{bmatrix} 1 \text{ when the price is } \$20 \\ 0 \text{ otherwise} \end{bmatrix}$$

$$\text{thirty} = \begin{bmatrix} 1 \text{ when the price is } \$30 \\ 0 \text{ otherwise} \end{bmatrix}$$

Traditionally, ordinary least squares are used to estimate the dummy regression model described above and the parameter estimates β_1 to β_6 are used to calculate the added utility of the radio being a Sony, being made by AT&T, being a.m., being a.m. and f.m., being priced at $20, and being priced at $30.*

A commonly encountered problem with conjoint analysis is that the utilities generated by the procedure described above do not always follow proper signs and/or order. For example, in the alarm clock/radio case, consider a respondent whose feature-level utilities estimates suggest that she or he prefers an unbranded alarm clock/radio over an AT&T or that she or he prefers a product with just f.m. over the one with both a.m. and f.m. Ordinal violations of this type, which are inconsistent with reasonable prior beliefs, raise doubts about the usefulness of conjoint analysis to construct market segments or to predict market shares of new products.

Recently, a solution to this problem has been proposed wherein a simple Bayesian approach is used to ensure that the estimates of feature-level utilities are the correct sign and ordinal ranking.** The proposed procedure allows for incorporating reasonable prior beliefs about the sign and ranking of the parameter estimates. For example, in the alarm clock/radio case, the following prior management beliefs about consumer preference can automatically be incorporated in the estimation procedure:

Management Prior Beliefs about Consumer Preference	Interpretation
1. $\beta_1, \beta_2 > 0$	AT&T and Sony brands are preferred over an unbranded product, given that all remaining attribute levels are the same.
2. $\beta_4 > 0$	Presence of both a.m. and f.m. is preferred over a.m. alone, given that all remaining attribute levels are the same.
3. $\beta_5, \beta_6 < 0$	A price of $15 is preferred over a price of $20 or $30, given that all remaining attribute levels are the same.
4. $\beta_5 > \beta_6$	A price of $20 is preferred over a price of $30, given that all remaining attribute levels are the same.

It has been shown that incorporating such reasonable ordinal prior beliefs about the parameter estimates, as suggested above, results in measures of feature-level utilities with superior face validity and consistency.[†]

*Paul E. Green and V. Srinivasan, "Conjoint Analysis in Consumer Research: Issues and Outlook," Journal of Consumer Research, vol. 5 (September 1978), 103–23.
**Greg M. Allenby, Neeraj Arora, and James L. Ginter, "Incorporating Prior Information into the Design and Analysis of Conjoint Studies" (Work in progress, Columbus, OH: Ohio State University, College of Business, 1993).
[†]For further discussion of the use of conjoint analysis, see Paul E. Green and V. Srinivasan, "Conjoint Analysis in Marketing: New Developments with Implications for Research and Practice," Journal of Marketing 54 (October 1990), 3–19.

nation cannot be found, then the project must be considered a doubtful venture. A thorough QFD reanalysis must be done to determine ways that new features can be added to increase the QA competitiveness of the offering. Alternatively, efforts can be made to change the design so that variable and fixed costs are reduced and the product can be sold at a target price suitable to generate the required sales. This is possible—P&G did it with Pampers.

Some Japanese companies start with price in their positioning strategy (see Chapter 9). They set a target price that they know will be value-for-the-money competitive, and then they use QFD to design a product at a cost that will achieve the desired financial goals. Such a competitive positioning strategy is not new. Henry Ford gambled that a huge, unmet market existed for the automobile—the middle-class consumer.

Without using any fancy market research techniques, he set $360 as the magic price for his 1916 Touring model, the price that he felt middle America could pay for a car and were willing to pay for a car. He then designed and built a factory that could produce a car that sold for this specific price point—at a profit. The car was spartan, simple, rugged, and came in only one color—black. Most importantly, the price was right. The original Ford Mustang was also built to a specific price point of $2,500 and was very successful. Price is often one of the *first* considerations in positioning a product or service.

The Limiting Assumptions

Feasible positioning analysis is the most useful and sound procedure a company can employ to determine the feasibility of a new positioning or repositioning strategy. It also offers an excellent basis for marketers, designers, engineers, and financial officers to work together. The analysis may result in only very approximate numbers, but the process enables all the parties to learn a great deal from each other. However, the following assumptions limit its validity and effectiveness:

1. As the volume of production and sales increase, fixed costs do not stay fixed. Ultimately, a new plant and more management are needed. Fixed costs may therefore increase in very large steps as production and sales increase.
2. It is unlikely that variable costs will increase in a straight line as the volume of production and sales increases. Cost economies will create a curve that may also have steps in it, such as at points where suppliers give volume discounts.
3. Price does not stay constant as sales volume increases because sellers give sales volume discounts to major buyers.
4. Inventory holding costs and costs of receivables (which finance buyers' payment tardiness) are not easily incorporated into break-even analyses.

Most of these problems can be addressed by making the formula and spreadsheet more complicated. However, the incremental advantage of adding such extra requirements to the decision-making model may not be worthwhile, particularly if it complicates the understanding of what is going on so much that users give up on the technique.

Positioning Issues in Global Markets

The global marketplace can be viewed in many ways. The traditional way was to view each country as a separate market with separate import regulations, tariff regulations, distribution systems, communication, and transportation systems. The likely first venture into export marketing for a U.S. company is to an English-speaking country, such as Canada or the United Kingdom, with very similar consumption cultures and competitive behavior.

Cross-Cultural Segmentation

The modern global marketing view is to see market segments first and countries second.[20] The question is not so much what is the market potential in Norway, but what is the sales potential among all the college educated 19- to 29-year olds in Europe, or among those who support the strong environmental movement in Europe? Major com-

20. For an even more provocative view of the collapse of borders and the development of interlinked economies, see Kenichi Ohmae, *The Borderless World* (New York: Harper Perennial, 1990).

panies are now describing and targeting global market segments and niches that transcend national boundaries. They may be reached physically using very different communication and distribution channels, but they are psychologically targeted the same way. They are assumed or identified by testing to share similar ideal product concepts. This allows a firm to design the same product line for such segments, and the product line is sold to the same targeted benefit segments in numerous countries.

The Americanization of world culture through science, entertainment, and business has helped to reduce the cultural differences, particularly among countries with highly educated populations.[21] This opens up the possibility for global segmentation and positioning, where the segmentation spreads across cultures rather than within cultures. In a way, even the word *culture* is inappropriate because the very process is premised on the assumption that cross-cultural differences are no longer as strong as within-culture differences. In short, cultures no longer follow national, political, or cultural borders as much as they did even 100 years ago.

However, through and beyond the year 2000, many countries will still vary in their consumer wealth, buying power, price elasticity, experience with the product category, and competitive behavior. Consequently, relatively few products can be positioned exactly the same way across the global marketplace. Those that *can* normally have a strong symbolic or intangible image that transcends cultural, technological, and economic differences (for example, Coca Cola has such an image). There is a special set of products made in the United States whose positioning should be the same in all global markets. This set is made up of products that symbolize and embody the American culture. It includes movies, rock music, television programs, clothing, outdoor equipment, motor bikes, automobiles, and much more than many economists and marketers recognize. These brands should maintain their American image positioning, but also match the foreign quality on other performance dimensions.

Different Competitors—Different Positioning

Global marketing often requires that the same product be positioned somewhat differently in each of its foreign markets, reflecting the positioning of the different competition in each market. So even though a global segmentation approach is used, the positioning and design of the product may have to be different because of competitive pressures and the higher consumer quality standards in some cultures. For example, U.S. products sold in Japan must be of the very highest quality because the Japanese market demands higher quality in many product-markets than do other global markets. This is true even if the determinant differentiation feature is the trendy American brand name (that is, a cultural symbol).

Asymmetric Counterattacking

A standard counterattack to the entry of a new competitor from a foreign market (that is positioned close to a firm's established products) is for the firm to launch its own products in the foreign rival's home market. If it cannot, then it is at a severe positioning and competitive disadvantage.[22] The foreign competition can position, QFD, and lower prices in the new market, knowing that the great percentage of its sales are not at risk. In fact, it can subsidize the cost of entering the new market, because the major players in the new market cannot strike back at the entrant's major market. This is why restricted access to the Japanese market has effectively given Japanese companies an unfair advantage in the United States—the U.S. manufacturers did not find it

21. Benjamin R. Barber, "Jihad Vs. McWorld," *The Atlantic*, March 1992, 53–65.
22. Gary Hamel and C. K. Prahalad, "Do You Really Have a Global Strategy?" *Harvard Business Review*, July/August 1985, 139–48.

at all easy to strike back at the Japanese market. The major presence that Japanese companies have established in newly industrializing countries provides another uncontested profit source for these companies to use when attacking Western markets.[23]

Companies must understand and account for such asymmetries in the ease of counterattacking when responding to foreign competitors and becoming the new competitor in foreign markets. These asymmetries result, in part, from the fact that trade is freer in some political economies than it is in others.

Repositioning Skills in Global Markets

Repositioning involves changing the perceived and actual characteristics of a service to better fit a changing marketplace environment. It can be gradual, such as when Pepsi-Cola repositioned itself from the second-class soft drink defined by its slogan, "Twice as much for a nickel" in the 1950s to its more contemporary "Take the Taste Test" image of the 1970s. Or it can be moderately fast, such as the Gap's repositioning from "the denim store in the mall" in the early 1980s to a seller of high-quality sportswear and casual wear in the late 1980s. Repositioning can be dramatic, such as when Ronald Reagan, a long-time Democrat, switched parties and became a Republican. Or it can be constant, such as the Japanese Kaizen approach, in which everyone in the enterprise is constantly thinking of ways to make minor improvements in a product or service. When four or five Japanese companies compete using Kaizen in any market, anywhere in the world, one can assume that their efforts will completely change the product designs over the next two to three years.

Sometimes, changing technology forces an entire product-market to shift positions. Computer manufacturers now position their products on their software compatibility, software availability, and connectability. Previously, they had emphasized speed and capacity, which are no longer as important because all companies offer satisfactory speed and capacity for almost all users, at an ever lower cost.

The entry of foreign clones into the United States PC market in the 1980s was somewhat predictable as their manufacturers had been supplying the parts for U.S. branded computers for several years. What was surprising was their ability to launch sophisticated notepad PCs into the U.S. market in the early 1990s. Whereas previously they had been making lower-cost, me-too imitations, now they were marketing uniquely positioned and differentiated portable PCs. The major U.S. brands of PCs were very slow to react to this repositioning of foreign competition—a serious mistake.

The new global competitive reality is teaching marketers a competitive law developed by Charles Darwin. Native species (products) are never so perfectly adapted to their domestic ecology (market) that foreign species (products) cannot find a foothold. Indeed foreign products often take hold and come to dominate.[24] For example, Japanese TV manufacturers entered the U.S. market focusing on portability and designing small, high-quality, black-and-white and color televisions. They were able to use private label distributors, such as Sears, who were very keen to help them sell their sets. Now they also own the big-screen televison market.

Darwin's law of competitive positioning places a premium on reacting quickly to the entry of new foreign products and services. It should also encourage U.S. manufacturers to enter new global markets. As global competition increases, new, differentiated products are entering markets at an increasing rate. Often strong positions in

23. Hamel and Prahalad, "Do You Really Have a Global Strategy?" 139–48.
24. Philip Appleman, *Darwin* (New York: W. W. Norton, 1979).

foreign markets are lost because senior executives neglect to pay attention to competitive threats in the specific market. This is an argument for decentralized decision making, which allows the local management to make major strategic repositioning decisions.

Triangulating Hunches in Foreign Markets

In global marketing, the most desirable positioning decision process is one in which the potential of the tentative strategy is confirmed from several different sources (such as experts, channels, suppliers, and consumers). It is called triangulation and helps increase the validity of the hunch. Triangulation is very important when deciding how to position a product or service in an unfamiliar foreign market. A cross-functional team must spend a great deal of its available time and effort arriving at a consensus on the fundamental choice of target segment (market niche) and basic positioning. The options will emerge as the environmental analyses are being undertaken in each foreign market, but the final choice should not be made until the planning environment reports are completed and thoroughly understood. This is because the planning team needs information about consumers and competition to identify the opportunities. Information about distribution channels may reveal whether a new product can reach and supply such new market niches.

Evolution of Global Positioning in a Firm

As mentioned above, a U.S. firm often starts to export to foreign markets that have 1) segments that desire the firm's current offering and 2) weak competition. As it gains international experience, the U.S firm recruits local managers and expands its product line with products uniquely developed (positioned and QFD designed) for the foreign market.[25] Ultimately, a global positioning strategy evolves where the same positioning concepts and products are used to target similar segments that exist in all countries, domestic and foreign. Some foreign markets will still have uniquely positioned products in the product line catering to a unique culture-specific or climate-specific benefit segment or competitive situation. But when the benefit segment transcends culture and geography, then standardized positioning, standardized design, and the same differentiation theme can be used to promote the positioning to the target benefit segment. Such a global positioning strategy requires a commanding understanding of consumer behavior and the benefit segments in the many countries and cultures around the world.

1. Many packaged-goods markets are mature, and executives bemoan the fact that their market has become a commodity market, meaning that the rival products are all close substitutes for one another. When price becomes the major factor that drives consumer choice between alternatives, then the product and image differentiation of competitive offerings has been reduced or lost altogether. A commodity market is a market where there is high substitution between alternative products: price is all-important and the lowest cost producer is most competitive. It is called a Walrasian price-competition market. What can a seller do in such a market?

Discussion Questions and Minicases

25. Susan P. Douglas and C. Samuel Craig, "Evolution of Global Marketing Strategy: Scale, Scope and Synergy," *Columbia Journal of World Business* (Fall 1989), 47–59.

2. An enterprising manufacturer of filing cabinet hanging folders makes them in several bright, modern colors rather than the standard, dull, cardboard green. Why was this a very successful and profitable differentiation strategy?

3. Please describe the unique positioning of each of the following brands.

Brand:	Positioning:
Polaroid cameras Honda cars Apple computers Perrier mineral water Target breakfast cereal Tandem computers Harvard Business School VISA credit card	

4. In the 1950s, Rayovac had a 35 percent market share of the consumer battery market, but it missed the alkaline boat and slumped to a 6 percent share. New owners in the 1980s introduced 6 to 8 battery packages. Rayovac also designed new types of flashlights with superbright krypton lights and lithium power. These flashlights stay functional for up to 10 years.[26] What usage segments did Rayovac target?

5. The advertisements at the top of this page present examples of successful and unsuccessful differentiation. Identify which is which and explain why.

26. Steve Weiner, "Electrifying," *Forbes*, November 30, 1987, 196–98.

6. Segmentation analysis should reveal the user and usage segments that seek different benefits from the use of a product. A seller can then position its offering differently to such segments. To segment *A* it will position its product as delivering the benefit most desired by segment *A*, and to segment *B* it will describe the way its product delivers the benefit most desired by segment *B*. Consider a manufacturer of buffered aspirin. How might it take the same product and position it differently to two different segments? (Hint: Think about a recently discovered new benefit of aspirin.)

7. *Consumer Reports* evaluates brands and models of products. How might a market planner use such information to develop a positioning strategy? What are the risks of using this information?

8. Using the figure below, describe what each segment wants. Evaluate the positioning of each of the brands. In particular, how would you rate the positioning of Chivas Regal? Do you think it is profitable? Do you think it is vulnerable?

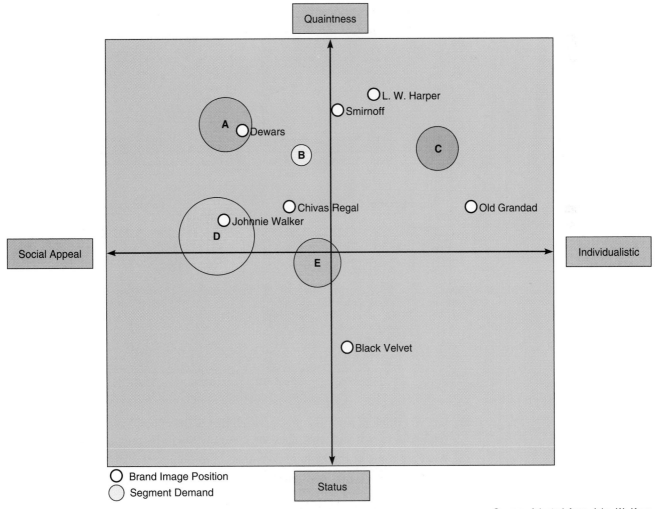

Source: Adapted from John W. Keon, "Product Positioning: TRINODAL Mapping of Brand Images, Ad Images, and Consumer Preference," *Journal of Marketing Research* 20 (November 1983), 380–92.

9. How might you apply QA analysis to a drug developed to help prevent infections in cancer sufferers whose immune systems have been weakened by chemotherapy? What statistical data would you need and how would you use the data?

10. Managers working for a developer building houses for professional couples in the $95,000–$125,000 price range could not agree on whether to build houses with three bedrooms, four bedrooms, or three bedrooms plus a study. How important was the exterior finish, how important was the ceiling height, and how important was the price? Seventy-one prospective buyers were recruited and divided into groups where they discussed drawings and details and then ranked, in order of preference, 32 cards describing hypothetical homes. The resulting conjoint analysis of their answers produced the added utility ratings of each feature (on a 100-point utility scale) presented below. What type of house should the developers build? (Hint: Use your commonsense knowledge of building costs.)

Source: Adapted from Richard R. Batsell and John B. Elmer, "How to Use Market-based Pricing to Forecast Consumer Purchase Decisions," *Journal of Pricing Management* 1.2 (Spring 1990), 5–15.

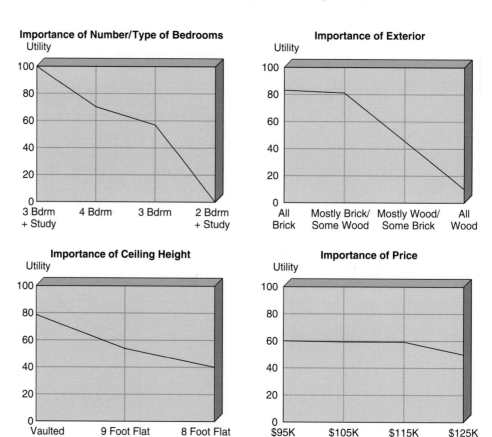

11. Can you think of a positioning approach that is the opposite of quality-added analysis? Who uses it and what does the company say in its promotion?

12. What are some of the basic reasons that a positioning strategy fails?

13. Think of any new product positioning that combines benefits and features that previously were considered incompatible. Explain why the two features seemed implausible in the minds of some consumers.

14. Interpret this breakfast food competitive map using the ideal points information as well as the positioning of the different foods.

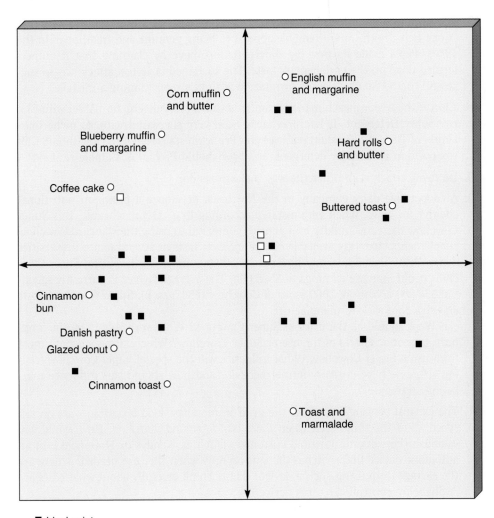

Corn muffin ○
and butter

○ English muffin
and margarine

Blueberry muffin ○
and margarine

Hard rolls ○
and butter

Coffee cake ○
□

Buttered toast ○

□
□ ■
□

Cinnamon ○ ■
bun

Danish pastry ○
Glazed donut ○

Cinnamon toast ○

○ Toast and
marmalade

Source: Paul E. Green, and Abba M. Krieger, "Recent Contributions to Optimal Product Positioning and Buyer Segmentation" (Working Paper, Wharton School, University of Pennsylvania, 1989).

■ Ideal point
□ Multiple ideal points

15. The demand equation for segment A is

$$Q_a = F_a(p_a, X_{1a}, X_{2a}, X_{3a}, \ldots, X_{na})$$

where Q_a is quantity demanded, F_a is the demand function unique to segment A, and $<p_a, X_{1a}, X_{2a}, X_{3a}, \ldots, X_{na}>$ are segment A's perceptions of price and the n features of the product. These perceptions determine demand through their influence via the F_a function.

When a seller modifies the demand of segment A by changing segment A's appreciation of specific features, what would change in the above equation? When a seller changes its product design and product differentiation, what would change in the above equation? If a seller changes its target to segment B, what would change in the above equation? Illustrate your answer by describing a market where marketers' have pursued these strategies.

16. Make a copy of Figure 8-4 and use it to explain how Tylenol undertook the mobile counterattack described in the chapter.

17. For decades, Coca Cola promoted its drink as "The Real Thing" and claimed that "Coke Is It"; both were intangible appeals to being genuine and traditional. In the 1980s, Pepsi made its first big differentiation move by claiming that it outperformed Coke on the core benefit: taste. The sustained taste-test attack was so successful that Coke changed its formula. Was Coke's repositioning a mistake?

18. Clorox, the major bleach marketer, entered the laundry detergent market with Clorox Super Detergent. It had previously been very successful with its niche marketing of Tilex mildew stain remover and Pre-wash stain remover. How should Clorox position its laundry detergent, and how should Procter & Gamble respond?

19. Do firms attack each other the way that armies do?

20. A cooperative dairy company in the Northeast developed a premium nutritional additive for cows. When administered according to a careful schedule, this Super Cowchow increases milkfat by 5 percent compared to using the standard Cowchow supplements currently available on the market. Tests at several major universities demonstrate that if a farmer now earns $500,000 in milk sales, using Super Cowchow could increase earnings to $525,000. The average farmer is currently spending $50,000 a year on 1,000 sacks of Cowchow ($50 a sack). Super Cowchow costs an extra $5 a sack to manufacture.

    What should be the price of Super Cowchow? What are likely to be the long-term economic effects of the use of Super Cowchow? Which farmers benefit most from using Super Cowchow? What influence will the special Super Cowchow feeding schedule have on dairy farmer behavior and how should this influence marketing strategy?

21. The exhaust venting fans above the grills in most fast-food restaurants are on full speed all of the time, even when there is no cooking going on. How would you establish the value to potential customers (such as Wendys or McDonald's) of an automatic device that switches the fans on only when they are needed? Where are the savings from using such a device? (Hint: Think carefully about what costs are really being controlled by this device.)

22. The feasible positioning analysis computes the cost of making and marketing the QFD positioning concept. It then includes these costs and the competitive price suggested by the QA analysis and inputs them into a TARGET spreadsheet. This spreadsheet computes what sales and market-share goals will have to be achieved to meet the input financial goals.

    How is the realistic achievability of the required sales and market share then assessed? What is to stop an executive from lowering the required sales and market share by simply plugging in a higher price? How are costs likely to be fudged so as to make the project look more feasible? (Hint: Read the section on cost analysis in Chapter 2.)

23. Several market research techniques and visual frameworks are available to help make the positioning decision. One approach is to use a person-situation usage segmentation matrix (see figure). The cells in the P-S matrix represent potential target market niches. The potential depends on the uniqueness of the benefits sought by the users in the situation, how much of the product category is used by the particular group of users, and whether competitors are already serving the niche.

    a. Consider the upper-left segment cell. Develop a new suntan lotion for the children/beach/boat market segment that has a new attractive benefit and feature.

b. Position the product lines of several brands in the matrix by studying their packaging and advertising. Where are the gaps in their positioning and product lines?

Person-Situation Segmentation Procedure

Step 1. Use observational studies, focus group discussions, and secondary data to discover whether different usage situations exist and whether they are determinant, in the sense that they appear to affect the importance of various product characteristics.

Step 2. If step 1, produces promising results, undertake a benefit, product perception and reported market behavior segmentation survey of consumers. Measure benefits and perceptions by usage situation as well as by individual difference characteristics. Assess situation usage frequency by recall estimates or usage situation diaries (Belk 1979).

Step 3. Construct a person-situation segmentation matrix. The rows are the major usage situations and the columns are groups of users identified by a single characteristic or combination of characteristics.

Step 4. Rank the cells in the matrix in terms of their submarket sales volume. The situation-person combination that results in the greatest comsumption of the generic product would be ranked first.

Step 5. State the major benefits sought, important product dimensions, and unique market behavior for each nonempty cell of the matrix (some person types will never comsume the product in certain usage situations).

Step 6. Position your competitor's offerings within the matrix. The person-situation segments they currently serve can be determined by the product feature they promote and other marketing strategies.

Step 7. Position your offering within the matrix on the same criteria.

Step 8. Assess how well your your current offering and marketing strategy meet the needs of the submarkets compared to the competitors.

Step 9. Identify market opportunities based on submarket size, needs, and competitive advantage.

Speculative Person-Situation Segmentation Matrix for Suntan Lotion

	Persons:								
	Young Children		Teenagers		Adult Women		Adult Men		
Situations	Fair Skin	Dark Skin	Fair Skin	Dark Skin	Fair Skin	Dark Skin	Fair Skin	Dark Skin	Situation Benefits/Features
beach/boat sunbathing					summer perfume				a. windburn protection b. formula and container can stand heat c. container floats and is distinctive(not easily lost)
home-poolside sunbathing					combined moisturizer				a. large pump dispenser b. won't stain wood, concrete, or furnishings
sunlamp bathing					combined moisturizer and massage oil				a. designed specifically for type of lamp b. artificial tanning ingredient
snow skiing					winter perfume				a. special protection from special light rays and weather b. antifreeze formula
person benefit/ features	special protection a. protection critical b. non-poisonous		special protection a. fit in jean pocket b. used by opinion leaders		special protection female perfume		special protection male perfume		

Source: Peter R. Dickson, "Person-Situation: Segmentation's Missing Link," *Journal of Marketing* 12 (1982), 56–64.

24. The following table presents a CANNIBAL spreadsheet, which can help a single-product company estimate the effect of introducing a second product. The first column estimates what will happen to annual sales and ROI if the new product is *not* introduced. It assumes that the firm will gain one whole percentage point of market share from its rivals, that the market will grow by 10 percent, and that the firm will gain 10 percent of the growth. The second column estimates what will happen to the old or existing product if the new product is introduced. It will gain half of a share point from rivals but will lose a whole share point to the new product (a quarter of its existing sales will be cannibalized). The market will grow by 15 percent (an extra growth because the new product and countering efforts of competitors will expand the size of the entire market), but the old product will only get 5 percent of this growth. The third column presents the expected performance of the new product. It is forecast to take two share points away from competitors, one share point from the old product, and a fat 50 percent of the entire market's growth. The fourth column adds columns two and three together to present the overall results.

a.   The Marginal Analysis column presents the marginal effect of adding the new product. Describe the effects in a memo. In the memo, indicate which estimates or forecasts of the new product's performance you think the profit and ROI increase projections are most sensitive to (that is, what affects bottom-line income forecasts most?).

Product Line Extension Analysis: The Effect of Cannibalism

	Single Product	Old	Extended Line: New	Combined	Marginal Analysis
Current market (000)	14,000			14,000	
Current share	4.0%	4.0%	0.0%	4.0%	
Forecast change in share: Share points gain/loss over competitors	1.0%	0.5%	2.0%	2.5%	1.5%
Share points gain/loss to own cannibalism		−1.0%	1.0%		
Forecast market growth	10.0%	15.0%	15.0%	15.0%	5.0%
Share of growth	10.0%	5.0%	50.0%	55.0%	45.0%
New market size (000)	15,400	16,100	16,100	16,100	700
New market share	5.5%	3.7%	9.1%	12.8%	7.4%
Sales volume (000)	840	595	1,470	2,065	1,225
Unit price	$2.00	$2.00	$1.75		
Total revenue (000)	$1,680	$1,190	$2,573	$3,763	$2,083
Gross margin/unit	$1.00	$1.00	$0.75		
Gross margin (000)	$840	$595	$1,103	$1,698	$858
Marketing costs (000)	$200	$200	$350	$550	$350
Allocated overhead (000)	$100	$100	$100	$200	$100
Profit before tax (000)	$540	$295	$653	$948	$407
Investment (000)	$4,500	$4,500	$1,000	$5,500	$1,000
Return on investment	12.00%	6.56%	62.25%	17.23%	40.75%

Source: The above spreadsheet is an extension of method discussed in Roger A. Kerin, Michael G. Harvey, and James T. Rothe, "Cannibalism and New Product Development," *Business Horizons*, October 1978, 25–31.

b. Use the spreadsheet to test the assumptions by changing each of the estimates (reducing each one at a time, leaving the others the same) by 20 percent in an unfavorable direction; that is, the gain in share points from competitors would drop to 1.6 percent, the cannibalization would increase to 1.2 percent, market growth would be only 12 percent, share of growth would be 40 percent, and marketing costs would be $420,000. What forecasts have to be most accurate?

25. QFD analysis of a service requires the mapping of the service process script (activity sequence) and the identification of activities that most determine customer perceptions of service quality. This can be done using survey research and structural equations analysis, but most of the time the determinant quality activities are identified using executive experience and judgment. Below is the activity sequence for a bank's installment lending procedure:

Installment Lending: Bank X

Source: G. Lynn Shostack, "Service Positioning Through Structural Change," *Journal of Marketing*, January 1987, 34–43.

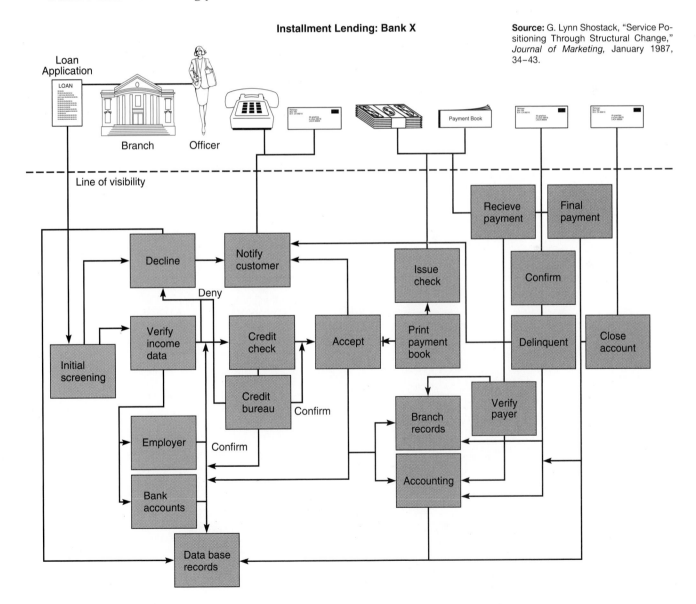

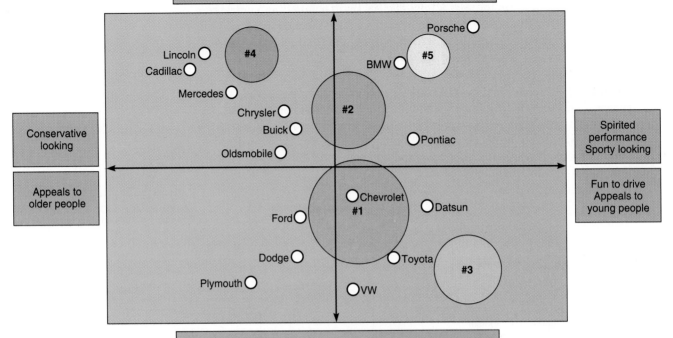

Source: Adapted from John Koten, "Car Makers Use 'Image' Map As Tool to Position Products," *The Wall Street Journal,* March 22, 1984, 31.

The Planned Repositioning of Pontiac

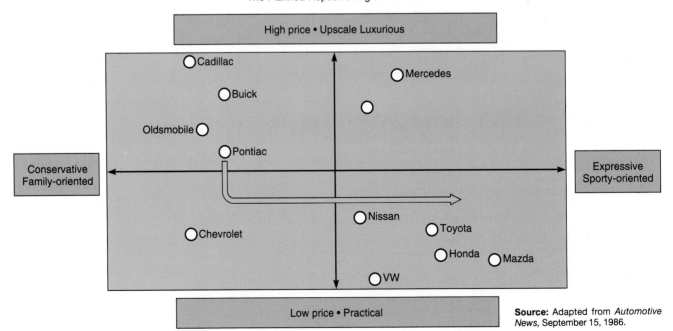

Source: Adapted from *Automotive News,* September 15, 1986.

a.   Which activities do you think most determine customer perceptions of overall service quality?

b.   In recent years, some banks have attempted to speed loan approval. How could the activity sequence be modified to speed up approval?

26. In 1991, the Goodyear tire company introduced the Aquatred brand (see advertisement). What is the target market and why is it such a clever, differentiated positioning? (Hint: Successful differentiation is in the minds of the consumer.) Which brand do you think will be most hurt by Aquatred? (Hint: Think of the different positioning appeals of brands.) The Aquatred actually works best with ABS braking systems. How might you use this information in future product-line positioning strategies?

27. The figures on the opposite page show two competitive maps of auto brands. The first also has segment ideal points identified. Give a name to each of the segments. Where would you place Acura? Where would you place Lexus and Infiniti? In the second map, what is the problem with Pontiac's ("we build excitement") efforts at repositioning. Do you think Oldsmobile's ("not your father's car anymore") campaign was a good one in the light of these maps?

Managing Products

"No gain is so certain as that which comes from the more economical use of what you already have."

Latin Proverb

"The empires of the future are the empires of the mind."

Winston Churchill

As discussed in the previous chapter, a product or service is a bundle of valued features, both tangible and intangible, that satisfy customer needs. While other marketing programs also add value, the remainder of the marketing mix cannot stand on its own without a competitively viable product.[1]

After important needs are identified and a product idea is generated to meet those needs, the process by which the new product is designed and developed must be managed so that the quality features are emphasized. Features that provide intangible attributes must also be designed. Product brands help to fulfill this role because the management of the brand image helps to establish the positioning of the product in the minds of buyers. Intangible benefits are also supplied by warranty assurances. Packaging, labeling, and services provide both tangible and intangible benefits. New product strategy does not have a clear beginning or ending. To stay competitive, the firm must constantly reevaluate its definition of quality if it hopes to continue developing quality products.

Keep these key ideas in mind as you read this chapter:

■ Product management depends on where the product is in its current innovation-imitation life cycle. Much of the redesign and modification takes place during the introductory and growth stages of the life cycle.

■ New product development is best viewed as an ongoing, continuous process.

■ New ideas can come from many outside sources. An attitude that says "forget it if it's not invented here" is competitively irrational.

■ When managing the development and introduction of new products, constantly test the new product idea with customers and get their feedback; keep improving the product after it is introduced.

■ A brand name is a valuable asset that needs to be carefully managed.

■ The positioning of a new brand is enhanced by choosing a brand-name logo that is attention getting, distinctive, memorable, and communicates the product's benefits.

■ When brand reputation is uncertain, performance guarantees or warranties are very important to assure customers of quality performance.

■ Package and product labeling persuade and educate the customer and distribution channel, thus providing communication that reduces risk and enhances the ease of use.

■ The product's packaging must meet the requirements of the distribution channel.

■ It is easier to design and launch new services than new goods.

■ Operations management plays a dominant role in new service development because the operations' people work *for and with* the customers. They are closest to the customer. It is their job to also understand the human engineering involved in designing a service that delivers high satisfaction to the target market.

■ Global marketing has greatly increased the rate of innovation and imitation in new product design. International marketing also poses special problems for brand management, packaging, and labels.

Throughout this chapter, the reader should keep in mind that goods and services are intended to provide value for buyers. The opening section of the chapter discusses the

---

1. The phrase *product* is used generically here to include both goods and services.

management of the new product development process. This process is not perceived by the buyer, but when it is well managed it allows the product to provide more value to the consumer. The latter sections of this chapter discuss brand management, packaging, labeling, and warranties. These factors also directly provide value for the buyer.

Managing new product development is also crucial if a firm wants to take an entrepreneurial approach to formulating and executing strategy. The theories of competitive rationality and creative destruction, which provide the underpinnings for this text, state that the use of innovation-imitation in the development of a product drives its long-term survival and performance. The implication for product management is that a company must take risks when offering new products and it must continually upgrade the products and services it already provides. This chapter discusses both the desired outcomes of innovation and the management of the process used to produce this innovation.

The environment, its changes, and the implications for marketing managers may all be thought of in the context of the product life cycle. This idea likens the life of a product to that of a living organism, exhibited by a birth stage, a growth stage, a mature stage, and a decline (death) stage.[2] The analogy has its limitations. As explained in Chapter 1, most products go through many innovation-imitation life cycles. Only fad products have a single life cycle. However, the life-cycle concept provides a useful way for many managers to think about managing their products. Our discussions below concern the management of the *product* element of the offering. Guidelines for the management of other aspects of the offering through the life cycle are summarized in Figure 9-1 and addressed in later chapters.

The product life cycle can be examined at various levels, from the life cycle of a whole industry to the life cycle of a single model of a specific product. It is probably most useful to think in terms of the life cycle for a product form, such as supercomputers, photocopiers, or hand-held calculators. Life cycles for product forms include definable groups of direct and close competitors, a core technology, and broad groups of users/buyers. These characteristics make life cycles for product forms easier to identify and analyze and would seem to have more stable and generalizable implications.

Product Management and the Product Life Cycle

Introduction Stage

In the initial stage (or birth stage) of the product life cycle, customers often do not have a good idea of what needs will be addressed by the new product technology or design. Very few prospective customers can tell a market researcher or product designer how they would use the product and what value it will give them. Consequently, segments are not well defined, nor are product features fully specified, let alone developed. In addition, there are few or no competitors.

During the introduction stage, marketers must focus on 1) involving several first users in design discussions, 2) distinguishing between first and early adopters, 3) getting prototypes and first versions of products into the hands of first users, 4) obtaining extensive feedback from first users, and 5) specifying later versions of the product quickly. Involving first users makes it possible to obtain helpful design considerations

---

2. George S. Day, "The Product Life-Cycle: Analysis and Application Issues," *Journal of Marketing* 45 (Fall 1981), 60–67; and Mary Lambkin and George S. Day, "Evolutionary Processes in Competitive Markets: Beyond the Product Life-Cycle," *Journal of Marketing* 53 (July 1989), 4–20.

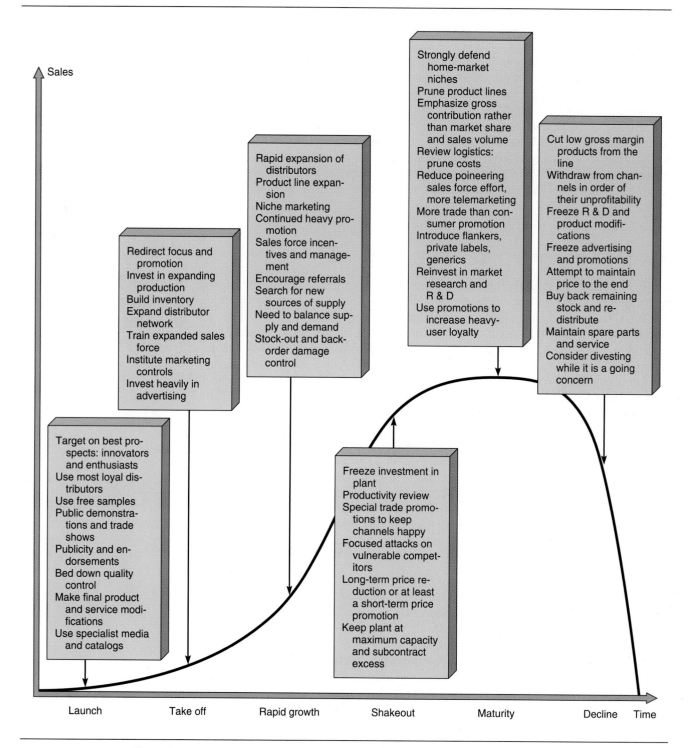

Figure 9-1
Product Life-Cycle Stages and Marketing Tactics

Some of the commonly prescribed competitive tactics are listed at each stage of the innovation-imitation life cycle. The figure illustrates that marketing programs should fit the competitive situation and that marketing programs also determine the next stage of the market.

from the user's viewpoint. It also provides the chance to get feedback from the next group of early adopters.[3] It is they who can tell the marketing manager what needs should be met by the product in a larger market. The innovator may simply buy the product for its novelty—to see if it works—without caring much about practical usage. The idea is to offer first versions for sale and obtain enough feedback to bring out upgraded revisions quickly. This is called the *exploratory* approach to new product development. Firms that offer more versions while focusing on learning from customers will obtain more information than their competitors.[4] The upgraded versions will more accurately reflect the customer needs that become evident as the customers try the product, find new uses for it, and suggest new or better features to meet related needs. Since customers often have difficulty discussing specific needs for specific features, obtaining quality feedback is key.[5]

Growth Stage

By the growth stage of the life cycle, the buyers of the product have more information on the product's uses and value. In addition, more competitors begin to see opportunities in the market and produce similar offerings. Channels of distribution begin to shape themselves to address end-user markets. The product itself is beginning to coalesce around a dominant design, or at least a relatively few dominant designs.[6] Segments are becoming more evident, yet they remain fluidly defined. While innovative activity producing wholly new designs has largely disappeared, feature innovation can progress at a rapid pace. The temptation at this stage is to add features that buyers do not want or to improve the features beyond the point where customers obtain additional benefit. Quality function deployment (QFD, discussed in Chapter 8) can keep the management team focused on the dimensions of customer needs that are most important.

In general, the marketer should strive to build as much customer loyalty as possible during this stage. Once the market stops growing, a shakeout is likely to occur and only the strongest competitors will survive. The marketing manager should focus on building a strong brand name and convincing buyers this particular brand meets important customer needs. In addition, the manager should look for ways to innovate within a dominant design to continually add new value for the customer.

Mature Stage

In a mature market, users of the product generally understand the product, understand its usage, and have established expectations for quality and performance. In addition, the competition has stabilized around a number of competitors with established performance records. These competitors continue to innovate, but much of the product innovation is incremental, often related to cost reductions.

Management of the product at this stage comes down to the continuous improvement of product features. Extensive contact with customers over the life of the product to this point should have given the firm a strong understanding of customers' desires and expectations for product performance. Using this information, the product manager will, by now, have a very detailed QFD analysis. This QFD analysis can then be

3. Geoffrey A. Moore, *Crossing the Chasm* (New York: Harper Business, 1991).
4. Preston G. Smith and Donald G. Reinertsen, *Developing Products in Half the Time* (New York: Van Nostrand Reinhold, 1991).
5. Since customers have limited knowledge of their needs and uses, quality function deployment (QFD) can be difficult to implement. A firm should still use QFD at this stage, but only as a general guide.
6. William J. Abernathy and James M. Utterback, "Patterns of Industrial Innovation," *Technology Review* 80.7 (June/July 1978).

used to focus the company's efforts on improving the features of the product that contribute to the most important customer benefits.

In addition, the firm should look for ways to add intangible benefits to the product. In many mature product markets, the competitors reach a technological wall—they cannot produce more benefits for customers without incurring unacceptable costs. Often it is not just the leading competitor who reaches this point; all the major competitors have the technical capability to match each other, product feature for product feature. If no competitor has a clear cost advantage, then competitors in a market such as this will face eroding margins until they barely cover their costs. When the market reaches this point, the firm must find some other way to differentiate its product or it will have to continue to compete on cost and price. Besides focusing effort on improving product quality, the firm can improve such intangibles as image, warranties, and service added to tangible goods. Service, in particular, has become a major method for firms in mature markets to differentiate their tangible products.

Mature markets also require the competitors to rationalize their product lines. Market segments become clearer and more stable during this stage. The variation in customer desires that exists will produce some very distinct market segments, with well-defined boundaries that require special offerings to meet their needs.[7] These needs will often be met by astute specialists. An alert larger company could also add special products within its line of products to address these market segments.

Decline Stage

In a decline stage, usually some technical innovation has been introduced that has made the product form obsolete for many of its customers, or customer preferences have changed to favor an alternative. Consequently, market segments are shrinking as their members switch to a new product. The product decisions to be made in this stage of the life cycle focus on downsizing the product line and determining how to shift the company's emphasis to other products. Obviously, as segments disappear, products aimed at those segments will have to be discontinued. When it is no longer feasible to offer the line at all, the firm should keep in mind that most products, particularly industrial goods, require long-term service well beyond the discontinuance of the line. For the purposes of maintaining strong relations with existing customers, the firm would do well to find a way to make this extended service available. It may sell service contracts to third-party service providers, or it may choose to maintain an ongoing service department within the company itself. The firm may face the same decision with the provision of spare or replacement parts. Thus, it may decide to license the manufacture of these parts to a third party or may manufacture the parts itself.

In any event, the company facing the decline stage of its mainline products does not want to be caught in the situation of not having new products to fulfill the revenue and profit roles of the old product. This concern reinforces the need for an active and effective new product development process.

New Product Development

A major theme of this book is the constant development of new technologies, the translation of new technologies into new products, and the continual modification and adaptation of existing products—that is, Schumpeterian creative destruction. If the firm is to survive and perform well, it is crucial for the marketer to understand the processes

7. Mary Lambkin and George S. Day, "Evolutionary Processes in Competitive Markets: Beyond the Product Life-Cycle," *Journal of Marketing* 53.3 (July 1989), 4–20.

Benefits from designing manufacturability, quality, and ease of maintenance into the product at the start		When design changes are made	
	Percent		Cost
Development time	30%–70% less	During design	$1,000
Engineering changes	65–90 fewer	During design testing	10,000
Time to market	20–90 less	During process planning	100,000
Overall quality	200–600 higher	During test production	1,000,000
White-collar productivity	20–110 higher	During final production	10,000,000
Dollar sales	5–50 higher		
Return on assets	20–120 higher		

Figure 9-2

The Competitive Advantages of Concurrent Engineering

Concurrent engineering by a cross-functional team emphasizes a heavy investment in design at the outset of the project because the costs of changing the design late in the development process are much greater. Concurrent engineering also saves time, increases quality, and is generally a far more rational decision-making and implementation process than bureaucratic new product development processes, which require that tasks by marketing, R&D, manufacturing, and finance be addressed sequentially.

Sources: These charts are based on data from Dataquest, Inc., the National Institute of Standards & Technology, the Thomas Group, Inc., and the Institute for Defense Analyses. See Otis Port, Zachary Schiller, and Resa W. King, "A Smarter Way to Manufacture," *Business Week,* April 30, 1990, 110–17.

that produce new products and, further, to understand how to manage and facilitate them.

One of the most salutary lessons that American marketers have learned in the last decade is that new product development can no longer be undertaken on a project-by-project basis. It has to be a constant activity. In the past, companies may have tried to manage their costs in part by periodically increasing and decreasing new product development activities. However, the lessons learned from competing with innovative Japanese and European firms, as well as from competing with aggressive domestic firms, suggest that companies must continually innovate to remain viable in the long term. Nowadays, the innovation process, and hence launching of new products, is more often a continuous business planning activity.[8] The management guru Tom Peters has suggested that a company should be producing at least a dozen new ideas *each month* on how each of its product lines should be improved. The process in which everyone in the enterprise is constantly thinking of ways to make minor improvements to the product, service, or production is called *kaizen* in Japan.

A frequently presented sequential model of the new product development (NPD) process divides the process into six stages: idea generation, idea screening, concept development and business planning, product development, market testing, and product launching. The process can be discussed in these terms, but it is important to keep in mind that, in practice, this process is much messier than the step-wise progression suggested by a simple listing of these stages. In concurrent engineering, several of these stages are deliberately undertaken at the same time. The emphasis is on designing quality, ease of maintenance, manufacturability, and low cost into the product and service at the very start of the process. The resulting increase in efficiency and competitiveness can be great (see Figure 9-2). The concurrent engineering process is also very adaptive, as it often encounters dead ends, redundancies, and mistakes, as well as the occasional breakthrough or "Aha!" experience. The people involved come from widely different backgrounds, ranging from technical to business orientations, and thus may have differing motivations and language barriers to contend with. To make this process

8. Tom Peters, *Thriving on Chaos* (New York: Alfred A. Knopf, 1987); and "Strategy Follows Structure: Developing Distinctive Skills," *California Management Review* 26 (Spring 1984), 111–25. See also George S. Day and Robin Wensley "Assessing Competitive Advantage: A Framework for Diagnosing Competitive Superiority, *Journal of Marketing* 52 (April 1988), 1–20.

productive, management must take a facilitating or shepherding approach rather than a directive approach.[9]

Before delving into the specifics of the NPD process, a few words need to be said about the frame of reference that the marketing manager can bring to this process. Experience and research have shown that the best new products are developed when extensive customer contact occurs throughout the process.[10]

Scientists and engineers in the firm's research and development department must understand the needs of the users of their products. In a start-up company, often the new product developers were themselves potential users who recognized an unmet need. This explains why their first products are so well targeted to satisfy customers. However, as time goes by, and a firm follows its first success with other new products, the developer must continue to learn about the target customers' needs. The original understanding becomes outdated as customers' situations change. The marketing manager and cross-functional team must keep the development process aimed at finding ways to meet customers' needs by making sure that the designers and engineers in the team continue to talk to their customers.[11] The objective, however, is not simply to convert customer suggestions into new products, but to develop a sufficient familiarity with the customer and the usage situation so that the designers can *anticipate* and *imagine* what technologies customers will want to use in the future.[12] Understanding the customer requires going well beyond listening to their current suggestions.

Idea Generation: Sources of New Ideas

In recent years, the pressure to innovate has opened firms and their planners to sources that they may not have paid much attention to in the past. Figure 9-3 presents potential sources of new product ideas or new uses for old products. Some of the most important sources for new product ideas are customers, competition, channels, the company's own R&D organization, and the company's sales force, as well as ideas generated by company employees.

A large number of the firm's ideas for successful product innovations should come from customer suggestions. An increasing number of companies are realizing this and working with customers on new product development.[13] This should not be surprising. In business-to-business markets, customers often possess a great deal of knowledge about the products that they buy. The number of inventive suggestions that come from users will be related to the importance of the product to them and their understanding of the product's technology. Consumer markets are another matter. Comparatively speaking, a homemaker's interest in buying a better dishwashing liquid is low, and his or her likely understanding of what is chemically possible is even lower. However, even in this situation, such consumers can give detailed descriptions of problems that occur when the product is used. They can also give detailed descriptions of how they would like to live their lives. Such discussions can lead to ideas for new products that solve

9. A major duty of marketing managers in Japanese companies is to play such a facilitating role to encourage cooperation and harmony. See William Lazer, Shoji Murata, and Hiroshi Kosaka, "Japanese Marketing: Towards a Better Understanding," *Journal of Marketing* 49 (Spring 1985), 68–81.
10. See, for instance, Robert G. Cooper, "Predevelopment Activities Determine New Product Success," *Industrial Marketing Management* 17 (1988), 237–47.
11. Edward F. McQuarrie and Shelby H. McIntyre, *Implementing the Marketing Concept Through a Program of Customer Visits* (Cambridge, MA: Marketing Science Institute, 1990).
12. Kim B. Clark and Takahiro Fujimoto, "The Power of Product Integrity," *Harvard Business Review* (November/December 1990), 107–18.
13. Eric Von Hipple, "Successful Industrial Products from Customer Ideas," *Journal of Marketing* (January 1978), 39–49; also Eric Von Hipple, "Lead Users: A Source of Novel Product Concepts," *Management Science* 32, no. 7 (July 1986), 791–805.

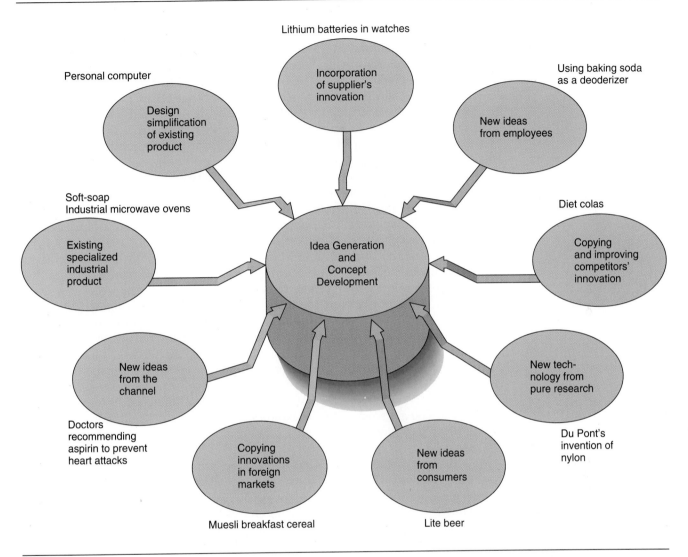

Figure 9-3

Sources of Innovation-Imitation Ideas

Some companies only develop new products from in-house R&D. They do not even seek out the suggestions of all of their employees. As can be seen from this figure, those firms are at considerable risk of losing their markets to competitors who seek new ideas from all possible sources.

problems and enhance a customer's life-style. Then, when an idea for a product is initiated or a product is improved, they can provide designers with valuable information.

Other outside sources of new ideas should also be examined with an open mind. The not-invented-here culture can be a serious barrier to adopting customer suggestions or competitors' new features. Few firms can afford to be so arrogant in today's competitive marketplace. To remain competitive, they must actively open themselves to all of the feedback they can get from every possible source, including ideas developed in other industries. For example, the use of the Velcro fastener has spread from furnishings to clothes, shoes, sporting gear, and many other product-markets, introducing new convenience and durability. Interestingly, its Swiss inventor got the idea from nature—the cocklebur's spurs.

New Product Policy: Company Cultural Attitude to Innovation-Imitation

The direction and tone established by top-level management shapes the way that the firm will pursue new product opportunities. A company can pursue two general strategies with its product development activity.[14] In the first continuous approach, the firm attempts to achieve a continuous stream of modestly successful new products. Each of these new products builds on the firm's knowledge of its customers and its technology; the firm never strays far from its core competencies. Individually, these new products do not remake the market or the organization itself. However, in sum, they add up to a consistently successful company performance.

The second strategy is to search for a revolutionary product that changes the market and the company. Such an approach—a *big hit* approach—often requires a substantial commitment of resources and a relatively long development period. The result, though, is discontinuity in the performance of the firm. This is probably accompanied by the reshaping of the product-market or even the creation of a new one. A hybrid approach can also be pursued, in which the firm attempts to produce the occasional discontinuous innovation, while generally pursuing a series of incremental ones. Such an approach will take even greater resources than the big hit approach.

The divergence between these approaches has implications for top-level policy making as well as for idea screening. At the top level, the firm must decide which approach it will direct its cross-functional teams to pursue. The principal criteria that will drive the choice are the firm's resources, financial goals, (see Chapter 7), and the nature of the market. The big hit approach holds the promise of making the firm into a market leader. Yet, to be successful in the approach, the firm must either be lucky or it must fund several R&D efforts to offset the risk of failure associated with a single effort to find a discontinuous breakthrough. If the firm does not have the resources sufficient to do this, the incremental, continuous stream of innovations is a more viable approach.

However, if the market is not yet well defined or the technology is still in its infancy, there may be an insufficient base from which to pursue even the incremental approach. In this case, the cross-functional team may wish to pursue an alternative approach—called an *exploratory* approach (see Figure 9-4)—which allows firms with limited resources to bootstrap an innovation in an emerging market.

This approach, a variant of the incremental approach, involves using considerable customer contact during the initial design stage, quickly launching the first version of a product to a relatively small initial market, receiving substantial feedback quickly, redesigning the product, and launching the revised version in a form that customers have indicated has a high level of value to them. Compared to a traditional approach to product development—in which considerable effort is spent performing market research, product testing, and subsequent redesign, all before the product is introduced—this approach offers several advantages:

- ◆ A faster inception-to-market speed, permitting a faster creation of positive cash flow.

- ◆ The potential for a lower expenditure of resources to get a first version out.

- ◆ The potential for a more efficient use of resources in redesign efforts.

- ◆ More efficient and accurate learning about customer desires, since the feedback is based on an actual offering rather than market/product research instruments.

14. Robert G. Cooper, "The Impact of New Product Strategies," *Industrial Marketing Management* 17 (1988), 237–47.

Interviews with marketing managers and founders of technical companies suggest that several approaches are used to develop marketing strategies for new products:

1. **Exploratory.** With this approach, the company gets a product to market quickly, so that it can receive feedback from customers. The company revises the strategy rapidly and gets a new version of the strategy launched, usually to a somewhat different and larger market. The company may go through several iterations of the product and the strategy. This approach involves informal customer contact while the strategy is being developed initially and also after the product is offered.

2. **Experimental.** With this approach all portions of the marketing strategy are developed and tested before the launch, using both formal and informal market research. The company launches the product with the idea that it is the right product for the market and does not expect to make major adjustments to the strategy after launch.

3. **Incremental.** This approach is often used in markets where a company has an established technology and a built-in relationship with an existing group of customers. The approach builds upon the established base to offer this customer group more and more value. New products are designed based on extensive customer contact. The product is offered and little adjustment is needed after launch.

4. **Over-the-wall.** This is the direct antithesis of the experimental approach. The company develops a product with little or no input from customers. The product is still believed to be the right product for the market, but this is often a matter of speculation until customers in the market either buy the product or not.

Figure 9-4

Approaches to New Product Risk Taking

Source: Joseph J. Giglierano and M. Jeffery Kallis, "Marketing Strategy Development in New Products and New Companies in Technical Industries," *Proceedings* (American Marketing Association Summer Educators Conference, 1991), 504–11.

The exploratory approach can even produce the big hit. An extreme example of the use of this approach was the Apple Macintosh computer. Guy Kawasaki described the "Macintosh Way" of getting the right product this way: lead, take a shot, listen, respond, then lead again.[15] Apple can argue legitimately, with only minimal exaggeration, that the Macintosh changed the world. It did so by producing an initial product, listening to the market, and producing subsequent revisions as fast as possible to rectify short-comings identified by customers. While the use of the approach for the Macintosh computer was apparently not entirely intentional, it still illustrates the capability of this approach to establish a product or product line with great impact. Smaller companies complete the same sort of process all the time, sometimes even on purpose, with less dramatic but certainly successful results.

Cross-functional New Product Development

For an idea or a concept to advance, it helps if it is championed by an individual who is constantly hustling inside and outside the company to keep up the enthusiasm and momentum.[16] She or he must also have the support of an influential senior manager. The problem is that although such a product champion must believe in the new product idea, he or she must also be impartial enough to assess the risks and problems that may cause the project to be abandoned. Even while representing the concept, the champion must also be responsible for seeing that a balanced environmental analysis is used to assess the product's opportunities and potential problems.

To help the product champion keep perspective, a cross-functional team should be assembled with the following skills: product design and engineering, market research, marketing, production, purchasing, and cost accounting. The major advantage of such team decision making is the constant, frank interaction between members of the group

15. Guy Kawasaki, *The Macintosh Way* (Glenview, IL: Scott-Foresman, 1990), 54–56.
16. This suggests that companies should create legends out of product champions that fought the nay-sayers. Such champions should also be financially rewarded. Such economic and status rewards will spur inventive ways of breaking down institutional blindness and barriers to change.

with different skills that enables marketing, design, operational, and cost problems to be solved at the same time, rather than sequentially.[17] Such teamwork greatly increases the shared insights, learning, and control, and, most importantly, reduces the time it takes from when a product is conceived to when it breaks even in the marketplace (BET).

To make the team function effectively, top management should appoint a team leader. Without such leadership, the team may flounder, wasting the time, skills, and patience of the team members. The team leader preferably should be someone with broad experience and a broad business outlook, but most importantly the leader should have the confidence of the team and be its *informal,* as well as *formal,* leader. This leader should have the authority to make crucial decisions and the willingness to make tough decisions. To provide the incentive necessary to compensate and motivate, many companies give a team leader a stake in the outcome. The team also often receives compensation based on the outcome. Many companies, such as 3M, leave the team intact after its introduction to run the new product as a fledgling business. There is some disagreement on whether this is always useful. Working out the format for operation of the new business unit may take away effort that could be spent bringing the product to market.[18] However, if the members of the team are to move on to other assignments, there is the potential for marketing mistakes when the project is handed to an existing operating unit.

Initial Screening, Planning, and Design: Investing in the Front End

The problems that companies have creating new products—problems such as missing cost targets or taking too long to develop a new product—often stem from mismanagement in the early stages of the new product process.[19] In the early stages of the new product process, information is uncertain. If screening is done in a way that penalizes all ideas except the most conservative ones, the competition will eventually crush the conservative company's competitive position. On the other hand, too loose a screening process (or none at all) may allow projects to proceed when a closer examination would reveal obvious flaws, either market related, technology related, or both. A rigorous process may also cause problems. Time may be wasted if a new idea has to be evaluated as part of the firm's yearly planning process. Even if there is a standing committee that evaluates new product ideas, it may take a long time to get an evaluation if the committee is composed of senior managers who are so busy they cannot find a time to meet.[20]

Probably the speediest way to accommodate new ideas as they arise is through an ad hoc committee formed to evaluate new ideas as they come up or when a critical mass of new ideas has accumulated. Top management gives this committee a good set of guidelines and some authority. Then management chooses the ideas for the team to pursue as they see fit. Cooper suggests the use of a fairly rigorous set of criteria in evaluating new ideas that involves two passes: the first pass employs "must have" criteria and the second pass employs "should have" criteria.[21] Use of such an approach will force management to gain an understanding of where the market and technical

17. Hirotaka Takeuchi and Ikujiro Nonaka, "The New Product Development Game," *Harvard Business Review,* January/February 1986, 137–46.
18. Smith and Reinertsen, *Developing Products in Half the Time.*
19. See Kim B. Clark and Steven C. Wheelwright, *Managing New Product and Process Development* (New York: The Free Press, 1993); Robert G. Cooper, *Winning at New Products* (Reading, MA: Addison-Wesley, 1986); and Smith and Reinertsen, *Developing Products in Half the Time.*
20. Smith and Reinertsen, *Developing Products in Half the Time.*
21. See Cooper, *Winning at New Products,* Chapter 6.

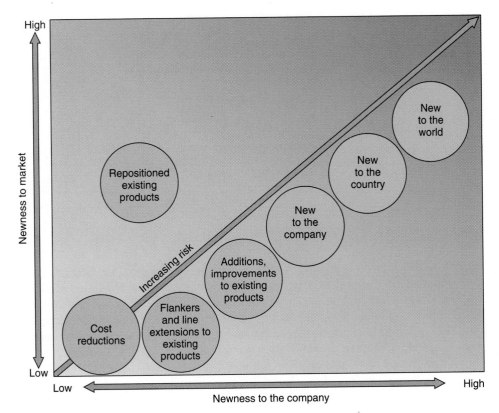

Figure 9-5

Newness and Risk of Failure

Newness has two dimensions—new to the market (consumers, channels, and public policy) and new to the company. As this figure shows, the greater the newness to the market, the more thorough the external environmental analysis and screening must be. The greater the newness to the company, however, the more thorough the internal company analysis and screening must be.

Source: Booz Allen & Hamilton, Inc.

risks are likely to arise and, further, will induce them to make an initial commitment to the projects that pass this phase.

The market analysis and screening for a new product idea should follow the procedure described in Chapters 1 and 2. Figure 9-5 illustrates how the risk of market failure increases with the newness of the product. The greater the newness of the idea to the world, the greater the need for a thorough external environment analysis (see Chapters 3 through 6). The greater the newness of the idea to the company, the greater the importance of the internal company analysis (see Chapter 7). A product must have extraordinarily clear and sustainable competitive advantages (for instance, patent protection) if it does not fit with current manufacturing, distribution, target market, and marketing image strengths. If such synergies do not exist, it might be better to have the innovation manufactured, distributed, and marketed under license by a company that has such strengths.

Once a new product is approved for development, manufacturing strategy planning design should be done concurrently so that time is not wasted.[22] At the very outset, point out that designers need only a rough idea of the product vision, its purpose in the marketplace, and the situations in which customers will use the product. Planning would begin by developing a rudimentary idea of the product, its customers, and uses. These initial product plans would be fed to the designers, who would in turn

---

22. Smith and Reinertsen, *Developing Products in Half the Time.*

Figure 9-6
The Design-Testing Loop

A new product idea may come from R&D or from the marketplace. A prototype must be designed, manufactured, and tested using trusted customers. The feedback from the testing modifies the design by adding features or reducing costs. Engineers also have to design for manufacturing, and this may involve working with suppliers. The result is then retested by customers and evaluated against competitive products. The loop continues until both the customer and manufacturing are satisfied. The speed of this looping is an important characteristic of competitive rationality as it determines how alert the firm is to the needs of the customer, its willingness to experiment, and its ability to implement. This looping speed becomes even more important the greater the number of loops that have to be completed—that is, the newer and more difficult the technology.

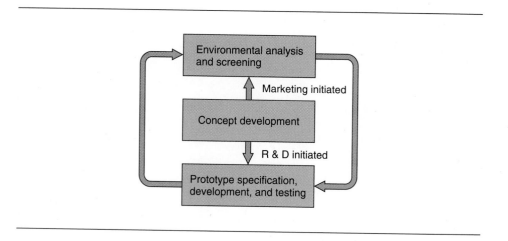

provide feedback on costs and capabilities as these become evident, allowing more precise planning as the project progresses. The recommended modification-screening approach to new product development, illustrated in Figure 9-6, requires a close and effective working relationship between the cross-functional team and trusted customers. This relationship is greatly helped by senior management leadership that encourages cooperation between the R&D, manufacturing, and marketing functions.[23]

A word needs to be said at this point about new product costs, profitability, and how these factors are incorporated into decision making for new products. Japanese companies seem to consider projected costs in a fashion different from the costing approaches taken by western companies (see Figure 9-7).[24] The favored model in the West is to design the product, build the prototype, and then estimate what it will cost to make such a product. The company then examines whether the product can be sold for a price that incorporates this cost, plus a desired profit margin. If the answer is no, then the product is redesigned or killed.

Japanese companies take a much simpler approach. At an early stage, a target price for the new product is determined, based on an understanding of customers and a quality-added analysis that determines what price range the product will have to sell for. Target profitability is determined based on the company's financial requirements. Working backward, target costs are set for the new product. Manufacturing and distribution are then designed to meet these target costs. This process involves considerable negotiation between the various functions of the company, as well as with the company's suppliers. The resulting product not only meets customer needs, but it is usually a cost leader as well. Considering the time it takes western companies to redesign if initial cost estimates are unsatisfactory, the Japanese approach can be much faster. A further difference between the Japanese approach and the western approach lies in the go/no-go decisions based on expected profitability. Western companies tend to kill products based on projections of the individual product's profitability. Oftentimes, expected profitability calculations are really no more than creative fiction based on imprecise cost and revenue projections. Japanese companies seem to be much more

23. Ashok K. Gupta, S. P. Raj, and David Wilemon, "A Model for Studying R&D—Marketing Interface in the Product Innovation Process," *Journal of Marketing* 50 (April 1989), 7–17; Hirotaka Takeuchi and Ikujiro Nonaka, "The New Product Development Game," *Harvard Business Review*, January/February 1986, 137–46; and Abbie Griffin, *Evaluating Development Processes: QFD as an Example* (Cambridge, MA: Marketing Science Institute, 1991).
24. Ford S. Worthy, "Japan's Smart Secret Weapon," *Fortune*, August 12, 1991, 72–75.

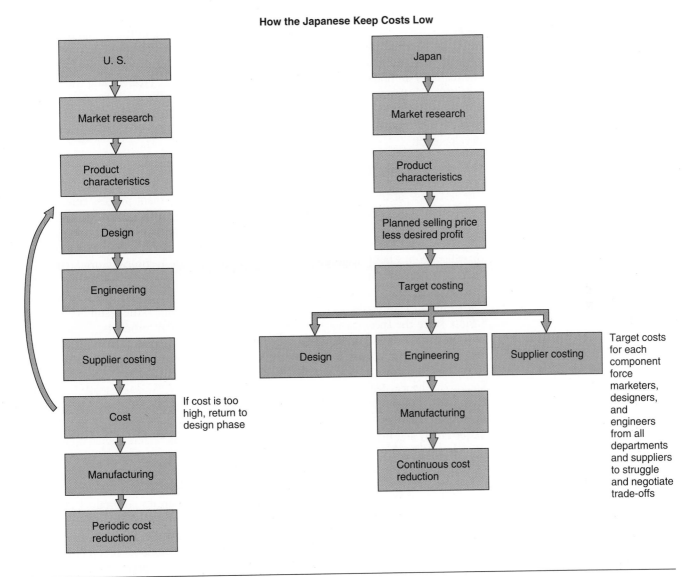

How the Japanese Keep Costs Low

In the traditional approach followed by many U.S. companies, cost is considered too late in the new product development process. Japanese firms often use price, along with other product features, to position the product. They then set a profit margin and subtract it to determine the target direct cost. This target cost, along with QFD-determined features, drives the concurrent engineering process. Afterward, the drive to reduce costs continues unabated.

Figure 9-7
Contrasting Approaches to New Product Design

Source: Reproduced with permission from Ford S. Worthy, "Japan's Smart Secret Weapon," *Fortune*, August 12, 1991, 72–75. © 1991 Time, Inc. All rights reserved.

willing to look at the total picture, seeing the product's likely contribution to an overall strategic position. Consequently, many more products are introduced because they are viewed to play a specific role in a product line or in the company's total offering (see Chapter 8).

This discussion reinforces two considerations that marketing managers should keep in mind when developing new products: an understanding of the customers and the role of an individual product in the company's total offering. Having contact with prospective customers during the development process will help the cross-functional team understand desired price ranges, as well as the product features desired (see Figure 9-6). If the team knows how customers will value a product, it can have a better sense of the correct trade-off between input quality and costs in the design process. As for thinking about the company's total offering and an individual product's role in that offering, having contact with customers will help here as well. Such contact can give the manager an understanding of how the whole offering is perceived and the manager will have a better sense of the quality differences between the products offered by the company. It should also be noted that the positioning procedure described in Chapter 8 combines the best features of Japanese and western approaches to new product development.

Product Specifications and Prototypes

The last stage of the front end of the new product development process concerns the production of detailed specifications for the new product. This step is crucial and often becomes the source of complicated problems if it is not done well. If the specifications are overly ambitious, the product that results will be too costly, will not perform well, or will take too long to develop. If the specifications are technically oriented rather than customer oriented, the result will be a product that is not well suited for the market. If, as often happens, the specifications are written in duplicate—once from a marketing viewpoint and once from an engineering viewpoint—the result is often confusion, since the specifications, in fact, describe two different products.

Specifications should be written jointly by the cross-functional team. A QFD process, illustrated in Figure 9-8 and discussed in Chapter 8, is a good way to work out these specifications, even during the introductory stage of the life cycle. Marketers should be concerned about two principal aspects in this process. First, marketers should avoid pushing for a product that does everything. A product that takes the best features of competitors' products and combines them into a grand design will probably be too costly and may prove too tricky to design. Rather, marketers should concentrate on determining the most important needs of the target customers and focus on these. The second consideration is determining when to freeze the design. In many instances, particularly in new and uncertain markets where customers have little knowledge of the product and its uses, it is more important to launch an initial product and learn from the launch than it is to get exactly the right design the first time. New features and functionality can be added in future versions of the product. Immense amounts of time and money may be wasted, though, if the marketers come in at the last minute with a list of desired design changes intended to meet the competition (without really understanding whether customers want these functions or not). Such antics will also be viewed by engineering and production colleagues on the cross-functional team as obstructionist and will strain future working relationships.

From the original idea, designers and engineers make an initial model or service routine (called a prototype) that meets performance specifications and comes in at or under cost projections. Computer-aided design (CAD/CAM) has dramatically increased the ability of a company to move quickly from concept to detailed engineering specifications and design blueprints. The manufacturing of prototypes for laboratory and market testing is often a problem unless the firm already possesses the manufacturing resources. If not, it must go outside to have the prototypes made.[25] Its innovation then becomes vulnerable to discovery by competitors. This may be a necessary risk to take,

25. Advances in CAD/CAM software already enable the testing of new product design appearances by having consumers view two- and three-dimensional, computer-generated, full-color prototypes. The computer can also test the *functional* performance of the design through computerized usage simulations.

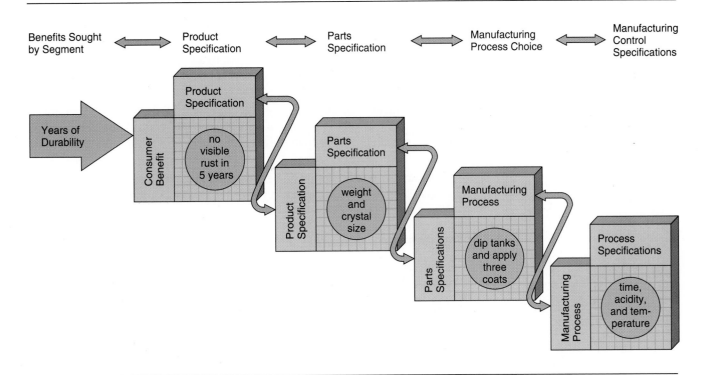

Benefits Sought by Segment ⟷ Product Specification ⟷ Parts Specification ⟷ Manufacturing Process Choice ⟷ Manufacturing Control Specifications

The QFD process flows from consumer benefits sought, to product requirements, to part or module specifications, to manufacturing operations, to process specifications. All of the manufacturing implementation issues surface in this QFD flow.

Figure 9-8
The QFD Process

Source: Adapted from Vincent P. Barabba and Gerald Zaltman, *Hearing the Voice of the Market* (Cambridge, MA: Harvard Business School Press, 1991), 54.

for confidentiality ceases to be a concern if test marketing is undertaken. In today's world, the best way for a firm to protect itself from the risk of competitors discovering its plans is for it to have a new product development process that moves faster than its competition.

Product Development and Engineering

It would seem that development and engineering of the new product is largely out of the hands of marketers. Such an approach, though, can lead to failure of the product in the marketplace. Engineering is a process in which product design is accommodated to the realities of materials, costs, production requirements, and product usage, and service design is accommodated to logistics limitations or employees' capabilities. To ensure that designs do not drift away from meeting customer needs, the sales and marketing people on the cross-functional team should continue to make sure that customers are consulted and that prototypes are tested by customers during the development process (see Figure 9-6).

Some other considerations to keep in mind when planning the development process,[26] particularly if it is important to introduce the product quickly, are listed here:

1. Divide the development of the product into component modules so that concurrent development of the modules can occur.

26. See Smith and Reinertsen, *Developing Products in Half the Time*.

2. Build robust interfaces between the modules. Time will not be lost in redesigning interfaces when module designs change or when new modules are upgraded in future product designs.

3. Concentrate technical risk in relatively few modules. If technical risk is spread across several component modules, total risk is greatly increased. It also diffuses the firm's ability to adapt if some technical goals cannot be met.

4. Establish controls that do not hinder the development effort. It is important for accountants and project managers to decide early what controls are necessary and what controls are no more than bureaucratic backside coverage and thus are not necessary.

5. Involve suppliers in the design and engineering process. They, better than anyone else, should know how their product performs. This is a very sensible type of competitive rationality routine.

Market Testing Consumer Products

The value of market testing consumer products before full commercialization is debatable. Market testing is much more than product testing, which is essential. A proper market test reveals what will happen if the product is launched in the entire target market. This may be very difficult to achieve without great expense, and if test marketing is considered, how will using such an initial "test" market differ from launching the product nationally? Often the only difference is in the phasing of the launch. It starts in one regional market, and if it is successful, it is rolled out into other markets. In short, a test market is often a partial or regional launch. If it works, the launch continues. If it does not, then a lot of developers will be burning the midnight oil. If the decision is made to pull the plug on the product, then the title of the project or exercise reverts from a phased rollout to a failed test market.[27]

If in-depth interviews with customers, prototype testing, and comparative field trials against competition (perhaps repeated several times in different regional markets) produce evidence of clear superiority on cost-competitive performance, and the proposed marketing strategy passes the STRATMESH screening test (see Chapter 2), then test marketing is probably not needed. For example, the hugely successful Gillette Sensor was not test marketed. The reality is that test marketing is needed when the prior evidence suggests that a firm does not have a clearly winning innovation and marketing strategy. The question then is why the project is going ahead at all, rather than whether or not the product or service should be test marketed. Test marketing will determine if the company has a clear winner on its hands, but so will prototype field testing. Here is the catch: test marketing is sometimes not reliable enough to establish whether consumers will detect marginal improvements in performance and will switch their long-term loyalty because of such differences. From this perspective, test marketing may offer few benefits and some important disadvantages.

The Risk of Test Marketing

The first risk of test marketing is that the delay will increase the risk of being beaten to the market by a competitor (Figure 9-9). Test marketing can take a year to complete, giving competition plenty of time to respond. In 1983, while Beatrice was carefully evaluating the results of its test marketing of a cat treat called Bonkers, Puss 'N' Boots

27. Ironically, a company that pursues this approach will have a sorry history of market test failures and a great history of roll-out launches. If this is so, market tests are likely to get a bad name.

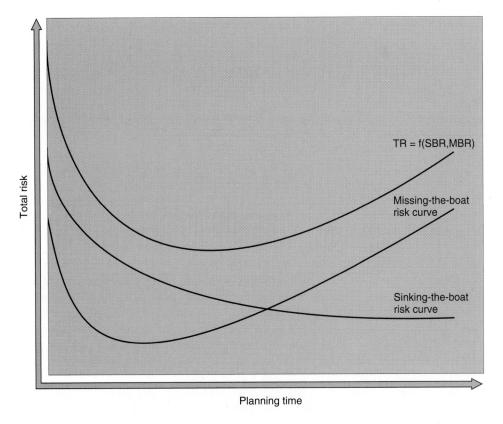

TR = f(SBR,MBR)

Missing-the-boat risk curve

Sinking-the-boat risk curve

Total risk

Planning time

Figure 9-9

Risk Reduction through Planning Time and Effort

The initial time spent analyzing the environment and screening strategy and tactics reduces the risk of product failure, or "sinking the boat." However, when further risk cannot be reduced by undertaking more research or planning, then the firm has reached the limits or bounds of its competitive rationality. At this point, the delay caused by continued testing can allow a competitor to beat the company into the market and gain a first-mover competitive advantage. Rather than spending too much time on planning, the firm would be better off launching the new product and then following up with redesigned models.

launched its competitive treat called Pounce. Five years later, Pounce owned 60 percent of this market.[28]

The second risk with test marketing is that it ends up being unrealistic. There is a temptation to give the product far more marketing support in the test than it would get when rolled out nationally. The product champion and the venture team launching the product have much at stake and are naturally keen to see the product succeed. Whether intentional or not, the results are sometimes biased by selecting a test market that is much more receptive than average, by encouraging extraordinary sales support, or by proffering unprecedented advertising campaigns or promotional incentives. Although statistics are not available, the chances that a product could pass such a market test and still fail in the marketplace are probably quite high.

The debate over whether to test or launch a new product further underscores the importance of systematically screening a proposed strategy against the known marketplace facts. Such careful planning described in Chapter 1 may be arduous and boring, but it may also be the best way to reduce the risk of new product failure. It is also a lot less expensive than a test market that fails, less damaging to the firm and less damaging to careers.

28. Thomas D. Kuczmarski, *Managing New Products* (Englewood Cliffs, NJ: Prentice-Hall 1988), 37. For a general discussion, see Peter R. Dickson and J. Giglierano, "Missing the Boat and Sinking the Boat: A Conceptual Model of Entrepreneurial Risk," *Journal of Marketing* 50 (July 1986), 58–70.

Brand Identity and Brand Equity

For thousands of years, men and women have been putting their names on everything from cattle and pyramids to children and ideas. Product branding is a variation of these very basic ownership and self-expressive human behaviors. Product branding, though, has another important use from the standpoint of meeting customer needs.

Customers, whether they are individual consumers or organizational buyers, must handle an enormous amount of information in the course of their daily activities. Consequently, people develop efficient ways of processing information—including the use of selective attention, memory shortcuts, and rules of thumb—in order to make decisions.[29] With that reality in mind, potential buyers will often use symbols, such as brands, to stand for larger chunks of information and simplify information handling.

A brand is a conditioned cue that, through its long association with a product or service, comes to stand for something, be it quality, reliability, craftsmanship, exclusive styling, status, or value. The brand name is also one of the most fundamental pieces of information consumers use to simplify choices and reduce purchase risks. Brand names assure customers that they will receive the same quality with their next purchase as they did with their last. Consequently, buyers are willing to pay a premium for such quality and assurance. On an impressionist painting, the name Vincent Van Gogh can add tens of millions of dollars to the price. The brand name on a mass-produced item can seldom make that much of a difference, but the principle is the same. For this reason, branding has emerged as an essential element of product strategy, be it for expensive sports gear, cars, or commodities (such as Morton's salt, Chiquita bananas, or Perdue chickens). Some of the more subtle characteristics of consumer brand knowledge are presented in Figure 9-10.

In fact, some brands are, in the aggregate, actually worth a great deal more than a great artist's signature. Kohlberg Kravis Roberts purchased RJR Nabisco for $25 billion—over double its book value. Philip Morris, Inc., paid $12.9 billion for Kraft (four times book value) and $5.7 billion for General Foods (again over four times book value). Nestle paid $4.5 billion for Rowntree (five times book value). Even under the generous assumption that the tangible assets of all these companies were undervalued by 50 percent, this still means that the goodwill and reputation of their brand names (brand equity) were worth billions. The enormous value of the equity of some brands indicates that today there is a clear disenchantment with the risks involved in spending hundreds of millions of dollars to launch new brands and a growing interest in marketing new products under the umbrella of well-established brand names that have become part of our cultural heritage. The management of brand equity has many aspects, as Figure 9-11 illustrates, some of which we now explore in more detail.

The Durability of Brand Names

Brand names can be very durable. Booz, Allen and Hamilton, Inc., compiled a list of the 24 leading consumer brands of 1923. Fifty years later, 19 were still leaders and the others placed in the top five. For example, 10 of the top 20 candy bars (including Snickers and Hershey's) have been around for 50 years and today account for 80 percent of all candy bar sales. The histories of four great brands are presented in Figure 9-12.

Strong brand equity is not only used to roll out new products and break into new markets. It also can serve as a formidable barrier, making it difficult for competitors

---

29. James R. Bettman, *An Information Processing Theory of Consumer Behavior* (Reading, MA: Addison-Wesley, 1979).

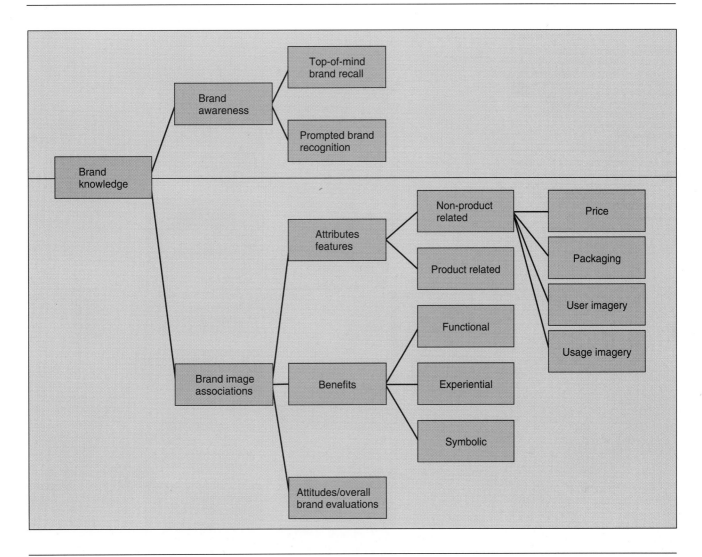

There are two basic types of brand knowledge: awareness and image. A brand for a candy or soft drink seeks high, top-of-mind brand awareness. It wants to be the first brand consumers think of when they get hungry or thirsty. Brand image describes consumer beliefs about a brand. These brand associations (attributes, features, benefits provided, and overall evaluations) vary in their *favorability, strength, and uniqueness.* A highly competitive brand creates strongly positive associations in the mind of a consumer that are unique or differentiated. Other brands do not have the same strongly positive associations.

Source: This figure is adapted from Kevin Lane Keller, "Conceptualizing, Measuring, and Managing Customer-Based Brand Equity," *Journal of Marketing* 57.1 (January 1993), 1–22.

Figure 9-10
Dimensions of Brand Knowledge

to enter or expand in the market. However, some great brand names do die from neglect and mismanagement. Magic Markers, introduced in the 1950s, were the first felt-tipped markers, but later entries improved the technology and expanded the market to include pens. Magic Marker's quality image slipped and a decision to drop its premium positioning and compete on price hastened the slide into oblivion. In the 1980s, the Italian luxury shoe handbag manufacturer Gucci stretched its brand name, reputation, and equity to a breaking-point by indiscriminantly putting its brand logo on 14,000 different products, including T-shirts, keychains, sunglasses, watches, and coffee

Figure 9-11

The Many Aspects of Managing Brand Equity

Brand equity has many aspects, including brand loyalty (discussed in Chapter 3), brand awareness, image and perceived quality, brand associations, and extensions. If managed well, these traits add value to the product or service and create additional customer satisfaction, which, in turn, provide a number of benefits to the firm.

Source: Reprinted with the permisson of the Free Press, a Division of Macmillan, Inc. From *Managing Brand Inquiry: Capitalizing on the Value of a Brand Name* by David A. Aaker. Copyright © 1991 by David A. Aaker.

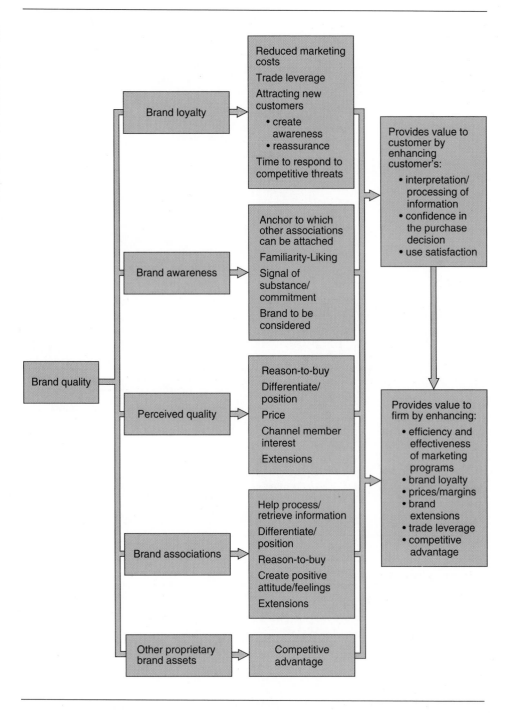

mugs. It has not been able to recover its reputation, equity, sales, and profits.[30] It is difficult to destroy a great brand name, but it can be done.

On the other side of the coin, new brand names can be launched successfully. Compaq computers became a billion dollar company in three years. Reebok, with sales of

30. "Upmarket Philosophy," *The Economist,* January 8, 1993, 98.

IVORY SOAP

The 108-Year-Old Soap

One Sunday morning in church 108 years ago, Harley Procter wrestled with a nagging problem. At 32—determined to retire at 42—he was in charge of Procter & Gamble sales, and wanted the perfect name for the white soap his cousin Jim Gamble had just invented.

He found himself listening to the congregation reading Psalm 45, verse 8: "All thy garments smell of myrrh, and aloes, and cassia, out of the ivory palaces. . ." The word straightened Harley like a ramrod. "Ivory!" Smooth—white—hard—long-lasting. Like Jim's soap. That was it!

In October, 1879, the first bar of Ivory soap went on sale as a trademarked product. Since then Americans have bought 30 billion more.

99 44/100% Pure

Harley wanted people to know how pure Ivory was. In 1882, he commissioned laboratory analyses of Ivory and three costly Castile soaps. As he suspected, Ivory, with only 56/100% impurities, scored highest. He subtracted the fraction from 100. Ivory was "99 44/100% pure!" Ever since, Ivory's classic slogan has told why it leaves the skin so clean, so fresh.

"It Floats"

At first, Ivory *didn't* float. But it

seems a workman left a batch of the soap in a mixer and somehow, the machine whipped tiny air bubbles into the mix—just enough to make the soap buoyant. People wrote in that they *liked* floating soap; when it slipped into murky river or tub water, it popped back up to the surface all by itself. Keep making it float, Harley ordered. In 1891, Ivory advertisements began telling the world, "It floats."

What happened to Harley? Just as he had planned, Harley retired at 42, and spent the rest of his life in Massachusetts. And what happened to Ivory soap? It became America's No. 1 soap. And it still is today, because Americans just can't get enough of that pure clean.

KLEENEX®

From Wisconsin to the World

People respected Charles B. Clark of Neenah, Wisconsin. So, in 1872, when the Civil War veteran talked about building a paper mill, John A. Kimberly listened. Clark, Kimberly and two other men invested $7,500 each to form Kimberly, Clark & Company. Their first product was newsprint made from rags.

The mill prospered on principles set by the founders: make the best possible product, serve customers well, and deal fairly with employees. In 1928, when Kimberly, the last of the four founders, died, the paper company was reorganized as the Kimberly-Clark Corporation.

Meanwhile, the company's chemists had developed CELLUCOTTON®, a revolutionary breakthrough in absorbent material, used extensively during World War I for gas mask filters and surgical dressings. After the

The four founders of Kimberly, Clark & Company

war, Kimberly-Clark refined CELLU-COTTON and marketed the new product in 1924 as KLEENEX® Facial Tissue, the "Sanitary Cold Cream Remover." And Broadway stars, such as Helen Hayes and Gertrude Lawrence, endorsed the product.

Six years later, surveys showed that most consumers used KLEENEX Facial Tissue as disposable handkerchiefs rather than as a cold cream remover. Kimberly-Clark responded by developing such advertising slogans as, "Don't put a cold in your pocket." Sales boomed.

Today, Kimberly-Clark's annual sales are over $4 billion. KLEENEX, the most popular facial tissue in the world, is sold in more than 130 nations. Through leadership in fiber-forming, absorbency, and other technologies, Kimberly-Clark has evolved from a small Midwestern newsprint manufacturer to a highly diversified international company best known for its quality consumer products.

An elegant KLEENEX tissue box from the 1930s, and the current classic foil package design.

TYLENOL®

The trusted pain reliever

One hundred years ago, a young pharmacist opened a shop in the Kensington area of Philadelphia. The community marked the occasion with a dinner. The pharmacist was happy to celebrate. It had been a successful first day, with sales totaling $5.79.

At about the same time, across the Atlantic, a European pharmacist was in no mood to celebrate. Young and inexperienced, he had incorrectly sent an obscure drug to two doctors who had given it to a patient. The pharmacist worried what the outcome might be.

Fortunately, the new medication quickly reduced the patient's pain and fever, working better than the drug the doctors had originally prescribed. Later, it was discovered that in the body, the drug became acetaminophen, the active ingredient in TYLENOL.

Today, we do not even know the name of that European pharmacist. But the young Philadelphia pharmacist, Robert McNeil, went on to found McNeil Laboratories, the company that turned a brand of acetaminophen called TYLENOL into the country's most popular pain reliever.

In 1951, scientists at McNeil, now a member of the Johnson & Johnson family of companies, became interested in the unique benefits of acetaminophen. After four years of tests and study, they concluded that acetaminophen effectively relieved

headaches, fevers, and body pains generally without the side effects commonly associated with aspirin.

In 1955, the FDA approved TYLENOL as a prescription drug, and five years later, as a nonprescription pain reliever. Success came quickly. Within a few years, TYLENOL became the pain reliever used most by hospitals. It continues to be dispensed today more than all other leading pain relievers combined.

Proof of the public's trust in TYLENOL was put to an almost impossible test during two tampering incidents of the 1980s. McNeil acted with model corporate behavior in rapidly and responsibly dealing with the problem, quickly restoring the brand to the marketplace in tamper-resistant packaging and product forms.

But it is clearly consumers', doctors', and hospitals' trust in the brand that

McNeil's original pharmacy.

has allowed TYLENOL to regain its place as the largest brand of pain reliever in the country.

KODAK

'You Press the Button, We Do the Rest'

This year, picture-takers around the world will "press the button" almost 40 billion times. Perhaps that's astonishing, but it's also understandable. Photography fills a vital human need. It allows us to preserve a visual image of the people, places, and events in our lives; to keep a record of our family joys and our children's growth; to revisit the scenes of our travels. Without photography, the world would have only half a memory. And no one has done more to advance the art in the last century than Kodak, which in 1988 celebrates the 100th anniversary of its first camera.

George Eastman, founder of Eastman Kodak Company, didn't invent photography, but he made modern photography possible with several breakthrough inventions. Perhaps most significant was his development

George Eastman

of flexible roll film, which served to bring photography to amateurs. Eastman also set about reducing cameras' weight. That first camera bearing the Kodak name, introduced in 1888, not only could be held in the hand, but delivered "snapshots" at the push of a button. "You press the button, we do the rest," was the advertising slogan. The camera came loaded with film for 100 pictures. After taking all 100, the photographer sent the camera to Rochester, New York. The pictures were developed and the camera was reloaded and returned.

But the camera that truly put photography within the financial reach of everybody was the famous box Brownie, sold for $1 in 1900. It introduced generations of people all over the world to the lasting joys of picture-taking, changing forever the way we look at ourselves.

These simple beginnings spawned a long line of spectacular photo-

How "Kodak" Came to Be

In 1888, George Eastman sought a brand name for his first camera, a short word that could be easily recognized and pronounced in any language. The letter "K" was a favorite of his, and he used it twice to coin a name that has become world-famous in photography.

Figure 9-12

The Histories of Four Great Brands

$3 million in 1983, greatly expanded its line of products during the first six months of 1986 and sales have grown to a billion dollars. Having acquired Rockport, the leading maker of walking shoes, Reebok faced an interesting embarrassment of riches. Should it make Rockport walking shoes, Reebok walking shoes, Rockport Reeboks, or Reebok Rockports? Much depends on who the target market is and the respective images and equities of the two brands in the target market.

Brand Clout in the Channel

In addition to signaling quality, a high-status brand name gives a manufacturer clout over retailers. Ralph Lauren franchised his own Polo men's clothing stores that capitalize on the image of his designer label—old money, panache, and understated, WASP-ish conspicuous consumption. While clearly irritated at Polo's downstream integration, the major department stores continued to sell the Polo label because of customer demand. Ralph Lauren's logic was that if the exclusive department stores can integrate upstream and push their own exclusive designer labels to compete with manufacturer designer labels like Polo, then he was perfectly entitled to retaliate by integrating downstream. Now Levi Strauss is test marketing Levi and Dockers stores.

The success of the The Limited women's clothing chain suggests that when retailers combine their merchandising skills with creative and competitive product design, quality control, and exclusive private brand imaging, they can often beat manufacturers in the brand war. The battle between retailers and manufacturers for dominance of the channel may well be won or lost on the crucial issue of whether, in the end, consumer *store* loyalty is greater than consumer *manufacturer brand* loyalty. If manufacturers lose their brand equity and end up manufacturing retailer's brands under license, then they can say good-bye to their marketing departments and most of the profits from innovating. Such a trend may be occurring in food retailing.

The Pros and Cons of Family Brands

The first advantage of a well-known brand is that it can be used to launch new products. Table 9-1 presents a list of successful brand extensions into new product categories and a list of failed extensions. There are two keys to successful brand extension:

1. Extend into product categories that are used in the same situation as the original branded product or used by the consumers of the original branded product.
2. Transfer the unique quality associated with the original brand (the characteristic that comes across as a strong benefit) into the new product category.

Brand extensions fail when the association between the products is not obvious, when the original brand has too unique an image, when already dominant brands exist in the product category, or when the quality of the new product is not as high as that of the existing product under the same brand name.[31]

A strong brand name will grab the consumer's attention and may lead to new product trial. It will provide a foot in the door—but that is all. A rose is a rose by any other name, and so is a ho-hum, me-too product. Brand name extension is most effective when it is applied to a product that is complementary in usage to the original, branded product. For example, Mr. Coffee, the brand name for the original automatic coffee machine and filter, has been applied to a premium brand of ground-roast coffee.

31. C. Whan Park, Bernard J. Jaworski, and Deborah J. MacInnis, "Strategic Brand Concept-Image Management," *Journal of Marketing* 50 (October 1986), 135–45; Peter H. Farquar, "Managing Brand Equity," *Marketing Research*, September 1989, 24–33; and Joshua Levine, "But in the Office, No," *Forbes*, October 16, 1989, 272–73.

Table 9-1
Successful and Unsuccessful Brand Extensions

Successful Brand Extensions to New Product Categories

BIC disposable shavers	BIC disposable lighters
Kodak film	Kodak cameras and batteries
Coleman camping lamps	Coleman cookers, tents, sleeping bags
Winnebago campers	Winnebago tents, sleeping bags
Ivory soap	Ivory shampoo, dishwashing liquid
Woolite detergent	Woolite carpet cleaner
Jell-O gelatin	Jell-O pudding pops
Rubbermaid housewares	Rubbermaid farm food bins
Barbie dolls	Barbie games, furniture, clothes, magazines
Odor-eater foot pads	Odor-eater socks
Dr. Scholl's foot pads	Dr. Scholl's shoes, socks, wart remover
Bausch & Lomb optics	Bausch & Lomb contact lenses, shades
Minolta cameras	Minolta copiers
Honda bikes	Honda cars, lawnmowers, rototillers, generators
Fisher-Price toys	Fisher-Price playwear
Lipton tea	Lipton soup mixes

Unsuccessful Brand Extensions to New Product Categories

Jack Daniel's bourbon	Jack Daniel's charcoal briquets
Dunkin' Donuts	Dunkin' Donuts cereal
Jacuzzi baths	Jacuzzi bath toiletries
Harley Davidson bikes	Harley Davidson cigarettes
Rubbermaid housewares	Rubbermaid computer tables
Stetson hats	Stetson shirts, umbrellas
Levi jeans	Levi business wear
Certs candy	Certs gum
Mr. Coffee coffee makers	Mr. Coffee coffee

Despite the strength of the brand and access to its excellent filter distribution system, the success of Mr. Coffee's new entry was still not assured. The $2.4 billion dollar market already had very strong brand names, such as Folgers, Maxwell House, and Hills Brothers, which dominated the market (60 percent).

Often, the company name can be used as the brand name (for example, Kodak, IBM, and Xerox). The often overlooked advantage of using the company name is that product advertising has a twofold impact: it promotes the corporate image to the stock market as well as the product to customers. In this day and age, when companies are so concerned about adding shareholder value and obtaining new financing, this is an important advantage. The advertising agency Ogilvy & Mather has pointed out that if a company's strong brand images are not tied to its corporate identity (which can occur when the company name is not the brand name), then there will be a difference between the value of consumer goodwill toward the company and the way the stock market values the company.[32] A number of companies that adopted separate corporate names are now returning to original brand names to represent the company.[33] During the 1970s and 1980s, company names were general and nonlimiting. This age of

32. "Two Different Animals: Brand Awareness and Corporate Image," *Forbes,* March 6, 1989, 20.
33. "Company Names Go Back to Basics," *San Jose Mercury News,* August 30, 1991, 12D.

acquisition and diversification has passed, though, and benign names such as Allegis and Amstar no longer hold meaning for customers, particularly when the parent company has divested itself of all the businesses except the original branded product line. Now the names that held strong brand equity, such as United Airlines (Allegis) and Domino Sugar (Amstar), are being rejuvenated.

Brand Name, Logo, or Trademark Tactics

As discussed above, brands serve important communication functions and, in so doing, establish beliefs among customers about the attributes and general image of a product. After a brand has been established, the brand name, logo, and trademark serve to remind and reinforce the beliefs that have been formed. To arrive at this point, the firm must have made good on its promises. The case for a new brand, however, is different. A well-chosen brand name and a well-designed logo can give a new brand a real boost. A good brand name, trademark, or logo for a new product should have four important characteristics:

1. It should attract attention.
2. It should be memorable.
3. It should help communicate the positioning of the product.
4. It should distinguish the product from competing brands.

Brand names and logos can help form memory associations. Names that are short, pleasing, easy to pronounce, and distinctive are more memorable. Ideally, brands and logos should be symbolic of one or more of the most important product benefits. Many brand names in the supermarket describe the unique benefit of the brand (for example, NoDoze, Easy Off, Handy Wipes, Band-Aid, Weight Watchers, Spray-N-Wash, and Healthy Choice). Insurance companies use very concrete images in their logos and slogans, such as umbrellas, good hands, or solid rocks, to symbolize their intangible services and their differentiation. It is important to keep in mind that buyers choose products based on their perceptions of the benefits. A brand or logo that promotes a feature will only work if the target customer understands the link between the feature and the benefit.

Changing Logos and Repositioning an Image

From time to time, a major company's brand logo is rejuvenated. This is undertaken at no small expense, as it requires changing everything from packaging and advertising to letterhead and vehicle decals. Many argue that some logos must remain contemporary, particularly if they are to symbolize the futuristic, high-tech image of the company. That is why, for over 50 years, Ma Bell kept modernizing and, in the process, simplifying its famous logo. Other companies that want to convey a conservative, traditional image (such as law firms and stockbrokerages) maintain old-fashioned names and logos. The John Hancock Mutual Life Insurance Company for a time dropped the famous signature from its logo in an overzealous spirit of modernization. The effect on attention and symbolism was very negative. The figure on page 317 shows how the Prudential Insurance logo has changed over the years. The company has kept the "solid as a rock" symbolism but has modernized it to represent its innovative financial services. What is interesting is that Prudential decided that its logo became too modern looking, and in the late 1980s, it reverted back to a more traditional logo.

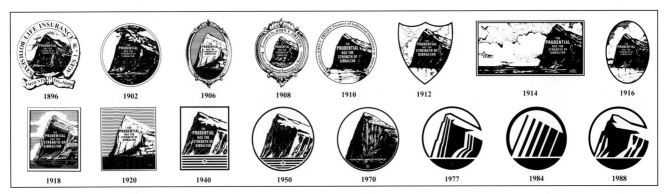

The Prudential logo has been revised many times, becoming progressively modern, until it became *too* modern.

The common law is that any good or service is automatically sold with an implied warranty of merchandisability and fitness. A product must be of merchandisable quality—that is, it will do what a reasonable person would expect it to do. An oven should cook food, an oven cleaner should clean the oven, and rubber gloves should protect hands from the oven cleaner. A product must work. The basic law is quite simple. Why then do we have warranties? There are two reasons: the first is to protect the seller and the second is to protect the customer.

Warranties: An Acid Test of Goodwill

Protecting the Seller

Some firms wash their hands of responsibility for a product's nonperformance by offering a limited warranty, or *antiwarranty*. A limited warranty is for the protection of the seller, not the consumer. The following is an example of an antiwarranty:

> Opening this software package indicates your acceptance of these [following] terms and conditions. If you do not agree with them, you should promptly return the package unopened and your money will be refunded. LIMITED WARRANTY. The program is provided "as is" without warranty of any kind, either expressed or implied, including but not limited to the implied warranties of merchandisability and fitness for a particular purpose. The entire risk as to the quality and performance of the program is with you. Should the program prove defective, you (and not Standfast Software, Inc., or any authorized Standfast computer dealer) assume the entire cost of all necessary servicing, repair, or correction.

This example, with only the name of the company disguised, was used by *Consumer Reports* to demonstrate that, when it comes to warranties, buyer beware. It also demonstrates how some manufacturers refuse to stand behind their marketing claims.[34] It is understandable for a firm to protect itself against customers who have unreasonable expectations, misuse the product, or act in bad faith. However, many warranties protect the seller against the claims of consumers who are acting in *good faith*. When this happens, it is now the seller who is acting in bad faith. For this reason, at least eight states do not allow sellers to offer such limited warranties. A company pursuing this kind of a warranty policy is also behaving irrationally in a competitive sense, because it has dropped even the pretense of serving the interests of consumers.

34. "Is That Warranty Any Good?" *Consumer Reports*, July 1984, 408–10.

Figure 9-13
An Effective Warranty

This warranty is written so that the buyer understands it, and it creates an image of product quality and customer service. It is a very effective marketing and merchandising tactic. It is also a clever production tactic, as it expresses Levi's confidence in the quality of its workmanship and, hence, sends a positive signal to its suppliers and employees. Note that this warranty is used even though Levi's is a well-established and reputable brand.

Another criticism of warranties is that they cannot be understood by most consumers. Figure 9-13 presents an exemplary Levi Strauss warranty. It is refreshingly open, honest, and generous. Who would not have confidence and trust in a seller that offers such a warranty?

Warranties As a Point of Competitive Differentiation

On the positive side, warranties like the Levi's warranty, often go well beyond protecting the consumer interest. They are used as a marketing tactic to reinforce product quality or performance claims.[35] This type of warranty strengthens a company by focusing attention on design and production process quality control that match the warranty.

35. C. L. Kendall and Frederick A. Russ, "Warranty and Complaint Policies: An Opportunity for Marketing Management," *Journal of Marketing* (April 1975), 36–43.

Rather than having a warranty constrained by engineering and production limitations, an ambitious warranty strategy acts as a spur to improve quality control and design. A significant reason for Chrysler's recovery in the early 1980s was its offer of a five-year, 50,000 mile warranty on its line of K cars and other models. At the time this was significantly and noticeably better than other manufacturers' 12-month, 12,000 mile warranties. Research has shown that an outstanding warranty has an impact on consumers, particularly for a new brand.[36]

Chrysler did more than simply offer and promote its outstanding warranty. It supported Lee Iacocca's promise to stand behind every car that his company built, and many believed that Chrysler could offer such a warranty only because it built "the best cars made in America." The connection between the warranty and quality was spelled out. The inferior warranties of competitors also implied, whether true or not, an inferior product. The Chrysler dealers also liked the warranty because the terms required maintenance and repair to be provided by an authorized dealer, which generally encouraged dealer loyalty. Chrysler's big gamble achieved two important objectives: it helped differentiate Chrysler in terms of quality and it helped its dealers combat the aggressive after-sales service competition of the emerging auto service specialists such as Sears and Firestone.

Following Through on Claims

A customer whose complaint is handled promptly and graciously can become a more vocal, loyal customer. It is therefore essential to process a warranty claim quickly and efficiently. A warranty may look good on paper and still not stand for much. All the good faith strategies in the world amount to nothing if the consumer faces an incompetent or unresponsive complaint-handling process. This is because the consumer will interpret the nonperformance as obstructionist or antagonistic to his or her grievance. The consumer may then end up angrier than if the promised warranty had never been offered.[37]

The keys to implementation are accessibility to a sympathetic ear—not a questioning or even adversarial customer service representative—and a speedy response. An 800 number connecting users to a person trained to receive warranty claims provides the accessibility and speed of response. A problem can often be defused by a sympathetic, knowledgeable, and diplomatic customer complaints manager with the authority to rectify problems. A good customer service manager often has to recognize (but does not point out) that customers often do not read the instructions, and that *product* nonperformance is often actually due to *user* nonperformance. Tracking such complaints may further reveal a problem with the product design or the readability and clarity of instruction manuals.

Packaging: Much More Than Protecting

Each year, companies spend more on packaging than on advertising. As markets have matured and competitive differentiation narrowed, packaging has become a very important component of marketing strategy. Sometimes a firm forgets that it is the packaged product, and not the product alone, that is sold and purchased. A product's packaging is often also its most distinctive marketing effort. This is not just because most

36. Geoffrey Heal, "Guarantees and Risk Sharing," *Review of Economic Studies* 44 (1977), 549–60; and Rao Unnava, "The Effect of Warranties on Strong Brand Names and Unknown Brand Names" (Working Paper, Columbus, OH: Ohio State University).
37. William O. Bearden and Jesse E. Teel, "Selected Determinants of Consumer Satisfaction and Complaint Reports," *Journal of Marketing Research* 20 (February 1983), 21–28.

consumer decisions are made at the point of purchase. The package often makes product usage easier and therefore adds to the value of the product (for instance, opening and resealing, pouring, mixing, processing, and cooking may all be enhanced or made easier by creative packaging). A package also continues to communicate on the kitchen shelf, workshop bench, and, most importantly, during product use. This explains why instructions on the package are very important.

Instructions and Better Performance

Caring about the customer includes paying attention to details. Providing easy-to-understand instructions is such a detail. Instructions make for a more informed and skilled user. A more informed and skilled user gets the very best performance out of a product. In this way, carefully presented and written instructions lift the performance and, hence, the quality of a product. If poor package instructions lead to misuse and less than optimum performance, then no matter how superior its ingredients or material composition, the perception of a product's quality (and not the user) will suffer. Consequently, making a few simple improvements to usage instructions probably offers more potential return on investment than any other marketing activity. The very success or failure of a new product may turn on the clarity and quality of its usage and care instructions. To not recognize this fact is a major tactical blunder.

Packaging and Classical Conditioning

The most powerful example of classic conditioning occurs when the consumer's satisfaction with a product is transferred to its package. The next time that consumer visits a retailer or looks at a catalog, he or she will respond to that package, including its design features and shape, more positively. And each satisfactory use reinforces the learning. Consequently, the package must be distinctive, and not just to attract initial attention. It acts as a distinct after-trial cue—the package is liked because the contents are liked.

Performing in Transit

A package must perform in several different situations: in the manufacturer's warehouse, during shipment to the wholesaler and retailer, in the reseller's warehouse, on the display shelf, during customer use, in the user's storage, and during reuse or disposal. Competitive advantage can come from superior performance at any one or more of these stages, and poor performance at any of these stages can be fatal. Consequently, each of these situations needs to be studied before a package is designed.

Cubic efficiency is a term that describes how efficiently a package occupies storage, transportation, and display space. Boxes are more cubic efficient than cans and cans are more efficient than most bottles. When shipping and storage space are expensive, the cubic efficiency of the package can become very important. New shipping and warehouse handling technology may also require standard package dimensions that neatly fit into a container and product code information on the package that keeps track of inventory in transit and in storage.

Performing at the Point of Purchase

A package may also have to be designed to fit a unique display location. For example, if a product is an impulse purchase item to be displayed at the checkout counter, then its packaging must be compact and fit the standardized display racks; otherwise the retailer will not display it. The classic case of an eye-catching display was the L'Eggs point-of-purchase stand with its hundreds of plastic eggs in different colors. More recently, DIM, a French hosiery manufacturer (and subsidiary of the BIC Company), took the fashion hosiery market by storm with its patterned, silky textured stockings that were displayed in a patented package with a hole through which a swatch of the stocking protruded. The package allowed the shopper to not just see, but feel "la difference."

Display packaging should reinforce the positioning of the product, but sometimes this does not happen. Johnson Wax, in one of its few false marketing moves, launched Clean and Clear (a cleaner) in an opaque bottle. The packaging confused both retailers and consumers, leading some to believe it was a polish. The bottle should have been sparkling clear. Cans or plastic or cardboard packages may be less expensive and easier to handle, but packaging industry research has shown that for some beverages and foods, a glass bottle or jar can significantly enhance the quality image of the brand.

Packaging to Enhance Usage

Just as distributors, retailers, and other channel intermediaries realize value from product packaging, the consumer can realize value from product packaging in the usage situation. If, for example, frequent users of eyedrops carry the product in their pockets or purses, then the consumer will receive value if the package is small and easy to open (perhaps with one hand). If jam manufacturers want their product to move from the refrigerator to the breakfast table more often, then the container should be made attractive enough to take its place on the breakfast table. When a product is transferred from its original package into a more attractive or convenient-to-use container, then much of the point-of-usage behavioral conditioning will be lost.

Several very innovative packages have added real convenience to product use. For example, when Beech-Nut apple juice switched from cans to bottles (onto which plastic nipples for babies could be attached), sales quadrupled. The taste improved as well. Minnetonka, Inc., was the first to introduce the soap and toothpaste pump dispensers to the U.S. market. Colgate-Palmolive, Lever Brothers, and Procter & Gamble all followed, concerned more about losing market share to each other than to the original packaging innovator, Minnetonka. Chesebrough-Ponds put nail polish in a special type of felt-tipped pen. The new convenience packaging helped increase the company's nail-polish sales by over 20 percent, and demand for the new product was twice what was initially forecast.

Even disposal can become a dominant concern. A package that is biodegradable will appeal to environmentally concerned market segments and, in fact, may be mandated by future public policy. Once upon a time, foods were sold in glass jars that could be reused by the homemaker. Today, very few packaged goods marketers in the United States seek to add value by providing a package that has a life beyond its ingredients.

Labels: A Further Test of Customer Orientation

Whether or not a company is really customer oriented can often be determined by an examination of its product's label. If the label appears to be an afterthought, with the bare minimum information (that is, it contains only what is legally required), then the conclusion is obvious. On the other hand, a customer-oriented label is likely to serve the following functions:

1. Identify the manufacturer, country of origin, and ingredients or materials comprising the product.
2. Report the expiration date and the contents' grading based on a prescribed government standard (as appears on cartons of eggs).

3. Explain how to use the product.
4. Warn about potential misuse.
5. Provide easy-to-understand care instructions.
6. Serve as an important communications link between the user, eventual buyers, and the company.

A quality label signals a quality product. Often the label must also be designed for the market segment. For example, the elderly need labels with large lettering. Furthermore, because many customers toss instructions and packaging away, the only way a customer can reach a manufacturer is through the information provided on the label. This suggests that a customer service–oriented company should always place its 800 service number on its labels.

Designing and Marketing Competitive Services

In the preceding sections, we have sometimes referred to services as products. While the various concepts discussed are applicable to services as well as to tangible products, it is also necessary to make note of the unique nature of services and the service components of product offerings and to discuss how this uniqueness must be managed.

A great deal has been written about the shift in the U.S. economy away from traditional manufacturing and toward services. Services such as education, medical care, entertainment, financial advice, and legal consultation have always been important, but recently they have grown in demand. Information processing and communications services have also greatly expanded in the last two decades. The marketing of services has come under the spotlight, not just because services have grown, but also because many Americans believe that the service they get from many manufacturers and retailers is not satisfactory.[38] A further concern is that productivity in the service sector increased very little during the 1980s.

The Unique Problems of Service Management

A service is *intangible,* which means that a consumer cannot see, touch, and feel a service before purchase, making it harder for a sales representative to sell the quality aspects of a service. Intangibility causes customers to have nothing concrete to evaluate—they must trust the provider's word that the service was done as well as it could be done for the money the customer paid. In addition, if the customer has little idea of how a service is performed or what cost they would incur if they attempted to do the service for themselves, very often they will undervalue the service. For these reasons, a service's brand image, reputation, and equity are particularly important in selling a service and introducing new services. Because of their intangible natures, services try to choose brand names and logos that are rich in tangible imagery (for example, the Prudential rock). The appearance of the service provider, such as grooming and uniform, are also important tangible signals of service image and a very important component of service management because a service is more *personal* than a product.

A service company also must strive to employ people-oriented staff members to undertake its services. Employees who like helping other people are ideal service providers because their interest in serving others is a fundamental feature of their

38. Jeffrey A. Trachtenberg, "Shake, Rattle and Clonk," *Forbes,* July 14, 1986, 71–74; Stephen Koepp, "Pul-eeze! Will Somebody Help Me?" *Time,* February 2, 1987, 48–57; and "Making Service a Potent Marketing Tool," *Business Week,* June 11, 1984, 164–70.

characters. What they say and do conveys their genuine caring and concern. People-oriented employees will go the extra mile, they will innovate and adapt the service to the unique needs of the customer. This is important, because a service must be designed to meet the needs of the customer even more than a product must. A service varies more in its execution than a product does in its manufacturing. It is a little easier to excuse a product for not exactly doing what you want or expect. The product does not know any better and cannot change its form or function. It is much more difficult to excuse a service provider who is not being responsive. There is no point in asking a product why it is not meeting your needs, but such a question is often directly or indirectly raised with a service provider. An unsatisfactory response is both embarrassing and unprofitable. It requires excuses and rationalizations. What it reveals is either the incompetence of the service provider or the crass economic motivation of the exchange. A product will never say "lady, you got what you paid for."

While intangibility makes a service harder to sell, it makes it easier to introduce new services by simply varying the nature of the service, changing the service production routine, and retraining the service provider. However, if overdone, this practice can lead to a proliferation of new services that ultimately confuses the customer and hurts a service firm's positioning (for example, in 1985 British Rail created so many new types of tickets [travel services] that it ended up confusing its consumers.)[39] It also places tremendous stresses on operations and delivery, so much so that the quality of all services can suffer. Establishing the cost of a new service is also more difficult than establishing the cost of a new product because so many costs are shared with old services (for example, they share the same human delivery system). Consequently, a service firm has to study carefully the image and operational implications of a new service.

Services are also consumed at the same time they are produced. This *simultaneity* allows a service company to increase customer satisfaction by uniquely tailoring the service to the needs of a specific customer. The problem with such special service is that it creates tremendous quality control and cost control problems for the operations managers in a service company. If a service is not standardized, then standards are difficult to set and conformance is hard to control. It seems that operations managers play an even more important role in designing new services than they do in designing new products because they are often in closer contact with the customer than are marketing managers (via their operational field forces), they know the mechanics of how a service is delivered, and they can determine whether the existing field force can deliver such a service. With services, QFD involves engineering of human behavior. In the benefits × features of the QFD matrix for a service, engineering design features are replaced with specific activities undertaken by the service provider.

Operations management has to break down a service into a sequence of activities, each of which contributes, in a different way, to a different component of customer satisfaction. Just as mechanical engineers understand the mechanics of a product, service operations managers understand the mechanics of a delivered service. But unlike mechanical engineers, they are closer to their customers ("manufacturing" occurs in the presence of the customer); therefore service operations managers have a better first-hand, intuitive understanding of the link between service features, consumer benefits sought, and consumer satisfaction. Thus, operations people often exercise more influence in new service management than they do in new product management. Some experts have gone so far as to suggest that service companies should cut back their

---

39. Christopher J. Easingwood, "New Product Development for Service Companies," *Journal of Product Innovation Management* 4 (1986), 264–75. Much of this section is based on the insights gained from this excellent article.

marketing departments and boost the size of their front-line operational team so that it can manage the new service.[40] In fact, many service companies have a separate department, a permanent cross-functional team made up of marketing and operation's top guns, that develops and manages new services.[41]

Test marketing also requires that the field force execute the new service activity sequence within the desired quality and cost standards. These tests often are low key and involve exploratory, on-the-job refinements of the service. A final important difference between service and product marketing is that the service provider is the best marketer for a service company. A product can use its packaging as a sales aid. A service company's service providers are often its packaging, its product, and its sales force combined in one. Thus, a service company depends a great deal on its service providers. Service quality is also notoriously difficult to control because service organizations involve people and not machines. The quality performance tolerances of a machine can be much more readily monitored, adjusted, and maintained.

Service providers differ in the degree to which a service is customized for each client. At one end of the spectrum are professional services such as legal or management consulting firms that are highly adapted to the client's individual circumstances. At the other end are services that are mostly routinized, such as dry cleaning or mass transit. The distinction between customization and routinization is an important one. In customized services, the importance of people is emphasized. People providing the service should have strong training, be adaptable, and be thoroughly competent in the area of their expertise. Routinization can be used for some aspects of customized service, such as billing, but these aspects are not the primary focus of the service. Routinized services, on the other hand, depend on well-designed systems and activity sequences that deliver the principal service. The service systems and scripts should be designed to perform the required tasks with efficiency and speed. Employees should be well trained to perform routine tasks efficiently. Equally important, they should also be trained to handle exceptions, problems, or breakdowns in the service system and script.

Product and Service Issues in Global Markets

Over the past twenty years, many U.S firms have come to rely more and more on foreign markets for a sizable portion of their revenues. When it considers a particular foreign market, a company must decide how much to adapt its product to the new market. In "The Globalization of Markets," Theodore Levitt says that basic needs are the same or very similar from country to country.[42] Accordingly, he suggests that little or no adaptation need be made for many products. This contention has raised considerable disagreement.[43] It is argued that cultures differ so much from country to country that a "one size fits all" product will tend to lose out to offerings that are more tailored to individual needs. It is also hard for a firm to argue for global standardization when it allows regions of its domestic U.S. market to offer specialized products, advertising campaigns, and promotions. In either case, the product manager considering the

40. Christian Gronroos, "Innovative Marketing Strategies and Organization Structure for Service Firms," in Leonard L. Berry, G. Lynn Shostack, and Gregory D. Upah, eds., *Emerging Perspectives on Services Marketing* (Chicago: American Marketing Association, 1983).
41. Easingwood, "New Product Development," 270.
42. Theodore Levitt, "The Globalization of Markets," *Harvard Business Review,* May/June 1983, 92–102.
43. For a discussion of standardized versus targeted global products, see Sak Onkvisit and John J. Shaw, *International Marketing: Analysis and Strategy* (Columbus, OH: Merrill, 1989); and Sak Onkvisit, and John J. Shaw, forthcoming, "Standardization versus Localization: The Need for the Compromising Perspective."

move into a foreign market must evaluate local needs, preferences, and buying behavior (as well as channel requirements, competition, and the regulatory environment) before deciding how much to customize the product.

At the same time that U.S. companies have expanded their operations in foreign markets, companies competing in the domestic market have discovered that the U.S. market attracts a lot of foreign competition. In light of this trend, even companies that compete only domestically must pay attention to competitive trends in other countries. Many global companies launch products in their home markets first (for example, the Volkswagen Golf was first launched in Germany and then was exported to the United States as the Rabbit). After gaining domestic experience, they launch the product in attractive foreign markets, particularly the United States. Consequently, a company that watches foreign markets for developments in their product categories can anticipate that these innovations will soon appear in the U.S. market. The solution is to become globally vigilant and to imitate overseas innovations *before* they reach the U.S. market. American companies must also rid themselves of their complacency, which is based on the belief that Japanese and other foreign competitors are able to imitate, but American firms are way ahead when it comes to real innovations. According to the National Science Foundation, in the early 1980s, new U.S. patents were more likely to refer to prior patents issued to Japanese inventors than they were to refer to patents issued to U.S. citizens.[44] American companies now seem to be behind in *both* innovation and imitation and need to improve their new product development management accordingly.

The issue of global branding was discussed somewhat in Chapter 8. A cross-cultural reality is that sometimes a global brand name cannot be used because the name (or a very similar name) is already owned by another company in the foreign market, or because the name loses its positive image in the translation to a different language. This explains why Pert Plus, P&G's blockbuster shampoo in the United States, is Vidal Sassoon in the United Kingdom and Rejoy in Japan. When facing such a situation, the marketer needs to examine the perceptual and belief framework of target customers in the foreign country before an appropriate customized brand name is chosen.

Packaging and labeling issues are similar for domestic and international trade. Just as packaging within the United States must be functional and communicative, packaging for international markets must do the same. However, cultural, logistical, and regulatory differences result in packaging requirements that differ. In developing countries, for instance, packaging that can be reused by the customer is often preferred to disposable packaging.[45] Legal requirements may necessitate that packaging be of a specified material or meet certain size specifications. In addition, labeling may be mandated to have multilingual translations, specify contents or ingredients, or provide certain warnings. Regulations on packaging and labeling may also be promulgated in order to erect barriers to foreign-produced products.

International services have the same unique characteristics of all services. When marketing services internationally, though, the special problems of services become even greater. It is more difficult for providers to establish trust with their clients due to distance and cultural differences. The chances for the quality of service to vary become greater when foreign nationals—with different customs and training—are hired by an international service provider. Finally, making aspects of the service more tangible becomes difficult because the tangible cues may be interpreted differently across cultures.

44. Neil Gross, "Back to Basics," *Business Week,* special issue on Innovation, 1989, 30.
45. Sak Onkvisit and John J. Shaw, *International Marketing: Analysis and Strategy* (Columbus, OH: Merrill, 1989), 490.

Finally, international marketers will face differences in regulations that affect their products beyond packaging and labeling. For example, individual countries may impose "domestic content" requirements on some products. In another example, ISO 9000 guidelines for quality management in products—published by the Swiss Organization for Standardization (ISO) in 1979—are being adopted by the European Community as it moves toward unification.[46] Products imported or manufactured in the EC will have to be certified as meeting these standards, which may prove difficult for many foreign manufacturers. EC unification also involves new standards for product design in many product categories. This may make it easier for importers in the long run, but may cause some trauma in the short term as product designs must be altered. Clearly, international marketers must do their homework before entering a new foreign market. In many cases, the marketer can do this by forming a joint venture with a company in the target country.

Discussion Questions and Minicases

1. Use the theory of competitive rationality to predict what will happen as CAD/CAM software improves.

2. The development and launch of Acuvue disposable contact lenses is a good example of what can be accomplished by a small, autonomous organizational unit. Prior to 1987, Johnson & Johnson's small Vistakon unit had concentrated on the market for contact lenses for patients with astigmatism. In 1988, Vistakon began marketing disposable contact lenses developed from technology that had been acquired in 1983 by Johnson & Johnson. Vistakon's sales have grown from $20 million in 1987 to $225 million in 1991. Much of the success of the venture would seem to stem from the autonomy that Johnson & Johnson gives its business units. Vistakon was not hindered by a lengthy and bureaucratic approval process. Consequently, Acuvue came out six months before major competitors, such as Bausch & Lomb, Inc. or Ciba-Geigy Corp., could respond.

   a. Acuvue lenses cost the consumer about $500 per year, considerably higher than the cost of other kinds of lenses. How is it that Vistakon can charge so much, particularly during the mature stage of the product life cycle?

   b. What suggestions would you have for Vistakon to continue its high level of performance into the future?

3. One way to extend the life cycle of a product is to find alternative uses for it. This is exactly what Vector Group has done with an unlikely product—Soviet missiles. In 1990, Vector approached the then Soviet Union's military to open talks about buying old Soviet missiles that had been obviated by the easing of tensions between the superpowers. After two years, Vector has closed a deal with the Russian Defense Ministry for 150 advanced submarine launched missiles. The new use for the missiles is simple—target practice. After removing the warheads, Vector will resell the missiles to the U.S. Navy. The Russian missiles are less expensive than target missiles produced in the United States. What suggestions would you have for Vector concerning its future operations in this market?

4. Several companies are looking ahead to the next wave of personal computers, called personal information managers. Apple has even announced its first such offering—Newton. Suppose you were a marketing manager for one of these com-

46. Kerry Pechter, "In Europe's Epicenter..." *International Business* 5, no. 8 (August, 1992) 46.

panies and you wanted to do a quality function deployment analysis for this new technology.

Discuss the problems you would encounter in doing such a QFD analysis this early in the life cycle for the PIM. How might you do a preliminary QFD analysis that would help you specify a product without getting bogged down in the problems you mentioned in the first part of your response?

5. The design for the Goodyear Aquatred tire is unique and effective. The tread design carries water away from the center of the tire so that better traction is maintained. This benefit is actually communicated in part by the tire itself—the tread design makes it very clear what the tire will do. The tire also is made out of a special compound that lasts longer. This allows Goodyear to offer a 60,000 mile warranty. The tire is priced about double the average price of other tires. Even so, sales for the tire have been high and the product introduction is a success.

    a. The impetus for this design came from Goodyear's advertising manager who returned from a trade show in 1989 lamenting that tires had become boring. The company then began an effort to create something that was exciting. One would generally not expect a successful new product in such a utilitarian industry to come from a development goal of creating an "exciting" product. Why do you think this product was so successful?

    b. One of the interesting aspects of this tire design is that the tread design itself enhances the communication of the benefits. What might a company do in its development efforts to incorporate communications elements into its product designs?

6. Increasing customer satisfaction with the photos taken by the basic lens-shutter camera (the poor cousin of the single-lens reflex camera) involved analyzing some 18,000 photos taken by such cameras and identifying why about one in 12 were not very good.[47] The reasons were fairly evident: 1) poor focus adjustment, 2) not enough light, 3) camera not set to the correct film speed, and 4) double exposures because the film was not wound forward. How do you think the design was changed to improve the lens-shutter camera?

7. What do you think are the specific ingredient characteristics and specific process characteristics that create great-tasting coffee?

8. The Autotest service plan does not present a benefit × activities QFD matrix for the proposed service. Please develop such a matrix. In doing so, think of all of the activities that Autotest might provide to assist the target market in buying a used car.

9. McDonald's Corp. has been investigating the possibility of adding new offerings to its menu. One of these is pizza.[48]

    a. Why would McDonald's want to try offering such items as pizza?

    b. What problems does McDonald's have in its efforts to extend its branded product line to include pizza?

    c. What do you think McDonald's should do to address these problems? What has it done so far? Explain your reasoning.

10. Suppose you are the product line manager for Weight Watchers frozen dinners. Your dinners are low calorie, "diet" meals. A newcomer to the frozen-food category, "Healthy Choice" from ConAgra, introduces a line of new products that offer not

47. Kenichi Ohmae, *The Borderless World* (New York: Harper Business, 1990).
48. "McRisky," *Business Week,* October 21, 1991, 114–22.

only reduced calories, but reduced sodium and cholesterol, as well. ConAgra's product introduction is a success, immediately taking a sizable portion of the market. What might you do to respond? What are the advantages and disadvantages of each of the following?

a. Introducing a Weight Watchers brand extension that has even better health characteristics than Healthy Choice?

b. Introducing a new brand of products intended to go head-to-head with Healthy Choice?

c. Increasing marketing expenditures for such factors as coupons and advertising?

11. Mips Computers, Inc., has an unusual approach to marketing its chips and computers. Mips is a premier designer and licenser of microprocessors based on RISC technology. RISC, or reduced instruction set computing, is a type of processor that performs calculations at least as fast as CISC (complex instruction set computing) processors and at a lower cost. RISC chips are being used in workstations, whereas personal computers—lower performance machines—primarily use CISC chips. While RISC has advantages over CISC, relatively little software (though a growing amount) is yet designed to run on RISC technology. Mips also incorporates its RISC chips into systems that it sells to OEMs (original equipment manufacturers) such as Digital Equipment, Prime, and Silicon Graphics.

The strange thing about Mips' marketing strategy is that the equipment manufacturers that Mips sells to are its *competitors* in the computer market. On the surface, it appears that Mips is competing against itself.

a. Why do you think Mips does this?

b. Why do you think Mips can do this without causing serious conflict with its OEM customers? What does Mips have to do to keep from causing such conflict?

c. Should Mips consider branding its systems products and selling them directly to businesses who buy workstations? Why or why not?

12. In 1991, Levi Strauss & Co. decided that too many counterfeit pairs of its 501 jeans were appearing, particularly in Eastern Europe. Cheap jeans of variable quality, not manufactured or licensed by Levi Strauss, were being sold with the Levi's logo. Obviously, this situation is intolerable. Levi's is an established brand name with an established quality image. Too many counterfeit jeans could undermine that quality image. A second problem is, of course, the loss of potential sales.

a. Should Levi Strauss be concerned about the deterioration of its image? Could it not it be argued that if buyers recognize that there is a difference between the fake jeans and the real thing, then Levi's quality image will be reinforced—not undermined?

b. One might argue that there are two market segments being addressed. A cost conscious market segment will buy the fake Levi's and a quality conscious market segment would purchase the real Levi's at a premium price. In this case, wouldn't the loss of sales actually be negligible?

c. What might Levi Strauss do to address the problem?

13. Bruce McLaren, a New Zealander, founded the McLaren racing team that won eight Formula One world championships during the 1980s. The company has been heavily financed by corporate sponsorships, but the McLaren brand name has not been used on other product or service extensions. Suggest some licensing opportunities and explain why.

14. Comment on the strengths and weaknesses of the logo for a luxury woolen mattress pad.

15. Why are warranties less often used in business-to-business selling and advertising? Does it mean they are less important?

16. Ford effectively responded to Chrysler's extended warranty by extending its warranties to 70,000 miles and seven years. What did this have to do with its campaign, "Ford, where quality is number 1"? Why did the Japanese manufacturers not extend their warranties beyond 12,000 miles and 12 months?

17. What does a service contract signal to the buyer of an appliance?

18. "We are social animals who live in families and communities. We work together, play together, and sleep together. We willingly give ourselves to those whom we love. Unselfish service to others is one of the greatest human virtues, almost deified in heroes and heroines." Does this statement describe a characteristic common to almost all religions and cultures? Many humans derive great satisfaction out of giving to other people, but what does this have to do with services marketing?

19. TRM Copy Centers Corp. of Portland, Oregon, runs a service for small retailers. TRM installs copiers in the store for $95 and then provides repairs and supplies. Customers make their own copies for 5 cents per page. The retailer keeps about one fourth of the proceeds.

    TRM makes this business profitable by centralizing and standardizing. Supplies and repairs are centrally dispatched from one location in each of the 34 cities where TRM operates. The copiers are secondhand, so their cost is low. They only come in two models, so their repair service is inexpensive. Of course, TRM buys supplies in bulk, so it controls this cost as well.

    a. What is it about TRM's service that makes it attractive to the retailer? The retailer can always purchase or lease its own machine and keep all the proceeds from copy sales without giving up 75 percent of the revenue. Discuss this in terms of how TRM overcomes the traditional problems of service providers.

    b. What problems might TRM encounter as it expands? How would you address these problems?

20. Retail giant Sears Roebuck has had difficult times of late. Competition and changing consumer behavior put Sears in a position of needing drastic changes. In the late 1980s, Sears changed its merchandising slogan to "everyday low prices." In the early 1990s, Sears concentrated on cutting costs and improving its bottom line.

    In 1992, Sears' efforts reaped unwanted results. The Consumer Affairs Department of the state of California brought charges against Sears for fraudulent activity in its auto repair business.[49] In the course of a year-long investigation, Sears was

---

49. Kevin Kelly and Eric Schine, "How Did Sears Blow This Gasket?" *Business Week,* June 29, 1992, 38.

caught systematically performing unnecessary repairs. Sears made reparations and took actions to correct the organizational incentives that brought on the problems.

Even with Sears' quick action to fix the problem, it suffered a loss of sales. What do you think will be the long-term effect on Sears' service businesses? Is this service snafu likely to affect Sears' other business? Please explain.

21. In the early 1990s, Apple Computer Inc.'s efforts in overseas markets included a targeted approach to Japan.[50] Apple contracted with several Japanese companies to sell Macintosh computers to both consumer and business customers in Japan. From a product strategy standpoint, Apple initiated agreements with Japanese companies to manufacture current or future Apple products: Sony Corp. manufactured Powerbook 100s (the smallest Apple laptop computer); Sharp agreed to make Apple's Newton, the palmtop "personal information manger"; and it was anticipated that Toshiba would make a Macintosh-based multimedia product that combined computing, video, text, and sound. The overall effort was aimed at getting Apple software into multiple products offered in Japan. Macintosh sales in Japan lagged sales elsewhere in the world prior to 1990. Apple's strategy for the future, though, seems to view Japan as a leading market, with rollout efforts of products to originate in Japan and the United States.
   a. Why would such a shift in Apple's global product strategy be attractive? What would Apple hope to accomplish with such a strategy?
   b. What risks does Apple face in following such a strategy? How might these risks be mitigated?

22. Intel, the leading manufacturer of microprocessors, based in Santa Clara, California, faced increasingly tough competition in the early 1990s.[51] Other semiconductor companies began offering their own versions of Intel's 80386 microprocessor, either by winning court cases (for example, Advanced Micro Devices) or by designing "clone" 386 chips that do not violate Intel's patents (such as those designed by Cyrix Corp. and Chips and Technologies, Inc.). Apple and IBM united in a joint venture to develop their own version of a microprocessor (to be manufactured by Motorola) to handle future multimedia processing requirements. Also, RISC (reduced instruction set computing) microprocessor manufacturers, which make the chips that drive higher-end workstations, were increasingly eyeing the upper end of the personal computer market.

In response to this competition, Intel took a number of measures. On one front, the company continued to fight the patent cases in court. Internally, it revamped its product development and marketing strategies.

On the product development side, Intel began to introduce products in half the time it had taken prior to these developments. Instead of beginning work on the 686 microprocessor when the 586 was introduced—a process that took about four years—Intel began work on the 686 two years into the development cycle of the 586. Thus, it hopes to introduce the 686 only two years after the 586. As the chips, and hence the development process, become more complex, new ways must be found to speed the process, even just to keep the process under four years in duration. Toward this end, Intel has instituted more concurrent engineering, computer-aided engineering, and prototype simulation.

Perhaps the biggest cultural change for Intel's development process is a new approach to accommodating customers. Instead of providing computer manufac-

50. Neil Gross and Kathy Rebello, "Apple? Japan Can't Say No," *Business Week,* June 29, 1992, 32–33.
51. *Business Week,* June 1, 1992, 86–94.

turers with chip specifications only near the end of the development cycle, Intel began seeking customer input from the very beginning of the process. Early on, with the help of new simulation technology, Intel was able to offer computer manufacturers virtual prototypes that they could use in planning new computer designs.

a. Discuss how Intel's change in product development gave it new competitive leverage. What threats will Intel have to watch for in its competitive efforts in the future?

In addition to changing the customer focus of the product development process, Intel also changed its branding strategy. In the past, Intel had focused on building brand equity among computer manufacturers and resellers. In 1992, Intel began advertising directly to consumers through television and print. Its "Intel Inside" campaign for 486 processors was the first major effort of a component manufacturer to build equity at the end-user level.

b. Why would Intel do this? What problems could potentially torpedo this effort? Student exercise: Read the business periodicals to find out what has happened to Intel's effort to build brand equity among end-users. Where do you think Intel and its competitors will be heading in the future?

23. April 2, 1993, will forever be known in the history of marketing management as "Marlboro Friday." This was the day that Philip Morris slashed prices on its leading brand of cigarettes. In one day investors reacted by wiping $13.4 billion off the stock market value of the company and many further billions off the value of major brand companies such as RJR, P&G, Quaker Oats, Coca-Cola, PepsiCo and Gillette.

But the writing was on the wall even at the time of the huge takeovers of the late 1980s when the consumer brand companies were purchased for hugely inflated prices (described in the chapter). The heavy use of price promotions undermined the brand equity by encouraging shoppers to buy on price (see Chapter 13). Retailers were also investing heavily in their own private labels that imitated the latest innovations. For example, Totes, Inc., launched its slipper socks in 1988 and sales of the socks peaked at 14 million a year, over 10 percent of which were made by Wal-Mart and Kmart alone. Within two years Wal-Mart and Kmart had found suppliers to make their own brand of slipper socks and their knockoffs were sold at a price 25 percent below Totes, which were dropped by the giant discounters. Several recent market research studies have shown that fewer consumers are shopping for a particular brand. More shoppers perceive little difference between products (perceived product parity), and the combined market share of the top three brands in many food retailing product categories has dropped. What should the senior executives of major consumer goods companies do to rebuild their brand equity and the market value of their stock? What do the above events tell you about the rationality of the stock market?[52]

52. The above facts were drawn from "Shoot Out at the Check-out," *The Economist,* June 5, 1993, 69–72; and, Zachary Ziller and Wendy Zellner, "Clout!" *Business Week,* December 21, 1992, 66–73.

Managing Distribution

"Prosperity makes friends, adversity tries them."

Maxim, Publilus Syrus

"Friendship is an arrangement by which we undertake to exchange small favors for big ones."

Baron de Montesquieu

*F*or many manufacturers and suppliers, the fight for survival and profits increasingly depends on the choice of distribution channels, channel relations, and the implementation of channel tactics. This chapter discusses each of these issues as components of the marketing plan's distribution tactics. The problems in channel management today are not trivial. In their attempts to become more competitive in their own markets, business buyers are exercising increasing power over suppliers and wholesale distributors. Firms are pushing inventory-carrying risk up the channel, and demanding much better service by instituting just-in-time delivery and quick response work-flow processes. Retailers are demanding more allowances, not passing on price discounts meant for the consumer, and often buying new products only on consignment (that is, they pay for it some time after they sell it; otherwise they return it). Many retailers are actively developing their own exclusive brand names and using established brands to sell off their own brands.

In many markets, resellers are being squeezed out, or into new shapes, by competitive pressures both up and down the channel. On top of all this is the globalization of supply sources. The U.S. domestic market is the demand vortex for the rest of the world. In the global trade war that has replaced the cold war, everyone wants to sell to America. American manufacturers and retailers have no alternative but to seek out the highest quality, lowest cost sources of supply from around the world. If they do not, then competition will find such off-shore sources and reap the competitive advantage. It would be competitively irrational for them to do otherwise.

In the first section of this chapter we discuss the choice of channel structure. This is a long-term strategic decision that involves the building of significant trading relationships. The rest of the chapter explores tactics that can be used to manage channel relationships. The concepts discussed in this chapter refer to a generic "reseller." Resellers can be wholesalers, retailers, industrial distributors, industrial dealers, or other channel intermediaries. The concepts are general enough to apply to all sorts of resellers, even though the resellers' circumstances are vastly different. Keep the following key ideas in mind as you read this chapter:

■ Trading channels often have traditional practices, margins, and routines that are hard to change. A company uses its competitive skill to innovate by finding a way of changing these practices to its own advantage.

■ The competitiveness and success of a distribution system depends on the fit between a retailer's positioning and consumer franchise and a product's positioning and target market. This unique trading fit between the seller and the reseller is hard for competitors to imitate.

■ Trading relationships are often destroyed by one party's greed and the diffusion of the relationship's innovative competitive advantage. Vertical integration or long-term trading contracts are ways of reducing such economic treachery.

■ Resellers are managed through the creative use of incentives and the extensive sharing of information.

■ Managing multiple channels requires adherence to well-defined performance targets that are consistent across the various channels. Channel members should feel that they are being treated equitably. To the extent possible, the target market segments addressed by each channel should be kept separate so that the channels are not competing against each other.

■ The logistics of inventory carrying, transportation, and order processing have to be managed together in creative ways that result in improved customer service and reduced costs. Distribution logistics are an important source of competitive advantage.

- Terminals and software can link suppliers and customers in ways that speed order processing, which greatly reduces inventory carrying costs and provides many other added-value services. Better information simplifies distribution.

- Retailers and distributors are not simply concerned with price margins. They often care more about how quickly the product will sell and the quality of the merchandising program.

Channel Cultures and Conventional Practices

One reason why many firms do not continually analyze their channels and change their distribution management is that a channel culture tends to develop over time. In many product-markets, the channel strategy seems very straightforward because trading channel tradition and customer expectations prescribe it. Managers come to view their existing distribution system and practices as a given that they will not even think of changing, thus presenting the classic opportunity for the innovator. Such market cultural norms are likely to have developed over several decades or, in some trading channels, over hundreds of years. Very often this tradition makes a lot of sense, reflecting a supplier-reseller fit that has developed and strengthened over time. It has produced functional specialization and reflects the cooperation, trust, and bonding that has evolved to fit the economic, political, and social environment. The buyers and sellers in traditional channels have learned, from mentors and on the job, to understand the strengths and weaknesses of the companies with whom they customarily deal. Over the years, a fabric of professional and personal relationships is woven that maintains the channel relationships and customs.

Trading channel culture and norms are continually evolving, being enriched with new legends and rituals. A lack of appreciation of the channel's customs and legends is often what experienced salespeople are talking about when they refer to new graduates as being wet behind the ears when it comes to the real world. Personal bonds and interpersonal behaviors are developed and reinforced by sales successes. This results in customary interaction patterns, selling protocols, order processing, duties, roles, margins, and payment terms. Each channel of distribution has its own subcultural norms, etiquettes, practices, and agreed terms for the exchange of favors, all of which set prior behavior-outcome expectations. They provide some predictability, which give the participants a sense of control and make channel relationships manageable. Distribution management must recognize these realities. However, an entrepreneurial approach to distribution begins with the recognition that competitive advantage and profits come from questioning and changing conventional distribution practices. The manager should constantly be seeking ways to more effectively and efficiently distribute the firm's product and services, including finding completely new channels.

The barriers to mobility in distribution are often greater than the barriers to mobility in production. Alternative channels are often occupied, if not choked, by competitors. The building of trust and goodwill in a new channel relationship can be a slow process, particularly if a firm is coming off a well-publicized falling out with a previous reseller. Consumers may also be slow to respond and switch their purchasing behavior, and aggrieved parties (for example, ex-distributors) can create a great deal of bad will. In fact, it is often easier to scrap and replace obsolete production equipment and plants

The Choice of Channel Relationships: Achieving a Supplier-Reseller Fit

than to scrap obsolete channels. Consequently, a great deal of very careful thought must be given to the choice of a distribution channel.

Accordingly, when choosing *overall channels* of distribution (before choosing specific resellers), a supplier should keep the following in mind:

1. Choose or construct a channel configuration that reaches the right target customers.

2. The channel should be able and willing to properly position the supplier's products and enhance the value of the offering for the final buyer down the channel.

In other words, the supplier choosing or constructing a channel structure should seek to reach a *fit* (that is, a consistency) between the supplier's marketing strategy and resellers' consumer franchises. A consumer franchise is a reseller's targeted buyer segments and their expectations of value to be provided by the reseller.

Unique Relationship Effectiveness

Figure 10-1
The Supplier-Distributor Fit

The trading relationship between the supplier and the reseller actually involves several fits and types of synergy. There is the synergy between the marketing programs and the synergy or overlap in the target markets. Then there is the fit of the reseller's marketing and positioning to the supplier's target market and the fit of the supplier's product positioning and marketing programs to the reseller's consumer franchise.

The fit of the supplier's target markets to the resellers consumer franchise is critical. When a natural fit occurs, the outcome is powerful. When the value of the supplier's product is combined with the image and service values provided by the resellers, buyers often perceive they have received more value than the sum of the parts; in other words, unique relationship synergy or symbiosis has been created.

Figure 10-1 illustrates, for a single supplier-reseller combination, the problem of fitting the supplier's target market and elements of competitive differentiation to the

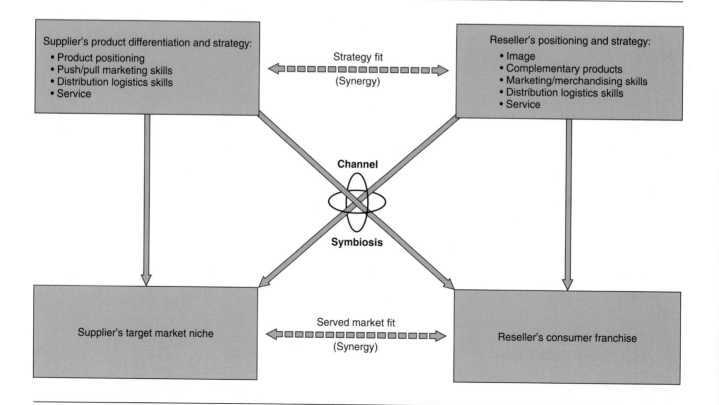

reseller's consumer franchise and competitive differentiation. The two vertical arrows on either side of the diagram represent what is commonly taught in basic marketing and retailing courses: suppliers must fit their product positioning strategy to their target market and retailers must fit their positioning to their consumer franchise. In reality, things are a lot more complicated when suppliers and resellers have to work together.

The two diagonal arrows cutting through the middle of the diagram represent the desired symbiosis between the supplier's strategy/market and the reseller's strategy/franchise. This symbiosis determines the competitive viability of this specific supplier-reseller relationship. The left-to-right arrow represents the fit that needs to be achieved between the supplier's product differentiation and marketing strategy and the reseller's consumer franchise. This means that the supplier must design its strategy to *sell its products through the reseller, keeping in mind the expectations of the reseller's targeted customers* at the point of purchase.

This seems obvious, but the emphasis is added because suppliers often forget this. Many suppliers, particularly in business-to-business markets, become focused on selling only to the next level in the channel, treating distributors as their final customers.

Similarly, the right-to-left arrow represents the fit between the reseller's positioning, service, and pricing strategies and the supplier's target market. It is particularly important for the supplier to understand this fit when the fit is not perfect. Then the supplier can adjust its overall marketing strategy to reach and provide value for the targeted final buyers.

Best results, then, are obtained when the relative fit of the target market and consumer franchise (the bottom horizontal double arrow in Figure 10-1) and the consistency between the supplier's and reseller's competitive competences and strategies (the top horizontal double arrow) are very close. Final buyers receive value from all elements of the combined offerings. The Rationality in Practice box on page 340 discusses four examples of companies that formed channel partnerships in which a great deal of synergy was created.

Complications arise when there is not a total overlap between the supplier's target market and the reseller's consumer franchise or when there is inconsistency in their strategies. When the fit is not perfect, the parties must work toward purposefully developing such consistency. Methods for doing this are discussed later in this chapter in the section dealing with managing channel relationships.

Unique Relationship Efficiencies

A unique advantage of a supplier-reseller relationship can also come from lower costs, if both parties work together very well in reducing the costs of doing business. If the cost reduction drives and efficiency efforts of both parties are synchronized, as illustrated in Figure 10-2, and if the synchronization between the supplier and resellers is better than other trading relationships, then trading relationship costs will decline at a faster rate than the trading relationships the supplier has with other resellers and the reseller has with other suppliers. If both supplier and reseller are competitively rational, they will value this cooperative competitive advantage and seek to promote, preserve, and protect it so as to strengthen their joint positioning advantage.

Selecting Specific Channel Partners

So what can a supplier do to select specific channel members so that the necessary fit between strategies, target markets, and consumer franchises is achieved? The distributor audit undertaken in the channel analysis should make selection a relatively straightforward, though not easy task. A reseller's *consumer franchise* can be assessed

Figure 10-2

Supplier-Retailer Efficiency Loops

The cost efficiency drive of the supplier helps drive the cost efficiency of the retailer, and the cost efficiency drive of the retailer helps drive the cost efficiency of the supplier. If these two loops can be synchronized, then they will drive each other to ever higher levels of efficiency—to the benefit of both parties.

Source: Reproduced with permission from Management Horizon's *Consumables Retail Review,* August 1992, 10.

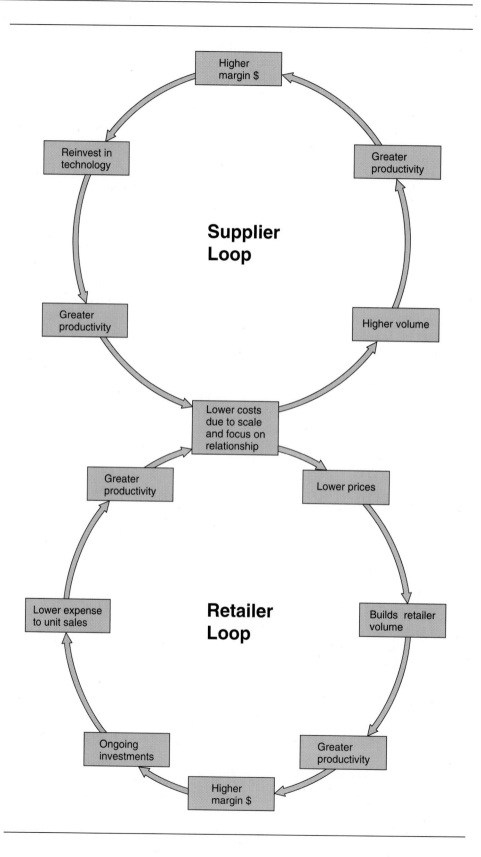

in terms of market coverage, current success selling into the target market segments, and relations with particular key accounts. A key competitive differentiation of a reseller is its *off-the-shelf delivery of product* to its customers. Despite all the bells and whistles that a reseller may claim to provide, its major responsibility to customers is to carry inventory. Consequently, one of the most important selection criteria is a channel partner's inventory holding policy. The appropriateness of a holding policy is indicated by its *fill rate* (the percentage of customer orders that are fulfilled off the shelf versus the percentage that are back-ordered). A supplier will also want to find out about the special back-order services, if any, that a retailer offers its consumers.

Resellers also provide value to their customers through their *selling efforts*. The importance of a reseller's selling efforts depends very much on how much a supplier is going to have to rely on resellers to push its product. When evaluating the fit between the supplier's strategy and the reseller's consumer franchise, the supplier should consider both the level of selling a reseller is likely to give the supplier's products and the ways in which the products will be sold. The reseller's enthusiasm for the supplier's products will depend very much on how important the supplier's line is to the reseller and its sales force for generating profits and commissions. Consequently, the supplier should look for resellers who sell an appropriate assortment of products in which the supplier's product fits nicely in terms of positioning and price points. In examining the reseller's selling methods, the supplier should look for the ways that the reseller enhances the positioning of the supplier's products. The reseller's sales force should have appropriate selling skills, an adequate level of product knowledge, and a sense of how the product will provide value for the targeted customers.

The supplier's choice of resellers needs to be tempered by three considerations:

1. Partners should be those whose expectations can be met.
2. The likely power relationship with the partners should be favorable to the vendor, or at least should be tolerable.
3. Partners should be chosen who can—and do—pay their bills.

First, the distributor audit will provide information on resellers expectations in terms of margin, allowances, incentives, delivery, training, and so on. The supplier who takes on resellers whose expectations cannot be met will, at the very least, be doing business with resellers who will not provide adequate sales support. At worst, disgruntled channel partners can generate enough ill will by word of mouth to ruin future relationships with other potential channel partners.

Second, the distributor audit will also give the supplier a sense of the likely power relationships between the supplier and potential resellers. From the supplier's point of view, the principal concern about resellers' power is their ability to affect the supplier's bottom line. Wal-Mart, for instance, took steps in late 1991 to curtail dealings with manufacturers' reps and product brokers. Such a move toward dealing only with manufacturers is likely to give Wal-Mart more direct control and power over its suppliers.[1] If the distributor audit indicates that the likely relationship with a reseller is not tolerable, the supplier must consider whether it should choose that particular reseller. In many cases, such as with Wal-Mart, it really has little or no choice, but at least it can think ahead and look for ways to shift the balance of power in the future (such as developing an exclusive deal with Kmart).

Third, it is absolutely essential that a credit check be run on the reseller. A strict company policy of requiring such a check saves embarrassment and also saves a com-

---

1. Karen Blumenthal, "Wal-Mart Set to Eliminate Reps, Brokers," *Wall Street Journal*, December 2, 1991, A1.

Examples of Channel Synergy

The right product united with the right reseller can be a powerful combination whose effect on the customer and the competition is more than the simple sum of its parts. The combination is not additive, but interactive. The incremental advantage over simply summing the parts is the unique synergy that exists between the strategies and target markets of the partners. This proposition is critical in distribution. The greater the competitive uniqueness of this combination, the greater the potential bond between the enterprises involved. The following are four examples of such synergy:

♦ **Nexus hair-care products with hair salons:** The regular patrons of a hair salon are most likely to find premium hair-care products attractive, so the consumer franchise-target market fit is excellent. In addition, the endorsement of a trusted hairdresser combined with the proven performance of the product creates a powerful integrated strategy.

♦ **Swatch watches with boutiques and high-class department stores:** This successful bond, launched in 1983, resulted from Swiss product quality, trendy design, and a good pull advertising campaign perfectly fitted with the exclusivity, endorsement, and consumer franchise of the select stores.

pany from a bad debt that could affect its bottom line. This is particularly true for start-up companies. For example, the entrepreneurial manufacturer of a plastic spout attachment that fits on plastic milk jugs and makes a nifty houseplant watering can lost $15,000 in bad debt during its first year of operation when a major wholesale distributor in the hardware and convenience store market went bankrupt. Not checking the credit rating of this well-known distributor cost the start-up manufacturer almost all of its first-year profits.

The final selection of resellers, if there is a choice, should occur in *two stages*. First, a reseller should meet the supplier's minimum performance criteria. Its consumer franchise, as indicated by its sales to major customers, should reasonably fit the target market; its credit rating must be good; its inventory carrying policies and order fulfillment must be at least satisfactory; its enthusiasm for the product line must be genuine; and the power relationships that are likely to result should be tolerable. If several alternative resellers meet such criteria, then the selection should proceed to the second stage. The reseller that scores highest on the average of the three key dimensions—consumer franchise, inventory policy, and selling enthusiasm—should be chosen. Obviously, if one of these three dimensions is deemed more important than the other two, then that dimension should be given more weight.

Managing Trading Relationships

Once channel partners are selected and initial agreements signed, the parties must work to develop a relationship that is mutually beneficial and will last into the future. Just as the main goal in choosing trading partners was to find partners that present the opportunity for establishing a fit between strategies, consumer franchises, and supplier target markets, the goal in managing ongoing channel relationships is to develop and maintain stronger synergistic competitive positioning. Managing channel relationships requires paying attention to an enormous amount of detail, and much of this detail will be specific to the particular industry in which the channel exists. However,

- **Compaq with independent computer retailers:** Compaq offered a focused support system, very competitive margins, and, in its early years in the market, superior product features (such as faster processing, more memory, and more reliability). The independent stores worked with Compaq enthusiastically because Compaq's success gave the stores more clout with IBM, Wang, and DEC, whose direct sales tended to undercut the computer stores' sales and market efforts toward small and medium-sized businesses.

- **IBM with software manufacturers and value-added resellers (VARs):** IBM opened its PC architecture to software companies and VARs at a time when the personal computer market was growing rapidly. IBM gave a number of entrepreneurial software companies, such as Microsoft, credibility and access to a huge consumer franchise. In return, IBM's PC image and competitive position were greatly enhanced because its hardware was very quickly supported by a large number of software programs. This put competitive pressure on other PC manufacturers who had proprietary operating systems—and thus little software support.

several general ideas can be applied in almost any setting, dealing with any level of the channel. These ideas fall under the following topics:

1. Support programs
2. Incentives
3. Formal and informal communications
4. Control procedures

Managing Support Programs

Despite differences among distributor types, there are some common drivers. One of the most important for a supplier to understand is that all distributors, whether large, small, wholesaler, retailer, or whatever, are preoccupied with TIM: turn, implementation, and margin.

Turn, Turn, Turn

The stock-turn of a product is often the key to success for a reseller—its most important competitive advantage. High turn means a reseller is working its money and floor space harder. It means that the reseller has the right products and presentation for its consumer franchise. Rapid stock-turn also creates excitement among the salespeople and conveys an atmosphere of energy and vitality to the customer. Suppliers often incorrectly assume that stock-turn will not be such a concern when a product is sold on consignment because the reseller has no money tied up in the stock. They overlook the fact that the reseller still has rent, salaries, and expenses to pay, and slow-turning stock pays the bills very slowly. Part of the addictive appeal of sales promotions is that they accelerate stock-turn. When used too frequently, however, the reseller trains the consumer to buy only on special, and the consumer trains the reseller to offer regular sales. The result is that stock turns only when it is sold at a reduced margin.

The first step toward boosting reseller merchandise turns is to make sure the match between supplier strategy and reseller consumer franchise achieves a good fit. Supplier products should fit the reseller's product assortment. Also, cooperative advertising, where both the product and the reseller are promoted together, is the traditional way of using pull to build reseller loyalty and increase stock-turn. One of the major problems with co-op advertising today is that it is becoming an automatic allowance or discount offered to all resellers, with little consideration for the nature of the campaign or even for whether such advertising will actually occur. This leads us into a discussion of the importance of the implementation of merchandising programs.

Merchandising Support

Many resellers have neither the time, the will, nor the skill to initiate and implement specific merchandising programs. Planning a product's merchandising program, setting up displays, and training salespeople can involve quite a high fixed-cost investment in time and effort. This means that there are considerable economies of scale and scope in implementing a merchandising program that involves many reseller outlets. It is seldom worth the supplier's investment in time and effort to support a program when only a small number of the employees at the outlets learn and meticulously execute the merchandising program for a product or product line. Neither is such a program cost-effective for the resellers, since such merchandising effort on their part is applied to only a small portion of their assortment. After all, the reseller will only set up the program once. On the other hand, if the supplier puts its own people out in the field to set up such programs in a large number of outlets, then it is worth the supplier's investment in time and effort to make such individuals expert at setting up and orchestrating the programs in multiple outlets. For similar reasons, resellers greatly value suppliers' strategies to orchestrate and implement special merchandising programs. They may not be prepared to invest in point-of-purchase displays or to train their sales staffs, but they are almost always willing to have a supplier set up such displays and to have a supplier's customer representative train their salespeople on the job.

The advantage to the supplier of reaching down the channel and overseeing such field activities is that the joint marketing program gets done and gets done right. A well-orchestrated and implemented reseller merchandising program enables the marketing "push" to extract the very most out of advertising's "pull." The inevitable improvisation and damage control can also be undertaken on the spot, ensuring the coordination of activities and events. In addition, when a competitor "pulls," the artful supplier can counter with a point-of-purchase "push." A supplier can undercut the competitor's merchandising effort by distracting and stealing the customers drawn to the reseller by the competitor's advertising.[2]

Too few suppliers appreciate that many resellers will trade margin for superior stock-turn, lower costs, and fewer hassles when a supplier presents a can-do attitude and follows through with its merchandising program. A further advantage of sending project coordinators out into the field is that they develop relationships with buyers, department managers, advertising executives, floor managers, and merchandising managers who are working together to execute a program. The resulting relationships are much stronger than those that result from negotiating price, delivery, and returns across a table or over the phone. In addition, field representatives give the supplier a much richer understanding of the day-to-day operating procedures, the key influences in the reseller's management, the strengths and weaknesses of its clients, and, finally, competitive intelligence.

2. Coca Cola accomplished this in the summer of 1991. Heavy retailer promotions, passed on to consumers, offset the effects of Pepsi's "Summer chill out" and "You've got the right one, baby, Uh-huh" advertising campaigns. Both campaigns achieved extremely high levels of viewer awareness. However, Pepsi's market share remained virtually unchanged. See *Business Week*, "Pepsi: Memorable Ads, Forgettable Sales," October 21, 1991, 36.

Incentive	Circumstances	Form
	Table 10-1	
	Some Common Forms of Reseller Incentives	
Functional discounts	Long selling cycle Extensive post-sale service Supplier wants functions reseller normally wouldn't perform	Discounts on merchandise given for reseller performance of specific activities (advertising, telemarketing, or point-of-sale displays, for example)
Bonuses	Rewards superior performance on specific criteria; can be used to reward individual reseller employees, too	Money paid for performance above targeted levels on such things as sales, order fulfillment, new accounts, or service may take the form of contests
Special events	Impact of bonuses or contests enhanced by special award event	Any form of special recognition event appropriate for the occasion

The two examples in the Rationality in Practice box on page 344 demonstrate that the innovative implementation of merchandising programs can be the way to obtain and maintain influence over retailers who, in their general relations with suppliers, seem to be becoming increasingly demanding, obstinate, and uncooperative.

Managing Distributor Incentives

The most important determinant of the effort a reseller will invest in a supplier's product is the amount of short- and long-term earnings the reseller expects from the product line. The customary trade discount will be sufficient for a line that is expected to increase a reseller's total sales or produce an above average stock-turn. If the reseller expects neither of these outcomes, then the supplier will be pressured to give extra allowances and discounts. Such extra concessions are tempting, particularly when a supplier is desperate to get its foot in the door.[3] However, such concessions can be very sticky. Even if sales performance exceeds expectations, it will be difficult to remove the above-average allowances because the reseller will have become adjusted to the margin, and a reduction of the allowances will come right off its bottom line. To avoid this trap, initial special entry allowances should terminate once a prespecified volume of business has been transacted.

As discussed above, the marketing manager should be aware of traditional practices in the channel, and this extends to reseller's customary incentive schemes in the industry. If the supplier offers an incentive that is lower than the reseller's customary expectations, then the reseller will be quick to point out the difference and the supplier will be perceived as ignorant, less competent, or a tightwad. If the incentive scheme is above customary practices, then the supplier may be seen as a "patsy" who can be taken advantage of in other ways. Whenever a supplier's proposed terms and agreements deviate from industry practice, the supplier should make it very clear that it is aware of the deviation and has a compelling reason to make the unusual offer.

One benefit of offering incentive schemes is that the practice tends to induce the supplier and reseller to take time to plan and execute a joint marketing campaign. When such cooperation exists, the supplier-reseller fit is, of course, enhanced. Table 10-1 gives some common methods of providing incentives to resellers.

3. For a study of vendor activities involved in gaining new product acceptance in the retail grocery channel, see Vithala R. Rao and Edward W. McLaughlin, "Modeling the Decision to Add New Products by Channel Intermediaries," *Journal of Marketing* 53.1 (January 1989), 80–88.

Rationality in Practice:

Innovative Retail Merchandising

Gallo Wines has a number of very strong brand names. When it delivers its cases of wine to a retailer, it delivers a consumer franchise produced by quality, targeted products, and good advertising that pulls. This gives Gallo's field force more than a foot in the door. Gallo further exploits its market strength by reaching down the channel with a merchandising program that is irresistible, sometimes even overwhelming. Gallo first requires that its distributors have the resources to employ separate, aggressive Gallo representatives. These reps build floor displays, lift cases, dust bottles, and "if you turn your back on them for a minute they will turn your store or department into a Gallo outlet."*

Gallo's field reps execute according to a 300-page training and sales manual. The manual covers such topics as the sales call and maintaining shelves, and each chapter ends with a quiz. The manual contains detailed checklists and advice: place the most highly advertised Gallo products at eye level; place impulse purchase items on shelves above the belt; the width of the display should be no more than seven feet (the largest width the eye can easily scan); if there is a large size that offers a decided unit price advantage to the consumer, then place it to the immediate right of the smaller size. The key to Gallo's merchandising success is its concern over details and staying on top of its distributors and retailers.

Another example, probably the most well-known textbook case of innovative retail merchandising, was the classic 1971–1972 Hanes L'eggs campaign. Again, the product and its advertising created a large pull, but this pull was matched by the push in terms of supply. Four hundred fifty young women in red, white, and blue hot pants set up and stocked the displays in supermarkets and drugstores. They

Margins Are Not Chiseled in Stone

Although there are customary pricing margins in many reseller markets (such as turn-key, which is a 100 percent markup on cost, 50 percent of retail price), the reality is that margins are negotiable. In a supermarket, the margins for different products often vary from 15 percent to as much as 67 percent of the price the consumer pays. Much depends on the stock-turn of the item, whether it is sold on consignment, the merchandising program, and proven sales success. With a strong, supplier-run merchandising program, a product can sell at a 30 percent margin, where without the program it would not be considered by the reseller even if it were offered at 55 percent of the same retail price. The message is simple. Negotiate from strength with executives who are able to negotiate terms. Many junior buyers are simply not allowed to deviate from the prescribed terms and margins. They are also not as sensitive as senior managers are to the value of a comprehensive merchandising program or the importance of measuring a line's profitability by its GMROI (gross margin return on inventory = margin $\times$ stock-turn), not by its simple percentage margin.

A second general recommendation is that a supplier must insist on getting the full value out of its margins. Today, resellers insist on product quality control and timely delivery. Similarly, suppliers must demand that extra functional discounts deliver the promised special service. An insidious custom emerging in supplier-reseller relations, especially with retailers, is that discounts for such things as cooperative advertising, consumer sales promotions, and early payment are often given even though *both* the retailer and the supplier *know* that the retailer may or may not comply with the terms. The retailer may end up not including the product in its advertising, it may pocket the price discount that was intended to be passed on to consumers, or it may deduct the early payment price discount and still settle its accounts long after they are overdue. A reasonable explanation for such retailer nonperformance is a lack of coordination

were helped by an early computerized stock control information system that managed warehouse inventory, sales, billings, and accounts. By 1969, pantyhose had become almost a commodity item, and the traditional sales-promotion entry would not have been enough in a market where there was already constant specializing. Hanes—with its "Our L'eggs fit your legs" slogan, its differentiation claim (based on the greater stretch and elasticity of the material used), and its eye-catching, symbolic packaging—was able to enter at a price of $1.39, compared to some private labels that were selling at 39 cents or three for a dollar.

A direct mail introductory coupon offer was made, but the real attraction to retailers was that Hanes required almost nothing of them except that they count the profits. The supplier asked for two-and-a-half square feet of display space, which was rented. The stock was sold on consignment and the display stockers did the rest, including mak-

ing every effort to have the striking display positioned in a heavy-traffic location. It should be noted that similar campaigns did not work as well for Hanes L'aura line of cosmetics, its line of men's underwear, and its line of socks, perhaps because of entrenched, strong brand-name competition in these markets, weaker product differentiation, and competitors' whose distribution and merchandising skills were already good and got better.

*Jaclyn Fierman, "How Gallo Crushes the Competition," *Fortune,* September 1, 1986, 23–31.

between retail buyers, the merchandising and department managers that set prices and make promotion decisions, and the advertising department. It is very difficult for a buyer to keep track of whether other executives in his or her company are keeping to the terms of a deal. At least, this is the standard excuse buyers give to suppliers for nonperformance. Another reason retailers do not fulfill their side of the promotional program is that they have been getting away with nonperformance for so long that they believe (and it may be true) that they are powerful enough to extract the discounts. In such a situation, the only hope a supplier has of getting value for its money is to keep on top of the retailer and not give an inch. One thing is certain: it is hard to remove a functional discount on the grounds that the service is not provided if the retailer has become accustomed to not performing and the supplier has signaled, by its lack of previous concern, that it has accepted such nonbehavior. Like all marketing tactics, distribution is far more than developing a program on paper. It has to be executed, which means finding a way of getting distributors to cooperate.

Managing Communication Relationships

It may surprise many marketing managers to learn that effective communication and coordination between a supplier and a reseller can be as important as financial incentives in motivating distributors.[4] Although there may be very little variation between suppliers' margins and credit terms, there is often a lot of variation in the quality of the communication programs offered by alternative suppliers. As a result, the suppliers with truly superior communication programs stand out. Another reason that effective communication is important is because it involves people—and, after all, it is people,

4. David D. Shipley, "Selection and Motivation of Distribution Intermediaries," *Industrial Marketing Management* 13, (1984) 249–56.

Suppliers improve the communication between themselves and their resellers by using the following techniques:

- Asking individual resellers and reseller advisory councils for advice and feedback on new product ideas and new marketing programs.
- Passing no market intelligence about the reseller's customers and competition.
- Explaining new marketing and promotional programs.
- Training reseller inside sales people in-house and outside sales people out in the field (using customer service representatives).
- Providing product promotional literature, training manuals, product demonstration videos, and service guides.
- Offering order/delivery and inventory management/shipping advice.
- Acknowledging orders and communicating promptly on order fulfillment delays.
- Providing an 800 number to handle reseller and customer problems and inquiries.
- Giving the reseller regular feedback on its performance letting it know how it compares to resellers in other markets.
- Providing a computer link and software that can help the reseller train its staff and manage its business.

Figure 10-3

Types of Communication Programs Directed at Distributors

not accounting systems or trading agreements, who determine the behavior of a reseller. It must be remembered that a channel of distribution is as much a social system as it is an economic one. Figure 10-3 presents a list of the many types of communication programs a supplier can develop with its resellers. Increasingly, innovative suppliers are using computer communication systems to tie down their relationships with resellers. They are offering free ordering, inventory management, and billing software to resellers, which not only eases the routine communication between supplier and reseller but also increases the quality of performance reporting between the parties.[5]

While the introduction of such communication programs can greatly improve a reseller's cooperation and performance, above all else a supplier must be responsive to reseller requests for information. A surprising number of companies waste thousands of dollars knocking on doors that are never opened and yet spend very little on improving service when customers come knocking. The test of whether a company really understands the value of communication is whether its employees, from telephone receptionists to the CEO, understand the importance of a prompt response to customers and resellers.

Order-Processing Communication

Computerization has dramatically reduced the cost of order processing. It has also greatly reduced the variability in order-processing time. Electronic order entry often allows immediate notification of item availability and potential substitutes that may be on special (See Figure 10-4). Orders can be checked against master files to prevent mistakes in item codes and the size of the order. The computer can also produce courtesy confirmation letters that are automatically sent to buyers. Examples of such electronic systems are listed here:

- Federal Express provides heavy users with terminals and software that enable them to track the movement of orders sent to customers via Federal Express.

5. Raymond E. Corey, "The Role of Information and Technology in Industrial Distribution," in Robert D. Buzzell, ed., *Marketing in an Electronic Age* (Boston: Harvard Business School Press), 29–51; Louis A. Wallis, *Computers and the Sales Effort,* Report No. 844 (New York: The Conference Board, 1986).

Figure 10-4

An automated ordering inventory system provided to retailers by a supplier.

Automated systems have greatly reduced the cost of order processing and improved stock control. They have also reduced the amount of stock that needs to be carried.

♦ American Airlines provides corporate travel departments access to its Sabre reservation system.

♦ Drug wholesaler McKesson provides terminals and software that are used to manage stocking and almost all other operational tasks in a drugstore.

♦ Kodak provides terminals and software that allow for photo-finishing training and manage other aspects of a photographic retailer's business.

♦ Inland Steel developed a computer network that keeps customers informed of order status and provides other added-value services such as electronic billing, funds transfer, and technical advice.

♦ The Norton Company supplies its distributors with information on order status, pricing, and products.

♦ The 3M Company provides a videotext system describing existing and new products.[6]

In some cases, salespeople and buyers are eliminated. Bose Corp., for example, has created an in-plant vendor program in which representatives from vendors reside in Bose's purchasing departments. These representatives manage the inventory of vendors' component parts on-site, ordering new supplies when needed. This system cuts inventory costs and eliminates much of the cost of selling and order processing.[7] Figure 10-5 presents a radical approach to buying and selling used cars that relies on a computer network.

6. Rashi Glazer, *Marketing and the Changing Information Environment: Implications for Strategy, Structure, and The Marketing Mix,* Report No. 89–108 (Cambridge, MA: Marketing Science Institute, 1989); and Louis A. Wallis, *Computers and the Sales Effort,* Report No. 844 (New York: The Conference Board, 1985), 13.
7. Walter P. Wilson, "High-Tech Firms Need Basic Business Sense," *San Jose Mercury News,* November 4, 1991.

Figure 10-5

An EDI Used-Car Market in Japan

Electronic Data Interchange (EDI) has advanced to such a point that Japanese used car dealers can now buy quality used cars via Aucnet, an electronic used-car auction network. Rigorous national inspection standards and disclosure reduce buyer risks. The next step will be to allow individual car sellers (but not buyers) to use Aucnet. Do you think such a system will be introduced in the United States?

Source: Neil Weinberg, "Moving the Iron," *Forbes,* December 7, 1992.

Reseller Feedback

The direction of communication should not be one way, from supplier to reseller. It should be reciprocal (reseller-to-supplier as well), and there are some types of information that a supplier should insist be passed back up the channel immediately. The first is information that indicates a major design flaw or quality control problem. It is in the interest of the reseller to quickly inform a supplier about product performance problems. But sometimes a reseller is reluctant to report being approached by another supplier or to give feedback about the plans of a competing supplier whose line it carries.

The second type of information a supplier should insist on is news about competitive threats. There are two very good reasons why a supplier should request—both in a contract and personally—that it be informed when a new supplier approaches the reseller. First, it places the onus on the reseller to respond in good faith. Any delay in passing on news of such an approach is a clear warning that the relationship is weak. Second, the competitor's actions can be preempted. The classic counterplay is to use short-term, forward buying discounts to choke the channel with inventory and protect the consumer franchise with a defensive promotional campaign.

Controlling Distributors

Controlling a channel involves information feedback and statistical process control. Effective control also involves the management of personal relations. Statistics on monthly sales, orders, inventory, stock-outs, back orders, delinquent debt, returns, and other allowances for each reseller and among all resellers are obviously necessary for control. Overall, distribution control statistics, such as canceled back orders, ordering and delivery errors, and promotional allowance payments, also indicate how well you as a supplier are servicing your resellers. It is very important for a supplier to plan to exceed its preset performance targets in its service to its resellers and to communicate such superior service quality to the trade. Otherwise, it is almost impossible for a supplier to sanction and control reseller nonperformance if it does not perform itself.[8]

Once the facts are on the table, the key to control is consistency in the granting or not granting of bonus awards, allowances, and so on, dependant upon the reseller's conformance to performance standards. Consistency in meeting reasonable performance expectations and consistency in rewarding such performance leads to further supplier-reseller cooperation and trust,[9] which in turn should build a better fit between the supplier's strategy and the reseller's consumer franchise. Response inconsistency, on the other hand, dilutes the focus of a supplier's strategy and creates impressions of poor management, capriciousness, unfairness, and unreasonableness. In such a situation, an enterprising troublemaker can ridicule a supplier and, worse, poison the whole channel network. Resellers who receive extraordinarily bad or good treatment are apt to either bitterly complain about it or brag about it to other distributors. In such cases it is particularly important not to confuse personality with performance, as it is easy to forgive people you like and play by the rules with other people. Word of such dissimilar treatment will almost certainly get around at future trade shows or association meetings. Preferential treatment based on personalities may also violate unfair competition laws. Taking disputes or grievances to an informal or formal reseller advisory board may help to give all parties a broader perspective and produce fair resolutions.

Managing Multiple Channel Relationships

As a company grows in size and adds new products to its lines, it will undoubtedly begin to want to distribute through new channels. It will consider strategies in which different channels will target different segments or will carry selected portions of its product lines. In managing this evolution in its channel strategy, a firm must consider how it will best sell to and service its targeted customers while minimizing the undermining effects of channel conflict.

Problems often arise as a market and industry change and a supplier attempts to go from exclusive to selective distribution.[10] As new segments emerge or as old segments change their preferences, a manufacturer may decide that new channels should be used. What, then, becomes of the established channel relationships? On the one hand, dropping the existing resellers is a betrayal of faith and may hurt future relationships. On the other hand, the supplier must expend scarce resources on new channels to take advantage of the new consumer franchises that are being built. A key to operating multiple channels is to establish and adhere to well-defined performance criteria. By tying support to well-defined criteria, the channel members will at least perceive that they are being treated fairly.

8. Punam Anand and Louis W. Stern, "A Sociopsychological Explanation for Why Marketing Channel Members Relinquish Control," *Journal of Marketing Research* 22.4 (November 1985), 365–76. Franchisees' beliefs about the reasons for supplier's past success were found to influence the franchisees' participation. Control is easier if a supplier can increase the intermediaries' expectations about positive performance outcomes.
9. James C. Anderson and James A. Narus, "A Model of Distributor Firm and Manufacturer Firm Working Partnerships," *Journal of Marketing* 54.1 (1990), 42–58.
10. Allan J. Magrath and Kenneth G. Hardy, "A Strategic Paradigm for Predicting Manufacturer-Reseller Conflict," *European Journal of Marketing* 23.2 (1989), 94–108.

In recent years, the joint consideration of selling and distribution strategies has led some suppliers to abandon their traditional reseller networks. Instead, they have begun to use direct distribution and selling for their major accounts and manufacturers' reps and public warehouses for their smaller or remote accounts. The linking of the company's computer with the public warehouses' computers and further networking into the rep's computerized order-processing system has provided integration and control not otherwise possible, making this an increasingly attractive selling and distribution alternative.

When a supplier sets up such a new channel, the same advice applies. The supplier should treat the new sales force and established resellers fairly. Both channels should have the opportunity to earn fair bonuses or commissions. The target markets that each are assigned should be well defined and separated as much as possible. Where there is overlap, specific rules should determine who is compensated and how much compensation should be awarded, and these rules should not be changed at the whim of management.

Protecting Trading Relationships

A manufacturer brings the uniqueness of its product differentiation, its push-pull selling skills, and the quality of the fit between its strategy and its target market to a channel relationship. The quality of its consumer franchise plus its image, competitive selling skills, distribution, and service competencies are assets the reseller brings to a channel relationship. A simple theory of relationship dependency and power is presented in the exhibit on page 352. When both parties receive extra profits from the market though working *together* on satisfying the customer and reducing costs, it is very difficult to determine who is more dependent on whom and who owns the advantage from working together. The market fit and differentiation fit described in Figure 10-1 and the efficiency synchronicity described in Figure 10-2 are unique to a particular channel relationship and often contribute considerably to the competitiveness of the trading relationship and resulting revenues and profits earned by both parties. The more unique and superior the fit between the supplier and reseller, the more differentiated the resulting trading relationship, and the greater the ability of the relationship (through the cooperative efforts of the supplier and reseller) to increase its market share (see Chapter 4) and earn monopoly profits. This is because no other existing trading relationship (combination of supplier and reseller) available to either the supplier or reseller is similar.

The *competitive uniqueness* of a channel relationship is the residual component of joint competitive advantage that either party cannot take with them to another trading relationship. The narrower the target market niche of the supplier, the narrower the focus of the reseller's consumer franchise; the better the fit of supplier and reseller strategies to such markets, the lower is the likelihood that either party will benefit from substituting or switching trading partners. Another implication is that the more that the two parties recognize the unique advantages of their cooperation, the greater their mutual understanding and cooperation will be, as evidenced in their day-to-day interactions and use of formal contracts.[11]

---

11. Erin Anderson and Barton Weitz, *The Use of Pledges to Build and Sustain Commitment in Distribution Channels* (Cambridge, MA: The Marketing Science Institute, 1991).

Imitation through Treacherous Diffusion

Channel strategy must not only create such unique competitive channel competencies. It must also foster an appreciation of these shared competitive advantages among the key decision makers working for both the supplier and reseller. The Rationality in Practice box on page 354 describes what can happen when executives depreciate the value of a unique trading relationship. It is almost inevitable that an especially productive trading relationship will ultimately be hurt by revealing trade secrets, designs, or marketing practices to other parties, even when the initial positional power of the two parties was asymmetric (greatly in the favor of one over the other). The destabilizing forces come from the transfer of expertise and consumer loyalty between the two parties and the opportunism of competitors.

To illustrate the problems of protecting a consumer franchise, let us assume that a small supplier is adopted by a very successful retailer. Over time, the retailer's consumer franchise will develop loyalties to the supplier's brand by a process of classical conditioning (from the constant association of the new brand with the retailer's very positive image) and direct instrumental learning (from the reinforcement of the positive outcomes of brand usage). If the supplier and reseller ever part company and the supplier finds another reseller, then the robustness of the reseller's consumer franchise is put to the test. Some of its shoppers will follow the supplier to the new reseller because their brand loyalty has become stronger than their store loyalty. How many depends on the relative attractiveness and competitiveness of the old supplier–new reseller channel relationship compared to the old reseller–new supplier relationship.

A problem with technology transfer down the channel can occur when an innovative supplier teaches its resellers merchandising and logistics skills and transfers knowledge about products and distribution systems. Such an investment is potentially transferable to the marketing of other suppliers' substitutes or even the reseller's own private label. Both Apple and IBM did this while developing the personal computer market. Likewise an innovative reseller teaches a supplier about merchandising skills that are potentially transferable to other resellers. Other resellers clearly are interested in exploiting the enterprise and investments of an innovative supplier-seller channel. They will be prepared to pay a premium to tempt disloyalty as the original supplier brings additional assets to the partnership, specifically a consumer franchise and special knowledge, insights, and skills. Likewise, other suppliers will be prepared to give additional allowances to a reseller to gain access to a market initially developed and served by another supplier.

As detailed in the box, a betrayal by a trading relationship partner creates imitation that makes the market more efficient, but in the process the original monopoly profits earned by the original channel partnership (shared by the original supplier and reseller) are lost forever. What can a firm do to protect the unique advantages of the channel from short-sighted opportunism and also to protect each party's investment in the other party's transferable competitive differentiation and advantage? The obvious strategies are to either integrate vertically or sign long-term nondisclosure agreements and binding exclusivity contracts.[12] More difficult to accomplish is the creation of a strong social bond between the channel partners based on their mutual respect for each other's management skills. In reality, legal contracts only augment personal relationships created by working effectively together over an extended period of time.[13]

---

12. Oliver Williamson, *The Economic Institutions of Capitalism: Firms, Markets, Relational Contracting* (New York: Free Press, 1985).

13. George John, "An Empirical Investigation of Some Antecedents of Opportunism in a Marketing Channel," *Journal of Marketing Research* 21.3 (August 1984), 278–89.

The Balance of Power in the Channel

In a trading relationship, the balance of power tilts in the direction of the party that is *less* dependent on the other. Supplier power is increased when environmental change increases the reseller's dependence. Reseller power is increased when environmental change increases the sup-plier's dependence. Asymmetric dependence (when A is more dependent on B than B is on A) *should* drive power. Perceived asymmetric dependence *actually* drives power.

Supplier Power		Reseller Power

Vertical Integration and Long-term Contracts

Developing a long-term, binding relationship with suppliers or resellers, either through investment or legal agreements, may appear to be a sensible way of protecting a unique relationship, be it from a shared differentiation advantage or logistics efficiencies. It can also be a way of bypassing or changing the cultural inertia and the lack of cooperation of established channels. Vertical integration (owning your supplier or reseller) offers the promise of potential efficiencies gained from a reduction in management overhead, integrating information systems, and better management and control of marketing campaigns and physical distribution logistics. It is sometimes the only way of introducing new technological advances into a channel. Integration enables unilateral decisions on who is going to do what and the more direct rewarding of key personnel down the channel for responding to the changes. It also gives the integrating firm more control over training and management succession. However, competitive market forces often make the use of independent channel agents more efficient, and vertical integration should only be employed when the market fails—when gross inefficiencies result from working with independent channel participants.[14] The conditions that are most likely to favor vertical integration are listed in Figure 10-6.

It needs to be emphasized that vertical integration and long-term exclusive trading agreements are not the same. Exclusivity is very desirable. Channel intermediaries that are not exclusive agents can manage the marketing of their several suppliers' products to their consumer franchise so as to maximize their own profits and not the profits of all or any of the suppliers. They often do this by developing a supplier promotion cycle that reduces the average gross margin of each supplier and increases their logistics and promotional costs. An exclusive legal contract buttressed by frequent, close, interpersonal contacts often gives as much control as vertical integration at much less cost and financial risk. However, even legal contracts have their limits. Research suggests that the trust and understanding built by working together over time (an implicit social contract) counts for more than clauses in a contract.[15] The unique human and financial investments that manufacturers and resellers have in a relationship, trading exclusivity, and a harmonious and cooperative trading history are likely to hold a relationship

14. Erin M. Anderson and Barton A Weitz, *A Framework for Analyzing Vertical Integration Issues in Marketing*, Report No. 83-110 (Cambridge, MA: Marketing Science Institute, November 1983).
15. Ian R. MacNeil, *The New Social Contract: An Inquiry into Modern Contractual Relationships* (New Haven, CT: Yale University Press, 1980).

The supplier is less dependent on the reseller when	The reseller is less dependent on the supplier when
1. There are many other resellers of similar quality.	1. There are many other suppliers of similar quality.
2. The reseller creates little of the supplier's competitive advantage by its selling services or cost efficiencies.	2. The supplier's product/services contribute very little to the reseller's value for money competitive advantage.
3. Sales to the reseller do not generate a large percentage of the supplier's overhead recovery and profit.	3. Sales of the supplier's products do not generate a large percentage of the reseller's overhead recovery profit.
4. Switching costs are low.	4. Switching costs are low.

together better than a legal contract.[16] When a trading partner has to resort to the clauses of a legal contract to gain the other party's cooperation, it often means that the relationship is on the rocks.

Integration to Defend against Competitive Entry

Upstream vertical integration is a way of ensuring supply when there is a chance of shortages or of limiting a competitor's access to a radical innovation. Procter & Gamble protected the product differentiation of its new line of Ultra Pampers by helping to finance the supplier of the absorbent polymer that provided the competitive advantage. Downstream integration ensures access to a particularly desirable consumer franchise and can choke off competitor's access to these consumers. No doubt Porsche had this in mind when it attempted to set up its own auto dealerships in the United States. Using antitrust law, current dealers, who often sell other luxury cars to potential and former Porsche owners, were able to stop the move and protect their consumer franchise.

Figure 10-6

Conditions That Favor Vertical Integration

Source: Reprinted by permission of Harvard Business School Press from *A Framework for Analyzing Vertical Integration Issues in Marketing,* Report #83-110 by Erin M. Anderson and Barton A. Weitz. Boston: 1991, p. 54. Copyright © 1991 by the President and Fellows of Harvard College.

1. When the level of customer service competition in the supplier market decreases, thus encouraging upstream integration.
2. When it is hard to measure the output performance of the channel and hence control is reduced.
3. When competitors can take advantage of a firm's investment in developing the channel's skills and efficiency.
4. When the environment is uncertain and there is a need for the quick adaptation of strategy.
5. When the transactions are large and/or frequent enough to produce economies of scope and scale that the firm should exploit rather than give away to the channel.
6. When unique products, trade secrets, and marketing processes need to be protected.
7. When the channel culture and norms appear to tolerate reneging on agreements, shirking duties, and the deceitful representation of one's competencies.

16. Erin Anderson and Barton Weitz, *The Use of Pledges to Build and Sustain Commitment in Distribution Channels* (Cambridge, MA: The Marketing Science Institute, 1991).

Rationality in Practice:

The Sweet Smell of Channel Success and Its Bitter Fruits

Once upon a time there was an innovative supplier and an enterprising reseller. The initial pioneering cooperation and joint efforts of the supplier and reseller led to a unique competitive triumph for the trading relationship in the marketplace. In combination, the supplier and reseller broke the rules and together introduced many different innovations. Everything was wine and roses. Both parties handsomely profited and the key individuals in the organization were promoted and rewarded.

As the pioneering era passed, routine set in. The personal interaction between the original executives was no longer necessary. These individuals started listening more to ingratiating subordinates telling them how smart they were (or vice versa). History started to be rewritten. New executives who were appointed to represent the buyer and seller had little or no appreciation of how much the joint venture's success had depended on working together and how it was the product of the interaction of both parties' efforts. In their attempts to distinguish themselves and gain promotions within the respective firms, these new representatives increasingly attributed the success of the venture to their firm's past and current efforts and depreciated the contribution of the other party. Even worse, in renewing the contracts and adapting to market changes, the two enterprises started to believe their own posturing.

Vertical integration by acquisition or joint venture can be very risky. The company cultures and senior management styles may turn out to be incompatible. Much also depends on what is predicted to happen to the competitiveness of the supply and resale markets. If the demand in the ultimate market is very uncertain, then a further investment or commitment to supply the end market (which is what downstream vertical integration means) greatly increases the stake and the risk exposure. If the reseller consumer franchises are unstable or technological innovation is changing the relative competitiveness of both suppliers and resellers, then committing to a single, long-term relationship (strategic partnering) limits the integrating firm's ability to switch to the most innovative supplier or reseller. Even if the integrating firm, be it supplier or reseller, could break the relationship, the desirable new supplier or reseller is likely to take a very jaundiced view of the integrator's overtures.

When integrating vertically, a firm believes that it is loading the dice in its favor for the long term because the supplier or reseller that it is acquiring or setting up will maintain its technological leadership, cost leadership, image, and management competence. Sustaining this may require heavy investment if market forces produce great volatility in the relative competitiveness of the players.

Physical Distribution Logistics

Distribution logistics is the management of the flow of materials and goods from the point of origin to the point of final consumption. The customer benefits from a channel's logistical system by receiving goods on time, at the right place, in the right quantity, in the right condition, and at the lowest total cost. Among marketing management functions, logistics may be the Cinderella whose time has come. A number of recent events and trends have led managers, if not marketing academics, to pay much more attention to this dimension of the marketing and exchange process. In many industrial markets, managers are finding it very difficult to sustain a long-term, competitive advantage through differentiating the physical product. Successful new features, styles, and models are quickly copied by competitors adept at monitoring the market, reverse

A belief that no one is indispensable, including the other party, started to take hold. Gradually it turned into a belief that other suppliers and resellers were just as good, if not better. This belief was fostered by the attempts of competitive suppliers and resellers to form relationships with the original reseller and supplier. Almost imperceptibly at first, valuable, shared information was leaked by both parties to other competitive parties. Other parties planted and nourished the idea that encouraging and even actively developing other alternatives would reduce dependency and increase power and profits. The inevitable disclosure of such activities precipitated a series of escalating actions and reactions. Eventually, the original relationship fractured.

The genuine need on the part of both the supplier and the reseller to protect self-interest, powered by feelings of personal betrayal, led to an abandonment of exclusivity. The reseller began a new strategy of multiple sourcing, and the supplier began a new strategy of non-exclusive distribution. The original channel's competitive advantage was completely undermined by both partners as its manufacturing, marketing, and merchandising innovations were shared with other parties, who, in turn, shared them with their other suppliers and resellers. Not everyone lived happily ever after.

engineering, and sidestepping patent protection. The increasing automation of production processes has also led to a narrowing of the variance in production costs, productivity, and quality between competitors. Many firms are well down the manufacturing learning curve, but most are only starting down the logistics learning curve. New distribution technologies are also creating whole new learning curves. The study and application of new systems of logistics is a dynamic and exciting new field of study.

In mature industries, where sustainable product differentiation is difficult, sales growth minimal, and advertising and promotional campaigns produce marginal returns, there is often considerable potential for introducing logistics efficiencies and innovations (see Figure 10-7). The returns are often not trivial. Physical distribution costs often constitute 25 percent or more of each sales dollar and many firms have up to 40 percent of their capital tied up in inventory. There is a lot of profit leverage in trimming distribution costs or inventory carrying costs. There is also increased sales potential from superior customer service.

In the terms of logistics, customer service means product availability and the length and variability in order-delivery cycle time. The normal practice is to determine what is an acceptable service level (such as the ability to ship 90 percent of orders received within 48 hours) and then search for a way of providing such a service level at minimal total cost. Later in this chapter, we will discuss designing a delivery service to a customer that minimizes customer costs. But first we will discuss the problem from the supplier perspective of providing a standard service level most efficiently. This requires identification of each of the different types of physical distribution activities and costs.

Inventory Carrying

A large part of the working capital of many manufacturers, wholesalers, and retailers is tied up in raw materials or finished goods inventories. The cost of this investment is calculated by multiplying the average inventory for the year (figured at cost) by the firm's target rate of return on investment, which is usually between 20 percent and 25 percent, before taxes (this is the rate of return the company could have made by invest-

Figure 10-7

High-Technology Warehousing

Wal-Mart used its high-tech, low-cost distribution centers as a major competitive competence and advantage during the 1980s and is continuing to do so in the 1990s.

ing these funds elsewhere, hence making this an opportunity cost). While this cost is often the major inventory carrying cost, it is only one of several costs. Added to the cost of capital tied up in inventory are storage costs (including all warehousing costs), the cost of labor involved in storing and handling, inventory shrinkage from damage, pilfering, and deterioration, and finally obsolescence depreciation. Obsolescence depreciation is the cost of writing off or writing down inventory that can no longer be sold or must be sold at a greatly reduced price because it has been made obsolete by new product innovation.

Increasing Inventory Velocity

An important way to reduce inventory carrying costs is to increase the velocity of the inventory throughout the entire business logistics system. Inventory velocity is the speed that a unit of raw material moves through the whole added-value system, to the end user. The higher the stock-turn of raw materials, goods in process, finished goods, and the field inventory (including inventory carried by the wholesalers and retailers), the faster the system's overall inventory velocity will be. An analysis of the differences in the stock-turns at various points in the system where inventory accumulates will indicate where momentum in the flow is lost. The extreme application of this approach is the JIT (just-in-time) system where raw materials, components, and goods-in-process inventories are completely done away with throughout the system. The more inventory in a channel that flows continuously and regularly, the faster the system's overall inventory velocity will be. Channel bottlenecks and wide fluctuations in flow dissipate the energy and momentum of the system. However, JIT is an extreme delivery option that requires a great deal of cooperation and close control. A simpler solution is to use financial and logistics information readily available on today's computers to pinpoint the costly trouble spots in a distribution system. Unfortunately, solving the problem cannot be left to the computer. Methods of moving inventory faster often come from the employees and contract operators who are frequently already aware of the inefficiency spots in the logistics system.

Quality circles have been used extensively in production to harness the ingenuity and cooperation of production-line employees. A multitude of small refinements in work flow, plant layout, and work assignments have often amounted to major gains in production efficiency. There is every reason to believe that similar efficiencies can be gained by employing quality circles to streamlined order-entry practices, picking and packing, dispatch, transportation, and warehouse storage. In summary, system inventory velocity can be increased by using information—information from customers about their purchase needs, information from the computer about changes in distribution costs, and information from employees about the cause of problems and how they might be solved—to substitute for inventory in supply pipelines as a buffer against uncertainty.

Transportation

The major concern with transportation management (managing inventory on the move) is the value received for the money spent on transportation. Air travel and trucking are faster, thus reducing in-transit inventory carrying costs (which can become large when goods travel by rail or water) and enabling express or expedited delivery. Air and road transportation are also more reliable, more convenient, and more flexible. Air transportation also has the lowest incidence of pilferage and damage. Transportation by rail or water is inexpensive, and the volume discounts can be great. The transit time and reliability of these services are less attractive, but improving. The deregulation of rail, air transportation, and trucking has led to the introduction of new services, price competition, and the possibility of negotiating better deals.

Full Service Freight Forwarders

The emergence of integrated shippers and full service freight forwarders has enabled these new channel entities to offer multimode transportation service packages (for example, truck to rail to truck) that combine the advantages of the modes without the disadvantages. It has also made the different modes more substitutable and hence more price and service competitive. Containerization has also contributed to the ease of switching modes as well as reducing handling, damage, and pilferage. A further advantage of containers is that they can often serve as temporary warehouses. Consolidation warehouses have evolved to take advantage of full truckload or container efficiencies. Located strategically close to the buyer, the warehouse receives goods from a number of suppliers, consolidates them, and ships full truckloads to the buyers. Some innovative companies are using the information systems of their shippers to keep track of goods in transit, identify sources of delay and unreliability, and control the performance of the transport supplier. The future extension of the universal product code (UPC) into industrial goods will enable a supplier to know exactly where an order is (and where it is not!) in the distribution channel and also enable a supplier to monitor its overall distribution system's inventory velocity. The introduction of such scanning technology will also greatly increase the automation of warehousing. For example, Helene Curtis' new distribution warehouse in Chicago cut distribution costs by 40 percent, enabling the company to reduce the price of Suave Shampoo by 5 percent and still increase company profits and improve on-time order delivery.[17]

Integrating Logistics Costs and Management

The total cost of physical distribution is a combination of inventory carrying costs, transportation costs, and order processing costs. Channel members can incur other opportunity costs as well; for example, a poor information system can lead to missed volume discount opportunities, and inadequate service levels can lead to missed sales opportunities. These costs are not mutually exclusive. For example, a reduction in transportation costs often results in an increase in costs somewhere else in the distribution system. This interrelationship in costs is complicated by organizational structures and management authority that assign different individuals responsibility for controlling different components of the costs of physical distribution. A warehouse manager attempts to minimize warehousing and inventory carrying costs, a shipping manager minimizes shipping costs, administration is concerned with order processing, buyers are concerned with getting the best bulk purchase deal, and, finally, the sales manager is driven frantic by out-of-stocks and canceled orders. Costs are squeezed in one area only to pop up in someone else's area to that person's surprise and consternation. Such conflicts of interest can result in turf wars, tit-for-tat retaliations, and an almost certain increase in overall costs. Senior executives often must intervene to bring the parties together and gain efficiency through cooperation and coordination. Also, group rewards should be given for overall system improvements, rather than simply rewarding individual initiative (which is good) and individual, ill-considered selfishness (which is bad). Having discussed the cost elements of physical distribution, we now turn to some of the new strategies that have been developed in recent years to reduce costs and enhance customer service.

New Logistics Tactics

In their attempts to gain competitive service and total cost advantages, an increasing number of companies are going beyond the conventional approaches to improving logistics (such as changing transportation modes and warehouse location) and are adopting one or more of the strategies discussed below. Each of these strategies fundamentally involves using information from customers, employees, and cost accounting to increase a distribution system's general and selective velocity, reliability, and responsiveness.[18] It should be noted that, in most cases, adoption of these strategies is enhanced by electronic data interchange (EDI). EDI involves direct electronic connection between channel members and channel facilitators, such as banks and transportation firms. Information is shared among channel partners on such factors as customers, orders, goods in transit, financing, and payments. Such sharing of information

17. Rita Koselka, "Distribution Revolution," *Forbes*, May 25, 1992, 54–62.
18. Bernard J. LaLonde, "Some Thoughts on Logistics Policy and Strategies: Management Challenges for the 1980s," (Working Paper Series, Columbus: Ohio State University, 1984), 84–100.

makes it possible for channel partners to act and react quickly in coordination with each other. Thus, this information is being used creatively to reduce costs and increase customer service, often both at the same time.

Targeted Service

It often does not make sense to give all customers the same delivery service on all products. Offering a superior service based on the importance of the business and the risk involved in losing the business (by not delivering) is a prudent alternative strategy. The 20 percent of customers or 20 percent of products that generate 80 percent of the profits should be given special treatment. In practice, this usually means carrying more inventory for select items and offering an expedited delivery service to particular customers when needed. Expediting an order that cannot be filled from stock may involve an interwarehouse transfer, a special production run, and the use of high-speed transportation. An out-of-stock order should be expedited if the expected loss of profit from not expediting is greater than the cost of expediting.

The EXPEDITE spreadsheet presented in Table 10-2 is designed to assess the profitability of offering an expedited service for a particular item. It demonstrates that the real long-term cost of not expediting an order can be much higher than expected. In making this judgment call, it should be recognized that the loss is potentially much more than the gross margin on the order. It includes the bad will created, which could lead to a loss of future business. The alternative to expediting is to increase inventory levels of the item and costs. An advantage of expediting is that expediting costs can be used selectively to serve important customers.

Developing regular order-delivery relationships with customers can reduce both inventory levels and the need for expediting. A supplier offers its customers automatic expediting, provided they cooperate by systematizing the timing, the content, and the size of their regular orders. It is easy to ensure delivery when the timing and nature of an order can be anticipated. The regular orders can be shipped by a slower, less expensive mode of transportation, and the occasional special order that needs to be expedited can be shipped by express mail, UPS, or air. A two-tier combination of normal and expedited operations is almost always more profitable than a single system of delivery.[19]

Assembly Postponement

Think of how expensive it must have been to offer a range of paint colors in different sized cans before the "tint, mix, and shake" process at the counter was developed. Considerable savings resulted from only having to ship and carry a base white paint to which color was added in the retail store. Stock obsolescence, often a problem with a fashion shade of paint, was also minimized. The consumer benefited because a much wider range of colors was now offered. Some of the cost savings were also passed on to the customer. For similar reasons, it is no accident the soft-drink industry spawned powerful regional bottlers. Very early on, soft-drink suppliers determined that it made no sense to ship water long distances when they could send concentrated syrup to the bottlers, who could then add the water, carbonation, and packaging.

Even durables can benefit from the postponement of assembly. Some dishwasher manufacturers have their colored panel facings added at a warehouse when the order is received. Refrigerator doors are similarly swung on the left or right depending on the consumer's choice. An increasing amount of furniture (particularly imported

19. David P. Herron, "Managing Physical Distribution for Profit," *Harvard Business Review*, May/June 1979, 121–32.

Table 10-2
Assessing the Value of a Special Delivery Service
Using the EXPEDITE Spreadsheet

	Specific item
Gross margin	30.0%
Average order size (in dollars)	$20.00
Average number of future orders lost with bad will	0
Discounting of future order income	2.0%
Margin penalty if order goes to competitor	5.0%
Order cost	$ 1.00
Back-order cost	$ 2.00

All possible outcome events	Without expediting estimated likelihood	With expediting estimated likelihood
Customer reorders	0.27	
Item back-ordered	0.20	
Item back-ordered with bad will	0.05	
Lost sale to competitor	0.38	0.08
Lost sale to competitor with bad will	0.10	0.02
	1.00	
Total cost/loss comparison	$4.13	$2.17

Step 1: Estimate gross margin, average order value, reorder cost, and back-order cost from accounting records.

Step 2: Estimate the likelihood of events when order cannot be fulfilled off the shelf. These probability estimates can be made from records or the opinions of employees working in order processing and sales.

Step 3: Determine whether to consider the impact of bad will in terms of loss of future orders. This is achieved by estimating how many future orders will be lost. The loss in future profit from this business is discounted by a percentage, which, in effect, is the target return on assets employed expected in the period between orders (for example, if the average order is placed every 12 months, it might be 20%; if it is every 3 months, it might be 5%).

Step 4: The margin penalty allows you to factor in the cost of the competitor gaining your business. This is over and above your lost profits as the competitor gains market share and profits at your expense. You make it stronger and this hurts you.

Step 5: The cost of expediting the order has to be estimated.

Step 6: Start playing "what if" on most uncertain factors, which are the likelihood of events (that must always sum to 1), the number of future orders lost, and the margin.

furniture) is shipped broken down to be assembled by the retailer or even the consumer. For several decades now, consumers have been battling with the assembly instructions for bicycles, exercise equipment, gas barbecue grills, and lawn mowers. While some of the savings in final assembly costs are passed on to the consumer, they are often not as great as the savings the manufacturer and retailer make in storage and transportation costs.

Postponement of assembly can increase consumer choice, reduce the inventory, transportation, and obsolescence costs, and, by requiring the channel to add value, increase channel cooperation. On the down side, sometimes postponement can lead to a reduction in the quality of the final product and a reduction in assembly economies of scale. The teaching of assembly-line skills to channel members may also increase competitive freeloading (competitors may also use the assembly skills that the supplier has taught the channel member) and in the long run encourage the channel to integrate upstream and become a competitor.

Delivery Differentiation

Up to this point, delivery concerns have focused on finding the lowest cost method of delivering a standard service and developing special expediting criteria and procedures. Another, more aggressive way of viewing logistics is to see it as a powerful point of competitive differentiation. This requires understanding the ordering and delivery process from the perspective of the individual customer, be it an OEM (original equipment manufacturer) or a reseller. Helping a dealer manage its inventory is one of the more important services a supplier can use to gain customer and dealer cooperation and performance.[20] Creative logistics differentiation can be seen in the following examples:

♦ A supplier of cartons developed a unique competitive relationship with a customer based on a joint feasibility study. The manufacturer eliminated its 19 annual auction bids and consolidated its buying with the supplier, who was able to introduce savings in freight, warehousing, and order systems efficiencies. The supplier immediately reduced prices by 7 percent and guaranteed additional price reductions of at least 10 percent over the next three years. A tracking system and steering committee were created to look for ways to introduce further savings and to monitor the resulting benefits. The supplier increased its margins by over 10 percent and increased its sales to the customer by 267 percent.[21]

♦ For four years, the medical supplier Baxter worked with a hospital to reduce inventory levels by $200,000 and reduce logistic costs by $1.9 million. The working relationship involved overhauling the ordering system, standardizing supplies, improving storage systems, and even introducing a delivery system for homebound patients.[22]

One of the first steps toward developing such a customer relationship is to sit down with the customer and attempt to tailor a service that is most efficient and effective given the customer's objectives. This requires considering the purchasing, transportation, inventory carrying and stock-out problems, and costs of the customer. It is not an easy task, because these factors must not be considered separately but treated as an interacting set of functions. Sometimes the customer may not appreciate the extent of the trade-offs involved in improving one of these delivery features at the expense of another. Such trade-offs are often unique to a particular supplier-customer relationship and must be treated as such. The development of such a new logistics relationship requires the following:

1. The development of new attitudes that change old habits.
2. Enough trust to be able to work together to develop competitive added value.

20. John F. Gaski and John R. Nevin, "The Differential Effects of Exercised and Unexercised Power Sources in a Marketing Channel," *Journal of Marketing Research* 22 (May 1985), 130–42. A strong relationship with dealer cooperation also existed in this sample for advertising support.
21. Harry Strachan, "Partnership Innovation," in *Creating Customer Satisfaction,* Earl E. Bailey, ed. (New York: The Conference Board, 1990), 19.
22. Terrence J. Mulligan, "Customer Alliances–1," in *Creating Customer Satisfaction,* Earl E. Bailey, ed. (New York: The Conference Board, 1990), 21.

3. A willingness not to try to exploit the new relationship at the expense of long-run cooperations.

4. Patience—payoff often takes time.

5. The supplier must be willing to adapt and change more than the customer.[23]

The spreadsheet DELIVERY, presented in Table 10-3, can be used to explore ways of improving the delivery service of a product purchased regularly FOB (free on board) by an individual customer. Basically, it identifies the optimal order quantity and transportation method that minimizes the customer's annual delivery and inventory costs. It allows the supplier to identify the advantages to its customers of 1) reducing or increasing its standard order quantity, 2) using a new order processing system, and 3) using a new method of transportation. The model considers the effect of a number of customer consumption statistics and cost estimates and the customer's risk aversion to stock-outs. DELIVERY then produces a table that identifies the customer's annual combined transportation and inventory holding costs for different order processing systems, transportation alternatives, and standard order quantities.

23. Mulligan, "Customer Alliances–1," 22.

Table 10-3
Customizing a Delivery Schedule Using a DELIVERY Spreadsheet

Supplier order processing	Time in working days:		
	Minimum	Average	Maximum
Order preparation and communication	1.00	2.00	3.00
Order entry and processing	1.00	2.00	3.00
Warehouse picking and packing	1.00	2.00	3.00

Order quantity	Customer packing, shipping, and delivery costs:				
	Method A	Method B	Method C	Method D	Method E
100	$ 20.00	$ 30.00	$ 20.00	$ 25.00	$ 30.00
200	$ 40.00	$ 40.00	$ 35.00	$ 50.00	$ 60.00
300	$ 60.00	$ 50.00	$ 50.00	$ 75.00	$ 80.00
400	$ 80.00	$ 60.00	$ 65.00	$100.00	$100.00
500	$100.00	$ 70.00	$ 80.00	$120.00	$120.00
600	$110.00	$ 80.00	$ 95.00	$130.00	$140.00
700	$120.00	$ 90.00	$110.00	$140.00	$160.00
800	$130.00	$100.00	$125.00	$150.00	$180.00
900	$140.00	$110.00	$140.00	$160.00	$200.00
1000	$150.00	$120.00	$155.00	$170.00	$220.00
Delivery Time:					
Minimum wds.	2.00	2.00	1.00	1.00	1.00
Average wds.	3.00	4.00	3.00	2.00	2.00
Maximum wds.	7.00	7.00	7.00	5.00	3.00

Continued

Continued from previous page

Customer information

Consumption per working day (average, maximum)	20	26
Number of working days in year	250	
Cost per unit (customer valuation)	$32.00	
Administration cost of placing each order	$20.00	
Annual inventory cost as a percentage of unit cost	25.0%	
Annual intransit inventory cost as a percentage	20.0%	
Do you want to include intransit inventory cost in the model? (No = 0, Yes = 1)	0	
Concern over a supply created stock-out (No concern = 0, Moderate = 2, High = 4)	4	
Concern over a consumption created stock-out (No concern = 0, Moderate = 1, High = 4)	4	

Table 1 — Average inventory required by customer

Order quantity	Method A	Method B	Method C	Method D	Method E	# Orders
100	193	167	193	167	125	50.0
200	248	223	248	223	182	25.0
300	303	278	303	278	237	16.7
400	357	332	357	332	291	12.5
500	411	386	411	386	345	10.0
600	464	439	464	439	399	8.3
700	517	493	517	493	452	7.1
800	570	546	570	546	506	6.3
900	623	599	623	599	559	5.6
1000	676	651	676	651	611	5.0
O-D Lag (#wds)	9	10	9	8	8	

Table 2 — Customer's total annual transportation and inventory carrying costs

Order quantity	Method A	Method B	Method C	Method D	Method E
100	$3,540	$3,837	$3,540	$3,587	$3,504
200	$3,484	$3,284	$3,359	$3,534	$3,454
300	$3,755	$3,389	$3,589	$3,806	$3,562
400	$4,105	$3,657	$3,918	$4,157	$3,831
500	$4,485	$3,987	$4,285	$4,487	$4,163
600	$4,796	$4,349	$4,671	$4,766	$4,526
700	$5,139	$4,728	$5,067	$5,085	$4,905
800	$5,501	$5,117	$5,469	$5,429	$5,295
900	$5,875	$5,512	$5,875	$5,790	$5,691
1000	$6,258	$5,912	$6,283	$6,162	$6,091

Coordinating Marketing and Logistics

Better integration of marketing and logistics strategies can also deliver major cost savings. For example, packaging should first be designed for convenience and its ability to attract attention when on display in a retail outlet. However, even within such specification constraints, many packages can be better designed for storage and transportation. Fruit juices are increasingly being packaged in cardboard boxes, which save space, and there is a trend toward concentrated liquid detergents and fabric softeners, which, again, save weight and space. A little commonsense cooperation can also reduce handling, shipping, and carryover costs. The huge sales spikes of price promotion programs can put tremendous stress on a company's distribution system leading to 1) a huge inventory buildup that is often expensive to store, followed by 2) expensive back-ordering, expedited delivery, and stock-outs down the channel that competitors can exploit. Volume promotional discounts should be offered on bulk packaged and stored quantities (for example, many products are sold by the pallet) to handle the sales spike problem. Special promotions can also be used to move seasonal items that otherwise would have to be carried over to the next season.

Channels and Services

Many of the ideas in this chapter are discussed in terms of the distribution of tangible goods. There are also channels of distribution for services, although differences between goods and services severely restrict what kinds of channels are available for services. The most important of these differences is that services cannot be inventoried. A firm marketing a service can build its operating capacity to handle peak loads, but this is not the same as creating inventories. Tangible goods that can be inventoried can be sold by an intermediary at a distance from the company's headquarters and from the manufacturing facilities. A service, on the other hand, usually must be delivered by someone who is physically located near the recipient.

This inability to be inventoried dictates that channels for services be limited to three kinds: direct, sales agents, and franchise operations. The type of channel chosen by the firm will depend upon the geographic dispersion of potential clients and on the complexity or degree of customization required for the target market.

A principal concern is the degree of control that the firm has over the selling and delivery of the service. If the firm is dealing with a localized market, it can probably offer services directly to all geographic regions through company-owned and managed branch offices. This is how local and regional banks operated before deregulation made national banking possible. Complexity or customization will also tend to require more direct channels. Thus, banks such as Citicorp have maintained ownership of branch banks as they have extended their services geographically. Other service organizations, such as accounting services or consulting services, also use the firm-owned local or regional offices as models for geographic distribution. The firm has much more control over the quality of the service if the local offices are owned by a central entity.

On the other end of the customization spectrum, firms with a good service system can expand geographically by franchising their operations. As long as the service can be taught and control mechanisms easily implemented (and the nature of the service demanded does not vary too much by geographic area), the original recipe for the service can be duplicated in multiple locations. This has been done with such services as carpet cleaning, office cleaning, and day care.

In between is the type of service that requires some customization and expertise on the part of the provider, but not so much that control is a serious issue. These types of services can be offered through sales agents, who take a commission on the service that is sold. This model has been used in such businesses as insurance and temporary personnel services.

In each of these channel formats, the keys to success remain choice, training, and the motivation of quality personnel. Where the service relies on standardization, having a well-designed and documented system is also key. In many services—financial services, for instance—having a well-designed electronic information system also provides a competitive advantage. Beyond this, the suggestions for managing trading relationships apply equally to distribution systems for both goods and services.

Global Distribution

Global distribution management is one of the most important issues facing a firm in the global marketplace. It involves special information management, transportation management, and inventory management. The more that global distribution can be managed through superior electronic communications, the less of a problem transportation and inventory management will be. Thus, developing a superior communications system with foreign subsidiaries, resellers, and customers is the first imperative. Freight companies such as Federal Express are able to supply such an information system, along with its global, overnight, or second-day service (see Figure 10-8). Federal Express expects to have some 100,000 "powership" computer terminals installed in its customers' offices by the year 2000.[24] These terminals enable the supplier to keep control over a shipment, reducing the need for a global warehousing network. FedEx has also developed a computerized customs clearing system that speeds custom clearance. Other freight companies, such as United Parcel Service and integrated freight forwarders, are developing similar tracking systems (see Figure 10-9).[25]

International air freight increased from one billion kilometer-tonnes a year in 1960 to 25 billion kilometer-tonnes in 1983.[26] Since then it has grown at even faster rate. Clearly, air freight has become the preferred mode of transportation for small, high-added-value products from computers to cut flowers. But international shipping has also increased and become much more efficient as the result of the globalization of port container facilities. It has reduced spoilage, waste, and theft; sped up shipment delivery; and increased the regularity and reliability of delivery times and schedules.

Figure 10-8
The Federal Express Global Overnight or Second Day Distribution Network

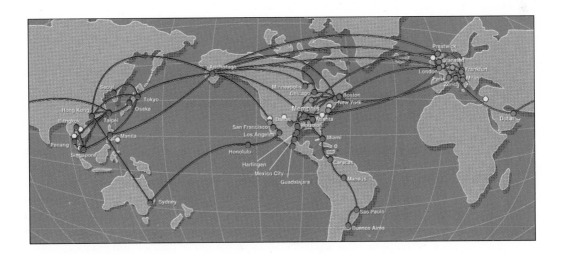

24. Seth Lubove, "Vindicated," *Forbes*, December 9, 1991, 197–202.
25. See the discussion of channel analysis in Chapter 5.
26. Gunnar K. Sletmo and Jacques Picard, "International Distribution Policies and the Role of Air Freight," *Journal of Business Logistics*, 6.1 (1984), 37.

Figure 10-9

A Seamless Worldwide EDI Communication System

Fritz Companies has developed an EDI system that gives it the ability to see and control the entire international transaction process in a seamless service, including paperless customs processing and clearance, before the goods land in the United States. Companies such as Boeing, Dow, Sears, and many of the Fortune 1000 importers and exporters use Fritz as a partner to reduce their investment in channel logistics, reduce overall costs, simplify and speed up the international order-delivery cycle, track orders, and increase their choice of offshore suppliers. Soon these companies could have access to each others' electronic sales catalogs, and price lists, through the Fritz system. When this happens, companies will be able to sell, buy, and ship through this electronic global marketplace.

Source: Fritz Companies, Inc., San Francisco.

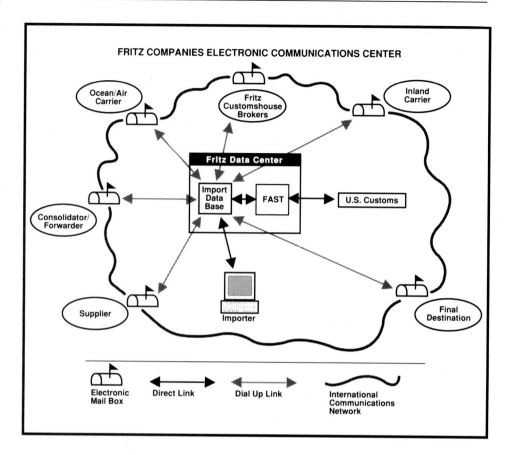

Containers have also become important as emergency warehousing facilities, particularly in markets that lack an adequate warehousing infrastructure. Warehousing is a problem in many markets, including, most surprisingly, Japan, where warehousing is very expensive and requires long-term contracts.[27]

In this chapter, we discussed the unique cultures and conventional trading practices of trading channels. Nowhere is this more important than in global marketing. First, a channel analysis, as described in Chapter 5, should be taken in the foreign market. This analysis should involve the extensive participation of consultants who are very familiar with the distribution infrastructure of the target economy, its culture, and its trading practices. Only then should a firm make the decision to use independent agents or to build its own distribution system. Some risk is involved in either case, more so if its own distribution is pursued rather than sales agents. One way to reduce the risk is to sell to a reseller at first, then if the relationship seems to work, make an offer to buy the reseller. A study of the global distribution practices of U.S. firms found that once a firm sets up a distribution system it tends to build on this system, no matter how shaky the initial foundations and the current inappropriateness of the sup-

---

27. Michael R. Czinkota and Jon Woronoff, *Japan's Market: The Distribution System* (New York: Praeger, 1986), 86.

plier-reseller fit.[28] This suggests that the initial distribution system decision making in a foreign market should be made from a long-run perspective. The study also found that

♦ Firms tend to rely on local resellers in cultures that are very foreign, and this is generally a good strategy. It is often encouraged, even mandated, by the foreign government. Such a trading relationship has the potential to grow into a production joint venture if protectionist government policies are introduced, such as in the European Common Market.

♦ Firms will consider building or buying their own distribution systems when their competitive advantage depends on confidential marketing processes, unique patents, product differentiation, or secret production processes that they do not want to have disclosed to the market. Treacherous diffusion and other types of opportunistic behavior are often serious risks in foreign markets because there is not a lot of competition in the distribution system to keep the players honest.

♦ Distribution decision making is also not very systematic and is often based on a weak channel analysis.[29]

All of this suggests that distribution management in the global market is particularly difficult, involving long-run commitments, conflicting guidelines (such as when introducing a very differentiated product in a very foreign market), and investment in high-technology control systems. However, it is in precisely such complex, uncertain, high-stakes decision-making situations that the firm with superior competitive rationality excels. All competitors are moderately good at distribution management in a familiar economy with very stable and rigid trading practices and systems. The superior firm does well in uncertain and volatile environments, such as in international markets. Global distribution presents tremendous opportunities for the astute, alert competitor who is able to adapt and implement quickly, particularly when using the new communication technologies.

---

1. The Woolrest Company, an innovative manufacturer and marketer of the first luxury woolen mattress pads, identified its target market as the over-50, traditional, upscale married woman. She was more likely to have a positive attitude toward wool as a natural fiber, to be aware of the sleeping problems the product addressed, and to be able to afford to buy the product for herself, her husband, and their parents. What types of retailers would provide the best fit for this product and contact segment?

2. What are the advantages of launching a new product through specialty catalogs?

3. In the early 1980s, there was a boom in designer labels on clothes, small appliances, even cars. Use the seller-reseller fit model to explain what ultimately went wrong with the marketing of most of these designer labels.

4. A supplier and reseller are having preliminary discussions as to whether they should develop a long-term, preferential relationship. Each party's enthusiasm

Discussion Questions and Minicases

28. Erin Anderson and Anne T. Coughlan, "International Market Entry and Expansion via Independent or Integrated Channels of Distribution," *Journal of Marketing* 51 (January 1987), 71–82.

29. Stephen J. Kobrin, John Basek, Stephen Blank, and Joseph La Palombara, "The Assessment and Evaluation of Noneconomic Environments by American Firms: A Preliminary Report," *Journal of International Business Studies* 11 (Spring/Summer 1980), 32–46.

depends on that party's perception of the other's current competitive strengths or assets, discounted by its uncertainty that such strengths or assets will be sustainable over the long term. Consequently, each firm must convince the other that it has sustainable strengths if it is to extract the most from the contractual arrangement, merger, or takeover. The party that is operating in the most uncertain competitive environment is very likely in the weakest negotiating position. Why is such negotiation very complicated? How might the issues be addressed by the supplier and reseller?

5. Often, it is the *impression* of relative dependency and power that is most important in negotiations and channel control—not the actual power. Describe how such impressions are formed. Illustrate your response by drawing a figure, if you can. (Hint: Think about what players in the market influence the creation of such impressions).

6. Home Depot has grown rapidly to dominate the do-it-yourself hardware store business. Home Depot accomplishes this feat with a combination of strong merchandising and a knowledgeable selling staff. Store employees go through extensive product and sales training. They go out of their way to help customers find items they are looking for. They can even provide demonstrations and advice.

   This approach to providing customer service, along with extensive product choice and availability, produces superior value for the customer. Not only do customers get the deep and wide merchandise of a warehouse store, but they also get a level of service uncharacteristic for such stores.

   Suppose you are a supplier of garden implements. What key issues would you face in trying to sell your products to Home Depot for resale? What sorts of things could you do to address these issues?

7. In the late 1980s, Garden Way, Inc., faced a classic case of having to manage multiple channels. Its garden tiller business had been built by selling direct, through mail order. Tillers were shipped directly to the customers, who tended to be serious gardeners living outside urban areas. As Garden Way added new products to its product lines—chippers, mulchers, snow throwers, and so forth—new target market segments were also added. The company still targets serious gardeners, but many are geographically located in suburban areas. Also, some segments, such as the segment for snow throwers, are not necessarily gardeners at all.

   To reach these new targets, Garden Way sought new channels, including independent dealers and, eventually, Sears. Consequently, the seeds were sown for a three-way conflict as Sears and the dealers could potentially sell to some of the same segments, and Garden Way itself still sold direct.

   If you were the vice-president of marketing for Garden Way, what could you do to minimize conflict, to build relationships with all your channels, and even to get them to work synergistically?

8. An entrepreneurial manufacturer of insulated, leaded, bevelled art glass (see the photo on page 369 and the figure on page 370) developed a very attractive product line for entrance doorways in residential homes that were valued at $150,000 and up. For several years, the manufacturer had sold exclusively to OEMs (original equipment manufacturers), and its sales were dependent on how well their doors sold. In an attempt to gain more control over its destiny, the company decided to initiate an aggressive marketing strategy. One of the first steps it took was to analyze the distribution channel for its product. The figure on page 370 presents the selling prices, margins, and added value provided at each step in the channel for the most popular item in the manufacturer's line. Should the company change its distribution system?

9. Frecom is a manufacturer of low-cost fax boards for personal computers. In an effort to reach as many buyers as possible, Frecom uses multiple channels. It advertises in computer magazines and provides an 800 number for buyers to call direct. It also signs up as many independent dealers as possible. One way that Frecom finds new dealers is by asking 800-number customers what dealer is closest to them. Then the company sends the fax board to the dealer and allows the dealer to install it, charging a service fee. Frecom then approaches the dealer about carrying the Frecom line.

   Frecom does a few things to provide support for its dealer channel, such as helping the dealer build its service business. On the whole, however, Frecom does not do much to maintain separation of the channels. Yet, dealers do not seem to complain. Why can Frecom do this and be successful? What pitfalls are there in Frecom's approach to the market? What would you suggest the company do about these pitfalls?

10. The benefits of information technology for logistical systems are not always obvious and this creates barriers for the implementation of an IT system. While Federal Express was successfully developing computerized tracking systems in the late 1970s and early 1980s, United Parcel Service (UPS) was having difficulties making investment in information technology pay off. It was only through a ten-year investment period, in which UPS methodically improved its information handling,

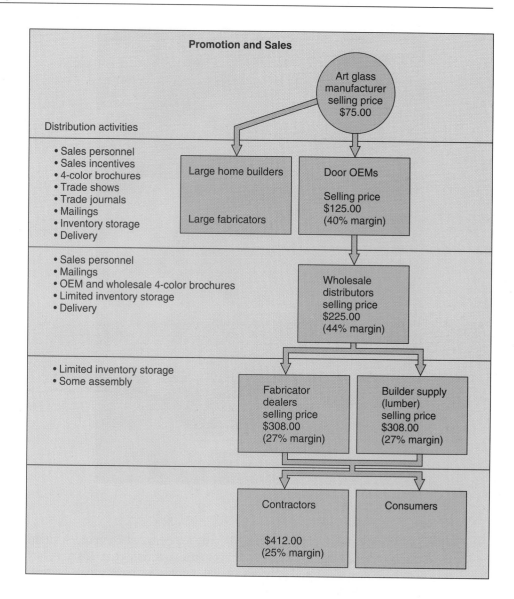

that it was able to reap rewards. By 1992, UPS had in place a global data tracking system that included centralized processing, hand-held input devices for truck drivers, and a label code system that carried more information than current bar code systems. At that time, UPS was able to compete with Federal Express on delivery time and customer information.

Why would UPS have such a difficult time implementing IT systems before it began its successful effort in 1983? If you were a systems integrator, how would you now attempt to sell information systems to companies that have been "burned" in the past by systems that never paid off?

11. The Disney Store, started in 1987, is a successful effort on the part of the Walt Disney Company to sell Disney products at retail. Each of the more than 140 stores has a consistent theme and atmosphere. The main purpose of the design is to make shoppers feel that they are in a Disney theme park. Service is friendly and helpful. The decor gives the feeling of being on a movie set. Merchandise is correlated with Disney movies and other promotions.

Why would Disney integrate forward to sell its merchandise, instead of licensing the name and logo or selling Disney merchandise to selected resellers?

What conditions do you feel have led to the success of such a venture? What factors might arise that would threaten the continued success of the Disney Store chain, and how should Disney respond?

12. A company can encounter a host of problems when it seeks a distributor or agent to sell its products overseas. Distance alone makes it difficult to meet and scout good dealers. Often, the only direct contact a fledgling exporter may have with a prospective distributor is a meeting at a trade show. Then the exporter may find itself locked into an agreement that does not result in sales. The distributor may carry competing products or its business may go in another direction. In addition, the legal system in the distributor's country may be different from what the exporter is used to, and it will be surprised when it finds that the relationship cannot be dissolved.

What are some ways that a prospective exporter might reduce the risks involved in finding a reliable distributor in a host country?

13. Please explain the essence of the LOSTSALE spreadsheet.

The LOSTSALE Spreadsheet

A Distribution System Capital Budgeting Comparative Analysis

Table 1 Operating characteristics	Present system	Proposed system A	Proposed system B
Warehouse replenishment time (in days)	16	8	8
Average customer order-cycle time from warehouse stock (in days)	5	5	4
Average customer order-cycle time for back orders (in days)	25	18	16
Percentage of total orders back-ordered	25.0%	10.0%	8.0%
Percentage of back orders cancelled	20.0%	20.0%	20.0%
Lost sales (% of total orders)	5.0%	2.0%	1.6%
Fixed operating expenses ($000)	$2,000	$2,000	$2,000
Variable operating expenses: sales, production, and general (% net sales)	80.0%	80.0%	80.0%
Physical distribution expenses			
Fixed transportation and warehousing ($000)	$285	$310	$325
Variable transportation and warehousing (% net sales)	5.20%	3.80%	3.00%
Fixed inventory costs ($000)	$60	$40	$50
Variable inventory costs (% net sales)	0.50%	0.30%	0.40%
Depreciation, buildings, and plant ($000)	$10	$40	$52
General physical distribution administrative expense ($000)	$25	$35	$40
Order handling ($000)	$15	$40	$50
Investment required			
Inventory fixed costs ($000)	$300	$200	$250
Inventory variable costs (% net sales)	2.5%	1.5%	2.0%
New warehouses ($000)	$0	$500	$600
New equipment ($000)	$0	$300	$400
Land ($000)	$0	$75	$100

Continued

Continued from previous page

Table 2 Present system	Cost and profit analysis of present system				
	Year 1	**Year 2**	**Year 3**	**Year 4**	**Year 5**
Total orders received	$20,000	$21,000	$22,000	$23,000	$24,000
Orders cancelled	$ 1,000	$ 1,050	$ 1,100	$ 1,150	$ 1,200
Net sales	$19,000	$19,950	$20,900	$21,850	$22,800
Production, sales, and administrative expenses	$17,200	$17,960	$18,720	$19,480	$20,240
Physical distribution costs	$ 1,478	$ 1,532	$ 1,586	$ 1,640	$ 1,695
Net profit before tax	$ 322	$ 458	$ 594	$ 730	$ 865
Tax at a 50.0% rate	$ 161	$ 229	$ 297	$ 365	$ 433
Net profit after tax	$ 161	$ 229	$ 297	$ 365	$ 433

Step 1: All of the cost estimates in the first table must be made and inserted into Table 1.

Step 2: The all-important reductions in back order cycle time, percentage of total orders back-ordered, and percentage of back orders cancelled must be estimated for the current and proposed systems and inserted into Table 1.

Step 3: The investment costs for the new systems must be estimated and inserted in Table 1.

Step 4: The tax rate percentage and target rate-of-return percentage must be estimated and included in Table 2 and Table 3, respectively.

Step 5: You are now ready to play "what if" with the cost estimates and estimates of improved performance.

Table 3	Cost and profit analysis of proposed system A				
	Year 1	**Year 2**	**Year 3**	**Year 4**	**Year 5**
Total orders received	$20,400	$21,420	$22,220	$23,230	$24,240
Orders cancelled	$ 408	$ 428	$ 444	$ 465	$ 485
Net sales	$19,992	$20,992	$21,776	$22,765	$23,755
Production, sales, and administrative expenses	$17,994	$18,793	$19,420	$20,212	$21,004
Physical distribution costs	$ 1,285	$ 1,326	$ 1,358	$ 1,398	$ 1,439
Net profit before tax	$ 714	$ 873	$ 997	$ 1,155	$ 1,312
Tax at a 50.0% rate	$ 357	$ 436	$ 499	$ 577	$ 656
Net profit after tax	$ 357	$ 436	$ 499	$ 577	$ 656

	Return on investment of proposed system A				
	Year 1	**Year 2**	**Year 3**	**Year 4**	**Year 5**
Physical distribution cost savings ($000)	$ 193	$ 206	$ 229	$ 242	$ 256
Contribution margin on sales gained by better service ($000)	$ 158	$ 166	$ 139	$ 146	$ 152
Total increase in before-tax profits from system A	$ 351	$ 372	$ 368	$ 388	$ 408
Tax	$ 176	$ 186	$ 184	$ 194	$ 204
Net increase in after-tax profits from system A	$ 176	$ 186	$ 184	$ 194	$ 204

Continued

Continued from previous page

Add:

Depreciation and capital recovery ($000)	$ 40	$ 40	$ 40	$ 40	$ 715
Difference in annual inventory carrying ($000)	$ 275	$ 284	$ 296	$ 305	$ 314
Increase in funds available with system	$ 491	$ 510	$ 520	$ 539	$ 1,232
PV of total funds flow with IRR 20.0% ($000)	$ 1,819				
Total investment ($000)	$ 875	Profitability index			2.08

Cost and profit analysis of proposed system B

Table 4	Year 1	Year 2	Year 3	Year 4	Year 5
Total orders received	$20,500	$21,525	$22,220	$23,230	$24,240
Orders cancelled	$ 328	$ 344	$ 356	$ 372	$ 388
Net sales	$20,172	$21,181	$21,864	$22,858	$23,852
Production, sales, and administrative expenses	$18,138	$18,944	$19,492	$20,287	$21,082
Physical distribution costs	$ 1,203	$ 1,237	$ 1,260	$ 1,294	$ 1,328
Net profit before tax	$ 832	$ 999	$ 1,113	$ 1,277	$ 1,442
Tax at a 50.0% rate	$ 416	$ 499	$ 556	$ 639	$ 721
Net profit after tax	$ 416	$ 499	$ 556	$ 639	$ 721

Return on investment of proposed system B

	Year 1	Year 2	Year 3	Year 4	Year 5
Physical distribution cost savings ($000)	$ 275	$ 295	$ 326	$ 346	$ 367
Contribution margin on sales gained by better service ($000)	$ 195	$ 204	$ 160	$ 167	$ 175
Total increase in before-tax profits from system A	$ 470	$ 499	$ 486	$ 514	$ 541
Tax	$ 235	$ 250	$ 243	$ 257	$ 271
Net increase in after-tax profits from system B	$ 235	$ 250	$ 243	$ 257	$ 271
Add: Depreciation and capital recovery ($000)	$ 52	$ 52	$ 52	$ 52	$ 892
Difference in annual inventory carrying ($000)	$ 122	$ 125	$ 135	$ 139	$ 143
Increase in funds available with system	$ 408	$ 427	$ 430	$ 448	$ 1,306
PV of total funds flow with IRR 20.0% ($000)	$ 1,626				
Total investment ($000)	$ 1,100	Profitability index			1.48

Source: This spreadsheet is based directly on the following article: John R. Grabner and James F. Robeson, "Distribution System Analysis: A Problem in Capital Budgeting," in David McConoughy, ed., *Business Logistics: Problems and Perspectives* (University of Southern California Research Institute for Business, 1969), 143–56.

Managing
Personal Selling

"A good name, like goodwill, is got by many actions and lost by one."
Lord Jeffrey

"Good listeners generally make more sales than good talkers."
B.C. Holwick

*I*n many business-to-business markets, the heart and soul of the organization's marketing is its sales force and selling strategy. In such markets, competitors such as Du Pont (chemicals) or Merck (pharmaceuticals) have put together inspired, disciplined sales forces that are respected, even feared. But even the very best sales forces cannot afford to rest on their laurels. Changing market conditions have made some sales management strategies and tactics obsolete. IBM, which once possessed a sales force without peer in the pioneer selling of computers, has reorganized its sales force three times in the last ten years. Meanwhile, an upstart, Dell Computer, has taught the industry that personal computers can be sold very successfully by a well-trained telemarketing sales force. Now, every major computer player is seeking to expand its telemarketing operations. Sales management may not be the most popular course in business schools, but it can be argued that more exciting innovations, technologies, and ideas are being introduced in sales than in advertising or other marketing functions. Table 11-1 lists some of these innovations.

In this chapter we discuss personal selling, sales strategy, and sales management. The overall message is simple. If a company does not hire people with excellent personal selling skills and cannot organize and lead such people, it cannot win in the marketplace. No matter how good it is, a new product or service will not sell itself. In fact, a new product or service must always go through several selling efforts. First, it must be personally sold to investors or senior executives. Then it has to be personally sold to production and the sales force. Only then does the sales force get the chance to personally sell the product to distributors, retailers, or end users. Distributors and retailers, in turn, have to sell the idea of buying the product to their companies. Often

Table 11-1
The Continuing Evolution of Personal Selling

Change	Sales Management Response
Intensified competition	More emphasis on developing and maintaining trust-based, long-term customer relationships.
Greater emphasis on productivity	Increased use of technology (for example, portable computers, electronic mail, cellular phones, fax machines, telemarketing, and sales support systems).
Fragmentation of traditional customer bases	Sales specialists or support staff for specific customer types. Multiple selling approaches (such as national accounts programs, traditional territory sales force, manufacturers' reps, and telemarketing). Globalization of sales effort.
Customers dictating vendor quality and delivery standards	Team selling. Compensation based on team performance and customer satisfaction.
Demand for specialized knowledge as an input to purchase decisions	Team selling. More emphasis on customer-oriented sales training. More highly educated sales recruits.

Source: Based on Thomas N. Ingram and Raymond W. LaForge, *Sales Management* (Fort Worth, TX: HBJ Dryden, 1992), Exhibit 2.1.

buyers even have to sell the idea of buying the product or service to their superiors! As we can see, moving a new product or service from idea to production and final usage involves a lot of personal selling.

Personal selling is the most expensive and powerful communications strategy a marketer can employ. There are several basic objectives of personal selling:

1. To persuade a potential customer to try a new product or service.

2. To keep current customers happy and buying.

3. To persuade a current customer to buy more.

4. To feed back ideas on customer needs, improved product positioning, and the success of company and competitor marketing tactics.

Personal selling involves much more than making a sale. Salespeople know more about their slice of the marketplace than anyone else in the company. They know customers and distributors on a personal level and are constantly crossing paths with the competition. Their livelihood often depends, more than anyone else in the firm, on their personal ability to change the way that both the marketplace and their firm think about the products and services they must sell. During the selling process, the customers questions or objections may suggest changes that will greatly improve the competitiveness of the offering. The salesperson may also recognize design problems not anticipated by the inventor or producer. It is the salesperson's role to make sure such information is passed on to those in a position to adapt the offering. In short, salespeople are often the change agents in the marketplace. They hasten the adoption of new innovations and the adaptation of their company to environmental realities. They are a key element of the competitive rationality of a firm. They also often have to unravel the marketing mistakes made by others. They are pioneering sellers and problem solvers. Keep these other key ideas in mind as you read this chapter:

- The size, nature, and organization of the sales force very much depends on the nature of the product and the behavior of the marketplace.

- In industrial markets, the cost of personal contact with the customer has soared to about $200 per call.[1] The order-taking function is being increasingly taken over by mail, telephone, or even computer services, meaning that the amount of time a salesperson once had to influence and change buyer behavior has all but disappeared. As a result, the salesperson must become more skilled at problem solving and time management.

- The allocation of territories in a rapidly changing market is not easy. It requires careful consideration of the service needs of different types of accounts.

- A large part of sales management is investing in human capital. Making a sales force faster and smarter, through training, technology, and leadership, greatly increases the competitive rationality of the firm. A customer orientation requires a sales management orientation.

- Sensible marketing planners involve salespeople from the very outset. The trick is for a cross-functional team to work with sales to plan and monitor the implementation and success of the marketing programs without getting too much in the way of the routine functioning of the sales force.

1. William A. O'Connell and William Keenan, "The Shape of Things to Come," *Sales & Marketing Management,* January 1990, 36–41.

The Objectives and Functions of a Sales Force

The most important objective of the sales force is to help achieve product-market share goals. The sales job should be carefully designed so that the selling activities are congruent with corporate strategy. For example, if the firm's primary strategy is to build market share, then the primary sales tasks will be prospecting, supplying high levels of service, and providing feedback from the market.[2] If the objective is to protect and develop existing business, salespeople should spend more time with existing accounts, particularly those that appear to have been targeted by competitors. When a company has the dual objectives of developing new business and expanding its existing business, it often employs separate, highly skilled developmental salespersons to achieve its first objective and a regular sales force to achieve its second objective. Advertising agencies, for instance, often use a new business sales force to identify and develop clients and then assign an account team to service the client and maintain a productive relationship between the client and the agency.

On the other hand, some sales forces spend much of their time selling to distributors. An important objective of such a sales force is to motivate the distributor, implement various selling programs, and maintain service levels. On important accounts, these trade salespeople often make calls with a distributor's salesperson to help develop new business or handle specific usage and service problems. A sales force that calls on retail accounts often has the multiple objectives of introducing new product lines, making sure merchandising displays are put in place, attempting to increase the amount and quality of shelf-space given to its product, and encouraging the account to cooperate with promotion programs.

Typical Functions of a Sales Force

A list of some of the varied activities salespeople may undertake in a day is presented in Figure 11-1. As you can see, much of a salesperson's time is spent away from the customer. A company considers sales force efficiency to be very high if salespeople spend 50 percent or more of their time actually selling.[3] Additionally, high-performing salespeople often go beyond the typical functions in ways that increase their sales and their efficiency. For instance, the list does not include creative activities such as buying a gift for a customer's secretary who has been very helpful or writing a computer spreadsheet program to monitor expenses. Yet these types of activities can help a good salesperson become a super salesperson.

Each industry has a set of expectations about which functions in Figure 11-1 salespeople should perform and how they should interact with customers. For example, a computer salesperson is likely to take an audit of customer needs, suggest and sell a system, install it, train users, upgrade the system, and handle any service problems. In other industries, other technical service specialists may undertake these functions, if they are performed at all. This is not to suggest that an enterprising firm cannot buck industry conventions and change the role and responsibilities of its sales force to give it a new competitive edge. Regardless of industry conventions, a salesperson must be competent and must develop a friendly, helpful, trusting, responsive relationship with the customer.

2. For a more complete discussion of how market-share strategies are related to selling objectives and tasks, see William Strahle and Rosann L. Spiro, "Linking Market Share Strategies to Salesforce Objectives, Activities, and Compensation Policies," *Journal of Personal Selling and Sales Management* (August 1984), 14–15.
3. O'Connell and Keenan, "The Shape of Things to Come." The average salesperson spends only 33 percent of his or her time selling face-to-face; 16 percent of a salesperson's time is spent selling by phone.

Figure 11-1

Typical Functions and Activities of a Salesperson

Source: Based on William C. Moncrief, "Selling Activity and Sales Position Taxonomies for Industrial Salesforces," *Journal of Marketing Research* 23 (August 1986), 261–70.

Selling Function

- Searching for leads
- Call planning
- Setting up appointments
- Developing a call schedule and organizing time
- Reading customer account histories
- Writing proposals
- Making sales presentations
- Overcoming objections

Working with Orders

- Handling shipping problems
- Handling back orders

Customer Service

- Problem solving, designing solutions
- Writing product or systems specifications
- Installing equipment
- Ordering accessories
- Demonstrating and training
- Undertaking minor maintenance
- Providing market intelligence on customer's competitors
- Taking customers on tours of company production and service facilities

Working with Distributors

- Establishing relationships with customers
- Collecting past-due accounts

Servicing Retail Accounts

- Setting up displays
- Stocking shelves

Administration

- Completing call reports
- Documenting and filing expense reports
- Meeting with sales manager
- Receiving feedback

Conferences/Meetings

- Attending sales meetings
- Attending exhibitions/trade shows

Training/Recruiting

- Traveling with trainees
- Planning sales activities
- Attending special training seminars
- Listening to tapes
- Reading product manuals

Entertaining

- Dining with clients
- Arranging parties

Travel

Fitting Function to Customer Buying Behavior

The first step in determining the role of personal selling and the basic selling strategy for a product or service is to study the way customers make their decisions. The customer's buying behavior (as described in Chapter 3), will define the selling role of top management, the salesperson, technical specialists, and office staff. Managers must also know how the competitors' sales forces are organized and managed. Is there evidence that the competitors' sales forces are not well adapted to the way their customers now make purchasing decisions? Does this suggest an opportunity for us? Management looks for a new angle that increases the effectiveness and the efficiency of its sales force.

The selling function will also differ depending on the nature of the customer's buying task.[4] For instance, when dealing with a customer who is buying a product or service for the first time (a new task), the salesperson must serve a missionary function. He or she must establish a relationship with the customer to understand the customer's needs. If the customer is planning a simple reorder (rebuy), the salesperson serves an order-taking function and must make sure that the order is correct, is handled efficiently, and is delivered when promised. The customer's needs dictate the salesperson's job, and the salesperson must do each job effectively to maintain customer loyalty. Years of hard selling effort can be wasted when a salesperson neglects to complete paperwork with the same care and energy that was devoted to selling. For example, a shipment that reaches the customer a day late because the salesperson did not carefully check shipping schedules can cost the customer dearly in terms of upsetting production schedules or working overtime to meet a deadline.

Fitting the sales function to buyer behavior means that the whole company adapts to the way a customer makes his or her buying decision. When every employee in the selling firm recognizes the importance of the customer, the entire company becomes a sales team. For example, a truly marketing-oriented company recognizes that whenever a customer calls for information, he or she talks to a sales representative, even if the person who answers the phone is an accountant or an after-hours maintenance worker. All the salesperson's efforts to win new customers can be squandered by sloppy support that costs very little to attain and maintain. The importance of handling customers must become part of the company culture, bred into the firm and nurtured from the top to the bottom. No one from the selling firm should be allowed to be rude to a customer, and every person must consider himself or herself a salesperson. Many individuals in the modern customer-oriented firm will be involved in personal selling at some time or other, and sometimes even special sales teams will be formed with employees who are not formally part of the selling function.

The relationship between the sales representative, the selling firm, the buying firm, and the purchasing agent is shown in Figure 11-2,[5] which depicts the multitude of communications (sources of influence and tension) between these entities. You can see that selling is more than just the interaction between a salesperson and a purchasing agent. Figure 11-3 shows how complex the situation becomes because competing sellers are also communicating with the buying firm. Figure 11-3 can be used to identify the system tensions and torsions that may exist, such as when the PA–SR1 link is strong but the SF3–BF is also strong. Having emphasized that a competitive firm must view its whole organization as a sales organization, we now turn to a discussion of the essentials of personal selling and relationship management.

---

4. For a discussion of how salespeople view the customer's buying task, see Erin Anderson, Wujin Chu, and Barton Weitz, "Industrial Purchasing: An Empirical Exploration of the Buyclass Framework," *Journal of Marketing* 51 (1987), 71–86.

5. T. V. Bonoma, G. Zaltman, and W. J. Johnston, *Industrial Buying Behavior* (Cambridge, MA: Marketing Science Institute, 1978).

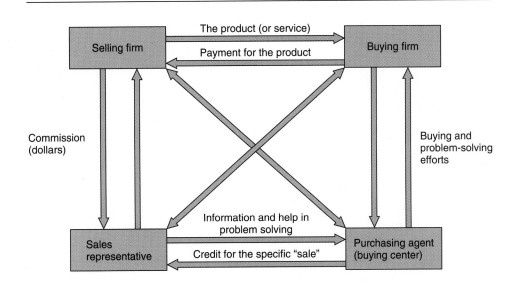

Figure 11-2

The Four-Way Relationship Model of Organization Buying

In addition to the dyadic relationship between the sales rep and purchasing agent (SR–PA), five other relationships exist that may influence the sale. The politics of selling are complicated because they involve the internal politics of both organizations and the politics between the organizations.

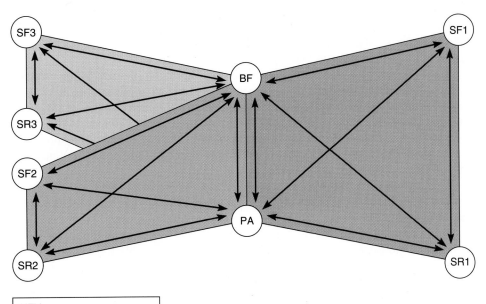

Figure 11-3

The Axle Model of Competitive Relationships

This model places the PA–SR relationship within the context of a whole set of seller relationships, tensions, torsions, and forces revolving around the buying firm–purchasing agent axle.

Personal Selling Skills and Relationship Management

There are two basic reasons why a company will spend up to several hundred dollars on a personal sales call. The first is to enable the salesperson to get a better understanding of the needs of the customer. No other type of contact with the firm offers the same opportunity. However, to take full advantage of customer contact, the salesperson must carefully question, listen, and interact with the potential client. We often view successful salespeople as smooth talkers, but they are more likely to be excellent listeners and acute observers of human behavior. The second advantage of personal sales calls is that they enable the salesperson to exercise his or her most effective persuasion skills. The salesperson must convince the customer that what the firm has to offer meets the needs of the customer better than any other competitive alternative. The mechanics of personal selling can be reduced to the following steps: prospecting, qualifying, presentation, negotiation, closing, and service. Each of these steps is now discussed.

Sales Prospecting

Prospecting for potential customers involves searching the yellow pages, trade listings, government reports, and magazines. It also involves relying on word-of-mouth networks to pass on information about new prospects. Prospects are often categorized as *A, B,* or *C* leads. *A* leads are immediately sent literature and called by a sales rep. *B* leads are likely to be sent literature and called by a telemarketing salesperson. A *C* lead is likely to be sent literature only. As the global marketplace opens up, the art and science of prospecting, particularly how to work trade shows, the major source of new customer leads, has taken on new significance.

The trade show has very ancient and honorable roots that go back to the medieval fairs where buyers and sellers gathered together to create an annual marketplace. With booths, demonstrations, and hawkers, trade shows are a modern version of the medieval fair. Thousands occur each year, and they occur in every country. At their best, they can provide an opportunity for a new company to break into a market by providing access to new customers and a chance to generate leads. In some specialized markets, the annual trade show is "an absolute must attend."

A successful trade show strategy starts with a list of goals. These will determine who will attend, the nature of the display, the appropriate sales approach, and the development and implementation of post-show follow-up activities.[6] Apart from the development of a traveling exhibit, the major expense in trade show marketing is the rental of the space and the cost of salespeople's time. As early as possible, a list of trade show attendees should be obtained from the trade show organizers. A friendly "see you at the show" letter with accompanying trade literature should be sent to prospective buyers.

A good trade show team employs at least two people: a screener and a good closer. The screener is at the front of the exhibit to meet people and to sort out the serious prospect from the inquisitive competitor and the general public. The closer spends his or her time at the back of the booth or in a hotel suite with serious prospects. Such selling efforts, followed up by a telephone call, often result in orders. The companies that take a very hard-nosed selling approach to trade shows may gain the reputation

---

6. It has been argued that trade show selling requires a selling approach that says "Thanks for coming in. What prompted your interest in our product?" However, this approach is unfamiliar to most salespeople. See Betsy Wiesendanger, "Are Your Salespeople Trade Show Duds?" *Sales and Marketing Management,* August 1990, 40–46.

of being party poopers, but they will differentiate themselves in terms of their professionalism and efficiency.

Many companies dilute the effectiveness of their trade show efforts by not promptly following up on leads. Follow-up personal letters should be sent and dated the day after the end of the trade show. The period after a major trade show is a time when customers and distributors judge the service of a company against the efforts of competitors who will also be following up on leads. That is why it pays to be the first to follow up. If a trade show does not draw new business, then it should be dropped. In general, trade shows are much more important selling tools in high-growth industries that are attracting new customers and new competitors.

Qualifying the Customer

Qualifying is a term used in personal selling to describe the process of learning to understand a customer's needs. The keys to personal selling are being able to put oneself in the shoes of the customer and to convince the customer that you are trustworthy. If you succeed, then customers will open up and start talking honestly about their concerns about the product and, particularly, your offering. When this happens, the salesperson can take the most advantage of interpersonal communication by answering the questions that really need to be answered and giving advice that the customer wants. The salesperson then becomes a problem solver on the buyer's side, rather than an adversary engaging in a verbal and intellectual wrestling match. As the dialogue continues, the buyer's confidence in the expertise and sincerity of the salesperson will increase. At some point, the customer will start disclosing preferences, the reasons for those preferences, and the true objections. The following is an excellent example of a master salesperson at work:

> A major research laboratory wished to purchase 200 potentiometers from Honeywell to measure temperatures, pressures, and speeds. Denzil Plomer, a 36-year veteran salesperson, recommended the company not buy Honeywell potentiometers but instead buy a data acquisition and analysis system that Honeywell could not even supply! Six months later, Honeywell had developed a data acquisition and analysis system, but the research lab only wanted to buy the potentiometers. Plomer convinced the lab to allow him to bid on both the potentiometers and the system. The competitors only bid on supplying the potentiometers. After a careful review, the lab opted for the Honeywell system and potentiometers that offered a superior solution. Plomer believes that integrity, listening, and creativity enabled him to serve his customers rather than simply make the quick sale. He seeks to build long-term relationships.[7]

The best way to establish customer needs is to ask questions and *listen* very carefully. A salesperson who does not listen will not fully understand a customer's needs. There is an art to asking questions.[8] A study conducted by Xerox learning systems established that successful salespeople use words such as *what, where, why, how,* and *tell me,* which allow the customer to respond more freely. Such questions are called open probes. Closed probes, the use of words such as *is, are, do, does, have, has,* and *which,* often limit answers to yes or no or a choice of alternatives. They do not get to the reasons behind the answers.

7. This example comes from Christopher Harvey, *Secrets of the World's Top Sales Performers* (Holbrook, MA: Bob Adams Inc., 1990) 99–106.
8. Camille P. Schuster and Jeffrey E. Danes, "Asking Questions: Some Characteristics of Successful Sales Encounters," *The Journal of Personal Selling and Sales Management* (May 1986), 17–27; see also Jeremy Main, "How to Sell by Listening," *Fortune,* February 1985, 52–54.

Qualifying the Selling Situation

Salespeople also need to learn to correctly categorize the selling situation, which includes the personality and competence of the buyer, the nature of the buying task (new or rebuy), how close the buyer is to making a purchase, and the organizational culture within which the buyer operates. They then must have the experience to choose the selling strategy that best fits the situation.[9] Experienced salespeople can help by holding group training sessions where they discuss how they deal with different types of customers when selling the company's products. This exchange of knowledge can be tape-recorded and circulated among the sales force so that salespeople can listen to the tape when traveling to sales calls.

A simpler way of sharing knowledge is to use a desktop system to write and publish a selling guide that is full of advice and anecdotes from successful salespeople. Such a book will help the novice and enhance the status of the quoted experts. This book might even form the foundation for a computer-based expert advice system that helps all salespeople to adapt their selling techniques on a continual basis.

Presentation

Videotapes, full-color brochures, and flip charts can greatly improve the quality of sales presentations. Many firms have no sense of proportion when it comes to investing in presentation aids for their sales force. After spending $200 or more to place the salesperson in the office of a buyer, they are reluctant to spend a few additional dollars to improve the quality of the presentation. It bears repeating that a quality sales presentation will increase direct communication and persuasion and will also act as an indirect cue to the overall quality of the selling company and its products.

A salesperson must have superior quality overheads or slides to use during a sales presentation to a buying group. It is probably better to invest in this sort of high-impact presentation tool, which a rep can adapt to his or her audience, than to present the sales pitch on a sales video. A sales video is unchangeable, difficult to update, and expensive to produce to the quality expected by the audience. Modern movies and TV commercials have set presentation and communications standards that few industrial selling videos can match.

A video is best used to demonstrate the on-site applications of the product or service and to explain how and why the product is used by other buyers. In short, it is used to present credible endorsements that also demonstrate the product in use. Videos can be taped onsite, inexpensively, and with little editing (which will add to its credibility). Again, a sales rep must learn to adapt the use of sales presentation aids to the unique selling situation. There is a right and a wrong time to introduce them. Forcing a canned sales presentation may alienate the customer and indicate the salesperson's lack of composure and command of the selling situation. The skilled sales presenter orchestrates the interaction so that the customer requests such a presentation.

A good sales presentation leaves a strong, concrete visual image in the customer's memory around which abstract information and arguments for buying the product or service can be stored and built up over time. It is better to leave one very strong visual image of the product's superior performance on a particular dimension than to overwhelm the customer with a multimedia song and dance show. The literature that is left behind should reinforce the key product differentiation advantages.

9. Barton A. Weitz, Harish Sujan, and Mita Sujan, "Knowledge, Motivation, and Adaptive Behavior: A Framework for Improving Selling Effectiveness: The Importance of Declarative Knowledge to the Personal Selling Concept," *Journal of Marketing* 52 (January 1988), 64–77.

Adapting Presentation Pitch to Personality

The personal approach used to gain the confidence and trust of a buyer must be built on the natural personality and interpersonal skills of the salesperson. This is one of the reasons why it is so hard to identify the successful salesperson from personality tests.[10] The successful salesperson makes the most of his or her personality by adapting it to the selling situation.[11] As humans, we are more comfortable being ourselves than trying to be someone we are not. However, some basic rules apply to all personal selling situations. For example, salespeople who do their homework and who can display detailed knowledge of their customer's business will create the impression that they really want to understand the buyer's needs. If a customer account profile is not available, then the salesperson should prepare by consulting the company's annual report or articles about the company in trade magazines. Ideally, the salesperson should also have access to the product plan's environmental analysis, which describes the customer, the competitor, and other market trends.[12]

Furthermore, it is important to recognize that the perceived expertise of a salesperson is judged relative to the buyer's own expertise. Hence, sales calls to expert buyers require greater than normal preparation. This explains why Merck and other leading drug companies spend over a year training their college-educated sales recruits, and why they often prefer to hire pharmacy majors. Merck's sales force is interacting with doctors who must be expert in the judgments they make about what to prescribe to a patient. Another rule is that good manners, politeness, courtesy, and old-fashioned charm are universal keys to creating an impression of competence and trust.

Negotiating and Bargaining with Customers

Any discussion of personal selling would be incomplete if it did not consider the topic of negotiating and bargaining. This activity occurs when the customer is satisfied that the supplier has a viable product or service and now wishes to negotiate on terms and price. It most often occurs at the closing stage of the selling process, but negotiating and bargaining tactics can occur at other stages as well. A good salesperson must be a good negotiator, even if the negotiating involves the most minor details.

All salespeople should be assigned to read several of the popular paperbacks on negotiation strategies as part of their general training.[13] However, a number of simple rules and tactics can often be successfully applied during negotiations with customers or distributors. Most of the following suggestions can be applied by either party involved in any trading negotiation. It therefore pays to assume, until proven wrong, that your adversary has read the same books on negotiation that you have read.

1. Trading relationships are built on personal commitment, enthusiasm, communication, and trust. Threats to discontinue dealings or not renew a contract are a poor way of managing a relationship and should only be made as a last resort. Reaching for the fine print in the contract is often the same as reaching for the

10. Another reason is that the duties of a salesperson vary greatly among industries and firms; see William C. Moncrief, "Selling Activity and Sales Position Taxonomies for Industrial Salesforces," *Journal of Marketing Research* 23 (August 1986), 261–70.
11. Barton A. Weitz, Harish Sujan, and Mita Sujan, "Knowledge, Motivation, and Adaptive Behavior: A Framework for Improving Selling Effectiveness: *Journal of Marketing* (October 1986), 174–91.
12. In presentations, purchasing executives are most critical of salespeople who are poorly informed about their business, poorly informed about competitors' products and services, run down competitors, are too aggressive, and who deliver poor presentations. See Milt Grassell, "What Purchasing Managers Like in a Salesperson . . . And What Drives Them Up the Wall," *Business Marketing* June 1986, 72–77.
13. Roy J. Lewicki and Joseph Litterer, *Negotiation* (Homewood, IL: Richard D. Irwin, 1985); and Roger Fisher and Scott Brown, *Getting Together: Building a Relationship That Gets to Yes* (Boston: Houghton Mifflin, 1988).

exit door. Contracts are used as insurance and protection against flagrant fraud and scoundrels. Unfortunately, they can also be misused, which occurs when one party unscrupulously uses a contract to take advantage of the other. Most executives, particularly senior executives, pride themselves on their word and woe-betide the junior executive who misunderstands this ethical code. Such unwritten understandings are, in fact, necessary for the U.S. and world economies to continue functioning. Most commercial trading relationships operate on informal quid pro quos (favors done and owed), which are called up from time to time, rather than the letter of the law.

2. However, a seller should protect its products, processes, and trade secrets with all the power of the law it can muster before negotiating with distributors and customers. Such actions signal that the company is being managed with an iron hand, even though it is extended in the velvet glove of friendship. It also signals that the supplier has an important competitive advantage that is worth protecting, the benefits of which will be shared with cooperating customers or distributors. Patents, copyrights, trademarks, and nondisclosure agreements arouse interest, discourage temptation, and engender respect.

3. Increasingly, what is negotiated is not a single sale, but a customer-supplier joint venture whose terms involve much more than price. Such negotiations can best be handled in a way similar to negotiations between superpowers. Senior executives meet and reach an accord or understanding. They then withdraw from the negotiation, leaving it up to their subordinates to work out the details. Their accord forces the subordinates to make settlements they would otherwise not make because they will face sanctions if they fail. As a last resort, senior executives can also get together again and work out any final impasses.

4. Always enter negotiations knowing the minimum terms that you will accept, below which you walk away from the negotiations. When such terms are not offered, walk away. Know the options of your rival and decide beforehand when and if you are going to reveal such knowledge and attempt to back them up against the wall. If you declare what you believe are your customer's options and you are right, then you are in a very powerful position. However, if you are wrong you will lose credibility and will be in a weaker situation. When an industrial buyer calls for bids or tenders for supplying a product or service, the accepted bid is often the starting point for negotiations: "We will award you the bid, if you change these areas." The response is, "We will accept if you address the following issues not contained in the initial Request for Proposal."

5. It often pays to let the other party make the initial offer and to justify it. If it is absurdly low, politely explain why, using marketplace facts. Ask the other party, in the light of the facts, to consider making a more realistic starting offer. If the other party does so, then it is conceding that you are in command of your facts. Do not counter absurdity with absurdity. When you do, you lose some control by implicitly agreeing to play by the other party's rules and by disconnecting the negotiation from reality. Questionable bargaining tactics that inconvenience or embarrass you should be challenged and confronted. If not, you admit that you lack bargaining power. Always maintain your cool. Take a time out if things appear to be getting heated.

6. There is some disagreement as to how much your initial offer should deviate from your reservation price or terms (the minimum that you would accept). Some experts claim you end up with a better deal if you start high. However, this tactic does not work when your opponent knows your alternatives. Making a better offer later in the negotiations may also be seen as bad faith at the outset.

7. In complex negotiations with an unfamiliar party, you should make an initial attempt to establish whether a settlement is possible on the most important issues. Each party makes a positional statement that describes the type of product and/or services it is seeking from the other party. A detailed negotiating agenda should then be discussed and followed. When an issue cannot be agreed upon immediately, then it should be left and returned to later. By doing this, both parties then know what is up for trade. The next topic for discussion should be how to proceed with these remaining contested issues. At this stage, items are often coupled together to help produce a compromise. Sometimes, each party alternates in making concessions. The last issue is normally price or margin, because each party now knows the exact nature of the bundle of products and services it will be delivering and receiving. Each has also developed an understanding of the negotiating skills and style of the other party, which is information that each will prefer to have before settling the most negotiated issue—price.

8. Try to find new solutions that satisfy the basic objectives of both parties when you reach a block. The more you explore each other's fundamental objectives, the more likely you will come up with new solutions.

9. It is a gesture of courtesy and an acid test of good faith to invite the other party to draw up the first draft of the final contract based on his or her understanding of the agreements reached in the discussions. It also reduces your legal costs. If the other party is going to attempt to exploit the relationship, he or she will use the fine print in the contract to do so. With the help of notes from the negotiations and a lawyer who can translate legalese into English, such booby traps can be defused or sometimes made to explode in the face of the perpetrator. More than likely the contract will pass the test and confirm the goodwill and trust developed in the negotiations.

Handling Objections and Closing the Sale

The art of handling objections is to anticipate all or most of the objections in the sales presentation. A skilled salesperson can turn an unanticipated objection into a problem that the salesperson and the customer can solve together ("How can we find a way through or around this problem?").[14] A salesperson should never dismiss an objection immediately ("Don't worry, that's not a problem."). To do so might cause the buyer to counterargue or simply politely clam up. Such outcomes have to be avoided at all costs because they change the negotiating parties from joint problems solvers to potential adversaries. At the least, the customer becomes embarrassed and defensive over voicing such an easily dismissed objection. It is much better to respect the concerns of the buyer by going over the issues step by step to let the buyer discover, with a little prompting, how they can be handled.

The fear of being unable to close the sale can give inexperienced salespeople nightmares. However, closing can be simple if the following suggestions are used. The key is to make a request to which the customer responds positively. For example, if a buyer quickly dismisses the salesperson's request for a trial order, the salesperson must work with the customer to determine the most useful next step. It is a human tendency to want to make some other concession to someone to whom you have just refused a request, particularly when there is social rapport between the negotiators.[15] Even if the salesperson only elicits an interest in receiving further information or bringing another

14. Paul H. Schurr, Louis H. Stone, and Lee Ann Beller, "Effective Selling Approaches to Buyers' Objections," *Industrial Marketing Management* 14 (1985), 195–202.
15. Robert B. Cialdini, *Influence* (Glenview, IL: Scott, Foresman and Company, 1988).

person into future discussions, it is important to end the meeting on a positive note. A definite and committed negative response closes the door to any future positive advances.

Building Relationships through Service

The relationship between a customer and a salesperson is like a marriage. There is a courtship period, when both parties begin to get to know each other. Then there is a ceremony, or contract to do business, which binds both parties to certain terms. The relationship is then maintained by developing high levels of trust and service norms that guide future interactions. If the relationship becomes unsatisfactory for either party, there is a divorce.

Developing strong relationships with customers gives a salesperson a sustainable competitive advantage in the marketplace. If a customer feels a certain level of commitment to the relationship, which has been fostered by the salesperson's attention to detail and willingness to go the extra mile in after-sales service, then, when a problem does occur, the customer will not immediately seek another supplier. Even though there may be many attractive potential partners in the marketplace, the customer will be loyal to a salesperson who has shown commitment and dedication over the long term.

To develop a long-term relationship, it is important for the salesperson to first understand the customer's needs and then to adapt selling techniques to those needs. However, the relationship has to be sustained, and it is sustained through attention to service, such as promptly returning calls, making special deliveries quickly and personally, seeking out answers to technical questions, and working with the customer to design the next generation of products and services that the customer will wish to purchase.

Sales Force Organization and Strategy

Any sensible marketing plan will give special service to the few major customers who constitute most of the business (often called house accounts).[16] It is a truism of selling that 80 percent of a firm's business comes from the top 20 percent of its clients. This top 20 percent is the firm's bread and butter. The level of support and the caliber of the selling team must be comparable with the importance of these largest customers. Senior executives will often be expected to develop personal relationships with their equals in these buying firms and take care of the day-to-day relations for such key accounts. When a major key account is lost, then the blame often rests squarely on the shoulders of senior management.

The development of special sales teams for the largest, most complex customers is called national account management (NAM). NAM programs assign special sales teams to coordinate major accounts at the national (or global) level. The NAM team works closely with corporate-level personnel to develop corporate-wide customer purchasing policies (and the accompanying significant quantity discounts) but communicates through local salespeople to sell and service at the customer's individual locations. Special national account management may go so far as to place a salesperson on site in the buying organization to be available on a day-to-day basis to help with

16. Jerome A. Colletti and Gary S. Turbidy, "Effective Major Account Management," *Journal of Personal Selling and Sales Management* (August 1987), 1–10; and Benson P. Shapiro and Rowland T. Moriarty, *Organizing the National Account Force* (Cambridge, MA: The Marketing Science Institute, 1984).

designing, installing, and servicing. As explained in the Rationality in Practice box on page 390, this salesperson's role is to expand and protect the business relationship.

Problems with key or national account management occur when several suppliers take such an approach with a single customer. An account representative is then under constant pressure to jostle the competition aside to get the attention of the important customer. The customer is in a position of power—multiple sellers are rushing to meet the customer's every need, and the customer knows that the seller cannot afford to lose his or her business. These types of NAM or house customers are often called "lost for good" customers, because once they are won over by the competition, it is difficult or impossible to win them back.[17]

High-Growth Account Management

Most of the literature on key account management has assumed that it is used in a relationship with a very large buyer. But a good case can also be made for developing a key account relationship with a company that is small but has great prospects. Indeed, many companies have earned great success by working and growing with customers who were treated as a special account from their start-up. Microsoft took this approach with IBM as IBM "started up" in the personal computer market.

The loyalties established with the entrepreneurial executives in such growth companies are likely to be much more enduring than those developed with professional executives in large companies who often move up or out, leaving an account representative stranded. Some entrepreneurial risks may have to be taken to give heavy support and service to high-growth prospects that may become very large customers in the future. Once the key house accounts have been identified and personnel selected to service and sell to this segment, salespeople can be assigned to the rest of the firm's customers. The following sections discuss the more general sales force organizational issues of territory design and assigning salespeople to territories.

Organizing the Sales Force

The field sales force can be organized in several different ways: by product, geographic region, customer, or stage in the selling process. Regardless of the approach used, the selling firm must recognize several important environmental realities. Some customers deserve (and must get) better sales service than other customers. The nature of the market and the competition in the market must be considered. In a growth market, the firm must be able to hire and train new salespeople to keep up with demand. In a market where the competition has a stranglehold, less selling effort might be used than would be used in markets where there was more opportunity to gain market share. The territories must also be large enough, in terms of sales potential, to motivate the salesperson to work hard, but small enough so that potentially important customers are not ignored. Finally, all salespeople are *not* equal, and the skill and experience of each must be considered when deployment decisions are made.

Keeping these issues in mind, the old-fashioned geographical territory is generally preferred over organizational structures designed around customers or products because it offers the firm the greatest control at the lowest cost.[18] Creating a specialized customer or product-based sales force drastically decreases the efficient time utilization

17. Barbara Bund Jackson, "Build Customer Relationships That Last," *Harvard Business Review,* November/December 1985, 120–28.
18. Gilbert A. Churchill, Jr., Neil M. Ford, and Orville C. Walker, Jr., *Sales Force Management* (Homewood, IL: Irwin, 1990), 36–44, 132–34.

Rationality in Practice:

Effect of EDI and CF Teams on Sellers

What effect will the joint venturing between two businesses that were previously in a traditional supplier-buyer relationship have on sales management? As discussed in Chapters 3, 5, and 10, electronic data interchange (EDI) enables automated just-in-time delivery and the close monitoring of quality conformance. It greatly reduces the need for a salesperson to serve an account, because a lot of the communication and order-delivery problems are eliminated or dealt with by other executives. Thus, the order-taking, customer-service, and the quality-selling components of a salesperson's job are greatly reduced or even eliminated in business-to-business or vendor-to-retailer markets. The upfront negotiation, however, required to set up the EDI configuration, software, expediting procedures, and quality conformance assurance and monitoring must be undertaken by more senior executives. In their interactions, the talks often expand in scope and what starts as a discussion on how to link EDI systems becomes much more of a joint venture. For example, at

one time, Procter and Gamble was selling to Wal-Mart and talking about how to develop an EDI order-delivery logistics system; now P&G and Wal-Mart are talking about developing new products and working together to reduce both of their costs (see Figure 10-2). Essentially, the traditional salesperson may not play an important role in such relationship discussions, except as a good-natured and credible facilitator.

Cross-functional team management is also having a dramatic effect on the sales management of key accounts. A cross-functional team in Motorola or Apple almost always invites a representative of a selling firm, such as a chip maker (a major supplier), to attend a special or occasional meeting with the cross-functional team. However, some cross-functional teams invite a JIT supplier to *become* a permanent member of the cross-functional team (see Chapter 1). The person chosen immediately becomes the primary account manager, and often the person is an engineer, rather than a sales person. A traditional, pioneering salesperson may make the relationship breakthrough, but once the relationship moves to close cooperation on product development and reducing joint costs,

of the sales force unless types of customers or product sales already cluster together by territory. This often can occur when a particular industry is concentrated in a region (such as computers in Silicon Valley or automobiles in Detroit). Whatever the structure, management must determine the size of the territory and must assign salespeople to territories.

Determining Sales Force and Territory Size: A Workload Approach

Territory design decisions must be made when starting a new firm or new division, when adding a new product line that increases the work load of the existing sales force, or when reorganizing a sales force because of major environmental changes. A common procedure for designing territories is illustrated in Table 11-2. It starts with the assessment of the type and number of present and potential accounts in the firm's target market. First, customers are categorized by their importance (the most important are AA; the next, A; and so on through D).[19] Remember that corporate goals determine which criteria are used to rank customers and also determine which customers rank highest. In addition, NAM customers may be handled by special teams, and house accounts may be handled by specific senior executives.

19. For other criteria, see Henry Porter, "The Important Few—The Unimportant Many," *1980 Portfolio of Sales and Marketing Plans* (New York: Sales and Marketing Management, 1980), 34–37; and Rosann L. Spiro and William D. Perrault, Jr., "Factors Influencing Sales Call Frequency of Industrial Salespersons," *Journal of Business Research* 6 (January 1974), 1–15.

the engineers and senior management take over account management.

Likewise, the same cross-functional team may include executives from major buyers of the product or service that the cross-functional team is responsible for marketing. The whole cross-functional team then becomes a selling-team, selling to and servicing the major buyer representatives from companies such as General Electric or Boeing. This always occurs in business-to-business markets involving the supply of complex plant, equipment, and construction where the delivered product package is uniquely designed and customized for a special buyer (for instance, a shopping mall, an oil refinery, a weapons system, a large computer system) or for markets that require a special component designed to be a part of another product (for instance, auto parts suppliers to Ford, Chrysler, GM or Honda). If a separate salesperson is responsible for selling to such a customer, and that customer has a representative as a member of a cross-functional team, then presumably the salesperson will be very keen to sit in on all such meetings. This is particularly so if the account is a large one (which is a safe assumption, given the importance of the buyer to the cross-functional team). Otherwise he or she risks losing control of a relationship on whose success his or her commission and livelihood depend (see Figure 11-2).

The alternative is for the cross-functional team to become the sales team for the account, responsible for all account selling and servicing. This would appear to be a more efficient solution. Thus, across the American and global economy, any increase in EDI and cross-functional teams that include major supplier representatives and major buyer representatives immediately impacts the nature of the players' key account sales management and incrementally changes the overall nature of selling in the economy. Two such interesting aggregate effects may be that traditional sales forces will be reduced in size, and engineers will be preferred over MBAs and marketing graduates for many of the positions in the organization relationships just described. These changes also explain why it is difficult, but not impossible, to have independent sales reps continue to play a role in such changes in relationships (see Discussion Question #20 at the end of this chapter).

Table 11-2 presents an example of a set of criteria that can be used to rank customers. In this case, the firm has a corporate strategy of rapid growth. Therefore, the most important accounts (AA) are large, with high growth potential and an opportunity for increased sales (low current penetration). Other very important accounts (A) are those with high growth rates and opportunity for growth, and medium accounts with opportunity for growth and increased sales. The number of each type of customer in the firm's target market is then estimated. Typically, a firm will have fewer AA, A, and B customers and more C and D accounts (the 80/20 rule again!). The next step is to establish a company norm for the average call frequency on each type of account in a year and the average time that should be spent on each call to each type of account. These norms should be based on past experience and the current selling objectives. More time will be spent with AA, A, and B accounts, but C and D accounts should not be ignored because, with effort, they could become more important (they could also become high-growth accounts, discussed previously). AA accounts might, for example, receive 30 minutes every other week, while A accounts receive 30 minutes every three weeks.

Next, the total amount of time required in a year to service all accounts should be calculated by multiplying the number of each category of account by the minutes per year to service that account, and summing the totals for AA, A, B, C, and D accounts. This will result in the total amount of selling time needed to reach corporate objectives. At this point, the number of salespeople required is determined by dividing the total time required to service accounts by the selling time available to the average salesperson (remember that many salespeople spend less than 50 percent of their time

Table 11-2
Determining Sales Territory Workload*

1. Categorize all current and potential accounts using a table such as the following:

Current penetration	Competitor activity	Large Growth: High	Large Growth: Low	Current Size Medium Growth: High	Medium Growth: Low	Small Growth: High	Small Growth: Low
High	High	A	A	A	B	B	C
	Low	A	B	B	C	C	D
Low	High	A	B	B	C	C	D
	Low	AA	A	A	B	B	C

2. Identify the number of minutes spent per call and the total number of calls per year for each account.
3. Calculate the total time, total number of accounts, and total hours per year for each account type.
4. From this information, determine the number of salespeople needed to service these accounts each year.

How to grade accounts from D to AA:
- On size (how much they contribute to gross profit)
- On growth (how fast are they growing)
- On penetration (how much of their business do we have)
- On competitor activity (level of calling/service, etc.)
- Highly innovative customers should receive special attention from R&D and service people to facilitate improvements in user training, maintenance, and product design.

*The WORKLOAD spreadsheet executes the following process.

actually selling). For example, suppose a firm has a total of 1,500 of all types of customers, and the time required to service those customers totals 13,000 hours per year. The firm's salespeople have 25 hours of selling time a week multiplied by 48 weeks (remember to subtract vacations, holidays, and sick days) for a total of 1,200 hours of selling time a year. Thus, 13,000 divided by 1,200 equals 10.8, or 11 salespeople needed to cover the market.

The number of salespeople may or may not be the same as the final number of territories. Territories are units of control for which objectives are set and results evaluated. Management may combine several individual work loads into a territory for reasons of product usage, customer similarity, geographical proximity, or competitive factors. The customers within one territory must be similar on an important characteristic (such as geographic location or type of business) so that a cohesive set of sales goals can be set for each territory. Continuing the previous example, the firm's 11 salespeople may be divided into five territories based on five geographic areas of the state (for example, northwest, northeast, central, southwest, and southeast). Once the number of salespeople needed and the number of territories has been determined, the next task is to assign salespeople to territories.

Assigning Salespeople to Territories

The important job of assigning individual reps to territories must focus on the needs of the territory and the abilities of the sales representatives. Not all salespeople have equal abilities, experience, preferences, or backgrounds. An attempt should be made to match salespeople with territories in such a way as to assure maximum customer service and the utilization of the salesperson's best skills. For instance, a salesperson with a highly technical background should be assigned to a territory with the most technically sophisticated customers. An inexperienced rep should not be placed in a territory with large accounts that demand high levels of expertise. Increasing a salesperson's efficiency should be the constant goal of management and is a major consideration in territory design. However, a fundamental limit to the efficiency of a salesperson is the distance between sales calls. If customers are geographically close, then a salesperson can make two, four, or more sales calls per day; but if customers are distant, then the salesperson's productive selling time is greatly reduced.

Many companies have well-established sales territories. These have historically evolved based on concentrations of customers, geography, and transportation services. Some companies employ consultants who use sophisticated computer programs to create territories that minimize travel, balance workload, and maximize profit.[20] Changing a sales territory is a significant event because it disturbs established customer relations and has repercussions on other territories. However, environmental events sometimes necessitate even a complete restructuring of sales force territories. The introduction of convenient and faster air travel in the 1960s led many companies to reconsider their sales territory strategy. In the 1980s, the growth of telemarketing again forced many companies to reevaluate how they should define their sales territories.

Field Staff Support

Field staff support (which is often made up of engineers) can greatly increase the efficiency and productivity of the sales force. The expertise of corporate customer and product specialists can be used on an as-needed basis by all salespeople. The specialists are always available to the customer or the salesperson by telephone. The field staff can make calls with the local salesperson, particularly when selling to new accounts. A serendipitous advantage of having such customer or product service specialists is that they are the ideal people to interact with R&D and production on the development of new products, quality control, or service problems. Their role in developing new business keeps them on the edge of product advances and discovering new customer applications. Most of a company's new product and service innovations are likely to be suggested by such boundary-spanning product specialists. They should be particularly rewarded for working with customers on new products and product modifications.

High-Growth Stresses on Sales Force Structure

A high-growth company faces particular problems because it constantly has to adjust its sales territories as its sales expand.[21] However, when it responds by reorganizing and subdividing its initial territories, a company has to be very careful not to alienate its experienced sales force. If it does not respond quickly on a region-by-region basis, then it leaves itself vulnerable to aggressive small competitors who focus on a region and do a much better job in their pioneer selling of new accounts. It is also vulnerable to the entry of a large company with a well-organized sales force that is already calling on potential customers. In a high-growth market, a company is often not sure how many potential customers exist out there. An aggressive approach to determining sales

20. Arthur Median, "Optimizing the Number of Industrial Salespersons," *Industrial Marketing Management* 11 (1982), 63–74; and Andris A. Zoltners and Prabhakant Sinha, "Sales Territory Alignment: A Review and Model," *Management Science,* November 1982, 1237–56.
21. David W. Cravens, William C. Moncrief, Charles W. Lamb, Jr., and Terry Dielman, "Sequential Modeling Approach for Redeploying Selling Effort in Field Sales Forces," *Journal of Business Research* 20, (1990), 217–33.

The notepad computer with a modem has greatly increased the productivity of salespeople who have learned to take advantage of all of the software and to communicate directly with the firm's information system (see Figure 11-9).

force size in such a situation is to keep adding salespeople until they no longer generate enough contribution to justify their employment. This way the true potential of the market is tested and pushed to the limit.

The Politics of Multiple Sales Forces

Although there are sound arguments for a single territorial-based sales force supported by customer and product specialists, the reality is that many companies operate parallel sales forces. The most valid reason for operating two or more separate sales forces is that the products are so specialized or so different that they need different experts to sell them. The need for expertise overrides the increased cost and control problems.

In practice, a parallel sales force organization is often created as the result of a takeover or merger. The companies may still operate as separate divisions and keep their own sales forces rather than face the organizational problems that might occur if an attempt at integration was made. An even more cynical view is that many large companies prefer to maintain the separate sales forces they inherited in the acquisitions because of organizational politics. With a risk-averse view of the future, management may also prefer to maintain the separate sales forces until it is sure the merger or acquisition has worked. It is easier to sell off a division as a self-contained enterprise with its own sales force if the acquisition or merger goes bad.[22]

22. The difficulties of managing multiple sales forces are further discussed in Richard H. Cardozo and Shannon Shipp, "How New Selling Methods Are Affecting Industrial Sales Management," *Business Horizons* 30 (September/October 1987), 23–28.

Managing the sales force involves recruiting, selecting, training, rewarding, and leading. The purpose of this section is to only acquaint the reader with such management functions, as entire chapters of sales management texts and scores of trade books are often devoted to each of these topics.

Recruiting

Recruiting is very important because hiring and training a salesperson is a considerable investment in human capital. In high-technology and pharmaceutical markets, a company is likely to spend over $100,000 in the salary and direct expenses involved in training. There are three basic costs involved in hiring ineffective salespeople. The first is the wasted cost of spending a great deal of time and effort training such a person. The second is the cost of exposing the customer to a poor salesperson. This is largely the opportunity cost of lost sales that would have been made by a more competent employee. The third cost, which is related to the second, is the strain on the enterprise and its management because the ineffective salesperson does not cover his or her compensation and expenses.

The first step in recruiting is to develop a sales representative's job description (see Figure 11-4). Job descriptions are not only used for recruiting and selecting; they are often used to set objectives and to evaluate performance. Recruiting is an area that is fraught with legal difficulties for the sales manager (see the Rationality in Practice box

Managing the Sales Force

Figure 11-4

Example of a Salesperson's Job Description

A good job description details the specific responsibilities of the position, the skills required, and the person to whom the new hire will report.

Source: Gene Garofalo, *Sales Manager's Desk Book* (Englewood Cliffs, NJ: Prentice-Hall, 1989).

Job Description	
Position: Territory sales person, Southern California	Division: Office equipment

Summary:
Sell office staplers, paper shredders, and mail room supplies to office equipment dealers and major account end users in Southern California territory.

Specific Responsibilities:
Cover Orange, Los Angeles, and Riverside counties. Call on dealers and important end users. Meet quota projections. Check dealer inventory. Discuss promotions/incentives. Help train dealer sales staff. Product-train dealer, supply dealer literature. Work with dealer on store displays and advertising. Work product shows. Enter orders and follow through with order entry system. Call on major accounts. Make demos, surveys, and proposals. Report on competitive activity. Report calls and sales activity. Suggest new products.

Reporting Structure:
Report to district sales manager.

Knowledge, Skills, and Experience:
Requires two years college, some mechanical aptitude, good verbal and writing skills, and four years outside sales experience, preferably in office equipment industry. Experience calling on dealers mandatory. Experience calling on end users highly desirable.

Rationality in Practice:

Avoiding Discrimination by Sticking to the Job Description

"I don't want to hire any salesperson who's been arrested." Sales managers or recruiters who ask about a potential employee's arrest record may be in for legal trouble themselves. Such a question may be discriminatory, because our legal system assumes innocence until guilt is proven, and an arrest is not considered evidence of guilt. Questions about arrests (without a conviction) are never appropriate in the recruiting and selection process.

Seeking other types of information during the recruiting process can also lead to charges of discrimination. A series of legal decisions from the Civil Rights Act (1866 and 1964) to the Americans with Disabilities Act (1992) prevents employers from discriminating against persons on the basis of race, color, religion, national origin, sex, physical or mental handicaps or disabilities, Vietnam-era veteran status, or disabled veteran status. Questions that might lead to discrimination against any of these groups should be avoided.

on page 396). Anyone who will be involved in the interviewing process has be aware of what can legally be asked of a job applicant.[23] For instance, you cannot ask about a job applicant's age, marital status, or religion. In addition, during recruiting the candidate must be fully informed about company procedures and expectations. Important topics include the term of employment (there may be a trial period or a year-long contract), the compensation plan, company policies, and steps taken in the termination process. Both the prospective salesperson and the employer should try to eliminate all uncertainties about expectations before the job offer is extended and accepted.

Selecting Salespeople

It is clearly worth making the very best attempt to increase the effectiveness of sales force selection, but a company must realize that the screening and selection process merely increases the odds of making a good decision and reduces the odds of making a bad decision. Psychologists and personnel specialists have earned hundreds of millions of dollars over the last 100 years attempting to help companies identify successful salespeople. They have not had a lot of success. It does not take much skill to recognize the very bad and the very good candidate. The problem is to discriminate among the bulk of applications in the middle of the range.

Because the environment in which most firms operate is rapidly changing, it is important to conduct a job analysis at regular intervals to identify the typical salesperson's actual day-to-day activities. An outside consultant will often observe and analyze salespeople at work and will develop a list of the tasks that must be completed to succeed on the job. These tasks then become part of the job description. Sales managers can work with the consultant to develop this list of necessary skills. The more a firms selection procedures mimic the realities of the work environment, the greater the probability that the salespeople will have the skills to succeed. The investment in the job analysis and job description will pay off in the quality of the recruits and in the larger percentage of recruits who succeed at the job.

Many sales managers have gut-level feelings about what makes a good salesperson. All would agree that the most important characteristic is the self-confidence to cope with the rejection that is characteristic of selling. A resume may tell a lot about an

23. C. David Shepherd and James Heartfield, "Discrimination Issues in the Selection of Salespeople: A Review and Managerial Suggestions," *Journal of Personal Selling and Sales Management* 4 (Fall 1991), 67–75.

While most employers do not knowingly discriminate, some typical job interview questions may be considered discriminatory. For example, questions about height and weight may discriminate against females or Americans of Asian or Spanish descent. Courts have ruled that qualifications such as race, gender, or age (or other physical characteristics) can only be justified if "no person of a particular sex, race, color or religion can adequately perform the given job." This has become known as the Bona Fide Occupational Qualifications criterion, or BFOQ. The sales manager or recruiter is on safest ground if all job qualifications are derived from written job descriptions that define the specific tasks, duties, and responsibilities involved in the sales positions to be filled. While totally avoiding discrimination is difficult, managers should take a proactive approach to nondiscrimination in selection.

Source: C. David Shepherd and James C. Heartfield, "Discrimination Issues in the Selection of Salespeople: A Review and Managerial Suggestions," *Journal of Personal Selling and Sales Management,* vol. 11, no. 4 (Fall 1991), 67–75.

individual's experience, but the personal interview is probably more important when selecting salespeople than any other criteria. If candidates cannot demonstrate confidence when selling themselves, then they are unlikely to be able to sell other products and services. Another important characteristic is adaptability.[24] Confrontational interviews that incorporate role playing are often used in the later rounds of the selection process to see how adaptable and enterprising the potential salespeople are under fire. Some companies, such as Ford, also test the time-management skills of potential recruits using problem-solving exercises.[25]

Training the Sales Force

As the cost of making a personal sales call rises, many companies are trying to find ways of increasing the return from each call. Training is an investment in human capital that can produce a more profitable return. It increases the day-to-day efficiency and effectiveness of a sales force. Some companies look at the high turnover of their sales force and regard the investment in up-front training costs as a waste. This can become a self-fulfilling prophecy as turnover increases because of inadequate training. If a company hires a salesperson in good faith to service its customers, then it must, in good faith, follow through by giving the sales recruit the training to do the job. Moreover, on-the-job specific training may be a more important determinant of sales performance than any personal characteristics.[26] Some companies might be better off spending more on training and less on selecting and buying raw talent.

There are two types of training: basic behavioral sales training that is common to many markets and company-specific sales training. Basic sales training increases the general competence of salespeople, making them generally more valuable to any enterprise. Company-specific training increases human capital or skills that can only be applied in their current employment situation. Both types of training are needed to increase a sales rep's effectiveness, but the second type of training has an added advantage—it increases the loyalty of the salesperson and reduces turnover.

24. For further information on salesperson adaptability, see Rosann L. Spiro and Barton Weitz, "Adaptive Selling: Conceptualization, Measurement and Nomological Validity," *Journal of Marketing Research* 27 (February 1990), 61–69.

25. For a comprehensive guide, see *Selection and Evaluation of Salespersons* (Princeton, NJ: Educational Testing Service, February 1985).

26. Gilbert A. Churchill, Jr., Neil M. Ford, Steven W. Hardly, and Orville C. Walker, Jr., "The Determinants of Salesperson Performance; A Meta-analysis," *Journal of Marketing Research* 22 (May 1985), 103–18.

A good sales training program should encourage curiosity and the desire to learn on the job and to share such learning. Many sales training programs do not succeed because they are so concentrated in time that they produce a mental meltdown. On the other hand, another common problem with sales training is that much of it is made up of entertainment with far too little on-the-job follow-up.[27]

Basic Behavioral Sales Training

The universally important skills needed for basic selling can be obtained from sources outside the organization. Dale Carnegie-type courses are offered everywhere to provide such training. These sources are expensive, but through them the trainee realizes that he or she is not the only salesperson working hard to develop skills. The competition is learning them, too. A much less expensive approach would be to combine a package of books, audio tapes, and videotapes on selling with round-table discussions with the sales manager and some of the successful salespeople. Many firms overlook the fact that much of sales training is inspirational. All salespeople need to hear "you can do it, too." The inspirational part of training should be continued throughout the salesperson's career, and new inspirational audio tapes are often the most cost-effective way to provide this type of inspiration because the salesperson can listen to the tapes while driving.

Specific Content Training

Figure 11-5 presents a list of possible training topics and recommended training methods. They are organized in terms of company specificity, starting with the general and progressing to the very specific. Perhaps the most controversial topic is the proposal to teach the trainees how to train others. There is method to such madness. The best way of preparing people for training and learning is to place them in the shoes of the teacher. They are then forced to confront themselves and the problem in a nonthreatening way. By learning how to teach, they learn better how to learn. They will also be better able to teach other salespeople, teach customers, and become better mentors.

Mentoring

The company culture must encourage salespeople to help each other. A variation on this theme is the development of a mentoring program to supplement on-the-job coaching. It is difficult for sales managers to be good mentors because they are also the boss, nipping at the heels of the salespeople to make sure they do their jobs. Ideally, a new recruit should be paired with an experienced mentor who can make calls with the new salesperson, observe the newcomer's selling style, and provide valuable advice formally and informally.[28] The chemistry cannot be forced, so such a mentoring program will always have varying success. A mentoring program also addresses a classic social group problem in sales force management—the polarization between the old guard and the new recruits. The old guard view the new salespeople as hopelessly ignorant about the specific market, arrogant, and opportunistic. The recruits view the old guard as dead-end stick-in-the-muds. A mentoring system forces members of both parties to see the others as interesting and capable individuals. The mentor has a great deal of wisdom to share, and the mentored can provide enthusiasm and respect that

27. Jack R. Sander, "Why Most Sales Training Doesn't Work . . And What You Can Do about It," *Business Marketing*, May 1984, 90–96.
28. David Marshall Hunt and Carol Michael, "Mentorship: A Career Training and Development Tool," *Academy of Management Review* 8.3 (1983), 475–85.

1. **Goal:** Basic selling and presentation skills that increase self-confidence, poise under fire, manners, and dress.
   Solution: Special how-to courses, books, and tapes such as Xerox's Planned Selling Skills (PSS). Role playing can be videotaped to identify mannerisms and mistakes.

2. **Goal:** Time and territory management.
   Solution: Game playing exercises. On-the-job advice from successful salespeople and mentor. Read company *Standard Operating Procedures Manual.*

3. **Goal:** How to train others.
   Solution: A lecture-type course that explains learning and teaching techniques. Vicarious learning from mentor.

4. **Goal:** Customer knowledge.
   Solution: Read marketing plan environmental analysis on consumers, market segmentation analysis, history of customer industry from trade magazines, books on customer, customer account profiles on computer. Most importantly, learn from a mentor about the rituals and legends in the industry—the who's who in the customer industry. Read sales territory account book that reports number of calls each customer should receive, personal contacts, products purchased, and so on.

5. **Goal:** Competitor knowledge.
   Solution: Read marketing plan environmental analysis on competition. Study company market research reports. Learn from mentor and on-the-job monitoring. Read and become familiar with trade press.

6. **Goal:** Company knowledge.
   Solution: Company public relations films, annual reports, in-house magazines/newsletters. Discussions with sales manager and mentor.

7. **Goal:** Product knowledge.
   Solution: Hands-on practice, marketing literature, product use manuals, packaging, videos, production plant tours, and tours of the service department. The latter reveals what is not in the marketing literature.

8. **Goal:** Systems training.
   Solution: Built into reporting software, sales manuals. A boot-camp style two-day course in following instructions down to the very last details. Discussions with sales manager.

9. **Goal:** Specific short-term product sales programs.
   Solution: The teaching of standard scripts, strategies for coping with common objections through videotaped role playing. On-the-job mentor observation.

10. **Goal:** Adaptive selling techniques.
    Solution: Videotaped role playing. On-the-job mentoring.

Figure 11-5
Sales Training Needs and Recommended Methods

helps fire up the mentor. The best way of teaching an old dog new tricks is to use a young dog to do the teaching. The salespeople fresh out of college are likely to be more computer literate and, hence, will be able to teach their mentors how to use high-technology products, while their mentors can teach the recruits the soft touch of selling. A mentor can also teach the new salesperson about the firm's culture, its values, and the roles played by key people. The standards, norms, and expectations of the culture are also often established at this time through example and through the legends and stories that make up the firm's folklore.[29]

Rewarding the Sales Force

Basically, motivation is how hard a salesperson wants to work to accomplish a task or achieve a goal. Salespeople often strike out when they go to the plate, but motivation is what makes them continue to swing. There are many theories and explanations for what motivates people based on the idea that people want to work hard when outcomes

29. Alan J. Dubinsky, Roy D. Howell, Thomas N. Ingram, and Danny N. Bellinger, "Salesforce Socialization," *Journal of Marketing* (October 1986), 192–207; and Richard Pascale "Fitting New Employees into the Company Culture," *Fortune,* May 28, 1984, 28–40.

Some innovative companies are using instructional software to increase the product knowledge of salespeople. In time, firms will build libraries of information that the salesperson will be able to access during sales calls by using a notepad computer. This information will also be available to telemarketing salespeople to answer service questions.

are valued and when effort is linked to performance. For one salesperson, money may be the strongest motivator, while for another, receiving an award at a banquet is the best incentive. Motivation has always been of interest to sales managers because it is the link between the rewards offered by the sales compensation system and the salesperson's performance.

Sales Compensation

Salespeople are motivated to work by the reward system they are offered. No other dimension of sales management directs, controls, and encourages the initiative of a sales force more than the way a sales force is rewarded. The starting point for the compensation package must be the market rate in the industry, including the customary incentive schemes used by the industry, if they exist. If a company pays less, then it will not attract talent from competitors. If it pays more, then it is potentially placing itself at a competitive cost disadvantage. The trick is to carefully design a compensation scheme that matches the competition and, more importantly, achieves specific objectives.

The Advantages of Clarity and Simplicity. Perhaps the most fundamental rule of sales compensation is to keep it as clear and simple as possible. When a scheme becomes too complicated or is changed too often, then confusion and uncertainty about the reward schedule will increase. A scheme can become too complicated when it has multiple objectives and rewards the salesperson for performance on several different dimensions (obtaining new accounts, running special customer training programs, increasing sales on existing accounts, controlling expenses, and so forth). A company may desire to change its incentive schedule to adapt to the new competitive realities of the marketplace or company constraints, but changing the scheme has two negative effects. First, it is likely to confuse the more experienced salespeople who have worked under several different schemes. Having adapted to them, they may find it difficult to break their behavioral adaptation, as well as distinguish between the schemes in their memory. Second, a history of such changes increases the expectations that the scheme will be changed again in the future, thus reducing commitment to the new scheme.

The Salary versus Commission Debate.   Should a sales force be paid a salary or a commission? Much depends on the realities of the marketplace environment. Most companies pay a base salary with bonuses for exceeding quota or a commission on all sales. For the first year, a salesperson may be paid a much higher base salary to compensate for time in training and the time needed to build commission sales. From the salesperson's perspective, salary provides the security that comes with a regular income to pay the bills. It signals the company's belief in and support of the salesperson, whether sales are good or bad. But it also is attractive to insecure or lazy salespeople who see it as a way of maintaining a comfortable income, no matter what they do. Also, a salary is unattractive to the motivated and capable salesperson who views the salary as an unfair ceiling or cap on rewarding his or her efforts. The antithesis of competitive rationality is a plan that encourages poor performance and discourages superior performance. When an organization does not recognize differences in skill and drive in its compensation scheme, it places the organization in a position of devaluing the highly competent salespeople.

From an organizational perspective, a salary compensation scheme is simple to administer. By disconnecting compensation from selling performance, it also encourages salespeople to perform important, but nonincome-generating tasks, such as service and administrative duties. When these tasks are important, salary should make up a larger percentage of the compensation package.[30] Industry studies have shown that in markets where personal selling is not so important in making the sale, a sales force is more likely to be paid a salary.[31] The general advantages of a commission approach are obvious. It focuses the attention and behavior of a sales force on selling, perhaps even to the detriment of other activities the company would like the salesperson to undertake. The company only pays for performance, so, in a sense, all of the compensation risk is shifted from the company to the individual. The more that personal selling is needed to move the product, the greater a firm's enthusiasm for a commission reward system will be. A commission plan is cost/performance efficient—it encourages greater selling effort from all of the sales force, and will automatically screen out the poor performers.

The importance of personal selling is likely to change as a market matures, and this affects the compensation plan. During the introductory period, a salesperson is likely to have spent a lot of time learning and prospecting—necessary functions, but financially unprofitable in the short run. Unless the salesperson is one of the entrepreneurial founders of the company, it is unfair to ask him or her to bear a lot of risk by working solely on commission. But as the market enters its growth period, it is

---

30. George John and Barton Weitz, "Salesforce Compensation: An Empirical Investigation of Factors Related to Use of Salary Versus Incentive Compensation," *Journal of Marketing Research* 26 (February 1989), 1–14.
31. Charles A. Peck, *Compensating Field Sales Representatives,* Report No. 828 (New York: The Conference Board, 1982); and Lesley Barnes, "Finding the Best Compensation Plan," *Sales & Marketing Management,* August 1986, 46–49.

Figure 11-6

The Effort, Success, Compensation Connection

It is fair to link compensation directly to dollar sales or measures of customer satisfaction, providing factors beyond the control of the salesperson do not greatly affect sales or customer satisfaction. However, when changes in the economy or a change in the competitiveness of the firm's products or services have a major effect on outcomes, then no matter how hard the salesperson tries, he or she has little influence on the final result of those efforts. In such circumstances, linking rewards to outcomes is unfair and competitively irrational.

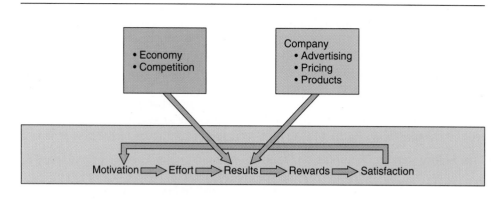

particularly important that an enterprise sells as fast and hard as it can. To gain a larger slice of a rapidly expanding sales cake, a company must grow faster than the industry average. It is not good enough for sales to keep growing; the rate of growth must increase. This suggests that tying commissions and bonuses to not just sales growth but *increases* in the *rate* of sales growth will help to increase market share. In a mature market, competitors jealously protect their major customer accounts, so it is very unlikely that an extra sales push will have much effect. It may then be appropriate to return to a largely salary-based compensation scheme with large one-time bonuses for stealing an account from a competitor.

The Effort-Performance Connection.   The more rewards are tied to performance, the more a sales force will perform. However, for a reward-for-performance compensation scheme to be really effective, the salesperson's effort and skill must determine performance. In markets where a company's sales are highly volatile because of frequent and dramatic changes in the trading environment or the company's marketing strategy, a straight commission approach may not work because there is an uncertain link between effort and results (see Figure 11-6).[32]

For example, let us consider how sales are affected when the economy booms and then busts. During the boom period, even the salespeople who are cruising will be rewarded; but when the economy busts, even the super seller may not be fairly rewarded. Such market volatility has a net negative effect on the salespeople because it creates the correct perception (particularly among the most aware and capable salespeople) that compensation is no longer under their own control. When specific actions taken by the company, such as an increase in the production of inferior products, weaken the link between effort and performance, then the sales force is likely to become very upset. In summary, a company cannot expect its sales force to carry all of the risk in the compensation scheme when the marketplace and the company's marketing strategy are uncertain.

Commission on What?   The standard approach is to base the commission or bonus on sales. This encourages a sales force to sell more and to increase market share. However, this approach may only be appropriate in special circumstances, such as during times of rapid growth. Generally, the overall objective of an enterprise is to increase profitability over a certain time horizon. This suggests that the sales force's compen-

32. Amiya K. Basu, Rijiv Lal, V. Srinivasan, and Richard Staelin "Optimal Compensation Plans: A Theory" (Working Paper, Graduate School of Business, Stanford University, 1984).

sation scheme should perhaps be connected to the gross margin earned on sales rather than dollar sales.[33] Basing compensation on gross margin requires that salespeople be informed of the relative profitability of the items in the product line in order to focus attention on higher margin products. Salespeople should also get regular feedback on their performance, which can be provided by notebook computer software on a regular basis. Other issues of sales force control are discussed in Chapter 15 on forecasting, budgeting, and control.

When the potential of sales territories varies, it is clearly unfair to use the same commission or bonus plan for every territory. One way of handling this is to set a different base quota (sales performance target) for each territory determined by its potential and sales history. Any sales above quota are then rewarded using the same commission or bonus schedule. However, even under this scheme, some territories are likely to be more financially attractive than others. The dilemma for the sales manager is how to assign unequal territories among salespeople. If the goal is to keep turnover low, then the most senior salespeople should receive the best territories. If the goal is to maximize performance, then the sales manager should assign the best territory to the best salesperson, whatever that person's seniority. Longevity may be best rewarded by giving special bonuses to salespeople at the end of every second year. In many industries, salespeople only last three or four years, so few such bonuses will be paid. But bonuses may encourage a salesperson to stay that extra three or four months.

When team selling is a common practice in a particular industrial market, the company must determine whether to pay a separate commission to each member of the group. It may be better to pay salaries and a group bonus that is divided up equally among the group members or based on the judgment of the group leader. At a more fundamental level, there is a lot of merit to incorporating the sales force's incentive scheme into a general company-wide bonus system, as discussed in Chapter 15. A general bonus scheme encourages overall cooperation and creates a company culture where everyone is aware that the company's competitiveness depends on everyone's performance and risk is shared by every employee.

A final problem with direct compensation schemes is that they tend to encourage a very short-term and selfish perspective. They motivate salespeople to sell rather than service accounts. Some firms have overcome this problem by giving a salesperson part of the commission on all sales made to a new account in the future, whether the rep is serving the account or not. This encourages the salesperson to view obtaining new business as an investment activity. The compensation scheme should also be flexible enough to allow the payment of split commissions to two or more salespeople who worked together to obtain a sale that otherwise would not have been made. Finally, the compensation scheme must attract and keep the superstar (see the box on page 404).

Sales Force Leadership

A sales force must be led from the front.[34] What this means is that salespeople should not be asked to do things that the sales manager and senior management would not do. One of the reasons that CEOs have been so successful as spokespeople in advertising is because they are able to convey the same enthusiasm to the public that they use to inspire their sales forces. Most senior managers wine and dine the executives of major

33. Douglas Dalrymple, P. Ronald Stephenson, and William Cron, "Gross Margin Sales Compensation Plan," *Industrial Marketing Management* 10 (July 1981), 219–24; Alan J. Dubinsky and Thomas E. Barry, "A Survey of Sales Management Practices," *Industrial Marketing Management* 11 (April 1982), 133–41.
34. Sales force budgeting and control, important elements of sales force leadership, are discussed in Chapter 15.

Rationality in Practice:

Attracting and Keeping the Superstar

Most compensation schemes are designed to reward mediocre to average performers because they make up a large part of any sales force. What such schemes tend to overlook is that some companies owe their existence to the efforts of one or two super salespeople who developed major business. As markets concentrate into fewer, but bigger buyers seeking to develop a more long-term trading relationship with single suppliers, the importance of the stellar salesperson is likely to increase.

The firm's compensation scheme can encourage the emergence and continued presence of selling superstars.

Any company, particularly a start-up operation, can offer its sales force an attractive stock option bonus scheme for extraordinary performance. A scheme that kicks in at a certain level of performance and is graduated to provide even higher rewards for higher performance offers several advantages. The rewards to the salesperson do not come off the current bottom line. Stock option bonuses encourage the salesperson to take a more long-term perspective and, hence, service accounts as well as sell. Also, it differentially recognizes the superior competence of such a salesperson over his or her peers. As peer recognition has been found to be an extremely important motivator of salespeople, this last advantage is probably the most important in this type of bonus scheme.

---

accounts at country clubs and in stadium sky boxes, but the inspired senior manager joins the sales force on the hot and dirty shop floors and the cramped back offices of the smaller accounts. Requiring the senior executive team to spend time out on the road with salespeople calling on small accounts has three major benefits. First, it gives executives a firsthand sense of the market. Second, it helps senior executives understand the effects of their decision making on the salesperson. Third, it fosters a belief in the sales force that senior management really cares. Salespeople will feel more comfortable talking to a senior executive after a day on the road than they ever would on the executive's corner-office turf. The benefits to the production efficiency of a "walkabout" leadership style has been well-established. It can be equally applied to sales management.

Sensible marketing planners also involve salespeople in their planning from the very outset. They often test the implementation of proposed selling tactics in several high-potential territories or in a sales region. The trick, then, is to work with sales to closely monitor the implementation and success of the program without getting in the way of the routine functioning of the sales force. The goal is to have salespeople 100 percent behind the marketing plan. Anything less reflects badly on the quality of the planning effort.

Ultimately, it is the responsibility of the sales manager to motivate the sales force. It is not an easy job because sales managers have three major responsibilities that can often conflict: 1) they are involved in the marketing planning for key product-markets; 2) they execute the different selling strategies for different products as directed by senior management or cross-functional teams; and 3) they maintain the general enthusiasm of the sales force, all of whom are individuals with different needs. Since most sales managers are former salespeople, their natural tendency is to be very loyal to their sales force. However, when sales managers share their frustrations with the sales force, the contagious dissatisfaction that can result hurts both morale and cooperation with other functional areas. Instead of taking such risks, sales managers often blow off steam with trusted senior salespeople who they know will not spread the dissatisfaction.

Instead of supporting and nurturing its super salespeople, some firms make the mistake of leaning in the opposite direction—and they pay dearly for it. In the early years of a new product line or during the company's start-up days, firms are very grateful for the selling success of the superstars. But over time, the firm's financial officers or senior executives, who often personally resent the annual commissions of the major salespeople compared with their own salaries, may be tempted to change the sales commission scheme to rectify the situation. They may argue that the reps no longer earn their compensation, even though they created much of the wealth for the owners of the company that is being divided out among senior management in stock options. What sometimes happens is that the salesperson who found and nurtured the key accounts takes his or her case to the customers who then, along with the salesperson, switch their loyalties to a competitor. A good salesperson hired by a good competitor will take as much as a third of his or her accounts over to the competition. On top of this, the firm has to hire and train a replacement. (The reverse applies when a firm steals a good salesperson from a rival.) When these kinds of situations arise, the company has made the mistake of viewing the salesperson as an unnecessary *expense*, when in fact he or she was a highly valued and irreplaceable *asset*.

Characteristics of a Good Sales Manager

Not all sales managers are born inspirational leaders, but they should compensate for it by building a personal library of inspirational audio and videotapes that can be loaned to their reps. What they must have is the ability to understand the unique personalities they manage. Everyone has a button that will motivate them if pushed. The major job of the sales manager is to find the right button.[35] To do this, a good sales manager gets to know his or her salespeople. Accompanying the salesperson on sales calls and discussing sales objectives provide opportunities for the manager to find out what the salesperson needs and values.

As the managerial link between the organization's objectives and the implementation of those objectives through the sales force, the good sales manager must have both a macro and a micro perspective. He or she must be able to deal with the economy's effect on corporate strategies one minute and bungled paperwork the next minute. In addition to being good at one-on-one interactions, a manager must also be good at conducting weekly sales meetings. Table 11-3 lists some of the suggestions made by salespeople as to how sales managers can improve such meetings.

Annual Sales Conferences. Annual sales conferences are important venues for managing and leading a sales force. The objectives of these conferences are to boost morale, build camaraderie, educate, and brief the sales force on plans for the year ahead. These objectives are achieved in varying ways. Holding the annual conference in an exotic setting is a signal of appreciation to both the salesperson and the spouse or family. An annual trip to a resort location is an additional compensation that the

35. For discussions on the use of contests as incentives, see William C. Moncrief, Sandra H. Hart, and Dan H. Robertson, "Sales Contests: A New Look at an Old Management Tool," *Journal of Personal Selling and Sales Management,* (November 1988), 55–61; and for how motivation changes as a salesperson's career progresses, see William L. Cron, Alan J. Dubinsky, and Ronald E. Michaels, "The Influence of Career Stages on Components of Salesperson Motivation," *Journal of Marketing* (January 1988), 78–92.

Table 11-3
Sales Force Suggestions As to How Sales Managers
Can Improve Sales Meetings

1. Make brief technical presentations using visual aids, followed by breakout discussion groups to maintain interest and get quality feedback.
2. Keep the sales force informed of changes in corporate, marketing, and sales strategies and plans.
3. Have key members of cross-functional teams, such as advertising and customer service executives, make brief presentations on issues of direct relevance to sales.
4. Don't try to squeeze too much into a meeting. Allow salespeople to share experiences so that they learn from each other.
5. Circulate the agenda beforehand so salespeople know the purpose and content of the meeting.
6. Ask salespeople to add their own items to the agenda and suggest speakers.

Source: Rayna Skolnik, "Salespeople Sound Off on Meetings," *Sales and Marketing Management,* November 1987, 108.

salesperson and the family can enjoy. Similarly, paying $10,000 to $20,000 to have President Ford talk about the current situation in the Middle East to five hundred salespeople who sell industrial adhesives signals that the company thinks its sales force is important. Salespeople can take photos, shake the man's hand, and be hit on the side of the head with a golf ball if they are so lucky. The annual conference is also the time to give out lots of awards. The more applause the better. It feeds the competitive and status drive of all, from the super rep to the novice. The ceremonies, initiations, rites of passage, and knighting of the superstars that occurs at sales conferences all contribute to the growth of the company culture.[36]

New Selling Technologies

Telemarketing is a systematic and continuous program of communicating with customers and prospects via telephone and interactive computer software connected to a database.[37] Telemarketing can be used to identify prospects and qualify leads, take orders for active accounts and reactivate inactive accounts, promote special offerings, provide information services, and take customer surveys.[38] The two basic advantages of telemarketing are its tremendous cost advantages over an outside sales force and the control it offers. The problems arise when integrating telemarketing with the outside sales force and introducing too many telemarketing programs that end up harassing the customer or that cut too many corners off the overall sales effort. Figure 11-7 spells out the advantages and disadvantages of telemarketing.[39]

36. Mark Thalenberg, "Rituals and Rewards," *Sales and Marketing Management,* June 3, 1986, 72.
37. See Cardozo and Shipp, "New Selling Methods."
38. The role of telemarketing in selling is examined in depth in William C. Moncrief, Shannon Shipp, Charles W. Lamb, Jr., and David W. Cravens, "Examining the Roles of Telemarketing in Selling Strategy," *Journal of Personal Selling and Sales Management* 9 (Fall 1989), 1–12.
39. For several case studies on the advantages of telemarketing, see Howard Sutton, *Rethinking the Company's Selling and Distribution Channels* (New York: The Conference Board, 1986); and Denise Herman, "Telemarketing Success: A Tough Act to Follow," *Telemarketing,* March 1987, 25–28.

Advantages:
  1. Increased speed and accuracy of order taking (by flagging inappropriate responses).
  2. Increased service image (customer orientation).
  3. Much greater control over customer interaction.
  4. Much less expensive than outside selling.
  5. Allows salesperson to specialize in customer field service and pioneer selling.
  6. Tremendous source of leads.
  7. Clever selling/service approaches can be quickly adopted by all members of the inside sales force.

Disadvantages:
  1. Coordination breakdown between inside and outside sales force.
  2. Can result in harassing customers with too much teleselling: "Don't call us, we will call you."
  3. Can really hurt if primarily seen as a cost-cutting substitute for an outside sales force. Firm is vulnerable to the personal selling skills of the competition.

Figure 11-7

Advantages and Disadvantages of Telemarketing

Telemarketing grew out of telephone order taking, when customers placed an order from a supplier's catalog. The operator entered the order into a computer and was able to give the customer immediate information on the order's status, such as the shipping date. Rather than waiting for orders from customers, some enterprising marketers started to initiate calls to customers on a regular, arranged basis. The development of software that described each customer's purchase history enabled the operator to run down a checklist of items that the customer regularly ordered.[40] Figure 11-8 presents the typical evolution of teleservicing and teleselling in a firm.

Many companies use their outside sales force to undertake telemarketing programs. A study by McGraw-Hill revealed that in 1986 salespeople spent 25 percent of their time in face-to-face selling and 17 percent of their time prospecting and selling by telephone.[41] A similar survey taken in 1977 reported that salespeople spent 39 percent of their time in face-to-face selling and minimal time selling by telephone. A good telemarketing operation is positioned to support the pioneering sales efforts of an outside sales force. It is seldom capable of totally replacing the personal contact and service of a field rep. In fact, what telemarketing does is *increase* the importance of the personal interaction and problem-solving skills of the field sales force. If the telemarketing operation is high tech, then the field sales force should provide the human interaction balance by becoming high "touch." (Note that this type of telemarketing is quite different from the telemarketing calls consumers receive at home offering aluminum siding or carpet cleaning.) As a company adjusts to this new sales technology, it will produce major changes in the functions undertaken by the field sales force, which may ultimately lead to a reorganization of the sales force.

40. William C. Moncrief, Charles W. Lamb, Jr., and Terry Dielman, "Developing Telemarketing Support Systems," *The Journal of Personal Selling and Sales Management* (August 1986), 43–49.
41. "Are Salespeople Gaining More Selling Time?" *Sales & Marketing Management,* July 1986, 29.

Teleservicing:
The evolution of the use of the telephone to service customers.

 1. Direct input of order into computer.
 2. Immediate notification of stock availability and shipment date.
 3. Real-time information on status of order.
 4. Information on possible substitutes.
 5. Information on related sales specials.
 6. Trouble-shooting advice from manuals stored on computer.
 7. Advice on equipment purchase, improved maintenance, and product utilization from Artificial Intelligence (AI) expert system software.
 8. Integrated faxing service to send diagrams and other documents.

Teleselling:

 1. Call screen and code prospects.
 2. Refer hot leads to salespeople.
 3. Call low-grade prospects with sales promotion offer.
 4. Call particular customer segments with a preferred clients special offer, based on recent sales history.
 5. Develop an Expert System software program that prompts responses to objections (provides selling scripts based on responses to previous questions).

Figure 11-8
Stages in the Evolution of Teleservicing and Teleselling

Telemarketing in Control

Telemarketing provides excellent control in terms of the sales presentation content, the accuracy of order taking, and the generation of new leads for salespeople. An interactive set of software programs can prompt the operator with the actual words he or she should use in various selling situations so that mistakes are avoided. The astute company will place its most knowledgeable and expert salespeople in telemarketing for several weeks to record their conversations with customers. From this database and related group discussions over what the salesperson could have done better, a whole set of scripts can be developed and integrated into the selling software. In this way, operators who are paid $5 to $10 per hour will bootstrap their perceived competence and selling effectiveness by increasing their sales by several hundred percent. The introduction of innovations in selling approaches that can improve the company's telephone selling techniques can be quickly adopted by all of the operators. The telephone selling learning curve is much steeper (faster) than the outside selling learning curve.

The introduction of artificial intelligence into order taking and customer service software programs will introduce even greater power and control into telemarketing. The basic advantage of using the computer and its prompting power is that it can make telephone selling almost as adaptive to the purchase situation as face-to-face selling. Operators can be prompted to offer special price deals on complementary products that the customer is currently not buying from the supplier. These price deals will be set according to account potential and current company pricing strategy. Programs can also suggest express delivery services, inquire about deviations from usual order sizes, and suggest novel solutions to out-of-stock problems. They may also point out volume discount advantages to the customer if it increases its order size.

A typical telemarketing workstation.

Not only does telemarketing provide control over aspects of selling, it also increases the accuracy of order taking (by having exception routines that query any unusual entries and insist that all information is entered before accepting the order), increases the speed of order processing, and reduces the order-delivery cycle time. It also can provide end-of-the-day, end-of-the-week, and end-of-the-month control over the implementation of a selling program.

Telemarketing's most important benefit may be that it can revitalize an outside salesperson. Specialized telemarketing prospectors are capable of making 100 calls a day by identifying prospects from the Yellow Pages, directories, or mailing lists. Telemarketing prospecting is low cost and provides a boost to salespeople. A morning of unsuccessful prospecting will kill a salesperson's enthusiasm for selling, but a list of fresh leads from the telemarketing center is bound to create excitement. A company has greater control over its outside sales force when its hands a rep a list of positive prospects and says "go get 'em." The salesperson can no longer claim the leads are not there and will have to produce call reports that measure his or her sales conversion ability.

Telemarketing Out of Control

Despite its current and potential power, telemarketing has been so mismanaged or abused by some companies that it has become a competitive disadvantage. These firms view telemarketing as an opportunity to drastically cut back the outside sales force, which makes the company vulnerable to the personal selling skills of the competition. A second common problem with telemarketing is that it is so inexpensive that some companies are tempted to implement too many special telemarketing sales promotions

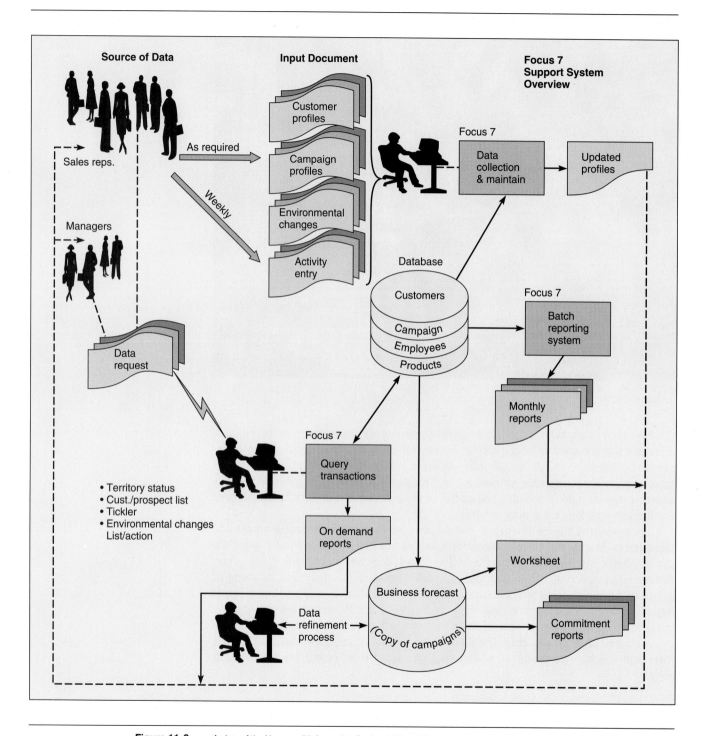

Figure 11-9

A Typical Computerized Support System for a Sales Force

A view of the Honeywell Information System's Focus 7 support system.

Source: Reproduced with permission from Louis A. Wallis, *Computer and the Sales Effort,* Report No. 884 (New York: The Conference Board, 1986). Such a system increases the competence and efficiency of the salesperson and also increases the competitive rationality of the firm.

to customers. Telemarketing then changes from customer service to the hassle of a hard sell. Once a company's telemarketing operation becomes overbearing, it is very difficult to recover from the negative image. The "don't call us, we will call you" customer attitude is a sure signal that telemarketing is out of control and can mean death to a telemarketing operation. Telemarketing must attempt to maintain its image as a customer service by orchestrating and sticking to customer calling schedules in the same way that personal sales calls are scheduled.

A major disadvantage of having a separate telemarketing and outside sales force is the problem of coordinating customer selling and service. One organizational solution is to have the salesperson do the telemarketing to his or her major accounts and have separate telemarketing salespeople handle all the small accounts. In fact, many companies are pleasantly surprised by the growth in their business that comes from telemarketing selling to small accounts that the field sales force often ignore. After all, a friendly telephone call is better than no call at all.

Selling Decision Support Systems

Each customer or product group sales force involves administrative overhead that increases the coordination of sales management not by a factor of two, but by a factor of four. A single sales force reports to senior management directly. Two separate sales forces have to coordinate their activities, in addition to reporting to management. Now there are four vital communication activities involved in sales management rather than one. Thus, the potential for loss of control is greatly increased. However, just as the introduction of computers has increased the span of a senior manager's control, the introduction of a decision support system connected to notebook computers used by the sales force has increased the sales manager's span of control over a number of salespeople.

Selling decision support systems have also increased a salesperson's control over diverse customer types and products. This is because customer account profiles can describe the unique needs and buying approach of a customer (see Figure 11-9 and Table 11-4). Product information can be accessed quickly, limiting the need for the salesperson to keep current on changes in product lines and the availability of individual items. Hence, advances in information technology should reduce the need for customer and product specialization on the part of the sales force. A sophisticated information system such as that described in Figure 11-9 could be used by both the inside sales force and the outside sales force who would download the customer file onto their notebook computers, including the latest information on a customer's telemarketing interactions with the firm.

All firms must decide whether they are going to develop and fully support their own sales force, use manufacturers' reps, or a combination of the two. There are some 50,000 manufacturer representative businesses or partnerships that service hundreds of industries and thousands of markets in the United States and Canada. They are often family businesses that sell 10 to 12 product lines manufactured and marketed by several different producers. Usually they operate as exclusive commission agents who have been granted exclusive rights to sell to their territory (typically a few states). They do

Deploying and Managing a Manufacturers' Rep Sales Force

Table 11-4
Effects of Computer Information Systems on Selling

Percent of Companies Reporting Favorable Effects of Support Systems

Information such as customer account status, sales or order summaries, sales in process, and bids outstanding provided to salesperson	80%
Individual time and territory management	58%
Faster order to shipment time	56%
Sales volume per salesperson	51%
Increased calls per salesperson	36%
Control of sales expenses	31%

Typical Information Contained in Computer-Prepared Sales-Call Reports

♦ Name, address, and key contact at prospect or customer visited

♦ Purpose of call—prospecting, qualifying, closing

♦ Outcome of call—more information needed from whom and when, business lost and why, business won (order details), business on hold (why, details on recontacting, waiting)

♦ Competitive information obtained

♦ Date of next scheduled call

Effect of Honeywell's Introduction of its Focus 7 System

♦ In the first year, overall sales force productivity rose 31%

♦ Shipments rose 33%

♦ Sales force turnover dropped 40% (it cost $50,000–$75,000 to train a salesperson)

Source: Louis A. Wallis, *Computers and the Sales Effort,* Report No. 884 (New York: The Conference Board, 1986).

---

not carry competing lines but often will sell the complementary lines of other manufacturers. Their typical sales commission is around 7 percent, but this varies by product line.[42]

The advantages and disadvantages of employing a sales force made up of manufacturers' reps are listed in Table 11-5. Some small companies must use reps because they do not have the start-up resources or the breadth of products to build and support their own sales force, particularly in distant markets. Even large companies see cost advantages in employing a rep sales force that is often more cost-effective (see the box on page 414).[43] The major risk of employing a rep firm to cover a territory is that the rep firm may not perform. This risk can be minimized by running a credit check, calling the other companies whose products the manufacturer rep sells, and talking to some of its major customers. A day's work will establish the credentials of a rep organization. Another form of insurance is to sign a short-term, three-month contract that can be terminated for nonperformance. If it takes a rep longer than three months to start moving the product, then the rep is not selling your products to its existing customers but is instead trying to use your product to break into new markets. When this happens, much of the advantage of using a manufacturer's rep is lost.

42. Henry Lavin, "When and How to Use Manufacturers' Representatives," in *The Handbook of Modern Marketing,* 2nd ed. (New York: McGraw-Hill, 1986).

43. Thayer C. Taylor, "The Raging 'Rep'idemic," *Sales & Marketing Management,* June 8, 1981, 33–35; and Erin Anderson, "Strategic Implications of Darwinian Economics for Selling Efficiency and Choice of Integrated or Independent Sales Forces," *Management Science* 4 (Summer 1988), 234–54.

Table 11-5
Advantages and Disadvantages of Employing Manufacturers' Reps

Advantages over a Company Sales Force	Disadvantages over a Company Sales Force
◆ Fast way of building consumer franchise—reps open doors.	◆ Some customers prefer to deal directly with the company.
◆ Low start-up investment costs.	◆ Diseconomies of scale—relatively expensive to use with major customers (high commission payments).
◆ Low risk—reps get paid for what they sell.	◆ More difficult to manage and control.
◆ Improved cash flow—you pay when you get paid.	◆ Harder to train on product knowledge.
◆ Higher average selling skills and lower turnover of salespeople.	◆ Difficult to fire—may lead to loss of customers and betrayal of confidences and trade secrets.
◆ Good advice from reps on product design and marketing for a new venture.	◆ Less continuous feedback.
◆ Easier to establish proven performance.	◆ Current customers may not fit the rep's consumer franchise.
◆ The halo effect—the company benefits from the other brands the rep sells.	◆ Paid on commission so will push products that are easiest to sell.
◆ Sales territories with fewer customers are covered more efficiently.	◆ Selling time is split among several lines.
◆ Lower average selling costs.	

The Fit of the Rep's Customer Franchise

In the previous chapter we discussed the importance of the fit between the supplier's target market and the channel intermediary's consumer franchise. The same concerns apply to manufacturers' reps. Reps should be screened in terms of the amount of business they currently do in the target industry and with important major accounts in that industry. If the distributor or rep is selling leading brands of other, complementary products to the industry, it is evidence that the rep has a legitimate, desirable consumer franchise (strong credibility and deep ties with the desired target market).

A supplier should never lose sight of the rep organization's basic strategic objective, which is to represent well-known, very strong supplier's brands. The smart thing for the rep to do is to build a stable of well-known, noncompeting lines that are all sold to the same buyers. A little of the brand loyalty of each line then rubs off on the rep, and a little can amount to a lot. The rep also builds loyalty directly through service and personal friendships. The rep firm's security is its confidence that if the trading relationship with its major principal (supplier) fractures, most buyers will adopt the rep's new replacement line rather than continue to buy the original supplier's line through a new sales channel. In other words, the initial positional power of the two parties that was clearly so in favor of the original supplier may, in time, become quite uncertain.[44] This risk, plus the trust and relationships that develop over time, is likely to lead a manufacturer to stick with its manufacturer reps rather than replace them with its own sales force.[45]

---

44. In fact, it has been argued that independent agents may ultimately exploit this transfer of goodwill at the expense of the firm. This risk is an argument for a firm creating and supporting its own sales force. See Oliver E. Williamson, *Markets and Hierarchies: Analysis and Antitrust Implications* (New York: The Free Press, 1975); and Jan Hiede and George John, "The Role of Dependence Balancing in Safeguarding Transaction-Specific Assets in Conventional Channels," *Journal of Marketing* 52 (January 1988), 20–35.
45. Allen M. Weiss and Erin Anderson, *The Effects of Switching Costs on the Termination of Distribution Channel Relationships* (Cambridge, MA: The Marketing Science Institute, 1991).

Rationality in Practice:

Choosing between Direct Reps and Independent Manufacturers' Reps

How might a firm make the fundamental strategic decision to create its own direct sales force or use an independent manufacturers' rep sales force? The competitively rational approach is to estimate which course will be most effective and make the most contribution to operating margin. Effectiveness can be predicted by estimating the penetration of the two approaches. Penetration is the percentage of an account's business the firm can expect to get, using its own direct sales force or reps. A direct force would be expected to achieve higher penetration because its selling efforts are not divided across several different manufacturers' product lines, as is so with reps. Penetration also depends on the number of sales calls and service efforts. The number and size of potential accounts (customers), the average cost of each sales call, and the commission paid to independent reps also need to be estimated.

When provided with all of these estimates, the OWN-VREP spreadsheet presented here does the appropriate analysis. In this spreadsheet the cost of each call and the commission paid to reps can be varied to see what impact they have on the decision. Based on the information in the tables, an all-rep sales force will earn $623,500 in contribution and a direct sales force will earn $591,300. An even better option is to use a direct sales force to serve accounts above $100,000 in potential and let independent reps serve the smaller accounts. This generates $785,000 in contribution. However, this combination can only be achieved if the firm started with a direct sales force serving all accounts. A firm that started with reps serving all accounts can hardly take the big accounts away from reps once they have developed the business. Several firms have tried this tactic, and it so upset their reps that the reps went to work for the competition, taking many of their large and high-growth accounts with them. A firm also has to be concerned about the rep's ability to add accounts (increase penetration). The spreadsheet should be used to forecast what the penetration and contribution will be five and ten years down the line using a direct sales force and what they will be using an all-rep sales force.

Owner versus Rep Sales Force

Contribution to Operating Margin (COM) of a Direct Sales Force
(assuming a cost per personal sales call of $110)

Account potential (in thousands of dollars)	Number of accounts	Average penetration	Estimated sales (in thousands of dollars)	Average gross margin	Average gross margin (in thousands of dollars)	Acct. calls per year	Sales force cost (in dollars)	COM (in thousands of dollars)	COM/acct. (in thousands of dollars)
800–1200	1	40%	400	39%	156	50	5,500	150.5	150.50
500–800	1	40%	260	39%	101	50	5,500	95.9	95.90
300–500	3	40%	480	39%	187	50	16,500	170.7	56.90
100–300	6	40%	480	39%	187	45	29,700	157.5	26.25
50–100	7	35%	184	41%	75	35	26,950	48.4	6.91
25–50	22	35%	289	41%	118	35	84,700	33.7	1.53
12–25	14	35%	91	41%	37	20	30,800	6.4	0.45
6–12	18	30%	49	43%	21	10	19,800	1.1	0.06
3–6	28	30%	38	43%	16	6	18,480	−2.2	−0.08
1.5–3	25	30%	17	43%	7	6	16,500	−9.2	−0.37
0.5–1.5	21	30%	6	43%	3	6	13,860	−11.2	−0.53
0–0.5	80	30%	6	43%	3	6	52,800	−50.2	−0.63
			2,299		912			591.3	

Contribution to Operating Margin (COM) of an All Rep Sales Force
(assuming a manufacturer's rep commission of 5%)

Account potential (in thousands of dollars)	Number of accounts	Average penetration	Estimated sales (in thousands of dollars)	Average gross margin	Average gross margin (in thousands of dollars)	Sales force cost (in dollars)	COM (in thousands of dollars)	COM/acct. (in thousands of dollars)
800–1200	1	30%	300	39%	117	15,000	102.0	102.00
500–800	1	30%	195	39%	76	9,750	66.3	66.30
300–500	3	30%	360	39%	140	18,000	122.4	40.80
100–300	6	30%	360	39%	140	18,000	122.4	20.40
50–100	7	30%	158	41%	65	7,875	56.7	8.10
25–50	22	30%	248	41%	101	12,375	89.1	4.05
12–25	14	30%	78	41%	32	3,885	28.0	2.00
6–12	18	25%	41	43%	17	2,025	15.4	0.86
3–6	28	25%	32	43%	14	1,575	12.0	0.43
1.5–3	25	25%	14	43%	6	703	5.3	0.21
0.5–1.5	21	25%	5	43%	2	263	2.0	0.10
0–0.5	80	25%	5	43%	2	250	1.9	0.02
			1,794		713		623.5	

Contribution to Operating Margin (COM) of a Mixed Sales Force
(assuming that a cost per personal sales call is $110, the manufacturer's rep commission is 5%, and the reps are given accounts with potential less than or equal to [in thousands of dollars] 100)

Account potential (in thousands of dollars)	Number of accounts	Average penetration	Estimated sales (in thousands of dollars)	Average gross margin	Average gross margin (in thousands of dollars)	Sales force cost (in dollars)	COM (in thousands of dollars)	COM/acct. (in thousands of dollars)
800–1200	1	40%	400	39%	156	5,500	150.5	150.50
500–800	1	40%	260	39%	101	5,500	95.9	95.90
300–500	3	40%	480	39%	187	16,500	170.7	56.90
100–300	6	40%	480	39%	187	29,700	157.5	26.25
50–100	7	30%	158	41%	65	7,875	56.7	8.10
25–50	22	30%	248	41%	101	12,375	89.1	4.05
12–25	14	30%	78	41%	32	3,885	28.0	2.00
6–12	18	25%	41	43%	17	2,025	15.4	0.86
3–6	28	25%	32	43%	14	1,575	12.0	0.43
1.5–3	25	25%	14	43%	6	703	5.3	0.21
0.5–1.5	21	25%	5	43%	2	263	2.0	0.10
0–0.5	80	25%	5	43%	2	250	1.9	0.02
			2,199		871		785.0	

Source: C. Davis Fogg, and Josef W. Rokus, "A Quantitative Method for Structuring a Profitable Sales Force," *Journal of Marketing* 37 (July 1973), 8–17.

Reps and Customer Service Problems

Difficulties between reps and customers arise from two sources. The first arises when customers want to deal directly with the company. The firm has no choice but to respond to the customer's desires. However, the company is still bound to pay the rep his or her commission on the sale unless it was specified in the original agreement that this business was to be treated as a house account. Recently, some "power" retailers, such as Wal-Mart, have decided that they will no longer deal with manufacturer reps because they feel they are a large enough customer to deserve direct sales service from a supplier. In such cases, the contracts with the rep who previously handled the account must be renegotiated.

The second difficulty occurs when the reps do not follow up on leads. One way that a firm supports its rep sales force is by passing on referrals and leads from advertising, trade shows, publicity, and other marketing activities. However, hot leads are not always followed up by the manufacturer rep. Manufacturers' reps are good at responding to their regular customers but sometimes do not like having to go out of their way to chase inquiries.

Reps need to check on the status of such leads on a regular basis, but managers are also often frustrated when reps do not report their progress to the home office.[46] Out of sheer exasperation, some companies start to follow up on leads themselves, chase down the sale, and bypass the rep. It may keep the rep on the tail of the leads, but it also undermines the relationship. The fair and honorable way of handling nonperformance is for the firm to inform the rep that it will chase down any leads on which it does not receive call reports within a specified time. When potential customers are left waiting, their image of the company's service diminishes.

Global Sales Management

Global selling is no different, in principle, from selling in the U.S. market. In practice, however, much greater care has to be taken in selecting selling agents. The compensation scheme should fit the local market conditions and be competitive with local salaries and commissions. The expense allowance structure is also likely to be very different in categories such as travel and entertainment. Whatever the stage of a country's economic development, if electricity and telephone are available, a computerized sales support system can be introduced. Such a system provides tremendous communications and control advantages. Training is likely to be expensive, because it is best to use training facilities at the universities and engineering institutes within the foreign market rather than to train in the United States. Local training ensures a cultural fit and also is geared to the competitive expectations of the foreign market, not the United States market. Finally, it is very important to have a technical advisor in the market as soon as possible who can troubleshoot and keep a close watch on the selling programs, pricing practices, and after-sales service programs of the local manufacturers' reps or distributors. Preferably, such a sales manager should be a national or someone who is, at the least, very fluent in the language and culture of the foreign market.[47]

46. The problem is that reps often resent close supervision and controls. See Jayashree Mahajan et al., "A Comparison of the Impact of Organizational Climate on the Job Satisfaction of Manufacturers' Agents and Company Salespeople: An Exploratory Study," *Journal of Personal Selling and Sales Management* (May 1984), 1–10.
47. For additional insight, see John S. Hill and Richard R. Hill, "Organizing the Overseas Sales Force: How Multinationals Do It," *Journal of Personal Selling and Sales Management* 100 (Spring 1990), 57–66.

Selling skills that work in the home market might not be effective in the foreign markets. Training salespeople in the market in which they will be selling is helpful because salespeople must become very familiar with local selling customs. In cultures that are quite different, it is imperative to hire nationals to do the selling because they understand the culture and selling customs. Salespeople cannot impose their own standards on a customer from a different culture. For instance, many typical American selling customs, such as asking for the sale when it looks as though a customer is ready to do business, are perceived as too aggressive in Japan. Just as a good salesperson will work hard to gear a sales presentation to suit the specific customer in the home market, a good salesperson should work even harder to gear the presentation to suit the customer in the foreign market.

Discussion Questions and Minicases

1. What problems may arise if senior management believes that its sales force is made up of "compulsive wooers" and "impression managers"?

2. Why might it be argued that sales is the area where a firm will be able to gain the biggest advantage over its competition during the 1990s?

3. Please redraw Figure 11-3 to demonstrate 1) the advantage that a small family firm (in which the head of the firm is the salesperson) has over a large rival in selling to a large company and 2) the mutual advantage a small family firm has in selling to another small firm, compared to two very large firms trading with each other. What implications does this have for the practice of relationship marketing?

4. How can a salesperson directly and indirectly influence the quality and economy images of the product he or she sells?

5. In addition to providing information about a product or service, a sales presentation includes two persuasive elements. The first is an attempt to ingratiate the buyer by praising the buyer's skills, personal appearance, good taste, personality, and so on. The second is a salesperson's subtle attempts at self-promotion through emphasizing his or her experience, success, and so forth. Little is known about how these two elements of persuasion should be combined in a presentation. Do you think a sales presentation should involve self-promotion first and ingratiation second, or the other way around? Should they be mixed together throughout the presentation? Justify your answer. Would your suggested tactic change if you were dealing with buyers who were excellent at impression management themselves?

6. Role playing during sales training, where salespeople are videotaped while taking turns playing the role of buyer or seller in a simulated sales call, has recently become a very important way of training recruits and providing refresher training of experienced salespeople. Whole books have been written on the subject. Explain all of the reasons why role playing is so effective.

7. Mentoring is a great idea if it can be done well, but its success depends very much on the fit of personalities between the mentor and the rookie. Make a practical suggestion as to how a sales manager might make such pairings. (Hint: Do not suggest the use of personality tests.)

8. In developing an objective method of categorizing an account as AA, A, B, C, and D, such as described in Table 11-2, what should determine whether size, growth, current penetration, or competitive activity is more important in ascertaining the

rating? Explain your answer by changing the table in the text to reflect company X's emphasis on growth? How would you change the table for a company Y whose emphasis is on attacking competition?

9. How might a sales manager handle imbalances in sales territory work loads in the short term?

10. The text presents a list of bargaining rules or tactics. Describe the one you most disagree with and explain why.

11. In major negotiations with a foreign buyer, it often may help to play the "simple Jim"—that is, behave in a way that leads the other party in a negotiation to underestimate your ability. Why?

12. Some companies use very complicated compensation schemes to achieve multiple objectives, and they change them frequently. What problems can this create?

13. Why should a commission schedule be progressive (increasing as a salesperson's sales increase) rather than regressive? That is, rather than sticking with a straight-line (constant) commission, why not increase commission from, say, 8 percent to 10 percent of gross margin at a point where a certain level of sales has been achieved?

14. Why does stealing a super salesperson from a rival result in a great triple play (that is, what are three competitive rationality advantages from making such a steal)?

15. How might a firm increase the sharing of good ideas and the competitive rationality of its sales force and the firm in general?

16. Why do annual sales conferences often make or break aspiring young marketing executives?

17. By analyzing the costs and returns from serving the different sized accounts described in the OWNVREP spreadsheet in the box on page 414, explain the inherent advantages and disadvantages of using the company's own salespeople versus using manufacturers' reps.

18. Some people have argued that the most important recent technological revolution in sales has been the widespread use of the cellular/mobile telephone. Detail all of the ways that mobile telephones have been used by salespeople to increase the effectiveness and efficiency of their performance.

19. How should the notebook computer be introduced to enhance its use by a sales force?

20. The following statement presents the advocacy position of a lobbying group representing the interests of independent reps. From what you have read in Chapters 10 and 11, argue the merits of the reps' case, the power buyers' case, and the case of the supplier who seems to be caught in between.

   Power buyers are large volume purchasers who use their buying power to obtain unfair competitive advantages. A recent survey conducted by the Council of Manufacturers Representatives Associations estimated that 101 companies are power buyers.[48]

   ♦ **Issue:** These power buyers use their market power to force suppliers to sell direct, denying suppliers the benefit of independent sales representatives, in order to obtain a discount in price in lieu of brokerage.

48. Coalition of Americans to Save the Economy, 1100 Connecticut Avenue, N.W., Suite 1200, Washington, D.C. 20036, (800) 752-4111.

- **Manufacturers are harmed:** Suppliers and manufacturers who have chosen to market and sell their products through independent sales representatives are being required by power buyers to sell direct in order to continue to sell to such buyers. Suppliers and manufacturers who continue to service the power buyer accounts by redeploying or hiring personnel face increased costs of doing business. Thus, power buyers obtain discriminatory price reductions, which other buyers do not receive, and force increased costs on suppliers.

- **U.S. economy is harmed:** Power buyer actions harm the U.S. economy. Small and medium-sized businesses who compete with the power buyer face higher costs for products as suppliers' marketing costs increase. These businesses find it more difficult to compete with the power buyers, reducing consumer choices and increasing consumer prices. Power buyers fail to return their savings to consumers, often raising prices in areas where competition has been driven out. Lastly, independent sales representative companies face the loss of their highest volume accounts and often must lay off employees or go out of business completely.

- **How abuse occurs:** Power buyers abuse their market power in several ways. For example, a large discount chain that has refused to deal with independent sales representatives has unilaterally increased its new store discount from 5 percent to 10 percent. The same chain also requested a price discount of 2 percent to 3 percent on all orders it placed during June and July with the understanding that noncomplying manufacturers will no longer do business with the chain. A large supermarket chain demanded that a supplier eliminate its sales representative and reduce its prices by 10 percent, the commission the chain claimed the representative was earning, or lose the account.

- **Violations of law:** These practices of the power buyers force the suppliers and the manufacturers to violate Sections 2(a), (c) and (f) of the Robinson-Patman Act, which prohibits price discrimination and discounts in lieu of brokerage received by a buyer from a seller. The practices also violate Section 2 of the Sherman Act, which prohibits the abuse of market power.

21. Please review the questionnaire appearing on the next two pages that was developed to select manufacturers' reps. How would you improve it?

FANMISER CORP.
MANUFACTURING REPRESENTATIVE EVALUATION FORM

Company Name _____
Street Address (no P.O. Box numbers) _____
City _____ State/Province _____ Country _____
Zip Code _____ Telephone _____ Fax _____
Contact Person _____ Position _____

For Prospective Canadian Distributors:
Federal Sales Tax Exemption Number (if applicable) _____
Provincial Sales Tax Exemption Number (if applicable) _____

For Prospective U.S. Distributors:
Employer Identifier Number (I.R.S. Tax Number): _____

If you wish to register more than one office, please provide on a separate typewritten sheet a summary of all locations for which you would like authorization. For each location provide the name of the office, its address, phone number(s), and key personnel.

Company Information

History
1. Are you a . . . _____ A) Corporation _____ B) Partnership _____ C) Sole Proprietorship
2. How long have you been in the business? _____
3. What was your gross sales volume last year? _____
4. Have you ever been terminated by a manufacturer for violation of a reseller agreement? _____
   If yes, by what manufacturer? _____
5. What professional company organizations does your company belong to? _____

Territory
6. What territory do you cover? _____
7. Will you accept deviations from this territory? _____
8. Who are your major accounts? _____
   _____
9. Will you provide references from some of your key accounts, if requested by FANMISER? _____

Office Facilities
10. What are your normal business hours of operation? _____
    What percentage (%) of time, in a typical business day, are your office telephone lines presently covered by:
    _____ Trained sales staff   _____ Trained technical support staff
    _____ Secretary or Office Personnel   _____ Outside Answering Service
    _____ Answering Machine   _____ Nobody or nothing
    _____ Other
    Do you expect these %'s to change if you are appointed as a FANMISER manufacturing representative? _____
    (if Yes, write in the revised percentages to the right of the ones noted above.)
11. Do you have a fax machine? _____
    If not, do you plan on getting one in the near future? _____

Personnel
12. How many full-time salespeople does your company have? _____
13. Will you provide resumes of your salespeople upon request of FANMISER? _____
14. How do you compensate your salespeople? _____
    How are commissions paid? _____
    How often? _____
15. Do you have incentive programs or profit sharing for employees? _____

Product Lines
16. Please furnish a list of your principals and product lines you currently represent including the territories covered with each principal and the number of years you have represented them. Attach this information to this evaluation form.
17. Please describe any of the products you manufacture for distribution _____
    _____
    _____
18. How well do you understand the FANMISER product? What type of information or training would help make you more comfortable in presenting it? _____
    _____
    _____
    _____

MARKETING AND SALES
1. Which industries do you sell to?
   _____ HVAC   _____ Food Service   _____ Other, please list
   _____
2. How well do you know FANMISER's market and customer? _____
3. How does FANMISER fit into your core business? _____
4. What do you feel is the average call cycle needed to make a FANMISER sale in your territory? _____
5. Which of your current or future contacts could benefit from FANMISER? _____

6. What type of support will you require from FANMISER? _____
7. What do you see as your sales potential for FANMISER? _____
   _____ Year 1 _____ Year 2 _____ Year 3 _____ Year 4 _____ Year 5
8. How would you sell our product? Distributors or direct? _____
   _____
   _____
9. Where do you plan to be in five years? _____
   _____
   _____
10. How will you handle sales leads from the factory? _____
    _____
11. Would you agree to send monthly sales activity and/or booking report to FANMISER? _____
    _____

PROMOTIONAL EFFORTS

12. Do you have a direct mail program? _____
13. How many people are on your mailing list? _____
14. Do you participate in any local trade shows? _____
    _____
    _____
15. Do you have your own catalog? _____

SERVICE AND TRAINING

16. Do your salespeople perform minor service or customer education? _____
    _____
    _____

ADDITIONAL INFORMATION

1. Please provide any additional information on your company (resume, brochures, etc.) that may assist us in the evaluation process and attach along with this application.
2. Summarize your business plan, including special market focus, capabilities, facilities, or other value-added features offered by your organization. Attach this information to this evaluation form.
3. Please complete page 6.

Credit References

Please provide one Bank Reference.
Bank Name _____
Address _____
City _____ State/Province _____ Country _____
Account Number _____ Telephone _____

Please provide three Supplier references (companies you currently purchase from an open account basis).

1. Company Name _____
   Address _____
   City _____ State/Province _____ Zip _____
   Contact Person _____ Position _____
   Telephone _____
2. Company Name _____
   Address _____
   City _____ State/Province _____ Zip _____
   Contact Person _____ Position _____
   Telephone _____
3. Company Name _____
   Address _____
   City _____ State/Province _____ Zip _____
   Contact Person _____ Position _____
   Telephone _____

I HEREBY CERTIFY THAT ALL INFORMATION CONTAINED ON THIS FORM IS CORRECT AND I REALIZE THAT ANY FALSIFICATION MAY RESULT IN THE IMMEDIATE CANCELLATION OF ANY RESULTING AGREEMENT.

Signature _____ Date _____

For consideration on an authorized FANMISER manuf. rep., please complete and return this form to:

> FANMISER CORP.
> 1053 E. Fifth Ave.
> Columbus, OH 43201-3099

In order for FANMISER to process this application, it must be accompanied by a cover letter and a business card.

Managing Communications

*"You cannot antagonize and influence
at the same time."*

J.S. Knox

"Well done is better than well said."

Benjamin Franklin

*C*ommunication management is the process of developing and supervising strategies that keep targeted consumers informed about a product's competitive superiority. Promotion emphasizes the *communication* of benefits already contained in the product, including those images that symbolize the product's quality. Thus, while product management might decide to package toothpaste in a pump for convenient dispensing, communication management has the responsibility of making consumers aware of this benefit and persuading them to buy the target brand. Marketers not only communicate product positioning through advertising, but also through their product, price, and distribution decisions. For example, selling a product at a prestigious store communicates the product's prestige value to the target market. In this chapter, we separate a marketer's decisions about product, price, and distribution from the strategies and programs that are adopted to communicate those decisions to the market. Our discussion will be confined to what a marketer's communication options are and how they should be managed profitably.

In the North American market, consumers are exposed to hundreds of commercial messages every day. These messages may come from commercials we hear on the radio as we drive to and from work, billboards that we see along the way, a coupon given out by a nearby cafe owner as we enter the office building, or the telephone solicitor who calls us in the evening to see if we are interested in buying a water purifier system. For convenience, academics and practitioners divide these various techniques into four general categories:

Advertising is the dominant method marketers use to reach consumers. Through advertising, marketers attempt to make consumers aware of their product's positioning (unique benefits or low price) in the hope that this information will lead the consumers to choose their product.

Sales promotions, discussed in Chapter 13, are temporary incentives, monetary or otherwise, that enhance the perceived value of the product or service. Manufacturers offer coupons, retailers have regular sales, and service establishments promise additional services for the same price. Sales promotions, you will notice, have to be conveyed to consumers through advertising. However, they are different from advertising because of the short-term value they add to the product.

Personal selling, discussed in Chapter 11, is used to promote a product that is complicated and that demands a substantial information exchange between customers and sellers. Some marketers (such as Avon or Tupperware) use this form of communication even for relatively simple products, because they wish to develop a long-term, personal relationship with the customer.

Publicity involves having the news media communicate information about a product to the marketplace. While publicity cannot be bought, it may be managed carefully to the advantage of a marketer. If a product is made interesting, it may provoke the curiosity of the news media who may want to report this to their audiences in the form of news. In addition, the last decade has seen a dramatic increase in direct marketing and the use of public relations for image-building purposes. Several advertising texts, therefore, include discussions on direct marketing and public relations management.

The Important Decisions

Improving the advertising strategy begins with identifying the important decisions. Positioning defines the desired audience, called the target market. It establishes the suitability and cost-effectiveness of various media choices. Once marketers choose the type of media used most by their target market, they can then use positioning strategy to develop the message strategy. The positioning strategy determines the message theme. The advertisement should communicate the desired competitive positioning, otherwise time and money are wasted. The message theme also influences the media choice. The theme and media decisions together influence the creative techniques that are used to communicate and persuade. The media schedule determines the campaign's reach (the percentage of the target audience that will be exposed to the advertising) and intensity (measured by the number of times that the target customers who are reached are exposed to the advertising).

The following sections discuss each element of the advertising strategy, beginning with message themes and creative tactics. Developing an advertising strategy requires marketers to consider several different communication and persuasion theories. However, the most important advertising decision a seller will make is its choice of an agency. Keep the following key ideas in mind as you read this chapter:

- The success of a firm's advertising crucially depends on hiring a creative and capable ad agency that understands the market and provides fast turnaround.

- The agency cannot be held responsible for a firm's weak target-positioning strategy.

- A basic theme has to be chosen from one of the following: a news theme, a logical persuasion theme, an image/feeling theme, or a trial theme.

- Much of the effectiveness of advertising campaigns depends on the impact of creatives. Advertising strategy is an art. Brilliantly distinctive campaigns that convey strong selling points stand out as much as dreadfully inept campaigns. The rest of the ads get lost in the clutter.

- The competition for the consumer's attention is intense. The modern consumer is wedded to habits and loyalties. Effective new creative concepts (for instance, the "Iacocca Pitch"—using the CEO of the company as the pitchman who promises satisfaction or your money back) are quickly copied by other advertisers.

- Point-of-purchase advertising is very important when the target consumers are under time pressure and a "trial" message theme is used.

- Creating a more efficient marketplace is important, but the sobering reality of consumer trial still remains. A great advertising campaign cannot sustain a weak product for very long.

- Just as it is often better to orchestrate several regional advertising campaigns, it is also usually better to have different campaign creatives and use different media in different international markets. The global market is not yet a single culture.

Advertising at a Crossroad

Advertising is so pervasive in our culture that most consumers passively accept it in all its myriad forms. The competition between advertisers to get our attention is far from passive. Television and radio stations, magazines, and newspapers fiercely compete to serve as an advertiser's communication channel. The reason that the broadcast media focuses on ratings and the print media focuses on circulation is because their advertising rates are dependent on the number and types of consumers who patronize their product. Over 150 billion dollars are spent in this country every year on advertising. The cost of a 30-second commercial on Super Bowl XXVI in 1992 was $850,000. The advertising business is big business.

From 1950 to 1980, U.S. companies increased their advertising to an extent never seen before in any economy. The Depression and World War II had dramatically reduced consumer spending, and there was a great deal of pent-up demand. Consumers cashed in their war-bond savings and increased their consumption of durable goods, such as new cars and appliances. Along with this new age of consumer affluence came the population increase we now know of as the baby boom. Sellers responded accordingly and the growth in new magazines, radio, and, most importantly, television encouraged and catered to the soaring demand. No other culture in history had ever been exposed to so many new products or so much advertising.

In the golden advertising era of the 1960s, new persuasion theories and tactics were developed by legendary advertising executives such as Rosser Reeves, David Ogilvy, and Bill Bernbach. Some myths about advertising's effectiveness were also created, such as the power of subliminal advertising. However, in the 1980s, attitudes toward advertising started to change. The major problem with advertising was not that it was dangerously and insidiously persuasive. The problem was that it too often had little to say and became lost in the clutter of other advertisements. Recognizing this, marketers shifted spending from brand and retail image advertising to short-term sales promotions.

The advertising industry is at an important crossroad. If advertising cannot be made more effective, then the money spent on advertising will continue to decline. This chapter discusses ways of making advertising more effective. It can be done.

Creative campaigns, intelligent execution, appropriate media selection, and proper scheduling will all contribute to successful advertising. To manage advertising successfully, one has to know the advertising process. How does advertising work? Your instinctive answer might be that consumers see or hear an ad and then go out and buy the product. Basically, that is correct, but other steps occur between the time a consumer is exposed to an advertisement and the time he or she purchases the product. Also, not all advertisements involve the same persuasion process.

Understanding How Advertising Works

The development of an advertising message strategy is more of an art than a science, because it involves the creativity of one or more artists. Despite decades of research on numerous aspects of advertising and persuasion, we are still a long way from settling on a general theory of advertising effectiveness.

The majority of people pay attention to only a limited amount of the information to which their five senses are exposed. Attention is important because it determines the number of advertisements consumers view in a magazine or newspaper and whether the consumers are switched on or off in front of the television set. Psychologists are not at all sure how individuals are able to subconsciously direct their attention. Clearly, people must use some "orientation" cues.[1] The unknown factor is how these cues are processed before one decides whether or not to pay attention to them.

An advertisement's first objective, therefore, is to gain its audience's attention, particularly if audience interest and product involvement are low. Most products face this problem. The attention-grabbing feature of an advertisement may be a pretty face, a familiar picture, a bright color, or a warning sound, such as a baby's cry or an emergency vehicle siren. These features may have nothing to do with the product being advertised and are included simply to gain audience attention. If an advertisement fails to attract the attention of its target audience, then the entire advertising campaign has failed. Given the enormous amount of advertising clutter that exists today, this can be a difficult task.

The second objective of advertising is to do something useful with the audience's attention once it is acquired. There are three basic approaches to persuasion.

1. Magda B. Arnold, *Memory and the Brain* (Hillsdale, NJ: Erlbaum, 1984), chapter 9.

The Buy-Feel-Learn Model of Advertising Effectiveness

The *Buy-Feel-Learn (BFL)* model applies to impulse purchases. Because of the routine nature of most purchases, consumers are not highly involved. For example, grocery shopping is often viewed as a repetitive chore, and most products bought at a grocery store are neither expensive nor complicated. Consumers tend to get habituated to certain brands in these situations, which saves them from having to think about what to buy every time they go to the store. At the same time, most consumers like variety in what they eat and wear. Therefore, they succumb to their impulses when they are confronted with something new and appealing, such as a new flavor of super-creamy ice cream. The BFL model of advertising recognizes this tendency in us to buy things that we don't know much about. This model suggests that as long as marketing management can inform a consumer about the existence of its brand, either through media or point-of-purchase advertising, there is a high likelihood that the consumer will *buy* that product on impulse. The consumption experience will result in positive or negative *feelings* about the product. Simultaneously, the consumer will *learn* about the attributes of the product (see Figure 12-1).

Figure 12-1

Advertising That Launches a New Product

The BFL "I have arrived" message theme used here encourages consumers to buy and try the product before they determine how they feel about it or change their beliefs.

The Learn-Feel-Buy Model of Advertising Effectiveness

The *Learn-Feel-Buy (LFB)* model of advertising proposes that consumers learn about a product when they are exposed to advertising. For example, assume you did not know much about the new Lexus automobile. You read an advertisement that tells you about the car's most important and unique features. You thus first *learn* about the Lexus from an ad. This information is designed to make you like the brand. Now assume that you like Toyota because of your positive *experiences* with it. Until you read the ad, you did not know that Lexus was made by Toyota. Now that the ad has passed along this information, you may develop additional positive *feelings* about Lexus. Assuming you have the money to buy a Lexus (and you may not find this out until you *visit a dealer*), the LFB model proposes that the positive feelings that the ad has developed in you toward the Lexus will make you take a serious first step toward buying the car, which is a visit to a Lexus dealer. Thus, the LFB model assumes a sequence of operations that must take place for an ad to result in the purchase of that brand (see Figure 12-2).

Figure 12-2

Problem Identification Advertising

This advertisement using the LFB "Have you got this problem?" message theme attempts to increase demand by educating the consumer about both the problem and the solution.

The Feel-Buy-Learn Model of Advertising Effectiveness

The *Feel-Buy-Learn (FBL)* model of advertising recognizes the fact that it is sometimes difficult to describe a product in words and that an ad need not always contain substantial amounts of information for it to work. Instead, a properly executed ad is capable of evoking feelings and desires in a consumer that will lead to a purchase. For example, advertisements for perfumes and vacation resorts usually contain very little information. However, they contain pictures rich in imagery that are pretested to evoke strong positive *feelings* in consumers (see Figure 12-3). This is consistent with the experiential nature of the product, which is often difficult to describe (see Chapter 3 on experiential consumer decision making). Marketers hope that the feelings generated by these ads will be associated with the name of the brand (which, in practice, does not always occur). Therefore, a consumer is led to believe that one way to attain those desirable feelings is to buy the advertised brand. The consumer actually *learns* about product attributes just prior to consumption (when he or she reviews such characteristics as price) or after buying (which is when the consumer finds out whether a perfume lingers or whether the mist attachment works efficiently).

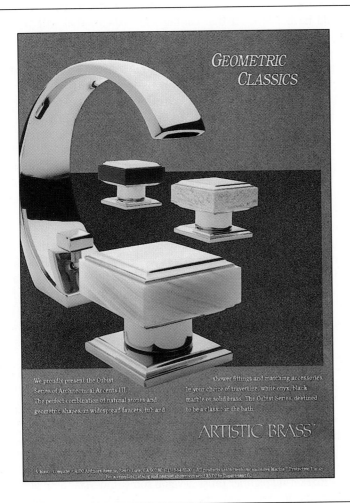

Figure 12-3

Image Advertising

The impact of this advertisement using the FBL "I'm chic, you can be too" message theme depends on the feelings that it creates toward the visual appearance of the product's design.

The three models of how advertising is expected to work cover situations that range from impulse purchases to well-thought-out and reasoned actions. We now discuss the three types of message themes that advertisers use to address the situations identified by each of these models.

The Choice of a Message Theme

Message strategy addresses the problem of what to say about the product and how to say it. Generally speaking, an advertisement for any product should promote the unique differentiation or selling proposition of that product. This is where the link between segmentation, product positioning, and message strategy becomes clear. When a marketer segments a market, a segment is identified that is either presently unoccupied or is not being served well. The segment that becomes the focal point for future marketing attention is first described by the required benefits and outcomes that are sought from the product. The product that is developed, engineered, and manufactured based on such research is expected to contain the attributes necessary to provide the desired benefit to the segment. For example, if consumers in the sensitive-teeth segment are looking for a toothpaste that tones their gum lines, then the marketer addressing that segment should have a product that contains ingredients that will provide this attribute, and it should be positioned based on its ability to help fight weak gum lines.

The message that is conveyed to a targeted consumer should automatically emphasize the unique benefit that is provided by the promoted product. In the above example, any advertisement should necessarily inform the consumer that the advertised brand of toothpaste will help him or her fight sensitive gum lines. The repetitive education provided by advertisements is expected to create a unique position in the minds of consumers for the advertised brand—in this case characterized by the problem situation (having sensitive teeth) and the available solution (the advertised brand).

The advertiser and its advertising agency share the responsibility for developing the message theme. It should evolve naturally from the positioning strategy and persuasion model that seems best, given the likely choice behavior of the target segment. If the message theme is not based on such a foundation, it can result in campaigns that are irrelevant to the product or service's competitive positioning or, even worse, damage it. For example, Burger King did not intend its message theme to portray its target customer as a nerd nor its hamburgers as nerdy in its infamous Herb campaign. However, this was the viewers' perception of the $40-million campaign that was launched on national TV during the 1986 Super Bowl. The ad presented Herb the nerd as "the only person who hasn't tasted a Burger King burger." The ad was attention grabbing, weird, funny, talked about—and a disastrous flop. Burger King would have been much better off using a message strategy that emphasized its long-standing product differentiation, which is better-tasting, flame-broiled hamburgers.

The agency should participate in all marketing planning meetings so that it understands the desired positioning strategy. It will also come to appreciate the need to fit the creatives, media choice, and media scheduling to the market facts. If the agency ignores the environmental analysis, which the marketing strategy is meant to fit, then it has demonstrated it cannot work within the decision-making process, and it should be replaced. The primary role of any agency is to develop a message theme and creative tactics that execute the positioning strategy. To be able to help the agency complete this mission, a marketing planner must develop some understanding of how advertising works. The majority of advertisements fall into one of three basic message categories, listed in Table 12-1, which are discussed and illustrated throughout the chapter. In fact, Table 12-1 is a framework or mental model for thinking about advertising.[2]

Newsworthy—BFL Themes

The first and most basic message theme presents the advertisement as a newsworthy announcement. This theme succeeds as long as the ad's message is "news." This type of message strategy is most commonly found in "FOR SALE" display advertisements in newspapers (see Figure 12-4), classified advertisements, advertisements announcing a new product or service (see Figure 12-1), and advertisements announcing visiting entertainment shows (such as where to get tickets for a U2 concert).

2. Another interesting dichotomy exists between the advertising theme that promises the removal of a problem and the theme that promises more satisfaction. See John R. Rossiter and Larry Percy, *Advertising and Promotion Management* (New York: McGraw-Hill, 1987), chapter 7.

Table 12-1
Message Themes: Repetition, Reach, and Media

Themes	Repetition needed	Reach needed	Best media*
1. News, informational themes (BFL)			
"I'm for sale,"	Low	High	N,R,TV
"I have arrived"	Low	High	N,R,TV
"I'm a bargain right now"	Low	High	N,R,TV
"Time to use me now"	Medium	High	D,N,R,TV
"Try me, like me."	High	High	TV,M
2. Logical persuasion themes (LFB)			
"Have you got this problem? I have the solution."	Medium	Medium	TV,M
"This is more of a problem than you think."	Medium	Medium	TV,M
"This is how I work."	Low	Medium	TV,M
"I am . . . I have . . . "	Medium	Medium	TV,M
"I'm better than them because . . ."	Medium	Medium	TV,M
"I'm better than them in this usage situation."	Medium	Medium	TV,M
"Don't believe what they say."	Low	Medium	M,TV
3. Image and feeling persuasion themes (FBL)			
"Remember me."	High	High	B
"Look at me, like me."	High	High	TV,M
"Smile, like me."	High	High	TV,R
"Think *X*, think me."	High	High	B,TV,M
"I'm chic, you can be too."	Medium	Medium	M,TV
"I'm a dream, a mood, a good-time product."	Medium	Medium	TV,M

*These recommendations are only general and would depend on the creative approach employed and cost per 1,000 exposures to the target audience. (B = Billboards, M = Magazines, R = Radio, TV = Television, N = Newspaper, D = Direct mail.)

Figure 12-4

**Example of an "I'm for sale"
News (BFL) Theme**

Another type of news message reminds consumers that this is the time to use the product or buy the product (such as lawn-care company advertising in the spring). The advertisements present basic facts with minimal persuasive creatives. The description of the product's characteristics is considered sufficient because the target audience is moderately to highly involved and is willing to read or listen to the details of the advertisement in order to interpret the attractiveness of the offer.

A news theme does not try to create new feelings because the audience already has well-established feelings about the subject (for instance, the announcement of a rock concert date or a department store sale is not expected to create *new* fans of the band or shop). Little attempt is made at elaborate product differentiation because brand differentiation has been established from the consumer's previous experience with the product, or because the differentiation is clearly newsworthy and does not need elaboration ("50% off!"). Consumers learn of the news, understand it, and react to it. They react either positively (by buying the product), or negatively (by not buying the product). Advertisements using this type of message strategy need to reach a high percentage of the target audience. Most of their news is in the headlines, and the audience takes only one or two exposures to get the message. The message speaks for itself and does not require much elaboration or attention-grabbing gimmicks. Consequently, newsworthy advertisements do not need a high frequency of exposure in order to be effective. Radio, newspapers, and television carry a lot of this newsworthy advertising.

Finally, a simple message theme whose intent is to get the consumer to try the product ("Try me, like me"; see Figures 12-1 and 12-7) is empowered by a free sample or by the words or images of a satisfied user (one example is the Alka-Seltzer classic "Try it, you'll like it" message). This theme is often used by new low-involvement, experience goods. Experience goods are products and services whose performance can really only be judged through trial. The advertising neither informs nor creates lasting feelings. It simply prompts trial.

A pertinent example for this type of strategy is the California raisins ad. For six years, raisin growers experienced flat sales. The raisin market appeared to be in the last stages of maturity and nearing decline. Then came the California raisins television ad created by Foote, Cone & Belding, which added excitement to a previously dull product. The ads did not promote raisins as a convenient, nutritious snack. They simply encouraged kids and adults to try raisins again—and it worked. The ads won awards and were the most popular advertisements among viewers in 1987. More importantly, industry sources estimate the campaign increased raisin sales by 14 percent.[3]

Logical—LFB Themes

The second major category of advertising message strategies uses a similar influence path, but it is a much harder sell. It relies on logical arguments, expert evidence, and test demonstrations—similar to the way a lawyer or scientist attempts to argue his or her case by the use of facts (see Table 12-1). Words and language are more prominent in this type of advertising. Examples of such advertisements are presented in Figure 12-5. These strategies generally assume a high level of interest and involvement from the target audience.

If the product category is new, the message strategy often attempts to raise interest and involvement by teaching consumers about the problem the product solves (see the Listerine ad). If consumers are familiar with the product category, then the message strategy must credibly explain why the promoted brand provides superior performance or value for the money.

Some evidence suggests that there has been a trend away from the use of mood and emotion in creatives and back to the bread-and-butter techniques selling of superior performance. For example, Procter & Gamble changed its Bounce fabric softener ad from the commercial featuring the hit song "Jump" (which was a finalist for the 1986 Clio Award for best ad) to an ad that discussed how and why its brand made clothes feel, smell, and wear better.[4] The advertisement shifted from explaining how Bounce makes you "feel" to a promise of "softness with no static cling," a functional, logical message strategy.

Increase Demand

The first subcategory of this message strategy attempts to increase consumer demand for the product or service by increasing the importance of the problem that it solves or highlighting a problem that to date had not been solved (see Figure 12-2). Arm & Hammer did this with its brilliant "Have you got this problem? I have the solution" campaign that raised household awareness of the use of baking soda as a refrigerator deodorant from one percent to 57 percent. Over three years, the company's baking soda sales increased by 72 percent.[5]

---

3. Edward F. Cone, "Terrific! I Hate It," *Forbes,* June 27, 1988, 130–32. The California Raisins ads were also rated number 1 in popularity in 1988 and 1989 and number 3 in 1990.
4. Edward F. Cone, "Image and Reality," *Business Week,* December 14, 1987, 226–28.
5. Jack J. Honomichl, "The Ongoing Saga of 'Mother Baking Soda,'" *Advertising Age,* September 20, 1982, M-2, M-3, M-22.

(a)

A second subcategory of logical persuasion attempts to increase the attractiveness of the brand by explaining the uniqueness or superiority of its features and/or performance ("I am. . . I have. . . "). Another type of message strategy spells out the competitive product differentiation ("I'm better than them because . . . "—such as the microwavable Saran Wrap ad in Chapter 8).

The most argumentative and combative type of logical message strategy attacks a competitor's advertising claims or product weaknesses either explicitly or implicitly (such as the "Bring your Visa card . . . because they don't take American Express" advertisements). The final and most ambitious ad is the direct marketing ad that attempts to take the consumer from attention to action (ordering) in one advertisement, although not necessarily in one exposure (see the Susan B. Anthony coin advertisement in the Chapter 1 Discussion Questions).

Image—FBL Themes

The third general type of message theme is one that connects or associates an image, feeling, or mood to a brand (see Table 12-1). In its most basic form, image persuasion can be seen in the billboard that simply states the brand name and illustrates the product attractively (as if it were saying, "Remember me" or "Look at me, like me"). The theory is that repeated exposure to an attractive presentation of the brand will build

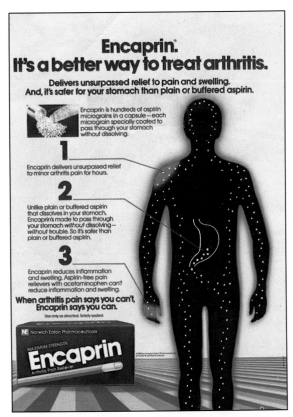

(b)

(c)

up familiarity, top-of-mind brand awareness (mind share), product appeal, and trial among nonusers and bolster the appeal of the product with current users. Rather than using information to persuade consumers, it uses emotions and feelings to change opinions and attitudes.[6]

In reality, most feeling or mood advertising is probably best at maintaining current market share by maintaining top-of-mind awareness for the brand, but does not do much more. The idea is that familiarity and recency of exposure to brand names will increase the probability of purchase. This tactic is likely to be pursued in a mature market where there is little product differentiation. In a sense, it is an alternative to price competition. The brand that has the highest top-of-mind familiarity is most likely to be chosen. Consequently, continuous advertising is needed to maintain "remember me" brand familiarity and loyalty, and it can become boring.

A more complex type of feeling ad attempts to evoke images and feelings from the memory of past usage experiences that are positive and reinforcing. The effect is to remind consumers of positive feelings associated with the brand that may prompt consumers to buy it. The Hallmark greeting card ads often use this technique.

6. W. R. Nord and J. P. Peter, "A Behavior Modification Perspective on Marketing," *Journal of Marketing* 44.2 (1980), 36–47.

Figure 12-6

Example of the Image, Feeling (FBL) Theme

Example of a "Think *X* (softness), think me" theme. By repeatedly associating teddy bear softness with the brand, the advertiser hopes to increase the belief that using Snuggle will make clothes, towels, and sheets softer.

Love softness?
Then you'll love me.

Snuggle® Fabric Softener.
I get clothes more than snuggly soft. With me, they're "cuddle-up" fresh, too. And your whole wash is static-free. For a snuggly soft wash, try me! **Snuggly softness that's really less expensive.**

Snuggle®
SNUGGLY SOFTNESS THAT'S LESS EXPENSIVE!
CONCENTRATED FABRIC SOFTENER

Association through Repetition

A classical conditioning persuasion strategy is the basis for a "Think *X,* think me" message strategy.[7] Advertisers hope that by constantly associating their product with *X,* the ads will encourage the target audience to associate *X* with their product (see Figure 12-6). Advertisers who want their products to possess a glamorous, exciting image pair themselves with glamorous, exciting celebrities or sports events (such as Wimbledon). The frequency of repetition needed to establish the connection depends on the target audience's level of involvement. In high-fashion women's clothing advertisements, the chic looks, arrogant posturing, and pouting of the model are associated with the outfit. One exposure to such an ad can have the target buyer reaching for the bellpull to call the Mercedes to the front door. Another hundred thousand consumers exposed to the advertisement dream of doing the same. On the other hand, it may take many repetitions for a brand of fabric softener that wants to convince consumers of its snuggle softness to obtain the advantages of associating itself with a snuggly soft teddy bear (see Figure 12-6).

7. M. L. Rothschild and W. C. Gaidis, "Behavioral Learning Theory: Its Relevance to Marketing and Promotions," *Journal of Marketing* 45.2 (1981), 70–78; and J. P. Peter and W. R. Nord, "A Clarification and Extension of Operant Conditioning Principles in Marketing," *Journal of Marketing* 46.3 (1982), 102–7.

A "Smile, like me" strategy is meant to work in a similar way (see the photos on page 440). The internal feeling of amusement and external smile or even laughter created by a cute or humorous ad is designed to transfer to the advertised product.[8] The result should be an increase in warm, fuzzy feelings toward the product. In this case, we are attempting to connect the product with positive feelings rather than an image or performance attribute. The qualifier is that many very humorous advertisements create emotions and feelings for the ad itself that never do transfer to the product.

Bringing the Dream World into the Real World

The most complicated form of the learning-reinforcement message strategy uses a feeling transfer persuasion theory. In this type of ad, product use is shown to create highly desirable feelings, moods, or outcomes. For example, perfume advertisements often present dreamy, high-imagery scenes. The connections between products and feelings or images in such advertisements can be so powerful that not only do such promises lead to purchase, but when the product is used (be it perfume or a Porsche) the actual moods and emotions portrayed in the ad are recreated in the user's mind and learned. The user of the product role plays what he or she saw in the ad and the feelings created by the ad reemerge in acting out the fantasy. Because the user feels, through fantasizing, more confident, assured, cool, attractive, sensual, hot, or macho, the dream becomes the reality. The feeling created by the advertisement not only leads to purchase and use, but it also influences the feelings that result from actually using the product. Such advertising does not need much exposure if it is connected to powerful needs, such as the needs for social power and sexual attraction (see the ad on page 442).

Creative Tactics

Once a company has chosen its basic message theme, it begins the often difficult process of translating its theme into a creative concept and final advertisement. Like any artists, the creative people in advertising agencies sometimes dislike direction. The dilemma for them is making sure that the product's desired positioning and message directs their artistic skill without crushing their enthusiasm and creativity. The critical test is the creative execution. If the message comes through loud and clear, then the theme has been executed successfully. If it does not, then the creative execution has failed. While almost all the decisions regarding creative tactics should be made by the advertising agency, an advertiser can influence the creative process in important ways. One way is by ensuring that the creatives do not eclipse the product positioning message. This can particularly happen when humor or celebrity endorsers are used. The advertiser also makes certain that the advertisement does not attempt to achieve so many communications objectives that in the process it achieves none. Most successful advertisements attempt only to convey a single message, a single image, a single claim of superiority, or a single reason to buy.

Simple Messages for a Low-Involvement Audience

Some advertisers and their agencies believe that an advertisement must contain ten good reasons for buying the product. In reality, readers, viewers, and listeners are usually a thousand times less involved in both the product and ad than the advertiser. Although the consumer might glance at the headline, he or she is very unlikely to read every one of the sales points detailed in the ad. The advertisement may work because

8. B. Sternthal and C. S. Craig, "Humor in Advertising," *Journal of Marketing* 37.4 (1973), 12–18.

As the competitive clutter around ads increases, advertisers are struggling to find creative executions that will stand out from the rest. While modern graphics and loud sounds cease to attract audience interest, advertisers have found truth in the adage "Old is gold."

AdvantEdge Television Advertising in New York sells old award-winning television advertisements that can be customized to a new client's product. Often, all the client needs to do is change the logo at the end of the commercial, and she or he is ready to air it within a week. What is the price? Often as low as 10% of what it cost to produce the commercial originally. Buyers like True Quality Phar-

the audience believes *the claim* that ten good reasons exist for purchasing the product, even though they do not read them. In short, the headline should execute the message theme. An exception is when advertisements are targeted at highly involved consumers who are in an active search and shopping mode. In this situation, the entire advertisement is likely to be read.

Building on Classic Themes

Another way an advertiser can positively influence the creative process is to encourage the agency to build on successful past themes. This technique is frequently underutilized. An old campaign's familiarity to customers can often be an excellent way to launch a new creative approach and help integrate the advertiser's product. Creative directors have also discovered that, in general, nostalgia sells (see the Rationality in Practice box above) or at least appeals to some market segments.

Young and Rubicam cleverly built upon Ogilvy and Mather's "Merrill Lynch is Bullish on America" theme, which had been used for seven years. They created the slogan, "Merrill Lynch, a breed apart," using one bull (symbolizing a sustained stock market rally) in a china shop (symbolizing the need to be careful and cautious) instead of a herd of bulls thundering out of the TV screen. The bull was put out to pasture prematurely (dropped) in 1985 by Y&R, which may have been the reason why the agency lost the account the following year.[9] The bull has since returned to Merrill Lynch's advertising. It is likely that an agency may be unreasonably resistant to acknowledging and building on successful past creatives, particularly when they were produced by other agencies. However, it is also true that while some nostalgic themes should remain buried when they become culturally passe, others should never have been brought to life in the beginning.

Describing the elements of a successful creative is like trying to describe artwork. The use of the elements or techniques can be identified, the process of how they are put together can be explained, but exactly how the artist derives the right combination of pieces remains part of the mystery of creativity. Consequently, all that we can and should do as marketers is try to understand the strengths and weaknesses of the following creative elements that are used in advertising.

Images

Seeing and hearing come naturally. We have to learn to read and listen to words.[10] Natural pictures and sound are therefore easier to process than words and are powerful

9. Christine Dugas and Paul B. Brown, "How Five Advertising Agencies Ran for the Bull," *Business Week,* April 14, 1986, 90–91.
10. J. R. Rossiter and L. Percy, "Visual Communication in Advertising," and R. J. Harris, ed., *Information Processing Research in Advertising* (Hillsdale, NJ: Lawrence Erlbaum Associates, 1983), 83–125.

macy of Texas agree that old wine in a new bottle does taste good, especially at these prices.

Meanwhile, Coca-Cola has made a splash with Paula Abdul, who is shown pitching Diet Coke as she dances with old, and now dead, celebrities like Louis Armstrong and Humphrey Bogart. It appears as though the old and forgotten are not as old and forgotten as one might assume.

If consumers truly are turned off by the new and turned on by the old, maybe this is an avenue creative directors should start thinking about.

Source: Excerpted from Stuart Elliott, "More Scenes from the Past Sell Products in the Present," *New York Times,* April 24, 1992; and Melanie Wells, "Old Ads Get Recycled by Different Retailers," *Advertising Age,* February 15, 1993, 12.

communicators. A picture is worth a thousand words, particularly when it makes a hero out of the product. Although visuals and sound can arouse attention, they work best when they execute the message strategy. Otherwise, attention-grabbing sight and sound images may distract consumers from the actual product message.

Picture-Word Integration

The integration of images with a written message has been shown to increase consumer memory for brand names and themes.[11] For example, an ad for the Rocket messenger service that includes a logo showing a flying messenger with a rocket tied to his back results in greater recall on the part of consumers than would result from presenting the same information as words alone. Similarly, the campaign by Nationwide Insurance, in which its tag line "Nationwide is on your side" is depicted by the movement of the word Nationwide to one side on the TV screen, is another example of how pictures and words can interact to produce a memorable effect on the viewer. Federal Express launched its fast delivery service by using a fast-talking spokesperson (Mr. Spleen) who described the benefits of using Federal Express. Many remember this ad for its humor, and the theme of speed is conveyed very effectively at the same time.

Multiple Sensory Channels

The use of multiple media has also been shown to increase consumer memory for the advertised information.[12] Thus, an ad presented on radio and in print is remembered better than the same ad presented through radio or print alone. Marketers who have realized this are now ensuring that their campaigns in various media are coordinated to present a unified image.

Headlines

Headlines should promise a benefit through product use, identify the target audience, name the brand, and be newsworthy and dramatic. They can pose questions to an involved audience that will arouse curiosity and thought. They can be humorous, such as the directive "Go to Elle" from the women's fashion magazine called *Elle.* Computer graphics are opening up exciting new opportunities for enhancing headlines, copy, and logos.

11. Kathy A. Lutz and Richard J. Lutz, "The Effects of Interactive Imagery on Learning: Application to Advertising," *Journal of Applied Psychology* 62 (August 1977), 493–98.
12. H. Rao Unnava and Robert E. Burnkrant, "Mode Specific Representation in Memory," College of Business, Working Paper series, The Ohio State University, Columbus, OH, 1989; and Julie A. Edell and Kevin L. Keller, "The Information Processing of Coordinated Media Campaigns" *Journal of Marketing Research* 26 (May 1989), 149–63.

Left: A BFL "Try me, like me" message theme. Right: An FBL "Like me" message theme. This print ad was supported by a humorous television advertising campaign.

Structure

The most important messages are generally placed at the beginning of an ad and repeated at the end. The layout and flow should be designed so that the audience processes the ad in the intended order. Advertisers should beware of creative distractors that interfere with this flow.

Music

Familiar tunes can grab attention and induce a mood.[13] They are even better if their lyrics reinforce the message strategy. Sprint's "I just called to say I love you" ad produced an immediate 25 percent increase in inquiries to the new long-distance phone company. It is possible for an advertising jingle to become so popular that it is fleshed out and released as a song. For example, Coca Cola's 1972 ode to brotherhood, "I'd like to teach the world to sing," became a top-40 hit. Coca Cola now airs the singing ad every Christmas as a nostalgic masterpiece.

13. Gerald J. Gorn "The Effects of Music in Advertising on Choice Behavior: A Classical Conditioning Approach," *Journal of Marketing* 46 (Winter 1982), 94–101; P. Sherrid, "Emotional Shorthand," *Forbes,* November 4, 1985, 214–15; and Gordon C. Bruner II "Music, Mood and Marketing," *Journal of Marketing* 54.4 (October 1990), 94–104.

The clever use of publicity in advertising adds credibility and creates a news message theme.

Humor

Humor can attract attention, create a good mood, or be passed on by word of mouth (Who can forget the slogan, "Where's the beef?"). Humor can be very powerful if it reinforces the basic message strategy, but that is difficult to do. One successful example was the Federal Express ad mentioned earlier, "Fast Paced World," which featured the fast-talking Mr. Spleen as a symbol of the need for speed and Federal Express's ability to meet a demanding executive's standards. Another example is Miller Lite's "Tastes great, less filling" shouting matches. The downside is that humor can overwhelm and distract.[14] Many people can remember the ad by its punch line but not the brand. Jokes also wear out very quickly.

Varied Executions

Brand name memory has been shown to increase when advertising executions are varied. For example, Dewar's whiskey ads present profiles of various people who consume that brand of whiskey. Each ad portrays a different person. Such variations in advertising execution are expected to help people remember the brand name better.[15] In the

14. B. Sternthal and C. S. Craig, "Humor in Advertising," *Journal of Marketing* 37.4 (1973), 12–18.
15. Robert E. Burnkrant and H. Rao Unnava, "Effects of Variation in Message Execution on the Learning of Repeated Brand Information" in *Advances in Consumer Research* vol. 14, M. Wallendorf and P. Anderson, eds., 1987, 173–76.

An FBL "I'm a dream, a mood, a good time product" message. While attention grabbing, is such sex in advertising appropriate for this product?

bunny-drummer Energizer ads, the pink bunny interrupted more than two dozen different fictitious commercials and, in this way, maintained high audience interest.

Sex

The steamy ménage-à-trois scene in the photo above may help sell Calvin Klein's Obsession (it at least fulfilled some fantasies; within a year Obsession became one of the top three fragrances). Sexual cues are great attention grabbers. However, they must be used in a setting relevant to the product, or else they can backfire. If an ad is viewed as crass, cheap, exploitive, and tasteless by the target audience, then all of these characteristics may then become attached to the advertiser and its brands.

Fear

Fear can be turned into a powerful tactic for drawing attention to a problem, but only if a credible solution is offered.[16] If the message is too strong, people will avoid future exposure to the ad, and the effect of repetition will be reduced. It may also create negative emotions and feelings that become associated with the brand. The most recent

16. Peter Wright, "Concrete Action Plans in TV Messages to Increase Reading of Drug Warnings," *Journal of Consumer Research* 6 (December 1973), 256–69; and J. J. Burnett and R. E. Wilkes, "Fear Appeals to Segments Only," *Journal of Advertising Research* 20.5 (1980), 21–24.

example of a successful fear campaign was President Bush's anti-Dukakis prison furlough TV ad. Normally the media will not accept ads that create fear about using a competitor's product.

Slice of Life

The slice-of-life creative approach is more readily integrated into personal experiences of product use and can help teach consumers how to use the product. It can also increase use (AT&T's successful "Reach out and touch someone" campaign) and reinforce the user's later experiences with the product. Slice-of-life creatives rely on vicarious learning strategies (learning by watching), which everyone employs from birth. Slice-of-life ads can be very powerful if they ring true in the same way that a great movie rings true.

Spokesperson

Over half of Japanese TV ads use a spokesperson who is immediately recognizable to the public.[17] The most successful ads use western pop stars and actors. Using a spokesperson draws attention and transfers the celebrity's image to the brand. It is best if the spokesperson's image complements and reinforces the desired brand image and the audience's perceptions of the product category. Spokespeople can also establish claim credibility, providing they are not exposed as being ingenuine. The problem is they are very expensive and can overwhelm the basic message.[18]

Two-sided Ads

Ads that are not all positive provide credibility with more highly involved audiences that enhance the positive claims made about the product or service.[19] This approach can be used by new entrants to inoculate against the competitor's arguments. A classic example is Avis's "We are #2, but we try harder."

Comparison Ads

Comparisons should only be used when competing against a market leader or when a product has compelling advantages over a competitive brand. They are good to use when the target audience is involved and can compare the benefits of one product against others. About 30% of TV ads are comparative (see the advertisements on pages 444 and 445).[20] This tactic carries the risk of identifying worthy competitors and raising their mind share ratings by identifying them as alternatives.

Competitive Interference

Interestingly, advertising can also be used to make consumers forget competitors' brand names. When consumers see advertising information for a brand, they appear to

---

17. See Andrew Tanzer, "The Celebrity Is the Message," *Forbes*, July 14, 1986, 88–89.
18. See D. Ogilvy and J. Raphaelson, "Research on Advertising Techniques That Work—And Don't Work," *Harvard Business Review* 60 (1982), 14–18. Their evidence suggests that a spokesperson can distract attention and reduce learning. Another study suggests that audiences are becoming bored with celebrity spokespeople. See Joanne Lipman "When It's Commercial Time, TV Viewers Prefer Cartoons to Celebrities Any Day," *The Wall Street Journal*, February 16, 1990, B1, B4.
19. Michael Etgar and Stephen A. Goodwin, "One-Sided Versus Two-Sided Comparative Message Appeals for New Brand Introduction," *Journals of Consumer Research*, 8 (March 1982), 460–65; Edward Giltenan, "Confronting the Negatives," *Forbes*, April 27, 1987, 83–84.
20. Chow-Hou Wee, "Comparative Advertising: A Review with Implications for Further Research," *Advances in Consumer Research* 10, R. R. Bagozzi and A. M. Tybout, eds. (Ann Arbor, MI: Association for Consumer Research, 1983); and "Red in Tooth and Claw," *The Economist*, May 18, 1991, 79–80.

Left: An LFB "I'm better than they are in this usage situation" message theme combined with a "Try me" coupon campaign. Right: An LFB "I'm better than they are because . . ." message theme, combined with a "Try me" promotion.

forget some competitive brand names compared to when they do not see advertising information for any brand.[21] This suggests that attention-getting point of purchase materials can make a consumer think about his or her brand to the detriment of competitive brands. This idea is especially appealing because advertising has become cluttered with competition—42 percent of the products advertised during a regular prime-time hour of programming have a competitive ad present in the same hour.[22]

Media Choice

For some new products, the choice of communication channels can be as important as the choice of distribution channels. Much targeting and contact segmentation involves choosing a media type with the most attractive and distinctive audience profiles. In this section we discuss the media in terms of its suitability for carrying different creative messages as well as its ability to reach different market segments at different levels of message repetition. This information is needed to assess the effectiveness of a media schedule and to execute a contact segmentation strategy.

21. Joseph W. Alba and Amitava Chattopadhyay "Salience Effects in Brand Recall," *Journal of Marketing Research* 23 (November 1986), 363–69.
22. Joe Mandese, "Rival Spots Cluttering TV," *Advertising Age,* November 18, 1991.

Check the figures.

Compare Schwab One to similar accounts.	Annual Fee	Initial Deposit Required	24-Hour Service	Commission Discounts
Schwab*ONE* Brokerage Account with Checking	FREE	$5,000	Yes	Yes
Merrill Lynch Cash Mgmt Account	$80	$20,000	No	No
Dean Witter Active Assets Account	$80	$10,000	No	No
Shearson Lehman Financial Mgmt Account	$100	$10,000	No	No

Based on a survey conducted by Charles Schwab & Co., Inc. in June, 1990. Available upon request.

Then decide.

Schwab One isn't the only brokerage account with free checking that lets you trade securities, earn income on idle cash, and access your funds with a VISA® debit card.

But after you glance at the numbers above, you may just decide it's the only one for you. We're here to help. To learn more about Schwab One, stop by any branch or call:

1-800-442-5111 Ext. O

Charles Schwab
We give you more ways to succeed.

Member SIPC · ©1990 Charles Schwab and Co., Inc.

Each media type possesses unique strengths, weaknesses, and cost structures. Potential advertisers receive a great deal of information from each advertising medium stating why it is the ideal communication vehicle, all supported by detailed and often contradictory audience and impact research. The problem centers on identifying the shortfalls of each media type. Table 12-2 summarizes the generally accepted advantages and disadvantages of each major media type. These assessments should be qualified by the unique circumstances of the advertiser. Media suitability depends on the target market, the basic message strategy, and the creative tactics used to execute the message strategy (see Table 12-1).

Minor competitors are often advised to bypass the medium dominated by a major competitor unless their advertising creatives are very strong. Otherwise, advertising becomes saturated. This causes a company's media voice share (its percentage of industry advertising that is seen on the medium) to be too small to register a significant impact. There is also the risk that the minor competitor will appear unflattering compared to the market leader.

Media Trends

Technological advances are changing communication channels as well as physical distribution channels. These changes are likely to affect the relative performance of the

Table 12-2
Advantages and Disadvantages of Major Advertising Media

Media	Advantages	Disadvantages
Newspapers	◆ Creates greater urgency ◆ Excellent for local retail sales and specials ◆ Major private ads media (classifieds) ◆ Short ad-placement lead time ◆ Co-op advertising with retailers ◆ High credibility	◆ Limited reach ◆ Limited targeting (can use suburban papers) ◆ Poor reproduction ◆ Section readership varies greatly
Television	◆ Intrusive, attention getting ◆ Most persuasive media ◆ High reach ◆ High frequency ◆ Offers visuals, sound, and movement ◆ Best for demonstrating new products, features, problem-solutions, and for highlighting zany humor ◆ Believable—what you see is what you get	◆ Networks deliver a mass audience ◆ Narrow casting limited to cable TV, specific programs, and local TV ◆ High production and running costs ◆ High ad clutter ◆ Information limitations
Direct mail	◆ Highly targeted from lists ◆ Personalized message ◆ Enables direct selling ◆ Very important in industrial marketing	◆ Clutter of junk mail ◆ Only a single exposure ◆ High per-exposure cost
Radio	◆ High intimacy ◆ Can reinforce TV ads ◆ Can use announcer, DJ endorsements ◆ Highly targeted audiences by age and music tastes ◆ Low production and running costs ◆ Short ad-placement lead time	◆ Lack of visuals limits learning and linking to point-of-purchase displays ◆ Difficult to buy national coverage
Magazines	◆ Very specific targeting, particularly for industrial markets ◆ Credible source effects of some magazines ◆ Allows detailed information for new products and comparison ads ◆ Extended life of magazine and readership over time ◆ Can direct market and include coupons in ad	◆ Needs high involvement. ◆ Long ad-placement lead time ◆ Difficult to get high frequency within purchase cycle time ◆ For some magazines, running costs of full-color ads are high ◆ Location of ad in the magazine is critical
Outdoor (Billboards)	◆ High frequency ◆ Less clutter ◆ Primarily for image and brand awareness ◆ Low running costs ◆ Moving parts create attention	◆ Limited attention span ◆ Limited reach ◆ Limited targeteing ◆ Quite high production costs
Point of purchase	◆ Closest to purchase ◆ Can be powerfully integrated with TV and magazine ads ◆ Useful for both high- and low-involvement products ◆ Three-dimensional effects	◆ Depends on retail cooperation ◆ Poor frequency ◆ Occurs too late in choice cycle ◆ Quite high production costs

media and provide significant competitive advantages to the advertiser who first recognizes and exploits this technology.

Television

Television is the medium preferred by national advertisers. It is the most persuasive, flexible, and expensive communication medium. Many advertisers spend much of their budget on television advertising in spite of the fact that rates keep increasing as television audiences shrink. The major television networks are under siege from cable television and video cassette recorders. During the 1980s, the three major networks' share of the prime-time audience dropped from 92 percent to 67 percent, while the cost of a 30-second commercial in a choice spot rose 85 percent to $185,000.[23] Many advertisers have since recognized niche marketing advantages by advertising on cable channels such as MTV and ESPN.

A major trend in television commercials during the 1980s was the advent of the 15-second commercial. About 35 percent of all television commercials are 15 seconds long. Some advertisers claim that a 15-second news or logical persuasion advertisement has 80 percent of the effect of a 30-second commercial, at about half of the cost.[24] They are much less effective for emotion-feeling themes. This increase in shorter advertisements has lead to increased clutter that over the long term may reduce the effectiveness of all television advertising.

Radio

The major trend in radio has been the increasing domination of stereo FM technology and the specialization of radio stations by the type of music played (hard rock, light rock, alternative rock, easy listening, country, and so on). Radio advertising directed at commuters can be very effective.[25] The impact that car phones have on the listening habits of upscale commuters has not been determined, but it is likely to be negative, unless the advertisement encourages listeners to call in for further information or to make a purchase. More generally, radio is a secondary advertising medium that supports advertising of primary media such as television and newspapers. Labeling it secondary does not mean that the dollar effectiveness of radio advertising is lower. Often it is higher because it inexpensively boosts the effectiveness of more expensive television and newspaper advertising.

Newspapers

High technology is also affecting the production and delivery of newspapers, although it is not so obvious to readers. The launching and surprising success of *USA Today* would not have been possible without the use of satellite technology and computerized printing. This newspaper poses a long-term, legitimate challenge to other newspapers and the other media because it offers advertisers national coverage with a heavy predominance of readership among traveling businesspeople. Newspapers will remain dominant in local classified advertising and retail display advertising, but they are losing exposure for national brand advertising because they have limited reach and limited

23. Zachary Schiller, "Stalking the New Consumer," *Business Week,* August 28, 1989, 54–62; and Jeffrey A. Trachtenberg, "The Revolt of the Couch Potatoes," *Forbes,* January 11, 1988, 260–61.
24. Jill Andresky, "Time and Emotion Studies," *Forbes,* November 18, 1985, 254.
25. Joshua Levine, "Drive Time," *Forbes,* March 19, 1990, 144–46. A major advantage of radio is its low cost per thousand of $2 compared to a television's cost per thousand of $14 and a surprisingly high $23 cost per thousand for newspapers.

reproduction quality in terms of their graphics. *USA Today* addresses some of these problems and targets itself to a very attractive market segment.

Magazines

The trend in magazines is toward focused topics. Color television killed many general-interest magazines, but sports, recreational, business, and highbrow magazines continue to flourish. The more narrow a magazine's focus and the more in-depth its coverage for a particular recreation or sport, the more likely it is that its subscribers will be real enthusiasts, early adopters of related products, and opinion leaders. Such media should be used first when launching a new product or service for which the real enthusiasts are expected to be the initial adopters who will spread the word. Having discussed the characteristics of the media, we now consider how to buy media space and time.

Combining Media

The increased cost of national television advertising (higher than $10,000 per second for ads during the Super Bowl), has led many advertisers to reduce their television spending and run complementary booster ads in other media such as magazines, radio, and billboards. Booster ads use scenes or sounds from the television commercials. Consumers are reminded of the complete television ad. They complete the story in their mind by using recall elaboration. This is a clever way of using different media together to increase the efficiency of an advertising campaign.

Supermarkets and department stores have used the combined-media technique in their local advertising for a long time. They announce a sale and create excitement with their radio and television advertising, which explicitly encourages consumers to look for further details in local newspaper advertising. The combined use of media whose advertisements have different message objectives—one to create excitement about the news and the other to provide logical persuasive detail—is an excellent example of synergy in strategy. The total effect of different message strategies is far greater than the sum of their separate effects.[26]

Media Scheduling

The great percentage of advertising expenditure (80 to 90 percent) is spent on buying media time or space. This suggests that the productivity of advertising expenditure can be improved by one or more of the following approaches: 1) finding the media that delivers the lowest cost per thousand members of the target audience, 2) achieving the most effective mix of reach and exposure frequency, 3) switching from national to regional campaigns, and 4) improving the timing of the campaign. Each of these media scheduling issues is now discussed.

Minimizing Cost Per Thousand of the Target Audience (CPM)

Media costs are generally measured in CPM (cost per thousand of delivered audience). The problem with this industry standard is that there is no audience discrimination. A nonuser of an advertised product category is weighed the same as a heavy user of the product category in this measure of delivered audience. Anheuser-Busch has pub-

---

26. The same message first read and then heard (or vice versa) may also be more memorable than the message only read, or only heard, several times. See H. Rao Unnava and Robert E. Burnkrant, "The Effect of Input Modality on Memory" (Working Paper, Columbus, OH: Ohio State University, 1991).

licly admitted that in the mid 1970s it misjudged the attractiveness of the *ABC Monday Night Football* package.[27] Anheuser looked at the cost of the package on a total dollar basis rather than on a cost per thousand beer drinkers' basis. Miller recognized the program's attractiveness on a cost per thousand of target audience. There were also very attractive advertising context effects. Not only was a large portion of the audience made up of heavy beer drinkers, but many were drinking beer while watching football and the Miller Lite Beer ads. They were primed to respond.

Increasingly, more sophisticated advertisers and agencies are measuring the cost per thousand of a specific target audience (TA) that the media delivers—abbreviated CP(TA)M. This refined statistic indicates the cost efficiency of the media vehicle's reach of the desired target market segment. This requires knowing customers' media usage and evaluating the cost effectiveness of different media based upon this information, (see Chapter 3 on media contact segmentation). For advertisers who purchase millions of dollars of advertising space per year, such a study is worth the cost.

Achieving Effective Reach and Frequency

Advertising campaigns often are measured by their reach and frequency. *Net reach* (NR) refers to the percentage of the target audience that is exposed to an ad message one or more times during a given time—usually four weeks. NR is a useful measure when only one exposure is needed to relay a message or when the goal is to have as many people as possible hear it. This applies to advertising—such as special clearance sales— that are newsworthy advertisements with a simple compelling message that generates further word of mouth. But what happens when experts tell us that consumers need to be exposed more than once to an ad for it be effective? Marketers should then use a measure of *effective reach*. The effective reach of a proposed media schedule is the percentage of the target audience exposed to an ad the minimum number of times (frequency) that is judged necessary for the ad to be effective.

Frequency measures the total number of times a person or household is exposed to an advertising message. The necessary frequency of exposure required for an ad to be effective depends on the brand's competitive position, consumer behavior, and the basic message strategy. Dominant, established brands with high brand loyalty need less frequency. A number of researchers have argued that three exposures within a purchase cycle (time between purchases) is optimal.[28] But this advice applies mainly to ads using a logical persuasion approach. Ads that attempt to imprint associations and feelings are likely to require many more repetitions. Figure 12-7 explains when to use higher exposure frequency.

The average frequency of an ad's exposure to the target audience is often used as a measure of a campaign's effectiveness or potency.[29] It is usually measured in GRPs (Gross Rating Points = Average Frequency × 100). Note, however, that this measure includes potential buyers who were exposed to the ad only once or twice, which may have been too low to have any effect. As a measure of effectiveness, average frequency weighs ten exposures as twice as potent as five exposures and ten times as potent as

27. Anheuser reacted by becoming the nation's top event sponsor. By 1987 it sponsored 80 percent of all professional sports teams in the country. See Michael Oneal, "Anheuser-Busch: The Scandal May Be Small Beer After All," *Business Week,* May 11, 1992, 72–73. In 1992 Miller hired away Anheuser's top marketing executive to be its new CEO.

28. Michael J. Naples, *Effective Frequency: The Relationship between Frequency and Advertising Effectiveness,* Association of National Advertisers, 1979.

29. Peter R. Dickson, "Gross Rating Points: A Case of a Mistaken Identity," *Journal of Advertising Research* 31.1 (1991), 55–59; and "Simplicity and Parsimony versus the Status Quo Definition of GRP," *Journal of Advertising Research,* June 1992. These articles explain that how the industry defines GRP as Net reach × frequency is average frequency × 100.

Figure 12-7

When Higher Advertising Frequency Is Needed.

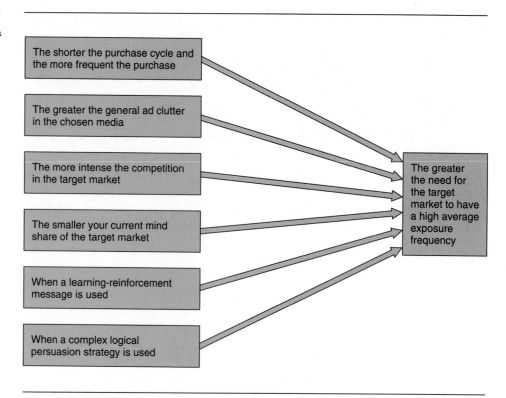

one exposure. This is a very unrealistic assumption. It assumes that each exposure is equally valuable; that is, the tenth has the same impact as the first (see the Rationality in Practice box on page 452).

Regional Advertising Campaigns

Increasingly, campaigns are being regionalized. Small, local companies have always used regional advertising, but even bigger companies such as Campbell's Soup are finding it more cost-effective to control and manage regional campaigns than a national campaign.[30] Managing market-specific campaigns also allows the use of creatives and media that are tailored to a particular regional market's tastes and life-styles.

As the marketing efforts of many companies become more focused, the decision as to which markets to develop next can make or break a firm's growth. The market potential of a city or region is an important factor. A number of market research companies can provide sales of a product category by city or county. When dealing with a new product category, census data can provide information on the markets with the highest concentration of the target audience as measured by various demographic characteristics. However, the costs of reaching the target audience can also vary considerably between cities and other factors such as retail support and climate may have to be considered when making the choice (see the Rationality in Practice box on page 454). Increasingly, national advertisers are using local advertising agencies to buy their

30. Christine Dugas, "Marketing's New Look," *Business Week,* January 26, 1987, 64–69; and Glen L. Urban, "Allocating Ad Budgets Geographically," *Journal of Advertising Research,* December 1975, 7–16.

media space, even if they use a national agency to produce the creatives. The logic is that local agencies are better buyers because of their knowledge of the local media.

Improving the Timing of a Campaign

There is more to media scheduling than CPMs, reach, frequency, and going regional. Over the planning period, marketers must decide whether to concentrate advertising seasonally or give it greater continuity. Much depends on the nature of consumer demand and whether selling seasons exist. Many consumer products have their major selling season in the three months before Christmas. For these products, most advertising is concentrated in the last quarter of the year. Other advertisers have peak selling seasons associated with the seasons. For instance, plant stores and their associated products have major spring and fall selling seasons. Advertising is often concentrated in two seasonal flights lasting six to eight weeks. It is likely to be intensive and use several media at the same time. The company's tactical objective is to dominate its share of voice (the total ad dollars spent by the individual company as a proportion of the dollars spent by the industry as a whole) without producing wearout (consumer boredom).

Low-involvement products that sell as much on their brand name as on their product features, and which have short repurchase cycles (for instance sodas that are repurchased weekly), need to have a constant advertising voice share to maintain their mind share and market share. Continuity is therefore very important to maintain the desired awareness and brand preference levels. This may require the company to rotate the ads frequently (using several variations on a theme) to avoid creative wearout.

Smaller companies that cannot afford a continued high-advertising presence often adopt a pulsed approach. They keep a low level of advertising, often in a single media (for instance, in a magazine read by heavy users), and then they use pulsed bursts of increased television or radio advertising to bring them up to the level of the market leader. These pulses are normally timed around peak demand periods or special promotions. The higher level of advertising is primarily aimed at gaining market share, while the lower level of advertising is aimed at the company's core of loyal, heavy users.

Another problem faced by advertisers is how to sequence and schedule the different media. As previously discussed, television and radio advertising often is designed to create interest and excitement and must precede the print advertisement that provides the detailed persuasive message. The timing is critical because the powerful effect of advertising in the hot broadcast media on advertising in the cool print media depends on the time lapse.

An often neglected aspect of advertising occurs at the point of purchase (POP), which might be better described as the point of choice. In some product categories (such as candy), up to 85 percent of the purchases made by shoppers are made on impulse.[31] The decision to purchase from a product category and the choice of brand within the product category is frequently made at the POP by today's busy shopper. The impulse shopper tends to be exposed to less media advertising and is not very impressed with

Point of Purchase: The Last Word in Advertising

---

31. "P-O-P Spending Increases 10%," *Marketing News,* October 10, 1988, 22. P-O-P spending increased 12 percent a year between 1983 and 1985; John A. Quelch and Kristina Cannon-Bonventre, "Better Marketing at the Point of Purchase," *Harvard Business Review,* November/December 1983, 162–69.

Rationality in Practice:

Choosing the Best Campaign

An advertising campaign has two major components, a creative execution of the theme and a media schedule. Often advertisers will choose between two or three creative executions and sometimes they will choose between two different media schedules (for instance, between a short, intense campaign or a longer, drawn out campaign). Almost never does a firm choose between advertising campaigns that have different creatives and different media schedules. A firm normally chooses the creative (the ad) and then chooses a media schedule that is best for the creative. A more competitively rational approach would be to choose the best combinations of creatives and media schedules; that is, choose between alternative campaigns that sensibly combine the creative ad and the media schedule.

For example, what if a company decides it should spend $5 million on TV advertising. Campaign option A is to buy 20 15-second prime-time slots at $200,000 per repetition and spend $1 million on ad execution, including paying a spokesperson. Campaign option B is to spend $2 million on a 30-second ad execution featuring a better-known spokesperson who is more attention grabbing and credible and to buy only 100 30-second prime-time slots at $300,000 per repetition. To determine which campaign should be chosen, the firm needs to know what percentage of the audience will notice or see Ads A and B once, twice, five times, and so on. Media schedulers or even the medium itself can provide such exposure frequency estimates. The advertiser also needs to know the relative

The impact index is scored from 1 to 20. An impact score of 20 for one of the ads that the target audience is exposed to a certain number of times (vehicle exposure frequency) means that it is 20 times as effective in its general impact (from attention to behavior) than an ad-vehicle exposure frequency with an impact score of only 1.

The impact scores are derived from the two impact graphs that are the best estimates of the planning group or the ad agency of the two ads (A and B).

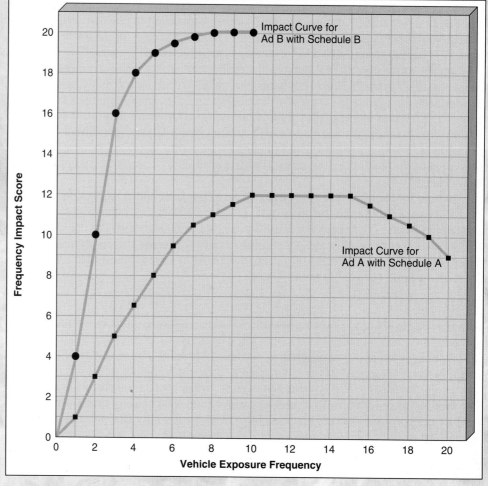

The ADIMPACT Spreadsheet

Comparison of Two Ad Campaigns Based on Reach, Frequency, and Impact
The percentage of the target audience exposed to the number of ads is estimated from audience statistics. The exposure frequency impact is an educated estimate of the cumulative impact of exposure on attention, beliefs, attitudes, and behavior.

Vehicle exposure frequency	Percentage of audience reached: Schedule A	Exposure frequency impact for Ad A	Percentage of audience reached: Schedule B	Exposure frequency impact for Ad B
1	16.3%	1.0	9.0%	4.0
2	13.8%	3.0	6.7%	10.0
3	9.9%	5.0	5.6%	16.0
4	8.9%	6.5	4.8%	18.0
5	6.7%	8.0	4.2%	19.5
6	5.1%	9.5	3.7%	20.0
7	4.1%	10.5	2.7%	20.0
8	3.3%	11.0	2.3%	20.0
9	2.7%	11.5	1.8%	20.0
10	2.2%	11.8	1.4%	20.0
11	1.7%	12.0	0.0%	0.0
12	1.4%	12.0	0.0%	0.0
13	1.1%	12.0	0.0%	0.0
14	0.9%	12.0	0.0%	0.0
15	0.7%	12.0	0.0%	0.0
16	0.6%	11.6	0.0%	0.0
17	0.5%	11.0	0.0%	0.0
18	0.4%	10.5	0.0%	0.0
19	0.3%	10.0	0.0%	0.0
20	0.2%	9.0	0.0%	0.0
Net reach	80.8%		42.2%	
2+ Exposure Reach	64.5%		33.2%	
3+ Exposure Reach	50.7%		26.5%	
4+ Exposure Reach	40.8%		20.9%	
5+ Exposure Reach	31.9%		16.1%	
6+ Exposure Reach	25.2%		11.9%	
8+ Exposure Reach	16.0%		5.5%	
12+ Exposure Reach	6.1%		.0%	
Average frequency	3.83		1.69	Critical Ratio
GRP	383		169	2.26
Impact weighted GRP	495		599	0.83

Step 1: Insert reach at each level of vehicle exposure frequency for Campaign A and Campaign B (in columns 1 and 3 above).

Step 2: Estimate impact curves and insert impact weights (in columns 2 and 4 above). Press F10 to see curves.

Step 3: Play "what if" with the estimates of reach and impact.

impact on the target audience of seeing ad A and B once, twice, five times, or more.

The firm and its advertising agency can then use this ADIMPACT spreadsheet to compute the overall effectiveness of campaign A and campaign B. For example, given the exposure frequency estimates and impact estimates presented in the table, campaign A is only 83 percent as effective as campaign B, using an impact weighted GRP score (the sum of each percentage of target audience that sees an ad n times weighted by the impact of seeing the ad n times). However, using the standard GRP measure, campaign A is more than twice as effective as campaign B.

Rationality in Practice:

Choosing Regional Markets

If a firm cannot afford a national advertising campaign, how does it choose the cities or regions on which to focus its campaign, and which should be the roll-out cities (that is, the cities that will follow the initial launch city)? A firm making luxury woolen mattress pads called Woolrest launched a very successful 10-week fall campaign in Seattle, Washington, in 1984. It wanted to know what new markets it should enter (roll-out in) in Fall 1985. To improve the quality of its decision making, the spreadsheet on the right was developed.

A number of cities were compared to Seattle in terms of campaign cost for a standard media schedule (estimated by seeking advice from local ad agencies), media reach and fit with the target market (provided by local ad agencies), the rating of the quality of the supplier-reseller fit (mainly department stores) in each city, the suitability of the cli-

mate and attitude of the region toward wool, and the number of households with a head of household over 55 years old and with an income over $15,000 (from the 1976 census data). The latter was as close to the target market as could be measured. Some of these ratings were quite objective, others were very subjective.

The simple cost-effectiveness rating (target market size/cost) was computed by dividing the number of target households by the media cost and standardizing the rating so that the Seattle score would be 100 (the known standard). Using this calculation, Baltimore, Pittsburgh, and Philadelphia all look as attractive, if not more attractive, than Seattle. However, when all the other attractiveness factors were considered (by multiplying the size/cost rating by each of the attractiveness ratings), then only Philadelphia looked about as attractive as the known standard, Seattle. The company used this spreadsheet to choose some of the cities for its fall 1984 campaign.

the quality of advice and service offered by today's low-skill retail salespeople. Consequently, POP advertising is often the first and last chance to influence the consumer.

How effective is point-of-purchase advertising? For a start, it is much more cost-effective per thousand target *shopper* exposures than any other media. Second, the advertising exposure often occurs only moments before purchase, so it is much more timely than any other advertising. Actmedia, the company that hangs ads on shopping carts, promises average sales increases of 8 percent or more for the four weeks a product is advertised in the store. Sales increases on impulse items such as ice cream can be 20 percent. The store gets 25 percent of the ad revenues and sells more product.[32] By contrast, a retailer often has to give away margin on a price promotion to get the increased volume in sales. POP advertising also often has the effect of a billboard—it prompts the consumer to recall a television or a magazine ad. In combination with media advertising and packaging, POP advertising can be doubly effective.

32. Russell Mitchell "An Upstart Is Upsetting Actmedia's Shopping Carts," *Business Week,* September 7, 1987, 28–29.

Woolrest Market Potential: USA 1985 Fall Season

Standard Metropolitan Statistical Area	Target: 55+ and $15,000+	Wool-aware & right climate	Rating of retail dist.	TV reach	Newspaper reach	Radio fit	Ten-week media cost index
Seattle	81,228	100	100	92.0%	47.0%	100	100
Baltimore	92,610	90	100	81.0%	39.0%	90	110
Boston	129,634	85	70	81.0%	50.0%	90	216
Cleveland	97,345	90	110	91.0%	39.0%	80	140
Denver	64,397	95	60	91.0%	58.0%	90	122
Hartford	36,495	90	100	65.0%	40.0%	90	128
Milwaukee	63,665	90	80	93.0%	46.0%	80	107
Minneapolis/St. Paul	85,138	90	100	93.0%	46.0%	100	158
Providence	35,391	90	50	67.0%	49.0%	80	76
Pittsburgh	112,087	85	85	82.0%	44.0%	100	126
Philadelphia	214,253	85	100	90.0%	40.0%	100	199
Portland	54,570	100	85	89.0%	45.0%	90	72

Standard Metropolitan Statistical Area	Size/cost rating	Size/cost (dist. adj.) rating	Size/cost (media adj.) rating	Size/cost (clim. adj.) rating	Size/cost (dist. & media adj.) rating	Size/cost (all adj.) rating
Seattle	100.0	100.0	100.0	100.0	100.0	100.0
Baltimore	103.6	103.6	68.2	93.3	68.2	61.3
Boston	73.9	51.7	62.3	62.8	43.6	37.1
Cleveland	85.6	94.2	56.2	77.0	61.8	55.6
Denver	65.0	39.0	71.4	61.7	42.8	40.7
Hartford	35.1	35.1	19.0	31.6	19.0	17.1
Milwaukee	73.3	58.6	58.0	65.9	46.4	41.7
Minneapolis/St. Paul	66.3	66.3	65.6	59.7	65.6	59.1
New Bedford	57.3	28.7	34.8	51.6	17.4	15.7
Pittsburgh	109.5	93.1	91.4	93.1	77.7	66.0
Philadelphia	132.5	132.5	110.4	112.7	110.4	93.8
Portland	93.3	79.3	77.8	93.3	66.1	66.1

Direct Marketing

In the last decade, the practice of contacting consumers directly has experienced substantial growth. You have very likely received offers for books, tapes, or compact discs from the people who produced them. What is interesting is that the scope of this type of direct marketing has grown to an extent that there now exists a Direct Marketing Association, which helps companies involved in direct marketing to standardize their practices and have a collective voice in dealing with legislation. Robert Coen from McCann Ericson estimated direct mail expenditures for the year 1991 to have been $24.3 billion, which is over 16 percent of all advertising expenditures in this country. The Direct Marketing Association defines direct marketing as "an interactive use of advertising media which stimulates (immediate) behavior modification in such a way that this behavior can be tracked, recorded, and analyzed, then stored in a database for future retrieval and use."

Direct marketing has become as popular as it is today for many reasons. The most important one, of course, is the availability of computer hardware and software, which has enhanced its contact efficiency. For example, the manufacturer of a water purifier system may want to reach only new home buyers. An ad on a popular prime-time television show is a waste of dollars because it reaches many people who do not form part of the target market, yet the advertiser is required to pay to them. A direct phone call or a mailer to current or recent home buyers is more efficient because it targets the market very precisely.

The availability of computerized databases today allows sellers to choose their prospective buyers. Manufacturers increasingly rely on direct marketing for other reasons as well, including time pressures on consumers (especially in two-income households) that preclude them from allocating precious hours for shopping thereby forcing them to shop from home; the increased use of 800 and 900 numbers that allow easy ordering; an explosion in the issue and use of credit cards, which facilitate purchases by phone; and, importantly, the growth of quality sellers (such as L.L. Bean and Dell Computers) who provide impressive guarantees and deliver quality merchandise.

The heart of any direct marketing system is the "list." The list consists of the names, addresses, and telephone numbers of those people in whom a manufacturer may be interested. In some instances, lists contain psychographic information that has been obtained through surveys (for instance, a magazine may conduct a life-style survey of its subscribers and store it in a database). Publicly available data, such as tax records and home buying activity, are also included on some of the lists. Recent estimates indicate that are over 30,000 lists are available for rent. These lists have been prepared by various parties involved in business activities. For example, when you send in your warranty registration card for a new product that you just bought (say, a humidifier for the winter), you may have written in some information about yourself as you answered some questions on the registration card. This information will be stored by the company and very likely sold to other sellers who might be interested in it. There will be a host of other manufacturers (perhaps, dehumidifiers) who would be very interested in getting those names and addresses so they can reach customers like you directly. Similarly, your credit history contains information on your purchases and even brand choices. The few companies that monitor your credit history have access to substantial amounts of information about you, which they sell to outside parties. Of course, certain rules prevent them from selling highly private information, but there is still plenty of information that they can sell that many people are interested in buying. Also, some companies prepare lists as part of their business. These companies typically have hundreds of lists and earn revenues in the millions of dollars by renting out those lists.

In choosing a list, two criteria are often viewed as critical. First, how old is the list? That is, does the list contain names of individuals whose records have been updated with their most recent purchase activities? If the list was compiled earlier, it may not be a good predictor of market potential because users of the list will not know how those consumers have been making their purchases in recent months. Second, the amount of money that has been spent on direct buying by each individual on a list is a critical piece of information. The more money an individual has spent on direct buying, the greater the likelihood that she or he will spend more when approached with an interesting product. List sellers know this and often charge higher prices for the names and addresses of individuals who have spent large amounts of money buying directly from manufacturers.

Direct marketing seems to be most beneficial for selling very specialized products. The low costs of printing and distributing catalogs and address letters or of advertising on a specialized cable channel (so as to predominantly reach only the members of the target market) enable sellers to realize higher margins on their products. When Dell Computer Company started selling computers by catalogs, it was scoffed at by analysts because consumers were not expected to make such expensive purchases by catalog.

However, by offering low prices and proven technology, Dell has managed to become one of the most profitable personal computer sellers in the low-margin, cut-throat computer market. Thus, there really is no limit on what type of a product you can sell directly to the customer—including services. In fact, direct marketing is often used by dentists, doctors, veterinarians, eye doctors, tax preparers, pest control companies, and many other services to remind their clients that it is that time of the year again. It is a crucial element of maintaining the relationship.

On the other hand, not everyone prefers to buy directly from manufacturers. Many consumers enjoy shopping and direct buying would deprive them of the pleasure of browsing. This is one of the reasons why catalog sales have grown rapidly but plateaued over the last few years. The growth potential for direct marketing is limited not so much by the type of merchandise but by the type of people who patronize direct sellers.

Finally, two problems face direct marketers that need immediate attention. As with any high-growth industry, direct marketing has grown faster than the supporting systems for this form of marketing could be put in place. Too many lists are available, too much duplication exists between lists, and too many manufacturers are jumping into the game without much market analysis. The excess competition causes clutter that is difficult to break through and attract consumer attention. Weak competition, by its inefficient and ineffective methods, will also upset consumers who may be pushed into avoiding all direct marketing attempts. The Direct Marketing Association plays a significant role in reducing damage to the industry through these processes.

Second, any time a list has been accessed and used, the issue of privacy is raised. Consumers may not appreciate getting letters that refer to their recent purchases because they may feel that the manufacturer from whom they bought the product has betrayed them. Direct marketers have to exercise a great deal of caution in this regard. Even when knowledge exists about a consumer's recent purchases, the consumer should be approached with suppressed enthusiasm, only referring to the purchase tangentially. Any feelings of privacy violation on the part of consumers can propel consumer advocates into pushing for legislation that might ban the use of lists. The Direct Marketing Association, once again, has acted proactively in this regard and provides consumers with options so they can remove their names from various lists.

In conclusion, much like the way scanner technology has provided important point-of-purchase sales information, computer technology has made selling directly to a choice group of consumers easier and cheaper. As long as the efficiencies of the process are maintained, and consumers continue to buy directly from manufacturers, this type of marketing is here to stay. Research should be aimed at ways of attracting consumer interest and cementing relationships by better use of the new technologies.

Generating Free Publicity

Publicity is advertising's Cinderella. Over 100,000 media editors in the United States and Canada are constantly searching for news and public interest stories, including stories about interesting new products, new product uses, and new services. The explicit or implicit endorsement given by the independent media when they publicize a new product can give a marketing campaign a powerful boost. Americans love to read or hear about Horatio Alger–type success stories. Consequently, nothing succeeds like success when it comes to publicity.

Coleco's publicity campaign for its Cabbage Patch dolls is a classic example of the power of publicity.[33] Planned almost a year before, the publicity campaign was carefully

33. Jerry Adler, "Oh, You Beautiful Dolls!" *Newsweek,* December 12, 1983, 78–81; and Lynn Langway, "Harvesting the Cabbage," *Newsweek,* December 12, 1983, 81–85.

orchestrated with the advertising and promotion campaign to peak in December 1983. The campaign started with the American Toy Fair in New York early in the year. In the fall, First Lady Nancy Reagan gave Cabbage Patch dolls to two South Korean children flown to the United Staes to undergo heart surgery. Jane Pauley gave the dolls much enthusiastic coverage on the *Today* show on November 18th and other media rushed to pick up the story about the 1983 "must have" Christmas present. This complemented the extensive coverage given in the Christmas gift ideas features of numerous November women's magazines. Coleco representatives appeared on TV talk shows, the dolls were featured on NBC's *Tonight Show* several times, and a Cabbage Patch Kid's sketch was presented in Bob Hope's Christmas show. Meanwhile, dolls were being given away to children in hospitals, and radio stations were distributing the dolls as contest prizes. The whole promotion actually got somewhat out of hand when frantic buyers started to make the news because of their wild attempts to buy a doll. Coleco then had to request that the news media cool the story—demand had exceeded supply.

The Advantages and Disadvantages of Publicity

The advantages of publicity over advertising are its greater credibility, the independent endorsements of media celebrities such as Bryant Gumbel on NBC's *Today* show, the speed of coverage, the creation of public interest, word of mouth, momentum, and excitement few advertising campaigns can match. In fact, often such media publicity stories are reproduced or mentioned in a company's advertising because as news they are so much more credible (see the advertisement on page 441). All of this can be achieved at a quite modest expense if the story is newsworthy.[34]

The disadvantages of publicity is that it is often an all-or-nothing proposition and there is a lack of control over the process and execution. If no editor takes the bait, then you are sunk. However, if one editor thinks your message is newsworthy, then others are likely to follow. If the wire services then pick it up, and other local media scramble to cover the story and extend it, then extraordinary reach and frequency can be obtained in a short period of time. Having several sources carry the story also increases credibility. The problem in terms of control is that the media are likely to change the angle of the story, particularly news releases. Photos and videotapes provide more control because they cannot be so readily edited. The skill of a good publicist depends, in part, on his or her friendly contact with the media. Because they are often ex-journalists or ex-editors themselves, many publicists have a network of contacts in the media.

The Importance of Implementation and Follow-through

Publicists have to walk a fine line with the media. They must package the message as conveniently as possible without removing the possibility for the media to create their own angle on the story. Some media will publish press releases as is. Others have a policy never to do this because they see it as surrendering editorial policy to thinly disguised advertising. In practice, firms often provide a company or, even better, an independent spokesperson that the press can call and build a story around. Publicity can also be generated through publicity stunts or media events or by giving the product or service away to prominent celebrities, to charities, or to be used as contest prizes. Rather than asking the media to approach company spokespeople, it is often better to put such people on the road so they can appear on local or national talk shows.

---

34. Another type of advertising-as-publicity that emerged in the 1980s made use of popular movies. Firms bought their way into movie scripts in order to have their products featured prominently and positively. In a sense, the stars are seen to be endorsing the product.

The media are very sensitive about the legitimacy of claims of performance superiority because they know that repeating them through the media will give such claims further credibility. Media professionals also know that they are likely to be besieged by complaints of editorial bias and demands that the story be retracted (tantamount to an apology and a lack of professionalism) from competitors if the claims are not watertight. That is why test performance results from independent researchers or testing labels are often more useful for obtaining publicity than for adding credibility to advertising.

Publicity in Industrial Markets

Publicity is often even more important in industrial markets because of the power of word of mouth. In industrial markets, the objective is to be featured in the new-products sections of trade, technical, and industry-specific magazines and newsletters. This kind of publicity is likely to draw far more inquiries from potential users and interested distributors or reps than any advertising (which, incidentally, the company may have had to purchase in the same magazine issue). Sometimes such publicity may be all that is needed to launch a new product or service into an industrial market.

Public Relations Management

When consumers buy products, they are essentially saying that they trust the products to satisfy their needs. This trust can result from their past experiences with products and the companies that make those products. In other words, what consumers think of a company or its brand name should have a significant influence on their buying habits. For example, while there were other reasons, consumers' positive attitudes toward IBM must have contributed to the success of the IBM PC in the early 1980s, even though IBM entered late into the PC market. Realizing the value of creating positive images for their companies in people's minds, businesses often undertake coordinated public relations campaigns that are targeted at various constituencies of importance to the businesses.

According to *Public Relations News,* public relations (PR) is "the management function which evaluates public attitudes, identifies the policies and procedures of an organization with the public interest, and executes a program of action (and communication) to earn public understanding and acceptance."[35] As can be seen from this definition, PR is a conscious and targeted attempt to align a company's image. Notice that it is the company's image that is being marketed, not any of its products. The expectation is that positive feelings about the company will translate into the increased patronage of its products. More importantly, if the company makes mistakes that could upset consumers, good public relations are expected to soften the negative impact of such mistakes. Public relations efforts are targeted at various groups of people. While the ultimate objective is to give people a positive feeling about the company, the feelings of different audiences will have different kinds of impact on the company's success. Therefore, the content of PR programs varies with the audience that is targeted.

The employees of a firm may often not be aware of key decisions taken at the top management level. Similarly, they may be so focused on their jobs that they are oblivious to the changes taking place in other divisions of the company. Employees may be unable to appreciate the vast and complex competitive environment within which the

35. Raymond Simon, *Public Relations, Concept and Practices,* 2nd ed. (Columbus, OH: Grid Publishing, 1980), 8.

firm operates and the firm's successful positioning in the industry. Communication, in the form of internal memos from the top management or announcements during informal company get-togethers, help provide valuable information to employees, boost their morale, and make them feel like a valuable part of the company. Such communication should strive not just to present the company in a positive light, but also to make the employees feel like an important part of it. Informed employees will stand behind their company, a strength that becomes especially critical during times of trouble or transition, such as General Motors in the early 1990s.

Public relations are also managed to convey an impression of financial soundness and well-being to stockholders and investors. The trust that develops in these constituencies will serve to insulate the firm from the vagaries of the stock market. The public relations management surrounding the departure of longtime CEO Ken Olsen from Digital Equipment Corporation, for example, might be one of the reasons that the market reacted very favorably to Olsen's departure and upped the stock price. Similarly, General Motors issued over five billion dollars worth of stock that was quickly purchased by investors, even when the company was posting colossal losses in 1991 and 1992. The public relations team that kept assuring people that everything was fine at GM must be credited for the automaker's success in drawing people's savings into the company.

Finally, the general public is addressed through corporate advertising. While the value of such advertising is controversial and unproven, intuition tells us that when consumers are positively predisposed to a company, they are more likely to pardon its mistakes and purchase its products. Dow Chemical Company, according to several newswriters, contributes to environmental pollution through the release of industrial effluents into the atmosphere. In this age of environmentalism, such negative information might hurt the company. While working hard, and successfully, to reduce industrial effluents released by its factories, Dow has also launched advertising campaigns that show how the company cares about the environment. This type of a campaign should aid in the development of positive attitudes that may later resist the effect of negative information.

Advertising and Publicity Effects on the Channel

The impact of an advertising or publicity campaign on the attitudes and behavior of channel members is rarely researched formally. This is surprising, because many retailers will not sell a new packaged good or durable unless it is supported by an advertising campaign. If the trade wants such a campaign, then most likely it is interested in the excitement to be generated by the campaign's creatives. Car dealers have been known to force automakers to return to old advertising campaigns by refusing to use new campaigns in their local advertising.

The effect of an ad campaign on channels has a personal side. Buyers, merchandising managers, and sales associates who are employed within the channel and like the campaign ads will become more knowledgeable and enthusiastic about a product's advantages and positioning. They will then be able to sell it more enthusiastically. This in itself can be an important secondary effect of an advertising campaign. The ad campaign can create its own synergy with distribution tactics. It clearly pays to pretest creatives on small groups of channel representatives or on the firm's own sales force.[36]

36. A surprising finding is that most Fortune 500 companies do not plan advertising campaigns with sales managers. See A. J. Dubinsky, T. E. Barry, and R. A. Kerin, "The Sales-Advertising Interface in Promotion Planning," *Journal of Advertising* 10.3 (1981), 35–41.

Advertising agencies are responsible for a majority of the decisions regarding their client's advertising strategy and tactics. They are the experts and are paid to show their expertise in these areas. Choosing an advertising agency with a good team is central to the success of an advertising campaign. Agencies that are creative, energetic, and that implement faster than on time constitute a very important and too rarely acknowledged competitive advantage. Choosing an advertising agency with a weak management team can be disastrous to a company's marketing efforts and competitive rationality.

As with any service provider, competition brings out the best in an advertising agency. It is not just the profit motive that is the driving force. Pride and rivalry are also at stake when agencies compete for accounts, even small accounts. An advertiser should solicit bids for its advertising accounts from several agencies about every five years. A new agency may demonstrate such an impressive new approach and team that it simply beats out the existing agency's proposal. On the other hand, the current agency that has performed well in the past should always have the inside track to reappointment. The current agency has a proven record, has developed personal trust relationships, and has an understanding of the client's product-markets and operating procedures. The risks and costs involved in switching are good reasons for favoring the current agency, whose efforts will be revitalized by the review. Unless another agency is clearly superior, it is best to remain with the current agency. The presentations of other agencies will offer fresh ideas and perspectives that can be incorporated into future campaigns. This may seem a little unethical, but it is part of the give and take of competing for accounts.[37]

Bigger May Not Be Better

Many mergers have occurred within the advertising industry in recent years, creating mega-agencies. It is unclear whether an agency's larger size is an advantage and, indeed, some of these new global agencies have failed.[38] Big agencies may be able to offer more media buying clout, but often the volume discounts they obtain are not passed on to the client. Instead, they are used to cover the agency's huge overheads and debts. It is true that global agencies are able to meet the global needs of a customer through their branch offices in other countries. On the other hand, smaller agencies can develop an affiliate network to cater to the multinational needs of a customer. The small boutique offers access to the principal creative talent and the boss of the agency. They are often more energetic, responsive, adaptive, and eager to do an excellent job because they have more to prove. Retaining an advertiser's account is also often more important to smaller agencies who are still establishing their reputations with new clients.

Beware the Bait and Switch

A concern in evaluating an agency is determining who in the agency will work on the account. Often an agency brings in an impressive and smooth presentation team. Those who sit quietly in the shadows, introduced with great fanfare at the end of the presentation, are the ones who will do the actual work on the project. The executives that initially dazzled the client may never be seen again. One way of avoiding this outcome is to insist that the agency employees who will work on the account make the sales presentation in the bidding process.

---

37. The market constrains this type of behavior because clients that abuse the bidding process in this way find that agencies will not bid for their business in the future.
38. See Joshua Levine, "Teaching Elephants to Dance," *Forbes*, March 15, 1993, 100–102.

Role Expectations

The tone of the presentation says a lot about the role the agency expects to play. If the agency talks down to a client, particularly about what the client knows about its business, perhaps that particular agency should not be hired. The agency-client relationship must be a partnership with mutual recognition of each other's competence. Some agencies adopt a patronizing approach to client relations and demand a free hand. From an historical perspective, this is somewhat understandable. Over the decades, advertising agencies have more often worked with executives who knew very little about marketing and advertising than with truly competent marketing executives. For many clients, the agency developed the entire marketing strategy and marketing plan. Today the situation is different.

The Importance of Media Management

It is common for advertisers to focus on the proposed creatives in judging an agency. The creatives will visually dominate a presentation. However, an agency's media selection and buying skill can be more important for two reasons. First, from 80 to 90 percent of the advertising budget is spent on media.[39] Second, in today's media market, many changes have occurred in the public's listening, viewing, and readership habits. Many sectors of the media market are hurting and are so desperate to increase their sales that many of the old rules no longer apply. Initiative and skill in this area can produce much more efficient contact segmentation and targeting, an important competitive advantage. Finally, the emphasis that the agency gives to the independent testing of copy on consumers and the trade before running a major campaign is a good indication of the professionalism that clients can expect from the agency (see Chapter 15 on advertising control).

Global Advertising

The major issue in global advertising is whether a single message theme and the same tactics should be used in all foreign markets or whether separate messages and tactics should be developed. As the availability and cost of media varies among markets, the media schedule will clearly have to be different. Some scholars have argued that the appeal of some products is cross-cultural and so generic that a single campaign theme can be used in many markets.[40] This has cost and positioning consistency advantages. Other practitioners believe that very few products have such general appeal. This is true with the exception, perhaps, of American products that have appeal precisely because they are American—such as Levis jeans and rock music. In that case, an "American" message theme that the target market will identify with may have great appeal. Otherwise, marketers should be very sensitive to differences in cultural values and the competitive environment, which demand different themes and persuasion tactics in different markets. The advertising agency chosen to buy the media in the foreign market will be able to help in judging the appropriateness of the appeal. This is a hard test, because it is in the agency's interest to work on preparing new creatives. Consequently, independent copy testing in foreign markets is very important. It is essential in non-English-speaking markets where the message has to be translated into a foreign language.

---

39. John R. Rossiter and Larry Percy, *Advertising and Promotion Management* (New York: McGraw-Hill, 1987).
40. Theodore Levitt, "The Globalization of Markets," *Harvard Business Review*, May/June 1983, 92–102.

Publicity and public relations also have to be handled with great sensitivity if the product poses a threat to domestic competition. Patriotic appeals to buy domestic occur in all world markets. It is here that distributors and retailers play an important role in advising a company on how to conduct such campaigns. In fact, in some cases it may be best to let the distributor or retailer develop the creatives and choose the media. One of the advantages of encouraging such initiative is that many new approaches may be tested, encouraging channel ownership of the marketing campaign. The campaigns that are very successful may be able to be modified and used with equal success in other markets around the world.

Discussion Questions and Minicases

1. Make up a terse list of dos and don'ts that an ad agency can use as a guideline when bidding for an account.

2. In which type of message themes and subthemes is the order of reading or flow of the ad most important?

3. In which type of themes and subthemes do you think peripheral cues (cues in the ad unrelated to the product) will be most influential?

4. Do you think people sometimes imagine that they are the person in the ad when they use a brand? What sorts of people do this with what sorts of products not mentioned in the text?

5. What type of message theme did the California dancing raisins TV ads use? What type of message theme did Nike use with Bo Jackson's "Just do it" ads?

6. The Energizer "It just keeps on going," campaign, featuring the pink bunny drummer, has become legendary. Describe its creative approach and explain why it was so effective. How does the campaign prompt people to think of the rabbit when watching other company's ads? How could the campaign be made more effective by a coordinated POP display? Does this have anything to do with remembering the brand name?

7. Since 1886, Coca-Cola company has used the following slogans: "Drink Coca-Cola," "Coca-Cola revives and sustains," "The pause that refreshes," "It's the real thing," "Look up America," "I'd like to buy the world a Coke," "Have a Coke and smile," and "Coke is it!" Categorize these themes and relate them to the product's life cycle.

8. Describe the results of the ADIMPACT spreadsheet in the box on page 452 and explain why one might choose A and another might choose B. What is the limiting assumption of GRP? Use and produce ADIMPACT spreadsheets and impact graphs to demonstrate the limiting assumption of GRP and its implications. If an effective reach criterion of 4+ exposures is used, campaign A is about twice as effective as campaign B. Which campaign do you think is the more competitively rational choice?

9. What is the underlying model used in the Woolrest spreadsheet in the box on page 454? Interpret the results. Boston was also chosen for political reasons (the American vice-president of Woolrest lived there). Given the judgments in this spreadsheet, what were some of the reasons why the Boston's market sales and profits were rather disappointing?

10. In an ad in *Vanity Fair,* a casually dressed young blonde slung over a young man's shoulder struggles as she is carried to a garage. In the next scene, her jeans are off, she is dazed and tousled and partially nude. The advertisement is selling Guess?

jeans. What do you think was the ad's message? What do you think Guess? wanted the message to be? Do you think *Vanity Fair* would have accepted an interview with a rapist promoting the pleasure of sexual assault? Who is responsible for this advertisement's effects?

11. The figure below presents the market test results of a special newspaper advertising campaign, an in-store coupon campaign, and a combined campaign where the availability of the in-store coupon was also promoted in the newspaper advertising. What does the table demonstrate? What does it tell us about managing communications?

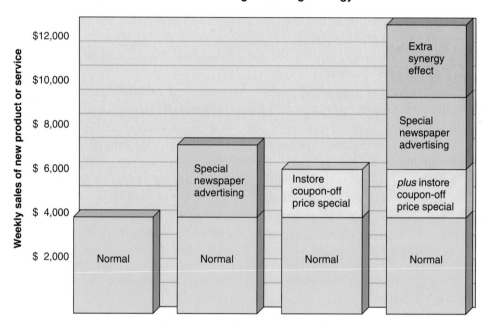

**Synergistic Effect of
Meshing Marketing Strategy**

12. In the early 1960s, the pioneering ad agency Doyle Dane Bernbach began teaming up the copywriter with the artist or art director. Previously they had worked separately on a campaign. What advantages come from such a team?

13. Present-day advertisers come up with very creative ways to get people's attention; sometimes the methods are crude, at other times they show great style. Why do you think much of modern advertising is good at gaining attention but not very good at informing its audience about a product's superior benefits and features?

14. Advertising is often criticized for its intrusive and formative influence on our culture, particularly on the values and ambitions of the young. Outside the business world, very few people consider that advertising has a positive influence on our culture. Placing the effects of advertising in the context of the effects of parents, schools, pop music, films, soap operas, and popular magazines, what can be done about the often unintended negative effects of advertising?

15. The Lincoln brand of Ford automobile runs an advertisement with an accompanying picture of President Lincoln. What persuasion theory is Ford using in its advertising? Do you think it works?

16. Service providers, such as dentists, eye doctors, tax accountants, pest controllers, carpet cleaners, lawn-care services, and hair salons, do a lot of local advertising in

newspapers and on door hangers. However, this should normally only be a minor part of their marketing communication program. What communication programs should they spend most of their marketing/advertising dollars on?

17. The department store Saks 5th Avenue always presents enchanting window displays at Christmastime that entertain shoppers but do not feature any merchandise. What emotional persuasion technique do you think the store is employing, whatever their genuine philanthropic intent?

18. In the last 50 years, sports heroes have made hundreds of millions of dollars from endorsing products. Do you think this will continue to happen, increase, or decrease over the next 50 years? Why?

19. Why do you think sweepstakes are used often in product markets with very little product innovation-imitation?

20. Which advertisement in the chapter do you think has the best picture-word integration? Why?

21. Why might it be a good idea for a company that makes suntan lotions or beachwear to run a premium whereby shoppers who buy the product can qualify for a sweepstakes prize of a hundred sailboards with the company logo on the sail?

22. Why is the Bacardi "Just add to everything, except driving" advertisement so efficient and effective? What cardinal rule of communication objectives and creative tactics does it break? Why can it break the rule?

Managing Pricing

*"Courageous managers raise prices,
desperate managers cut them."*

*"Accountants know the cost of everything
and the value of nothing. "*

Anonymous

D espite decades of study by economists and market researchers, price setting is still determined by a best-guess decision that is often quickly revised when the guess turns out to be wrong. For example, each year the giant automakers proudly roll out their new "priced-to-sell" models. If dealership waiting lists develop, then the manufacturers know they have priced the new models too low. To raise prices, they begin to manufacture and sell cars that have been loaded with high-priced options. If, on the other hand, a model moves off the lot slowly, then manufacturers devise various price promotions to make their offerings more attractive to buyers. The effect is lower prices.[1] The auto manufacturers use very sophisticated design and manufacturing techniques. However, when it comes to setting price, they revert to simple trial and error.

When the great packaged-goods manufacturer and marketer Procter & Gamble first market-tested Pampers, it priced the diapers at ten cents apiece. The product bombed, because mothers perceived disposable diapers to cost more than buying and washing cloth diapers. The convenience advantage of disposable diapers did not compensate for their higher cost. P&G returned to the drawing board and developed a new design for its product and package. It cut material costs and lowered production time. As a result, production costs decreased, as did profit objectives. P&G relaunched the product at a price of six cents per unit, and Pampers became a great success and hugely profitable.

How can companies reduce the uncertainty associated with finding the "right" price for either a new product or a product modification? Most marketing texts offer various price-setting methods but suggest that the appropriateness of each method depends on the company's individual pricing objectives. In this chapter, we present a procedure and mental model that build on the positioning-pricing technique described in Chapter 8 and link *all* of the major pricing methods and objectives. Keep the following key ideas in mind as you read this chapter:

- A marketer must understand the cost structure of a product (not just the costs, but the nature of the costs involved) because it will determine long-term profit forecasts of various proposed prices, and because the constant drive to reduce costs requires an understanding of cost structure.

- The positioning-pricing approach presented in Chapter 8 will determine the base price.

- Cost-based price setting is common, but true costs are hard to determine and competition dictates many pricing decisions.

- Demand curves have price points around which demand changes significantly. Such price points are created by competitive substitutes, custom, and buyer perceptions.

- Consumers do not always trade off price *against* quality; sometimes price helps signal and determine quality.

- Price changes should be based on their effect on long-term profit contribution and *not* on sales.

- The standard competitive response is to match prices quickly as they go down but to react less immediately as prices go up.

1. When demand is uncertain, the tactic of pricing high and then reducing price if sales are slow is not new but has only recently been developed into a formal economic theory. See Edward P. Lazear, "Retail Pricing and Clearance Sales," *The American Economic Review* 76 (March 1986), 14–32. The model describes a type of market clearance pricing that lowers the price to raise demand to the level of supply. The airlines have incorporated such a pricing approach into their revenue management system (RMS). If bookings come in quickly for a flight, the number of low fares offered is reduced. If bookings are slow, the number of low fares is increased.

- Discounts, payment terms, and a number of other tactics are used to offer different prices to different customers in different buying situations.

- Price promotions are used as an inducement to try a new product, without the introductory low price hurting the long-term quality image of the product.

- Price promotions of mature brands encourage loyal customers to stock up and customers loyal to other brands to switch.

- Price promotions are expensive because they involve extra marketing management, extra advertising, inventory management, and implementation expenses. They can also lead to a chronic promotions war, which may be difficult to stop.

Pricing Objectives and Decision Making

Price has to satisfy multiple objectives. At the very least, a firm's pricing strategy should

1. Support a product's positioning strategy,
2. Achieve the financial goals of the enterprise, and
3. Fit the realities of the marketplace environment.

Figure 13-1 describes a price-setting procedure that is designed to satisfy these objectives. A product's positioning strategy attempts to differentiate the product from

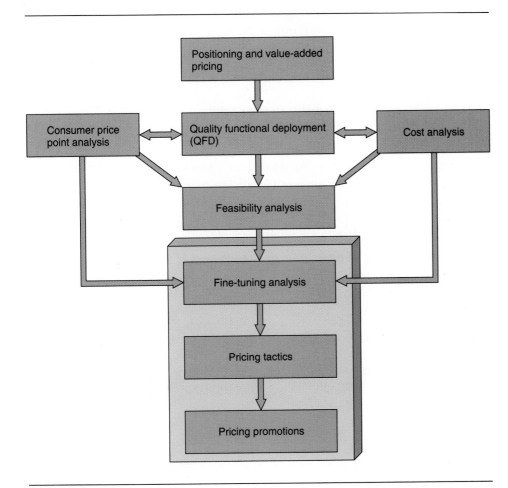

Figure 13-1

A Systematic Approach to Setting Price

This figure presents a mental model that integrates several methods of pricing, which are usually discussed separately. In this textbook, cost analysis is discussed in Chapter 2 (gathering and use of market intelligence). Positioning added-value pricing, QFD, and feasibility analysis are discussed in Chapter 8 (positioning).

its competition on at least one desirable choice feature. It specifies the product's target segment, desired benefits, and value delivered. These characteristics in turn determine the product's quality, cost, and price.

The competitively rational approach to setting the base price for a new product is described in Chapter 8. The positioning, quality function deployment (QFD), and quality-added analyses described in Chapter 8 produce an initial price that is tested in a feasibility analysis. This analysis determines the level of sales and market share needed to meet company profit goals. The feasibility of achieving such sales and market share is assessed in light of the overall environmental analysis and the anticipated effectiveness of the rest of the proposed marketing strategy, such as distribution, advertising, and personal selling. If the sales goals at the initial price are infeasible, then the decision-making team must go back to the drawing board. An alternative price may be tested in the target return analysis. If no price-sales combination is feasible, then something more fundamental has to change. Either the positioning, product design, or profit goals will have to be revised.

It is important to understand the full implications of this procedure. Price is not simply determined by positioning and costs. Often price determines positioning, product design, and costs as described in the P&G diaper example. The price had to be reduced, which required P&G to make changes in product design and in the production process that altered the cost structure and reduced cost.

In this chapter we expand on this positioning-pricing procedure by first discussing cost-based pricing and then demand-based, price-point pricing; penetration pricing; price skimming; and price-quality signaling. The last sections of the chapter discuss pricing tactics and promotions that *change* the base or list price into a price spread.

Cost-Based Pricing

While many pricing experts say that costs should never determine price, the fact is that costs determine the great majority of prices. Examples of real-world, cost-based pricing rules are listed here:

♦ A department store sets its prices based on a rule which states that the selling price should be twice the purchase cost. Retailers call this *turnkey* pricing.

♦ Defense contractors are required by law to detail their costs in each bid and apply a set profit margin to those costs. This is called *cost-plus* pricing.

One of the most widely known formulas for pricing professional services is to bill clients at an hourly rate of three times the hourly wage of the individuals performing the service. Payments then break down this way: one third goes to salary, one third goes to overhead, one third becomes profit. This is called the rule-of-three.[2]

Figure 13-2 presents the advantages and disadvantages of using cost rules to specify price. Good arguments exist on both sides of the issue. While it may not be wise to use a cost-based formula to set price, costs must be known and cost structure understood to ensure that the product can be manufactured and sold at the proposed price for a profit; if profit does not show up immediately, it should at least be evident down the road. Anything less than a thorough analysis of the present and future cost structure is folly.

2. Victoria Arnold, "Believe It or Not, Most Professionals Don't Charge Enough," *Journal of Pricing Management* 1.2 (Spring 1990), 57–59. This article points out the problem of applying pricing rules that may have worked in the past but are no longer appropriate because cost structures have changed and are always changing.

Advantages of Cost-Based Pricing Rules

1. A firm is in business to make a profit. Profit depends on the difference between unit price and unit cost. If this difference is negative, then profits are impossible. Hence, price must be set higher than unit cost.

2. It is fair to base price on costs. The Roman emperor Justinian, St. Thomas Aquinas, Karl Marx, and Adam Smith all proposed that the just or normal price of a product should be related to its costs. Modern economic theory and public opinion also agree that the fair long-term price is related to cost plus a fair profit.

3. Costs are both measurable and known. Modern purchasing, production, and marketing information systems can compute the past and current unit costs of producing and marketing products down to a "claimed" fraction of a cent.

4. Cost rules are easy to administer. Once a rule is specified, pricing can be delegated to lower management or even to a computer.

5. Cost rules stabilize prices in a market. If everyone uses cost rules (perhaps even the same cost rule), price increases can be predictable when input costs increase. No seller is going to upset the apple cart by doing anything crazy with its prices.

Disadvantages of Cost-Based Pricing Rules

1. Costs cannot be known at the time prices are set. Costs can only be known after they have been incurred. When future costs are uncertain, a cost-based rule does not assure a positive difference between unit price and unit cost. A firm's cost structure may change in such a way that the old pricing rule based on specific costs no longer works.

2. In some situations, a product can be sold at less than its average cost and still contribute to profits. This occurs when price exceeds the marginal cost of production and marketing.

3. Cost-based rules are economically inefficient. The forces of both demand and supply must be allowed to determine price for the marketplace to work efficiently. Charging a price the market will bear (rather than cost-plus pricing) may be considered unfair, but according to long-standing economic theory, it is the best way to ensure the efficient allocation of resources.

4. Costs are often managed. Many costs are shared between product lines and items within a product line. The apportioning of these costs to a particular product line or item involves a judgment made by cost accountants. The decision may be affected by noneconomic motives such as company politics that want the costs of a product to appear high or low.

5. A cost rule is based on a wrong perspective. It implies that product should be considered first, product-cost-price-consumer, rather than starting with the consumer, (that is, consumer, price, cost, product). The latter is the Japanese approach to pricing and product design.

Figure 13-2

The Advantages and Disadvantages of Cost-Based Rules

Demand Price-Point Analysis

Demand analysis uses positioning strategy to address the following questions:

1. Given the product's positioning, how sensitive is the target market to variations in price?

2. Do price points exist around which the target market is particularly price sensitive?

If a broad enough price range exists, then every market will be price sensitive. For example, no one will pay $100 for a can of Coke (unless of course it is the last can on the lifeboat), and almost everyone will pay a nickel (except those who hate the taste). However, when setting price, firms are constrained at the low end by their own cost structure and at the high end by the competition's prices. It is the price sensitivity of shoppers *within* these constraints that is important. Many of the issues that determine buyer price sensitivity are presented in Chapter 3, which analyzes consumer price sensitivity and consumer market segments.

In theory, the overall sensitivity of a product's sales to price is described by its demand curve. The demand curve specifies the quantity of goods sold at various price levels and the sensitivity of purchases to fluctuations in price. Demand curves, however, are very difficult to estimate. The only way to systematically derive a demand curve is to test the product at different prices in markets that have similar promotion campaigns, distributors, and consumers. The competition must also be similar across test markets and not change between measuring demand and making the final pricing decision. Unfortunately, very few marketers do this because such price tests are extremely expensive, and many factors that influence sales besides price cannot be controlled.[3]

What alternatives are we left with if we cannot estimate the demand curve successfully? At the very least, we can estimate the key price points on the demand curve. Key price points are those points around which many consumers enter (buy) and exit the market (no longer will buy), thus increasing or decreasing sales sharply. Marketing a product to a key price point can be a very successful positioning strategy. How did Henry Ford manage to sell so many Model T runabouts at $380 to $400 and still make a profit? Simple. He gambled that a huge unmet market existed for the automobile—the middle-class consumer. He thought he could have a profitable venture if he could sell a car that was affordable to the middle class. In 1916, without using any fancy market research techniques, he lowered the price of the Tourer from $440 to $360. He then worked on improving product design and reducing costs in the production process so that he could sell the car at the lower price (see Table 3-1 in Chapter 3) and increase his profits. The car was spartan, simple, rugged, and, most importantly, its price was right. The original Ford Mustang was also built to a specific price point of $2,500 and was very successful. Price is seldom the last marketing decision made in launching a new product. Rather than determining a price for a product, a product is often designed for a price—a price which, based on executive judgment and/or consumer research, will be attractive to the product model or service package's target segment (see Chapter 8).

Kinked Demand Curves

Economists usually represent the functional relationship between sales and price (Q = f(p)), as a continuous, smooth curve where the responsiveness of sales to changes in price is expressed as a mathematical function called price elasticity. However, the demand curve that the marketer actually faces has sharp kinks in it, as the figure in the Rationality in Practice box on page 474 illustrates. For decades, retailers and manufacturers have been talking about the price points that kink the demand curve. Market research supports the anecdotal experience of many executives.[4]

There is a very good reason for identifying a product's price points as illustrated in the box. It can be mathematically shown that the highest profits are earned at the price points on a demand curve. This is because sales fall sharply above a price point, thereby hurting profits. Below a price point, sales stay about the same; but because the price is lower, the profits are lower. Identifying price points can therefore narrow down the choice of various prices to charge. These hot price points in demand occur for three main reasons:

3. For examples of experiments that test demand at various price levels, see Alan G. Sawyer, Parker M. Worthing, and Paul E. Sendak, "The Role of Laboratory Experiments to Test Marketing Strategies," *Journal of Marketing* 43 (Summer 1979), 60–67; Gerald Eskin, "A Case for Test Market Experiments," *Journal of Advertising Research* 15 (April 1975), 27–33; John R. Nevin, "Laboratory Experiments for Estimating Consumer Demand," *Journal of Marketing* 11 (August 1974), 261–68; and Sidney Bennet and J. B. Wilkinson, "Price-Quantity Relationship and Price Elasticity Under In-Store Experimentation," *Journal of Business Research* 2 (January 1974), 27–38.
4. In the jargon of economics, if buyer reservation prices (the most a buyer will pay) are not distributed evenly along the price dimension but instead cluster at various prices, then such prices will be price points and the aggregate demand curve will kink at these points. Therefore, a price point is a discontinuity in the demand function Q = f(p).

Perceptual Price Points

Perceptual price points are those points that, if exceeded, simply make the price look larger because the actual expression of the price is larger. For example, $10.00 is a larger expression than $9.99. It is a four-figure number rather than a three-figure number. Likewise, $10,000 is a larger expression than $9,999. Consumers are therefore more sensitive to a $200 increase in a car initially priced at $9,900 than they are to a car initially priced at $9,700. For the first car, the increase pushes the price over the psychological $10,000 barrier. There is evidence that prices ending in a nine (just below a round figure) are hot price points. In a study done at the University of Chicago, researchers showed that reducing the price of Imperial margarine from 89 cents to 71 cents increased sales 65 percent. Reducing price to 69 cents increased sales 222 percent.[5]

Customary Price Points

Customary prices are those that shoppers have become accustomed to paying, perhaps because the price has remained the same for years (such as a 25-cent local telephone call). The price could be related to the convenience of using coins to pay for the product. Candy bars are priced at 25 cents or 50 cents. They used to cost 5 cents or 10 cents. The marketers of these products faced a problem when cost increases required them to raise the price of the 5-cent candy bar. Did they raise it to 6 or 7 cents? No, because customers would resist paying 6 or 7 cents for a 5-cent candy bar. Instead, they shrunk the candy bar's size, and then they later raised its price to 10 cents and once more increased the size of the candy bar. They increased its price again after people adjusted to the fact that the price of all candy bars had risen. The vending machine distribution channel also required any recommended price changes in its channel to move in steps of 5 cents.

Substitute Price Points

The third and probably most common explanation for the existence of price points is that they occur at or close to the price of competitive substitutes. When an item's price is raised above the competition's price, many buyers switch to the competitor's product, thus producing a sharp kink in the demand curve for the item. The extent of the kink depends on the perceived differentiation in image and performance between the two alternatives, which can be established by quality-added analysis (discussed in Chapter 8). If the item's differentiation on important quality-added features is significant, there will be no noticeable substitute price points. On the other hand, if the item is perceived as almost identical to a competitor's product, then demand for the item will change dramatically depending on whether it is priced above, at, or below the competitor's price; that is, a major substitute price point will exist in the item's demand curve.

Penetration Pricing

The feasibility pricing analysis described in Chapter 8 assumes that the major pricing objective is to earn revenues that at least achieve a target return on assets employed. Marketers need to determine the time horizon for the break-even analysis. With many new products and services (for example, Federal Express's overnight delivery service),

5. See Thomas Nagle, *The Strategy and Tactics of Pricing* (Englewood Cliffs, NJ: Prentice-Hall, 1986), 249. Nagle quotes Kenneth Wisniewski and Robert Blattberg, Center for Research in Marketing, University of Chicago.

Rationality in Practice:

Adapt-A-Jug and Eco-Spout Demand Pricing

Earlier in the textbook, we mentioned an entrepreneur in Columbus, Ohio, who invented a brightly colored pouring funnel that attached to small jugs and other plastic containers. Compared to conventional plastic watering cans, this funnel gives superior reach when watering house plants, but it can be used to pour higher viscosity liquids, such as motor oil, into hard-to-reach tanks. A further advantage is that when attached to a plastic container, the unit protects and stores liquid better than conventional plastic pouring cans.

The demand curve for Adapt-A-Jug was estimated by asking several hundred shoppers outside of a Kmart store what was the most they would pay for such a product.* The demand curve thus applies only to Kmart, the type of store

*For a method of measuring demand by asking buyers about the most they would pay, see Peter R. Dickson and Alan G. Sawyer, "Entry/Exit Demand Analysis," in Thomas C. Kinnear, ed., *Advances in Consumer Research*, vol. 11 (Ann Arbor, MI: Association for Consumer Research, 1984), 161–70.

The Adapt-A-Jug Demand Curve

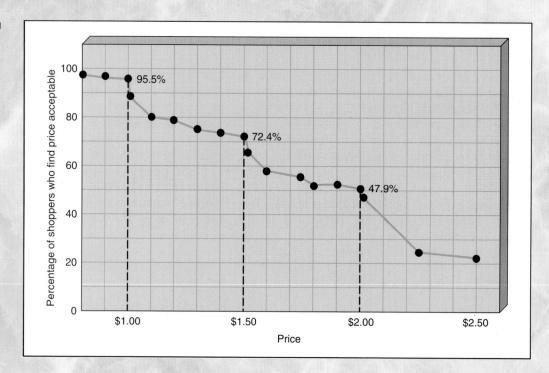

it takes several years before sales reach the break-even point and even longer before profit targets are achieved. When this happens, a marketing planner has to work backward from a long-term target return price that is based on future expected volume and costs. Until the desired sales volume is achieved, major losses must be accepted.

The goals of penetration pricing are to build market share and earn profits from future repeat sales and word of mouth. The effect on the target sales analysis is to require a much greater volume of sales and market share to achieve long-term profit goals. Penetration pricing can be a very effective pricing strategy.

1. It results in faster adoption and market penetration. This can take the competition by surprise. While scrambling to react, they may make major mistakes in their pricing and channel relationships.

2. It creates early adopter goodwill, which results in more word-of-mouth adoptions. Early adopters are often the most interested buyers and are more prepared to pay

The adaptor-jug with an earth-friendly
positioning as a watering can.

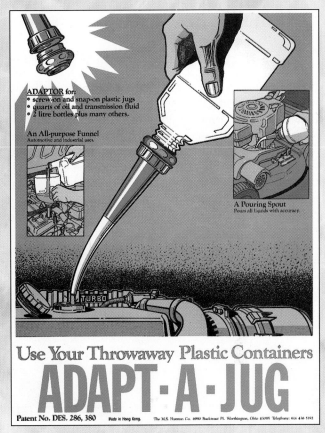

The adaptor-jug positioned as a useful
pouring spout.

where the product would be sold. Each shopper was first shown the alternative watering cans available in the Kmart store. Those cans were priced from $2.99 to $4.99. As can be seen, a kinked demand curve was found with critical price points for the watering spout of $0.99, $1.49, and $1.99. The price point that will earn maximum profits for the seller of the Adapt-A-Jug is $1.99.

a higher price. The lower price can create a great value-for-money image (providing price is not used by consumers as a signal of quality).

3. It creates tremendous cost reduction and cost control pressures from the very outset. It is much easier to tighten costs and increase productivity from the start. Costs will also reduce faster with improved economies, higher volume, and a cost-concern orientation. Penetration pricing is most attractive to a firm that believes it can become and remain the low-cost producer and seller.

4. It discourages the entry of competitors. Penetration pricing can be very intimidating and demoralizing to existing competitors because it signals that the new competitor is in for the long haul and will not be easily discouraged. It also signals that the firm believes it has a sustainable, cost-competitive advantage over the competition.

Rationality in Practice:

The Art of Penetration Pricing

It has often been said that Japanese companies used penetration pricing to gain their initial foothold in the North American consumer electronics markets. In reality, their targeting position strategy was much more complex than simply producing an economically priced model. For example, with the portable transistor radio, one of Japan's first manufacturing triumphs in the global market, Japanese firms introduced new features that added value and differentiated their radios in terms of sound quality and convenience features. At the same time, Japanese firms continued to reduce costs and maintained their penetration pricing strategy. Very quickly, consumer goodwill toward the brand and toward the retailer where the product was purchased began to grow. This consumer goodwill toward the retailer increased the Japanese manufacturers' influence and power in the channel. Japanese firms have repeatedly demonstrated how a market can be penetrated and then dominated when product and cost innovation-imitation techniques are used to build brand equity and sustain the penetration pricing strategy. However, it is clear from the figure that Japanese automobile manufacturers learned, or could have learned, from Mercedes-Benz how to use penetration pricing in the U.S. market.

5. The resulting higher stock-turn in the channel creates more channel support. A problem with penetration pricing is that it is difficult to keep the channel's dollar margin the same or more than the channel of distribution usually receives from competitors on each unit sale. A penetration pricing strategy may require giving a higher percentage margin on the wholesale price to the channel.

6. Penetration pricing of a secondary or export market is often based on marginal costing. However, it is not viewed as predatory or illegal until it has demonstrated its effectiveness. It is hard for an established competitor with a 20 percent or more market share to credibly complain about the unfair penetration pricing of a new competitor that starts with no market share.

There are several ways for a firm to offer a penetration price. At the extreme, new pharmaceuticals are often introduced at a zero price through free sampling. Computer software is also often given away to opinion leaders. The first adopter of a new aircraft is often given a special discount. Tactically speaking, setting a high base price and using an introductory price discount has two advantages. First, it allows the high base price to signal the quality of the product. Otherwise, a low penetration price may lead some buyers to suspect the quality of the product. Second, the expiration of a special early adopter discount will also produce less resistance than raising the price.

Price Skimming

Price skimming is an alternative strategy to price penetration. A seller price skims by launching a high-priced product targeted to the segment who most values the added features. After the initial sales boom to this segment levels off, the company launches

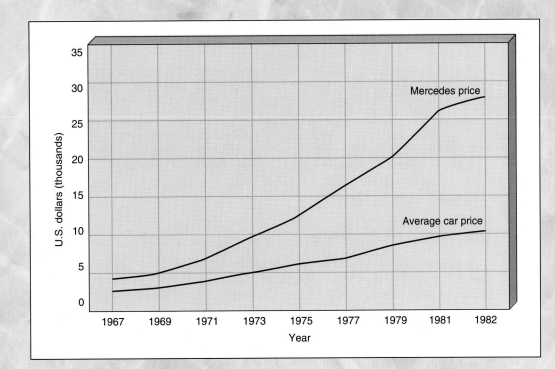

Mercedes-Benz's Price Penetration of the U.S. Market

In 1967, the Mercedes-Benz models were priced close to the average car price. This enabled the company to penetrate the consumer market segments that sought luxury, reliability, performance, and status from owning and using a car. Having penetrated the market, Mercedes-Benz proceeded to raise its prices at a faster rate than the average price increases throughout the 1980s.

Source: Reprinted from "Pricing Opportunities and How to Exploit Them" by Hermann Simon, *Sloan Management Review*, Winter 1992, pp. 55–65, Figure 5, by permission of the publisher. Copyright © 1992 by The Sloan Management Review Association. All rights reserved.

a lower-priced model targeted to the segment who also values the differentiation but who is not willing to pay as much for it as the first segment did. Once sales to this segment level off, the company introduces an even lower-priced model. With such sequential targeting, product positioning, and price skimming, a firm can convert more of the added value of its differentiation into profit. This clever strategy prevents the seller from giving away profits by selling at too low an initial price to those who most value the product, and it enables the seller to later sell to those who want the product but who do not value the differentiation enough to pay the initial high price. Many new technologies are priced this way.

For example, between 1963 and 1977, Polaroid came out with six successive camera models beginning with Model 100 priced at $164.95 and ending with the Super Shooter priced at $25. With each model it reduced some incidental features, and new design and production innovations greatly reduced production costs. The basic patented differentiation feature—the instant color photograph—was still offered. In constant dollar terms, the last model was less than one tenth the price of the initial model. Polaroid systematically controlled the market because its differentiation was protected by patents. Kodak did enter the market in the mid-1970s, but it was later judged to have violated Polaroid's patents. Polaroid was able to earn extra profits from its patented differentiation, and its sequential targeting-positioning strategy combined with its price skimming earned it even greater profits.[6]

6. See *The First Thirty Years, 1948–78: A Chronology of Polaroid Photographic Products* (Cambridge, MA: Polaroid Corporation, 1979). This initial skimming tactic, followed by the penetration pricing of lower value segments, charged those who initially valued the product most a higher price, and those who valued it less were charged a lower price. Thus, this long-term pricing strategy was very efficient in minimizing the difference between a buyer's reservation price, the most the buyer would pay, and the price paid.

Price Quality Signaling

If a claim of superior performance cannot be verified objectively by credible independent sources, then sellers must find other ways to bolster the credibility of their claims. One way is to associate their products with high quality brand images. Another way is to use higher prices as a signal of higher quality. When used together, trusted brand reputation and higher prices can play a vital role in supporting claims of superior quality. The reason they work so well together, at least in the short term, is because it is easier to believe a respected manufacturer basically saying "you get what you pay for," than it is to believe an unknown manufacturer making the same claim. Over the long term, consumers will eventually be able to verify the quality of most goods or services, independent of their prices.

Quality Assurance Pricing

In many instances, price reinforces a brand image of quality (as exemplified by the Curtis Mathes slogan, "More expensive—but worth it"). Price can also enhance the quality of a whole new product category when compared to established substitutes. Elegant, battery-run, electronic clocks and watches were priced too low when they first appeared on the market. Sales soared when prices were raised comparable to their mechanical substitutes. In actuality, they were not only less expensive to make but they also performed better than the spring-run timepieces they superseded. The problem created by the low price was that consumers did not believe they were getting more than they were used to paying for, largely because the cost and quality innovations were so radical and not visibly apparent to the shopper.

Price is a signal that extra effort has been put forth to produce a superior product that will perform to the buyer's satisfaction. A higher-priced brand provides assurance that an acceptable consumption outcome will result. Thus, quality assurance pricing is most likely in product-markets in which the following circumstances exist:

1. Product performance varies.
2. Search and inspection do not provide adequate certainty regarding product performance.
3. The cost of search and shopping is high compared to the cost of the product.
4. The product's true performance cannot be clearly tested through trial.
5. The cost of product malfunction is high (including direct consequences and the cost of wasted repair time).
6. The cost of remedying poor performance is high.

In these situations, many shoppers will be willing to pay more to get higher quality. They believe the risk of nonperformance far outweighs the risk of paying too much. The greater their uncertainty about the product's performance, the higher the price premium they will be willing to pay compared to economy offerings. For example, Pathmark Premium, priced at 89 cents, was a household cleaner with the same cleaning formula as Fantastik, the market leader, priced at $1.79. Despite vigorous point-of-purchase promotions including day-glo labels on the Premium packing stating, "If you like Fantastik, try me," the product did not move off the shelf and was finally withdrawn. In the household-cleaner market, the cost of the cleaner is small compared to the labor input. If it smears or does not clean, then the labor has to be repeated. Consumers believe they are avoiding such a risk by paying a few cents more per use for a high-quality cleaner. Of course, there is a limit to how much extra consumers will be willing to pay for the quality of a well-known brand name.[7]

Prestige Pricing

When buyers want the *very* best quality money can buy, their sensitivity to product performance increases more than their sensitivity to price. They believe you get what you pay for, and therefore they will pay more with the expectation of getting more. Owning top-quality goods gives people confidence in their purchases and security in themselves. High-priced products are more exclusive to own and, hence, become more desirable to those who want *only* the best.

The average consumer must live within budgetary constraints that limit the expression of individuality (or conformity) through the purchase of prestige goods. For wealthier individuals, prestige permeates their entire living environment. The products and services they buy authenticate their success or power. These products may also serve as signals of membership to an exclusive group. Wealthy people want exclusivity in their purchase of homes, cars, clothing, accessories, and vacations. The items they buy conspicuously signal their economic power and social prestige. High price assures such exclusivity.

Legend has it that several years ago Porsche made an attempt to price its aging 911 model out of the U.S. market as it introduced the new 928 model and planned for the 944 model. But something unexpected happened. As the 911's price rose, demand strengthened rather than weakened. At the higher price, the 911 became more exclusive and desirable among yuppie sports-car aficionados. Whether true or not, the underlying logic helps to explain why exclusive clothes and perfumes are often very expensive. Joy is advertised as the costliest perfume in the world (see Figure 13-3). It would not be nearly as "desirable" at half the price.

Pricing tactics and promotions convert a product's base price into a range or spread of prices called a price schedule. A price schedule enables a seller to cater to the different needs and price sensitivities of different customers. It also recognizes the varying costs of doing business with individual customers. Figure 13-1 indicates how the consideration of price tactics builds on a firm's basic pricing strategy. However, before discussing these tactics, we first explain a method of fine-tuning a target price.

Up to this point, we have discussed price setting for new or improved products. However, many pricing decisions involve an adjustment to the price of an existing product. They are prompted by disappointing sales caused by unexpectedly tough competition, a short-term economic downturn, or some other reason. In this section, we present a technique for testing whether such a price change should be initiated. Price changes can also be used to fine-tune a proposed base price. Fine-tuning involves increasing and decreasing the proposed or existing price and examining the advantages and disadvantages of the change. It involves calculating the percentage contribution margin at the current price and estimating price elasticity, how much sales volume will

Changes from the Base Price: Price Tactics and Promotions

---

7. Quality assurance pricing is important in some consumer markets but not in others. For example, Barbasol shaving cream sold very well as a low-price brand, but Barbasol deodorant did not. Consumers wanted to pay more for the peace of mind offered by a high-quality deodorant. See *Forbes*, February 24, 1986, 114.

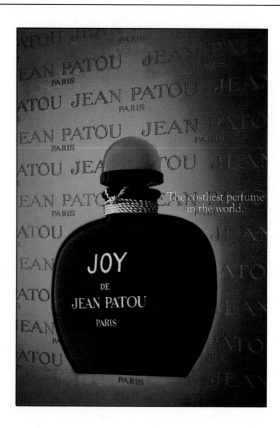

change with a change in price. These two pieces of information are combined to determine the potential gain from raising or lowering the price.

The Relationship between Price and Contribution

A company that is in business to make a profit is always concerned about profits. A
change in price, therefore, should be judged in terms of its effect on company profits.
A company is often prepared to forgo short-term profits to earn more profits over the
long term. However, bottom-line profit must always be a concern, at some point in
time. Contribution is the difference between price and average variable cost multiplied
by unit sales—$(P − V) \times Q$ (see Chapter 2). Profit is contribution minus fixed costs.
Therefore, in order to increase profit, contribution must increase. This means that
when thinking about changing a price, a seller is most interested in its effect on
contribution.

Changing price affects contribution in two ways that almost always work against
each other. First, lowering price decreases the contribution margin (the difference
between price and average variable cost) by the amount of the price decrease. Second,
in a price-sensitive market, a price decrease increases unit sales. Combining these two
effects, a price decrease increases contribution if the percentage sales increase is large
enough to compensate for the percentage decrease in contribution margin. Similarly,
a price increase increases contribution if the percentage increase in the contribution
margin is large enough to compensate for the percentage decrease in sales.

The Formula

The marketing planner needs only two formulas to fine-tune price. A price decrease increases contribution when:

%ΔQ is greater than {(%Δp)/(%CM−%Δp)} × 100%.
  where
  %ΔQ = percentage increase in quantity sold
  %ΔP = percentage decrease in price
  %CM = current percentage contribution margin

For example, if %CM = 50% and a 10 percent price reduction is being considered, then such a price reduction would have to result in a 25 percent increase in sales just to match the previous contribution ({10%/(50% − 10%)} × 100% = 25%). In many markets, a 10 percent reduction in price will boost sales by less than 20 percent so, in this situation, such a price reduction is not a good idea.[8]

A price increase increases contribution when:

%ΔQ is less than {%Δp/(%CM + %Δp)} × 100%
  where
  %ΔQ = percentage decrease in quantity sold
  %Δp = percentage increase in price
  %CM = current percentage contribution margin

For example, if %CM = 50% and a 10 percent price increase is being considered, then contribution increases if the estimated price increase reduces unit sales by less than 17 percent ({10%/(50% + 10%)} × 100% = 17%). The critical question then is what percentage of sales volume will be lost if price is increased by 10 percent. If the percentage is less than 17 percent, then the price should be increased. The FINETUNE spreadsheet box on page 482 explains how this decision making can be easily made.

In this section, we shift our focus from initiating a price change to responding to a price change. Just as marketers should not initiate price changes impulsively, response to a competitor's price change should also be carefully considered and measured. There are very few markets in which consumers react immediately to price changes. Commodity markets and the stock market are notable exceptions. Usually customers experience a great deal of inertia, caused by ignorance or loyalty, which allows time for sellers to think carefully about what their next move should be. Sellers can learn a great deal from watching and waiting. Impulsive reactions can disturb the equilibrium of a market and lead to price wars, which severely decrease all sellers' contribution margins and profits.[9]

Responding to a Competitor's Price Change

8. A survey of the price elasticity of 367 brands from 1961 to 1985 computed the average price elasticity to be −1.8. That means that, on average, a 10 percent reduction in price will lead to an 18 percent increase in sales volume. See Gerard J. Tellis, "The Price Elasticity of Selective Demand: A Meta Analysis of Econometric Models of Sales," *Journal of Marketing Research* 25 (November 1988), 331–41. The price elasticity of markets varies greatly depending on the similarity and availability of substitutes and the amount of innovation and imitation in the market.
9. For a discussion on price wars and price cutting momentum, see Joel E. Urbany and Peter R. Dickson (1991), "The Effects of Price-Cutting Momentum and Consumer Search on Price Setting in the Grocery Market," *Marketing Letters* 2.4, 393–402; and Joel E. Urbany and Peter R. Dickson, "Reactions to a Competitive Pricing Move," (Working Paper, Columbus: Ohio State University, 1991).

Rationality in Practice:

The FINETUNE Spreadsheet

The FINETUNE spreadsheet presented in this table makes fine-tuning price a very simple process. First of all, the price elasticity of the market must be estimated. Price elasticity is the percentage change in volume expected from a 1 percent change in price. All the executives involved in the pricing decision should estimate the percentage increase in sales volume (%ΔQ) for various percentage *decreases* in price (%Δp) and the percentage decrease in sales volume (%ΔQ) as a result of various percentage *increases* in price (%Δp). The highest, average, and lowest estimates can then be tested for different percentage changes in price. It is also very important to discuss the credibility of these estimates. For example, if the sales manager is advocating a 10 percent reduction in price, then at the very outset of the discussion the manager should provide his or her best guess of how a 10 percent reduction will affect sales. This must be justified in terms of where the sales will come from (from which competitor's market share or from which growth segment). Value-added analysis and general assessments of price sensitivity based on past price changes made by the seller or competitors should form the basis of the above judgments.

The second step in using FINETUNE is to estimate the current percentage contribution margin of the product. This figure is inserted into the spreadsheet. The spreadsheet then computes the minimum percentage sales increase needed for a price decrease to be worthwhile. It also computes the maximum percentage sales decrease needed for a price increase *not* to be worthwhile. The best estimates of the effect of a price change are compared against the FINETUNE limits. If the estimates of the effect of a price decrease do not exceed the minimum percentage sales increase needed, then price should not be decreased.

If the estimates of the effect of a price increase exceed the maximum percentage sales decrease allowable, then price should not be increased.

FINETUNE increases competitive rationality. Generally, it makes executives much more reluctant to reduce price and more willing to increase price. As the example shows, if a product has a 30 percent margin, then a modest 10 percent price reduction would have to increase sales by more than 50 percent for it to be worthwhile. A 10 percent increase in price would have to produce a loss in sales greater than 25 percent for it not to be worthwhile. The reason for the high price elasticity needed to make a price reduction profitable is fairly straightforward. A 10 percent price reduction on a $10 item with a 30 percent contribution margin comes right off the bottom line. It drops the contribution by 33.3 percent, from $3 to $2 per unit. To generate the previous contribution requires a 50 percent increase in sales. A 10 percent increase in price raises the per unit contribution from $3 to $4 per unit and therefore requires a 25 percent loss in sales to wipe out the advantage. If the current average contribution margin is uncertain, then more conservative and liberal percentages can be tested to see whether they materially change the decision.

The FINETUNE spreadsheet draws our attention to the importance of understanding competitor reactions. In the case of a price reduction, the competition is likely to match or even undercut it. This should result in more conservative estimates of likely sales volume gains from a price reduction. In the case of a planned price increase, on the other hand, there is a chance competitors will match it, and hence the loss in sales estimate will be too pessimistic. Consequently, long-term competitive reactions should make marketers even more reluctant to drop prices and less reluctant to raise them. The behavior of competitors depends greatly on their perception of how sensitive their loyal customers are to price and their own concerns over losing any market share.

The Price Increase Case

A competitor may initiate a price increase for several reasons. Demand may have suddenly increased. Past price wars may have lowered price to such a level that no seller is making a profit. The most frequent reason for price increases are cost increases. In this case, if the market leader and others initiate an increase, then all sellers in the market can raise prices. No change in market share will occur, but dollar contribution will increase, and that money can then be spent on gaining a future competitive advantage or distributed to shareholders. Sales will only decrease if buyers switch right out of the product-market to other substitutes. The major risk is that buyers will consider the price increase unfair, resulting in a loss of brand loyalty as well as a loss in sales.

How sales must change to match the effect of a price change on dollar contribution to overhead recovery and profit

Current contribution margin: 30.0%

Price reduction	Increase in sales needed to match the current dollar contribution	Price increase	Decrease in sales that wipes out the contribution gain of the increase
1%	3.4%	1%	3.2%
2%	7.1%	2%	6.3%
3%	11.1%	3%	9.1%
4%	15.4%	4%	11.8%
5%	20.0%	5%	14.3%
6%	25.0%	6%	16.7%
7%	30.4%	7%	18.9%
8%	36.4%	8%	21.1%
9%	42.9%	9%	23.1%
10%	50.0%	10%	25.0%
11%	57.9%	11%	26.8%
12%	66.7%	12%	28.6%
13%	76.5%	13%	30.2%
14%	87.5%	14%	31.8%
15%	100.0%	15%	33.3%
16%	114.3%	16%	34.8%
17%	130.8%	17%	36.2%
18%	150.0%	18%	37.5%
19%	172.7%	19%	38.8%
20%	200.0%	20%	40.0%
21%	233.3%	21%	41.2%
22%	275.0%	22%	42.3%
23%	328.6%	23%	43.4%
24%	400.0%	24%	44.4%
25%	500.0%	25%	45.5%
26%	650.0%	26%	46.4%
27%	900.0%	27%	47.4%
28%	1400.0%	28%	48.3%
29%	2900.0%	29%	49.2%
30%	0.0%	30%	50.0%

A more competitive tactic is to wait before raising prices. This will allow the firm to take market share from the competition by appealing to the price-sensitive market. If competitors pull back their price increases, a company may still keep some of its newly acquired customers. If the competition does not pull back, then when the increase in sales from new customers levels off, the company can raise prices. This price response tactic is called *price shadowing*. Often prices are not raised all the way up to the competitor's new higher level in order to retain most of the new business. Using this pricing tactic results in both a sales volume increase and an increase in contribution margin. The price increase initiator is vulnerable and will often signal its intention to raise prices with a pre-announcement. If the competitors do not send signals back that they intend to follow suit, then the initiator will be less likely to follow through its announced price increase. This has often happened with air-travel price competition among U.S. domestic airlines.

The Price Decrease Case

In this situation, a firm can end up losing contribution margin, sales volume, or both. Dealing with a competitor's price decrease is an acid test of a seller's confidence in its targeting-positioning strategy. If a firm responds immediately to a competitor's price cut, it may not lose any business and may, in fact, gain business from other competitors who have not yet dropped their prices. If a price decrease is delayed, then marginal customers will be lost. Much depends on which firm has initiated the price cut and the reasons for its move. If the initiator is a major competitor with long-term cost advantages, then the best strategy is to hold the current price, lose price-sensitive customers, but work harder to create a market niche through improvements in quality, service, and differentiation. This strategy does not play to the cost advantage strength of the competition. If the price reduction is the result of a design or production innovation that has reduced costs, and if this innovation can be imitated, then obviously a seller must do so and lower its prices as well. Many firms react to a competitor's price decrease by lowering prices but not to the level of their competitors' prices. This tactic, called *price covering*, is based on the belief that the remaining price difference will be unimportant to loyal customers.

Price Tactics That Create a Price Schedule

In this section we discuss a number of pricing tactics that are used to change the base price. They are mostly either price discrimination tactics or ways of adapting to the varying costs of doing business with different customers. In applying them, a seller creates a complex price range around the base price (see Figure 13-4). The following are some of the more common price tactics used.[10]

Price Shading

Price shading occurs when a salesperson reduces the list price during a sales negotiation. It is price discrimination based on buyer knowledge and negotiating aggressiveness. Buyers who are aware of the lowest prices offered in the market and who are very tough negotiators pay less. Common in industrial markets, it also occurs in some consumer product-markets such as the automobile market. Shading off the list price occurs for several reasons:

1. It allows sellers to give more favorable terms to attract the large buyer or important customer. The more such favorable terms are unexpected, the greater the effectiveness of shading price.

2. The list price can be adjusted up and down to adjust to seasonal fluctuations in supply and demand.

---

10. For excellent descriptions of various pricing tactics, see Thomas T. Nagle, *The Strategy and Tactics of Pricing* (Englewood Cliffs, NJ: Prentice-Hall, 1986); Gerard J. Tellis, "Beyond the Many Faces of Price: An Integration of Pricing Strategies," *Journal of Marketing* 50 (October 1986), 146–60; Andrew A. Stern, "The Strategic Value of Price Structure," *Journal of Business Strategy* (Fall 1986), 22–31; and Joel Dean, "Pricing Policies for New Products," *Harvard Business Review* 54, November/December 1976.

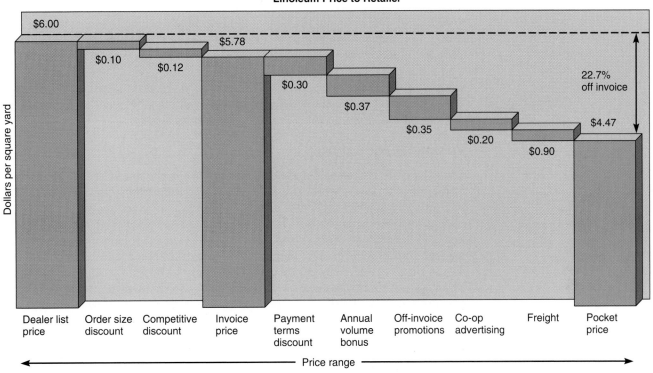

The granting of each of the above price discounts or marketing allowances to a retail account reduces the list whole-sale price down to the final selling price—the revenue left in the seller's pocket. The difference between the list price and the list price with all of the possible discounts and allowances given to the buyer is the price range or band. Managers are often surprised by the width of this range and also by which customers are getting which allowances and discounts and who is paying the highest and lowest prices at the end of the range. Some customers are also more sensitive to certain types of discounts than other customers, and this knowledge should influence pricing tactics and negotiations. The figure is adapted from Robert L. Rosiello "Managing Price, Gaining Profit," *Harvard Business Review,* September/October (1992), 86.

Figure 13-4

How Pricing Tactics Create a Price Range

3. It allows the salesperson to adapt to each customer's level of market knowledge. The buyer who is well informed about competitive suppliers will have to be offered a competitive price.

4. It is customary business practice for buyers to haggle with sales reps in an attempt to extract better buys. A buyer's sense of control, self-esteem, and job satisfaction are all directly related to the buyer's perceived success in such price shading negotiations. Some firms actually pay bonuses to their buyers based on how much they can shave off a seller's list price. If this happens, shading is clearly important.

Sellers who do not shade their list prices may be perceived as uncooperative and unreasonable. They risk alienating buyers who have become accustomed to receiving such discounts. Buyers might not believe that a firm does not deal. Instead, they assume that the seller chooses not to deal with them. To avoid such problems and allow the sales force some discretion over price, a firm should determine the average discount to be granted across all sales and add it back onto the base price to set the list price.

This new list price is then no longer the true base price because it includes a shading allowance to be given at the salesperson's discretion, provided the average final price does not end up lower than the target base price.

Although price shading is a very useful pricing and selling tactic, it must be controlled. Giving the sales force too much price shading discretion may result in lower sales and profits.[11] Many salespeople overestimate customer price sensitivity. Rather than overcoming objections by emphasizing product or service differentiation, such a salesperson often takes the path of least resistance and reduces the list price too much. If sales personnel are given discretion, it should be within strict guidelines and perhaps take the form of more generous terms or volume discounts.

Volume Discounting

Giving quantity discounts is a standard practice in many markets. It is price discrimination, in that buyers who place large orders pay less. Sellers can afford to initiate such discount schedules because larger orders result in lower per-unit selling, processing, and production costs.[12] Quantity discounts also help increase or maintain the loyalty of heavy users. On the down side, buyers may exploit volume discounts by placing large orders and reselling surplus units to smaller accounts. A variation of this buying tactic is achieved by groups of small customers who form buying groups to take advantage of volume discounts. A common problem with applying standard industry discount schedules is that no competitive advantage can be gained by offering them.

Volume discounting has become much more complicated with the introduction of just-in-time open contracts, in which products are supplied continuously. In such situations, a special price can be arranged that will apply to all products delivered for a three-, six-, or twelve-month period. Various clauses may allow for certain price increases that are related to input cost increases, and price decreases based on volume economies or the introduction of cost–saving innovations. Pricing may become particularly complicated when the arrangement extends to a joint investment in the plant. In this case, the buyer-partner is likely to be charged a contractual cost-plus price.[13]

Payment Terms

Payment terms price discriminate against slow-paying customers. Buyers who pay promptly, pay less. It is a standard practice in most industrial markets to give a discount for prompt payment. The money owed by customers for their purchases (called debtors or receivables in accounting terminology) can become an important working capital cost. In their efforts to reduce such costs, sellers give incentives for prompt payment. Many product-markets use the standard term "two-ten, net thirty," which means that a 2 percent discount will be given if the account is paid within 10 days; otherwise the full price must be paid within 30 days. What happens after 30 days is not made clear—in fact, very few sellers feel they are in a strong enough position to impose and extract interest penalties on delinquent customer debt. They are often happy enough to finally get paid. Aggressive buyers also sometimes deduct the 2 percent for prompt payment, even when they settle the account after 10 days.

Rather than accept the customary prompt payment terms (that have often eroded in effectiveness), can a seller develop a more effective, competitive way of rewarding

11. P. Ronald Stephenson, William L. Cron, and Gary L. Frazier, "Delegating Pricing Authority to the Sales Force: The Effects on Sales and Profit Performance,' *Journal of Marketing* 43 (Spring 1979), 21–28.
12. James B. Wilcox, Roy D. Howell, Paul Kuzdrall, and Robert Britney, "Price Quantity Discounts: Some Implications for Buyers and Sellers," *Journal of Marketing* 51 (July 1987), 60–70.
13. Nagel, *The Strategy and Tactics of Pricing*, 233.

prompt payment? One approach is to offer graduated terms based on the time it takes the buyer to pay. The tactic works this way: A customer is required to pay the full invoice price. On its next invoice, the customer is notified that it has earned a credit by promptly paying its last account. The terms are carried forward and applied to the next purchase. This pricing tactic is based on three behavior modification principles: increased reward for greater compliance, positive feedback based on actual performance, and reinforcement conditional on future positive behavior.

Prepayment Terms

A prepayment term is a form of price discrimination directed at customers who have no previous credit record or who are credit risks. The standard hard-nosed approach requires that orders to such customers are paid for before they are shipped or before service is provided. Customers with unknown or delinquent credit histories present a problem. A firm's future competitive edge may depend on fostering their business, but the high risk of bad debt associated with such business may also cripple a firm's competitiveness.

The nondiscriminating seller extends standard credit terms to such customers and attempts to keep a very close eye on the account. This is hard to do unless the firm has an ever vigilant sales force and credit department. Furthermore, once customers are in a financial hole, it is difficult to get their attention or cooperation. It is easier to keep supplying such customers, believing that they will improve their financed position and pay off their debts. It seldom happens.

Tied Pricing

Tied pricing is a price discrimination tactic based on captive markets created by the purchase of complementary products. It is normally applied to the pricing of accessories or supplies, and some companies make more money through tied pricing than they make selling the original equipment. Kodak film, IBM punchcards, and Xerox paper all had higher percentage profits than did the Kodak camera, the IBM card-punch machine, and the Xerox copier. Attempts to contractually require buyers of particular pieces of equipment to buy the operating consumable is called a tied pricing contract, and it is illegal. However, in practice, tied pricing often occurs informally. Either out of respect for the manufacturer, concern over compatibility between equipment and supplies, or lax purchasing management, billions of dollars of tied sales are made each year. A strategy of selling the original equipment at a very low price and profit margin and then making the profits on equipment is actually a form of cost allocation where the aftermarket sales are subsidizing the original equipment sales. It is economically sound in that it enables an initial penetration price and the creation of a captive customer market, which can then be exploited by the monopoly pricing of supplies and accessories.

Another variation of tied pricing occurs when suppliers use price to entice buyers into usage situations and then charge high prices for complementary products or services that are also commonly purchased and consumed in the usage situation. Movie theaters often advertise attractive, competitive prices in the local newspapers. However, the sales of high-priced soft drinks, popcorn, and candy made to captive customers account for a large percentage of a movie theater's profits.[14] Naturally, these prices are

---

14. Snacks and beverages sales account for 75 percent of movie theater profits. A Coke that costs 10 cents sells for 75 cents; candy that costs 35 cents sells for $1; popcorn that costs 30 cents sells for $2. See "Those Peculiar Candies That Star at the Movies," *Forbes,* May 19, 1986, 174–76.

not advertised. The loss leader specials run by supermarkets work on a similar principle. The losses on advertised specials are made up on the other purchases made by the shopper.

Segment Pricing

Some pricing tactics are blatant forms of price discrimination. Senior citizens receive transportation and entertainment discounts, children's seats on planes cost less than adult seats. Family recreational air travel is much more price sensitive than business travel. Because of this, airlines charge less for children and offer early booking discounts that effectively exclude business people from purchasing such tickets. As with all forms of price discrimination, segment pricing works best when buyers in the higher-priced target segment cannot buy the product or service directly or indirectly (through resale) at the lower price. The following are more subtle types of price discrimination directed at different customer/usage segments.

Geographical Market Pricing

Differential pricing between regional markets (location segments) is a long-standing form of price discrimination. Free on board (FOB) pricing requires customers to assume the cost and responsibility of transportation. It is equitable in that the buyers pay according to their distance from suppliers. The disadvantage to suppliers is that their product becomes incrementally more expensive and less price competitive as the geographical distance between themselves and the buyer increases.

The opposite of FOB is uniform delivery pricing. Here, the costs of transportation are averaged among all customers (the U.S. Post Office's domestic first-class postage charges, for example). It enables a marketer to be more competitive in distant markets at the expense of its competitiveness in local markets. Various zone pricing schemes, which are compromises between the above two approaches, are often adopted. Such delivery pricing schedules often are based on considerations of both transportation costs and the competitiveness of different regional markets. For example, a company entering a secondary geographical market where price competition is greater than in its primary market may use the profits in its local market to subsidize the extra transportation costs to the secondary market. The problem is that competitors are likely to retaliate in kind.

Usage Segment Discounting

Another form of price discrimination is based on product or service usage. How can a seller encourage new uses of a product or service without reducing the price of the product or service for existing uses? Electric utilities have developed usage segment discounting to compete in the home heating market segment. There are no substitutes for electricity to provide light and run home appliances, but there are alternative fuels, such as gas and oil, that can heat water and homes, and these alternative fuels are price competitive. How can the utility discriminate prices between these two uses in the same home? The answer is they charge a higher rate for the first 100 or so kilowatt-hours used each month (presumably for lighting and running appliances) and a much lower rate for the remaining kilowatt-hours used. This makes electricity competitive for heating. Research can establish how many kilowatt-hours the typical target household consumes per month on lighting and appliances. This information is then used to set the discount point, which might only apply in the winter. Otherwise, the heavy consumption of electricity for air conditioning during the summer would be priced at the discount rate. There is no competitive advantage to giving such a summer discount unless an increase in consumption is desired during the summer. This is unlikely as most utilities operate at their highest capacity levels at this time.

Off-Peak Demand Pricing

The most common form of usage segmentation pricing is based on the time of usage. Long-distance phone companies, electricity utilities, hotels, bars, restaurants, amusement parks, and movie theaters all use off-peak demand pricing. For firms like these, demand for their products and services fluctuates over time, and they cannot store their production. Consequently, they have periods of under-utilization and often low incremental variable costs. At off-peak time, such companies welcome any additional revenue, as long as it makes some contribution toward their high fixed costs. Off-peak demand pricing also occurs with items that can be inventoried, but the cost of inventorying the product to the next season is high (it includes storage cost, handling, working capital costs, and the risk of obsolescence). Off-peak demand pricing explains after-Christmas sales and end-of-season fashion sales. Unfortunately, some price-sensitive shoppers learn when these sales occur and wait for them. This has the effect of reducing the overall average selling price and contribution margin.

Antisegmentation Pricing

A number of pricing experts have suggested that a clever way to maximize revenues is to bundle products rather than sell them separately. However, unlike the above pricing tactics, which vary price according to variations in individual demand, this tactic reduces variability in individual demand, thus increasing the economic efficiency of a single price.[15]

The following example illustrates the approach.[16] Let us assume that 75 percent of the 1,000 patrons of a city's symphony orchestra prefer traditional orchestral pieces and 25 percent prefer avant-garde works. Each segment naturally would rather attend concerts whose programs are made up entirely of the type of compositions they prefer. Few are happy at the way program directors adopt an antisegmentation approach by offering programs that mix traditional with avant-garde. However, such product bundling allows the symphony to charge higher prices and fill more seats.

Consider the traditional patrons. They are prepared to pay $6 for each traditional piece played but only $3 to listen to avant-garde music. On the other hand, avant-garde patrons are prepared to pay $9 for each modern piece played but only $3 for each traditional piece. A $9 ticket to a concert featuring three traditional pieces or three avant-garde pieces sells out the 1,000-seat performing arts center and brings in $9,000. An $18 ticket to a concert featuring three traditional works sells 750 seats and earns $13,500 while a $27 price tag to a three-piece avant-garde evening sells 250 seats and brings in only $6,750 in revenue. However, because both segments will purchase a concert package, a bundled program of two traditional works and one avant-garde piece priced at $15 a ticket sells out and earns $15,000. The symphony, however, cannot do this if it faces a competitor who caters to the traditional segment and another competitor who caters to the avant-garde segment.

15. An efficient price is one that is very close to the most a customer is prepared to pay for the product (reservation price). High variability in individual demand means that buyers' reservation prices vary a lot and many are well above the price paid. Thus, the price is not very efficient.

16. This example comes from Thomas T. Nagle, "Economic Foundations for Pricing," *Journal of Business* 57 (1984), s3–s26.

Managing Price Promotions

Price promotions can be a very effective way of encouraging consumers to try a product, reaching price-sensitive segments, and moving inventory quickly.[17] They also now form one of the most common marketing tactics employed by companies. Sales promotion budgets are, on average, 50 percent greater than advertising expenditures. This trend toward greater price competition simply reflects the maturing of many consumer goods markets.[18] In mature markets, sales growth can only be achieved by gaining market share from competition; when this happens, price is the tactic usually used to achieve this goal.

Promoting a New Brand

Two basic learning theory principles have been used to explain how introductory promotions work. The first is that a reinforced behavior will persist. A price promotion is a form of behavior reinforcement, as well as an inducement to buy. The second is that repeated associations between a new product and its price promotions lead to a transfer of the positive feelings felt toward the promotions to the product.[19]

When it comes to launching a new packaged good and building a brand franchise, a free-sample promotion is clearly superior to both coupons and introductory discounts. Both the number of trials and the speed of response to a free trial is greater than the response to coupons. The problem with a free-trial promotion is the expense of providing and delivering the product. Direct mail ceases to be economical for large items, but companies exist in all urban areas that can deliver samples to the front door with the weekly package of advertising fliers. If a national campaign is too expensive, more limited local campaigns can give punch to a regional roll out. Niche markets can be reached by dispensing give-aways at special events that attract the potential users (for example, giving away MTV T-shirts at rock concerts) or through radio stations with distinct consumer franchises. Another focused approach is to give a free sample away with a complementary product (even one produced by another company) that is purchased by the target market. This promotion helps both products (see Figure 13-5) and is difficult for a competitor to imitate.

Promoting a Mature Brand

Few experts dispute the effectiveness of using price promotions to launch new products. The effectiveness of price promotions in mature markets, where category sales increase very little when price is reduced, can be questioned.[20] Price promotions in mature markets are a form of price discrimination across time.[21] The promotion price

17. For a guide to sales promotions, see Robert C. Blattberg and Scott A. Neslin, *Sales Promotion* (Englewood Cliffs, NJ: Prentice-Hall, 1990.) This is an excellent and comprehensive reference text on sales promotions.
18. In 1967, 45 of 50 consumer goods markets were still growing. By 1982, only 8 were still growing. See John Philip Jones, "The Double Jeopardy of Sales Promotions," *Harvard Business Review,* September/October, 1990, 145–52. This article presents an excellent discussion of the advantages and disadvantages of price promotions.
19. Robert C. Blattberg and Scott A. Neslin, *Sales Promotion,* (Englewood Cliffs, NJ: Prentice-Hall, 1990), chapters 2, 3, and 5. Whether these positive feelings are permanent is debatable.
20. Category sales refer to the primary demand, that is, sales of all brands in the category.
21. The theory is that with random reductions in price, a consumer must continue to search the market (as past experience cannot be used) or frequently pay a higher price. Thus, price promotions attract the price-sensitive shopper with low search costs. See Hal R. Varian, "A Model of Sales," *The American Economic Review* 70.4 (September 1980), 651–59; and Robert C. Blattberg and Scott A. Neslin, *Sales Promotion,* (Englewood Cliffs, NJ: Prentice-Hall, 1990), 95.

Figure 13-5

A Cross Promotion That Is Difficult to Copy

Combined price promotions are difficult for a competitor to imitate quickly, because it involves cooperation with another division or another firm.

attracts deal-prone switchers, as well as current buyers who want to stock up. The problem is that since promotions encourage switching, they can break down loyalty in a mature market.[22] If all competitors run promotions, then over time there are more promotions encouraging consumers to switch than there are promotions encouraging consumers to stay loyal. Thus, switching will increase (loyalty will decrease) in a market that uses high/low promotion pricing compared to a market that has stable prices set somewhere between the high/low prices of a promotion market. Promotions can further damage brand loyalty if previously loyal and insensitive shoppers start anticipating the promotions and adjust their buying and consumption schedule to the promotion schedule. They are not deal-prone switchers; they buy only one brand, but only when it is on promotion.[23]

22. See William Boulding, Eunkyu Lee, and Richard Staelin, "The Long-Term Differentiation Value of Marketing Communication Actions," Marketing Science Institute #92–133, Cambridge, MA, 1992. They found that advertising and sales force activities "increased a firm's ability to insulate itself from future price competition." Price promotion *decreased* a firm's ability to insulate itself from price competition. See also Chapter 8, Figure 8-1.

23. In effect, promotions can increase the selective demand elasticity of consumers (by increasing switching between brands) and also the primary demand elasticity of consumers (consumers only enter the market when a favored brand is on promotion).

The Timing of Promotions

The timing of promotions is an important tactical decision.[24] Promotions running late in the season are designed to reduce inventory carrying costs and the risk of fashion obsolescence. A promotion that is run at the beginning of a season has a very different objective. It extends the selling season by starting the season early. The sensitivity of the market to an early promotion will also be greatest, since it is the first price promotion of the season. On the other hand, it may also attract buyers who would otherwise buy later at the usual price.

In markets where all manufacturers offer trade promotions, retailers often manage the promotions by scheduling them. For example, Coke may be on special one week and Pepsi on special the next week. This ensures that the retailer always has at least one brand at a sale price all of the time, thus maintaining its low-price image. But it also makes it easier for consumers to schedule their buying around the promotions of their preferred brand or brands; that is, it encourages deal-to-deal buying.

The Advantages of Coupons and Rebates

Close to 80 percent of coupons directed at households are inserted into Sunday newspapers or flyers hung on doorknobs. They are used primarily to attract new triers and price-sensitive brand switchers, increase product category sales, and enable manufacturers to control the final price more directly.[25] As illustrated in Table 13-1, the number of coupons distributed has increased dramatically in recent years. In 1991, consumers redeemed 7.5 billion coupons with an average face value of 54 cents. This amounts to an overall savings of four billion dollars. Retailers received about $600 million in fees according to NCH Promotional Services, the nation's largest coupon processor. On the

24. For excellent reviews on promotion tactics, see Dudley M. Ruch, *Effective Sales Promotion Lessons for Today: A Review of Twenty Years of Marketing Science Institute-Sponsored Research* (Cambridge, MA: Marketing Science Institute, 1987), report #87–108. Kenneth G. Hardy, "Key Success Factors for Manufacturers' Sales Promotions in Package Goods," *Journal of Marketing* 50 (July 1986), 13–23; John A. Quelch, "It's Time to Make Trade Promotion More Productive," *Harvard Business Review*, May/June 1983, 130–36; and Michel Chevalier and Ronald C. Curhan, "Retail Promotions as a Function of Trade Promotions: A Descriptive Analysis," *Sloan Management Review*, Fall 1976, 19–32.
25. Robert C. Blattberg and Scott A. Neslin, *Sales Promotion,* (Englewood Cliffs, NJ: Prentice-Hall, 1990).

Table 13-1
Coupon Trends (1984–1990)

Year	Number of coupons distributed	Percentage change of coupons distributed	Number of coupons redeemed	Percentage of coupons redeemed
1984	163.2	—	6.25	3.8
1985	179.8	10	6.49	3.6
1986	202.6	13	7.12	3.5
1987	215.2	6	7.15	3.3
1988	221.7	3	7.05	3.2
1989	267.7	21	7.13	2.7
1990	279.4	4	7.09	2.5

Source: Donnelley Marketing Inc., "13th Annual Survey of Promotional Practices," 1991.

Figure 13-6

An In-Store Coupon Dispensing Machine

Manufacturers are seeking ways to make it easier for price-sensitive consumers to gain access to coupons. One approach is the use of coupon dispensing machines. Another is to issue coupons at the checkout stand, based on what has been purchased (this procedure allows many manufacturers to target their rivals' customers).

other hand, only about 3 percent of all coupons are redeemed, leading manufacturers to experiment with new ways of dispensing coupons (see Figure 13-6).

Coupons and rebates should be used instead of simple price discounts for several reasons.[26] Retailers may not pass on a price discount to the consumer. They may engage in a very common practice called *forward buying,* whereby they make the purchase at the trade discounted price and then hold much of the merchandise in inventory only to sell it later at the full price. They may also sell what they buy at a discount price to other retailers around the country (this is called *diverting*). However, retailers have to accept a coupon, and to gain any unique competitive advantage from a coupon promotion over the competition, an individual retailer must double or triple its value.

Coupons are also more efficient to offer than discounts passed on to consumers, because price-sensitive consumers, to whom the promotion is targeted, are the ones most likely to redeem coupons. Coupon and rebate redeemers select themselves as

---

26. Coupons are redeemed at a retail outlet. Rebates are redeemed by returning proof of purchase to a redemption center. Manufacturers often make the redemption task difficult to reduce the redemption rate. This enables rebates to have a much higher face value than coupons, making them a more powerful purchase inducement in advertising or point-of-purchase merchandising.

being highly promotion responsive. Coupons and rebates are not wasted on shoppers who do not use coupons and rebates. Experimental research also suggests that consumers may have a more positive feeling about coupons and rebates than an equivalent price reduction.[27] This is in part because they feel using coupons and rebates makes them smarter shoppers. Everyone gains the benefit of a general price reduction, but only the shoppers with initiative gain from clipping coupons or mailing in a rebate.

On the other hand, many price discounts are wasted because 1) about 50 percent are not supported by special point-of-purchase displays, 2) about 30 percent are not even passed on to consumers, 3) many are not noticed by buyers, and 4) they are automatically given to all buyers, including the price-insensitive shoppers who would have purchased anyway.[28] At the least, it makes sense to consider reducing the amounts of consumer and trade discounts and using the savings to increase the point-of-purchase promotion of the price reduction.

Promotional Differentiation

The best promotions are those that a competitor cannot copy quickly.[29] A tie-in price promotion with another product cannot be copied or countered quickly (see Figure 13-5). It also makes sense to build a promotion on a unique competitive advantage. GM, Ford, and Chrysler all have strong finance divisions. The Big Three use this strength to attack foreign competitors' market share—but not each other's—by offering low promotional financing, which is something the foreign competition cannot readily match. Toro, the snowblower manufacturer, designed a preseason trade-in promotion program with its dealers that competitors were not able to counteract effectively until the start of the next season. MCI's Friends & Family promotion launched in 1991 offered a 20 percent discount on long-distance telephone calls between friends and family. Its market share jumped from 13 percent to 17 percent. AT&T found it difficult to respond in kind because it lacked the sophisticated billing system needed to link customer accounts.[30] A promotion should, at the very least, market the product's competitive differentiation. Coupons should be placed in advertisements to attract attention to the product differentiation claims, and point-of-purchase displays should promote the item's basic points of competitive differentiation.

Sales Promotion Problems

As described above, when price promotions become the dominant tactic in a mature market, they increase the price sensitivity of the market, reduce loyalty, and increase the cost and difficulty of doing business. Some promotion campaigns will be extremely successful, others will not be very effective at all, but over the long term they will all average out. When all sellers are using the same promotion (and achieving the same average performance), then the promotion no longer confers any sustainable competitive advantage. So why do sellers keep promoting? They fear that if they stop promoting, then competitors' continued promotions will have a devastating effect on their market share and cash flow.

27. Robert Schindler, "How Cents-Off Coupons Motivate the Consumer," in *Research on Sales Promotion: Collected Papers*, Katherine E. Jocz, ed., Report #84–104, (Cambridge, MA: Marketing Science Institute, 1984), 47–62.
28. Peter R. Dickson and Alan G. Sawyer, "The Price Knowledge and Search of Supermarket Shoppers," *Journal of Marketing* 54 (July 1990), 42–53.
29. John A. Quelch, Scott A. Neslin, and Lois B. Olson, "Opportunities and Risks of Durable Goods Promotion," *Sloan Management Review* 28.2 (Winter 1987), 27–38.
30. Mark Lewyn, "MCI Is Coming through Loud and Clear," *Business Week,* January 25, 1993, 84–88.

Also, the only viable alternative marketing strategy, once a seller is trapped in an endless cycle of price promotions, is a back-to-basics product-differentiation strategy that rebuilds customer loyalty. This strategy depends on technological innovation, which is slow and risky. Additionally, the firm may not have the financial or management resources to put into the needed R&D because the discretionary financial and management resources are being spent on price promotions.

The marketing history of Procter & Gamble's Pert shampoo nicely illustrates the advantage of genuine differentiation over price promotions (see Figure 13-7). Pert was languishing with a market share of under 2 percent and price promotions were having no effect on long-term sales—even when combining the manufacturer's rebate with the retail discount meant that the shampoo was, in effect, being given away. The company shifted its strategy and concentrated on the product rather than its promotions. Pert's formula was changed so that it combined a shampoo and conditioner in one. This patented innovation gave Pert Plus an outstanding performance advantage over the several hundred competitive brands, and it was recognized in the *Consumer Reports* product testing. The brand's market share shot up to a market-leading 12 percent. Product extensions, such as an anti-dandruff version, also helped increase sales. Pert could never have achieved such success and profitability with promotions. Gillette's new Sensor shaving system is another example of a firm using product differentiation and superior quality to rise above the hurly-burly of price-promotion selling.

Changing Goals and Incentives

A careful analysis of a promotion's likely profitability can have a sobering effect and strengthen the backbone of a company or an executive who was once hooked on promotions but is now experiencing promotion withdrawal. The FINETUNE spreadsheet can be used to assess the profitability of short-term trade promotions or consumer price discounts. Another way of discouraging price promotions is to operate close to production capacity. This reduces the seductive appeal of the marginal, incremental promotional sale, which is most attractive when fixed costs are high and there is excess capacity. Sales force incentives should also be based on contribution rather than sales. Toughing it out requires everyone from the top down and bottom up to cut back on their use of promotions. A gradual, rather than precipitous, withdrawal from promotions is more likely to be successful. It gives everyone time to adjust.

Changing Channel Behavior

A problem with many trade promotions is that they are not linked to any specific behavior such as extra selling efforts, merchandising programs, or advertising. One solution is for manufacturers to pay special allowances to retailers for participating in a price promotion program after evidence of performance is provided, instead of unconditionally deducting the allowances off the initial invoice. The trade should be rewarded for proven performance rather than expected performance. Another even more positive approach is for the manufacturer to work with major retailers on the type of merchandising promotions they would prefer to offer. This flexible approach is based on the reasonable assumption that the retailer knows best what sells in its stores. Implementing unique price promotion programs with individual retailers will not only ensure they are implemented but will likely make those promotions more effective for both the manufacturer and the retailer.

To discourage deal-to-deal buying, manufacturers can place restrictions on the quantity of goods that retailers and wholesalers can purchase on the deal by tying deal purchasing to normal purchase quantities. However, cracking down on the resale and diversion of promotionally priced products to other geographical markets is not easy. The problems of an out-of-control promotion strategy and out-of-control channel partners go together because they both have the same root cause—weak product differentiation and brand equity. Procter & Gamble put its considerable brand equity (P&G controlled the number 1 and number 2 brands in some 30 product categories) to the test in 1992 when it announced its intentions to move away from promotion pricing, starting with its Luvs and Pampers disposable diapers.[31] The new program reduced the list wholesale price and provided retailers with brand development rebate incentives based on six monthly sales increases. The incentives were based on the recent sales performance of the brand. In this way, retailers are rewarded for past performance, rather than given trade promotion discounts, no matter how they had used such discounts in the past. P&G's approach is risky, because retailers who are upset at losing the profits from frequent promotions may favor other major brands or promote their own private labels. P&G's major competitors may also try to take advantage by increasing their promotions. Not everyone is following P&G's lead. Heinz increased its trade promotion expenditures in 1992.[32] How else, then, might a company get out of a price promotion war?

Changing Competitor Behavior

Once competition between promotions has begun, it is difficult to convince competitors to cease the promotion war. Only a market leader such as P&G, be it in a national, regional, or niche market, might feasibly implement the following strategy. First, the manufacturer publicly announces it intends to switch to a lower everyday list price and gradually reduce the size and frequency of its promotions. However, retaliatory promotions will be run if rivals do not follow the lead.[33] Such tit-for-tat promotions will attack any competitor in the major markets who continues to promote prices heavily. The term "tit×2" stands for a response that is twice as strong and effective as the initiator's promotional initiative. The success of such a tactic depends on targeting the rival's customers with a heavy comparative advertising campaign by doubling the face value of coupons, moving inventory quickly into the channel, and squeezing shelf space. The seller can even use direct marketing to pinpoint customers with special promotional offers.[34] If a seller is intent on ridding itself of the promotion yoke, then it must spare no expense and be ready to strike fast and very hard at a competitor. Establishing itself as such a credible threat is a sound investment.[35] But this strategy is only effective for market leaders with plenty of guts. It is not the best competitive strategy for others. The best competitive strategy, once again, is for a seller to develop product and service differentiation, which builds the kind of consumer loyalty that is immune to the promotional assaults of competitors (see Figure 13-7). This is not an easy task in mature markets, but it is *the* task.

31. Zachary Schiller, "Not Everyone Loves a Supermarket Special," *Business Week,* February 17, 1992, 64–68; Eben Shapiro, "P&G Takes On the Supermarkets with Uniform Pricing," *Wall Street Journal,* June 26, 1992; and Bradley Johnson and Jennifer Lawrence, "P&G Tests New Retail Plan, Cuts Diaper Price," *Advertising Age,* June 22, 1992.
32. Cyndee Miller, "Moves by P&G, Heinz Rekindle Fears That Brands Are in Danger," *Marketing News* 26.12 (June 8, 1992).
33. Game theory research has shown that the best way of eliciting cooperation from a competitor is to make an initial conciliatory offer (we will run no more price promotions) and then respond tit-for-tat to any aggressive responses. See Douglas R. Hofstadter, "Metamagical Themas," *Scientific American* 248 (5) (1983), 16–26. Tit×2 ups the ante.
34. Aimee L. Stern, "New Marketing Game: Stealing Customers," *Dun's Business Month,* February 1985, 48–50.
35. Research has demonstrated the value of a reputation for fierce combativeness in a market. See Paul Milgrom and John Roberts, "Predation, Reputation and Entry Deterrence," *Journal of Economic Theory* 27 (1982), 280–312.

The example on the left is a very costly price promotion. Procter & Gamble offered a $2.50 rebate and the supermarket reduced the price of the product to $2.50. In effect, the shampoo was being given away to shoppers who redeemed the rebate. An effective alternative to such costly price promotions is shown on the right: the introduction of a new shampoo innovation. Pert Plus was the first shampoo to successfully combine a shampoo with a conditioner. It was very well received in the market and its unique selling proposition (differentiation) was so strong that it did not need price promotions in order to compete.

Pricing Tactics in the Global Marketplace

Export pricing requires paying special attention to all of the issues discussed in this chapter. As far as costs are concerned, export pricing is often marginal pricing that uses the direct variable costs of producing, shipping, and selling the product in the export market. Some of the unique export costs are export tariffs, "consultants commissions" that end up as bribes paid to government officials, and special climate and transport packaging. The advantage of marginal pricing is that it enables penetration pricing. The disadvantage is that, as the export market grows, domestic sales will lose some of their competitiveness because they will still have to subsidize export sales' overhead costs.

This problem is often brought to a head when current production capacity is reached. If capacity is to be expanded to meet export demand, then the cost of the expansion must be borne by the export prices. Export prices will have to rise unless production efficiencies at the new plant compensate for moving from marginal to full-cost pricing. Otherwise, the domestic price will be loaded with the even greater burden of subsidizing export sales.

The more conservative approach is to adopt a rigid cost-plus approach to export pricing from the outset, with an added profit margin to compensate for the risk or frustrations involved in export marketing. Such a conservative, take-it-or-leave-it pricing approach is hardly conducive to developing global market sales. Once upon a time, American companies escaped the price competitiveness of the U.S. market by finding cozy export markets. Today, export markets are often more price competitive than the U.S. market because large companies from the U.S., Japan, and Europe are all behaving in the same way, which is to use marginal pricing in export markets.

Controlling distributors' pricing practices is difficult in any market, but in some export markets it is particularly difficult because of the lack of on-site control. The most cost-effective way of keeping tabs on the pricing practices of distributors is to keep in direct contact with end users. Marketers of consumer goods may have to employ a local market research firm to undertake occasional price checks without the "help" of the distributor. A further problem with channel pricing is that export channels have a tendency to become very long with many intermediaries adding their margins and very little value. The increasingly common "value-added" taxes (usually a tax on the selling price at each point in the channel) makes the problem even worse.

Financial terms are particularly important in export marketing because of the greater risk of bad debt (nonpayment) and currency fluctuations.[36] Payment risk is normally covered by asking for a letter of credit from a respected bank that establishes creditworthiness and serves as a legal claim on funds. As far as terms are concerned, instead of the seller offering terms to the customer or distributor in a distant market, it is often better for the seller to help the buyer obtain financing from its local banks or financial markets. They are in a better position to assess the risk of buyer default or changes in exchange rates—and to deal with the consequences.

The problem of foreign exchange fluctuations is most often handled by quoting all prices in U.S. dollars (the international exchange currency) and hedging. Hedging is when a firm uses a financial service that buys foreign currency futures in the same way that pork bellies futures are bought and sold. Through a complex formula, a firm can purchase a mix of such futures that reduces the effects of future foreign exchange fluctuations. If it does not hedge, then a firm inevitably winds up speculating on exchange rates. As that is not its business—nor should it be—such unskilled speculation adds a dangerous uncertainty to the profitability of a firm's export activity. Investing in hedging is like paying an insurance premium to protect against unfavorable currency fluctuations (such as a stronger U.S. dollar that effectively increases export prices). It is an added cost of global marketing.

Other ways of handling an exchange fluctuation that strengthens the U.S. dollar is to seek countertrade deals and keep earnings in the host country for the short term. A more long-term solution is to invest the earnings in expansions of local assembly, service, and distribution facilities. Such investments are best made when the dollar is strong. Some global companies are able to shift their sourcing of supply, depending on currency fluctuations. For example, Cummins Engine supplies the Latin American market from either the United States or the United Kingdom, depending on whether the dollar or the pound is weaker. It is hoped that as international financial markets merge into a single global financial market, currency fluctuations will be less of a problem. Global marketers will then be able to focus competitive rationality on making and selling better products instead of being distracted by the lure of making profits from outsmarting the foreign-exchange market.

---

36. Fred Cohen and Rhonda Price, "Competitive Pricing Strategies for Exporters," *Journal of Pricing Management* 2.2 (Spring 1991), 37–39.

1. During the Great Depression of the 1930s, prices rose even in markets where demand was down and business inventories had risen. This seemed inexplicable to economists and the politicians of the time because, according to the theory of supply and demand, prices should drop when demand decreases and there is an excess of supply. Congress set up a special investigation into prices. What did investigators learn about price setting that explained the unexpected rise in prices?

2. One price skimming tactic is to charge early adopters, who value the product most, a high price and then lower the price later. This tactic can have some very negative consequences. What are they?

3. In 1984, Noumenon Corp., a California software company, launched Intuit, priced at $395, to compete against Lotus' Symphony and Ashton-Tate's Framework, which both sold for $695. Despite a major ad campaign, Intuit failed to sell. The price was then dropped to only $50 and raised each week by $20 to test demand. At $90 sales peaked and fell off completely at $210. The company decided to relaunch Intuit at $89.95. What mistakes did this company make both before and after its initial launch?

4. Apple Computer launched its Macintosh computer at $2,500 in January 1984 (with the infamous Super Bowl ad). It was designed to sell at $1,000, but production cost increases raised it to $2,000 and John Sculley (the legendary PepsiCo brand manager) added $500 for a lavish marketing campaign. Mac's mouse/windows technology was child's play to use and made the Mac accessible to the general public. A more powerful, faster Mac with a color monitor was launched in 1987, again at a premium price. From 1986 to 1991, Apple's share of the world personal computer market was from 6 to 8 percent with a gross margin of 50 percent. In 1990, Microsoft launched Windows, which makes a cheap IBM clone as easy to use as a Mac. Did Apple make a mistake with its pricing approach? What was its alternative and how might the alternative have been more profitable?

5. Videotaped movies were initially sold to the public in the early 1980s at a price of around $79.95. In the early 1990s, they are being sold as low as $9.95. What do you think would have happened if the distributors had used a penetration price at the outset? Who benefited from the price approach that was adopted?

6. Along with consumer price sensitivity, how does the current contribution margin affect any future decision to price skim or price penetrate the market? (Hint: the FINETUNE spreadsheet can be used very effectively to answer the question by playing "what if" with the %CM variable.)

7. Sellers sometimes match competitors' price reductions, particularly the market leader's price reductions, when all the information indicates that buyers are not very price sensitive. Give some of the reasons why this happens.

8. Is it a good idea to reduce your price during a recession? What if you sell to businesses and they are pressuring you to reduce prices?

9. Most volume discount schedules are standard within an industry. All competitors follow the same schedule, which suggests an opportunity for an innovator to break in with lower volume discounts. Can a firm develop a more competitive volume discounting schedule that attracts growth business and does not hurt overall profitability? Develop such a proposal. (Hint: First draw a declining cost/volume curve and then impose the industry discount schedule as a step function on top of the curve; now draw your alternative step function.)

10. Create a spreadsheet that computes a graduated percentage discount that is equivalent to net 30 and depends on the seller's cost of working capital (expressed as an interest rate). How could this be assessed automatically by the seller's billing software?

11. The challenge for every business-to-business seller is to find a pricing tactic that attracts the business of start-up firms who may grow to be multimillion-dollar accounts without risking devastating bad debts. Extending credit is particularly dangerous in our economy, which regularly cycles from boom to bust. It is especially risky in global markets where the chances of recovering bad debts is much lower. Propose a prepayment scheme that is friendlier than simply putting up the money and that discriminates prices based on the buyer's creditworthiness.

12. How can a shrewd buyer extract more concessions from a seller who uses price shading? Do you think that price shading is economically efficient for the firm and for the economy as a whole? Do you think it is fair?

13. There is a ferry that runs between Martha's Vineyard and Cape Cod in Massachusetts. It is a popular mode of transportation for wealthy people who maintain summer homes on Cape Cod and for tourists. The ferry has developed quite a complex rate structure:

    The regular fare is $4 each way but travelers can buy a 10-ride card for $30. The name of the passenger is written on the card so that only one person can use the ticket. The ferry also carries autos at a rate of $25 each way. There are discount rates for round trips that originate on the island. A return trip on the same day costs $25 and a return trip within five days of departure costs $40.

    Why has the company developed such a scheme? How do you think it could improve the scheme by offering different discounts?

14. In 1991, Transmedia Network sold its charge card for $50 a year. The card offers a 25 percent saving on meals in some 1,000 restaurants in Florida, New Jersey, and New York. The deduction is made off the VISA or MasterCard bill. Transmedia actually advances the restaurant $5,000 in exchange for credits worth $10,000 in tabs. It rebates $2,500 to the patrons and keeps $2,500 for itself. Restaurants like it because they still clear $1,000 as the cost of food and beverages usually amounts to only 40 percent of the gross tab. Transmedia expects its membership to grow to 100,000 by the end of 1993. What is the long-term problem with this deal for the restaurants?

15. Why does the off-peak pricing of some services, such as long-distance telephone calling, have to be carefully set? What can go wrong?

16. Product/service bundled pricing (antisegmentation pricing) has many advocates, but it does not work well in some situations. What firms in what markets can best apply price bundling?

17. The metered pricing of the typical Xerox copier in 1974 was as follows:

Basic monthly use charge	$ 50.00
Monthly meter minimum	$135.00
Total monthly minimum	$185.00

    The meter rate per copy of the same original was as follows:

1–3	4.6 cents per copy
4–10	3 cents per copy
11 plus	2 cents per copy

    What type of price segmentation and discrimination is this and what consumer and competitive environment facts do you think led Xerox to adopt such a pricing strategy?

18. The proprietor of a small Mexican restaurant has come to you with the audacious idea of allowing customers to decide how much they will pay for their meals. He thinks it will be a great marketing gimmick and probably just as profitable as having to set prices. He offers the following menu: 8-Inch Mexican Pizza ($3.00), Smothered Burrito ($3.00), Plato de Sopapilla ($4.50), El Bandito ($4.40), Fried Clam Dinner ($4.50), El Puerco ($10). The prices in parentheses are the minimum prices he would charge if he were to fix his prices. Prepare a "Choosing Your Own Price" handout to customers that implements his idea. How would customers feel about the price they end up paying?

19. In 1982, the Windmere Corp. sold 670,000 hair dryers to retailers such as Eckerd drugstores for $6.50 each. In 1983, the company raised its price to retailers to $8.00 but offered a $5.00 rebate on each dryer provided the buyer got the rebate coupon, filled it out, saved the purchase receipt, ripped the proof-of-purchase mark off the box, and mailed them all to Windmere. Windmere paid an 80-cent processing fee. Normally priced at $12.99, the VIP Pro hair dryer was often featured in store advertising at a sale price of under $10, which meant that the price was below $5 with the rebate. The rebate campaign was a smashing success. How could this be? What was the critical statistic that determined its success?

20. Which of the full-page newspaper advertisements shown below do you think would be most effective? Do you think they appeal to different market segments? What do you think will be competitors' responses to each ad?

Organizing and Implementing

"It is not enough to be busy; so are the ants. The question is: What are you busy about?"

Henry David Thoreau

"Those who command themselves, command others."

Hazlitt

*I*mplementing marketing decisions requires many skills, two of which are featured in this chapter. The first skill is the ability to structure organizational resources in a way that increases competitive rationality. The second skill is the ability to schedule activities, allocate resources, assign responsibility, and monitor progress. Marketing strategy, organization, and implementation are closely linked issues. Good strategy with poor organizational structure or implementation, poor strategy with good organizational structure and implementation, or poor strategy with poor organizational structure and implementation can all result in failure.[1] Consequently, determining the cause of failure, learning from it, and correcting it can be very difficult.

Moreover, as a planned strategy is implemented, it often is changed by creative managers into a new strategy better adapted to the changing marketplace.[2] At other times, organizational structure and politics change the implementation of strategy in less desirable ways. In today's extremely competitive global environment, the ability to adapt to change, reduce costs, and maintain competitive levels of quality and service, all at the same time, are extremely important. Also, the ingenuity used to deploy organizational human resources and a network of working relationships with other organizations contributes to the successful implementation of new strategies. A firm must be nimble. Often profits and success come from the ability to react opportunistically to changes in the marketplace rather than from long-term product differentiation or other so-called sustainable competitive advantages.[3]

Keep the following key ideas in mind as you read this chapter:

- A cross-functional team, as defined and discussed in Chapter 1, should not only make market decisions; it should also manage and coordinate with the network of organizational alliances that are formed to implement the positioning, new product/service development, and all of the other marketing programs that make up a firm's competitive strategy.

- A clan culture is best for getting an organization to work together to get things done, continuously improve institutional routines, and implement special projects.

- A marketing organizational structure should be built around the sales force, if it exists. Any other organizational structure is less effective and less efficient.

- When an organization becomes too large, bureaucratic, and centralized in its decision making, it may be better off decentralizing into autonomous divisions that can form their own strategic alliances and relationship networks. Cross-functional teams are the embryos of future divisional organization and management groups.

- Critical path analysis is a useful tool for preparing action plans and activity sequence scripts.

- However, much of implementation depends on the intuitive, activity sequence-scheduling skills and time management skills of managers. These skills have to be understood before the individual manager, cross-functional team or firm can speed up and improve implementation.

---

1. Thomas V. Bonoma, "Making Your Marketing Strategy Work," *Harvard Business School,* March/April 1984, 69–76.
2. See the discussion on marketing management practice in Chapter 1, particularly J. B. Quinn's work on how strategy incrementally evolves from implementation decisions.
3. See Chapter 1 and also Amar Bhide, "Hustle as Strategy," *Harvard Business Review,* September/October 1986, 59–65; George Stalk, Jr., "Time—The Next Source of Competitive Advantage," *Harvard Business Review,* July/August 1988, 41–50; and Peter R. Dickson, "Toward a General Theory of Competitive Rationality," *Journal of Marketing,* Winter 1992.

The marketing organization in many established companies developed as a separate function because of the traditional, narrow focus of the sales organization. Exasperated by the inability of the sales force to adopt a long-term customer perspective, senior executives during the 1960s created a separate marketing function and organization to manage sales forecasting, market research, product development, advertising, promotions, and pricing. Product managers, who reported to a marketing vice-president or marketing director, were responsible for coordinating the marketing and selling in particular product-markets. In theory, they increased coordination, planned and implemented more effective and efficient marketing campaigns, and were able to react faster than a committee. In practice, their lack of authority limited their effectiveness and reduced them to the role of communication facilitators who sometimes created unnecessary reports, memos, and other paperwork. What is more, the product manager's lack of a specific functional skill (such as engineering, design, accounting, or sales) and high turnover (and hence low product-market experience) among product managers raised questions as to what they added to the competitive rationality of the firm and, hence, their value for the money.

Rethinking Marketing Management

In the 1980s, when senior management sought to reduce overhead by cutting out layers of middle management, it became apparent that most sales executives were equally well trained to manage regional marketing activities, such as market research, advertising, and promotions, as well as the sales force. In addition they were able to ensure coordination with sales and distribution, and they possessed the authority to ensure that things were implemented quickly and done right the first time. As a result, many firms began to rethink their organizational structures. More of the responsibility for implementing marketing programs was also delegated to outside consultants. Market research firms, advertising agencies, and companies that run sweepstakes contests, coupon campaigns, or other promotion programs were given more complete responsibility for budgets, deadlines, and results. Other marketing functions were delegated to regional sales managers or undertaken by divisional senior management, particularly new product development.

At the same time that the marketing function and organization was being rationalized, senior executives addressed the problem of poor communication and cooperation between sales, marketing, R&D, engineering, manufacturing, and distribution by forming cross-functional teams consisting of representatives from each functional area.[4] These teams were conceived of as junior versions of the senior executive team that manages a small firm or a division of a larger company. Some cross-functional teams are temporary, created to address a short-term problem such as speeding up the launch of an important new product or improving cooperation between marketing and manufacturing (as discussed in Chapter 7) or between marketing and R&D (as discussed in Chapter 9). Others are permanent and are used to team-manage a product market. Such cross-functional teams provide a constant and continuous interface between all of the functions in the firm. They have budgetary responsibility and the authority to get things done, and they develop and manage relationships with outside

The Evolution of Marketing Organization

---

4. Chapters 1 and 2 define and discuss at some length the role of cross-functional teams in planning, intelligence gathering, and intelligence use. Appendix 1 describes some of the key mechanics of setting up and leading a cross-functional team.

management service companies such as market research firms, advertising agencies, suppliers, manufacturing subcontractors, and freight forwarders. Successful cross-functional teams that grow a product-market are the embryos for future new company divisions or separate companies. The many reasons for the superior competitive rationality of cross-functional team management are described in Chapters 1 and 2. Put most simply, cross-functional team management creates a more adaptive, responsive, customer-oriented, learning organization that can apply total quality management. Teams break down the psychological, sociological, and political resistance to change that permeates the traditional bureaucratic organizational structure. Organizations that have adopted such an integrated team management approach include Hewlett-Packard, Ford, and British Airways. In the following sections, we further discuss how cross-functional team management is integrated into the traditional functional structures of organizations and how it is used to manage organizational networks.

Organizational Networks and Relationship Marketing

The organization and implementation of marketing programs and tasks involves the study of the economics and politics of how to do it best.[5] It is a special competitive rationality skill that the CEO and senior executives of the modern firm must possess. This skill has become crucial because the rules of the game have changed. CEOs with the old skills of charismatic leadership, cost control, or the shrewd buying and selling of assets must adapt to the new reality. The reality is that the American firms that use the new information and management technologies most innovatively will flourish. The new technologies increase the ways in which a firm can implement its innovation-imitation strategies most efficiently and effectively. How do the new technologies increase the firm's choices? The new information and management technologies allow firms to reduce transaction costs dramatically *and,* at the same time, increase control.

How EDI Increases Outsourcing Control and Choices

In earlier chapters, we explained how electronic data interchange (EDI) can reduce negotiation time and costs, contracting time and costs, shipping time and costs, inventory holding costs, obsolete inventory write-downs, in-transit monitoring costs, customs processing time and costs, back-ordering time and costs, expediting time and costs, and payment time and costs. But EDI can do even more. Most basically, EDI increases the opportunity of out-sourcing production, distribution, and the implementation of many other marketing activities and programs (see Figure 10-9: A Seamless Worldwide EDI Communication System). This greater range of "how to do it best" choices must ultimately confer a competitive advantage. As long as one firm has *more choices* of how to produce, distribute, and implement marketing programs, it will have a competitive advantage over its rivals. Furthermore, many modern products rely on so many different technologies that only the very largest companies can possibly be the best in all of them. All other firms must form strategic alliances to remain competitive.[6] Examples of such alliances are Apple and Motorola working to develop a new

5. Ronald H. Coase, "The Nature of the Firm," *Economica* 4 (1937), 386–405; Oliver E. Williamson, *Markets and Hierarchies* (New York: The Free Press, 1975); and Robert W. Ruckert, Orville C. Walker, Jr., and Kenneth J. Roering, "The Organization of Marketing Activities: A Contingency Theory of Structure and Performance," *Journal of Marketing* 49 (Winter 1985), 13–25.
6. Kenichi Ohmae, *The Borderless World* (New York: Harper Business, 1990), 4.

generation operating system and microprocessor; Xerox and Sun Microsystems developing new computer products; and Apple and IBM developing new networking software. Such alliances require special levels of shared-destiny, trust, and, in particular, the ability to communicate and share information through compatible EDI systems.[7]

How Cross-Functional Teams Best Manage Relationship Networks

Cross-functional team management, within an entrepreneurial clan culture, breaks down the so-called silo mentality of the bureaucratic organization.[8] These silos are the different organizational departments (such as finance, production, engineering, design, marketing, sales, and management information systems) that end up as political fiefdoms. Each one follows and serves its own traditions and legends, its own values created by its professional training and specialized responsibilities, and its own external constituencies.[9] The adoption of the cross-functional management approach goes a long way toward improving a firm's competitive rationality. It allows the collective inculcation of the three drives that are the foundation of competitive rationality: the drive to increase customer satisfaction, the drive to reduce costs, and the drive to improve the enterprise's decision-making and implementation behavior. Cross-functional team management also will increase the number and success of innovation experiments, increase learning from the experiments, and increase the ability of the firm to detect changes in the market environment.

But there are further, perhaps even more profound advantages of cross-functional team organization and implementation. Once a firm has learned the organizational skill of cross-functional team decision making, it can advance to the next major increase in its competitive rationality—selecting and managing a whole *network of relationships* with other firms in a way that results in higher customer satisfaction at a lower cost. EDI provides the potential ability to develop numerous new relationships with suppliers and customers. Cross-functional team management realizes this potential.

In essence, once a cross-functional team has learned to manage itself and completely change the firm's internal political economy, it can launch into the task of reaching out, selecting, and managing a whole set of strategic alliances, that is, managing its external political economy. Again, throughout this book we have talked about how a firm increases its competitive rationality by choosing to contract out important organizational functions. Firms frequently use market research firms to help scan the environment and create the executive's mental models of the market environment. Firms also work with important customers and suppliers, involving them in the decision making and working with them to improve the quality of decisions and the speed of implementing them. Advertising agencies are hired to develop communication programs. Design and engineering consultants are hired to create product and service design. Integrated freight forwarders provide global EDI networks that reduce transaction costs and increase control and choice. Information processing firms such as EDS can install or lease information systems. Sales reps are used to personally sell to customers. Distributors sell, educate, train, install, and inventory products, and are counted on for after-sales service. All of these firms form a network of strategic alliances

7. John A. Byrne, Richard Brandt, and Otis Port, "The Virtual Corporation," *Business Week*, February 8, 1993, 98–103. The term *virtual corporation* is similar in meaning to the shell or hollow corporation mentioned later.
8. Frederick E. Webster, *It's 1990—Do You Know Where Your Marketing Is?* MSI White Paper (Cambridge MA: Marketing Science Institute, 1989).
9. Paul F. Anderson, "Marketing, Strategic Planning and the Theory of the Firm," *Journal of Marketing*, 46 (Spring 1982), 15–26.

Figure 14-1 (a)

A Network of Organizational Relationships Managed by a Cross-Functional Team

As a group, the cross-functional team must manage a whole network of strategic alliances and working relationships. However, all members of the cross-functional team are involved in the management process.

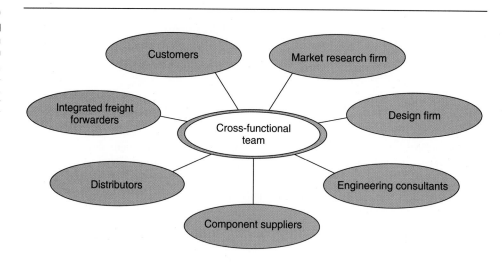

Figure 14-1 (b)

A Network of Organizational Relationships Managed by Functions

As illustrated, an organizational network that is managed by functional silos risks communication inefficiencies and political ineffectiveness. Brand or product management helps increase coordination but often is only a temporary solution to the internal organization problem.

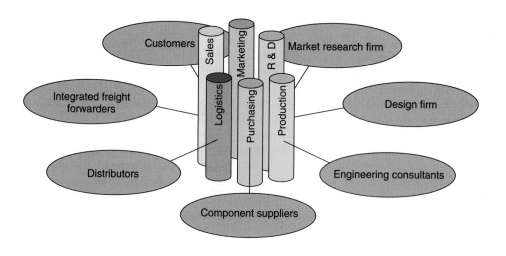

(a network of legal contracts and social contracts) used to make decisions and manufacture and market the product (see Figure 14-1).[10] Examples of other diverse functions that can be contracted out include warehousing, trucking, sales promotions, and new product R&D undertaken by universities or research organizations such as the Battelle Memorial Institute or Bell Laboratories. In short, many firms have been outsourcing many and varied key organizational activities for decades. What is new is that some firms have dramatically increased their out-sourcing of much of their manufacturing by working with new suppliers or by developing strategic alliances with competitors.

---

10. For an interesting discussion of network organizations, see Frederick E. Webster, "The Changing Role of Marketing in the Corporation," *Journal of Marketing* 56 (October 1992), 1–17. We, however, go much further in integrating marketing management into general business management (undertaken by a cross-functional team) than Professor Webster proposes. Internal organizational politics are greatly reduced by cross-functional team business management. This simplifies organizational politics down to the economics and politics of managing the strategic alliances in the network.

Hub-and-Spoke Relationship Management

At the center (or hub) of a network of strategic alliances or long-term, out-sourcing relationships is the cross-functional team. Some of the above economic agents may be important enough (such as designers, suppliers, customers, or the advertising agency) to be represented on the cross-functional team or cross-functional team working parties. Other relationships will be managed through the sales force or kept in constant contact through meetings, briefings, and EDI. The critical point is that a cross-functional team can manage a network organization much better than the traditional bureaucratic organization (see Figure 14-1). Bureaucratic organizations assign authority and responsibility to manage each of the external agents described in Figure 14-1 to different departments, which then proceed to manage them *inside* their separate silos. The result is an increase in the probability of significant communication breakdowns and political system friction in both the internal and external network, that is, a decrease in system competitive rationality. Over the long term, the above competitive realities point to a single conclusion. Firms that shift to cross-functional team management and EDI increase their own internal competitive rationality and are better able to harness the competitive rationality available from other organizations with which they have working relationships.

Why must the firm be able to use EDI and cross-functional team management to take advantage of the full forces of competition? The theory of competitive rationality demonstrates that competition creates suppliers who are very skilled at serving their customers. Competition among suppliers of production, distribution, and marketing services described in Figure 14-1 creates especially skilled executives and firms. In fact, this competition is likely to produce firms that are more efficient at certain production, distribution, and marketing functions and programs than the firm itself can ever afford to be. It is a matter of specialization and competitive survival of the fittest. Simply put, a firm often cannot improve on the efficiency of a market.[11] If this is so, then it is important that the firm choose a strategic alliance with the suppliers most jointly efficient and effective in the desired skill. If it does not, then a rival will choose a superior supplier. This link in the rival's organizational network will be stronger than the firm's link (perhaps because it has a better freight forwarder, design firm, or advertising agency). But making a superior choice when forming a strategic alliance is not enough. The firm must then create a working relationship that takes the most advantage of the partner's skills.

The Hollow Company

In extreme cases, the firm's essential organization and function may be purely administrative because all of the major production functions have been subcontracted out to external suppliers. For example, the company 1-800-FLOWERS subcontracts the delivery of flowers to local florists (see Figure 14-2). In this case, the firm's core competency is its ability to position a product, make market decisions, implement programs, and choose the right organization network alliances and manage them. Companies such as Casio, Nike, Liz Claiborne, and Emerson Radio have moved toward such marketing organizations. They are very flexible and adaptive because the production investment risks are carried by their suppliers.[12] MS-DOS, the operating system that Microsoft sold

11. Coase, "The Nature of the Firm"; Williamson, *Markets and Hierarchies;* and Ruekert et al., "The Organization of Marketing Activities," 17.
12. Ravi S. Achrol, "Evolution of the Marketing Organization: New Forms for Turbulent Environments," *Journal of Marketing* 55 (October 1991), 77–93.

Figure 14-2
A Network Organization Ad

Rather than sending flowers by UPS or FedEx, as some companies such as Black Tie Roses do, 1-800-FLOWERS subcontracts a network of local florists to arrange and deliver the flowers. In this way, all of the firm's manufacturing and physical distribution functions are out-sourced.

to IBM (and that was eventually responsible for Microsoft making a name for itself) was purchased from a small Seattle computer company. The system was initially called Q-DOS (quick and dirty operating system). Microsoft changed the name, for fairly obvious reasons, positioned the product superbly, developed the trading alliances, and managed the alliances very well.

However, most organizations continue to take on a great many production, distribution, and sales functions, either because they feel they can do it more cost-effectively or because they fear a loss of control. In-house manufacturing is likely to occur in the marketing of complex products, particularly innovations early in the product's life cycle, when a great deal of competitive advantage comes from secret processes, undisclosed formulas, or other information that needs to be kept confidential for as long as possible within the organization.[13] A firm that emphasizes *innovation*-imitation is not likely to out-source the R&D, design, and production of key components unless it has patents on its product and process innovations. A firm that emphasizes innovation-*imitation* may be more likely to out-source. Because it is less at risk, a company

13. Robert W. Ruekert, Orville C. Walker, Jr., and Kenneth J. Roering, "The Organization of Marketing Activities: A Contingency Theory of Structure and Performance" *Journal of Marketing* 49 (Winter 1985), 13–25; and Erin Anderson, "The Salesperson As Outside Agent or Employee: A Transaction Cost Analysis," *Marketing Science* 4.3 (1985), 234–54.

that emphasizes imitation may give away its vital technological secrets and customer contacts to a supplier. However, this may be a huge mistake, for if the firm is *not* an innovator, how does it compete if its suppliers treacherously become its competitors?

In global sourcing and marketing, a firm has to constantly transfer its design and manufacturing technology to suppliers in its organizational network. This inevitably increases the skills of its off-shore partners, which poses a very serious long-term competitive risk. For example, many Asian manufacturers are being given technology by U.S. companies and other multinationals that would have cost billions of dollars and taken a generation of management for them to have developed on their own.[14] For example, Schwinn Bicycle Co., now in Chapter 11 bankruptcy, taught its two Chinese suppliers (Giant and China) how to become its major competitors and became a victim of global sourcing. [15] According to the theory of competitive rationality, this continuing give-away should spur the firms who give such technology to even *greater* innovation. To stay ahead of the potential competition from errant suppliers that they create by transferring their existing technology, they must always be several steps ahead in their experimentation, learning, and implementation skills (that is, they must practice superior competitive rationality). *Thus, the cumulative effect of such global sourcing and technology transfer is to speed up the rate of innovation-imitation in the global market, and this rate of change will continue to accelerate.*

Organizational culture is the pattern of role-related beliefs, values, and expectations that are shared by the members of an organization.[16] These beliefs, values, and expectations in turn produce the rules and norms for behavior, which have a powerful influence on the ways in which groups and individuals in the organization behave. The role-related values of an individual are a composite of an individual's personal values and the organizational values. Examples of personal values, organizational values, and role-related values are presented in Figure 14-3.[17] A high level of positive shared organizational values leads to a strong and positive organizational culture, which is essential to successful and speedy implementation.

According to theorists, when the market mechanism fails or is inappropriate, an organization can use two other major implementation systems: bureaucracies and clans.[18] A bureaucratic system relies upon a formal structural hierarchy, rules, and regulations, as well as close personal monitoring, to achieve control. Examples of tools that are used as bureaucratic mechanisms in marketing would be a formal planning process that grinds on for months through an approval hierarchy, a salesperson's daily reports, and formal customer credit policies. Some experts have argued that bureaucracies are appropriate when the implementation tasks are repetitive, routine, and unchanging in stable competitive markets.[19] But a stable, competitive market is an oxymoron. Competitive markets are not stable. They may be stable for short periods,

Bureaucratic and Clan Organization Systems

14. Robert Neff et al., "Multinationals Have a Tiger by the Tail," *Business Week,* December 7, 1992.

15. Andrew Tanzer, "Bury Thy Teacher," *Forbes,* December 21, 1992, 90–95. Schwinn was also not a leading innovator and, in fact, missed the boat on the mountain bike fad.

16. Rohit Deshpande and Frederick E. Webster, "Organization Culture and Marketing: Defining the Research Agenda," *Journal of Marketing* 53 (January 1989), 3–15.

17. G. J. Badovick and S. E. Beatty, "Shared Organizational Values: Measurement and Impact on Strategic Marketing Implementation," *Academy of Marketing Science* 15.1 (Spring 1987), 19–26.

18. William G. Ouchi, "A Conceptual Framework for the Design of Organizational Control Mechanisms," *Management Science* 25.9 (September 1979), 833–48.

19. Ruekert et al., "The Organization of Marketing Activities," 13–25.

Figure 14-3

The Shared Values That Make an Organizational Culture

Organizational culture is the pattern of role-related beliefs, values, and expectations that are shared by the members of an organization. These beliefs, values, and expectations, in turn, produce the rules and norms for behavior, which have a powerful influence on the ways in which groups and individuals in the organization conduct themselves. The role-related values of an individual are a composite of the individual's personal values and the organizational values highlighted here. A high level of positive, shared organizational values leads to a strong and positive organizational culture, which is essential to successful and speedy implementation.

Personal values	Role-related values	Organizational values
Ambition	Ambition	Customer satisfaction
Beauty	Competence	Efficiency and reduced cost
Compassion	Customer satisfaction	Excellence
Courage	Excellence	Entrepreneurship
Excellence	Helpfulness	Improved decision making
Fairness	Honesty	Internal competition
Family	Ingenuity	Outperforming competition
Happiness	Integrity	Respect for employees
Honesty	Loyalty	Service quality
Independence	Resourcefulness	Short-term profitability
Integrity	Responsibility	Teamwork
Kindness	Teamwork	Technological leadership
Loyalty		
Respect		
Responsibility		
Tradition		

but they will be disturbed by the innovation-imitation cycle. Bureaucracies are very bad at adapting to such change and, in fact, often strongly resist change. They are even worse at initiating change through market experimentation. Some claim that formalizing and centralizing tasks can lead to higher effectiveness and efficiency in implementation. This position, however, does not explain how a bureaucracy can discover or invent the most effective and efficient way of undertaking a task that is then formalized throughout the organization by centralized authority. An organization cannot discover the most effective way of doing things without experimentation, and creative experimentation is not a characteristic of a bureaucracy.

Why a Clan Culture Is More Adaptable and Effective

A bureaucracy smothers the heretic manager who, using his or her own skills, bypasses the systems, policies, and structure and finds better ways of doing things.[20] A bureaucratic organizational structure is particularly good at resisting change because it provokes conflict between functions and factions.[21] This conflict ultimately can be disastrous. Extremely adaptive and responsive firms with clan cultures can, through their sustained innovation, create such market turbulence that they drive their bureaucratically organized rivals into self-destructive modes of decision making and market behavior and, eventually, organizational nervous breakdowns. The rival's competitive rationality crumbles under the sustained pressure of change.[22]

A clan system, as opposed to a purely bureaucratic or market system, obtains motivation and control through socialization of the individual into an informal social

20. Thomas V. Bonoma, "Making Your Marketing Strategy Work," *Harvard Business Review,* March/April 1987, 69–76.
21. James Brian Quinn, "Formulating Strategy One Step at a Time," *Journal of Business Strategy* 1 (Winter 1981), 42–63; Paul F. Anderson, "Marketing Strategic Planning and the Theory of the Firm," *Journal of Marketing* 46 (Spring 1982), 15–26; and Richard R. Nelson and Sidney G. Winter, *An Evolutionary Theory of Economic Change* (Cambridge, MA: Harvard University Press, 1982).
22. Tom Peters, *Thriving on Chaos* (New York: Harper & Row, 1987); Lawrence R. Jauch and Kenneth L. Kraft, "Strategic Management of Uncertainty," *Academy of Management Review* 11 (4) (1986), 777–90; and Stephen L. Fink, Joel Beak, and Kenneth Taddeo, "Organization Crisis and Change," *Journal of Applied Behavioral Science* 7 (1) (1971), 15–37.

system that stresses teamwork. The level of shared beliefs, values, and goals among individual members of an organization (described in Figure 14-3) will determine the extent to which the clan mechanism operates. For instance, if all employees share the genuine belief that a high level of customer satisfaction is important both for their own and for their organization's survival, then this belief facilitates the implementation of marketing strategies that incorporate high customer service levels. In general, a clan culture is characteristic of most Japanese companies and in many ways it is most efficient. A clan culture results in faster and better implementation for several reasons:

1. Goals and beliefs of the organization are shared by most members so that goal conflict is reduced.

2. Clan members believe that team effort is the best way to achieve individual self-interest so they help each other.

3. The reduction in politics and conflict and the increase in commitment reduces resistance to implementation and reduces costs associated with formal controls, particularly supervisory middle-management costs.

Creating a Clan Culture

Much of the responsibility for creating the clan culture rests on the shoulders of senior management. Several organizational practices or policies encourage the development of a clan culture:[23]

1. Defining the desired philosophy and implementing it by creating a supportive structure and incentives.

2. Developing the interpersonal skills of organizational members.

3. Stabilizing employment.

4. Deciding on a system for equitable evaluation and promotion.

5. Providing broader career path development.

6. Seeking out priority areas to implement a participative approach to problem solving and decision making.

Marketing and sales departments are social organizations, and the personal interaction climate in the organization is a critical determinant of the organization's ability to implement its marketing plans.[24] A firm with "the right stuff" has a clan culture that encourages, motivates, and empowers people to both follow and lead. Such companies not only welcome the challenge of adapting to the changing marketplace, they initiate change.[25] Marketing strategy cannot be successfully implemented unless a firm's leaders create a clan culture of customer orientation, enthusiasm, and cooperation that is propelled by the three basic drivers of competitive rationality: the desire to improve customer satisfaction, reduce costs, and improve decision-making and implementation routines.[26]

23. William G. Ouchi, *Theory Z* (Reading, MA: Addison Wesley, 1981).
24. Tom Bonoma, *Marketing Management* (New York: The Free Press, 1984). In particular, see Chapter 1 and 39.
25. See the best-selling books, such as William G. Ouchi, *Theory Z* (New York: Avon Book, 1981); and Tom Peters, *Thriving on Chaos* (New York: Harper & Row, 1987).
26. A clan culture that stresses "don't rock the boat" cohesion will not perform as well as it will not be innovative and entrepreneurial. See Rohit Deshpande, John U. Farley, and Frederick E. Webster, Jr., "Corporate Culture, Customer Orientation, and Innovativeness in Japanese Firms: A Quadrad Analysis," *Journal of Marketing* 57 (January 1993), 23–27. For further general discussions of the advantages and disadvantages of different types of management organizations, see Richard Daft, *Organization Theory and Design*, 3rd ed. (St. Paul, MI: West Publishing); and Bedeian and Zammuto, *Organizations: Theory and Design* (Fort Worth, TX: Dryden, 1990).

Internal Organizational Structure That Enables Implementation

To cope with today's market environment, organizations have developed a wide variety of internal organizational structures that range from the simple functional organization, to the product-market organization, up to the more complex matrix organization. Each of these structures has its advantages and disadvantages.[27] The *functional* organizational structure creates functional specialists—such as a sales manager, advertising manager, and market research manager—who all report to a marketing vice-president. It is the most common form of marketing organization, and it is very simple and efficient in a stable environment. It cannot adapt to change very quickly, however, and breaks down as the number of products, market segments served, and functions increases. It is particularly unsuited for serving very different global markets. A *product-market* organization adds a layer of staff positions called product, brand, or market managers whose responsibility is to coordinate all of the functional activities associated with each brand, product, or specific market. A *matrix* organization is designed to form teams of functional and product-market managers that can focus on a specific project.

New product development highlights the difference between functional and matrix organizational structures. The bureaucratic, functional management of new product development involves cooperation among functional departments, such as marketing, R&D, and manufacturing, who together employ formal, bureaucratic channels of authority and communication. Management guidance is provided by senior management or a product manager who is responsible for orchestrating the new product development process but lacks the authority to make it happen. Cross-functional team management, on the other hand, involves the creation of a full-time or part-time team of executives with different functional skills who have collective responsibility and authority for the project. A team whose members are temporarily transferred from their functional departments to work on the project part-time is called a project matrix team. A project matrix team may be used by smaller firms that cannot commit full-time human resources to a single new product development cross-functional team. In fact, it is not unusual for a manager to be a member of several such cross-functional teams working on different projects.

The Superiority of Cross-Functional Team Management

Overwhelming evidence suggests that cross-functional team management of the new product development process is superior to the various forms of bureaucratic, functional management that are still common in large U.S. firms.[28] Cross-functional teams are particularly suited to projects involving concepts and technology new to the firm.[29] However, over a period of time, a structure built around too many matrix teams can degenerate into a chaotic communications nightmare by being too formalized, too inflexible, and too slow. The solution is to break the organization into decentralized divisions or product groups when a matrix organization becomes too big, unwieldy, and inefficient. For example, the return on investment in R&D by small firms is up to

27. Barton Weitz and Erin Anderson, "Organizing and Controlling the Marketing Function," in *Review of Marketing 1981,* B. M. Enis and K. J. Roering, eds. (Chicago: American Marketing Association, 1981), 124–42.
28. Eric W. Larson and David Wileman, "Organizing for Product Development Projects," *Journal of Product Innovation Management* 4 (1989), 284–97; F. Axel Johne and Patricia A. Snelson, "Success Factors in Product Innovation: A Selective Review of the Literature," *Journal of Product Innovation Management* 5 (1988), 114–28.
29. Eric M. Olson, Orville C. Walker, Jr., and Robert W. Ruekert, "The Impact of Structural Coordination Mechanisms on the Development of Alternative Types of New Products" (Working Paper, College of Business, University of Minnesota, November 1992). Interestingly, these researchers found that traditional bureaucratic new-product development processes work better for more straightforward existing product modifications and line extensions. Perhaps this is because the creation of a cross-functional team in a traditional bureaucratic culture takes some time and extra effort that hinders progress.

20 times that of large corporations, prompting firms such as 3M and General Electric to move to highly decentralized and autonomous divisional structures.[30]

When an organizational structure is designed, it is important to ensure that the structure is simple, can easily be changed, can adapt to changing market conditions, and encourages entrepreneurship. One of the best methods to ensure that an organizational structure can meet these requirements is to reorganize the structure on a regular basis.[31] Continuous reorganization means, for example, monitoring division size to keep it within reasonable limits, shifting products or product lines among divisions to take advantage of internal or external changes, forming temporary project teams to handle tasks like new product launches, and matching the administrative mechanisms and managers to strategy.[32] Such continuous reorganization improves the structure's adaptability to a changing environment and facilitates faster implementation. A simple basic structure, in combination with a clan culture, can result in extremely fast implementation since resistance to implementation of any particular task is minimal. In the case of a bureaucratic organization, however, constant reorganization can create high levels of stress and erode its efficiency even further.

Building the Marketing Structure around the Sales Force

One way to carry out structural reorganization while at the same time retaining the basic form of the organization is to build the marketing structure around the sales force. An example of such a structure is given in Figure 14-4. The advantages of such a design are as follows:

1. Marketing skills already exist in the sales force.

2. R&D technicians and product managers support the sales force.

3. Special project teams with the product manager as the executive officer facilitate coordination among different functional areas.

4. Most importantly, the sales managers responsible for implementing are also responsible for a major part of market decision making.

If a company has made the huge investment in creating its own sales force, then presumably the unique skills of the sales force and its management are very important to the firm's competitive advantage. Otherwise, why not out-source selling to independent telemarketing operations or manufacturers' reps?

Because the skills and competence of the sales force are so important to the competitive advantage of the firm, senior management should give serious consideration to assigning the management and implementation of many marketing functions to the sales force organization. After all, the sales organization has to play a prominent if not preeminent role in implementing the marketing programs.[33] If sales managers have line responsibility for helping to create and implement product market plans, then the plans will be implemented. Furthermore, as the eyes and ears of the firm, sales managers should constantly provide new insights as to how customers and distributors could be better satisfied as well as put forth a constant flow of competitive intelligence.

30. San M. Lee, "The Pan-Pacific Age and the United States," *Pan Pacific Business Association Newsletter* (Winter 1988), University of Nebraska, as quoted in Achrol, ibid.

31. Thomas J. Peters and Robert H. Waterman, Jr., *In Search of Excellence* (New York: Harper & Row, 1987).

32. Vijay Govindrajan, "A Contingency Approach to Strategy Implementation at the Business-Unit Level: Integrating Administrative Mechanisms with Strategy," *Academy of Management Journal* 31.4 (1988), 828–53; "Implementing Competitive Strategies at the Business Unit Level: Implications of Matching Managers to Strategies," *Strategic Management Journal* 10 (1989), 251–69.

33. If sales does not play the dominant role in the marketing program, then the firm should review why it has its own sales force. Thus the presence of a sales force defines the preeminent importance of selling in the firm's marketing strategy.

Figure 14-4

A Generic Marketing Organization Chart

If the skills and competence of the sales force are important enough to the firm's competitive advantage to justify its existence, why not build marketing management into and around the sales force organization? The sales organization has to play a prominent, if not preeminent, role in implementing the marketing programs. If sales management has line responsibility for helping create product-market plans and implementing them, then the plans will be implemented. It is hard to justify any organizational structure that does not have the sales force as its backbone. However, the senior executive team and the supporting cross-functional product teams dominate decision making. Note that this framework also gives considerable decentralized sales and marketing authority to regional sales directors.

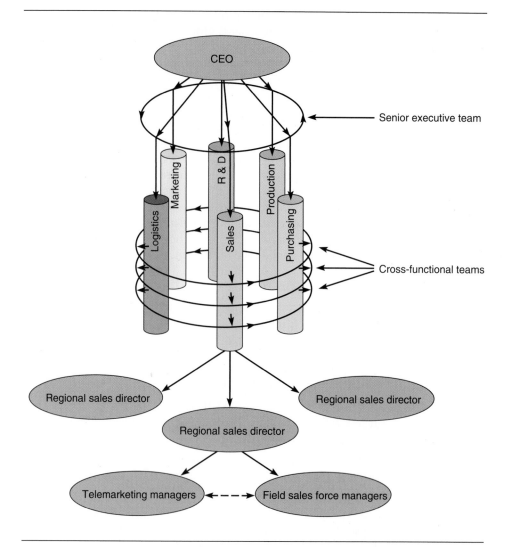

Marketing versus Sales Is Outdated

It is hard to justify any organizational structure that does not have the sales force, if it exists, as its backbone. In fact, many strategy implementation problems can be traced to a separation of the sales and marketing organizations. The fundamental argument against out-sourcing marketing functions is the loss of control. The very same argument can be used against creating a separate sales and marketing function. What competitive advantage can be possibly gained from such a separation? It is sometimes argued that the orientation of a sales force is too short term. Creating a separate marketing function with a longer-term perspective, however, is a poor and temporary solution. The appropriate solution is to address the short-term perspective of the sales force by changing incentives and the sales-force culture. Another fallacious argument is that the sales force management lacks sufficient marketing training or skills. However, most sales managers took marketing courses in college or have been sent to several executive education courses on marketing management. Moreover, it is the executive committee of a division or the cross-functional team managing the product group that develops, approves, and revises the marketing plan. The vice-president of marketing and sales or his or her delegate serves on this committee, plays a key role in formulating strategy, and is, of course, primarily responsible for its implementation.

A more serious problem with building marketing management around the sales force is that the sales force structure has to be somewhat adaptive, dividing its regions as the market grows and particularly as the company enters global markets. Whole new foreign sales regions will likely have to be created with supporting cross-functional teams. The general solution is to spin the whole unit off into a separate division. When in doubt, decentralize.

Implementation is the series of steps taken by managers to gain the cooperation and compliance needed to install planned changes in an organization's behavior. One study found the best implementation approach was for the manager to:

Individual Leadership That Facilitates Implementation

1. Have the seniority and authority to manage the change process and appraise performance.
2. Demonstrate the need for change through unfavorable benchmark performance comparisons of existing routines or behaviors with comparable organizations.
3. Demonstrate the feasibility of change by describing ways that current practices can be improved.
4. Form a participant task force to identify inefficient and ill-advised procedures or activities and to suggest ways in which they might be improved.
5. Approve suggested changes.
6. Monitor and demonstrate improvements in performance that were brought about by the implemented change.[34]

This approach was observed to be more effective than implementing by edict, persuasion, or, at the other extreme, more participative approaches. The successful implementer unfreezes old beliefs, norms, attitudes, and behaviors and actively supervises the change process. This approach is also consistent with decentralized, continuous, cross-functional management, which assumes that the sales and marketing executives are responsible for implementing the marketing strategy and projects. Interestingly, another study notes that in Japan the marketing manager "patiently advises, guides and persuades, and the members concerned develop a feeling that the decision is their own idea."[35] Marketing managers in Japan are not market specialists but rather are experts in *implementing change* in the organization. It seems that they can exert such informal influence because the whole organization shares the customer orientation norm, a cooperation rather than adversarial norm, and a consensus decision-making norm. In U.S. firms with less of a clan culture and more of a bureaucratic structure, a senior line manager is likely to be much more effective at implementation management than a junior staff manager such as a brand or product manager.

34. Paul C. Nutt, "Tactics of Implementation," *Academy of Management Journal* 29.2 (1986), 230–61.
35. William Lazer, Shoji Murata, and Hiroshi Kosaka, "Japanese Marketing: Towards a Better Understanding," *Journal of Marketing* 49 (Spring 1985), 69–81.

The Present and Future Product Manager

A product or brand manager can still play a very important cajoling, educating, coordinating, and monitoring role with sales, the advertising agency, and manufacturing. In a bureaucratic organization, a product or brand manager is responsible for overseeing the development and execution of marketing plans but cannot ensure the necessary cooperation from others in the organization. While this can be a problem even in bureaucracies, most of the time things get done through informal influence.[36] The product manager with good people skills and expertise can play a key role in ensuring the execution of product-market plans (see Figure 14-5). The informal communication and leadership of such product managers acts as the glue that binds the organization together. The problem is that they are often in the job for too short a time to effectively build the team or clan spirit. The role of product managers in an organization using cross-functional team decision making is less clear because the team, as a team, takes collective responsibility for implementing its decisions. The individual with overall responsibility is the team leader, who is just as likely to be a designer or engineer as he or she is to be a marketer. Perhaps the product manager evolves into the team's executive assistant and will come to play a dominant role in managing the product as it matures, consulting the cross-functional team on an as-needed basis.

Activity Scheduling Techniques That Facilitate Implementation

Many implementation concerns should have been addressed in the environmental-strategy meshing process. Strategy will already have been refined to handle production scheduling and capacity, the limited experience of the sales force, and other such constraints. The savvy marketing planner will also have lined up a senior manager to play the role of the *champion* or *fixer* if, as a last resort, someone needs to lean on someone else to gain resources or cooperation. However, the many details that are necessary to execute the marketing strategy still must be worked out. The box on page 520 presents an amusing story of what can happen when such action-planning steps are not taken. Over the years, techniques such as management by objectives have come and gone, but one management approach—management by profanity (MBP)—has stood the test of time. That is about the only test that it has stood. When things go wrong, MBP becomes the management approach of choice. It can be observed when a senior executive turns to a subordinate and asks a question such as, "We did send back the packaging artwork that we approved last month, didn't *you*?" The classic reaction to MBP is an exclaimed or muted oath, normally accompanied by a sinking feeling and clammy palms. Highly contagious, MBP can trigger in others an involuntary string of colorful phrases, vigorous arm-waving, hand washing, and the high-pitched shouting of directions down corridors to no one in particular. It is best avoided as it can become a chronic condition and is associated with high blood pressure, angina, short- and long-term hormonal imbalances, and premature aging. More seriously, the problems of poor execution go beyond the undermining of a particular strategy. The finger pointing that results can rip an organization's morale and harmony apart. It also can undermine an organization's confidence that it can do anything right and can lead to individual disillusionment with the company. The solution is systematic project action planning.

36. David L. Wilemon, "Interpersonal Influence in Product Management," *Journal of Marketing* 40 (October 1976), 33–41; and Steven Lysonski, Alan Singer, and David Wilemon, "Coping with Environmental Uncertainty and Boundary Spanning in the Product Manager's Role," *Journal of Business & Industrial Marketing* 3.2 (1988), 5–16.

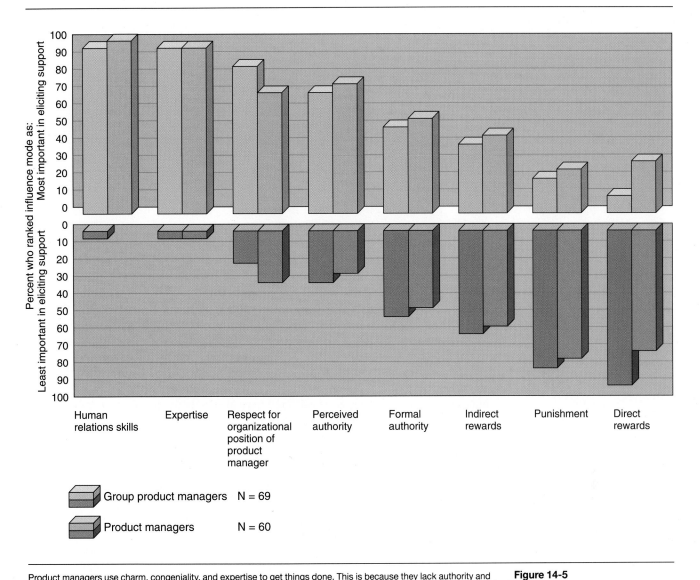

Product managers use charm, congeniality, and expertise to get things done. This is because they lack authority and reinforcement control.

Source: Adapted from Alladi Venkatesh and David L. Wilemon, "Interpersonal Influence in Product Management," *Journal of Marketing* 40 (October 1976), 36.

Figure 14-5
How a Product Manager Elicits Support

Project Action Planning

In our personal lives, we frequently undertake orchestrated behavioral routines in which certain activities must follow one or more others (for example, getting dressed in the morning must come *before* starting the car). If we do not perform these activities in the right order, then we do not achieve the desired goal, and not only do we end up looking stupid, but we often have to spend extra time and effort undoing the mistakes before starting over. The potential problems are even greater when organizations undertake major construction projects or attempt a major new product launch.

The use of scientific management in project scheduling probably occurred as early as the construction of the pyramids and was certainly well understood by the railroad

A Comedy of Errors

For a concatenation of comedic [implementation] errors confounding a single promotion, few can top Pan Am's ill-fated "Bottle in a Basket" campaign of a few years back. To demonstrate Pan Am's superior service on the hotly competitive New York–San Juan route, the airline's ad agency, J. Walter Thompson, hit upon the idea of serving passengers with a light repast: a small bottle of Mateus wine, sliced salami, cheese, and an apple, all served in a little plastic basket on a dainty gingham tablecloth. Cute.

"We got the thing all organized," a former J. Walter Thompson account executive recalls, "when all of a sudden we get this hysterical phone call from Pan Am: 'Don't run the ad! We just received 2,000 pounds of sliced salami—but our contract with the commissary requires that all meats must be sliced by them.'" Back went the sliced salami along with a rush order for a ton of whole salamis. At length, with the salamis received and duly sliced in the commissary, the campaign was ready to kick off again when another May Day call was flashed from Pan Am. It seemed that while the little plastic baskets were in New York, the bottles of wine were in San Juan. Hence, another delay to let the bottles catch up with the baskets. No such

---

contractors who criss-crossed the U.S. heartland in the 19th century. It was further refined during World War II when U.S. shipyards were able to produce liberty ships for the convoys faster than the German U-boats could sink them, which was very fast.

The modern origins of planned project implementation are usually traced to the use of Program Evaluation Review Technique (PERT) on the Polaris Weapon Systems development in 1958 and Du Pont's development of the Critical Path Method (CPM) at about the same time.[37] These critical path analysis techniques are commonly used in building and highway construction. They have also been used to dramatically increase the speed, efficiency, and profitability of new product launches. There are few good reasons why they should not be used as a matter of course in implementing marketing strategy and, hence, become an integral part of the annual marketing plan. Good managers go through an intuitive path or network analysis in their action planning and control anyway. CPM analysis can assist in planning and controlling the implementation of competitive strategy and, through a mental assimilation of the logic and structure of the process, improve the intuitive action planning of managers. Much has been made of the need to continuously increase manufacturing productivity by improving the production process. Little has been said about continuously improving the marketing production process. Critical path analysis assists in marketing action plans in a number of ways listed in Table 14-1. It is not *the* answer, but it is part of an answer.[38]

The Competitive Rationality of Activity Scheduling

The first step in a CPM analysis is to break down the marketing strategy into specific activities and activity sequences. Examples of a new product activity schedule and promotion activity schedule (AS) scripts are presented in Figure 14-6. The potential number of activities and complex sequencing emphasizes why having a staff create marketing plans does not work. Line managers must prepare the marketing planning for it is they who must develop a strategy or a project into a list of specific tasks (correctly sequenced), create milestone completion dates and progress reviews, and assign responsibility for the efficient and effective completion of each task to specific

---

37. As an aside, Du Pont is seldom given the accolades it deserves for the many outstanding innovations in management accounting and scientific management that its employees have developed over the last century.
38. An excellent example of the use of CPM in implementing a marketing plan is provided by Warren Dusenberry, "CPM for New Product Introductions," *Harvard Business Review,* July/August 1967, 124–39.

luck. A mix up in the order resulted in the baskets being shipped to Puerto Rico at the same time that the wine was being flown to New York.

With the logistical problems involving baskets, bottles, and salamis finally straightened out, Pan Am signaled the agency to run the kick-off ad—which pulled so well that the maiden 'Bottle in a Basket' flight was a sellout. Just as airline and agency were congratulating each other, however, word came from San Juan that the wine bottles aboard the first flight had cork tops, not screw-off caps, and the flight attendants had no corkscrews to open them. "We ended up with 180 frustrated passengers ready to break the bottle over our heads," reports the ad man.

Refusing to despair, the indomitable airline thereupon shipped cases of Mateus back to Portugal in exchange for screw-capped bottles. Unfortunately, by the time all the elements of the promotion were finally in place, Pan Am had switched its Puerto Rico service to much larger 747s, and the assembly and serving of 300 baskets of food was deemed too much of a hassle for Pan Am's stewardesses. So, the entire promotion was ditched.

Source: Quoted directly from Robert Levy and Lynn Adkins, "The Hypes That Failed," *Forbes*, September 1980, 74–75.

individuals.[39] To be able to do all of this they must believe in the plan or project, own it, know all of the activities and sequences involved, and understand it enough to adapt it in ways that more efficiently and effectively achieve the desired objectives. In short,

---

Table 14-1
Advantages of Using the Critical Path Method in Strategy Implementation

1. It enables decision makers to estimate how long it will take to roll out all of the components of the marketing plan, and it can be used to calculate the chances that the targeted deadlines will be met.
2. It greatly improves control over all of the integrated and interdependent activities that are required to implement the marketing plan.
3. It reveals interdependencies and human resource bottlenecks that would not be exposed by more intuitive action planning.
4. It encourages a greater degree of honesty and accuracy in the forecasting of the time necessary to enact specific activities.
5. It enables senior executives to delegate responsibility with confidence and to manage by exception.
6. It encourages more responsible time management from external participants, such as market research firms and advertising agencies.
7. It reduces confusion, duplication, false starts, and frustration, and it can significantly improve internal communication and morale.
8. It ensures that synergy gets a chance by orchestrating the timing of interactive marketing activities.
9. It enables sound decisions to be made about where to invest extra resources to speed up overall implementation.
10. It allows the detailed information on time and costs from those responsible for implementing specific activities to be used as a final check on the feasibility of the proposed marketing strategy.
11. It enables the timely scheduling of go/no-go decisions or contingency plan reviews.

---

39. John M. Hobbs and Donald F. Heany, "Coupling Strategy to Operating Plans," *Harvard Business Review*, May/June 1977, 119–24.

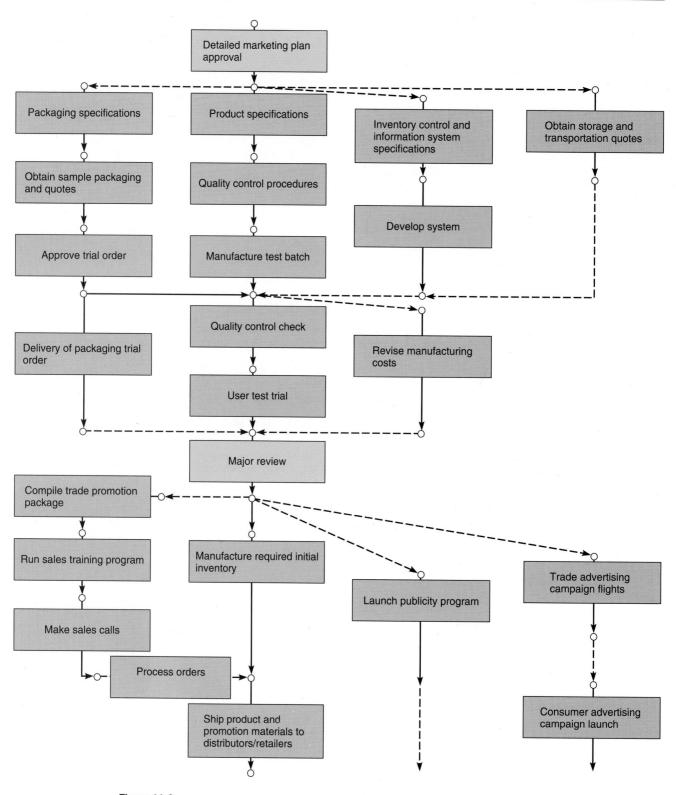

Figure 14-6
A New Product Activity Sequence
(AS) Script

Figure 14-6 continued.   **Promotional Action Plan**

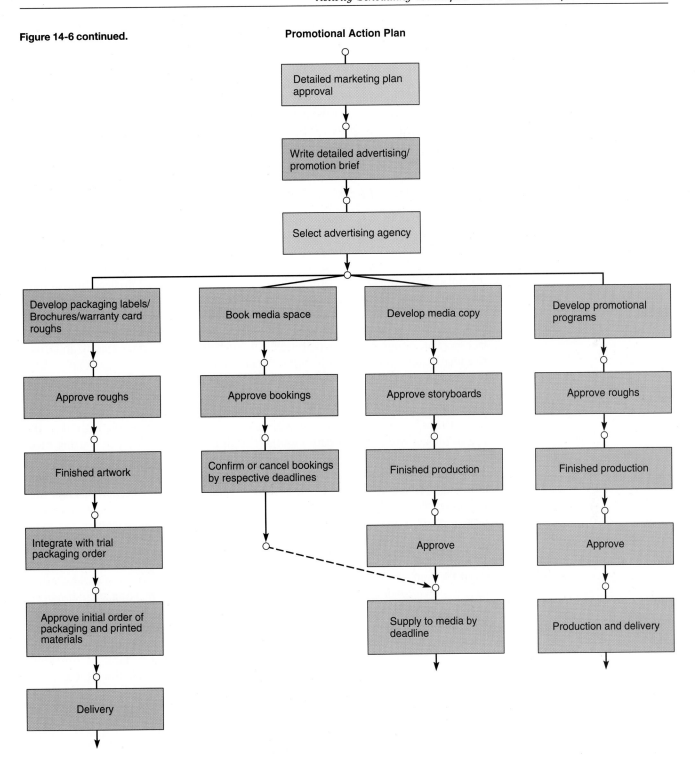

they must be involved in the initial planning. Once an activity schedule has been developed for an advertising campaign or sales promotion, it can be used as an activity sequence blueprint or script for future ad campaigns. The next step is to assign responsibility for implementing each activity to an individual or to an individual leading a team. This individual is then asked to indicate all the activities that absolutely must precede the task he or she is responsible for executing. He or she must also estimate the time needed to complete the task, given the resources that will be made available. CPM uses only one time estimate while PERT uses a most optimistic, most likely, and most pessimistic time estimate.

The Critical Path of Activities

All of the activities are now connected in their dependency sequences or paths. This produces a network of sequenced activities as illustrated in Table 14-2, which enables the computation of the earliest possible start time of each activity (EST) and the identification of a set of sequenced activity paths. The path that will take the longest time to implement is the critical path. All other paths have some float or slack time (a time cushion) in that there can be a time over-run on a noncritical path activity and it will not delay the overall roll-out of the marketing plan. Any time overrun on the critical path is *critical* because it will push the completion of the whole project back and, in fact, may mean missing important deadlines, such as the Christmas season, an attractive media supplement, or an important trade show.

Working backwards from the last activity on the critical path, the latest start time (LST) of all preceding activities can be computed. The difference between LST and EST gives the maximum possible slack or float for each activity. Of course, if all of the slack or float time on an implementation path is used by one activity on the path, then the rest of the activities on that path lose their slack time and any delay in starting them or time overrun then becomes critical. Procrastinators and dawdlers make no friends down the implementation path because the extra time that they take reduces the time cushioning of succeeding activities. When everyone is aware of the network and who is responsible for what and when, then the participants tend to come under increased peer pressure to perform on time. The system tends to be self-managing.

Crashing Time and Competitive Rationality

Often the implementation of a marketing plan requires the meeting of various externally imposed deadlines. An executive's career can depend on meeting such deadlines. After the construction of the initial CPM chart, it may become apparent that such important deadlines will not be met unless things are put into overdrive and the time taken to execute some of the activities is shortened. Reducing the time taken to execute the overall plan is called, rather colorfully, "crashing" the project. Table 14-2 presents a modified analysis of the crashing of a direct mail campaign for the NCR Century computer.[40]

The normal and crash time for each of the 16 activities was first estimated. The crash time is the minimum time that it will take to complete the activity regardless of the cost or resources expended. The average daily cost of crashing each activity also must be estimated. This is a best estimate of the cost of saving a day on each activity. In actuality, the daily cost of crashing each activity is likely to be a discontinuous step function rather than a continuous and linear function. The activities on the initial critical activity sequence path are crashed starting with the least expensive time savings

---

40. Edward J. Feltz, "The Costs of Crashing," *Journal of Marketing*, July 1970, 64–67.

Table 14-2
Speeding Up Implementation by Project Crashing

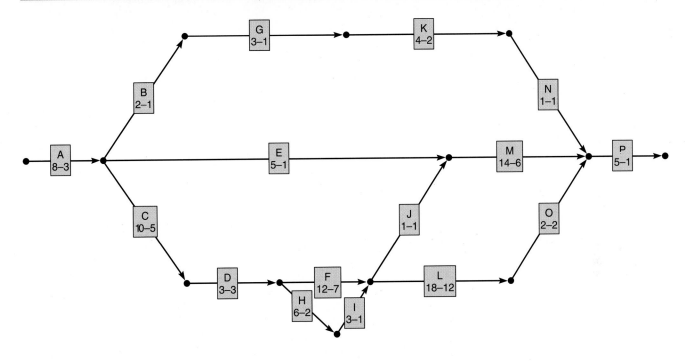

Network Plan for NCR Century Direct Mail Campaign

	Activity	Activity duration in days		Activity dollar cost		Rate of cost increase ($/day)
		Norm.	Crash	Norm.	Crash	
A.	Rough copy	8	3	$ 400	$ 650	$ 50
B.	Copy for announcement	2	1	125	225	100
C.	Layout	10	5	600	1,200	120
D.	Approval	3	3	—	—	—
E.	Research mailing lists	5	1	100	540	110
F.	Final art	12	7	750	1,500	150
G.	Approval—announcement	2	2	—	—	—
H.	Final copy	6	2	250	400	38
I.	Type set	3	1	350	535	88
J.	OK mailing lists	1	1	—	—	—
K.	Printing—announcement	4	2	150	400	125
L.	Printing	18	12	2,150	3,350	200
M.	Order mailing lists	14	6	500	620	15
N.	Deliver to mailing center—announcement	1	1	—	—	—
O.	Deliver to mailing center	2	2	—	—	—
P.	Mail material	5	1	1,150	1,650	125

Continued

Continued from previous page

Crashing analysis	Project duration (days)	Project cost (direct)
Normal time and cost	58	$6,525
Critical Path A-C-D-F-L-O-P		
a) Activity A reduced 5 days @ $50/day	53	$6,775
b) Activity C reduced 5 days @ $120/day	48	$7,375
c) Activity P reduced 4 days @ $125/day	44	$7,875
d) Activity F reduced 3 days @ $150/day	41	$8,325
Critical Paths now A-C-D-F-L-O-P and A-C-D-H-I-L-O-P		
e) Activities E and F can be jointly reduced 2 days @ ($38 & $150)/day	39	$8,701
f) Activity L reduced 5 days @ $200/day	34	$9,701
Critical Paths now A-C-D-F-L-O-P A-C-D-H-I-L-O-P- A-C-D-F-J-M-P A-C-D-H-I-J-M-P		
g) Activities M and L can be jointly reduced 1 day @ ($15 & $200)/day	33	$9,916

(that is, activity A, followed by C, P, and F). As the critical activity sequence is crashed, it may be sufficiently shortened so that it ceases to be the only critical path (that is, if F is crashed by more than three days). When this occurs, then an analysis of simultaneously crashing joint critical paths has to be taken (see Table 14-2). It should be noted that crashing all activities cost $11,060, while the selective crashing of activities on the changing critical paths produced the same effect (a 33-day project) at a cost of $9,916. Whether activity schedule crashing is done using a technique, such as CPM or done intuitively, a major component of competitive rationality is a firm's ability to speed up its implementation. Firms such as Toyota, Hitachi, Honda, Sharp, Sony, Mitsubishi, Benetton, The Limited, Federal Express, McDonald's, and Domino's Pizza have demonstrated the advantages of greatly accelerating their competitive action time (see the Rationality in Practice box on page 528).

Assigning Responsibility for Executing Activities

One advantage of the above action planning approach is that responsibility for completing a particular activity within the time and cost budget is clearly assigned. It can be taken a step further. To ensure early warning of potential implementation problems, a second individual can be assigned to critical tasks. This individual's responsibility is to ensure that the task is completed on time and within cost and to report any problems immediately if it becomes apparent that the targets will not be met. In a clan culture, such a control system may be overly bureaucratic. An alternative is to define the person responsible for the next task in the activity sequence as the customer. This "customer" has a considerable interest in receiving timely and quality service and therefore should be responsible first for reporting problems in receiving timely and quality service and second for helping devise a group solution to the problem.

The formal assignment of responsibilities should be sensitive to informal group leadership dynamics as well as to the formal lines of authority. A firm must use the natural dynamics within and between teams of employees. Firms are social organizations, and the firm that does not draw on social dynamics to empower its employees will be at a disadvantage to the rival that does. When employees volunteer to take on implementation responsibilities that would not normally be given to them individually or as a group, they may be seeking a chance to prove themselves and display initiative. Such initiative provides a way of identifying natural leadership and finding a leader for future formal teams.

Using the Best Human Resources in the Best Ways

The experienced implementor knows that there are always a few subordinates that are clearly superior. Consequently, they are assigned to the most demanding and critical implementation activities. But a problem can arise when an organization leans too much on such individuals at critical times. While the maxim "give a busy person the job" often holds true (they are busy because they are competent and can execute), such executives can be stretched in too many ways by too many tasks, all needing to be completed about the same time. The stress can tie them up and then break one of the most important resources an organization has—a potential leader. Such overload may also endanger the project's quality and customer satisfaction. The AS script analysis approach to action planning enables senior management to review the assignment of responsibility to make sure that key implementation bottlenecks are not created by making too many demands, at any one time, on the most conscientious and talented executives.

Activity Schedule Memory Skills That Facilitate Implementation

Experienced managers often do not prepare formal marketing action plans because marketing projects and routines are less structured than manufacturing projects and routines. They cannot be as clearly specified in engineering terms and have to be more flexible in the face of uncontrollable events. So how do experienced managers prepare action plans? They are able to map them out intuitively and store them in what is called the manager's prospective memory. Prospective memory is memory not of past events but of things to do in the future. Years of experience (making mistakes and watching others make even more) enables a manager to sequence a project's activities or tasks. A manager learns an activity sequence script by implementing or supervising the implementation of similar projects over time. Intuitive scheduling is perhaps the most underrated and neglected skill in marketing.

The Learning of Routine Activity Sequence Scripts

Production process activity sequences executed in the past are laid down on top of each other in episodic memory (memory of past episodes) as illustrated in Figure 14-7. The production process undertaken at time t-3 is stored on top of the earlier similar production process undertaken at time t-4. The sequence of activities and events of the project undertaken at time t-2 is added and so are the activities of the project undertaken during time t-1. When asked at time t to implement or supervise a similar project, the manager now possesses an activity sequence script that she or he has learned. The activities, actors, and physical surroundings are common to the four previous projects.[41] They become the basis for action planning. The very distinctive elements or

41. Roger Schank and Robert Abelson, *Scripts, Plans, Goals, and Understanding* (Hillsdale, NJ: Lawrence Erlbaum Associates, 1977).

Rationality in Practice:

Time-based Competition

Atlas Door, founded in the late 1970s, became the leading door supplier in less than ten years against long-established rivals. Traditionally, the industry had a 16-week order-delivery activity sequence cycle. Atlas computerized its order-entry, pricing, engineering, and manufacturing so that it could price and schedule 95 percent of its business while the customer was still on the phone. This saved 1 to 2 weeks. Just-in-time production cut manufacturing down to 2-1/2 weeks. Being able to access previous special orders on the computer greatly reduced reengineering time and shipping only complete orders forced a very efficient just-in-time logistics system, saving time associated with completing orders after the initial shipment. Atlas positioned itself as the supplier of last resort and penetrated the

Figure 14-7

How an Activity Sequence Script Is Learned

Production process activity sequences executed in the past are laid down on top of each other in episodic memory (memory of past episodes). The production process undertaken at time t-3 is stored on top of the earlier similar production process undertaken at time t-4. The sequence of activities and events of the project undertaken at time t-2 is added, and so are the activities of the project undertaken during time t-1. When asked at time t to implement or supervise a similar project, the manager now possesses an activity sequence (AS) script that she or he has learned. It is the activities, actors and physical surroundings that are common to the four previous projects. The AS script becomes the basis for future action planning.

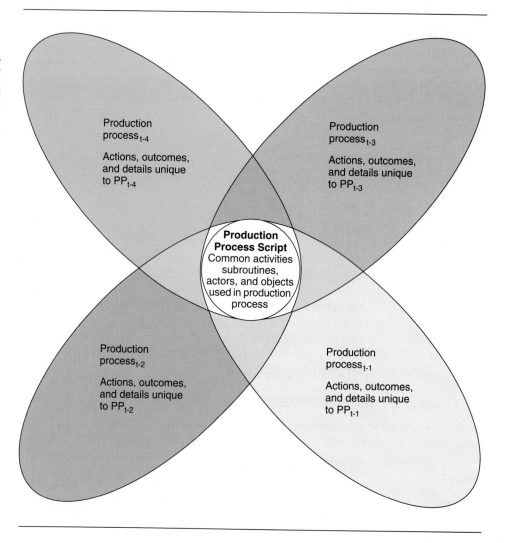

market when the competition could not deliver or missed key deadlines. This enabled Atlas to charge higher prices while the simplification that led to the faster service also reduced costs.* As mentioned in the discussion of company analysis in Chapter 7, firms are using benchmarking to discover ways that firms in other markets have simplified routines. What is learned is imitated or modified to shorten the time necessary to complete all activity sequences, be they routine or complex. The motive for the creative "crashing" of activity sequences is the belief that time is money. Taking too much time is a competitive disadvantage in many markets today.

*George Stalk, Jr., "Time—The Next Source of Competitive Advantage," *Harvard Business Review*, July/August 1988, 41–51.

outcomes of previous projects will be remembered, but they will be remembered separately and will not be part of the script. Like an experienced cook, the manager will use the AS script as a blueprint but will improvise by using the people and resources at hand. As events unfold in implementing a project's activity sequence, they will prompt recall of what happened in a specific past production process, reminding the manager of what worked and what did not work in the past.

Activity Scheduling Skills

Some managers and employees are only able to learn and follow particular production scripts.[42] The risk is that they become slaves of these routines, mindlessly executing their work-to-rule scripts. They cease to pay attention to new environmental information that suggests that the market is changing and that the old way of doing things may no longer be the best way.[43] Changing conditions can upset the effectiveness of AS scripts and routines that previously were very effective and efficient. Inevitably, routines must be adapted and changed creatively to meet the new conditions. Creative adaptation of routines can be taught and utilized on the job. For example, Scandinavian Airlines System (SAS) and British Airways have trained 24,000 and 37,000 employees, respectively, to respond creatively when it comes to pleasing the customer rather than to execute service routines mindlessly.[44]

Other managers with superior abstract thinking skills—or higher levels of curiosity, creativity, initiative, and motivation—advance beyond learning and improvising AS scripts. Their production scripts become the basis for learning rules about what to do and what not to do in implementing plans in a firm and in a market. These rules are stored in a special part of memory called the production rule memory store (see Figure 14-8). Managers use these rules to adapt old scripts to new situations, to transfer what they have learned in one situation to another, and to assemble completely new scripts. Such managers are also likely to have superior prospective memory—they have

42. Try reciting the alphabet backwards! For more complex examples of ASS rigidity, see Connie J. G. Gersick and J. Richard Hackman, "Habitual Routines in Task—Performing Groups," *Organizational Behavior and Human Decision Processes* 47 (1990), 65–97; and Ellen J. Langer, "Minding Matters: The Mindlessness/Mindfulness Theory of Cognitive Activity," in L. Berkowitz, ed., *Advances in Experimental Social Psychology* (New York: Academic Press, 1989).
43. Howard M. Weiss and Daniel R. Ilgen, "Routinized Behavior in Organizations," *The Journal of Behavioral Economics* 14 (1985), 57–67; Meryl R. Louis and Robert I. Sutton, "Switching Cognitive Gears: From Habits of Mind to Active Thinking," *Human Relations* 44.1 (1991), 55–76; and Abraham S. Luchins and Edith H. Luchins, *Wertheimer's Seminars Revisited—Problem Solving and Thinking*, vol. III (Albany, NY: State University of New York, 1970).
44. Karl Albrecht and S. Albrecht, *The Creative Corporation* (Homewood IL: Dow Jones-Irwin, 1987).

Figure 14-8

Activity Schedule Memory

There are three types of memory stores used by managers in their active working memory to plan and implement. The most basic is episodic memory of past routines or projects worked on, observed, or otherwise studied. An assemblage of similar activity sequences become an activity sequence (AS) script that is stored in script memory. Managers with superior abstract thinking skills advance beyond learning and improvising activity schedule scripts (ASSs). The production scripts they learn become the basis for learning rules about what to do and what not to do in implementing plans in a firm and in a market. These rules are stored in a special part of memory called the memory store for production rules. Such managers are also likely to have superior prospective memory.

Source: Kay Stafford, Rosemary Key, and Peter Dickson, "A Theory of Activity Schedule Memory," College of Home Economics Working Paper, 88-01 (The Ohio State University, July 1988).

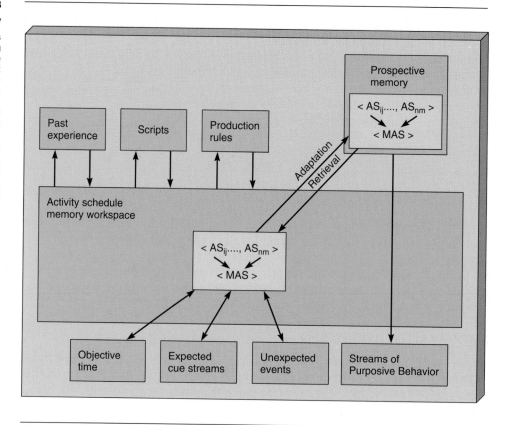

longer memory frames, they plan further into the future, and they are superior time managers.[45] An organization that continuously strives to learn how to do everything it does better must be led by managers with such skills.

Time Management and Remembering to Get Things Done

Prospective memory is a very special sort of memory that is needed in action planning. Episodic memory concentrates on past events. When using prospective memory, however, a manager deliberately plans, rehearses, and remembers to do things that will affect the future. Prospective memory requires recall of activities that have been done so far in an activity sequence, things that have yet to be done, the order in which they must be completed, and activities that have to be executed today.

The master activity schedule (MAS) is a manager's mental diary. It is called a master activity schedule because it combines, merges, integrates, and prioritizes activities from several different AS scripts that a manager is currently supervising or implementing (see Figure 14-9). Every day a manager is doing several things at once, making more or less progress on several production process activity sequences. It is akin to juggling several balls in the air at one time. The MAS does this juggling. It does so by first assembling the set of n (number) activity sequences that the manager is currently

45. Elliott Jacques, *The Form of Time* (New York: Crane, Russak, 1982); and Walter Kiechel, "How Executives Think," *Fortune,* February 4, 1985, 127–28.

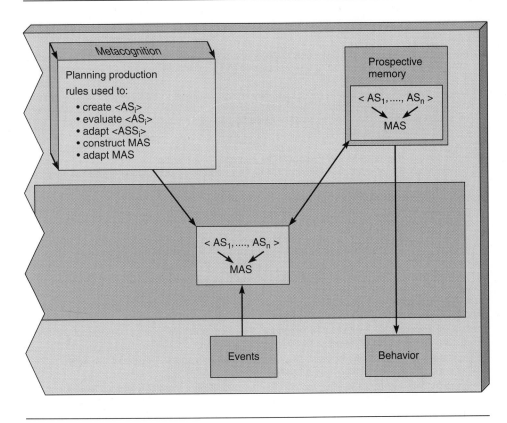

Figure 14-9

How a Manager's Prospective Memory Operates

This figure describes how a busy manager intuitively remembers what to do next. Prospective memory is the part of our memories that enables us to think and plan ahead, load such plans into a "what I/we have to do" memory store, and retrieve the activity sequences into working or active memory where they direct purposeful behavior. Metacognition is our self-awareness of our implementation planning and time management skills—how we use external prompts such as lists, diaries, and charts. These how-to-remember rules are stored in a tool kit in our memories. Some managers are very aware of their skills, are able to use their time management tool kits very well, and have very organized prospective memories. Other managers do not have tool kits of planning production rules or do not use what they have, and as a result they have very fuzzy prospective memories and are very bad time managers, always late and forgetful. The other terms in the figure are defined below:

ASi   = The ith production process activity schedule

$<ASi>$ = A set of production process activity schedules that the manager is responsible for executing or being executed by others.

$<ASSi>$ = A set of activity schedule scripts.

MAS   = The master activity schedule that merges a set of ASs.

undertaking. It then chooses which activities or tasks from different projects should be done first, which next, and so on. The DMAS is the daily master activity schedule for a working day.

A manager with a very routine job follows a single activity sequence each day, day in and day out. There is no variety and no need for MAS skills in prospective memory. On the other hand, the efficiency and effectiveness of a very busy executive involved in implementing a dozen projects at once depends on his or her master activity scheduling in prospective memory. Executives without such intuitive mental skills may be creative in terms of coming up with ideas, but will be hopeless at getting things done and coping creatively with unexpected events that disturb their routines. Such coping requires changing individual AS scripts and the MAS in response to new information from the environment. A manager with excellent production rule and prospective memory skills is commonly known as a good time manager. Some of the skills (and production rules) associated with good time management are described in Table 14-3.[46]

Combining Intuition and Scientific Management

Activity schedule memory theory also helps explain why quality circles and worker consultations are so useful in implementation. Managers and lower-level employees cannot

46. Table 14-3 is based in part on William Oncken, Jr., and Donald L. Wass, "Management Time: Who's Got the Monkey," *Harvard Business Review,* November/December 1974, 75–80; and Warren Keith Schilit, "A Manager's Guide to Efficient Time Management," *Personnel Journal,* September 1983, 736–42.

Table 14-3
Ten Time-Management Tips (Production Rules)

1. Develop long-range, major goals, and projects and a short-run "to do" master activity schedule (MAS), which is a combination of tasks related to the activity schedules of different projects that you are executing in parallel.

2. Make a list each day of the six most important things you have to do from your master activity schedule. Write them in a good pocket diary and update them each new day. Focus your day on the 20 percent of the activities that produce 80 percent of your productivity (Pareto's Principle). Concentrate your effort.

3. Group tasks around when they need to be done, and do all the most demanding thinking tasks at the time of the day that you think best (for example, if you are a morning person do them in the morning). Group other tasks around where they need to be done to avoid wasted traveling time.

4. Schedule and rehearse your day while you are exercising, washing, shaving, or applying your makeup in the morning. Think about starting and *finishing* each key activity or task. Try to anticipate and avoid problems.

5. If you are a procrastinator, do tasks you do not want to do first. They will then be off your mind and you will have a sense of achievement and a more positive attitude the rest of the day.

6. Do not take on more than you can manage. Good time managers know when they are over-committed; poor time managers do not and use the overload as an excuse for the lateness and sloppiness of everything they do. Reserve one or two hours a day for unexpected tasks, delays, and so forth.

7. Control interruptions. Use a muted telephone answering machine to eliminate distractions and to keep in touch with other people's activities.

8. Plan meetings, keep them focused, and conduct them with speed. Do not let the least prepared participants dictate how a meeting is run.

9. Do everything you do as well as you can. Better to do it right the first time than waste time and effort having to undo it and do it again (a basic principle of quality management).

10. Do not wait to be told to do something. Do not ask what to do. Suggest, recommend, act, advise, and report. Take the initiative. Do not do work that can be delegated to capable subordinates. Doing tasks others can do is often a way of avoiding what you know only you can do, and have to do (a form of procrastination).

be expected to show initiative and creativity if they do not understand how their tasks fit into the big picture, the larger production process, or AS script. When they develop such an understanding, what they do starts to make sense and they feel much more a part of a team and interested in the overall outcome. Everyone is on the same page of the same script. Participants are also then able to step back and suggest creative ways to speed up activity sequences (crashing the critical path), reduce costs, and increase output quality. Workers and managers also become each other's customers in the activity sequence as they recognize that their success depends on working with each other, rather than warring with each other. Not all managers and employees can be expected to respond equally to becoming involved in the bigger picture, just as few second lieutenants are capable of thinking like generals. But, at worst, it is likely that most suggestions will, at least, ever-so-slightly improve the efficiency and effectiveness of implementation.

The problem with managers relying on intuition to create action plans and activity schedules, as just described, is that these internal memory structures cannot be shared readily with all the individuals and teams working on implementation. A formal action plan path analysis allows everyone to know where, how, and at what time they fit into the roll-out (see the Rationality in Practice box on page 534). It also enables the organization to pass on to future managers the wisdom and action-oriented implementation insights that the experienced manager has in his or her head.[47]

1. What type of network organization might you set up to offer a nationwide cut-flower delivery service to compete against Teleflora or 1-800-FLOWERS, which link a network of thousands of florist stores? What other organizations and established companies might be part of the network? What would your firm actually do? What flowers would you concentrate on?

2. What sort of training should a marketing graduate be given to succeed in a company that uses cross-functional teams to manage a network of out-sourcing relationships? What specific technical skills do you think a marketing graduate should have in order to excel in such an organization? What marketing courses do you think should be required to train such a marketing graduate? What courses currently required for marketing majors might be dropped or made optional?

3. How would you organize the marketing of a start-up operation in a new country? How would you staff the organization in a way that would lead to the greatest competitive rationality?

4. How should a firm organize its marketing when it does not use direct selling but relies on direct marketing through mail order and magazine advertising? (Hint: Think about what marketing function is most important for such a firm.)

5. Banks are typically organized with their sales operations separate from marketing. Sales operations is the function that is in charge of branch management and tellers. In recent years, a number of banks have become dissatisfied with their marketing efforts. What might be the problem and how might it be addressed?

6. How might a firm improve the effectiveness of its product managers without switching to cross-functional team management?

7. In what order are tasks crashed in an activity schedule to increase the speed of implementation (that is, increase time competition)?

8. Figure 14-7 illustrates how we learn an activity schedule script. Use the figure to describe how we learn a golf swing, a tennis serve, to turn on skis, and to swim. According to the process described by this figure, when is it best to get expert coaching? What implications does this have for organizations and individuals developing implementation routines?

9. How might you test whether a manager has the desired intuitive action planning skills? What in a manager's thinking, personal planning, and past behavior might provide good evidence of the presence of such skills?

10. What games do you think require prospective memory skills?

11. What are the advantages and disadvantages of a manager having a secretary keep the executive appointment diary, screen incoming calls, type, open mail, and so on?

47. Benjamin B. Tregoe and Peter M. Tobia, "An Action-Oriented Approach to Strategy," *Journal of Business Strategy* 11.1 (January/February 1990), 16–21.

Rationality in Practice:

Scheduling Tools

To create an activity schedule document, inexpensive computer software can be used to describe the activity sequences, estimate the time and resource needs, and generate a critical path and Gantt chart, all in less than an afternoon. It can later be refined by consultating with the parties responsible for the different activities. At most, it will take about 10 to 20 work hours and is a task ideally suited to help a brand, product, or project manager with his or her planned marketing activities. In addition to the inexpensive computer software that is available, several worksheets and visual aids are available to help implement the product-market plan (see figures). The support systems exist to help a marketing manager and cross-functional team plan and implement a project's AS script. What is often absent is a greater *commitment* of time, training, and human resources to the rudimentary application of scientific management to action planning. Even a simple task matrix—with weeks across the top, tasks down the

Action Plans

Prepare *action plans* for programs which are required to achieve profit center five-year objectives and strategies. Identify:

1. *Why* the *action plan* will help achieve profit center objectives and strategies.
2. *How* the *action plan* will be executed (detailed explanation).
3. *Who* is responsible for the *action plan*, the *action plan* name and number, and identify the objective number if the *action plan* is based on an objective (and/or the strategy if the *action plan* is based on a strategy).
4. *When* each step of the *action plan* will be complete.
5. *What* will be the impact of completion of the *action plan* on sales, profit contribution, capital expenditures, and other areas of applicable (such as expense, cost savings).

ACTION PLAN INSTRUCTIONS

Prepare *action plans* for programs which are required to achieve five year objectives and strategies.

a. Identify who is responsible for the *action plan*, the *action plan* name and number, and identify the objective number if the *action plan* is based on an objective (and/or the strategy letter if the *action plan* is based on a strategy).

b. Provide a rationale indicating how the *action plan* will help achieve division or profit center objectives and strategies.

c. Provide a complete comprehensive explanation of how the *action plan* will be executed.

d. Provide a timetable for completion of intermediate steps and completion of the entir *action plan*.

e. Give estimated inpact of completion of the *action plan* on sales, profit contribution, capital expenditures, and other areas if applicable (such as expense, cost savings).

f. List support required from other areas of Multifoods or from outside the company to complete *action plan*.

Figure 14-9: Examples of Action Planning Worksheets

The worksheet on this page and the following page can help a manager construct an activity sequence script (ASS) and monitor it. Source: Reproduced with permission from Hopkins, David S. (1981), *The Marketing Plan*, New York: The Conference Board, Report No. 801.

Examples of Action Planning Worksheets

The worksheet on this page and the tools illustrated on the following page can help a manager construct an activity sequence script (ASS) and monitor it.

Source: Reproduced with permission from David S. Hopkins, *The Marketing Plan* (New York: The Conference Board, Report No. 801, 1981).

534

page, and the initials of executives responsible for implementation and supervision in the cells—is better than nothing. A firm should also require such action planning from its advertising agency and other outside contractors whose quality of service is increasingly judged on its speed as well as its content. A firm's routines are its genes. Improve its routines and you improve its genes and its chances of future success.* A company culture that emphasizes time management and rewards activity schedule memory skills will find that almost all of its routines will be improved. Action planning is not just necessary to execute strategy. It is a crucial competitive rationality skill that can improve a firm's production routines in all aspects of its business. A marketing manager who lacks such skills is a manager in name only.

*See Richard R. Nelson and Sidney G. Winter, *An Evolutionary Theory of Economic Change* (Cambridge, MA: Harvard University Press, 1982) and the theory of competitive rationality in Chapter 1.

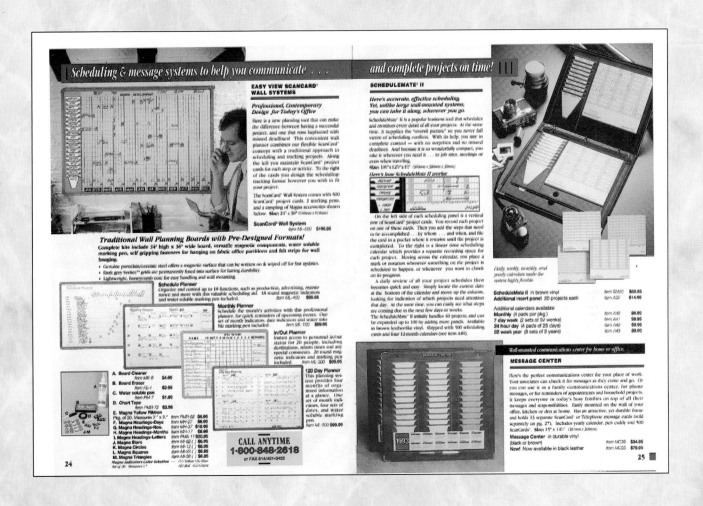

12. How are football coaching and directing of a ballet similar to planning and implementing a competitive marketing program?

13. The recent discovery of old takes of early Charlie Chaplin movies has revealed that cameo scenes were shot hundreds of times to produce the marvelous spontaneity and impudence of the little tramp. Chaplin was a perfectionist who demonstrated the value of really caring about execution and implementation. What lessons might marketers learn from Chaplin's work habits? In your answer, explain the crucial difference between making a movie and making a market.

14. Why will preparing a critical path and hanging it on the wall in a public place, where progress to date on the project can be seen by all, work particularly well in a clan culture?

15. Why should a chief executive of a company encourage all functional areas (such as accounting, procurement, distribution, manufacturing, employee services, R&D, design) in a firm to contract themselves out for hire to other companies that are not direct competitors? What are the risks, and how can they be minimized?

16. Some experts have argued that next to the president, the most important person in the modern organization is the vice president of Continuous Improvement, who is responsible for continuously improving organization structure, systems and processes. Other experts disagree. Please discuss both sides of the argument.

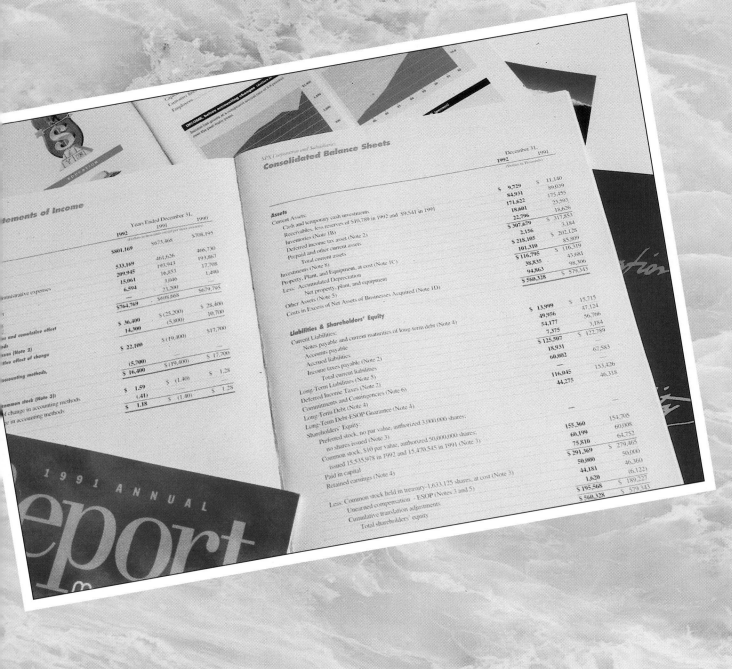

Forecasting, Budgeting, and Controlling

"Goals are dreams with deadlines."

Anonymous

"I hope that I may always desire more than I can accomplish."

Michelangelo

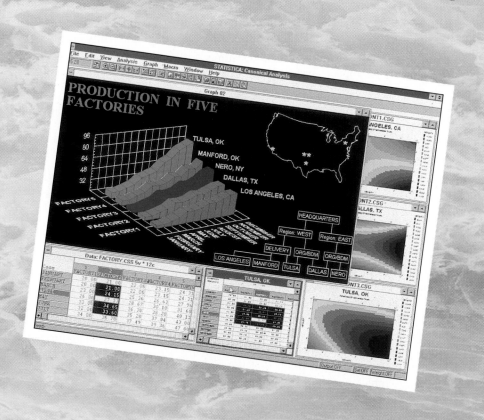

*B*udgeting is an organizational process that involves making forecasts based on the proposed marketing strategy and programs. The forecasts are then used to construct a budgeted profit and loss statement. An important aspect of budgeting is deciding how to allocate the last available dollars from all of the proposed programs within the marketing plan. The control section of this chapter explains the output control process; how to measure and report performance; and how to use the information to identify performance variances, diagnose problems, and improve the quality of future performance. This chapter builds on a number of discussions in earlier chapters, particularly, developing an understanding of cost structure (Chapter 2), discovering what the target consumer wants (Chapter 3), positioning and differentiating the product (Chapter 8), determining how the target consumer judges quality, and designing such quality and added value into the cost structure of the product (Chapter 9). Keep the following key ideas in mind as you read this chapter:

- It is important that the decision-making team understand how to use the various budgeting tools available. The use of such tools will result in a bottom line–oriented marketing plan that is likely to come closer to meeting financial objectives.

- Because budgeting is often a political process, a decision maker must be a skilled politician as well as competitively rational.

- A decision maker who lacks an understanding of basic management accounting can be easily bamboozled by numbers, charts, and budgeting procedures, which can reduce the decision maker's effectiveness at gaining resources and sensibly allocating resources.

- Accounting is sometimes a magical numbers game—now you see them, now you don't. Sales and costs are made to appear and disappear depending on whether the accounts are being prepared for tax purposes, the shareholder, or management. This must not happen in marketing control. It introduces dangerous biases and uncertainty that can dramatically reduce the competitive rationality of the firm.

- A firm that undertakes continuous consumer satisfaction surveys and has user-friendly decision support systems will behave with greater competitive rationality than its rivals.

- A firm's competitive rationality depends greatly on how closely its budgeting routines and control systems reflect reality.

The Profit and Loss (P&L) Statement

Since each business or marketing plan should end with a summary statement of the forecast sales, costs, and bottom-line profit for the year ahead, we begin this chapter with the profit and loss statement. In concept, the profit and loss (P&L) statement is simple; in practice, it is difficult to construct because its elements can only be estimated. Businesses first prepare a planned P&L statement; then at the end of the year the actual P&L will be computed and it can then be compared to the planned P&L statement. This kind of analysis contributes significantly to competitive rationality by providing the firm with an opportunity to learn about how and why actual performance varies from planned performance. A discussion of the specifics of such an analysis appears later in the section on profit and loss control. Here, we discuss how a P&L statement is assembled by using an example.

Table 15-1
Example of a Profit and Loss Budget Statement for the ACME Company

Inputs	Current year (actual)	% Change projected	Next year (projected)
Market sales (units)	700,000	10.0%	770,000
Our market share	28%		28%
Our unit sales	196,000		215,600
Unit price	$100.00		$100.00
Variable manufacturing costs	$50.00		$50.00
Variable distribution costs	$15.00		$15.00

Fixed costs (in $000s)

	Current year (actual)	% Change projected	Next year (projected)
Advertising	$1,707	0.0%	$1,707
Sales promotion	$2,568	0.0%	$2,568
Selling	$300	0.0%	$300
R&D	$175	0.0%	$175
Administration overhead	$1,300	0.0%	$1,300

Profit and loss estimates (all figures in $000s)		Current year (actual)		Next year (projected)
Total Revenue		$19,600		$21,560
Total Variable Cost		$12,740		$14,014
Total Contribution		$6,860		$7,546
Advertising	$1,707		$1,707	
Sales promotion	$2,568		$2,568	
Selling	$300		$300	
R&D	$175		$175	
Administration overhead	$1,300		$1,300	
Total Fixed Costs		$6,050		$6,050
Operating Profit		$810		$1,496

P&L projections for the ACME Company are presented in Table 15-1. The planned P&L statement requires several inputs. The projection of sales is based upon estimates of overall market size as well as company share. Planned price and estimates of variable and fixed activity costs come from company records and the marketing plan. A simple P&L spreadsheet provides the capability of playing "what if" by changing the inputs and determining the impact of such changes on the bottom line. Before moving ahead with a discussion of budgeting and forecasting, several accounting issues need to be discussed.

Allocating Costs

Cost allocation was discussed in Chapter 2. Cost distortions occur because joint factory, marketing, and administrative overhead costs are allocated using inappropriate methods, such as direct labor cost, materials cost, or production processing time. Once upon a time these may have been acceptable accounting practices. The cost distortions were minor because the direct costs were much greater than the shared or joint costs that had to be allocated. The problem today is that a much higher percentage of production and marketing costs are shared among many more product items and product lines. The solution is activity-based costing.[1] Shared marketing and other overhead costs are first attributed to activities (such as selling and service). An analysis is then done to determine how much of these activities (measured in time and cost) are spent making, marketing, and servicing specific products. The results may not be very accurate, but it is better to be within 20 percent when measuring how much of the actual organizational resources are allocated to a product than to be assuredly wrong (at times by as much as 100 percent) using outdated allocation methods. Competitive rationality depends on minimizing the biases that can obstruct the understanding of internal costs (and cost structures) just as much as minimizing the biases that obstruct an understanding of the external market environment.

Treating Marketing Costs as Income Generators

Many firms classify marketing costs as overhead expenses rather than as part of the cost of goods sold in their profit and loss statements. Direct marketing costs are just as much a part of the cost of goods sold as production costs; yet, for reasons of accounting convention, they are often not treated as such. It is difficult to determine how much the marketing function has suffered from having its costs categorized as overheads. Overheads are often considered less productive and necessary than direct costs. As a result, they tend to be trimmed first in hard times. In contrast, the manufacturing costs of goods sold are viewed as a necessary part of doing business and are less frequently questioned. How marketing costs are identified have strong implications for marketing budgets and control. Chapter 1 described the problems that can arise when managers become rigid in the way they view activities. A hundred years of P&L accounts characterizing marketing as an overhead cost rather than as a necessary, *productive* activity cost may have contributed to the extinction of more firms than any other bias in management thinking. The situation can be rectified by the realistic correction of some old-fashioned accounting practices.

Treating Marketing Costs as Investments

A further important problem with marketing costs is that the traditional P&L statement almost never treats any marketing expense as an investment to be depreciated over time rather than expensed in the current year or period. When a new product is launched, the initial investment in R&D as well as the additional product management, advertising, and sales promotion produce cash flows that extend beyond the current accounting period. Expenditures on activities that produce these effects are, by definition, investments. They produce a future income stream. According to conventional accounting practice, these costs should be spread over current and future reporting periods in proportion to the revenue generation in each period. Unfortunately, conventional accounting only appreciates tangible assets, such as plants and buildings. It seldom depreciates intangibles such as market development or R&D investments.

1. Robin Cooper and Robert S. Kaplan, "Measure Costs Right: Make the Right Decisions," *Harvard Business Review*, September/October 1988, 96–103.

Budgeting involves converting all of the planned programs, tactics, and tasks into costs and subtracting these costs from expected sales. Most firms have standard budgeting procedures and use standardized forms to capture information (see Figure 15-1). How budgeting is actually done in a firm depends upon the following factors:

1. **Organizational culture.** While there are budgeting fundamentals common to most firms, any given firm may have relatively unique procedures or budgeting routines.

2. **Organizational politics.** A firm's political structure determines who controls total expenditures and who allocates resources.

3. **Control over information.** Budgets cannot be constructed without the correct historical or current information.

4. **Decentralization of profit responsibility.** How the budgets for operating divisions and product groups are approved is related to a firm's profit responsibility structure.

5. **Composition of the senior management team.** The budgeting skills and career specialization of senior managers come into play.

6. **Importance of the project.** This is related to the rewards and sanctions associated with the outcomes for key people.

No single universal budgeting procedure is used by all firms. Figure 15-2 presents the results of a study on the use of three common budgeting procedures.[2] Only 7 percent of the firms use a bottom-up method, in which budgets are developed by line managers and submitted to higher-level managers. Sixty percent use a bottom-up/top-down procedure, in which a lower-level manager's initial budget recommendations are scrutinized by upper management before approval. About one in four of the firms surveyed use a top-down/bottom-up procedure, in which budget constraints are passed down from top management, and line budgets are then submitted by managers subject to such constraints. The remainder of the firms used a different method. Figure 15-3 presents the characteristics of each of these budgeting procedures. The bottom-up/top-down budgeting approach has more of a market orientation than the top-down/bottom-up approach because it is initially developed by executives who are closer to the market and, hence, more likely to understand the market.

Budgeting is both a rational and a political process. Rational budgeting attempts to allocate resources where they will produce the greatest contribution to financial and marketing objectives. Political budgeting enables those individuals with the most power and influence to obtain the most resources for their projects, whatever the financial or marketplace consequences. This may very likely lead to an inefficient allocation of resources.[3] Therefore, the decision maker must display a good political sense as well as a rational understanding. This also explains the great advantage of using a cross-functional team approach where major budgeting decisions in a division are made by

Forecasting and Budgeting

---

2. Nigel F. Percy, "The Marketing Budgeting Process: Marketing Management Implications," *Journal of Marketing* 51 (October 1987), 45–59. This study focused on U.K. manufacturing firms. The budgeting practices of U.S. firms may be different.
3. See Percy, "The Marketing Budgeting Process." Also see D.C. Hambrick and C.C. Snow, "A Contextual Model of Strategic Decision Making in Organizations," in *Academy of Management Proceedings*, R.L. Taylor, ed. (Ada, OH: Academy of Management Journal, 1977); and Richard M. Cyert and James G. March, *A Behavioral Theory of the Firm* (Englewood Cliffs, N.J.: Prentice-Hall, 1963).

Marketing Budget Proposal For: _____

Summary		19___ Actual	19___ Actual	19___ Original vote	19___ Estimated	19___ Proposed	19___ Approved
Sales	$						
Income before marketing	$						
Income before marketing to sales	%						
Marketing (A)	$						
Marketing to sales	%						
Marketing includ. allocations (B)	$						
Operating income before adj. (D)	$						
Operating income to sales	%						
Population	M						
Sales milex ($/1000 pop.)	$						
Marketing milex ($/1000 pop.)	$						

Marketing Budget Categories

	Actual	Actual	Original vote	Estimated	Proposed	Approved
1 Magazines						
2 Newspaper rop						
3 Newspaper supplements						
4 Radio						
5 Television						
6 Posters						
7 Special media						
8 Agency fees						
9 Trade media						
11 Consumer non-price incentives						
13 Consumer price incentives						
14 Sales conferences						
15 Merchandising materials						
17 Trade allowances						
18 Trade free goods						
19 Sundries						
Marketing (A)						
Allocations of publicity						
Alloc. of fgt. on unindent. merch. mat.						
Alloc. of military food marketing						
Marketing includ. alloc. (B)						
Package development (C)						
Market research (C)						

(A) Marketing — Total of budget categories.

(B) Marketing including allocations — Marketing plus allocations of publicity, freight on unidentified merchandising materials, and military food marketing.

(C) Already deducted via administration expenses in arriving at income before marketing.

(D) Operating income before adjustments — "Income before marketing" less "Marketing including allocations" before corporate adjustments.

Per _____

Date _____

Figure 15-1
An Example of a Marketing Budgeting Worksheet

Note that the estimates go through several revisions and some costs are allocated because these costs are expended on marketing several products and cannot be directly estimated.

Source: Reproduced with permission from David S. Hopkins, *The Marketing Plan* (New York, The Conference Board Report #801, 1981), 95.

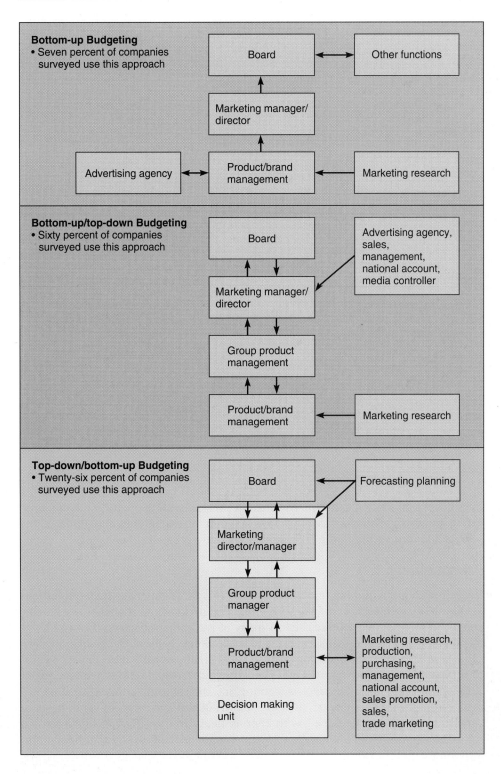

Bottom-up Budgeting
• Seven percent of companies surveyed use this approach

Bottom-up/top-down Budgeting
• Sixty percent of companies surveyed use this approach

Top-down/bottom-up Budgeting
• Twenty-six percent of companies surveyed use this approach

Figure 15.2

Three Different Marketing Budgeting Routines

In a study of marketing budgeting, 93 percent of the firms surveyed employed a budgeting process or routine that was either bottom-up, bottom-up/top down, or top down/bottom-up. The third process is clearly the most directive, and the researchers found that this approach was related to a situation of financial stringency and budget constraints.

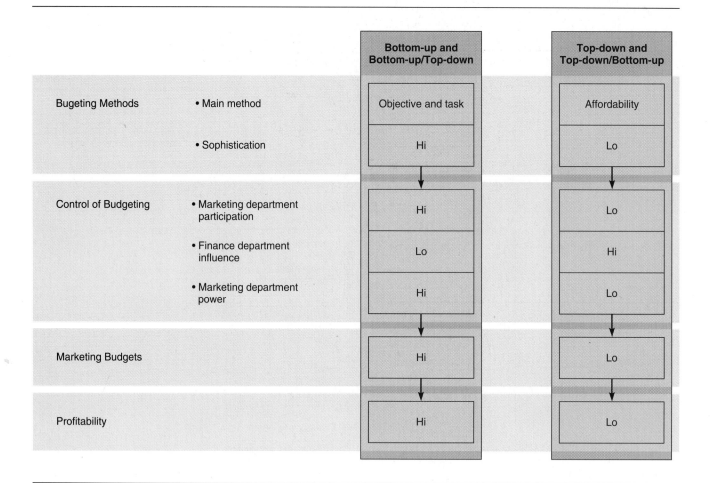

		Bottom-up and Bottom-up/Top-down	Top-down and Top-down/Bottom-up
Bugeting Methods	• Main method	Objective and task	Affordability
	• Sophistication	Hi	Lo
Control of Budgeting	• Marketing department participation	Hi	Lo
	• Finance department influence	Lo	Hi
	• Marketing department power	Hi	Lo
Marketing Budgets		Hi	Lo
Profitability		Hi	Lo

Figure 15-3

Characteristics of Bottom-Up and Top-Down Budgeting

The top-down approach displayed in this figure suggests that the finance executives are either politically dominant or possess greater competitive rationality skills than the marketing executives. The bottom-up approach suggests the opposite.

the CEO in consultation with a management team representing production, sales, marketing, purchasing, and finance. This approach minimizes, but does not eliminate, the politics and thus increases the chances of competitively rational budgeting.

Forecasting

Budgeting always requires a forecast of sales and costs. Traditionally these projections are based on the history of past sales and costs. Past performance should be the starting point of a forecast, but as discussed in many of the earlier chapters, the purpose of marketing planning and management is to make things happen, things like dramatically increasing sales and reducing costs. If the marketing plan has no impact on history, then it is very much a status quo plan. Many plans operate this way intentionally. If the marketing strategy in place is working and the company wants assured performance from the product-market, then the marketing plan and competitive strategy will very likely be more of the same—with improvements. In this situation, and assuming the external environment is not expected to change dramatically, then historical projections are quite reasonable and often quite accurate.[4]

4. For a comprehensive guide to forecasting, see David M. Georgoff and Robert G. Murdick, "Manager's Guide to Forecasting," *Harvard Business Review*, January/February 1986, 110–20.

Expert Opinion: People who have expert knowledge about an industry are surveyed to get their opinions of the industry's outlook. Their forecasts and justifications are often then circulated between them and experts are asked to adjust their estimates based on shared information. This is called the Delphi method of forecasting. Relative to other forecasting techniques, experts are best at scenario forecasting: estimating the effects of extraordinary events such as a change in government policy, technology, or the economy.

Survey of Buyer Intentions: Buyers are surveyed and asked to estimate their purchase intentions. This is appropriate when buyers have clear intentions and are willing to express them. Some trade associations, trade magazines, or market research firms undertake such surveys for an industry (for instance the Annual Survey of Buying Power taken by *Sales and Marketing Management*). When the state of the economy greatly influences sales, then surveys of buying intentions are quite useful for forecasting.

Sales Force Survey: Gathering feedback from the sales force is less effective than directly surveying buyers, but it is easier to do. The problem is that salespeople can be too optimistic or too pessimistic depending on their current enthusiasm and confidence. Sales force surveys can be useful in estimating the impact of new products, services, strategies, and programs that buyers are not yet aware of and in estimating likely changes in regional demand.

Historical Sales Projections: Past sales are plotted and statistical trend projections are made. This forecast is often broken down into a trend component, a cycle component, and a seasonal component. Historical projections are best when the market is stable and past marketing strategy will be continued in the future. Most forecasts start with such a sales projection and then are adjusted by the use of some of the other forecasting techniques.

Input-Output Modeling: Used by economists to project industry demand, a model is constructed using economic determinants of demand (inputs) that forecasts sales (output). It can be very reliable in stable economic conditions but not very reliable when major changes occur in the marketplace, such as the development of new competitive technologies or an unexpected global political event (a war in the Middle East or the collapse of the USSR, for example). The most sophisticated predictive modeling is done by experts called econometricians. In recent years they have had a hard time with their predictions because the major drivers of the economy have been very unstable.

Figure 15-4
A Summary of Forecasting Techniques

Forecasting becomes much more difficult when a sharp shift in marketing strategy is proposed, such as a shift in product positioning.[5] The other major contributors to the unreliability of historical forecasts are unexpected changes in the economy or in competitor behavior. Sales forecasts must then be generated from expert opinion as well as customer and sales force estimates (see Figure 15-4).[6]

The forecasting techniques described in Figure 15-4 are geared toward projecting demand without explicit consideration of changes in the firm's marketing strategy. The innovative manager faces the problem of estimating what the firm's share of market sales will be *if* the current strategy is changed. The spreadsheet format in Table 15-1 is an effective tool for marketing budgeting because it enables planners to conduct "what if" analyses; that is, "If the advertising budget is increased by 20 percent, and market share subsequently changes to 25 percent, what is the impact on profit?" The following section briefly describes methods of estimating how market share and sales will respond to changes in marketing strategy.

Forecasting Sales Response

Market response refers to the degree of sales change that occurs in response to changes in marketing strategy. It is more commonly referred to as *elasticity,* which is defined

5. David L. Hurwood, Elliot S. Grossman, and Earl L. Bailey, "Sales Forecasting" (New York: The Conference Board #730, 1978).
6. Kenneth R. Evans and John L. Schlacter, "The Role of Sales Managers and Salespeople in a Marketing Information System," *The Journal of Personal Selling and Sales Management,* November 1985, 49–58; and E. Taylor, "Using the Delphi Method to Define Marketing Problems," *Business,* October/November 1984, 16–22.

Table 15-2
Estimating Sales Response to Changes in Marketing Strategy

Approach	Advantages	Disadvantages
Judgment		
Based on managers' past observations of how sales are related to marketing effort.	Managers have good insight and a bird's-eye view of the market. Also, low cost and easy to obtain.	Subjective estimates can be very biased because managers only remember past programs that resulted in extreme outcomes.
Consumer Surveys		
Direct questioning of consumers. Examples: conjoint studies, copy testing, purchase intentions.	Only moderately expensive.	Not applicable to all tactics (such as very new product concepts or ad budget decisions).
Test Market Experiments		
Manipulate key marketing variables to evaluate their effects on sales and profits. Random assignment of test markets/subjects to treatment conditions.	Can isolate the effects of marketing effort on sales and examine interaction effects. High validity, if test not contaminated by competitor behavior.	Most costly. Usually outside expertise is needed. Slow.
Statistical Demand Analysis		
Mathematical model of demand that estimates relationships between demand and marketing.	With enough data, highly valid. Allows many factors to be considered and provides estimates of optimal effort and spending.	Extensive data needed. Very high cost. Only covers the efforts tried in the past. Usually requires outside expertise.

formally as the percentage change in sales relative to the percentage change in price or some other marketing variable. How can a manager develop estimates of how sales will change if marketing strategy (price, advertising budget, sales force allocation, and so on) is adjusted? There are four general techniques, which we describe below. The advantages and disadvantages of each method are summarized in Table 15-2.

Subjective Judgment

Subjective judgment involves obtaining a manager's best guess as to how sales or market share will change if marketing strategy is changed. Experienced managers are the most accessible source of market response information and can provide reliable sales response estimates provided they are asked properly. It is useful to interview several managers to obtain sales response figures, which can then be roughly verified. It is also important to provide them with explicit questions that cover all plausible customer and competitor reactions.[7]

---

7. Hermann Simon, "Pricing Opportunities—and How to Exploit Them," *Sloan Management Review,* Winter 1992, 55–65.

Consumer Surveys

This method involves telephone, mail, or personal interview surveys of consumers to obtain their reactions to alternative marketing strategies (such as different prices, ad campaigns, or product descriptions).

Experimentation

Experimentation occurs when the firm purposely manipulates marketing variables over time or in different regions to assess the impact of such changes on sales and profits. For example, a consumer goods manufacturer experimented with its price for a product over several months by using different price levels in three different groups of geographic markets. It is important to maintain as much control as possible in an experiment to eliminate the possibility of sales results being affected by any variables other than the one being manipulated.

Statistical Demand Analysis

This technique involves obtaining a statistical estimate of the relationships between sales and important marketing variables using actual sales and marketing data over time. It requires the relatively sophisticated econometric modeling of a great deal of data collected for many time periods. A statistical demand analysis generally provides the most accurate information on elasticities (because it uses actual sales data and accounts for the influence of many variables), but it is extremely complicated to implement.

Sales Force Budgeting

We now turn to a discussion of how to set the budget for each specific marketing activity. In doing so we focus on the two major components of marketing budgeting: sales force and advertising budgeting. Very similar issues and problems arise in setting the budgets for other marketing activities and projects.

If the work-load approach has been used to determine how sales territories should be staffed to meet the selling objectives, then this information can also form the basis of the sales budget. The budget can be built by estimating the likely compensation and expenses involved in servicing each territory. Historical information will help in this estimation but may have to be adjusted if call rates, call time, and other duties have changed. The cost of keeping the sales force in the field is the total cost of serving all of the territories. The sales management overhead expenses and salaries must be added to estimate the overall budget. The telemarketing group may operate under a separate budget that is funded from the direct sales it generates.

Rather than a line-item budget, which details expenses item-by-item, a regional sales manager is often given an overall program budget, which enables him or her to juggle expense overruns. This approach also gives the sales manager the opportunity to spend money where he or she thinks it will produce the greatest return. Average personal selling costs are about 14 percent of gross sales.[8] Because a significant percentage of personal selling expenses are directly tied to sales, personal selling budgets tend to be a little easier to estimate and control than other marketing expenses. Many firms compare selling expense-to-sales ratios between regions to help control costs and to estimate future budgets.

8. William A. O'Connell and William Kennan, Jr., "The Shape of Things to Come," *Sales & Marketing Mangement,* January 1990, 36–41.

Advertising Budgeting

An unresolved (and perhaps unresolvable) argument has continued for years over how to set an advertising budget. At the heart of the problem is deciding how best to estimate the effect of advertising on sales. As discussed above (and illustrated later in this chapter in the section on marginal budgeting), various techniques can be used to estimate sales response, but many firms are not familiar with them. Instead, they have concluded that if you cannot measure advertising's separate, unique effect on buyer behavior or sales, then what is the point of setting target performance objectives? This, in part, explains why a number of more traditional, simple rules are used, even by very large companies, to decide how much to spend on advertising during the planning period. Several of these rules are now discussed before an alternative approach based on the objective-task method is described.

Percentage of Sales

The most common way of determining how much to spend is to project sales and spend a prespecified percentage of projected sales on advertising. It is useful to find out how much, as a percentage of sales, the industry as a whole spends on advertising.[9] The amount varies considerably among product-markets. In the pharmaceuticals and cosmetics industries, a company may spend 20 percent or more of its annual sales on advertising; food, soap, and cleaner manufacturers spend about 10 percent of their sales on advertising; the two major U.S. soft-drink companies spend about 5 percent; retail chains spend about 2 percent; and automobile manufacturers between 1 percent and 5 percent, with the smaller foreign manufacturers spending a higher percentage.

If a market is efficient, then the competitors in the industry might be expected to learn to spend about the right amount on advertising. If they were spending too little or too much, then presumably a new or established competitor would discover this, through experimentation and gain a major advantage by doing something different. The Rationality in Practice box on page 552 presents two such cases. Each deviated from the standard percentage-of-sales method of setting the advertising budget, but one became a success story and the other did not. Note that if the competitors in a market stick to a percentage-of-sales rule, then they are setting their advertising voice share in proportion to their current market share. This is an implicit acceptance of the competitive status quo, and it implies a "don't rock the boat" collusion.

Again, if markets are efficient, then the reason that some industries spend more on advertising than others is presumably because advertising is more effective in those markets compared with other marketing expenses (such as promotions to distributors). If this is true, the percentage of sales an industry spends on advertising tells us something about the effectiveness of advertising and the importance of advertising innovations or a new brand image in that industry's market. Changes in spending, such as those revealed in Figure 15-5, also tell us something about the changing effectiveness of different marketing tactics over time. Perhaps spending has swung too far in favor of promotions, and in the 1990s, spending on advertising will increase again.

Competitive Parity, Plus

The problem with using the percentage of sales to determine an advertising budget is that it ignores many environmental realities. For example, a new entry attempting to penetrate a market must at least match the advertising expenditure of the competitor

9. Paul Farris and Mark Albion, "Determinants of the Advertising-to-Sales Ratio," *Journal of Advertising Research* (December 1981), 7–16.

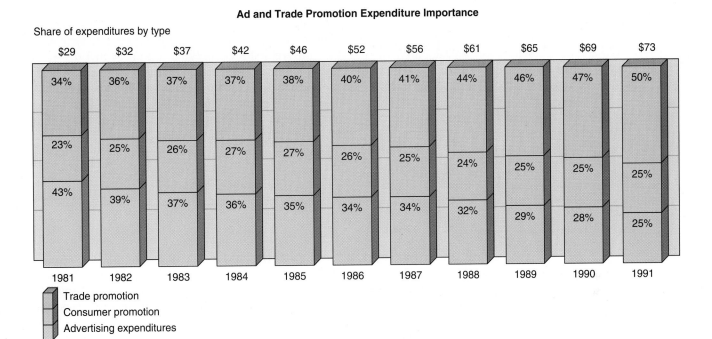

Ad and Trade Promotion Expenditure Importance

Share of expenditures by type

Figure 15-5

Changes in Spending on Advertising and Promotions

In the 1980s, consumer packaged-goods companies learned that, dollar-for-dollar, trade promotions were more effective at helping them achieve their goals than consumer advertising campaigns. They reallocated their spending accordingly.

Source: Neilsen Marketing Research, Donnelley Marketing, 1992.

whose market share it is attacking. This competitive parity approach to ad budgeting will mean the firm with low market share will have to spend a considerably higher percentage of its sales on advertising if it is trying to increase its market share. Some experts have proposed (without any strong empirical evidence to support their figures) that a new entry should identify the market share that it hopes to have at the end of two years and should spend one and half times that percentage during those two years on advertising. For example, if the goal is a market share of 10 percent, then the new entry should spend 15 percent of the industry's total spending on advertising during those two years. The theory is that a new entrant must gain mind share (consumer attention) before it gains market share, and it will take a higher voice share (advertising dollars spent) for a new entrant to achieve this.[10] In markets where competitive reaction is likely to be fierce, the amount spent may have to increase greatly to maintain a voice share and resulting mind share that is higher than the current market share.

Objective-Task

If a company does not have a strong competitive position and message theme, then it should spend less on advertising. On the other hand, if it has a lot to say, then it should spend a lot on advertising to inform consumers of its competitive advantages. If a company has a new product that it knows is clearly superior to the competition and will be profitable, then it should beg, borrow, and steal (figuratively speaking, of course) to

10. James C. Schroer, "Ad Spending: Growing Market Share," *Harvard Business Review,* January/February 1990, 44–48. In mature markets, a company has to outspend the competition by a huge amount to gain share and/or develop a brilliant new creative such as Diet Pepsi's Ray Charles "uh-huh" ads. See also Chapter 4 for a discussion of voice share, mind share, and market share.

Breaking with Tradition

There is always the possibility that the established players are wrong, and the level of advertising spending in a market is too low and could be greatly expanded if aroused by an aggressive campaign. In the fall of 1976, Canon introduced its fully automatic AE-1 SLR camera by radically departing from the industry's conventional advertising expenditure and media strategy. Using the Australian tennis pro John Newcombe, it ran pre-Christmas prime-time TV ads to demonstrate that it had solved the problem of expensive-camera complexity—"The Canon AE-1 is so advanced, it's simple." Over the next two years, Canon's spending on TV and magazine ads doubled each year to almost $10 million. Other manufacturers scrambled to keep up, and industry spending just on TV in 1978 soared to $50 million. However, Canon had gained a jump on the competition and over three years gained 32 percent of the 35-mm market, catapulting itself past market leaders Minolta, Olympus, and Pentax. Canon achieved this feat by breaking with industry advertising conventions and investing in a bold new creative and media strategy that greatly invest in a major marketing campaign that includes a large advertising budget. In short, how much a firm spends on advertising should be based on a thorough analysis of the market environment and an assessment of the competitive potential and profitability of the product or service that is to be advertised. Such an approach is detailed in Figure 15-6.

After the initial steps, in which the environment is analyzed, communication goals, a message strategy, and a media strategy should be developed based upon the positioning strategy and information about the competitors' advertising strategies and spending. The next step is to estimate the approximate cost of a campaign that will achieve the communication goals (expressed in terms of the basic message theme, timing, and the target audience's average frequency of exposure to the message). The approximate media cost and cost of developing the creatives should be estimated by the advertising agency. Step 5 in Figure 15-6 narrows down such estimates by specifying what will be spent in specific markets. This may lead to a decision to pull back from some markets, add other markets, or increase or reduce the advertising budget.

Looking at the overall advertising budget required to achieve the advertising objectives in *all* of the geographical markets, the company must decide whether it can afford the advertising budget it has developed and whether it appears to be a good investment. If the budget is too expensive, the decision makers must decide where to trim the fat. The budget might cut back on the overall reach and frequency objectives or on the creatives. But such pruning may weaken the overall campaign so much that it threatens its success in all markets. A better approach may be to cut back on the number of markets to ensure the potency of the campaign in the remaining markets. This occurred during the 1992 presidential election when, in the last two weeks of the campaign, the Democrats spent all of the money they had left in about 18 states where the polls suggested the race was close.

Marginal Budgeting	A very important element of competitive rationality is for a firm to recognize that buyer response to spending on different marketing activities varies by the activity. In other words, the response elasticity of buyers varies. The recognition of this fact is not enough. The firm with the superior insight to correctly estimate these response elas-

expanded both total demand and its own market share. The expensive-camera market segment had been asleep until Canon woke it up.

In a very different market, Heineken broke with tradition by slashing its advertising buying in 1987 to a quarter of what it was in 1985. Senior executives believed that Heineken's image would not suffer too much and the savings would compensate for the damage to profits resulting from a weakening dollar. They were very wrong. Heineken's market share of imported beers slipped from 38 percent to 23 percent. The advertising expenditure was needed to *maintain* its share of advertising voice, its share of mind, and its market share. Competing Mexican brands, in particular, gained a major advantage from Heineken's mistake.

Sources: Courtland L. Bovee and William F. Arens, *Contemporary Advertising* (Homewood, IL: Irwin, 1986); and Jeffrey A. Trachtenberg, "Beer Blunder," *Forbes,* February 8, 1988, 128–30.

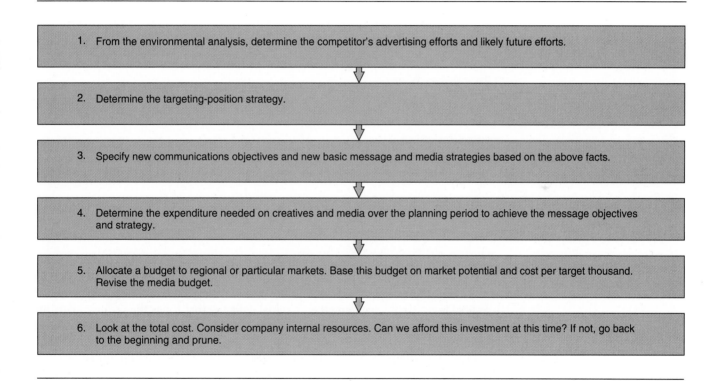

1. From the environmental analysis, determine the competitor's advertising efforts and likely future efforts.

2. Determine the targeting-position strategy.

3. Specify new communications objectives and new basic message and media strategies based on the above facts.

4. Determine the expenditure needed on creatives and media over the planning period to achieve the message objectives and strategy.

5. Allocate a budget to regional or particular markets. Base this budget on market potential and cost per target thousand. Revise the media budget.

6. Look at the total cost. Consider company internal resources. Can we afford this investment at this time? If not, go back to the beginning and prune.

At Step 3 in the usual objective-task method of determining the advertising budget, it is recommended that various objectives, such as a 40 percent brand awareness (mind share) be specified. The ad agency should have a gut feel for how many exposures of a particular ad are needed for it to be effective. This judgment will determine how much needs to be spent on media to achieve the needed exposure average frequency. If the budget has to be pruned, judgment should be again used to cut out the least effective spending. Note that this is not a top-down or bottom-up process but rather is based on planned objectives and marketing programs. The above process forces the team to ask whether it might be better to spend the dollars on some marketing activity other than advertising. This concern over the incremental return for dollars spent applies to all marketing spending and is called marginal budgeting.

Figure 15-6

Objective-Task Advertising Budgeting

Table 15-3
Inputs and Results for ACME's Marginal Budgeting Analysis

	Managers' Average Market Share Estimates Given Different Scenarios		
	Worst Case	Status Quo	Best Case
If the advertising budget is			
Cut 20%	24%	25%	26%
Maintained	28%	28%	30%
Increased 20%	30%	32%	34%
If the promotion budget is			
Cut 20%	26%	27%	27%
Maintained	28%	28%	29%
Increased 20%	29%	30%	31%

	Profit Projections (in millions) Using the Table 15-1 Spreadsheet		
	Worst Case	Status Quo	Best Case
If the advertising budget is			
Cut 20%	$0.76	$1.03	$1.30
Maintained	$1.50	$1.50	$2.04
Increased 20%	$1.69	$2.23	$2.77
If the promotion budget is			
Cut 20%	$1.47	$1.74	$1.74
Maintained	$1.50	$1.50	$1.77
Increased 20%	$1.25	$1.52	$1.79

ticities will, all other things being equal, end up being more competitive and profitable. This, of course, assumes that the firm follows through by investing in the activities that produce the greatest response. This type of investment decision making is called marginal budgeting—spending the marginal dollar so that it has the greatest effect on long-term profitability. Some experts believe that this is how all marketing budgets should be set.[11]

To explain the marginal budgeting process, let us assume that the initial planned P&L statement developed by the ACME company manager in Table 15-1 is to be used as a starting point for considering the relative impact of changes in the advertising and promotions budgets. The brand manager has asked several experienced managers to forecast market share for the company's product brand at different advertising and promotion budget levels (a 20 percent cut, no change, and a 20 percent increase) under each of three scenarios or future "states of the world": status quo (competition continues as usual), worst case (competitors introduce new brands), and best case (competitors cut back their marketing spending). Table 15-3 presents the average market

11. L.M. Lodish, *Advertising and Promotion: Vaguely Right or Precisely Wrong?* (New York: Oxford University Press, 1986); and John R. Rossiter and Larry Percy, *Advertising and Promotion Management* (New York: McGraw-Hill, 1987), 398.

share figures obtained from those managers and the projected next year profit obtained from plugging the market share and budget projections into the Table 15-1 spreadsheet.

The results in Table 15-3 suggest clearly that an increase in the advertising budget is perceived by the managers to have a substantially larger marginal impact on profit, regardless of which scenario occurs. Further, the 20 percent cut in promotion does not hurt profit much and even improves profitability in the status quo scenario. The manager could extend this analysis by asking her or his colleagues for market share estimates two or three years into the future and expanding the number of scenarios that might occur (for instance, scenarios that assume different economic conditions, like prosperity versus a triple-dip recession). The Rationality in Practice box on page 556 presents another marginal budgeting spreadsheet that can be used to allocate resources.

Control

The control systems of an organization are important to its competitive rationality because of the impact they make on its implementation and learning processes. Control refers to the firm's efforts to assess its performance and change strategy as necessary. A firm uses several types of control: *economic* reward control, *clan* control, *process* control (see Chapter 14), and *output* control. A highly competitive firm employs all four types of control. Its reward system encourages the achievement of the desired goals, its corporate culture and informal process controls encourage the self-monitoring and improvement of activity scripts, and its bureaucratic output control sets performance standards, closely monitors, and evaluates.[12]

Economic Reward Control

Business enterprises are economic entities. Employees work for economic rewards—not exclusively, but economic incentives assuredly motivate, direct, and, hence, control behavior. It is therefore logical that a major part of organizational control is achieved by linking financial rewards to performance. It then becomes critical to choose the right performance criteria to reward. In 1990, Edward A. Brennan, chairman of Sears Roebuck, shook up the company by making all employees focus on profits. In the Sears Tire & Auto Centers, this resulted in the setting of higher sales targets and quotas; sales commissions and incentives were based on the amount of repairs done.

Two years later, Sears agreed to pay $8 million to settle civil charges that it overcharged customers for repairs in California. Undercover agents were overcharged an average of $288 for unnecessary repairs.[13] The economic control mechanism encouraged the Sears employees to cheat their customers and cost the company hundreds of millions in the loss of future business and brand equity. More recently, an ABC news story about Food Lion highlighted a number of serious hygiene and sanitation problems in deli and meat merchandising that were apparently caused by the market managers' efforts to meet the company's cost and profit margin goals.[14]

12. There is evidence that a combination of informal process control and bureaucratic output control creates the highest job satisfaction. See Bernard J. Jaworski, Vlasis Stathakopoulos, and Shanker Krishnan, "Control Combinations in Marketing: Conceptual Framework and Empirical Evidence," *Journal of Marketing* 57.1 (January 1993), 57–69.
13. Seth Faison, "Sears Will Pay $6 Million to Settle Repair Complaints," *New York Times,* September 3, 1992, D5; and Kevin Kelly and Eric Schine, "How Did Sears Blow This Gasket?" *Business Week,* June 29, 1992, 38.
14. *ABC News Primetime Live,* November 5, 1992, Transcript #270.

Rationality in Practice:

Marginal Budgeting

The table that follows presents a marginal budgeting (MARGINAL) spreadsheet that can help determine whether the firm's resources should be used to increase the advertising budget or for some alternative marketing activity. MARGINAL's purpose is to act as a focus for the cross-functional team working on the final stages of the entire marketing budget for a product market. Prior to the meeting, each member of the group should be asked to prepare an estimate of the likely return over the next five years of investing an additional amount (such as $10,000), over and above what was tentatively planned, in each of several marketing budget items. These estimates can then be Delphied (circulated among the participants and then revised until some consensus is reached) and used in the MARGINAL analysis. Variations in the original estimates say a lot about the firm's understanding of current market response elasticities. How a firm arrives at the final estimates also says a lot about its competitive rationality decision-making procedures.

Group profit sharing is a particularly effective control tactic as it encourages all sorts of initiatives to reduce costs and increase sales, stimulates information exchange, and encourages informal social controls between employees. An advantage of a general group incentive program is that it overcomes some of the problems of measuring performance in intermediary processes. As outcomes become a shared responsibility, as decision making becomes shared, as implementation requires organization-wide cooperation, and as results increasingly depend on uncontrollable factors such as competitor behavior and economic conditions, it becomes difficult to connect results to individual performance or to use bureaucratic forms of control. A firm has to rely more on collective economic incentives.

Profit sharing is usually understood to be a plan that uses an annual bonus or share to reward employees based on company or corporate profit performance.[15] The

15. Robert L. Heneman, *Merit Pay: Linking Pay Increases to Performance Ratings* (Reading, MA: Addison-Wesley, 1992), 95.

MARGINAL: A Marginal Budgeting Spreadsheet

Purpose: To determine the best allocation of funds by choosing investments offering the highest potential return.

The return on an investment must be higher than the minimum target return. The incremental (marginal) dollar amount should be invested in activities yielding the highest projected rate of return. All investments yielding returns above the minimum target return should be considered if funds are available.

Incremental amount available for investment: $10,000

Minimum acceptable target return on investment: 30.0%

Incremental investment	Cost	Estimated Gross Profit Increase ($ in 000s)					Return	Above target?
		Year						
		1	2	3	4	5		
Consumer advertising	($10.0)	$10.0	$2.0	$2.0	$3.0	$1.0	38.7%	YES
Trade advertising	(10.0)	8.0	4.0	2.0	0.0	0.0	24.9%	NO
Publicity promotion	(10.0)	6.0	4.0	4.0	2.0	2.0	30.3%	YES
Sales force training	(10.0)	5.0	4.0	5.0	3.0	2.0	30.5%	YES
Sales promotions	(10.0)	12.0	0.0	2.0	0.0	0.0	31.6%	YES
Packaging redesign	(10.0)	0.0	6.0	6.0	5.0	5.0	27.3%	NO
Product redesign	(10.0)	0.0	8.0	7.0	6.0	5.0	35.7%	YES

Instructions

Step 1: Set incremental investment amount and target return rate.

Step 2: Develop five-year income stream estimates for various marketing activities.

Step 3: Develop what-if analyses by choosing pessimistic and optimistic income projections.

Note: The return is the internal rate of return (IRR), which equates the present value of the initial investment to the present value of the cash flow stream.

employee's share is distributed either as cash or as a deferred payment into a retirement fund. Even though profit-sharing plans lack the ability to directly link individual employee or team performance to rewards, employers have successfully used profit sharing plans to improve company performance, reduce costs, and create a more cooperative work force. John V. Jensen, manager of employee benefits at Andersen Corporation, testifies to the effectiveness of Andersen's profit-sharing plan.[16] In 1987, Andersen's profit-sharing distribution reached 84 percent of pay, and business was booming. According to Jensen, employees do see a link between profit sharing and reducing expenses, holding down costs, and high-quality products. Hartzell Manufacturing in St. Paul, Minnesota, has also reported positive results from its profit-sharing plan.[17] Since its implementation, employees are more willing to work together to solve problems,

16. Polly T. Taplin, "Profit-Sharing Plans As an Employee Motivator," *Employee Benefit Plan Review* (January 1989), 10.

17. Rebecca Sisco, "Put Your Money Where Your Teams Are," *Training* (July 1992), 42.

correct each other's mistakes, cooperate with team members, and generally work smarter.

A final profit-sharing success story comes from the service sector.[18] Southwest Airlines had outstanding operating profits in 1990, reaching $81.9 million, while only one other United States carrier reported profits. Southwest employees were also reported to be the most productive employees in the airline industry in 1990, with employee revenues reaching $137,675. Employee turnover was also low, 7.8 percent in 1990, and according to Ann Rhoades, vice-president of personnel, all employees "question every change we make and watch every penny." Another type of economic reward control is described in the Rationality in Practice box on page 560 about employee suggestion systems.

Clan Control

The use of process control through action planning and clan control is important but has been discussed extensively in previous chapters, particularly Chapter 14 on organization and implementation. For example, CPM or Gantt charts are types of process control mechanisms.

Clan control in a firm, division of a firm, or even a functional department is actually self-control resulting from internalized organizational values and the social influence of colleagues. A clan culture creates shared beliefs and commitments to customer service, hard work, honesty, and cooperation.[19] It is helped by careful hiring, earned job tenure, training, admission to honorary societies within the firm, and low turnover. The commitment is passed on through the legends, ceremonies, and rituals of the firm. This form of internalized control is commonly found in family businesses, entrepreneurial firms lead by charismatic individuals (the firm as family), and professional firms.

A clan culture produces motivation and self-control that does not need nearly as much external monitoring as a hierarchical, bureaucratic, or autocratic organization. But even in a clan culture, individual rewards are still very important, particularly for coming up with an innovation-imitation and championing it through to successful adoption. Any economic enterprise also needs formal outcome feedback to direct control. Relevant output performance statistics, such as quality and efficiency standards, costs, volume, and profit margins, need to be provided to each cross-functional team and function. Such information keeps the firm alert, able to diagnose change, and to experiment, learn, and adapt. In the next section, we focus on output controls—the setting, monitoring and evaluation of formal performance standards.[20] They are an important part of a firm's competitive rationality.

Output Control

Output control involves converting objectives into specific, measurable standards, finding ways of measuring the standards, reporting the results in user-friendly ways, interpreting and diagnosing the exceptional results, taking corrective action, and documenting the diagnosis and action taken. According to quality guru Edward Deming, the first task is to focus and eliminate the *special* causes of exceptional negative results.[21] These are the one-time performance blips related to human or system failure.

18. Danna K. Henderson, "Southwest Luvs Passengers, Employees, Profits," *Air Transport World,* (July 1991), 32–41.

19. William G. Ouchi, "A Conceptual Framework for the Design of Organizational Control Mechanisms," *Mangement Science,* 25(9), September 1979, 833–48.

20. Bernard J. Jaworski, "Toward a Theory of Marketing Control: Environmental Context, Control Types, and Consequences," *Journal of Marketing* 52 (July 1988), 23–39; and Kenneth A. Merchant, "Progressing Toward a Theory of Control: A Comment," *Journal of Marketing* 52 (July 1988), 40–44.

21. Mary Walton, *The Deming Management Method* (New York: Putnam, 1986).

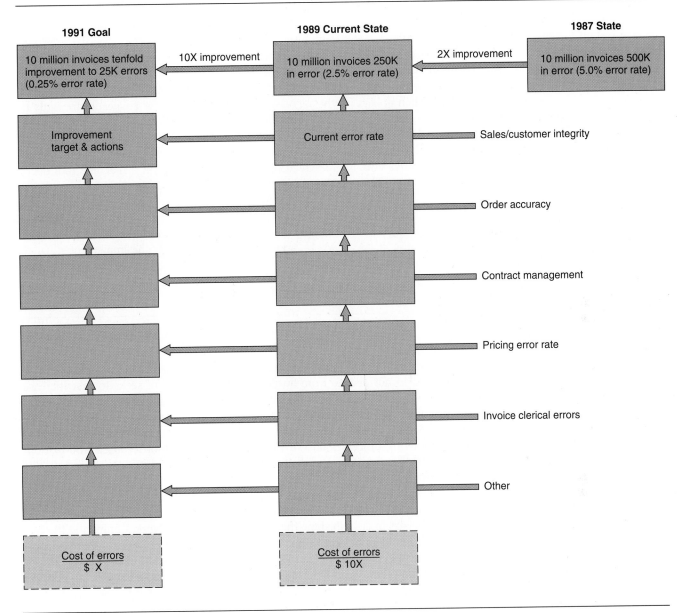

1991 Goal

10 million invoices tenfold improvement to 25K errors (0.25% error rate)

10X improvement

1989 Current State

10 million invoices 250K in error (2.5% error rate)

2X improvement

1987 State

10 million invoices 500K in error (5.0% error rate)

Improvement target & actions

Current error rate

Sales/customer integrity

Order accuracy

Contract management

Pricing error rate

Invoice clerical errors

Other

Cost of errors
$ X

Cost of errors
$ 10X

Figure 15-7

Identifying and Reducing Common Causes of Service Error Rates

The monitoring of output error rates for the overall billing system and its specific functions or activities leads to the identification of causes and to process control by changing subroutines and systems.

When these are reduced, management can then turn to the variation in performance created by *common* causes within the organization, such as worker ability and motivation, equipment, poorly designed activity scheduling, and basic management systems. These variations are much more difficult to reduce. They are within the control limits but still differ from the average. Figure 15-7 shows how Xerox went about eliminating the common causes of its billing system errors from 5 percent to the company's goal of 0.25 percent.[22] Xerox eliminated errors in each of the activities that made up its billing production routine by changing each activity so that it was less prone to error and by introducing new controls on each activity.

22. Norman E. Rickard, "Customer Satisfaction = Repeat Business," in *Creating Customer Satisfaction,* Earl L. Bailey, ed. (New York: The Conference Board, 1990), 44.

Rationality in Practice:

Employee Suggestion Systems

A reward system for employees' good ideas promotes and directs the three drives to increase customer satisfaction, reduce costs, and improve the decision-making and implementation routines of a firm. According to the Employee Involvement Association,* in 1991 over two billion dollars were saved by member companies who had an employee suggestion plan. The association recommends that employees should be involved as much as possible in the creation and implementation of employee suggestion systems, thereby creating a feeling of worker ownership. This should also increase acceptance and feelings of fairness. One method of evaluating employee suggestions comes from a nuclear generating plant of a southern utility company.** There are two types of suggestions: tangible ideas that result in measurable increases in profitability and intangible ideas that do not directly influence profitability but may address such issues as working conditions, employee safety, public relations, and internal communications. Intangible suggestions may be rewarded financially, but the reward is usually smaller than those for tangible suggestions, which most often equal a percentage of the increased profits. Eligibility for suggestion rewards is limited to employees whose normal job responsibilities do not include suggesting improvements. For example, a quality control employee may not receive a reward for an idea relating to quality control, but a machine tool operator could.

Once the employee has generated a tangible idea, he or she must complete a form that identifies the problem and the specific solution. This involves stating what, how, where, and when the solution can be implemented. Once the form is completed, it is given to the suggestion pro-

If performance is the overall average output, then conformance is the extent to which results do not deviate from an average. Quality control seeks to first increase conformance and then raise performance. However, it is much easier to monitor and adjust machines and production processes to eliminate common causes of variance than it is to adjust marketing control. A firm has greater control over its production process. Marketing processes do not have the same quality of feedback information, and they depend on variances in distributor and customer behavior that are very difficult to control.

The principles are, however, still the same: the firm must construct a flowchart of the activity schedule that describes how the process should work and then construct a second flowchart to describe how the process actually does work. Comparing the two activity schedules identifies the inefficiencies, makes simpler procedures more evident, and points out the sources and causes of variability in completion time or quality of output. Such flowcharts also help members of a cross-functional team organize their collective thoughts and come to a common understanding of what has been happening and what has to happen. The output performance and conformance of each task in the activity schedule needs to be tracked. Each subsequent task results from its antecedent tasks and so has a vital interest in the antecedent tasks' performance and conformance. In this sense, the system has some built-in internal controls.

Exception Reporting Systems

To avoid being buried in output data from routine, ongoing marketing activities, many marketers use an exception management reporting system. It reports only exceptional results, those that deviate significantly from what was planned or budgeted. When this occurs, the system reports the situation in detail. For example, it may present the results of the previous five reporting periods so that a visual trend analysis can be taken to help diagnose the cause. The benefits to a manager are obvious. He or she can now focus attention and management on the exceptions, good or bad. Many production,

gram administrator who judges the eligibility of the employee and the suggestion. If the employee and suggestion are both eligible, the suggestion is sent to the supervisor responsible for the area of concern. The supervisor analyzes the suggestion, estimates the costs of implementation, and determines the annual savings in operations. The supervisor then recommends or rejects the suggestion and the decision is sent back to the program administrator. Rejected suggestions can be appealed through the program administrator, and the administrator may resubmit the idea to another supervisor for reevaluation.

If the suggestion has been accepted and the reward exceeds $1,000, it is sent to the economic analysis section for final review and approval. If the reward is less than $1,000, it is automatically approved. Tangible suggestions accepted by the economic analysis section are awarded 20 percent of the first year's increase in "measurable net savings which result directly from the suggestion," with a maximum reward of $10,000. The reward given to the employee is based on an estimate of the first year's savings, so he or she can be rewarded immediately. At the end of the first year following the actual implementation of the suggestion, the reward may be adjusted, but it will never be decreased. Potential problems of suggestion systems are a lack of management support and monetary awards that are too small. If the company cannot afford larger rewards, points could be awarded and used in an annual lottery for a grand prize.

*Formerly called the National Association of Suggestion Systems, One Illinois Center, Suite 200, 111 East Wacker Drive, Chicago, Illinois 60601-4298.
**P. Michael Moore, "Employee Suggestion Systems Can Work," *CMA Magazine*, November 1988, 40–42.

accounting, and marketing information systems already have this capability and, if not, their report writing can be modified to accommodate such triggers. Immediate exception reporting is a crucial part of Total Quality Management because TQM requires that deviations from accepted performance be corrected immediately.

For example, Cypress Semiconductor Corp. in Silicon Valley has its computer-based purchasing system designed so that it completely shuts down if an order fails to arrive on time and no one has explained to senior management why it is late.[23] To start up the system again, the supplier has to be contacted, a new delivery date set, and the information has to be reported to the chief financial officer. This system goes beyond exception reporting—it demands a response and creates such inconvenience that it quickly eliminates such errors and increases just-in-time inventory productivity. It is an example of output control in that it responds to unfavorable information, but it is also an example of process control because it makes sure that the correct process routines are followed and that orders are received on time.

The way an intensive care unit operates in a hospital provides a good analogy of an effective exception reporting marketing information system. Patients using intensive care equipment have their vital life signs connected to several machines. The machines are preset to set off an alarm if, for example, the patient's blood pressure or pulse rate fell below a certain level. Intensive care machines do not ring alarms when the patient's vital signs become better than normal, but an exception management system *should* do this. Such cases may identify new cost-saving efficiencies or sales initiatives that should be adopted throughout the system. Under-budget spending is not necessarily a good sign, for it may indicate that a particular campaign is not being implemented. In seasonal businesses, fast exception reporting is crucial because it enables quick responses.

23. Richard Brandt, "Here Comes the Attack of the Killer Software," *Business Week,* December 9, 1991, 70.

Choice of Measure and Accountability

It is important to spend time thinking about which performance measures and level of analysis should be reported and what other statistics should have preset exception reporting triggers. The individual held accountable for particular performance measures should be the one to make the final choice of level of analysis and trigger points. Key marketing statistics are daily, weekly, or monthly forward orders, shipments, inventory, and critical expense-to-sales ratios. The reporting system could also include ratios of returns to sales, complaints to sales, and statistics from regular consumer and trade surveys.

Accountability should be considered when deciding on the level of analysis. If different line executives are responsible for territorial, region, and product group performance, sales and expenses should be aggregated by sales territory, region, and product group. An executive cannot be responsible for performance if what he or she is responsible for is not measured and reported by the firm's management information system. The upper and lower alert limits around planned (expected or budgeted) performance should also be the decision of the individual who must react to the information. Some types of trigger points (such as sales and inventory) may also have to be adjusted seasonally.

Control Charts

When a deviant operating statistic is flagged, a report should be produced that contains the recent operating history, perhaps in the form of a chart similar to that illustrated in Figure 15-8. In this simple control chart, it is clear that the marketing expense-to-sales ratio has been climbing steadily over time. It is not a one-time blip caused by a special event that led to under spending in a previous period, but it is a definite trend that probably can be diagnosed. It may also be useful to have the system report the previous year's performance as well as the last time the exception limits were exceeded.

Future sophisticated information systems will allow the manager to record the diagnosis and remedial steps taken for future reference. This would allow future management teams to find out when previous exceptional deviations occurred, what the diagnoses revealed, which remedial steps were taken, and how everything worked out.

Exception management systems will feed crucial information into an organization's computer files recording the history of a product or sales region. Given that many

Figure 15-8

An Output Performance Control Chart

This chart reveals a clear trend in the marketing expense-to-sales ratio. It suggests a comon problem that has a negative trend. An exception appears to be the drop expressed by the fifth X. Future sophisticated information systems will generate such control charts on a computer screen and allow the manager to record the diagnosis and remedial steps taken in a window for future reference. This would be a real advantage for the next brand or product manager who comes along. He or she will have access to information regarding when previous exceptional deviations occurred, the diagnosis of what caused them, the remedial steps taken, and the outcome.

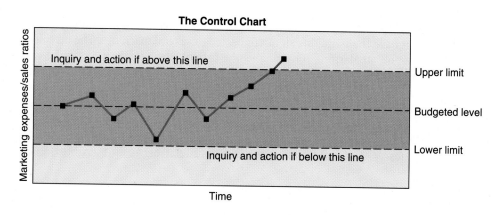

The Control Chart

Marketing expenses/sales ratios

Inquiry and action if above this line

Upper limit

Budgeted level

Lower limit

Inquiry and action if below this line

Time

people spend roughly five to ten years with the same company, there are fewer people around for younger executives to question regarding how problems were handled in the past. The greatly expanded storage capacity of computers will make it easy to capture and attach exception or contingency management decision information to critical past operating statistics and, hence, partially (but certainly not completely) compensate for the loss of the wisdom and insights of "old salts." Such archived information will also be valuable in evaluating management performance. We now discuss the application of these general control techniques to specific types of marketing systems.

Specific Types of Total Quality Marketing Control

The theory of competitive rationality suggests that customer satisfaction is a key output control measure. If the firm's customer satisfaction index rating is not higher or rising faster than its rivals, then the firm is in trouble. Another output control measure that is a critical determinant of the success of a firm's competitive rationality is the percentage of its sales and profits coming from new products (products introduced in the last five years). It is a measure of the firm's innovation-imitation success and suggests the new product control statistic. This and other quality control measures are described below.

Customer Satisfaction Control

The first and most important control for a company that focuses on its customers is a measurement of customer loyalty and current satisfaction. In a competitive market, customer loyalty and satisfaction are leading indicators of future sales. If they begin to decrease, then it is likely that future sales will also decrease. Therefore, in an effort to avoid losing customer sales, marketers are increasingly conducting surveys of customer satisfaction.[24]

Table 15-4 presents an example of such an analysis. It segments customers by their past loyalty. A slip in satisfaction from a company's most loyal customers is much more serious than a decline in satisfaction among customers who have never been very loyal. The most rigorous customer satisfaction index (CSI) counts the percentage of "happy" customers in the satisfaction survey. Happy customers are customers who say 1) they are *completely* satisfied, 2) they would *definitely* recommend the product or service to friends, and 3) they *definitely* plan to continue to be loyal customers.[25] Many firms would be lucky to have a score of 20 to 30 percent on this type of index. The advantages of such a demanding standard of satisfaction are that it leaves a lot of room for improvement and it is very easy for everyone, particularly senior management, to understand. It is useful for tracking change and, more importantly, the rate of change, and it is user friendly. It is useful for benchmarking and also making a follow-up diagnosis to determine why other customers are not happy, which customer segments are most unhappy, and how their problems can be resolved so they become happier customers. Tracking service requests is another way of identifying customer dissatisfaction. For example, the downtown Chicago Marriott hotel discovered that two-thirds of its guest calls to housekeeping were for an iron and ironing board. Instead of replacing

24. Robert A. Westbrook, "A Rating Scale for Measuring Product/Service Satisfaction," *Journal of Marketing* 44 (Fall 1980), 68–72; and Richard L. Oliver and John E. Swan, "Consumer Perceptions of Interpersonal Equity and Satisfaction in Transactions: A Field Survey Approach," *Journal of Marketing* 53 (April 1989), 21–35.
25. This measure was recommended in a talk given at an American Marketing Association and American Society for Quality Control Meeting, March 11–13, 1990, by D. Randall Brandt, "The Purpose and Prospects of Customer Satisfaction Measurement," of Burke Marketing Research.

Table 15-4
A Customer Loyalty and Satisfaction Matrix

	Current Satisfaction				
Past Loyalty	Completely satisfied	Somewhat satisfied	Neutral	Dissatisfied	% of Sales
Firm friends	7%	3%	0%	0%	10%
Core loyal	10%	5%	5%	5%	25%
Loyal switchers	10%	10%	10%	10%	40%
Buy-on-price customers	0%	5%	10%	10%	25%
Overall	27%	23%	25%	25%	100%

Just looking at the overall result, the situation looks rather grim. An analysis of the past loyalty figures, however, provides a little more assurance and explanation. Fortunately, the customers who are most loyal are generally still satisfied. There should be some concern with the 5 percent of core loyal customers who are currently dissatisfied. The customers who buy on price have a tendency to be less satisfied because they have not developed a continuous cooperative relationship and they will always be dissatisfied if they think they could have gotten a lower price.

the black-and-white TVs in the bathrooms of concierge-level guest rooms (housekeeping had received no calls requesting color TVs in the bathroom), the hotel spent $20,000 putting irons and ironing boards in all guest rooms.[26]

New Product Ratio (NPR) Control

The percentage of current sales coming from new or modified products introduced in the last three years (NPR) indicates how quickly and successfully the firm is reformulating itself by creating or entering new product-markets or creatively destroying its established product-markets. A highly innovative firm such as 3M has a goal of gaining over 20 percent of its sales from products launched in the last five years. The new product ratios are critical measures of the market success of a firm's innovation-imitation decisions and the rate of change within the organization. When new NPRs are high (and getting higher), then the firm is showing sure signs of superior competitive rationality (assuming costs are *also* being controlled). While it can be subject to fudging (small modifications to mature products are claimed to be new products), the ratio is an important internal and external indicator of a firm's ability to initiate change and adapt to change. As mentioned in the discussion of corporate mission and competence in Chapter 7, a 1992 survey of high-growth companies found that a firm's commitment and investment in new-product development resulted in a higher NPR. In a market with a great deal of innovation-imitation, NPR is one of the three most important measures of success, along with customer satisfaction and profits.

Sales Force Control

Sales force control involves a great deal of the informal or clan process control described in Chapter 14. The more successful such informal control is, the less the need for output control of the sales effort. In this context, the annual sales-force meetings can be seen in a very different light. Like the tribe meeting for a special religious

26. The bad news is that it took the hotel 15 years to discover the ironing problem! See Leonard L. Berry, "Improving America's Service," *Marketing Management* 1.3 (1992), 29–37.

ceremony, it is full of rites of passage, initiations, rituals, honorific recognition, the relating of legends, the creation of new legends, and, most of all, the reaffirmation of group values. Sales conferences are extremely important in creating and sustaining the clan culture and clan controls.

Controlling selling performance should be relatively straightforward if the reward system of salary, commission, bonuses, and contests is properly designed to direct the behavior of salespeople. The training program should make very clear how a sales rep's performance will be measured. Ideally, it should include instructions on how to use the company computer information system (having access to the performance statistics that the sales manager looks at daily or weekly can help the sales rep monitor his or her own performance on an ongoing basis). Such performance statistics should be compared to sales force averages and the individual's past performance. This approach utilizes a basic law of evaluation and control; self-monitoring and self-control are always more effective than externally imposed monitoring and control.

The three basic dimensions of performance direction and control that most concern sales management are 1) the allocation of effort to selling different product groups, 2) the allocation of effort to new versus old business, and 3) the control of various expense-to-sales ratios. Each of these will be now discussed in turn.

Selling Different Product Groups

The information system of the modern firm now enables it to compute the contribution of individual product sales to company growth and profitability. This information should clearly direct and be used to control the individual efforts of a salesperson. There is, however, a major constraint on directing the efforts of a salesperson toward selling a particular product line. The profile of customers in the salesperson's territory may be such that there is little or no potential or present demand for the company's most profitable or high-growth product lines. When this situation exists, the sales-manager and product managers must work with the sales rep to determine the appropriate allocation of effort across the product groups for the rep's territory. Sales performance goals and budgets are then developed, and performance is compared against these goals and past performance history.

New Versus Old Products

Steering a sales force toward new versus old business is problematic because even though most companies expect their sales people to come up with new business, they don't want this to happen at the expense of old business. It is almost impossible to achieve both goals in a highly competitive market where your new business is someone else's old business and your old business is someone else's future new business. Time spent attacking someone else's market share is, therefore, time spent away from defending your own current market share. Another problem is the uncertainty over the growth potential of a territory. A sales rep will tend to underestimate growth potential and senior management will tend to overestimate it. That is why the conversion percentage of leads (the percentage of new accounts resulting from leads provided to the sales rep) is such an important measure of a sales rep's motivation and ability to pioneer a sale. Here, there is no question that the leads exist in the territory. They have been generated through telemarketing, trade shows, advertising, or publicity and have been passed on to the sales rep to follow up and convert to new customers. If the conversion percentage is low because the sales rep is generating his or her own new leads and converting them into new accounts, then all is well and good (except that it suggests the territory potential is too large for one sales rep to handle). If, however,

Table 15-5
Sales Control Statistics

Name: R.G. Barry	Control and Evaluation of a Salesperson				
Annual performance	**1981**	**1982**	**1983**	**1984**	**1985**
Dollar sales ($000)	$900.5	$926.6	$978.2	$1,074.8	$1,121.8
Dollar sales quota ($000)	$800.0	$850.0	$900.0	$950.0	$1,000.0
Gross profit of sales mix ($000)	$198.4	$204.4	$216.8	$232.5	$263.3
Sales to new accounts ($000)	$64.7	$38.9	$55.6	$70.9	$80.6
Salary and/or commission	$35,444	$37,367	$42,378	$44,232	$44,566
Selling expenses	$19,567	$22,333	$24,678	$25,111	$30,233
Number of days worked	274	280	278	283	267
Calls on new prospects	132	105	126	135	124
Number of new accounts	17	9	12	14	18
Number of old accounts	225	235	233	238	239
Calls on old accounts	946	1115	1120	1098	1044
Number of accounts lost	7	11	7	13	20
Sales analysis ratios	**1981**	**1982**	**1983**	**1984**	**1985**
Dollar sales/Dollar sales cost	$16.37	$15.52	$14.59	$15.50	$15.00
Sales/call	$835.3	$759.5	$785.1	$871.7	$960.4
Cost/call	$51.0	$48.9	$53.8	$56.2	$64.0
New sales/new account	$3,806	$4,322	$4,633	$5,064	$4,478
New accounts/prospect calls	12.9%	8.6%	9.5%	10.4%	14.5%
Average cost of new account	$396	$571	$565	$542	$441
New business cost/sales	10.4%	13.2%	12.2%	10.7%	9.9%
Old sales/old account	$3,715	$3,777	$3,960	$4,218	$4,356
Old sales/old account calls	$884	$796	$824	$914	$997
Old business cost/sales	5.8%	6.1%	6.5%	6.2%	6.4%
Gross profit percentage	22.0%	22.1%	22.2%	21.6%	23.5%
Gross profit in dollars/sales cost in dollars	$3.61	$3.42	$3.23	$3.35	$3.52
Gross profit/call	$184	$168	$174	$189	$225
Sales to quota ratio	112.6%	109.0%	108.7%	113.1%	112.2%

there is no other reasonable explanation for the low conversion percentage, then the salesperson is probably misdirecting his or her efforts, is not working hard enough, or lacks the necessary selling skills.

Expense to Sales Ratios

Table 15-5 presents a simple sales control spreadsheet that computes some typical control statistics used to monitor the effort invested in new versus old business over time. It also monitors some of the selling cost ratios, the third important dimension of control. The value of such a simple spreadsheet is that it enables a sales rep, alone or with the sales manager, to observe the effect of changing his or her behavior on some of the important performance ratios.[27] This raises a common problem with sales force

27. Performance ratios measure output-to-input performance efficiency and can be compared with past performance or highest performers in the company. See Thomas V. Bonoma, *Marketing Management* (New York: The Free Press, 1984), 508.

control. It is very rare for a sales rep to improve performance on every possible ratio that can be computed, so the picky sales manager can surely find something to express concern about. Control is not simply finding fault in the detail; it is using detail to come up with recommendations to improve overall performance. When overall performance is superior, then a sales manager and the company should forget the minor transgressions and be much more interested in congratulating the salesperson and learning how the rep achieved the superior performance. That way, his or her tactics can be shared with marketing and the rest of the sales force.

Advertising Control

The first and most successful way of controlling advertising effectiveness and spending is to include an ad agency representative in the management team. The agency personnel must share the values of the organization and understand its culture, its politics, and its competitive rationality. It must become a believer in its client such that the firm can have confidence that the agency will exercise self-control and also can be informally controlled. The absence of such an understanding can lead to a nightmare of over-the-shoulder supervision and endless questions about expenses. The time and effort an organization spends monitoring the progress of its agency can be very counterproductive.

Admittedly, maintaining process control over the ad agency is not easy because an important characteristic of informal clan control is that the member feels its membership in the clan is not threatened. Members may be sanctioned but not rejected by the clan or firm. This is precisely what happens when a firm changes its advertising agency. Changing the agency people who work on the account also does not help. Moreover, the effectiveness of an advertising campaign still needs to be monitored by outcome measures. An agency's assurance that its proposed campaign will be a great success does not make it so. Evaluating effectiveness is part and parcel of most major advertising campaigns. It is how an organization learns about what works and what does not.

The ads whose outcome performance can be most easily and validly tested in the field are direct response ads sent to different samples drawn from mailing lists. The ad that generates the most orders or inquiries and keeps on pulling (after several repetitions) is clearly the most effective and should be used as the message theme and creative in a more general advertising campaign. The standard approach to testing a TV campaign is to use day-after recall (DAR). Representatives from the ad campaign elicit feedback from respondents who claimed to watch the TV program the previous day and ask them to recall specific copy points. Improved versions of this approach measure the delayed effects of multiple exposures on preferences as well as awareness. The survey conductors mask the brand name in an ad and ask respondents to recall it. These latter approaches are fairer tests of the effects of ads whose goal is to influence emotions rather than change beliefs.

The Starch Recognition Tests use a similar approach to determine the effectiveness of test ads placed in specific magazines. Despite some measurement problems, such recall tests do give a rough measure of the attention-grabbing or pulling power of an ad. The problem is that such tests encourage sensationalized ads. As one crusty advertising executive points out, if you want to score high on DAR or Starch ratings "Put a gorilla in a jockstrap" in the ad. His prescription for increasing sales is not as definitive.

Copy Pretesting

The objective of testing the potential effectiveness of an advertising campaign prior to launching it is to make sure the creatives achieve the target-positioning and message strategy objectives. Several approaches can be used. The minimal approach to pretesting creatives is to conduct one-on-one discussions with a small sample of consumers. The subjects are exposed to a test ad (either as a rough storyboard or in its finished form) along with several unrelated advertisements and competitive comparison advertisements. After exposure, subjects are asked to recall the content of the ad or to express thoughts about the ad.

If the subjects cannot play back the most important elements of the ad, cannot remember the brand name, or react negatively to elements of the ad, then the creative staff must go back to the drawing board. Pretesting is most useful for newsworthy or informational-persuasive strategies but is not good for ads that use image and feeling strategies. This is because subjects often have difficulty expressing emotional reactions created by an ad, and one exposure of such an ad is seldom enough to register any effect.

Theater testing is a more controlled approach to evaluating a finished TV ad. Respondents are recruited by phone or mail and invited to view new TV shows with commercials embedded in the programming. A raffle or drawing held before and after the exposure to the ads offers each participant a choice of "gifts" (the test and competitive products). This enables the survey conductors to measure the change in choice preferences that result from one, two, or three exposures to the ad. Written evaluations of the show and the ads are also obtained. The above two techniques are limited in their discriminative and predictive powers. Focus groups and theater tests are able to identify a very good ad and a very bad ad, but they do not discriminate well between good, average, and bad ads.

The most sophisticated approach to testing an ad is offered by Information Resources, Inc. (IRI). IRI's BehaviorScan approach can test various TV commercials by broadcasting them to selected homes in their test markets and tracking their effect at the local grocery stores using retail sales data. It can be used by packaged goods manufacturers to test market a new product and to test a new advertising campaign against an old campaign. A.C. Nielsen Co. and Burke Marketing Services, Inc., have developed similar monitoring systems. Recent research with tracking systems has produced some fascinating insights, including the conclusion that increasing the advertising of established brands more often than not has *no* effect on sales.[28]

Sales and Profit Variance Control

An important aspect of control is that it allows firms to compare actual bottom-line performance to planned or budgeted performance. A profit variance may be the result of things going right and things going wrong. Variance analysis attempts to untangle some of these swings and roundabouts. In particular, variance analysis untangles deviations from the plan that are the result of miscalculations in estimating total market size, market share, price, and costs. It identifies problem areas and, to a lesser degree, diagnoses problems to determine possible causes.

The variance analysis section of management accounting courses has traditionally been very intimidating for marketing majors. In part, this is because the potential to make compounding computational mistakes is very great when variance analysis is

---

28. Magid M. Abraham and Leonard M. Lodish, "Getting the Most Out of Advertising and Promotion," *Harvard Business Review,* (May/June 1990), 50–60.

Table 15-6
Performance Compared to Plan Variance Analysis

	Planned	Actual	Variance B/(W) Planned*
Market size	40,000,000	50,000,000	10,000,000
Sales volume	20,000,000	22,000,000	2,000,000
Market share	50.0%	44.0%	−6.0%
Price	$0.5000	$0.4773	($0.0227)
Unit variable cost			
Production	$0.2000	$0.2000	$0.0000
Marketing	0.1000	0.1000	0.0000
Total unit variable cost	$0.3000	$0.3000	$0.0000
Unit contribution margin	$0.2000	$0.1773	($0.0227)
Total revenue	$10,000,000	$10,500,600	$500,600)
Total variable cost	6,000,000	6,600,000	($600,000)
Total contribution margin	$ 4,000,000	$ 3,900,600	($ 99,400)

Variances	Actual to planned
Price/Cost $[(Ca − Cp) \times Qa]$	($499,400)
Volume variance	
Market share $[(Sa − Sp) \times Ma \times Cp]$	(600,000)
Market size $[(Ma − Mp) \times Sp \times Cp]$	1,000,000
Total volume variance $[(Qa − Qp) \times Cp]$	$400,000
Total contribution variance	($99,400)

*B/(W) = Better/Worse
C = Contribution margin per unit
S = Market share
M = Market size

Q = Quantity sold
a = Actual
p = Planned

done by hand. The VARIANCE spreadsheet (see Table 15-6) takes care of such concerns.[29] It extends the traditional variance analysis in two important ways. First, it separates manufacturing and marketing activity costs and enables researchers to determine how these costs deviated from plan-influenced profit. Second, it allows an after-the-fact adjustment of the initial plan's targets to account for totally unforeseeable events (for instance, a competitor entry or exit, bad weather, a plant strike or shut-out,

29. This spreadsheet is based on James M. Hulbert and Norman E. Toy, "A Strategic Framework for Marketing Control," *Journal of Marketing* (April 1977), 12–21.

or a dramatic rise in raw material costs). This helps explain performance variance that was completely beyond the control of management. Such variance from budget does not reflect on the quality of the environmental forecasts or the implementation and control of prices and costs. The remaining performance variance can then be traced to poor estimates of market size and market share or poor price, manufacturing costs, and marketing cost control.

The following examples will show the difference between price variance and volume variance. Suppose planned sales are 5,000 units at $10 per unit for a total of $50,000. Actual sales equal 5,000 units at $8 per unit for a total of $40,000. The $10,000 total variance is due entirely to the actual price being $2 lower than planned. Price variance can be found by taking the difference between actual price and planned price multiplied by planned units. Now suppose actual volume sold equals 3,000 units at $10 per unit for a total of $30,000. In this case, the $20,000 variance is due entirely to the actual volume being lower than the planned volume. Volume variance is calculated by taking the difference between planned and actual volume multiplied by planned price.

Contribution Variance

Normal variance analysis requires an explanation of variances in contribution margin. Remember that contribution is the profit left to cover fixed costs after accounting for variable costs. Contribution variance can be broken down into a price/cost variance and a volume variance. The calculation is similar to the above calculations except unit contribution margin is substituted for price to account for variable costs.

Volume Variance

Volume variance can be caused by two factors: market share and market size. To determine the share component of the total volume variance, take the difference between actual and planned share, multiplied by the product of actual market size times planned contribution per unit (see the calculation in Table 15-6). Similarly, market size variance can be found by taking the difference between actual and planned market size, multiplied by the product of planned share times contribution per unit. The sum of the market share variance and market size variance yields the total volume variance.

The first step in the variance analysis spreadsheet requires the entry into Table 15-6 of planned estimates and actual market size, market share, unit price, production variable unit costs, and marketing variable unit costs. The spreadsheet does the rest. In this example, the total contribution was $99,400 less than expected. It can be traced to the market share being much lower than expected (44 percent rather than 50 percent) and price being lower than expected. Clearly a drop in a deteriorating competitive position has occurred. A higher than planned price might explain the drop in market share. In fact, the situation would have been much worse had not the market size turned out to be much larger (25 percent higher) than expected. While this was a fortuitous compensating variance, it is really not good news as it may indicate a loss of new business to competitors. The only outstanding performance was the control of costs.

Uncontrollable Variance

The REVISVAR spreadsheet presented in Table 15-7 increases the sophistication of the analysis by allowing an after-the-fact adjustment of planned performance because of unforeseeable circumstances. In the example, the circumstances were an unexpected increase in market size, a drop in market share, and a drop in industry and company

Table 15-7
Revised Variance Analysis: Accounting for Uncontrollable Events

	Planned	Actual	Revised
Market size	40,000,000	50,000,000	41,000,000
Sales volume	20,000,000	22,000,000	20,090,000
Market share	50.0%	44.0%	49.0%
Price	$0.5000	$0.4773	0.4800
Unit variable cost			
Production	$0.2000	$0.2000	$0.2000
Marketing	0.1000	0.1000	0.1000
Total unit variable cost	$0.3000	$0.3000	$0.3000
Unit contribution margin	$0.2000	$0.1773	$0.1800
Total revenue	$10,000,000	$10,500,600	$9,643,200
Total variable cost	6,000,000	6,600,000	6,027,000
Total contribution margin	$ 4,000,000	$ 3,900,600	$3,616,200

Variances	Actual to planned	Actual to revised	Revised to planned
Price/Cost $[(Ca - Cp) \times Qa]$	($499,400)	($59,400)	($401,800)
Volume variance			
Market share $[(Sa - Sp) \times Ma \times Cp]$	(600,000)	(400,000)	(82,000)
Market size $[(Ma - Mp) \times Sp \times Cp]$	1,000,000	793,800	100,000
Total volume variance $[(Qa - Qp) \times Cp]$	$400,000	$343,800	$ 18,000
Total contribution variance	($99,400)	$284,400	($383,800)

C = Contribution margin per unit	Q = Quantity sold
S = Market share	a = Actual
M = Market size	p = Planned

price. The unforeseeable increase in demand resulted from a fire in a European manufacturing plant that increased industry exports by a million units. The underestimation in demand error should therefore be reduced by 1,000,000. A new competitor also entered the market and, if this had been anticipated, company market share would have been reduced by a percentage point. Because of the new competitor's entry pricing strategy, the planned average unit selling price would also have been revised down two cents. The overall lower market prices caused by the new entry may, in fact, have accounted for some of the unexpected increases in demand.

Overall, actual performance was $284,400 better than the revised expected performance, largely because of the underestimation of the market. Revised performance was estimated to be $383,800 lower than the initially planned performance mainly because of the price cost variance. The net effect was a shortfall of $99,400 in the actual as compared to the initially planned contribution. The diagnosis is that there was not a

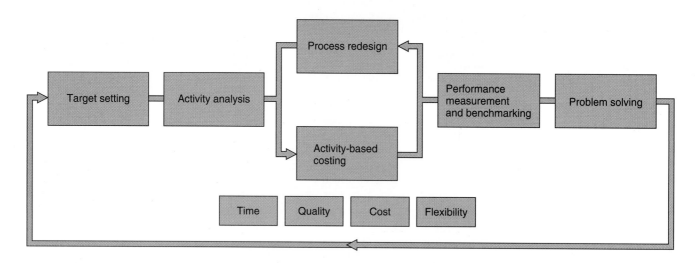

Figure 15-9

Using Benchmarking to Continuously Improve a Firm's Competitiveness

Benchmarking is best used in a management process that is continuously seeking to increase consumer satisfaction, reduce costs, and simplify the relevant manufacturing, logistics, or marketing activity sequence script (ASS).

Source: Reprinted from "A Tool Kit for Continuous Improvement," by Paul Sharman, May 1992, pp. 17–20, by permission of The Society of Management Accountants of Canada.

price control problem but there was a problem in the initial and revised estimates of market size and market share. This case study of the use of VARIANCE and REVISVAR demonstrates the power of variance analysis in diagnosing causes and assigning responsibility for variations in key performance measures.

Competitive Benchmarking

The ultimate evidence of superior competitive rationality should be superior performance on customer satisfaction surveys, greater productive efficiency, lower costs, higher NPR, and higher profits. A surprising number of firms are able to make such competitive benchmarking comparisons. They do so by purchasing the results of industry studies taken by independent market researchers or by participating in collaborative studies with competitors or like firms in geographically separated markets. The general procedure used in competitive benchmarking is illustrated in Figure 15-9.

Continuous Customer Satisfaction Benchmarking

The best-known example of an industry-wide study of customer satisfaction is the J.D. Power & Associates Customer Satisfaction Index for automakers. Each March, the company (which also offers similar surveys to computer manufacturers) sends out a six-page detailed survey to some 70,000 owners of new model cars. About one-third respond. Manufacturers receive very detailed reports of problem areas and benchmark comparisons with competitors. In the late 1980s, Honda drew a great deal of public attention to the J.D. Powers survey by promoting the fact that Honda was rated number one in customer satisfaction four years in a row. Now all of the premier brands such as Lexus and Infiniti are striving to achieve the top rating ahead of Honda and Mercedes (see Figure 15-10). In 1991, Lexus and Infiniti succeeded.

The measures and weighing system that J.D. Powers uses has changed over time based on the responses of consumers and the auto industry. For example, customer handling (before and after sales service from the dealer) has accounted for 40 percent of the score but this is likely to be increased to 50 percent or more because

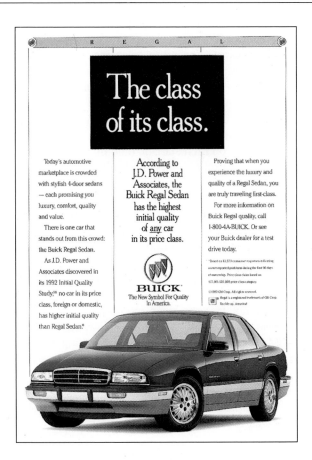

Figure 15-10

Promoting Customer Satisfaction

Honda was the first to use J. D. Power's satisfaction ratings in a very effective advertising campaign. Personal computer companies such as Dell have also featured customer satisfaction ratings in their advertising.

service has become more important to customers.[30] If this happens, then the manufacturers will work even harder to improve customer service. J.D. Powers' influence on the efforts of major auto suppliers to meet customer needs has grown extraordinarily since it started its rating service in the early 1980s.

Continuous Financial Performance Benchmarking

Financial performance can also be studied relative to other firms. It is an alternative method of identifying variance. Rather than comparing performance across time or against budget expectations, a firm participating in an interfirm comparison can compare performance across similar operating units. These units may be regions, divisions, or stores within a company; independently operated franchises; or even separate companies in the same line of business. The statistics compared are normally adjusted for sales and are performance statistics such as advertising and the selling expense-to-sales ratio, stock-turn, gross margin, and sales per employee. They provide an assessment of

30. Larry Armstrong, "Who's The Most Pampered Motorist of All," *Business Week,* June 10, 1991, 90–91.

competitive rationality in terms of cost management and operational efficiencies. Table 15-8 presents an example of an interfirm comparison analysis.

The participants in an interfirm or interregion analysis often are surveyed beforehand or have a working party choose the operating and output ratios they wish to benchmark with each other. There may be difficulty in setting a standard code of accounts as well as difficulty with consistency and honesty in reporting performance among the participants. Continuous benchmarking is much easier when undertaken within a company because confidentiality is critical when it is undertaken between firms. While the participant receives information about the overall median, lower, and upper quartile performances on each statistic (and maybe the average of the best three as well), no other individual firm's results are disclosed. This usually requires the participation of a trade association to gather the responses and an independent accounting firm to do the analysis. Such analyses of comparative production and accounting statistics have been undertaken annually in many industries for years. Comparisons of marketing performance measures are less common.

Determining where an organization ranks on various performance measures also requires an analysis of why variance exists. Reviewing the difference between the top performance and its own performance tells a firm how far it has to go to be the best. But it does not explain how to get there. In fact, it may simply not be possible because the top performer does not face the same internal and external environmental constraints: Analyzing sets of determinant performance ratios to diagnose the source of the inefficiency and to establish whether or not something can be done to improve a particular operating statistic is quite an art. But, at the least, a comparison of similar operating units can prompt a sobering reappraisal of current behaviors and standard operating procedures (production and marketing process routines). If the analysis was performed within an organization, high performing units can explain to less successful units how they managed to get to the top of the heap.

Control and Artificial Intelligence

Over the last two decades, the information problems of marketing managers have gone from famine to feast. When this happens, a manager's ability to discriminate between important and unimportant information is dulled or paralyzed by too much information and not enough sensible analysis. For example, a supplier of plastic bags had great difficulty determining monthly and quarterly sales of 1,000 different items in his product line (they varied in size, thickness, color, and composition). The problem for the company was that the monthly sales analysis was too thick to read (two inches thick, to be precise). The same information overload is occurring with retailers and manufacturers who try to use scanner data produced at the supermarket checkout. One of the reasons why Toys Я Us has been such a phenomenal success is that almost since it was founded it has used an excellent information system to track sales. This has enabled it to determine well before its competitors what is selling and what is sitting. For example, in 1980, Toys Я Us knew early in the Christmas season that handheld electronic games were not moving.[31] It canceled orders and quickly cleared its merchandise. In a market where over 40 percent of the products each year are new, such early exception reporting is a key to survival and profitability.

31. Connie Leslie, "Toy Stores: Profits 'R' Us," *Newsweek*, January 2, 1984, 54–55.

	Table 15-8			
	Interfirm Comparison Analysis			

Interfirm Comparison Unit,
Department of Management Studies, University of Waikato, Hamilton.
Jewelers' Association of New Zealand Survey 1980
Comparing You with All Other Participants

The Number of Participants in This Analysis Is 68

Participant Code No. Ratios Compared	Expressed as	Your result was	Difference between you and median result	Lower quartile	Median-middle result	Upper quartile	Average of best 3 in group	Rank/ out of
Was your PROFIT satisfactory?								
1. Your NET PROFIT/LOSS for each $100 of SALES was	$	1.87	8.31	4.17	10.19	15.99	24.83	60/ 68
Net profit is sales less cost of goods sold & expenses								
2. COST OF GOODS SOLD for each $100 of SALES was	$	69.00	8.07	64.41	60.93	54.82	53.92	63/ 68
3. EXPENSE for each $100 of SALES were	$	29.12	1.47	34.46	30.59	23.35	21.25	30/ 68
Were your EXPENSES too high? For each $100 of SALES the breakdown of expenses is as follows:								
4. SALARIES (excluding workshop salaries)	$	17.69	3.26	16.82	14.43	11.16	12.58	55/ 68
5. WORKSHOP SALARIES	$	N/A		11.28	8.79	4.17	8.79	
6. ADVERTISING AND PROMOTION	$	0.91	0.58	2.39	1.49	0.69	0.38	23/ 68
7. RENT AND RATES	$	4.17	1.99	3.46	2.19	1.43	1.58	59/ 68
8. OTHER OCCUPANCY EXPENSES	$	3.53	1.36	3.53	2.17	1.20	0.79	51/ 67
9. MOTOR VEHICLES	$	1.27	0.22	1.65	1.05	0.72	0.92	45/ 68
10. INSURANCE	$	0.68	0.14	1.15	0.82	0.58	0.64	26/ 66
11. TRAVEL AND ACCOMMODATION	$	0.00	0.22	0.61	0.22	0.00	0.70	1/ 68
12. OTHER OPERATING EXPENSES	$	0.87	1.03	3.64	1.91	1.12	0.72	14/ 68
Salaries (Ratio 4) and rent (Ratio 7) can be evaluated by an alternative method.								
13. AVERAGE SALARY PAID (excluding workshop)	$	13536	4387	11439	9149	6244	10621	58/ 67
14. AVERAGE RENT per SQUARE METRE of PREMISES	$	120.31	78.62	81.03	41.69	28.61	72.50	58/ 65
Was your STOCK CONTROL adequate?								
15. STOCKTURN The number of times you turned over your stock during the year was	Times	N/A		1.30	1.50	2.30	1.71	

Continued

Continued from previous page

Participant Code No. Ratios Compared	Expressed as	Your result was	Difference between you and median result	Lower quartile	Median-middle result	Upper quartile	Average of best 3 in group	Rank/ out of
The Number of Participants in This Analysis Is 68								
16. GROSS MARGIN Gross profit as a percentage of sales was	%	31.00	8.07	35.59	39.07	45.18	46.08	63/ 68
17. STOCK MARK-UP Gross profit as a percentage of cost of sales was	%	44.93	19.20	55.25	64.12	82.41	85.51	63/ 68
18. STOCK PROFITABILITY (Ratio 15 × Ratio 17) Gross profit as a percentage of average stocks	%	N/A		85	113	146	148	
How PRODUCTIVE was your STAFF? For each person:								
19. SALES were	$	76514	28855	35231	47659	66324	60593	10/ 67
20. GROSS PROFIT was	$	23719	4631	14577	19088	25340	27912	21/ 67
21. NET PROFIT was	$	1434	3305	2568	4739	7449	15137	55/ 67
For each $100 of salaries:								
22. SALES were	$	565	8	454	573	738	658	35/ 68
23. GROSS PROFIT was	$	175	50	184	225	271	302	37/ 68
24. NET PROFIT was	$	11	45	26	55	96	164	59/ 68
Was the value of your SALES adequate?								
25. TOTAL SALES	$	160680	48539	119188	209219	303042	343354	39/ 68
26. SALES per SQUARE METRE of PREMISES	$	2685	458	1473	2427	3424	4195	23/ 65

Within the next few years a new generation of computer software will be commercially available that produces exception reports, diagnoses problems, and proposes corrective action based on case histories. It will talk to the planner in precomposed sentences that present the results of the most sophisticated statistical models. At Duke University, one of the first prototypes of this program has been developed by Professor John McCann.[32] His Marketing Gates software contains the following components:

♦ *Data viewers* that extract and view data from huge databases that are continuously updated.

♦ *Analyzers* that test for trends and exceptional data points and ratios.

♦ *Designers* that help design and schedule the necessary strategic and tactical marketing response (such as a special trade promotion).

♦ *Monitors* that track the effects of corrective actions taken.

32. John McCann, Bill Lahti, and Justin Hill, "Marketing Gate: A Knowledge-Based System for Augmenting Marketing Intelligence," (*Working Paper,* Fuqua School of Business, Duke University, 1989). For further references on DSSs, see Louis A. Wallis, *Decision Support Systems for Marketing* (New York: Conference Board Report, #923, 1989).

Marketing Gates software is different from other types of software in the way it communicates with marketing executives. It communicates in words, sentences, inferences, interpretations, and conclusions about the marketplace environment rather than in numbers. The knowledge of general marketing experts and product market specific experts will ultimately be built into the software, making its ability to report marketing management diagnostics even more exceptional. It will become a market management system that will assist a cross-functional team in all aspects of market management, from analysis to strategy formulation to control. This type of marketing software is likely to be available to improve the efficiency and effectiveness of market management by the late 1990s.

Budgeting and Control in Global Marketing

Overseeing the budgeting and control of a number of regional or national markets is one of the more straightforward global marketing activities because it involves information processing and analysis that has been greatly simplified by global EDI (electronic data interchange). Using EDI, the performance of an international market can be compared to its approved budget as readily as the Southwest U.S. market. If budgeting and control required physically looking over the shoulder of the executives responsible for budgeting and control in different international markets, then controlling international markets would be very difficult. However, such a physical review is not required. If the same routines are adopted in all international markets, then not only is budgeting and control rather straightforward, but benchmarking between national markets can be used to further identify cost irregularities and the effectiveness of new initiatives taken in specific markets.

The major problem with budgeting in global markets is transfer pricing. Transfer pricing is the price that a production unit within a multinational company charges another production unit of the company in another country for components or services. The two factors that complicate such pricing (pricing to the first production unit, costing to the second) are tax laws and international exchange rates. Multinational firms naturally attempt to earn, account for, and report their profits in countries that have lower corporate tax rates. They do this by charging a lower transfer price to production units in the country with lower corporate tax rates. This lowers the reported profits earned by the production unit in the country with the high tax rates and raises the profits earned by the production unit in the country with the low tax rates. In effect, profits are exported to countries with low or no taxes on company profits. However, when this happens, the true costs of the component are distorted, which makes it difficult to properly control costs. Fluctuating exchange rates also add uncertainty to transfer pricing and cost control, particularly if the financial function of the firm is also attempting to make money for the firm by speculating in foreign currency transfers. One solution is to keep a second set of accounts and budgets that reports all true costs in U.S. dollars (the standard global currency). These accounts report the true cost of a component shipped to another country, rather than its tax reduction-driven transfer price.

The willingness of senior management to believe that some of the control measures described above simply do not apply to a specific international market is an invitation to a loss of control, waste, and even fraud. All of the above measures of control should be applied globally, with *no* exceptions. The point is that the expected performance standards on each of the measures will vary depending on the competitive nature of each market. Moreover, whatever the initial standard, performance on each of the control measures should be improving in all of the international markets. The adoption of so-called banana republic budgeting and control procedures (or more precisely *non*procedures) will almost inevitably result in a banana republic performance. In less colorful terms, competitively irrational budgeting and control procedures will lead to competitively irrational decision making and behavior.

1. The spreadsheet PROFIT, presented in the following table, takes standard accounting information and computes the traditional P&L budget statement and a more competitively rational P&L budget statement. Please explain the differences between the two statements.

Traditional and Rational Profit and Loss Budget Statements

Management Accounting Information

Sales	$15,000
Increase/decrease in inventory	(67)
Variable manufacturing costs	6,018
Fixed manufacturing expenses	870
Variable distribution costs	774
Fixed distribution costs	100
Actual selling costs	300
Selling costs to be charged to this period	300
Actual advertising costs	1,707
Advertising costs to be charged to this period	900
Actual sales promotion costs	1,568
Sales promotion costs to be charged to this period	1,200
Actual market research and development expenses	175
Market R&D expenses to be charged to this period	50
Actual product management expenses	210
Product management expenses to be charged to this period	200
Administration overhead expenses	1,300

Traditional Profit and Loss Statement

Sales		$15,000
Variable manufacturing costs	6,018	
Variable distribution costs	774	
Inventory adjustments	(67)	$ 6,725
Gross profit		$ 8,275
Fixed manufacturing expenses	870	
Fixed distribution expenses	100	
Administrative overhead expenses	1,300	$ 2,270
Profit before marketing expenses		$ 6,005
Selling	300	
Advertising	1,707	
Sales promotion	1,568	
Market research and development	175	
Product management expenses	210	$ 3,960
Net profit before taxes		$ 2,045

Continued

Continued from previous page

Rational Profit and Loss Statement
($ in 000s)

Sales		$15,000
Variable manufacturing costs	6,018	
Variable distribution costs	774	6,792
Gross manufacturing contribution		$ 8,208
Selling	300	
Advertising	900	
Sales promotion	1,200	$ 2,400
Gross marketing earnings		$ 5,808
Market R&D expenses	50	
Product management	200	$ 250
Net marketing earnings		$ 5,558
Fixed manufacturing expenses	870	
Fixed distribution expenses	100	
Administrative overhead expenses	1,300	
Inventory adjustments	(67)	$ 2,203
Net profit before taxes		$ 3,355

Costs Carried Forward to Be Charged to Future Periods

Selling	$0
Advertising	807
Sales promotion	368
Market R&D	125
Product management	10
Total costs carried forward	$1,310

2. Which of the budgeting routines in Figure 15-2 do you think shows the greatest competitive rationality? Why? What might your answer depend on?

3. The excessive construction of commercial offices in the United States during the 1980s was an economic disaster. Could it have been avoided by better forecasts? What forecasting techniques do you think could have been used?

4. Why might firms rely too much on forecasts of sales and costs that are based on computer-generated historical statistics?

5. What marketplace events are most likely to upset an economic forecast based on historical data?

6. The failure of almost all econometric forecasters to predict the 1990–1992 recession in the United States and Britain has added to the general skepticism about economic forecasting. A further concern is that the forecasts of different prestigious economic forecasting units often vary. How should an executive respond when 50 different economic forecasters make 50 different predictions?

7. The mental model that an executive uses to think about the impact of advertising expenditure on sales is a very important determinant of advertising budget decision making. Draw a graph of the relationship that you believe exists between advertising spending and sales. On the graph, indicate the optimum amount that should be spent on advertising. Would the relationship between spending on other marketing activities and sales have a similar shape?

8. Describe what economic theory the MARGINAL spreadsheet is based on and explain how it works (see the box on page 557). What problems may arise from using such a spreadsheet?

9. Another way to understand the output implications of a cost structure is to use the Du Pont Financial Analysis model. It breaks financial analysis into two streams: income and investment. The following table presents the RETURN spreadsheet, which enables planners to use the Du Pont model in "what-if" analyses under different assumptions and forecasts of sales, costs, and investments in new assets. What are the advantages of using such a spreadsheet?

RETURN: A Du Pont Financial Analysis Spreadsheet

Assumptions

Net sales	$1,000
Cost of goods sold	450
Variable expenses	150
Fixed expenses	200
Inventory	500
Accounts receivable	300
Other current assets	100
Fixed assets	2,000
Total liabilities	800

Income statement accounts

Net sales		$1,000
COGS		450
Gross margin		$ 550
Expenses		
Variable	150	
Fixed	200	
Total expenses		350
Net profit		200

Balance sheet accounts

Inventory	$ 500
Accounts receivable	300
Other current assets	100
Total current assets	$ 900
Fixed assets	2,000
Total assets	$2,900
Total liabilities	800
Net worth	$2,100

Financial Ratios

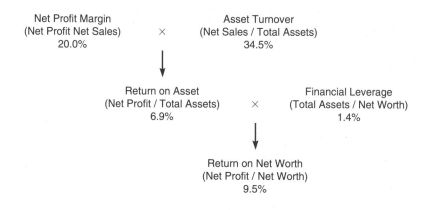

10. In 1992, upon discovering that its "Uh-huh" Diet Pepsi ads were ranked number one in Video Storyboard Test's ranking of the most popular commercials for each quarter of 1991, and that Diet Coke's forced preference advantage had slipped from 70–30 percent to only 52–48 percent, PepsiCo decided to increase its ad budget spending from $70 million in 1991 to $120 million in 1992.[33] What does this tell us about the competitive rationality of Pepsi's advertising budget and advertising budgeting in general?

11. Please justify the following propositions:
    Proposition #1. The greater the uncertainty about the external marketplace, the greater the use of informal controls.
    Proposition #2. The greater the dynamic change in the marketplace, the greater the use of informal controls.
    Proposition #3. The tighter the financial situation of the firm, the greater the use of formal controls.
    Proposition #4. The greater the consistency between marketing objectives and control measures, the greater the likelihood of attaining the objectives.

12. Monitoring customer satisfaction has become a very important marketing control measure over the last decade. But are there any other satisfaction indices that are important?

13. Monitoring customer dissatisfaction is a key component of competitive rationality, but often customers will not report their dissatisfaction. What marketing tactic can a firm employ to make sure that customer dissatisfaction reported by customers and is brought to the attention of senior management?

14. Why is the percentage of new products contributing to sales such a critical measure? Should it be an absolute or comparative measure?

15. Federal Express puts a scanner code on all its packages, and the code is scanned whenever the package is moved. Experts predict that all freight will have such codes in the future. What impact will this have on logistics control and logistics services?

16. If the clan culture is so great for implementation and control, then why don't more companies change from their current bureaucratic cultures to the clan culture?

17. What fairness and motivation problems might arise with profit sharing?

18. Some consultants have suggested that a better alternative to profit sharing is a profit-related pay plan where the employee's salary is supplemented if the company makes a profit, but it is also reduced if the company makes a loss. What control problem might result from such a scheme?

19. A program to reward employee suggestions seems to be a very sound idea, but how might it be difficult to implement so as to be useful in improving a firm's marketing management?

20. How can product managers present problems for a sales manager who is trying to control the allocation of his or her sales effort across product groups?

21. Diagnose the performance of the sales rep reported in Table 15-5. What action would you take if you were the sales manager?

33. Joshua Levine, "Affirmative Grunts," *Forbes,* March 2, 1992, 90–91.

22. Why might a firm pretest its advertising creatives rather than rely on measures that monitor a consumer's reaction (in terms of attention and recall) to advertising after it has appeared in the media? Who should do the pretesting?

23. The Geneva-based International Standards Organization has produced an extensive list of quality standards (ISO 9000) that apply to numerous functions within an organization.[34] Some examples are listed here:

   ◆ *Design:* Sets a planned approach for meeting product/service specifications.

   ◆ *Inspection and Testing:* Requires workers and managers to verify that all production activities are undertaken according to process specifications.

   ◆ *Training:* Specifies methods to identify training needs and keep records.

   ◆ *Purchasing:* Specifies ways of approving suppliers and ordering procedures.

   Independent ISO auditors inspect and certify that a firm meets the standards required by the Economic Community. Certification can cost hundreds of thousands of dollars and take as long as 18 months. The ISO 9000 certification has been adopted in 55 countries. What impact do you think it will have on global marketing?

24. In April 1993, the Kennedy School of Government at Harvard University launched a project designed to pass legislation that gives shareholders more rights and control over management. One of its proposed regulations would require firms to track customer satisfaction surveys and publish them in quarterly and annual reports. What has this activity got to do with shareholder rights? What effect do you think such a law would have on management?

25. The following is a true horror story about customer disservice. Describe the types of service process controls that you would implement to make sure that such an incident would never occur again.

On Thursday, 9 A.M., I made a call to CVI (Cable Vision Industries) to schedule a service call. I have two cable connections; however, only one was working. I was told the serviceman would be at my house between 8 A.M. and noon the following day (Friday). On Friday morning, I was up before 8 A.M. and ready for the serviceman. I worked on a project while sitting about 15 feet from the front door. My seven-year-old was home and playing and I also had four dogs indoors. At *eleven* o'clock, I received a call from CVI's office saying that the serviceman was on his way. At around *12:15,* I called CVI to find out why the serviceman hadn't arrived yet. I was told to hold the line. I did— for around 18 minutes. Being put on hold for five minutes is a very long time; 18 minutes is an eternity. Finally, I was told by the operator that she couldn't contact the serviceman because he wasn't answering her call. She said she knew he was going home at 1:30, so he should be at my place soon.

At 1:40 P.M., I again called CVI. A different operator answered the phone. I had to explain the entire situation again. But this time, I at least got a name—Linda. She puts me on hold for around 12 minutes. Back on the line again, she tells me they still can't contact the serviceman. I tell her that I would like to talk to a supervisor. I'm back on hold now for about 8 minutes. Back on the line she (Linda) tells me that the supervisor said they would try to contact the serviceman and let me know. I called back again at around 2 P.M. and asked to talk to a supervisor. I did not go through the story again. After waiting 14 minutes, I was told that there were three supervisors on duty now and until 5 P.M. However, the operator could not get in contact with any of them. She said she would keep trying and have one of them call me.

It's now 2:45 P.M. I am talking to another operator whose name is also Linda. I go through the entire story again. I waited another 12 minutes. Then I was asked if anyone had left a message on the front door. I said he couldn't have missed me. I hadn't even

34. Jonathan B. Levine, "Want EC Busines? You Have Two Choices," *Business Week,* October 19, 1992, 58–59.

left my working space by the front door long enough to take a shower, in fear of missing the serviceman. I also told her I had four dogs in the house that go crazy barking when the bell rings or someone knocks on the door. I was put back on hold. While on hold, I took the cordless phone to the door and there it was; a door-hanger message that read "Sorry We Missed You!" The serviceman wrote on the card, "Will need to be home." The time was also written in at 11:45 A.M. He never rang the bell. He just hung the note and left.

The operator came back on the line and I told her about the doorknob message. On hold again for four minutes and I'm finally speaking to a supervisor. I repeat the story, which is becoming a saga. The supervisor (Malena) says to me, "Wait a minute, let me check your . . ." she started saying "account" then mumbled it off. I could hear her punching the keys of her computer. I was saying to myself, *yes, please check my account and you will see it is flawless, a good account that you wouldn't want to lose.* I had the feeling that if our account wasn't just right (up to date payments, etc.) then she would have fluffed me off. When she came back on the line, I told her that I felt as a supervisor she should know that I was told over two hours ago that a service person would call me, and over an hour ago I was told a supervisor would contact me. I also told her that I have been given the runaround all day and that I had spent more than an hour just on hold, not counting interacting with the operators.

She then says, "We will have someone out today." I said, "Great, but when? I cannot sit here all day waiting." I asked her to give me a time and I would be back by then. She said she couldn't do that because she has no idea how long each service call would take and that they run anywhere from five minutes to an hour. She said she could set it for after a certain time, and someone will call 30 minutes ahead of time, so we set the time at *after* 5:30 P.M. Five minutes after getting off the phone with the supervisor, the first Linda I talked to hours ago called and asked, "I'm calling about the third cable hookup you need." I thanked her and said I did not want a third hookup, but that I had two hookups, one of which was not working. Before I could say anything else, she put me on hold. After another six-minute wait, she came back on the line. Before she could say any more, I cut in to tell her that I had just (10 minutes ago) talked to the supervisor and the matter has been resolved. The operator then wanted the name of the supervisor I talked to so that she could check with her and get her own records in order.

At 5:05 P.M., the serviceman shows at our front door. No call ahead and *before* the designated time. Would we have received another "Sorry We Missed You" had we not come home early from doing some chores? After checking a few wires and changing a few, he had the set working. In the middle of his working, he received a call from CVI's office. When he got off of the phone, he asked if someone from here called the office, "irate" about the service. I said I was not irate, however, I had been on the phone all day trying to get this matter resolved. He then said, "It must have been something, because they sent me from the other side of town to do this job." He was at our home for approximately one minute. However he did leave a tool at our house and had to come back an hour later to pick it up.

A Guide to Creative Decision Making

*"Genius is one percent inspiration
and 99 percent perspiration."*
Thomas Edison

*"Some men see things as they are and say 'why?'
I dream of things that never were and say 'why not?'"*
George Bernard Shaw

It is a Monday morning in June, show-and-tell time of the year. The brand manager has been delaying work on the annual marketing plan, rationalizing that the day-to-day implementation and fire-fighting problems of managing a brand must take priority. New strategy development has been postponed several times because it is such an unstructured, usually unproductive exercise. An inadequate environmental report containing various unrelated market research reports and some newspaper clippings on competitive activity and economic trends has been pushed around the desk, the way that a child plays with indigestible food on a plate. The manager actually knows a lot more about the environment, but even though this internal information is somehow stored in memory, the manager cannot readily access it. First, new facts have to be absorbed, and then the manager has to start creating ideas. The outward evidence of this process may involve a lot of head scratching, ear pulling, forehead massaging, hand clenching, doodling, and gazing out the window. What is going on inside the marketing manager's mind during such moments of intense cognitive effort, and what facts, structure, and procedures will help?

The lot of marketing decision makers is not easy. First, few universal marketing laws can be applied to the unique product-market each marketing manager faces. Second, all sorts of factors can bias a manager's perceptions and judgments of the marketplace. Third, competing marketing managers are continually disturbing the equilibrium. The moment one manager thinks the situation is under control, some other enterprising mover and shaker changes the situation. Creative decision making is like playing chess with multiple opponents who frequently change the rules by, for example, moving their knights four squares forward and two to the side instead of making the standard play. But, at least chess is played at only arm's length. The competitive market game is played from a greater physical, temporal, and conceptual distance. Furthermore, strategies are unreliably implemented, resulting in outcomes that are difficult to measure and that extend over an indeterminant length of time. Before these results can be observed, they are affected by poorly understood competitor and facilitator actions and reactions. The overlapping factors that influence creative decision making can result in quite a quagmire—one that the manager must often face alone.

The manager's mind must absorb, structure, and create at a very abstract level of perception and imagination. This is the *art* of marketing management. However, because it is an artistic skill does not mean we cannot apply logic and science to improve our understanding and managerial problem solving.

This appendix begins with theories of the organization and processing of information. The second section examines the use and misuse of history and experience. The third section describes the creative problem-solving process and presents suggestions on how to improve each stage of this process. The fourth section discusses the organization and management of group problem-solving situations and explains how to increase the productivity of group and team problem solving. Metacognition, an awareness of our own thought processes, was introduced in Chapter 14 in the discussion of activity sequence memory. Metacognition theory says that the more aware we become of *how* we think, the more we will be able to improve the *way* we think.

How Information Is Stored in Our Memories

Cognitive psychology has established that information is stored in memory in particular structures. These structures are learned and vary greatly among individuals. Experts have much richer cognitive structures than novices. While we may be born with some basic structures for visual perception and language, a very controversial assertion, we primarily build our memory structures from direct experience and second-hand knowledge (vicarious learning). It is this learning capability that enables people to vary so much in behavior and to be so creative, adaptable, and successful as a species.

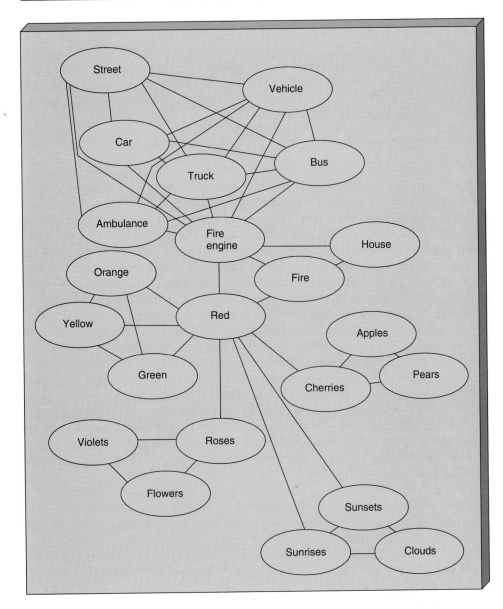

Figure 1

A Fragment of a Memory Network

This typical fragment of a memory network was developed by Collins and Loftus, the inventors of spreading activation theory. A shorter line indicates greater relatedness. If given a word association task, a person with this memory would say either *house, fire engine,* or *red* in response to the prompt *fire.* Facts about a market are organized in similar networks, and their organization determines what facts are recalled quickly when thinking about the market.

Source: Allan M. Collins and Elizabeth F. Loftus, "A Spreading Activation Theory of Semantic Processing," *Psychological Review* 82.6 (1975), 412. Copyright © 1975 by the American Psychological Association. Reprinted by permission.

Within these memory structures are stored facts and beliefs. The likelihood that an important fact will come to mind depends on whether critical doors are opened to gain access to the information in memory structure. The process of opening doors to important information or opening multiple doors down a network of memory stores is called *spreading activation* (see Figure 1).[1] When the nodes (or connections in memory between facts) are activated, they activate other nodes and, hence, knock on and open doors to other memory storage rooms or files. This is an important theory,

1. A. M. Collins and E.F. Loftus, "A Spreading Activation Theory of Semantic Processing," *Psychological Review* 5 (1975), 85–88; and J.R. Anderson, "A Spreading Activation Theory of Memory," *Journal of Verbal Learning and Verbal Behavior* 22 (1983), 261–95.

because it suggests that the way we gain access to and use information about the marketplace environment depends on how we have *organized* it in memory. If it is organized into sensible hierarchies, building from specifics to general facts, and if this structure is frequently used, then, all else being equal, we will be able to make extensive use of what we know. We will also be able to add both new information and new structures to our environmental knowledge. However, if it is loosely and chaotically organized and seldom activated, then the task of thinking about the marketplace environment will be a metaphorical and literal headache.

It's Not What You've Got, But How You Use It

Problem-solving is directly related to memory organization and structure. The famous Gestalt school of thought in psychology emphasized the structural understanding of facts—putting facts together in the right way and organizing them to create new meaning. This means that we must structure environmental facts so that we can use them better. We must organize how we think about the marketplace. The process of organizing environmental information prescribed by the STRATMESH procedure is such an attempt. This organization was called mental models in Chapters 1 and 2. Chapters 3 through 7 described a number of such frameworks and models. After repeated use of the same consumer, channel, competitor, public policy, and company environment frameworks or mental models described in Chapter 2, a marketing planner will adopt this general framework as his or her own way of thinking about any product-market. The more frequently such an organized way of thinking is used, the easier it will be for the manager to think about the environment this way.

New theories make the distinction between declarative knowledge (facts) and procedural knowledge (the skills we have learned, both physical and mental). John McEnroe developed exceptional motor responses for playing tennis. Albert Einstein developed brilliant mental motor responses for thinking about time, mass, and energy. Investigating competitive rationality thought procedure is important because it will help us understand what gives direction to a manager's thoughts and behavior and how thoughts and facts are connected.

Researchers at Carnegie-Mellon University, such as John R. Anderson, have created artificial intelligence computer programs with logic built on hundreds, even thousands of condition-action pairs, called *production rules*.[2] These rules are based on the concept of "if x then y." For example, *if* Hal is the father of Joel and Joel is the father of Paul, *then* Hal is the grandfather of Paul. For the rule to apply, the thinker must be aware of the facts contained in x (that Hal is the father of Joel and Joel is the father of Paul). This depends on whether such facts can be pulled from memory or from outside information. Systems of these production rules can model psycho-linguistic mental processes, mathematics skills, and problem solving. In the Rationality in Practice box on page 590 you are asked to solve a series of problems. By completing the entire water jug exercise, you will better understand the material presented later in this appendix.

Competitive Thinking Production Rules

An example of a marketing *strategy* production rule might be the following: *if* the consumers are price sensitive and our closest competitor drops its price, *then* we should consider dropping our price. It can be made more complicated by detailing the action, such as looking at the impact of a price decrease on other participants in the marketplace and on contribution margin. The importance of studying not only what

2. John R. Anderson, *The Architecture of Cognition* (Cambridge, MA: Harvard University Press, 1983).

managers know (that is, what they can access in memory) but also what mental procedures they apply to such knowledge now becomes clear. A particular planning process is actually a set of recommended planning production rules that should be applied to the suggested strategy and environmental information. The STRATMESH process, described in Chapter 1, uses very clear procedures that describe how information should be used. Most planning systems are not specific in regard to *how* information should be used. This means that individual planners must apply whatever intuitive information usage rules or procedures they have learned.

The Thinking Skills of Expert Marketing Decision Makers

Expert chess or marketing strategists are very different from novices on three interrelated components: they are more knowledgeable (have access to more facts), they have superior knowledge structure and organization that enables them to see the facts differently, and they possess many more plays, or procedures, that are triggered by their views of the facts.[3] The parallels between expert chess players, great entrepreneurs, and talented senior executives should now be clear and have been confirmed by research. Several extensive field studies provide strong evidence that skilled senior executives think differently from their lesser-skilled counterparts because they have richer, more complex, and more discriminating memory structures and well-learned, often intuitive ways of searching and using information. According to Daniel Isenberg in his article "How Senior Managers Think," senior managers can intuitively sense when a strategy-environment problem exists.[4] They have well-programmed and integrated implementation responses. This intuitive fluency in analysis and response is the result of well-organized and intra-related memory structures that interrogate the environment facts and prompt *ah-ha!* strategy and implementation solutions. Their pattern recognition is so superior that they are much better at identifying a *new* environmental fact and drawing higher-order implications from such anomalistic information.

Experienced senior executives are also capable of stepping back and seeing the big picture, a skill that comes from possessing high-order integrated information structures. In fact, some senior managers actively test strategic hypotheses to learn about the business. What appears to be action for action's sake is adding to experience and environmental information structures. Finally, senior managers appear to see the connections between problems and how solving one problem may create others. This suggests they are better at mentally meshing new problem solving strategy with all aspects of the environment because of the quality of their environmental information structure and their frequent use of this structure in their day-to-day thinking. To put it simply, they are paid a lot to think a lot and to put all the pieces together.

Other researchers have observed the greater cognitive power of the senior executive in terms of how perceptions and thinking are organized. Senior executives can conceptualize whole systems and reason through the multiple consequences of strategy on consumers and competitors. Like chess masters, skilled managers are also more capable of making subtle distinctions and differentiating between environmental phenomena. In particular, they are adept at seeing a strategy or a fact from *someone else's* point of view (for example, the different viewpoints of the different players in a market). As Walter Kiechel suggests in "How Executives Think," "thirteen ways of looking at a blackbird" may be routine thinking for a senior executives.[5] They also can think in more dimensions and are adept at going from the abstract *down* to the particular and

---

3. W.G. Chase and H.A. Simon, "Perception in Chess," *Cognitive Psychology* 4 (1973), 55–81.
4. Daniel J. Isenberg, "How Senior Managers Think," *Harvard Business Review*, November–December 1984, 81–90.
5. Walter Kiechel, "How Executives Think," *Fortune*, February 4, 1985, 127–28.

Rationality in Practice:

The Water Jug Problem

This problem will test your ability to think abstractly. Imagine that you are working at a kitchen sink and on the bench in front of you is a large plastic jug which, when filled to the top, has a capacity of 29 quarts, and a smaller jug which, when filled to the top, has a capacity of 3 quarts. There are no graduated markings on the containers. How can you use these two jugs to gather 20 quarts of water? Give yourself a minute to solve the problem.

The solution is to first fill the 29-quart jug and then fill the 3-quart jug three times.

The next problem is a little more complicated. You are now given a jug with a capacity of 21 quarts, a second with a capacity of 127 quarts, and you get to keep the 3-quart capacity jug. Using all or any of these three jugs, obtain 100 quarts of water. Give yourself two minutes to solve this problem.

One solution is to fill the 127-quart container once and then remove the excess by filling the 21-quart jug once and 3-quart container twice ($127 - 21 = 106$; $106 - 3 = 103$; $103 - 3 = 100$). Another solution is to remove the excess water by filling the 3-quart jug nine times ($127 - (9 \times 3) = 100$).

Now that you understand the nature of the task, solve each of the problems below. You may use any or all of the measuring jugs described in each problem. Write down your solution beside each problem using the alphabetical code for each jar. For example, the production-rule solution to problem 1 is $B - 3C$. Time how long it takes you to solve all of the problems.

back *up* again. This is further support that information is hierarchically stored and integrated by levels of abstraction, and that the paths in these networks are frequently traveled and restructured. Another interesting field observation is that experienced executives start to test possible strategies against environmental facts much earlier in the problem-solving process than do novices, perhaps because they already have the memory structures in place to do so.

Decision Making Is Not for Everyone

There is some evidence that most people, managers or not, can only cope with two abstract dimensions and about ten concepts at once.[6] When situations are described in three or more dimensions, or we have to juggle a dozen or more factors at once, then we become confused and start to simplify. The limitations in our capacity to think in the abstract may be even greater. Our evolutionary heritage influences our consumption decision making. It also influences our ability to make strategic decisions.

In his famous work on developmental psychology, Jean Piaget described the highest level of cognitive development as formal, operational thinking. A person with such a hypothetical-deductive skill can imagine and test possible hypothetical strategy against facts. He or she can also understand and fluently use abstract concepts, such as price-elasticity. The bad news is that decades of testing and research have shown that not all adults (maybe only 50 percent) are capable of such formal thinking, and even those who can often do not use the skill in their problem-solving tasks. It is clear that a planner/strategist needs such skills if he or she is going to use mental methods to test possible strategies against environmental information structures. Planning that

6. G.A. Miller, "The Magical Number Seven, Plus or Minus Two: Some Limits on Our Capacity for Processing Information," *Psychological Review* 63 (1956), 81–97.

Problem	Given containers with these capacities:			Obtain	Solution
	A	B	C		
1		29	3	20	_____
2	21	127	3	100	_____
3	14	163	25	99	_____
4	18	43	10	5	_____
5	9	42	6	21	_____
6	20	59	4	31	_____
7	23	49	3	20	_____
8	15	39	3	18	_____
9	28	76	3	25	_____
10	18	48	4	22	_____
11	14	36	8	6	_____

involves the understanding and creative development of strategy requires the skills of induction (taking specific experiences and information and generalizing, or integrating, them into a higher order structure) *and* deduction (applying the generalizations and structural understanding to specific situations). It also requires the additional prospective memory skill of thinking ahead (that is, conjecture about what will happen). Little is known about this important competitive rationality skill.

Two alternative methods of managerial problem-solving are available (see Figure 2). The *reproductive* approach recalls a successful past strategy and seeks to apply the same strategy to a similar situation. Its use of what is called a *transduction logic* goes from the particular to the particular. Like teaching a dog a trick, the reproductive approach is a learned stimulus-response, a reflexive problem-solving response that does not employ a higher-order understanding of the situation. One problem with reproductive thinking is that some short-term change in performance, such as a monthly downturn in sales, will produce a knee-jerk, fire-fighting response rather than careful reflection and a wait-and-see attitude. If sales bounce back the next month, then the outcome will reinforce the manager's shoot-from-the-hip style of decision making, even if the results are unrelated to the actions the manager took. Other problems with this approach will be discussed later in this appendix.

The *productive* thinking approach involves using abstract mental structures (which have been built by using past induction and current deduction) to mentally test hypotheses that explain the environment and that suggest strategy. The problem is solved through understanding, insight, and the use of formal thinking. It is a skill that not everyone has acquired or been given. Developmental concept learning studies have shown that average and below-average children use the reproductive method to solve problems, but children with high IQs and college students solve the same problems using more of a productive, hypothesis-testing approach. Marketing planning is, of

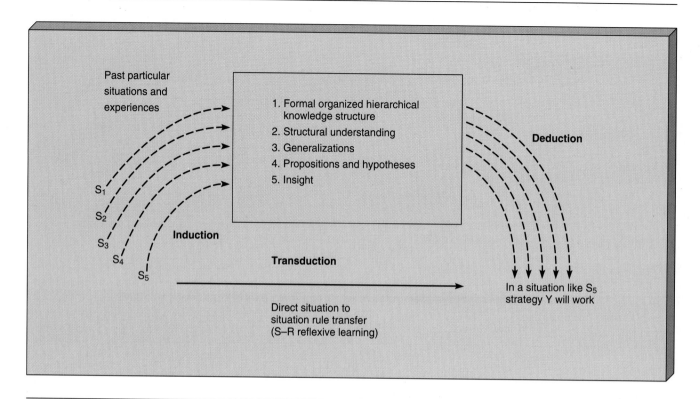

Figure 2
Two Methods of Managerial Decision Making

The transduction, or reproductive, approach to managerial decision making recalls a successful past strategy and seeks to apply the same strategy to a similar situation. Transduction logic, then, goes from the particular to the particular. The induction-deduction, or productive, thinking approach involves using past situations and experiences based on abstract mental models and structures to test hypotheses and suggest strategy. The problem is solved through understanding, insight, and the use of formal thinking.

course, a much tougher problem-solving exercise than those used by developmental psychologists.

Marketing planning is at least a two-stage hypothesis-testing exercise using incomplete and unreliable information. The first stage answers the question, "What is the future operating environment?" The question answered during the second stage (which is dependent on the answer to the first question) is, "What strategy best fits this future operating environment?" It is this type of demanding cognitive problem that the STRATMESH planning procedure was designed to help solve. To cope, managers often have to simplify the problem. But, this may create more problems than it solves. The application of the productive problem-solving approach to marketing planning is still better than the application of the reproductive, what-did-we-do-last-time problem-solving approach.

Recent research suggests that there is a higher-order mental skill that may be even rarer than productive problem solving—problem-*finding*.[7] Problem finding is the ability to see and anticipate problems. Compared to problem solving, this skill requires even more complicated and sensitive information structures in memory (broad and deep expertise) and the ability to imagine first-, second-, and third-order consequences. It also requires the ability to see a situation or a strategy from many different problem-

7. Patricia Kennedy Arlin, "Piagetian Operations in Problem Finding," *Developmental Psychology* 13.3 (1977), 297–98; and "Cognitive Development in Adulthood: A Fifth Stage?" *Developmental Psychology* 11.5 (1975), 602–6.

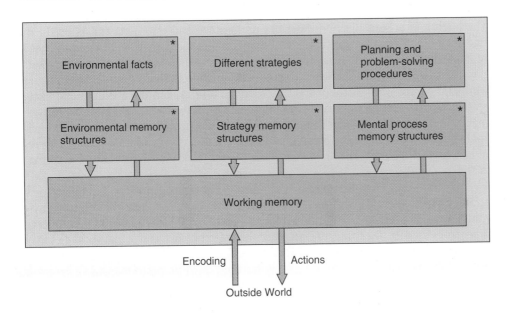

Figure 3

The Mental Models and Memory Structures of the Strategist

The environmental facts are stored in memory structure networks that we call mental models. The different marketing tactics and strategies that we have seen or read about are also stored in different knowledge structures. The way Chapters 9 through 13 are organized is likely to influence both your learning and the way you store the marketing strategies and tactics described in those chapters. We also have memory stores that contain the problem-solving procedures such as STRATMESH that we retrieve from long-term memory and use to process the environmental information and strategic information in our working memories.

*STRATMESH modifies these structures and content.

creating perspectives and to anticipate interaction (synergy) effects between variables. This skill probably results from a combination of individual mental skills (such as multiple role playing, "what if, then that" reflection, and projection) and specific industry or product-market experience. It is not necessarily related to high IQ or education. An individual with such skills is likely to have highly developed environmental and strategy memory structures, as illustrated in Figure 3. Such an individual may appear to be coldly logical. It is also possible for an individual with such skills to appear to make intuitive, almost impulsive, decisions. This is because of the frequency and fluency of his or her use of such skills. Like skilled generals or creative scientists, new information indicating slight changes are seen by problem-finding managers as anomalies that may require a radical change in the way they view the situation, the mental production rules, and strategy they apply to the situation.

Arthur Koestler has written about creativity in art, literature, humor, and science.[8] He has concluded that the common feature of creativity is the novel combination of ideas, the *juxtapositioning* of ideas and facts in new and surprising ways. The PC STRATMESH program attempts to foster creativity in marketing decision making by forcing managers to consider many different combinations of suggested strategic and environmental facts (see Appendix 2). It is evident, however, that many marketing managers and entrepreneurs are able to do this in their minds intuitively. Somehow, they are able to combine their information structures about the marketplace with their knowledge of alternative marketing strategies to develop new, creative strategies. They are endowed with especially creative mental processes, or production rules, that categorize and combine information.

8. Arthur Koestler, *The Act of Creation* (New York: Dell, 1964).

Using Experience and History

The history of an organization describes its heritage and traditions and is useful in understanding its current culture.[9] Most managers, particularly young managers, need to know the history of the company and the background of particular product-markets that predate their own experience. History can provide lessons about what strategies work and do not work in the marketplace. It can also explain the attitudes and likely reactions of competitors, distributors, and senior executives who, as junior executives, may have been responsible for some of the history. Placing past strategies in their environmental contexts helps the planner understand how the organization has found ways of adapting in the past. History can then be seen as a flow of interrelated events that is still evolving.

The immediate past strategy is often a useful starting point for developing new strategy. However, before testing the fit of this strategy to the anticipated future environment, several issues need to be explored. First, how did the implemented strategy differ from the planned strategy? Differences between planned and actual strategies may shed light on recent environmental changes and constraints that produced the differences and may not have been adequately factored into the projected product-market environmental analysis. When history is ignored, then history is likely to repeat itself.

On the negative side, history taken out of context and used to rationalize rather than learn, can be "bunk," as Henry Ford put it. Productive thinking uses history well by analyzing past strategy and adapting it to fit the new environment. History is likely to be misapplied by reproductive problem solvers who, in reaching for old saws and bandages, are trapped by tradition and ritual. During World War II, a British motorized light artillery unit sought to speed up its rate of fire. A careful slow-motion study of film of the firing procedure revealed that two members of the five-man team snapped to attention for three-second periods while each shell was fired. Puzzled by this meaningless act, a crusty old artillery colonel was consulted. After pondering it for some time, he finally exclaimed, "Ah-ha! I have it. They are holding the horses." While this is a bizarre example, many companies and executives seem unable to live in the present. A fitting epitaph for many companies, and even civilizations buried by competition, is that they did not *learn* from the past, they *lived* in the past.

Perceptual Rigidity

Einstellung, or problem-solving rigidity, is a common phenomenon (see the Rationality in Practice box on page 596). The famous philosopher David Hume called it mental inertia. It suggests that we should be very cautious in transferring solutions or production rules from one problem to another and strategies from one environment to another. The Ryder advertisement identifies a type of marketing decision-making Einstellung: companies seeing distribution as a cost rather than a source of competitive advantage (see Figure 4).

Recent events can distort perceptions about the marketplace in the same way that a driver's fear of having an accident is affected by witnessing a gruesome head-on wreck. Called a memory availability bias, it clearly has personal survival value. But, it can also distort decision making that has to place events and abstract issues in perspective. Other decision biases and traps are presented in Table 1.

Computer-based statistical analysis, decision calculus, and artificial intelligence (AI) can help us use all the information available (particularly the most recent infor-

9. George David Smith and Lawrence E. Steadman, "The Present Value of Corporate History," *Harvard Business Review*, November–December 1981, 164–73.

Is traditional thinking keeping you from seeing straight?

The horizontal lines you see here are, in fact, quite parallel. Yet, somehow, they seem askew.

In a sense, a similar phenomenon is evident in business today.

Take distribution.

Classically, for business, it's an expense. Rarely, if ever, a source of competitive advantage.

Take a different perspective, however, and new possibilities emerge.

Distribution can in fact be a source of capital. Capital you could allocate more efficiently, more productively, to your primary business. To improve your product. And with it, your market share.

If this sort of thinking—this kind of perspective—piques your interest, write M. Anthony Burns, our Chairman, at Ryder System, 3600 NW 82nd Avenue, Miami, Florida 33166.

Ryder System. A $5.5 billion leader in highway transportation services, aviation services and insurance management services. A new perspective.

RYDER SYSTEM

Figure 4
Decision-making Einstellung.

A clever ad that attempts to get customers to change their conventional thinking and practices.

Table 1
Ten Decision Traps

1. **Plunging ahead**—Gathering conclusions, forming beliefs and conclusions without thinking about the best way to make the decision.

2. **Frame blindness**—Solving the wrong problem because you have applied the wrong mental model or framework.

3. **Tunnel vision**—Applying too limited a perspective or not applying all of the mental models needed to solve the problem (such as the STRATMESH environment models). Being too influenced by conventional thinking or the thinking of others.

4. **Judgment overconfidence**—Failing to see reality because you are too sure of your facts or beliefs.

5. **Shortsighted shortcuts**—Using rules of thumb (simple information-processing production rules), such as relying too much on a certain type of available facts.

6. **Shooting from the hip**—Winging it, rather than following a more laborious, systematic, and careful decision-making procedure such as STRATMESH.

7. **Group failure**—Assuming a group of smart people will produce a collectively smart decision without a carefully managed group decision-making process.

8. **Fooling yourself about feedback**—Not learning from past mistakes because you are defensive and attribute failure to causes other than your poor decision making.

9. **Not keeping track**—Not tracking outcomes and, hence, being unable to assess success or failure.

10. **Failure to audit decision process**—Not recording the decision process so it is unclear what went wrong and it is impossible to know how to make better decisions the next time.

Source: Based on J. Edward Russo and Paul J. H. Schoemaker, *Decision Traps* (New York: Simon and Schuster, 1990).

Rationality in Practice:

Am I Dogmatic, Rigid, Myopic? Never!

If you have not tried the simple exercises in the box on page 590, then you might find it useful to do so before reading on. Completing those exercises will help you to better appreciate the following findings.

Problems 2 to 6 in the earlier exercise can be solved by the use of the rule B−A−2C. Two of the problems can be solved other ways: problem 5 can be solved by using the formula A+2C poured into B, and problem 6 can be solved with B−7C. Some of you may have discovered that problems 7 through 10 could be solved using production rules that were simpler than the B−A−2C procedure (problem 7: A−C; problem 8: A+C; problem 9: A−C; problem 10: A+C; problem 11: A−C). All of the problems (except problem 9, which was the extinction task) could be solved using the habituated production rule B−A−2C. The experiments conducted by Max Wertheimer and his students from 1936 to 1937 suggest that most of you would not have used the simpler rules, particularly if you were racing the clock.

In a wonderful stream of inductive, phenomenon-oriented research led by the Socratic Wertheimer, his students tested people from various age and education populations, varied the problems (jigsaw puzzles, geometry problems, mazes), concretized the problems by, for example, having subjects actually pour the water, varied the time pressure, varied the involvement and rewards, varied

mation) to make balanced predictions about the incidence and severity of marketplace events.[10] However, the use of artificial intelligence systems can also increase the risk of problem-solving rigidity. In most decision situations, AI is likely to reduce the perceptual and shortcut biases in decision making and improve the quality of the mediocre decision maker. However, if something new is introduced into the decision-making environment, then the task is made doubly difficult because both human and machine will then have to be reprogrammed. It is yet to be established which will adapt fastest, and it may not be the machine. If this is so, then we face the compounded problem of man and machine Einstellung. We now turn to a description of a creative problem-solving process designed to overcome rigidity in decision making.

Stages in Creative Problem Solving

As long ago as 1926, the stages of the creative problem-solving approach were defined as preparation, incubation, insight, and testing. There has been very little refinement of these steps since, but the anecdotal experiences of great minds have accumulated to provide guidance about enhancing the productivity of each of these stages.[11]

Preparation: Putting on Your Bifocals

During this stage, information about the problem is gathered and structured. In marketing management, it involves performing the environmental analysis and structuring the information in a particular way in the environment report. Information quantity, quality, type, and the way the information is organized shape the spotting of problems and opportunities in the current or proposed strategy, so this is a very important stage

10. For an excellent extended discussion of the problem of overconfidence in our beliefs and judgments based on past success, see J. Edward Ruso and Paul J.H Schoemaker, "Managing Overconfidence," *Sloan Management Review*, Winter 1992, 7–17. They prescribe a waiting period of critical analysis before commiting to a plan of action. The decision maker should decide cautiously and implement confidently.

11. See also Richard E. Mayer, *Thinking, Problem Solving, Cognition* (New York: W.H. Freeman and Company, 1983); and W.A. Wickelgren, *How to Solve Problems* (San Francisco: Freeman, 1984).

experimenters, varied the number of extinction tasks, varied instructions and framing, and included self-recited warnings after problem 6 that cautioned the subjects not to be blind to other solutions. They had to work very hard to moderate the Einstellung effect, which was dramatic under speed and stressed conditions, when the number of set-creating problems was increased, when subjects were encouraged to generalize the rule that solves the problem, and when very complex water-jug problems were used.

To paraphrase the major researcher Abraham S. Luchins,* whose dissertation was initially rejected because certain members of his committee could not believe the *strength* of his results, methods have to be developed to make problem solvers open to the evidence, to new prob-lem-solving procedures, and to the testing of new hypotheses. Otherwise, they will be slaves to the rote application of learned, mechanized rules that may work inefficiently most of the time and, when the situation changes sufficiently, may not work at all or worse, may block the problem solver's ability to develop creative, innovative solutions. Good advice for managers, don't you think?

*See Abraham S. Luchins and Edith H. Luchins, *Wertheimer's Seminars Revisited: Problem Solving and Thinking,* vol. III (Albany, NY: Faculty-Student Association, State University of New York at Albany, Inc., 1970).

(see Chapters 1 and 2). To keep perspective, it may be useful to restate a problem from several viewpoints. The decision maker should also keep asking, "Has the core problem been identified, or am I still treating the symptoms?"

Incubation and Meditation

Total preoccupation with a problem is not good. We work best on a problem if we adopt a pulsed concentration strategy, alternating between periods of focusing and concentrating on a problem the way a dog worries over a bone, followed by periods of mental relaxation, digestion, and lower-level thinking. The conscientious manager probably never stops thinking about the marketing strategy, the environment, or a particular issue or problem. Instead, he or she raises and lowers it in consciousness and conscious thinking. Some may only need to change their focus to another problem; but most of us may need to relax completely by, for example, fishing, hunting, partying, or cooking. The initial focus and concentration gets the external environmental facts and proposed strategy in our mind. The most effective next step is to turn inward and become introspective, contemplative, reflective, and projective—daydream the problem.

Focused concentration is probably best when one is mentally fresh and at maximum alertness. Sleep and waking research shows that maximum periods of alertness occur early in the morning, late in the morning, early in the evening, and later in the evening. The time in between is filled with mental slumps. It is not coincidental that these slumps occur at mid-morning coffee and tea breaks, at siesta time after midday lunch, and at game-show time on evening TV when we put our feet up. The night owl/early bird dichotomy is a documented individual difference characteristic, so periods of maximum conscious mental effort should match one's own personal arousal cycle. In fact, the pulsed concentration approach may be a way of simply accommodating our natural physical and mental alertness cycles.

There are several ways to "rev" concentration into overdrive. One is to write down the current solution, improved solutions, and the most novel solutions to a problem. The next step is to work these solutions over by elaborating them. Take the strategy apart component by component, inspect it, clean and polish it, and then reassemble it in your mind. While doing this, note any fringe thoughts and issues and come back to them later. Another way is to talk to a mentor or an equally involved colleague such as a cross-functional team member. The advantage of such discussion is that explaining a problem clearly to someone else often forces clarification of the issues and structure (a sounding board effect). The other individual's questioning and restructuring of the problem will often lead to a mental breakthrough. Working with someone else can also boost one's feelings of confidence, self-competence, and control.

When incubating a problem, it is important to stop consciously worrying about the problem, to reduce stress, and to relax. Everyone has a different method of relaxing that may include some of the following: exercise, soaking in a bath, drowning in music, taking a sauna, neck massage, deep breathing, and meditation. For example, one way to build confidence and feelings of competence and control is through exercise. Physical fitness often brings feelings of mental fitness and well-being. Another approach is to view the exercise as a game, a detective puzzle where just one new insight or fact may break open the case. The objective is to get the monkeys off your back.

Successful incubation results in deep thought reorganization in memory and perhaps a slow, laborious, high-torque, churning and meshing of information structures and mental models. The reason for the earlier assertion that we never stop thinking about a problem (it just drops from internal sight) is that often a surprising thought or solution to a problem will come to mind spontaneously, even when we were not thinking about it. When this happens while showering, shaving, or even sleeping, it is important to write the idea down. There is nothing more frustrating than trying to recall a brilliant, but forgotten, idea or insight.

The "Ah-Ha" Illumination

Illumination, or insight, is the exhilarating "ah-ha" or "eureka" experience that results when everything seems to fall into place. That may be literally what happens. Insight is a restructuring of perception and facts that brings new organization, perspective, hypothesis, and explanation. Tabatha Babbett, a Shaker woman, thought of the circular saw while working at her spinning wheel and watching two men saw wood using the traditional two-man straight saws. She connected two concepts almost subconsciously. The idea for the steel frame that enabled the building of skyscrapers came when the inventor's wife put a heavy book down on top of a fragile bird cage.

The mental meshing of disparate environmental facts into a cohesive higher-order concept and synchronicity, the clicking together of strategy and environmental facts, are keys to skilled competitive thinking. Much of our modern humor depends on assembling disparate facts and fitting them together in a perverse and unexpected way by the punch line. The "ha-ha" surprise of a good joke is not too different from the "ah-ha" insight that occurs during problem solving.

Insight often comes from the slow accumulation of facts or it can be produced by exposure to a single new fact or proposition that leads to a radically new explanation. While Darwin developed one of the great theories of modern philosophy and science, he had some fairly weird theories to explain the evolution and extinction of species before he developed his theory of the origin of the species. According to his own handwritten notebooks, in July of 1837, after undertaking one of man's greatest around-the-world observational research programs, his explanation for what he had observed involved *monads* (not to be confused with *nomads*)! Monads were small living particles that determined the characteristics of a species but that had their own life cycles. This explained the origins and extinction of species. Species died out because their monads reached the end of their life cycles.

In September of 1838, after reading Malthus's *Essay on Population*, Darwin understood that the limits to population growth were determined by environmental resources. He then was able to develop key insights: that competition for resources between species determines the limits of a species population growth, and that adaption to the environment is the key to survival of the fittest. In the process, he dropped his monad explanation and completely restructured how he organized all of his thoughts, perceptions, and facts. Marketing managers can experience similar dramatic insights and illuminations in understanding their competitive marketplaces, but most of their time is spent on the labor: the 99 percent perspiration component of creativity (versus the 1 percent inspiration) that Thomas Edison described.

Testing: Shucks, Another Dead End

Ensuring that a solution or a strategy works requires screening the idea for its fit. This is what STRATMESH is designed to help do. It may also be useful to bring in independent participants to evaluate the fit. The developers of a strategy may be too close to the problem and solution to see the implementation constraints. It is important to resist getting discouraged if the flaws in a strategy are exposed. Even Einstein admitted that he wasted two years on a stroke of genius that wasn't. It is comforting to know that this happens to even the very, very best minds. Testing builds the confidence needed to implement the strategy just as it exposes the overconfidence that can result from the euphoria of the initial idea.[12]

Team Decision Making

Marketing decision making often involves group consultation and team decision making. This can occur at the early stage of creative strategy development and at the senior management review stage (see Chapter 1). Team decision making has several advantages. Judicious selection of group members who represent different internal and external constituencies and who have different marketplace experiences will encourage multiple views of the environment and the fit of strategy. Cross-functional teams enable the efficient accumulation of creative ideas from a number of people. Teams can also produce greater comprehension, cohesion, focus, and more effective implementation. Effective planning is the multiplicative product of *quality* decision making and *acceptance* by those who have to implement the plan. Team decision making must not achieve one to the exclusion of the other.

The disadvantages of teams are that they can be unwieldy (more than ten members may be hard to control), difficult to manage, and, because of the presence of political moles, sandbaggers, and social loafers, can increase rather than decrease discord, rivalry, and organization frustration. They can also produce social pressures to conform, can be dominated by an individual, and, through a lack of personal accountability, can produce irresponsible decisions. A group's effectiveness critically depends on the role and performance of the group leader. The leader must, through formal status and/ or informal respect, direct and encourage the group, set the tone of discussion, maintain morale, manage meeting mechanics, and, most importantly, make sure the team

12. See Russo and Schoemaker, "Managing Overconfidence."

makes decisions.[13] One of the reasons why small entrepreneurial companies can compete against large corporations may be that the commitment to quality group decision making is greater in the small enterprise where team members are shareholders and all have a major stake in seeing the group work effectively. Some of the major group decision-making problems and suggested solutions are listed in Table 2.

Brainstorming, Blue-Skying, and Beyond

In the 1960s, group brainstorming sessions were very much in vogue. The procedure encouraged off-the-wall ideas and responses, encouraged free-association and fringe thoughts, used analogy, and encouraged the unusual combination of ideas and the concrete visualization of abstract ideas. The emphasis was on the production of new ideas, and any criticism was absolutely taboo. Later research showed that individuals given the same instructions, including those presented in the section on individual problem solving, but who worked alone and then pooled their ideas, were at least as productive, if not more productive, than brainstorming groups. The theory behind brainstorming is that one person's idea will spark another person's idea and a ripple of creativity will build into a torrent. At least three things can go wrong in practice. First, the discussion can fly off on tangents that send discussion out of control and into the wild blue yonder. Second, adversarial competitiveness and gamesmanship between individuals and/or participating constituencies, such as finance versus marketing versus production, can inhibit any additive creativity that comes from group dynamics. Third, lazy individuals can hide in groups and be less productive than if they had to develop something alone.

The advantages of the two approaches can be combined by first asking individuals to work alone and allowing them to discuss and circulate their ideas. Then, others can incubate on them before the meeting. This is likely to happen anyway as many executives will want to float trial balloons before the meeting. The meeting must be artfully directed back to the topic by the discussion leader without cutting off the creative process. Some level of criticism and evaluation is also appropriate. Pointing out an environmental constraint on a new marketing strategy is a necessary start to the problem-solving process. The group's intellectual resources must then be harnessed to come up with a solution. Criticism is not bad. It is essential to improve ideas and, if not present, will feed the concerns of group cynics who believe that team decision making wastes time.

The group leader can encourage creativity by showing confidence in the group's creative ability. Research has clearly demonstrated that groups whose leaders tell them that they have a reputation for being original thinkers produce better solutions to problems.[14] Instructions that ask for interesting, clever, and unusual ideas also work better than instructions that simply ask for a lot of ideas. Another way of increasing group creativity is to ask the participants to come to the meeting with solid ideas that will work and with at least one really off-the-wall suggestion. Part of the meeting should be set aside for discussing what may seem to be outrageous suggestions. It is likely that breakthrough advances in strategy, competitiveness, and profitably will come from radical rather than conservative thinking.

13. Jon R. Katzenbach and Douglas K. Smith, *The Wisdom of Teams: Creating the High Performance Organization* (Cambridge, MA: Harvard Business School, 1993). The authors emphasize the need to set specific targets for the team, such as getting a product to market in half the usual time.
14. M.A. Colgrove, "Stimulating Creative Problem Solving: Innovative Set," *Psychological Reports* 22, (1968), 1205–11.

Table 2
Summary of Group/Team Decision-Making Problems and Solutions

Problem	Possible Solutions
Lack of knowledge; reinventing the wheel	Add experience to team.
Lack of creativity	Add the best and brightest to the group; encourage the group's confidence in its own creativity.
Creative impasse	Break and incubate.
Narrow perspective	Vary the background and perspective of the team membership, even though it will increase management problems.
Groupthink	Bring in an individual, even late in the planning process, to be a perceptual heretic and a devil's advocate.
Premature closure	Separate "getting ideas out on the table" from "idea evaluation."
Paralysis by analysis	Set no-matter-what deadlines on decision making and implementation; use analysts who cut through the rhetoric rather than pile it on.
Lack of preparation	Circulate environmental report and proposed starting strategy beforehand; give plenty of notice; embarrass loafers and unseat them for second offenses.
Hidden agendas and politics	Encourage opening position statements and concerns; use heavyweights to increase cooperation and commitment to the overall planning goal.
Cheap shots in group discussions	Make team members pay $1 into a party pot for every cheap shot.
Low commitment	Make sure line and sales management implementers are heavily represented; develop a performance incentive payment scheme for all participants; make promotions dependent on team performance.
Arguing at cross purposes	Structure and direct discussion to deal with issues in an orderly manner.
Everyone talking at once	Pass or throw a ball around. Only the person holding the ball gets to talk.
Separation of creativity and responsibility in team membership	Never embarrass the major stakeholder. Allow him or her to direct the contribution of the spark plugs.
Diffused responsibility	Identify the manager with ultimate implementation and performance responsibility and give him or her the ultimate veto.
Top-down domination	Senior management should step back and play a supportive, nurturing role.
Physical distractions	Relocate, but pack the information-system supports before the suntan lotion.
Time stress	Don't make things worse by panicking; learn from your mistakes so that it doesn't happen again in the future.
Insoluble conflicts	Return to the basics instead of constantly trying to break the deadlock.

Good and Bad Criticism

Often it is not the criticism per se but the intent and tone of the criticism that creates problems. At the very outset, the group discussion leader must emphasize that the superordinate goal of the group is to develop a more competitive, profitable strategy. This objective must dominate all other personal or subgroup goals. It may require bringing in a senior executive to impress the group with the importance of burying hatchets. Care must be taken, however, to not produce an under-the-gun group siege mentality. The leader must be skilled at discouraging the adversarial, tit-for-tat game of pointing out flaws in each other's ideas and in identifying and flushing out hidden agendas. The group leader must do this without undermining the legitimacy of individuals voicing the concerns of the function or outside constituency that they represent. If avenues for such individual expression are not left open, then the organization runs the risk of groupthink, where people are afraid to voice criticism for fear of upsetting group cohesion. Historians consider groupthink a major reason for poor White House decision making in the early years of the Vietnam War.

The tone of the criticism can make a big difference (see Table 3). Expressing one's reaction with enthusiasm, "I quite like the idea, but I'm wondering how we can handle the concerns of distributors who . . " is very different from sneering, "I've never heard a more stupid idea in my life. You want to have our distributors hate us more than they already do." Good, useful criticism is not a gushing, Pollyanna style of communication, but a cooperative attempt to turn problems into advantages.

Decision Politics, Roles, and Responsibilities

Team selection and dynamics are often complicated when groups have three key players: a discussion leader, a creative leader, and the individual who is responsible for

---

Table 3
Idea Starters and Stoppers

Idea Stoppers	Idea Starters
♦ It's too much work.	♦ It's OK.
♦ We'll look silly.	♦ Tell me more.
♦ We're not ready for that.	♦ What are the options?
♦ We've never done that before.	♦ I'd like your ideas.
♦ It's not practical.	♦ What do you think?
♦ It won't work here.	♦ Let's give it a try.
♦ Be realistic.	♦ I've got a wild idea.
♦ It's not in the budget.	♦ What other ways are there?
♦ We've heard it all before.	♦ What if . . . ?
♦ We'll never get it approved.	♦ We might want to consider . . .
♦ That's really weird.	♦ Yes!
♦ Get serious.	
♦ Naah.	

Source: Based on Susan Butruille, Stanley S. Gryskiewicz, and Robert C. Preziosi, "Kaleidoscope Thinking for Creativity," *Training and Development,* September 1991, 28.

implementation and any resulting negative outcome. It is very dangerous not to have someone individually responsible for the product-market plan because the alternative, collective responsibility, is often no responsibility. In group decision making, success has many fathers but failure has none. Also, if the planning is important enough for the cross-functional team to consist of the top talent, then some of the participants may be more talented and creative than the person responsible for the project and overwhelm him or her.

At times it may be wise to appoint a discussion leader who is not the creative leader or person ultimately responsible for the plan because when the roles are combined such a group leader is likely to dominate the group. When this happens, decisions cease to be group decisions. For instance, a senior executive can impose the wrong decision on a group. Studies taken after World War II showed that high-status air force pilots were able to persuade the groups they led that their clearly incorrect answer was correct. Lower-status pilots were less successful at such persuasion.

For uncertain choices, a weighted average of opinions based on individual expertise is superior to both simple majority voting and leaving the decision up to the acknowledged expert. In other words, experts should be given more say, but even experts can benefit from the collective decision process. For example, expert consultants such as doctors, lawyers, accountants, and engineers, often form partnerships where the collective wisdom of the partnership can be readily provided to the client. Decisions in companies are often based on an informal weighing of group members' opinions. But this will only happen if the leader encourages the voicing of other opinions.

When a group member develops a brilliant, but risky, strategy that someone else will ultimately have to implement, the discussion leader's skills are likely to be stretched. The organization wants to utilize the mercurial brilliance of junior and senior executive spark plugs but cannot afford to undermine the position of the implementer who does not want to appear to be a pedestrian thinker. Clearly, executives who manage these discussions well, earn their pay.

Meeting Mechanics and Monkey Wrenches

The importance of managing the mechanics of a cross-functional team meeting are often underestimated. Frequently, group meetings get off to a bad start because the participants were given too little notice and do not have enough time to read and ponder preparatory reports. The meetings then end on a frustrating note because key participants have not scheduled enough time and have to leave the meeting early to fulfill other commitments.

The meeting surroundings can have a major effect on the process. Marketing strategy meetings are often lengthy. This means the chairs and room temperature must be comfortable, and external visual and audio distractions must be minimized. The meeting table should be designed so that participants sit face to face and support systems such as drinks, snacks, and bathrooms are conveniently available. The farther participants have to travel for refreshments, the more likely they will be bushwhacked in the halls while the discussion is hurt or delayed by their absences. Meeting interruptions must be minimized. This all may sound trivial, but the cost of executive time spent in planning meetings can be astronomical. Chapter 2 discusses more meeting mechanics specific to the STRATMESH planning procedure. Poor meeting mechanics not only increase organizational inefficiency but send bad signals to the participants about how seriously they should view the company's decision-making process.

Multiple Teams

For very important decisions it may be useful to create several cross-functional teams or to split a team into several smaller teams that each address the same problem. This approach, while expensive, has been shown in controlled studies to result in more creative advertising campaigns and other marketing tactics.[15] This appoach has also been successfully employed in new product development by Japanese companies such as Sharp, Casio, and NEC, who have hundreds of teams working on similar projects in the general product-market of office automation.[16] The external competitive rationality of these firms is increased by creating an internal competition among teams *within* the firm.

Teams That Reengineer Marketing Decision and Implementation Processes

A common theme running throughout this text is the need to increase the added value and reduce the cost of organization routines, particularly the new product development process, the procurement process, the sales prospect conversion process, the order-delivery process, and the after-sales service process. A team must harness all of the individual and group creative skills and suggested processes described above. Table 4 lists the additional unique requirements of an organization decision-making team that is given such a process reengineering task.

Companies such as Kodak, Motorola, Chrysler, and Western Digital have had considerable success in using such teams to reduce the time it takes them to come up with a new, improved product or the time it takes to imitate and improve on a competitor's new product. Both the cost and time taken to develop a new product have been greatly reduced. Even more importantly, the quality of the output of the new product development (NPD) process is greater, as measured by lower product cost and higher customer satisfaction.

The first stage of process reengineering is to create a process map, which describes the typical process such as the new product development activity sequence script. The second step is to reengineer the process completely to improve the quality and speed of decision making and implementation. The third step is to build into the process self-learning steps so that each new product development cross-functional team is constantly finding ways of improving the new product development process. If the new process does not have such learning built in, then the process cannot reengineer itself. Consequently, the competitive rationality drive of constantly improving organization decision-making and implementation routines will be frustrated because it will be, at best, intermittently satisfied.

In a world where global competition is constantly introducing new innovations and the life cycle of a new model is now measured in months rather than years, a firm cannot review and overhaul its marketing routines every five years or so. It must constantly improve its marketing processes. In such markets, creative team decision making involves much more than coming up with new products or marketing programs.

15. I. Gross, "The Creative Aspects of Advertising," *Sloan Management Review* 14.1 (1972), 83–109; Paul Saintilan and John R. Rossiter, "Gross' Theory of Creative Competition: The Time Is Right" (Working Paper 92-001, Australian Graduate School of Management, University of New South Wales, 1992).
16. Kenichi Ohmae, *The Borderless World* (New York: Harper Perennial, 1991), 65–71.

> ### Table 4
> ### Team Requirements for New Product Development Processing Reengineering
>
> 1. Must be championed by a senior executive who can persuade functional barons to accept changes in the new product development process that cross their boundaries. The champion must give process reengineering number one priority and must be energetic, enlightened, resolute, and prepared to take the certain heat that radical change will generate (the elimination of old reward systems, jobs, standard operating procedures, rules, whole processes, and even whole departments).
> 2. Must be a small team of five to ten members with two or three outsiders who are not afraid to ask the dumb questions, such as "Why do we do it that way" or "Why do we do it at all?" The team should have bottom-up involvement of the best people in the organization. When an organization does its own reengineering of its genes (routines), it needs to involve its very best people from the bottom up. All members must have excellent activity schedule memory (ASM) skills so they can create and critique new added-value activity sequences.
> 3. Must be led by a process-oriented senior executive who understands the entire added-value chain, from concept to after-sales service.
> 4. Must focus on changing the process, and nothing else (such as changing departments). Must move quickly and decisively. Do not accept watered down political compromises or attempts to delay.
> 5. Must be concerned about implementation: changing company information systems, culture, personnel, and reward systems so they fit the new process. Do not try to make everyone happy. It cannot be done. The objective is radical change and not consensus.
> 6. Must accept that fundamentally changing routines involves risk and conflict. Appoint team members who can deal with risk and conflict in a constructive, problem-solving way.
> 7. Must not quit, or accept only minor improvements. The team should use examples from other firms to inspire and teach.
> 8. The whole team must sell the whole exercise as well as implement it. It must not be sold as yet another management fad or flavor of the month.
>
> **Source:** Michael Hammer and James Champy, *Reengineering the Corporation: A Manifesto for Business Revolution* (New York: Harper-Collins, 1993).

It involves constantly improving marketing management processes through creative innovation and sharing the innovations throughout the organization. This is the essence of competitive rationality and competitive rationality is the essence of competitiveness.

Discussion Questions

1. Why is the problem-solving game that marketing planners must face harder than playing chess?
2. Argue the pros and cons of whether a marketing manager's creative skills are superior to that of a composer or artist.
3. Why is spreading activation a key theory underlying the way we organize the structure of the environment report and the strategy report? (Hint: What is directed spreading activation?)
4. How is the cognitive architecture of experts different from the cognitive architecture of novices? How does this difference enable the experts to think better?
5. What is induction and deduction? How are they used in marketing planning?
6. How can history work for you and against you in problem solving?

7. Name two thinking production rules that the STRATMESH process uses. Does it use any others? (Hint: See Chapter 1.)

8. What are the basic advantages and disadvantages of group/team decision making?

9. Why is it important to distinguish between the discussion leader, the creative leader, and the person responsible for implementation?

10. Why are meeting mechanics so important?

Classic Problem-Solving Exercises

1. A Kurdish peasant woman was kneading dough in front of the center pole of her tent. She wanted more flour and since the bag of flour was behind the pole, she bent forward, encircling the pole with her arms, plunged her cupped hands into the flour bag, and scooped out some flour. When she pulled back to get the flour to the dough that she had been kneading, she found the pole was in the way. Hearing her wailing, a passing Mullah popped his head inside the tent and, after stroking his beard for several minutes, gave her a suggestion that solved the problem. What was it?

2. A man bought a horse for $600 and sold it for $700. He then bought it back for $800 and sold it for $900. How much money did he make in the horse business? What was the value of the horse at the end of the dealing?

3. You are in a cell that is 16 ft. 8 in. long, 12 ft. 6 in. wide, and 7 ft. 9 in. high. The four walls, floor, and ceiling are made of solid concrete. Terrorist jailers open the steel door and throw in two sticks of wood and a large C-clamp. The first piece of wood is 2 in. by 1 in. and 60 in. long. The second piece is 2 in. by 1 in. and 42 in. long. You are given 30 minutes to make a hat rack on which a jailer can hang his hat, flak jacket, and submachine gun. If you cannot do this in the time allotted, you will be shot. How would you make the hat rack?

4. Count the squares.

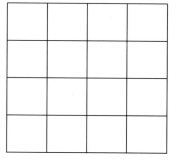

5. Link the nine dots with as few connected straight lines as you can.

6. In a knock-out tennis tournament involving only 64 players, how many games will be played? If there are only 55 players, how many games will be played?

7. A train leaves Detroit bound for Chicago every hour on the hour, and a train leaves Chicago for Detroit every hour on the hour. The trip takes 6 hours. How many trains will you meet coming from Chicago if you board the 8 a.m. train in Detroit bound for Chicago?

8. Divide the circle into as many parts as you can using only four straight lines.

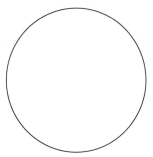

9. There are 12 books standing on a bookshelf. If a bookworm eats and crawls its way from page 1 of the first book to the last page of the last book, how many books has it eaten its way through?

10. Look at the old woman in the picture below. Try to guess her nationality. Next, see the young girl in the picture.

11. If the problem you solved before this one was harder than the puzzle you solved after you solved the puzzle before you solved this one, was the puzzle you solved before you solved this one harder than this one?

12. Below is a plot of land owned by Solomon.

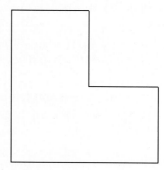

He has four sons. How can he divide the land into four plots of equal size *and* shape?

STRATMESH and Sample Plan

"When a man's knowledge is not in order, the more of it he has the greater will be his confusion."

Herbert Spencer

"Life is the continuous adjustment of internal relations to external relations."

Herbert Spencer

Executive Summary

The used car and auto repair markets have often been associated with unfair business practices that are largely the result of consumers' lack of information and expertise. This reputation is not reflective of the majority of the sellers within these markets but is nonetheless the burden that they must carry.

Automobiles are becoming more complex. This trend began with the adoption of the automatic transmission several decades ago. The state-of-the-art auto of today contains many microprocessors for control of the engine, transmission, and, most recently, the braking system. Thus the average automobile owner cannot know enough to judge the type and extent of necessary repairs to his or her vehicle, nor can he or she adequately judge the condition of a previously owned vehicle. This, when combined with the distrust of dealers and repairers, creates an opportunity for the independent auto diagnostician.

The major auto manufacturers, through their dealers, offer warranties on used autos for varying lengths of time depending on the vehicle age and condition. The independent used car dealer generally does not offer such warranties and is therefore at a competitive disadvantage. The independent diagnostician can help by certifying the condition of a used car to the potential buyer.

The proposed AUTOTEST service to be offered in Columbus, Ohio, will require an investment of some $700,000. It is projected to earn $60,000 a year on the owners' investment of $120,000. The bank loan of $600,000 will be paid off in 10 years, thus leaving the owners with the property and residual value of the premises and goodwill.

The viability of this venture, which will charge a premium price for its service, will depend crucially on the marketing campaign establishing demand for the AUTOTEST *seal of approval* among both buyers and sellers.

Environment Report

1.00 Consumer Analysis

The mechanical condition at the time of sale is reported as the single most important factor in purchasing a used car. Most used car buyers base their assessments of an automobile's mechanical condition and purchase value on the seller's oral representations and on the physical appearance of the car. In the Columbus, Ohio, market, demand would come from:

1.10 The Younger Careful Buyer Benefit Segment

The major benefit sought from such a service is reducing the cost and time involved in repairing a recently purchased used car. A number of consumers also mentioned avoiding the feeling of having been taken. The major target markets are teenagers (first car) and young, working women. They currently rely on family and friends to undertake such inspections with variable success. Young men think they are less at risk. The young consumers who have paid for an auto diagnostic in the past also report having fewer wrecks, are better credit risks, and are generally more responsible and conscientious.

Source: This STRATMESH case was prepared by P. R. Dickson with the assistance of the following group of MBA students: Matt Harlow, Bill Hunnicutt, Mark Knouff, Peter Polanski, Dale Sydnor, and Gary Wedlund. Copyright 1992. It is designed to help teach the importance of fitting proposed strategy to the reported environment facts. To learn how to use STRATMESH, see the Rationality in Practice box on page 618.

Over 50 percent of the consumers in the market for a used car would be seriously interested in such a service at the right money and time cost. More than 70 percent would prefer to have an independent firm (one that would not be doing any repair work) perform the inspection. Twenty percent of recent buyers of used cars actually did have their car inspected before the purchase. The mean expected price of diagnostic service was $50, with a large standard deviation of $10. More than 100,000 used car sales are made in Columbus and Franklin county each year. It is estimated that over half of them are more than four years old. Total potential demand is conservatively estimated to be 20 to 30 vehicles a day over 300 working days (7,500 vehicles).

1.20 The Quality Seller Benefit Segment

In his article, "The Market for 'Lemons': Quality Uncertainty and the Market Mechanism," George A. Akerlof convincingly argues that seller reluctance to tell the buyer of poor vehicle quality occurs often enough that most buyers always discount the stated condition of the vehicle and, hence, lower the amount they are prepared to pay for a car. This hurts the seller of a quality used car. Reducing the cost of discovering the truth about a car would make the used car market more efficient in that it would result in used car prices being more related to the quality of the individual car and, hence, benefit the seller of a 'gem,' a high-quality used car. This seller tends to be an older household who bought a new car and has owned and looked after it for more than six years and 60,000 miles and trades in the car for a new one. Such sellers are likely to encourage a prospective buyer to have their 'gem' inspected.

1.30 Independent, Honest Joe Used Car Dealers

Local used car dealers are generally in favor of the proposed service, even if it were legally mandated, with the understanding that most of the cost could be passed on to consumers. Such diagnostic information would benefit a dealer in negotiating a trading price and helping resell the car. These benefits are particularly attractive to small dealers who lack the capability of checking over a car and wish to position themselves as having higher integrity and higher quality cars than their competition.

Such dealers have an image disadvantage compared to the private seller that is often unfair. It is likely that non-disclosures of vehicle mechanical problems are as high if not higher in private sales made by "decent folks" because used car businesses have a word-of-mouth reputation and operating license to protect that keeps them a little more honest in their car dealing than a citizen disposing of a used car. Selling inspected vehicles would reduce the sleaze factor, which is often an illusion.

2.00 Competitor Analysis

The U.S. public has a cultural mistrust of auto repair facilities and car dealers, which will work against them. However, they can marginally price any diagnostic service down to cover the direct cost of the labor, if they have slack facility capacity, and if it leads to repair work. The major competitors are the following:

2.10 General Repair Service Chains: Formidable Price Competition

BP Pro-care and Goodyear Auto Centers are fully capable of performing diagnostic services. Well financed with significant brand recognition. Placed in convenient locations. Fully staffed with competent mechanics and advanced equipment. Possess multi-brand knowledge and have additional capability of repairing most problems found. Overall credibility is variable, with SEARS most suspect. The cost of a full diagnostic service from these competitors is about $50 to $60.

2.20 New Car Dealers: Credibility Problem

Fully capable of offering diagnostic services. Hampered by long waiting period if current style of customer queuing is retained. Establishment of separate facilities dependent on the strength of the individual dealership. Lack of consumer confidence would be the primary limiting factor because of interest in selling and servicing used cars. The offering of extended warranties on their new cars and near new cars is an indirect competitive threat to the proposed service. If a car with a 100,000 mile, 7-year extended warranty is sold after five years with 30,000 still on the warranty, then the buyer's perceived risks are greatly reduced. The cost of a diagnostic service package from a dealer varies from about $50 to $100. The higher priced service involves following a manufacturer prescribed diagnostic package.

3.00 Facilitator Analysis

Conventional channels do not apply in this service but the following players in the market can act as facilitators:

3.10 Lending Institutions: Their Car, But Do They Care?

Their risk is the possibility of an automobile malfunctioning after it has been tested and approved, resulting in customer repayment problems. However this did not seem to worry them. Perhaps more senior executives would be more appreciative of the concept since it may not only reduce lending risk but also enhance a bank's customer service if it supports its customers use of such a service. However, convincing lenders to encourage their borrowers to make more informed purchases will be no easy task. Many bank managers take a narrow and very conservative view of the service that they provide customers. Indeed, they almost scoffed at the idea that banks would become a facilitating agent for such a service.

3.20 The AAA: Little Local Interest

The AAA was also judged to be an important party in the diagnostic clinic environment. A local AAA manager expressed a lack of interest toward this venture. AAA offers such diagnostic services in several states as do its sister institutions in countries such as Australia and New Zealand. Despite the local disinterest, it should be remembered that the AAA was founded to provide automobile-related services to its members. Perhaps its members only buy new or near new cars.

3.30 Consumer Organizations: Will They Help or Hurt?

The popularity of consumer interest groups such as those founded by Ralph Nader has been in decline in recent years, but research indicates that the issues raised by such groups are still important in the consumer's mind. The problem with such groups is that they are often dead against anyone earning money and profiting from helping consumers make better choices (themselves excepted). They are chronically suspicious of the integrity and corruptibility of such a business, perhaps rightly so.

3.40 Interested Insurers Are Disinterested

The insurance industry makes a big marketing deal out of its concern over vehicle safety, but the fact is that it has seldom initiated economic incentives to encourage its customers to buy safer cars or keep their cars safe. To be fair, the greatest cause of accidents is driver malfunction! The insurance executives spoken to expressed little interest in the service. They see themselves in the insurance business. They did acknowledge that the most dangerous drivers (18–25-year-old males) are also likely to be buying older used cars, which may have mechanical problems that contribute to wrecks.

4.00 Public Policy and Legal Analysis

Public policy will play a vital role in determining the long-term potential of the service concept. In order to develop a successful strategy we must identify and monitor the likely moves of the following players:

4.10 Ohio State Regulations: No Safety and Pollution Inspections

Several states require regular vehicle safety and pollution inspections for older vehicles. Most of the inspection facilities are licensed by the state or are owned and run by the states, with resulting customer service and efficiencies that are typical of state-managed enterprises.The state of Ohio does not require such inspections, however, in recent years it has enacted or considered several consumer protection rules and acts governing deceptive sales practices, odometer tampering, lemon automobiles, and safety inspections. Jalopy pollution inspection regulations may also be enacted. The result is that Ohio has more malfunctioning, dangerous, dirty clunkers than say Florida or California, but this is likely to change.

4.20 FTC Federal Regulations: Down But Not Out

In 1984, the FTC proposed a trade regulation to discourage oral misrepresentation and unfair "omissions of material facts" by used car dealers concerning the coverage of warranties. The rule provided for warranty information through the required usage of a "Buyers Guide" sticker. The dealers had some legitimate complaints about how the program would be implemented, but instead of suggesting an information program that might work, the industry lobbyists attacked the whole concept. Congress killed the FTC efforts to provide more used car buyer information before the 1988 election. The used car industry was a major contributor to the 1988 political campaigns of incumbents. Future energy, pollution, safety, and consumer federal regulations are likely to encourage states to introduce new inspection programs. However, such programs will have to be very low cost and efficient or they will be politically unacceptable to both federal and state governments trying to reduce government and costs.

4.30 Customer Lawyers Seeking Damages

Consumers and their ambulance-chasing lawyers may attempt to sue the diagnostic service, claiming that a diagnostic error on the mechanics of a vehicle contributed to the cause of an accident. Worse, some insurance companies may encourage such litigation as a way of reducing their liability.

5.00 Organization Human Resources Analysis

Initial partners involved in this entrepreneurial start-up venture are three recent MBA graduates with varying business and technical backgrounds. One partner was employed by Midas Muffler as an assistant manager, another was a store manager and partner for a local Goodyear Tire and Service Center. The remaining partner has a father who is 60 years old, ran his own garage, and would work for five years and even employ some of his mechanic friends, part-time, to provide the expertise. The three partners prefer to keep their current jobs but will accept responsibility for marketing, public relations, accounting, personnel, and financial management on a part-time gratis basis.

6.00 Financial Resources Analysis

Each of the three partners are willing to support the start-up with $40,000 from their personal resources for a total of $120,000. The current lending ratio offered by local banks for asset-based ventures of this type, which are considered viable, is 6:1. In better times it has been as high as 10:1. Total capital available for the venture would therefore be $840,000. The owners agree to retain all net profit in the business for the first five years with a view to using the funds to first franchise the concept in other Ohio cities. They would like to earn interest on their investments at the same rate as the bank, which is 10% on a 10 year loan.

Strategy Report

1.00 Positioning: Impartial, Expert, Fast

AUTOTEST will provide diagnosis tests on older cars for buyers, sellers, and owners of the safety of the vehicle (brakes, steering suspension) and the worthiness of its drive-train (engine and transmission). Successful service differentiation will involve the following:

1.10 Added Value to Private Buyer: Wins Both Ways

The service is valuable to the private buyer whatever the outcome. If the car passes the tests with flying colors, it increases the likelihood that the car is basically sound and worth the price paid. If the car does not pass the minimum test, then the buyer has avoided problems. An in-between rating enables the buyer to get quotes for the cost of repairs. The service may also be valuable as a check-up before going on a major holiday or for a do-it-yourselfer who lacks the diagnostic equipment or an owner who wishes to question a repair estimate. Sellers of quality used cars will have their cars tested and use it as a selling point.

1.20 Added Value to Independent Used Car Dealers

The ratings can be used by an independent used car dealer, particularly those without workshops, to screen some prospective buys and to use as a selling feature on its cars. If 40 independent dealers used this service occasionally to regularly then they would differentiate themselves from the other 200 dealers in the county. We will list partic-ipating dealers in our launch advertising and offer contract rates to secure this "fleet" segment. Buyers of used cars who are prepared to pay a premium for a quality used car will seek out dealers who sell AUTOTESTED cars. Thus the positioning strategy relies a lot on self-selection segmentation creating a new type of dealer—a dealer in premium used cars.

2.00 Testing Services

A complete diagnosis of the engine, transmission, brakes, steering, and suspension will be offered as a package deal at a reasonable price. These services will be performed by friendly, skilled mechanics using state-of-the-art diagnostic equipment in a drive-through, four-station setting with an attractive lounge. Initial service will be offered by appointment (the inspection will take an hour) but a queuing service may be introduced at a later date. The features of the service are as follows:

2.10 Quality Seal: Minimum Acceptable Standards

An A (autotest) Seal will be issued only if the car meets all acceptable quality standards. Otherwise, a report will be issued identifying the car's condition without a sticker. The seal must be a very attractive, high-quality, dated decal that cannot be removed. All customers will be given computer-based, laser printer reports of their car's performance, which in reality will be a WINDOWS-based form that includes compression test results and a series of item checks. It just looks more credible coming from a computer, which can produce a certificate-looking report and also store the record, thus minimizing paperwork. The records can also be statistically analyzed to provide information to customers and publicity releases to the press in the future about lemons. It also makes the reporting faster and more foolproof. The seal will be attached to the car by the mechanic.

2.20 Quality Mechanics with Customer Service Skills

Employees will wear a distinctive uniform, somewhat classier than normally worn by mechanics—the wear and tear will be less because there will be no repair work. The average hourly rates for good auto mechanics is $15/hour in Columbus. The head mechanic will be one of the owners' father who is a very street-smart, experienced mechanic. The two other mechanics paid $15/hour should prefer diagnostic work to the hard-and-dirty labor of repairs. The two junior staff paid $7.50/hour should be apprentices in their late teens. Priority should be given to hiring a woman and minority to help in customer relations.

A two-week initial training period should occur on fleet sales allowing any operational problems to be worked out in relative privacy. If initial volume warrants, the fleet diagnostic services can be established as a second-shift operation, involving a retired, experienced mechanic and a young, part-time apprentice, thus increasing capital utilization, contribution, and profits.

3.00 Price

The service will have a premium image and can therefore command a higher price than competing service centers. Our primary appeal will be to middle income groups who are willing to pay a premium price for a fast, quality service. The key pricing tactics are as follows:

3.10 Consumer Prices: $60 and $35 for Safety or Drive Train

Our services will be sold in packages and pieces at the following initial price points:

Complete Package	$59.99
Drive Train Package	$34.95
Safety Package	$34.95

The budgeted price will be $57 after deducting credit card fees for about 67% of purchases.

3.20 Fleet Pricing: $45 for Complete Package

In order to receive the AUTOTEST quality seal, the dealers would have to purchase the Complete Package listed above. The contract price for dealers will be $45 per vehicle. Dealers will have to pay by cash or check—no credit.

3.30 Initial Half-Price Promotion Offering for First 1,000

During the market introduction we will offer a discount on a comprehensive diagnostic package in order to stimulate "first time" sales, and we will offer half price on first month of testing or private vehicles. As capacity for first month is 500 private vehicles, this will cost $15,000. We will offer half price off dealer price for first 500 dealer vehicles tested. This will cost $12,000.

4.00 Location and Premises

AUTOTEST will be located in a mall location near Morse Road close to many of the used car dealers and has a design similar to Goodyear, Sears, and Firestone auto-repair centers, except smaller. The mall location is attractive because of the parking space availability (30 spaces) and it is easy to find and get to. The four-bay building with a customer lounge will be able to be expanded to six bays. The lounge should contain the latest auto magazines, *Consumer Reports,* Blue books, and three cable TVs and coffee station for customer entertainment.

The AUTOTEST premises would be similar in design to the building below.

5.00 Personal Selling to Dealers

The founders will act as the initial sales force. Each will have 20 used car dealers to call on and will contact each one at least once a month. Eighty percent of the dealer business is expected to come from about 6 to 8 dealers having 20 cars tested a month. If 4 to 5 sign on initially, then we expect others to feel the competitive pressure to follow. The new car dealerships will use their own workshops to look at cars and therefore will not use the service.

5.10 Use Parts Suppliers As Volunteer Sales Force

Auto parts outlets such as NAPA and Nationwise provide minimal car repair advice as a value-added feature. Referrals for diagnostic service will only enhance their business while a reciprocal arrangement to auto parts stores should do little harm to our unbiased image. Fifty free tests should be given out to employees of ten of these stores and the program assessed in terms of referrals (cost of $3,000 to come out of initial advertising budget).

6.00 Advertising and Publicity Campaign

The initial three-month promotion will be very heavy. It will create a great deal of publicity, word of mouth, and will encourage a number of dealers to start using the AUTOTEST seal as a selling point. Once the service becomes well known, it will be sold by word of mouth and reminder advertising in the used car classifieds. The major program elements are as follows:

6.10 Communication Message: Look for the Quality Seal

Based on our promotional objectives, our communication message should focus on the following key points:

1. Look for the AUTOTEST Quality Seal.
2. Know what the AUTOTEST Quality Seal means: what its *absence* means.
3. We sell "goodwill." Any firm or individual that uses our services or recommends them will be perceived as caring and trustworthy.

6.20 Media Channels: Three-Month Big Bang on Print and Radio

Over the first three months, a campaign on local radio stations and the newspaper will promote the AUTOTEST service and look for the Autotest Seal of Approval. This will include 24 $500 ads in the auto section of the *Columbus Dispatch* and 12 full-page ads in the 12 issues of *Tradin Times*. The cost of the special print campaign will be $20,000. A $20,000 radio campaign will also be undertaken.

Another $10,000 will be spent on brochures and seals; $10,000 paid to an agency for creatives, design of seal, and PR work; and $200 per week will be spent on reminder ads in the classified used car ad sections of *Tradin Times* and the Saturday *Columbus Dispatch*.

6.30 Publicity

We will use every opportunity to create consumer awareness of AUTOTEST by obtaining as much free publicity as is possible, given the public service nature of our unique product. Some suggested outlets for free publicity will include television, radio, and newspaper outlets as well as publications such as *Business First, Columbus Monthly,*

Rationality in Practice:

STRATMESH

1.00 How to Use STRATMESH

STRATMESH (STRATegy MESHing) is a computer-based thinking framework that helps you evaluate planned strategy and tactics presented in a strategy report (SR) from the different perspectives of facts, beliefs about buyers, competitors, channels, regulations, and your company's goals, strengths, and weaknesses presented in an environment report (ER). It provides a simple method of evaluating a product or service's proposed positioning and marketing programs against existing or anticipated environmental conditions. Using a Strategy Report window above an Environment report window, you run your strategy by market facts, issues, constraints, and performance objectives. See Chapter 1 of Peter Dickson, *Marketing Management* (Fort Worth, The Dryden Press, 1994) for a detailed description of the STRATMESH planning procedure.

1.10 Advantages of STRATMESH Planning

In conventional marketing planning, an executive first reads an environment analysis and then the proposed strategy. Checking the fit of the strategy to the reported market realities would then require a great deal of flipping back and forth between the pages of an Environment Report and Strategy Report. Even so, issues are still likely to be overlooked or forgotten. STRATMESH makes this task much easier. STRATMESH does not do any thinking or computations for you. What it does is organize, access, and scan the information in the Strategy Report (SR) and Environment Report (ER) in a way that makes it easy for you to evaluate and comment on the fit of the proposed strategy to all components of the reported environment. It also makes you more creative by encouraging you to consider strategy and tactics from several different perspectives.

2.00 Starting Up STRATMESH

The STRATMESH program may be run on any DOS computer. The response and execution times are appreciably faster when running STRATMESH off a hard disk. To enter the program type SM and enter/return. This prompts a screen that asks you to input the name of your Comment Report (XXXX), Strategy Report (XXXX.SR), and Environment Report (XXXX.ER). You then type Mesh and the name of your Comment Report XXXX. The Strategy Report and Environment Report must be prepared on a word processing package and printed back onto the disk in DOS format as disk files. For example, Word Perfect 5.1 uses the Ctrl F5 key to store files in DOS format.

3.00 Naming the Reports

We suggest you name the WP files XXXXWP.SR and XXXXWP.ER where XXXX is the name you are giving to the project (your Comment Report). We further suggest you name the DOS versions of these WP files XXXX.SR and XXXX.ER respectively. If other people are STRATMESHing on the project and using the same computer and MESH subdirectory, make sure that your XXXX is a very different name. The current version of STRATMESH sometimes chokes if the meshing exercise names are similar. After creation of the WP reports and their storage as DOS files in the MESH subdirectory, it is a very good idea to make backup copies on a diskette.

4.00 The Required Report Headings and Layout

The logical organization of your SR and ER documents will have a great impact on your successful use of the STRATMESH program. It pays to spend time organizing the contents of your reports into sensible and meaningful hierarchical information structures. Think carefully about your grouping or "chunking" of environmental information and strategy because, down the road, it will influence how you come to think about the marketplace and your strategy. Try to think of headings that help you remember the content of the section.

4.10 Numbering Headings: 1.00–9.00

The major headings in the Strategy Report and Environment Report should start with a number (such as, 1.00, 2.00, . . . 9.00). This means you can have a maximum of nine major headings in your SR and in your ER. Within each major heading you can have nine subheadings, each with a number. For example, under the first heading you can have nine headings numbered from 1.10 to 1.90. These numbering formats *must* be followed.

4.20 Required Heading Format: Blank Lines Either Side

We recommend that the major headings be upper case and the subheadings be lower case. Every heading must be separated from the text by a blank line above and below the heading. Headings must also be only *one line* in length. For use in STRATMESH, the SR and ER documents must be single-line spaced and in DOS format.

4.30 Length of Paragraphs: Keep Them 8 to 9 Lines

Keep your report paragraphs down to about 8 to 9 lines. If you do, they will show up as a complete thought in the window. Write in a tight memo type format to yourself and colleagues. You are not trying to win a Pulitzer Prize. The conclusions of graphs and tables should be summarized. In a working plan, supporting tables and graphs are relegated to an appendix.

5.00 Operating Keys to Success That You Must Learn

There are several keys whose functions you must learn to successfully operate STRATMESH. After some practice you will find how easy it is to use them to scan the reports, move between the reports, access the Comment Report, zoom in on an entire report and wrap up your STRATMESH session. Press the F1 key for help.

5.10 Using the Right/Left/Up/Down Arrows to Scan a Report

You use the pointer that first appears in the top screen to move around the SR file. Pressing the → key will take you into the first major section of the SR. The Down arrow and Up arrow (on the far right of your keyboard) moves you down and up the headings. The ← key takes you out of the section and back to the subheadings. The right arrow takes you to detail, the left arrow moves you back up to summary levels. As you become very familiar with the various sections of the Strategy Report and Environment Report you will only need the report subheadings in the windows to act as a memory prompt.

5.20 Using the Far Right − Key to Move between Document Windows

The far right − (minus) key moves you back and forth between document (SR, ER) windows.

5.30 Using the Far Right * Key to Zoom In on an Entire Report

When the far right * key is depressed, you zoom in on the complete report that is in the active window. If you are in the top window you will zoom in on the Strategy Report, if you are in the bottom screen you will zoom in on the Environment Report, and if you are in the Comment Report window you will zoom in on the complete Comment Report. Press the far right * key again and you will return to your previous state. In the zoom mode you can scroll up and down using Home, PgUp, PgDn, and End.

6.00 Using the Comment Report as a Notepad (Far Right + Key)

Any comments about the environment-strategy fit or any new ideas can be recorded in a Comment Report accessed at the touch of the far right + key. Hit the key again and you return to where you were. These comments are automatically connected to the sections of the Environment and Strategy Reports that prompted the idea or comment.

6.10 Writing Comments about the SR/ER Fit

The Comment Report has its own very basic word processor. Please only use the following keys in writing your brief comments. If you use any others the program may freeze up on you.

a. The left, right, up, and down arrows move the cursor.

b. The insert key switches modes from INSERT to OVERTYPE.

c. Use the Del key to erase letters.

The printed Comment Report is a working document that is used to adapt strategy, to take to a cross-functional team meeting to discuss the proposed plan, or to pass on to someone.

6.20 Printing the Comment Report

To print the Comment Report, hit F10 and a menu will appear that enables you to Save, Print, or Quit. If you have not saved before printing, then the program will prompt you. The Comment Report is in DOS format so it can be stored on disk and entered into most word-processing packages. This enables you to dress it up in standard company memo format. Most of the time you will want to do this.

7.00 Using the F10 Key to Save, Print, and Quit

When you hit the F10 key, a menu will appear. Typing S will save the comments you have made in the Comment Report, which is in DOS format and can be used in almost any word-processing package. Typing P will prompt another menu, which will offer you the two ways of printing the Comment Report. Typing Q will exit you from STRATMESH (there is a check question that asks whether you really want to quit, to which you must answer yes (y) or no (n) and hit return). If you have not saved your comments, you will be prompted to do so. Finally, remember to press the F1 key for help. Press F1 again to return.

Columbus Alive, suburban newsletters, and the AAA newsletter. Part of the publicity will be that AUTOTEST is a free-market test of whether used car buyers are prepared to pay a fair market price to obtain important information about a car they want to buy.

7.00 Licensing and Insurance

Vendor licensing, incorporation, and zoning requirements should be dealt with immediately upon firming up the grand opening date. Required liability insurance binders should be obtained as soon as the operational details are established. Riders for building and equipment can be added as their values become known. An additional rider for business interruption should be included, with a large initial limit to cover the damage that could be done to image building if a loss of business occurs early in the process.

A Federal Employer Identification Number (FEIN) should be obtained upon receipt of the incorporation papers. Immediately following receipt of the FEIN, registration with the Workers Compensation Bureau and the Ohio Bureau of Employment Services should be accomplished.

8.00 Budget

The budgeting projects an annual profit of $60,000 on sales of $360,000 and an investment of $120,000. It is hard to see where costs can be trimmed unless inspection routines can be made even more efficient than estimated. To that end it is suggested that some of the projected profits can be used to reward employees for cost time/cost saving suggestions. Key elements of the budget are as follows:

8.10 Annual Sales Forecast: 7,000 services

4,000 private sales	at $57	=	$228,000
1,000 half sales	at $33	=	$ 33,000
2,000 dealer sales	at $45	=	$ 90,000
(Less $1,000 in bad debts)			
7,000 sales			$350,000

One-shift capacity is 4 bays × 8 hours × 5 days × 50 weeks = 8,000.

8.20 Financing: Buy What Appreciates, Lease What Depreciates

Immediately after determination of the locations suitable for the initial sites, options on the land should be acquired and mortgage financing sought from the bank. The building should be included in the financing, with both being owned by a separate, related corporation and leased back to AUTOTEST. This company will retain title to the property should the venture fail. Lease commitments should be sought for all equipment. Preferably the equipment manufacturers programs should be utilized, as they combine price discounts with market interest rates.

8.30 Annual Profit and Loss Budget Statement

Lease of $600,000 facility	$ 95,000
Equipment leasing	$ 10,000
Utilities and insurance	$ 20,000
Head diagnostic technician	$ 30,000
Two technicians	$ 60,000
Two junior technicians	$ 30,000
Employee benefits	$ 20,000
Employee suggestion incentives	$ 5,000
Employee performance bonuses	$ 10,000
Annual marketing expenses	$ 10,000
Total operating costs	$290,000
Sales	$350,000
Profit	$ 60,000

8.40 Capital Expenditure of $700,000

Major spending is $600,000 needed to purchase, renovate, and lease back facility, $60,000 on initial advertising campaign, $10,000 on initial legal and incorporation fees, and $30,000 on initial price discounts and free services. The reserve of $20,000 will be used as initial working capital and for contingencies.

Photo Credits

2 *bottom left:* © 1993, Comstock; *top left:* © 1993, Comstock; *right:* © 1993, Comstock. **6** © 1993 Copyright of The Reader's Digest Association, Inc. Reader's Digest. The Digest and the Pegasus logo are registered trademarks of the Reader's Digest Association, Inc. **7** © 1993 Copyright of The Reader's Digest Association, Inc. Reader's Digest. The Digest and the Pegasus logo are registered trademarks of the Reader's Digest Association, Inc. **12** © Butch Gemin. **13** Courtesy of HGM Corp. **40** *left:* © Rhoda Sidney, PhotoEdit; *right:* Courtesy of International Business Machines Corporation. **47** © Henry Groskinsky. **51** Courtesy of Find/SVP. **82** *top left:* © Derimais/Jerrican/Photo Researchers, Inc; *bottom left:* © Garry D. McMichael/Photo Researchers, Inc; *right:* © Mathias Oppersdorff/Photo Researchers, Inc. **85** Source: The Ford Motor Corp.; Source: The Ford Motor Corp.; Source: The Ford Motor Corp. **86** Courtesy of Chrysler, Inc.; Courtesy of Ford Motor Corp.; © Tony Stone Images; Courtesy of Mazda. **104** © Buddy Jenssen/Leo de Wys, Inc. **107** © David R. Frazier/Photo Researchers, Inc. **108** © '87 Blair Seitz/Photo Researchers, Inc. **119** © 1993 Copyright of The Reader's Digest Association, Inc. Reader's Digest. The Digest and the Pegasus logo are registered trademarks of the Reader's Digest Association, Inc. **122** *left:* Courtesy of the following: IBM, Inc.; Apple, Inc.; NCR, Inc.; Epson, Inc.; Compaq, Inc.; Hewlett Packard; Ricoh. **149** Courtesy of Blockbuster Entertainment. **152** *center left:* Stock Montage, Inc., Chicago, IL; *top left:* © Guiliano Colliva/The Image Bank; *top right:* Courtesy of International Business Machines Corporation; *bottom left:* Stock Montage, Inc., Chicago, IL. **169** Courtesy of The Limited, Inc.; Courtesy of the Sharper Image. **187** *top left:* © Photo Researchers, Inc.; *right:* © 1990, Roger Grace/Greenpeace; *bottom left:* © Leo de Wys, Inc. **195** Source: *Consumer Digest,* September 1992. **218** *bottom left:* © Jeff Isaac Greenberg/Photo Researchers, Inc.; *top left:* Courtesy of Honda of America Mfg., Inc.; *right:* © Wesley Bocxe/Photo Researchers, Inc. **240** *left:* © Butch Gemin; *right:* © Butch Gemin. **290** *top left:* © 1991 Steve Drexler Photography/The Image Bank; *bottom left:* © David Young-Wolff/PhotoEdit; *right:* © Butch Gemin; *center left:* Courtesy of Honda of America Mfg., Inc. **313** Copyright November 1987, a special advertising section—"What's Behind the Name?"—that appeared in Reader's Digest; Copyright November 1987, a special advertising section—"What's Behind the Name?"—that appeared in Reader's Digest; Copyright November 1987, a special advertising section—"What's Behind the Name?"—that appeared in Reader's Digest; Copyright November 1987, a special advertising section—"What's Behind the Name?"—that appeared in Reader's Digest; **317** Courtesy of the Prudential Insurance Companies. **332** *top left:* © Butch Gemin; *bottom left:* © Butch Gemin; *right:* © Butch Gemin. **347** © John Blaustein. **348** © Rei Ohara/Black Star. **356** © Butch Gemin. **365** Courtesy of Federal Express Corporation. **366** Courtesy of the Fritz Companies. All rights reserved. **374** *left:* © Barrie Rokeach/The Image Bank; *right:* © Grant Faint/The Image Bank. **400** © Robert Krist/Black Star. Courtesy Merck & Co. Inc. **409** © Bob Daemmrich/Stock, Boston. **422** *right:* © Butch Gemin; *left:* © George E. Jones III/Photo Researchers, Inc. **465** © Bacardi Imports, Inc. **502** *left:* AP/Wide World Photos; *right:* © Frank Herholdt/Tony Stone Images. **536** © Index Stock International Photography, Inc.; © Index Stock International Photography, Inc. **538** *right:* From Statistica/w, Copyright © StatSoft, Inc., Tulsa, OK; *left:* © Butch Gemin. **616** © Peter Dickson.

622

Name Index

COMPANY INDEX

SUBJECT INDEX

Stock
control, competitive analysis and, 145
obsolescence, 359
Stock-turn, 159, 341–342, 356–357
Storage
ease, price sensitivity and, 103
system, competitive analysis and, 146
Store loyalty, 314
Strategic alliance, 506–507
Strategic business unit (SBU), 228
Strategic marketing concept, 5–6
Strategy implementation, critical path method
and, 521
Strategy-marketing matrix, 26
Strategy report, 67, 614–621
Structure, advertising and, 440
Subjective judgment, 548
Subsidy, 190
Substitute price point, 473
Substitution, price sensitivity and, 102–103
Suburban shopping center, 160–161
Sunk cost, 60
Supermarket, 160–161
Supplier-distributor fit, 336
Supplier-reseller fit, 335–340
Supplier-retailer efficiency loop, 338
Supply, demand and, 11
Survey
consumer, 549
research, 55–57
comparison of techniques, 56
Swiss Organization for Standardization, 326
Symbol, 263
Synergy, 232
channel, 340–341
marketing and production, 234

Target audience, minimizing cost per thousand,
448–449
Targeted service, 359
Target market, 424
Tariff, 190
Tax break, 190
TBIS. *See* Transaction-based information system
Team, 18
decision-making, 599–604
cross-functional, 18–19
Team decision making, 599–604
Technology
established companies and, 135
market analysis and, 70
transfer, 28
Telemarketing, 406–411
advantages and disadvantages, 407
in control, 408–409
out of control, 409–311
workstation, 409
Telephone service, deregulation and, 192
Teleselling, 408
Teleservicing, 408
Television advertising, 447
10-K, 48–49
10-Q, 48–49
Test marketing, 308–309
Theater testing, 568
Tied pricing, 487–488
contract, 487

Time
management, 530–531
tips, 532
pressure, consumption and, 95–97
Time-based competition, 528–529
Total direct variable cost (TVC), 58
Total quality management (TQM), 20, 236,
260–268, 561
dimensions, 263–265
Total quality marketing control, 563–574
Total service quality management, 265–267
TQM. *See* Total quality management
Trade
promotion, channel behavior and, 495–496
relations, competitive analysis and, 146–147
show, 382–383
market intelligence gathering and, 47
Trademark, 316
Trading
channel, 156
partnership, 126
relationship
balance of power and, 352
contracts and, 385–386
evolutionary rigidity and, 172–173
long-term contracts and, 352–354
managing, 340–350
protecting, 350–351
vertical integration and, 352–354
Training, sales force, 397–399
Transaction-based information system
(TBIS), 55
Transfer pricing, 577
Transit, packaging and, 320
Transportation
competitive analysis and, 146
conglomerate, integrated, 163–164
management, 357–358
mode, containerization and, 164
Triangulation, 279
Tribal network, 180–181
Tribal relationship network, global, 180–181
Trucking, deregulation and, 192
Turnkey pricing, 470
Two-sided advertising, 442

Uncertainty
entrepreneurial firm and, 10–11
marketing planning and, 64
Uncontrollable variance, 570–572
Uniform delivery pricing, 488
Unique mind share, 250
United States Census Bureau, 49, 191
United States Congress, 151
United States Department of Commerce, 72, 110,
164, 191
United States Department of Justice, 13, 50
United States Patent Office, 212
United States Supreme Court, 11, 194,
200, 201
Universal product code (UPC), 199, 358
Unnatural monopoly, 190
UPC. *See* Universal product code
UPC-type coding, 163, 184
Usage segment discounting, price discrimination and,
488–489
Utility, 207